LIBERATION
(*JOSNA O JONONIR GOLPO*)

Humayun Ahmed

Acre Press

Josna o Jononir Golpo
Bengali original published by Anyaprokash, Dhaka, Bangladesh
www.anyaprakash.com
© 2004 Humayun Ahmed
First edition February 2004

This translation published by Acre Press, Stroud
rogwynn27@gmail.com
© 2014 Roger Gwynn
First impression February 2014
Revised edition November 2015
Improved edition October 2016

CONTENTS

Translator's Introduction	... ...	iii
Author's Foreword	... ...	v
Author's Dedication	... ...	xi

1.	Moulana Irtazuddin in Dhaka	... ...	1
2.	Shahed and Gourango	... ...	17
3.	Inspector Mobarak Hussain	... ...	28
4.	Nilganj High School	... ...	38
5.	Kolimullah the poet	... ...	47
6.	Mobarak Hussain and Mr Zohar	... ...	52
7.	Shahed and Naimul	... ...	58
8.	Naimul and the professor	... ...	67
9.	Moriam the bride	... ...	71
10.	Mobarak Hussain and Sheikh Mujib	... ...	77
11.	Shahed and Asmani	... ...	83
12.	The crackdown	... ...	89
13.	News item: Bhutto flees	... ...	96
14.	Eyewitness accounts	... ...	97
15.	Shahed and Asmani apart	... ...	101
16.	Shahed and Gourango again	... ...	110
17.	Moriam and Naimul	... ...	118
18.	Foyzur Rahman and his family	... ...	122
19.	General Tikka Khan's birthday	... ...	132
20.	Kolimullah in wartime	... ...	137
21.	Masuma meets Kolimullah	... ...	146
22.	Asgar Ali: a porter's tale	... ...	152
23.	Gourango	... ...	160
24.	Shahed under arrest	... ...	165
25.	News items: 13th April	... ...	177
26.	Asmani in exile	... ...	178
27.	Nilganj in wartime	... ...	185
28.	A brave policeman's fate	... ...	191
29.	Carnage in Darogabari	... ...	198
30.	Asmani in flight	... ...	202
31.	Foyzur Rahman's family on the run	... ...	206
32.	News item: 21st April	... ...	209
33.	News item: 26th April	... ...	210
34.	News items: 2nd June	... ...	211
35.	News items: 3rd June	... ...	212
36.	News item: 11th June	... ...	213
37.	Shamsur Rahman in the village	... ...	214
38.	A poet's heart	... ...	221
39.	Nilganj under military rule	... ...	222

40.	A Pakistani army captain's letter	229
41.	Eyewitness accounts	230
42.	Naimul and Surma Baba	235
43.	Foyzur Rahman family's odyssey	242
44.	Shahed on the road	245
45.	Agartala	250
46.	Diary extract: 30th July	253
47.	News item: 8th August	254
48.	Sheikh Mujib in jail	255
49.	News article: Begum Mujib in wartime	257
50.	Moulana Irtazuddin's last hours	262
51.	A wartime burial	268
52.	Asmani in the refugee camp	269
53.	Naimul the freedom fighter	273
54.	Major Zia	282
55.	News article: Zia's brother-in-law	284
56.	Kolimullah's new life	288
57.	Bacchu Miah the cowboy	294
58.	Moulana Bhashani in Calcutta	299
59.	A freedom fighter's letter	301
60.	Document: a wartime doctor	302
61.	Naimul in Dhaka	304
62.	Naimul and the professor again	312
63.	Gourango in custody	315
64.	Pakistan army council of war	316
65.	Ambush on the river	321
66.	An unsung hero	323
67.	Mindless brutality	328
68.	The tide turns	332
69.	Shahed and Asmani reunited	336
70.	News: call to surrender	337
71.	Kolimullah the chamaeleon	338
72.	The end	346

Notes	351
Glossary	361
List of Characters	367
Chronology	369
Map	371

TRANSLATOR'S INTRODUCTION

Humayun Ahmed (1948-2012) was the best known and most popular fiction writer in Bangladesh from the early 1980s until his death at the age of sixty-four. Apart from numerous novels and short stories he also wrote the screenplay for many successful films and TV serial dramas.

Humayun Ahmed adopted a simple, straightforward prose style which made his works easily accessible to the general reader. His greatest talent, which was probably the key to his popularity and certainly the reason for his success as a screenplay writer, was his ability to faithfully reproduce the speech of ordinary Bengali people of any social class and record their often eccentric mannerisms. His realism was at once breathtakingly accurate and delightfully humorous.

Josna o Jononir Golpo, 'a tale of moonlight and a mother', was different from most of Humayun Ahmed's other novels in that its primary purpose was to inform rather than to amuse. As the writer himself explains in his Foreword, the book took a long time in gestation and was created largely out of a sense of duty: the duty to make available for the common reader an honest and comprehensive picture of the political and social developments which led to the emergence of Bangladesh as an independent state.

With intercalated excerpts from other sources the novel manages to produce a vivid evocation of the chaos and wild emotions of an extraordinary moment in human history – "that ghastly, beautiful and surrealistic period" as the author himself called it.

Bangladesh is now, in its fifth decade, going through an identity crisis, as the war crime trials mounted by the Awami League government have reawakened the fiery emotions of 1971 and latent tension between secularist and Islamic schools of thought has been brought to the surface. The truth about what happened during the liberation struggle is sometimes in dispute. This is therefore a good time for friends of Bangladesh to take a fresh look at Humayun Ahmed's intelligent and balanced painting of the human landscape of East Bengal in 1971.

This translation is not a mechanical word for word reproduction of the original work; I have striven to reproduce Humayun Ahmed's colloquial voice in natural English. The deliciously spiced slang and dialect used by many of Ahmed's minor characters have been turned into English slang and dialect

Inevitably a number of exotic words, including names, have found a place in the English text. No consistent method of transliteration has been followed. Help with meanings can be found in the Glossary at the end of the book, and a List of Characters, Chronology and Map have also been included. Further information relating to specific points is available in the Notes section, each reference being signalled in the text by a circular symbol (°).

Roger Gwynn
Stroud, Gloucestershire

October 2016

FOREWORD

I was twenty-three years old when the Liberation War began, and a student of Dhaka University. I had already sat the theory exam for an honours degree in chemistry, and was awaiting the practical. Everything was going well – just one more year and I'd have my MSc, then I'd join the university staff as a lecturer, and go abroad to do a PhD.

The archetypical student swot is sometimes depicted in literature. I conformed to the type. The swot has no particular friends; I had no particular friends. The swot spends his time reading books; I spent my time reading books. In 1969, at an intensely exciting time of popular awakening, I was a singularly unexcited youth whose sole form of recreation was reading works of fiction in the Public Library, drinking tea at Shorif Miah's canteen, and sometimes going down to the Bangla Academy where concerts of Bengali songs were often held.

Wherever I happened to be, I always made sure I returned to my own room in Mohsin Hall before dark. As a scholarship student I had been allotted a whole room to myself, which I had filled with books of every kind. Knowing I was fond of music my father had provided me with a record player. While frightful scenes of upheaval were unfolding outside, there I sat, behind closed doors, listening to songs. "*Why so restless, oh dear wayfarer?*"

My familiar, nicely ordered little world was shattered in 1971. I was mentally quite unprepared for the situation in which I found myself. I was like a fish dragged from its quiet shady pool and flung all of a sudden onto a dry bank scorched by the fierce summer sun. A strange experience it was indeed. I fled for dear life from one place to the next, along with my brothers and sisters. I got enrolled as a student in a madrasah – a Quranic school run by the Holy Man of Shorshina – in order to avoid persecution. Pakistani soldiers placed a crate full of ammunition on my head, and made me walk in front of them with this incredibly heavy head load, all the way from Barhatta to Netrakona. I spent some time in an army prison camp, where the brutality was horrific. One morning a soldier came and handed me an unusually large banana, saying, "You're going to be lined up and shot tomorrow morning – but don't worry, that's the best thing that could happen to you. For if you're innocent you'll go straight to heaven, and if you're guilty of anything you'll just be receiving your rightful punishment!"

I later described these happenings in various newspaper and magazine articles. I also wrote quite a few short stories, and a novel or two, touching on the joy and pain, despair and ignominy of the Liberation War. But one day I thought, I ought to write a novel encapsulating the entire war period. Just as it behoves everybody to repay the debt they owe to their parents, so is it also our duty to repay what we owe to our motherland. As a writer I should do this through my writings.

So I took up my pen, and *Josna o Jononir Golpo* started coming out in instalments in a newspaper called *Bhorer Kagoj*. But whenever I start a serialization I fail to complete it, and this time was no exception. After six or seven instalments it ground to a halt. A couple of years later I resumed the series, but again after a few issues I dried up and couldn't go on. I wrote other things including various plays and films, but the story of the Liberation

War remained unwritten. Sometimes I felt guilty about it, and then I would soothe my conscience by assuring myself I would get round to it in due course when I was less busy. What was the hurry, there was still plenty of time!

Suddenly one day I realized that I didn't have all that time at all, in fact time had run out and *Josna o Jononir Golpo* was never going to be written. At that moment I was lying on a trolley in Mount Elizabeth Hospital in Singapore, and two nurses were wheeling me towards the operating theatre for open heart surgery. I had been given an injection of anaesthetic and my eyelids were growing heavy; the bright lights of the hospital were rapidly going dim.

Just as I was about to lose consciousness I thought, oh dear, I never managed to write *Josna o Jononir Golpo*. If I'm allowed to come back from this alive, I shall definitely complete the book. And a wave of joy flooded over me as I slipped into oblivion, for it had suddenly struck me that I must be a real writer: death was staring me in the face, and my one and only concern was for an unfinished manuscript.

On my return to Bangladesh I took the work in hand. I was still very weak and could write no more than a page or two each day, but I persevered and finished the book. And then I felt I had done what I could to repay my debt to my motherland; and the joy that gave me was boundless.

Josna o Jononir Golpo is a novel, not a historical study. Nevertheless in writing it I have tried to stay as close as possible to the historical truth. I may have erred here and there, but that is only natural. A novel is not gospel and any errors can be corrected if necessary.

I have borrowed some important figures of that era as characters for the novel. A novelist has the liberty to do such things. I apologize in advance if I have made any mistakes in my portrayal of these notable figures. I humbly call the reader's attention to the well known dictum that the truth is whatever is written by an author:

> *All thou narratest is true, while all that happens is not true;*
> *O poet, thy mind, where Rama took shape, is more real than Ayodhya!*

Almost all the incidents described in the book are true. Some are derived from my own experience, others have been borrowed from the experiences of other people. Before going for publication I asked many acquaintances to read through the manuscript of the novel. Those who had not seen the Liberation War (by which I mean readers from the younger generation) went through the book and objected that many of the incidents in it seemed fanciful; such things, they suggested, could surely never happen in real life.

There is only one thing I can say to them: those times were strange times indeed, and our world was an amalgam of dreams and nightmares. Everything seemed both quite real and quite unreal. I lived through that ghastly, beautiful and surrealistic period, and if I have succeeded in capturing even a little of its flavour my life will not have been in vain.

I wish to express my sincere thanks to all those who helped me in the task of writing *Josna o Jononir Golpo* by supplying various pieces of information. The books which have been published about the Liberation War were a considerable help to me; in particular I would like to mention

Rabindranath Trivedi's *Ekattorer Dosh Mash* (*Ten Months in 1971*). In it the writer has put together a fine day to day record of events covering the ten months of the war. Several chronicles by both men and women authors in the form of diaries were of service too. These made it possible to tell what had happened in Dhaka on each individual day of the conflict. However I could not refer to them without an element of caution, for on reading some of these diary-style narratives I realized that rather than having been written at the time they described, they had been drafted later and backdated. For one writer, in his record of a particular day, may have put down a remark like "heavy rain falling since early morning in Dhaka city," while another, for the same date, has made a comment about "Dhaka city broiling in brilliant sunshine". Or one may have noted "I just heard that the government in exile has performed an oath-taking ceremony," on a date which fell a couple of days earlier than that on which the said ceremony actually took place. Political bias has also affected some diaries; for example, one diarist gives a blow by blow account of every passing day, yet somehow fails to mention a certain Major Ziaur Rahman going on air from Kalurghat radio station and urging everyone to join the liberation struggle. The major's name is nowhere to be found.

The same problem is encountered in relation to the famous speech given on 7th March 1971 by the founder of Bangladesh, Bangabandhu Sheikh Mujibur Rahman. In the first edition of his celebrated work *Bangladesher Tarikh* (*Annals of Bangladesh*), Justice Muhammad Habibur Rahman states that Sheikh Mujibur Rahman ended his speech exclaiming "*Joy Bangla! Jiye Pakistan!*" ("victory to Bengal, long live Pakistan") but in the second edition he omits the words "*Jiye Pakistan!*" The laureate poet Shamsur Rahman, in his autobiography published serially in the daily paper *Dainik Janakantha* under the title *Kaler Dhuloy Lekha* (*Written in the Dust of Time*), also records that Sheikh Mujib's final words were "*Jiye Pakistan!*" And I have heard many other people say the same, people with Awami League sympathies. The problem is that after trawling through every newspaper published on 8th March and 9th March I have found no reference to any such words. If that is the case, why should a false notion have gained currency?

If Bangabandhu did say "*Jiye Pakistan!*" what harm was there in that? Whatever he said, he surely chose his words carefully before saying them. He knew he had to keep the door open for negotiations with Pakistan; he knew he had to play for time. On 7th March he was not in a position to make a full declaration of independence. I consider his speech of 7th March to have been even more significant than Lincoln's Gettysburg address. If there is any lack of clarity regarding its contents, that is to be regretted.

Out of the fifteen volumes of documents relating to the Liberation War which have been published by the Bangladesh Ministry of Information I have carefully perused seven, and I have made direct use of numerous sections of them. However in respect of these documents too I have my reservations. I will give just one example. Statements were taken from witnesses of the torture meted out to young female prisoners at Rajarbagh police quarters. It was stated that the policemen had tied the girls' ankles with rope and then hung them upside down by their feet. I cannot make out the logic behind anyone taking girls they were intending to rape and stringing them up in this way; nevertheless for the sake of argument I am prepared to accept that this was done. But what I find totally unbelievable is the claim made by some witnesses that the girls had had their satchels and textbooks with them, in other words that they had been on their way to school or college when they were arrested. Throughout the period of terror about which we are talking every school, college and university was closed. There was absolutely no question of any young person venturing onto the streets with their course textbooks. The impression I get is that those witness statements were never properly verified. I must add that as a nation we are all too fond of exaggeration.

We also have a tendency to understate the role played by the Indian Army. Anyone who, fifty years from now, attempts to get a picture of the Liberation War by reading the various novels and short stories about it published in Bangladesh will be unaware that the Indian Army even existed. The subject of this foreign army has been expunged from our literature. Maybe some writers think it would detract from the glory of our own freedom fighters.

There is nothing at all inglorious about acknowledging a debt. Great nations and magnanimous individuals do acknowledge their debts. I had in fact intended to include in this book a list of all the Indian soldiers who gave their lives for the freedom of Bangladesh, just so that those who read it could see how long the list was and at least utter a passing "oh dear!"

In the end I gave up the idea of the list, as putting it in would have increased the size of the book by a hundred pages or so, and anyway if I had included that list I would clearly also have had to have a list of all the martyrs from the ranks of the Bangladesh Army, the former East Pakistan Rifles (now known as the B.D.R.), the police force, the Ansars and the Liberation Army. But, you may be surprised to hear, no comprehensive list exists. The official list is still under preparation. Thirty-three years have passed since the war ended, yet the list hasn't yet been completed. When will it be ready, I wonder?

I frequently gaze at the list of *Bir Shrestha* – the Supreme Heroes of the Liberation War – and give a little sigh. Not one of the recognized heroes on this list came from outside of the armed forces. Yet I know full well, and the people who gave the awards knew too, that many irregular fighters in the Liberation War also displayed exceptional courage. The deeds they performed, without the benefit of military training or experience, were beyond compare. And yet none of them have been given official recognition. Why not, I ask?

Among the shortcomings of this book is my failure to include anything about the women abused by Pakistani soldiers during the war. The subject is so delicate and so painful, I simply could not bring myself to write about it. I hope others may do so, and then the tears of those hapless young girls may flow out of their pens.

Now I want to mention one very personal matter. About twenty years ago my wife Gultekin presented me with an exercise book for my birthday. It had a blue cover and a spiral binding, and contained five hundred pages. She told me I must write a long novel about the Liberation War in it, even if I only managed to do one page a day.

I have given Gultekin much unhappiness throughout her life, but I hope that today for once she will be happy.

The Almighty granted me the privilege of composing this work, and I hereby express my boundless gratitude to Him. Let me end this foreword with my hopes for a happy and glorious Bangladesh free from political, ideological and religious bias.

Humayun Ahmed
Nuhash Polli
Gazipur

2004

x

JOSNA O JONONIR GOLPO: A TALE OF MOONLIGHT AND A MOTHER

by

Humayun Ahmed

Dedicated to my mother
Begum Ayesha Aktar Khatun
and my father
(Shaheed) Foyzur Rahman Ahmed

1

Moulana Irtazuddin Kashempuri, the Arabic teacher from Nilganj High School, was standing in Komlapur railway station. He was a short, stocky man about sixty years old, with a luxuriant beard which was neither white nor black but somewhere in between. His skull was close shaven. A barber used to come round every Friday morning to shave it; for he was in the habit of wearing a turban on Fridays, and turbans are supposed to sit better on shaven heads. After that he would apply eye-black to his eyes and dab a small amount of perfume on his ear lobes. Wearing a long tunic-like shirt which went down to his knees he would then go to the mosque and act as the imam at Friday prayers. Such had been his custom for the past fifteen years. Although the Nilganj mosque had an imam of its own it was always he who officiated at the congregational prayers on Fridays.

Irtazuddin Kashempuri was holding a goose with pure white plumage. He was clutching it by the neck with his right hand while it struggled and flapped its wings. Mr Kashempuri's face wore a harried look, for the redoubtable bird had pecked him on the elbow while they were getting down from the train, and drawn blood. A small crowd had now gathered around them; people were watching curiously, waiting to see what would happen next. Mr Kashempuri and his goose had managed to arouse in their audience an expectation of entertainment.

Irtazuddin admonished them solemnly. "What's the matter? Haven't you ever seen a goose before? Please go away and get on with your own business. Why are you wasting your time? Don't you have anything better to do?"

None of the onlookers showed any sign of wanting to get on with their own business; very likely the fact was that they truly didn't have anything better to do. Instead they continued to stand there surrounding Irtazuddin. Several more people came and joined the crowd. At this point the goose aimed another peck at the same place as before, Irtazuddin's left elbow. "Ah!" exclaimed Irtazuddin, jumping almost clear off the ground. The crowd roared with laughter; their hopes had not been in vain, this was something worth watching. Ruefully Irtazuddin wondered why people derived so much pleasure from the misfortunes of their fellow men. He had been in pain – why should anyone be so pleased about that? What was at the bottom of it all? One day he must sit down and think calmly about the subject, but right now it was impossible to think, he was feeling too ruffled. Meanwhile a man was coming forward to offer some advice. He delivered his advice in a serious tone. As a nation, we Bengalis are very good at giving advice.

"Uncle, yer reverence, yer should 'old 'er by 'er throat. If yer 'old 'er by 'er throat she won't be able ter bite yer."

"I shall do whatever I think best," replied Irtazuddin wearily. "There's no need for you to trouble yourself about it. Please leave me alone."

But the purveyor of good advice was undeterred. Turning towards the crowd he declared, "Trouble is, she ain't got 'er mate wiv 'er. A goose as got 'er mate wiv 'er won't give no grief. Yer reverence, sir, where's 'er mate then?"

Irtazuddin glowered at him and said nothing.

It was mid February, and around eleven o'clock in the evening. In the village it would have been quite cold at this hour. In Nilganj he had to cover himself with a quilt at night. But here it was hot and humid. The sky was cloudy and there were flickers of lightning to be seen. It ought not to be so hot and humid at this time of year. Maybe it was because of the clouds that there was this unusual warmth. The way the lightning was flashing, there was probably going to be some rain. But that would be awkward, because he hadn't brought his umbrella with him. He never went out without his umbrella, but somehow this time he had forgotten to bring it. That was a sign of getting old. When people get old they start making various little mistakes. And once little mistakes have become a regular habit they start making major mistakes.

Irtazuddin was wearing a coat made of coarse silk with a tight collar, and he had a scarf round his neck. He was sweating in the heat. Who could have guessed that Dhaka in mid February would not be at all cold? There were an awful lot of people in the city, and the city stayed warm thanks to all those warm-blooded people. He wondered how many hundreds of thousands of people there were living in the city. He must find out the correct figure.

Irtazuddin was getting thirsty, but he had no idea where he could find any water. They'd built this enormous station and yet they hadn't installed any water taps. What with the encumbrance of his baggage, his thirst and the wound the goose had inflicted on his elbow, he was feeling most uncomfortable. Now he had to get to Malibag. The house was 18/6 West Malibag and it was in a side lane. He'd only been there once before, and now he wasn't sure he'd be able to find it again. All the side lanes in Dhaka looked exactly the same to him. Not only the lanes, the people also looked the same. They seemed more like shadows than real people. You could tell real people apart, but you couldn't tell one shadow from another. Yes, Dhaka was a land of human shadows, Shadow City.

Irtazuddin engaged a rickshaw to take him from Komlapur to Malibag; the fare was agreed at one rupee. He couldn't be sure whether the rickshaw puller had cheated him or not. He didn't often come to Dhaka, and he had no knowledge of rickshaw fares. He didn't wish to underpay anybody, but nor did he want to be rooked. In the city people were fond of getting the better of others.

"Brother rickshaw puller, may I know your name?"

"Badrul."

"Listen, brother Badrul, I'll give you two rupees instead of one if you'll find the house for me. I've got the address, it's 18/6 West Malibag. Agreed? If you're willing to do it you can say 'Praise be the Lord', but if not, you needn't say anything."

"The 'ouse is near the level crossing, right?"

"I have no idea. I've only been there once before. All I can remember is that there was an alstonia tree next to the house. But it was dead. The alstonia is a rural tree which can't survive in cities, that's why it had died."

"All right, guv, climb on board, let's go."

"But I asked you to say 'Praise be the Lord'. *Alhamdulillah*. Kindly say it."

"*Alhamdulillah*!" said the rickshaw puller, surprised.

It was quite a late hour, yet many shops were still open, people were thronging the streets, music was blaring from a teashop. What was the meaning of it? Would it be like that all night long? Didn't these people go to bed at night? After a while Irtazuddin's rickshaw got caught up in a procession. It wasn't anything big, just a demonstration with a couple of dozen men in it, but each of them was carrying a lighted torch. More smoke than light was coming from the torches. The men's faces were gleaming with sweat and their voices were hoarse; it looked as if they had been demonstrating for a long time and were now worn out.

Badrul pulled up his rickshaw at one side of the road and sat staring at the procession in fascination. The demonstrators were chanting the same slogan all the time, "Burn, burn, let it burn!" Irtazuddin frowned and thought to himself, what kind of slogan is that? "Burn, burn, let it burn" – that's no good. Slogans ought to be of a peaceable nature, something more like "Put out, put out, put out the flames!"

The goose had been alarmed by the sight of the demonstration, and was trying to jump down from the rickshaw. Irtazuddin sat there grim faced, clutching the bird's neck firmly. The goose was watching the torches in the procession with astonishment; all her life the only night lights she had seen were paraffin lamps and the moon, and like Irtazuddin she was quite unaccustomed to flaming brands. Every now and then she gave a flap of her wings.

Abruptly the procession turned into a side lane, and suddenly everything went quiet again. The rickshaw puller started pedalling once more. In a voice full of eagerness he enquired, "'Ow much did yer goose cost yer, guv?"

Irtazuddin was annoyed. These city people judged everything in terms of price. Whenever they saw anything of good quality the first thing they wanted to know was how much it cost.

"This goose is from my own farmyard," said Irtazuddin, "I didn't buy it. My younger brother lives in Malibag and I've brought it for him. At least, not exactly for him; he has a little girl who'll turn four in April, and I've brought it for her. Children are always fond of birds and animals."

"Ah."

"She lives in an urban area, so she never sees things like that."

Irtazuddin realized he was feeling hungry. He hadn't been aware of his hunger until this moment, thanks to all the emotion and stress, but now it was making itself felt. He hadn't had anything to eat at suppertime, and now it was really late, midnight at least. A person's ability to withstand hunger decreased with age, he reflected. It wasn't just the body which deteriorated in old age, the spirit which dwelt in the body also started decaying. It was because of this decay in their spirit that old men unwittingly drifted into a world of delusion. Maybe he himself had already drifted into that world. Only strict truthfulness could prevent a person from becoming deluded. That was why he always spoke the truth. He couldn't recall ever having told a lie in the last twenty-five years or so.

The rickshaw had been wandering around Malibag for quite some time now, but the house hadn't come to light. There was no rhyme or reason in the numbering: here you had number thirteen, and then the next house was number one hundred and eleven. Where had all the numbers in between gone? And if there was a West Malibag there should have been an East Malibag to go with it; yet there was no such thing as East Malibag. It was ridiculous. There were hardly any people about in the back-lanes, and those that could be found appeared to be from a different planet. When you asked them where 18/6 West Malibag was they would stare at you in astonishment for a few minutes and then yawn. A genuinely surprised person never yawns, so both the air of surprise and the yawn were entirely put on.

Irtazuddin's neck had begun to itch from the scarf he was wearing. Both of his hands were engaged, so he was unable to give himself a scratch. It would be so much better if people could have three arms, he thought. That third arm would come in useful time and time again... Then he was appalled with himself for having had such a silly thought. Almighty God had exercised great care and deliberation when He created man. If He had thought man needed three arms He would have given him three. Irtazuddin repeated to himself three times the formula of contrition: *tauba, astaghfirullah!* I beg God's forgiveness.

The goose was being really troublesome. Even though he was gripping her by the neck she was still endeavouring to peck him. He hadn't managed to bring both of the geese, although he had intended to. One of them had evaded capture.

It was the female goose that had been caught, while her mate had scooted away into the pond. The poor fellow was probably now wandering around searching for his wife. It had been wrong to break up the couple and bring only one. Irtazuddin felt bad about it. They were dumb animals, they would be unable to express their grief in words, but they would miss one another. They would be shocked by man's cruelty, and yet they would still have to go on living among human beings; that was their fate.

At last the house was found. There was the number – 18/6. There was the alstonia tree, looking just as dead now as it had last time. Irtazuddin gave the rickshaw puller an extra half rupee along with the promised two. He felt like presenting him with one of the tins of puffed rice too; but as he had brought them expressly for Shahed he could not do so.

"Brother Badrul."

"Yes, sir?"

"You have gone to a lot of trouble for me. I shall pray earnestly for you."

Wiping his face with his cloth Badrul remarked, "Yer a wonder, sir!"

"A wonder? Why do you say that?"

"Yer give me a tip and now yer goin' ter pray for me an' all. No-one else would."

Irtazuddin let out a long sigh. "We're all wonders," he said. "If I'm a wonder, then so are you. God Almighty likes wonderful things, that's why there's so much wonder in the world."

The whole household was fast asleep.

The house was in darkness, the gate was locked. Irtazuddin felt annoyed. It made him indignant to see how distrustful city people were. What need was there to lock gates?

After he had been rattling the gate and calling "Shahed! Shahed!" in a loud voice for some time, a light went on inside the house. A man he had never seen before opened the door and came out, asking, "Who is it?"

The man was tall and fair-skinned, and his voice was as soft as a woman's. From the way he sounded it was obvious that he was scared.

"Who are you?"

"I am Irtazuddin. I have come here from Nilganj. I'm the Assistant Headmaster and Arabic and R.E. teacher at Nilganj High School."

"Whom do you want?"

"I've come to see Shahed. I'm his elder brother. I'm sorry, I forgot to give you a *salaam*, please forgive my lack of civility. *As-salaamu alaikum*."

The man had been standing on the verandah, but now he stepped back into the doorway. However the door was open and he was still visible. For some reason he was afraid. Irtazuddin realized that he might indeed look a bit frightening, a thought which disconcerted him, but he couldn't think how to dispel the man's fears. The man had not returned his greeting, and that was bad: exchanging the *salaam* was supposed to be a sign of peaceful intent.

"Nobody of the name of Shahed lives here."

"He doesn't live here? How can that be?"

"He's left here. I'm the new tenant."

"Do you know where he's moved to?"

"No."

"Does anyone know?"

"I couldn't possibly say whether anyone knows or not."

The man was about to close his door when Irtazuddin called out in a weary tone, "Brother, would you please come over here and open the gate."

"Why should I?"

"I've got a goose here, which I wish to present to you."

"A goose?"

"I brought it for Shahed's daughter, but I can't go wandering around with a goose on my hands at this time of night, so I shall be grateful if you will accept it from me."

"Why ever should I start taking in other people's geese?"

"Surely there are some children in your family who would love it."

The man stepped forward out of the doorway. His wife's face was visible in the crack of the door; she was staring at the goose with interest. Irtazuddin smiled and addressed his next words to her. "If you will accept this goose and these other things I shall be really pleased. There's no need to feel embarrassed. I actually find having a goose with me rather a nuisance."

The face of a strikingly pretty teenage girl appeared in the doorway. The girl's name was Ratneswari° and she was a student of Class X at Viqarunnessa Noon Girls' High School. Ratneswari was filled with wonder, for nothing as remarkable as this had ever happened in her life before. A rather saintly looking old man had turned up in the middle of the night, saying he wanted to present them with a goose. Her head was already buzzing with ideas of how she would narrate the story at school; some of her friends wouldn't even believe it was true. It would have been great if she could have got a photo of the holy looking man.

Ratneswari whispered to her mother, "Are we going to accept the goose, Mum?"

"I don't know," replied Ratneswari's mother in a low voice, "wait and see what your Dad says."

"Who *is* that man, Mum?"

"I've no idea."

Looking at Ratneswari's father Irtazuddin said cheerfully, "Is that little girl your daughter? She has such a sweet face. What's your name, my dear?"

But before Ratneswari could reply her father spoke. "Kindly leave. We cannot accept your goose or any other of your things."

"Very well, don't take them," said Irtazuddin wearily, "but could you please open the gate, I need to go to the toilet."

"I can't open the gate," replied Ratneswari's father. "I haven't got a key."

This was untrue. The key was in the house, tucked away on top of a wardrobe.

"Why don't you open it," whispered Ratneswari's mother. "Poor fellow, he's an elderly man."

"Don't interfere in things you don't understand," said Ratneswari's father quietly. "Get back inside, now, go on." And hustling his wife and daughter into the house before him he slammed the door loudly.

The switch for the light bulb on the verandah was inside the house. Someone turned off the light from inside and the verandah was plunged in darkness. Hurt and surprised, Irtazuddin stood there feeling somewhat crestfallen. Why had they behaved like that? Couldn't people show a wee bit of kindness to their fellows?

He threw the goose over the gate into the yard. She could stay there. And what was the point in carrying the tins of puffed rice and other bits of baggage around with him either? If the rickshaw puller had still been there he might have given them to him. Anyway, they could stay there on the ground in front of the gate; needy people would surely find them and take them away. There was little sense in lingering outside a locked gate, but still he stood there. Somehow he had a faint hope the gate was going to be unlocked after all, and the girl who looked like a fairy was going to say to him, "Please come in, Mum has invited you to come inside."

The goose was craning her neck to look at him. "Goodbye, dear," Irtazuddin said to the goose. The goose emitted a grotesque squawk; perhaps she was giving him permission to leave. The more beautiful a bird was to look at, reflected Irtazuddin, the uglier its voice was. For example the peacock. It was splendid to behold, but its voice was unpleasantly strident. The sole exception was the crow, unprepossessing both in its appearance and in its voice.

Rain was starting to patter down. It was good to feel the rain after that stifling heat. Irtazuddin was getting gradually wetter as he walked along. The rain seemed to have an odd clamminess about it. Those areas on his body which it had reached felt quite sticky.

The rain stopped just as he was emerging from the side lane. Another torchlit procession was making its way along the main road, though this one was smaller than the one before. Or maybe it *was* that earlier procession, coming round again? Irtazuddin found himself walking alongside the marchers, as if he was taking part in the demonstration. He didn't know where the procession was heading, nor did he have any idea where he himself was going to go. If this had been a rural area he could have gone up to any farmhouse and explained his predicament, and be would have been offered shelter. They would have provided him with water for his ablutions, and they would have given him something to eat. Steaming hot rice with lentils, a hot chilli, an onion... Irtazuddin's stomach turned over. He hadn't realized quite how hungry he had become. That vision of steaming rice was refusing to go away.

Where was he going, along with these demonstrators? Why was he going there? He ought to be looking for a place where he could take refuge for the night. It wouldn't be possible to find a hotel so late at night, and besides, he couldn't afford to stay in a hotel. The best thing would be to go back to Komlapur railway station and spend the night lying on a bench or something. There were plenty of places near the station where you could get a meal. His first priority was to have a little wash and then have something to eat.

One of the torch bearers had moved closer to Irtazuddin; they were walking side by side, and the man was looking at him curiously. Irtazuddin felt like asking him if he realized that the word for torch, *moshal*, came from the Arabic *mash'al*; not in order to show off his knowledge, but as a way of starting a conversation. Once the conversation was under way he could ask him why they were holding a torchlit demonstration in the middle of the night. The elections were over. The Awami League° had secured 167 of East Pakistan's 169 seats in the national assembly. In West Pakistan Zulfiqar Ali Bhutto° had won 83 seats°. That was it, what more was needed? Why chant "Burn, burn, let it burn" in the dead of night? Had they got the idea of burning from the fact that they were carrying lighted torches?

When someone had a blazing torch in their hand they did feel like setting fire to something, just as a man with a sword in his hand felt like slashing something, or one toting a gun felt like shooting someone. Human nature was bizarre. So what would happen if you put a big bunch of flowers in a person's hands? Would they start handing out flowers to other people?

Irtazuddin pulled up in surprise. This was extraordinary. He was standing in front of Shahed's former residence again. The procession had gone round in a circle and brought him right back to where he had been before. The two tins of puffed rice he had left outside the gate were no longer there, but the goose was visible inside. She was crouching there in the darkness to one side of the house. Perhaps geese can recognize humans by smell; anyway the goose came out of her hiding place and ran towards Irtazuddin flapping her wings. What a wonderful sight!

Irtazuddin gave a small sigh and walked on. Now he must find out how to get to his destination – Komlapur railway station. The goose was craning her neck and staring at him. Was she surprised? Were geese endowed with a capacity to feel surprise?

It took Irtazuddin almost twenty-four hours to find out where Shahed lived. Virtually all of that time was spent combing the streets. He had passed the night at Komlapur railway station, then after performing his dawn prayers at a mosque near the station he had set off in search of Shahed. His quest had reached its conclusion at twenty-five past nine in the evening. The house was an old fashioned two storeyed building in a back lane in Rayer Bazar. The landlord lived on the ground floor. Strange to say, there was an alstonia tree in front of this house too, only this time it was a healthy one. Had Shahed perhaps made a resolution never to rent a property unless it had an alstonia tree to go with it?

Irtazuddin looked dreadful. The stress of searching for Shahed's house seemed to have aged him. His eyes were reddened, and even in the intense heat he was feeling cold, a sign that he was going to get a fever.

"What a state you're in, brother!" exclaimed Shahed in alarm. "You're looking really awful. What's the matter, are you ill?"

"There's nothing wrong with my health," replied Irtazuddin wearily, "I'm just worn out. I couldn't find where you lived. In the end I went to your office; I hadn't realized it would be closed today."

"So how did you find out my address?"

"From the doorman I got the address of a colleague of yours, Mr Rahman. He lives in a place called Bashabo. I went there and sought him out. He didn't know your address, but he knew of somebody else who did know. Oh, it's a long story and it's hardly worth listening to. Where is everyone? Where's Runi, where's her Mum?"

"Asmani has gone to her mother's house," replied Shahed rather hesitantly. "She set off only a short time before you arrived. Mother-in-law is ill. Asmani went as soon as she heard about it."

"Why didn't you go too? A mother-in-law is the same as a mother; anything you can do for her helps balance the debt you owe to your own mother. Mother died soon after you were born, and you never had a chance to repay your debt to her. It doesn't matter so much if you don't repay a father, but a mother's sacrifice must be repaid. Anyway, show me the way to the bathroom, I must have a bath. I've missed several of the prayers. Do you have a prayer mat anywhere?"

"No," admitted Shahed shamefacedly. "But there's a clean sheet which I can spread out for you."

"Regardless of whether or not you say the prayers yourself," said Irtazuddin gravely, "as a born Muslim you ought to have a prayer mat, a set of prayer beads and a prayer cap in the house."

"Do you want to use hot water, elder brother? Can I heat some up for you?"

"There's no need for hot water."

"Have you had anything to eat?"

"No. But I'm not going to have any supper, I'm feeling feverish, so I'll fast. Fasting is the only real cure for a fever."

"And you're going to have a cold bath when you're feverish?"

"I told you, I've got polluted. If I don't have a bath I can't say my prayers."

Shahed would have felt his brother's brow to see how much of a temperature he had, only he didn't dare to. There was a gulf separating the two brothers. After Irtazuddin had been born five other siblings had followed, before finally Shahed himself came into the world. Incredibly, each of the five intervening children had died within a month of his or her birth. They all had the same symptoms – their arms and legs went cold and they had convulsions and breathing difficulties. The very same symptoms appeared in Shahed on the fifteenth day of his life. His arms and legs went cold, and he had terrible convulsions. His father was driven half out of his mind, and he rushed to the mosque and said to the imam, "I once committed a great sin. There is only one reason my children keep dying – it's a punishment for my sin. I shall publicly confess to my sin, if only God will spare my son's life."

It emerged that he had once committed a murder. He confessed and handed himself in to the police, was tried and sentenced to life imprisonment. He went off to jail with a smile on his face, for the life of his youngest son had been spared. He died in prison. Irtazuddin had taken on responsibility for running the household from an early age. He brought up his younger brother almost as his own child. For many years Shahed was unable to get to sleep unless he was lying in Irtazuddin's arms. Once when he was in Class III Shahed had contracted typhoid, and for eight of the twenty-one days during which the fever raged Irtazuddin had sat nursing his little brother in his lap. The boy would start crying if Irtazuddin put him down even for a moment, then relax as soon as he was picked up again. The relationship that existed between Irtazuddin and Shahed was not so much that of two brothers as one of a father and his son.

"Listen, *bhai jan*," said Shahed now, "you just bolt the front door and go and have your bath, while I pop out and fetch Asmani. I won't take long, I'll just dash over there and come straight back again."

"But she's gone to see her mother, who is ill," protested Irtazuddin in irritation. "Why drag her back? What sense is there in that?"

"There's nothing wrong with my mother-in-law," confessed Shahed guiltily. "I was telling a lie. Asmani ran away because we'd had a quarrel."

Irtazuddin contemplated his younger brother with disfavour. What was all this, a husband and wife quarrelling? A woman is a giver of birth, a progenitrix; whatever she might say or do, one should never get angry with her. It was a form of cowardice to get angry with a woman; only weak, incapable men got angry with their wives.

"It won't take long, elder brother," said Shahed. "I'll get a baby taxi for the journey there and back."

"Very well."

The most trivial matter had given rise to this disagreement between Asmani and Shahed. That was the funny thing, all their major quarrels were sparked off by mere trifles. The origin of today's dispute had been the bolt on the bathroom door. It had recently become detached and fallen off. For several days now Asmani had been asking Shahed to buy three half-inch nails to fix it. Each time he had promised he would get them, and then forgotten to do so.

So a row had flared up between Asmani and Shahed over this bolt, a truly awesome row. After shopping at the bazaar in Mohammedpur that afternoon Shahed had returned home with some groceries, and the moment he had come through the door Asmani had said, "Have you got those nails?"

Shahed had started taking off his outdoor clothes. "You keep going on and on about those nails," he had said. "I'm fed up with hearing about them. You always have an axe to grind, don't you? You can't talk about anything except nails. Once you've got an idea into your thick head it won't budge."

"So that means you haven't actually got them?" Asmani had asked.

"No, I haven't."

"Why didn't you get them?"

"I forgot. It isn't everyone who has a memory like yours. Not all of us are elephants who can remember every damn thing."

"So I suppose you're never going to get them at all?"

"I'll go and buy them this very minute," Shahed had snapped grimly. "I can't bear any more of this."

"What have I said that you can't bear?"

"You've said more than enough."

Then Shahed had stumped off, slamming the door behind him as he went in order to show how displeased he was. And then Asmani had felt bad. Poor chap, she had thought, he'd only just come home with the shopping, I needn't have brought up the subject of the nails straight away like that. I could have given the landlord's little brother-in-law Moznu the money to go and get them instead. Seeing as Shahed always forgets things it was wrong of me to harass him unnecessarily. Asmani had got quite annoyed with herself, and she had decided that when Shahed came back she would do something to make him get over his anger and cheer up all in one go. She knew a way of making Shahed cheer up, though the awkward thing was she felt ashamed to do it.

Three nails would have been enough, but Shahed had bought a whole kilogram of nails, plus a hammer and a screwdriver. With much banging and clonking he had gone and fixed the bathroom bolt himself. Then he had said to Asmani, "There you are, your bathroom is back in order. Now you can jolly well go to the bathroom, fasten your bolt and sit there. Sit there for two whole hours, and make sure you time yourself. If you come out before the two hours are up watch out for the consequences."

"Why should I go and sit in the bathroom?" Asmani had asked in a pained voice.

"Because the nails have been purchased and the bolt has been fixed, that's why. Nails, nails, nails! My life has been made a misery. The country is in a parlous state, there's no knowing whether my salary is going to be paid or not, or even whether I'll still have a job, but no, those things don't matter to you, just nails, nails, nails! You've made my life a misery."

"Made your life a misery?"

"Yes."

Asmani's eyes had filled with tears, but she was determined not to let Shahed see this. She had looked away and said, "All right, I'll see to it that your life is no longer made a misery on my account. From now on your life shall be made a bed of roses."

So saying she had gone into the kitchen. If she had remained in Shahed's presence he would have seen she was crying, and that was something she could not let happen. Weeping all the while, she had put the lentils on to boil, then prepared a dish of hard boiled eggs in curry sauce. At nine o'clock she had come and said to him calmly, "I'm off now."

"Why, where are you off to?" Shahed had asked in surprise.

"To Mum's place in Kolabagan. From now on I shall make *her* life a misery. I won't make your precious bed of roses a misery any more."

"Asmani, don't you think you're going a little bit too far?"

"No, I don't think so at all. I'm leaving the cupboard key on the dressing table. Please send all Runi's things over, but there's no need to send any of mine."

"So this is goodbye for ever?"

"Yes."

Runi had been asleep in Asmani's arms, clinging to her neck. Normally she would stay awake until eleven in the evening, but this time she had fallen asleep by nine. If she had been awake it would have been more difficult for Asmani to get away, for Runi never willingly let herself be parted from her father. Shahed had said impassively, "If you want to go, then do, though I hardly see the point in traipsing off in the middle of the night. Why not wait until morning and then go?"

"It's not a problem," Asmani had said, "Moznu is going to accompany me. I've already asked him to get hold of a rickshaw."

"Oh? When did you ask him?"

"Half an hour ago. I walked right past you, but you were too busy reading the newspaper to notice me."

There had been no trace of anger in Asmani's voice, as though no quarrel had taken place between them and everything was perfectly normal.

Shahed had thought quickly. What ought he to do, he had wondered. He could always beg for forgiveness, that might be the wisest thing. But he doubted whether begging her pardon would do the trick. Asmani was exceedingly angry and would not easily be pacified. She wanted to make him suffer. The best thing would be to allow some time for her anger to subside. If he turned up in Kolabagan a couple of days later looking really miserable, that would go a long way towards softening her. He would need to go there pretty late at night, around half past eleven or twelve – the advantage of going in the dead of night being that Asmani would never dream of letting him return home alone at such a late hour.

Thus there was no need to go out of his way to propitiate her at this stage; quite the reverse, it might be a good thing to display a bit of hard feeling on his own account. So adopting a severe expression Shahed had glared sullenly at Asmani to show her how offended he was, trying not to blink as he did so. Asmani had totally ignored her husband's serpent-like gaze and said calmly, "I'm going now. Mind you lock the door before going to bed."

"It's a matter for me to decide whether I lock the door at bedtime or leave it wide open; there's no call for you to offer advice. Go on, get moving, go to your mother and snuggle up in her arms."

"And be so kind as to wait more than twenty-four hours before you start dropping in at some ungodly hour asking me to come back."

"I would hardly go to such lengths to get you, seeing that you'd already satisfied my appetite within five years of our marriage."

Shahed had been about to say a few more cutting words, but before he had a chance to utter them Asmani had made her exit. For the next five minutes Shahed had remained sitting there in a dream. A wonderful idea had occurred to him. Asmani had set off in a rickshaw – how would it be if he went out quickly, grabbed a baby taxi and headed straight for Kolabagan. It would be quite a laugh! Asmani would get down from her rickshaw and see Shahed sitting in her mother's verandah, calmly reading the newspaper with a cup of tea in his hand.

But Shahed had not been able to put his plan into practice, because just as he had decided to go out and look for a baby taxi he had heard the voice of Irtazuddin Kashempuri calling, "Shahed, are you there? Shahed? Is this Shahed's house?"

Irtazuddin completed all the prayer cycles which he had missed earlier. It took him about an hour to finish the prayers. Then he hunted for a newspaper, found one and read it through, without skipping a single item. It was all about meetings and demonstrations; there was practically no other news at all. Offices and factories were ready to shut down at a mere hint from Sheikh Mujibur Rahman°, girls were being trained as guerrilla fighters, radio and TV stations had stopped broadcasting the Pakistan national anthem. He finished reading the newspaper, another half hour went by, and still Shahed hadn't returned. Irtazuddin was considerably vexed. What was this, disappearing for an hour and a half after promising he would just go there and come straight back again? A person's actions should always match his words. Since taking a bath Irtazuddin had started to feel hungry, and the fever which had been threatening to overcome him seemed to have abated for the time being. He got up and went into the kitchen to see if there was any food around, in which case he might have a bite to eat. There was a dish of curried eggs and some *dal*, but no rice. Of course he could always do the rice himself; he was used to cooking his own meals, and boiling up a few handfuls of rice was child's play. But Asmani wouldn't really like that. Even if she didn't actually say anything she would be annoyed. For some obscure reason women couldn't stand male members of their family being in the kitchen.

To pass the time Irtazuddin went out onto the verandah. It was a small verandah furnished with two cane chairs placed next to each other. You could get a glimpse of the road from there. Irtazuddin sat down in one of the chairs.

There was a slight breeze in the verandah, and the chair was comfortable. It was very pleasant sitting there and he was feeling quite drowsy. But he mustn't fall asleep. Why ever was Shahed taking such a long time? He oughtn't to risk travelling home with Asmani if it got any later. Irtazuddin was almost dozing off. He must snap out of it, otherwise Runi would come home to see her uncle asleep on the verandah with his mouth wide open, snoring loudly, and the sight would upset her. The image would stay stuck in her mind for the rest of her life, and whenever she thought of her uncle that scene would spring to her mind. Anything which makes a strong impression on a person in childhood remains with them for good.

Irtazuddin was desperately trying to ward off sleep, so he thought back to his wedding day. That was an infallible antidote to somnolence, like an injection of Coramine. The moment he recalled his wedding day every vestige of sleep would vanish! He could see it all in his mind's eye. As the bridegroom, he had arrived in the bride's village, Borolekha, accompanied by his delegation. A ceremonial arch formed by a pair of banana trees had been set up, carrying the legend "Welcomb". The spelling on it was wrong, "b" instead of "e". But the whole place had seemed to be in a trance. All the bride's relatives were keeping very quiet.

People were whispering in each other's ears. After a while news had spread that the bride had contracted cholera, and after suffering all day from diarrhoea and vomiting she had passed away just as the late afternoon prayer was due. Then word had gone round that she hadn't died after all but had been taken into town for treatment, although there was little chance of her surviving. The real truth didn't come out until much later. The girl had not been suffering from cholera, nor had she been taken anywhere; she had run away. She had caught a late night train to some faraway place with a distant male cousin of hers.

After that Irtazuddin had never got married. Nobody had really tried to persuade him to do so either; for he had had no guardian or elders to guide him.

Occasionally Irtazuddin would dream of the girl who had fled in the middle of the night. In these dreams she behaved as if she were his wife. Irtazuddin would then feel embarrassed, both during his dream and after he had woken from it. Once it was over he would appeal to God in a tragic tone, "Oh Lord and Sustainer! Why do you play these tricks on me? I am your worthless servant. Why, after I have put that girl right out of my mind, do you bring her back to me again? Only children play cruel tricks like that, but surely you are no child?"

Irtazuddin had fallen asleep lolling sideways in the chair. The moment he was asleep he dreamed of that girl. This time she had a child of about four or five years of age in her lap, who looked like Runi but was terribly thin. She seemed to be ill.

"Are you still asleep?" the woman was asking him. "Don't you realize what's going on out there? They're setting fire to people's homes, and the soldiers are shooting people. Come on, take her, and let's run for our lives!"

Irtazuddin knew that he was dreaming and that the scene would disappear as soon as he woke up. He made an effort to rouse himself, though it was not a serious effort as he was rather enjoying the dream. He was amused by the frightened face of the young woman (she was called Asma Begum) because he knew it was all fantasy and there was no real reason for her fear.

"What are you doing, still sitting there like that! Come on, take the child, she's running a fever."

"What's her name?" asked Irtazuddin shyly.

Asma was furious. "This is a fine time for fooling about, amidst all this danger! Don't you know your own daughter's name?"

Then without a further word she thrust the little girl into Irtazuddin's arms. The hue and cry outside got louder and louder. Somebody was crying, "Fire! Fire!" People were rushing about all over the place. A burst of machine gun fire could be heard. Irtazuddin took the child in his arms and hastened down into the street, which was filled with hundreds of people. Asma was clinging tightly to Irtazuddin's left arm. A beautiful young woman holding onto him as they ran along – this scene was rather embarrassing; shocking, in fact, and quite inexcusable from an Islamic point of view. Still, there was one good thing: nobody was paying any attention to them. It was like a scene from the Day of Judgment – each person there was concerned only for their own survival. Everyone was going, "Help! Help!" They were expecting some awful calamity, and everyone was petrified.

To add to the chaos, just as they were all fleeing in one direction a different crowd of people came running from the opposite direction, shouting "*Joy Bangla! Joy Bangla!*" Their shouting woke Irtazuddin up. To his surprise he saw that there really was a huge procession going past, hundreds of people thronging the road. They were carrying staves and spears, and yelling "*Joy Bangla! Joy Bangla!*" loudly enough to make the clouds reverberate. There was also a porter's cart trundling along, with a man astride it holding a sword.

Irtazuddin sat staring at the procession with a frown on his face. He did not like this chant of "*Joy Bangla*" – it was redolent of "*Joy Hind*", and that was not a good thing°. And all those sticks and spears were useless. Even a century ago the bamboo fortress built by the village revolutionary Titumir had proved ineffective. It had been a complete waste of effort. That was a sad thing about the Bengali race, they never put any effort into worthwhile things, only into futile projects.

Shahed returned home around midnight, looking downcast. There was no-one else with him, he had come back alone.

"How is it you took so long?" asked Irtazuddin.

"I didn't find them," replied Shahed weakly, staring at the ground.

"What do you mean, you didn't find them?"

"My mother-in-law has a cousin who lives in a lane near Green Road. They had all gone off to see her. I was waiting all that time in the hope that they'd come back, but they didn't. I expect they're going to stay there overnight; they sometimes do. That woman is very fond of Runi. She doesn't have any children of her own, and treats Runi as a daughter. Doubtless she insisted on their staying."

Once again Irtazuddin felt annoyed. Shahed was telling lies, he was making things up as he went along. Why not simply admit that his wife had refused to come home? What was the point of spinning elaborate yarns? Lying was something that soon became a habit, and then a fellow would find himself saying things which were not true even when he had no reason to do so.

"Do you want to go to bed now, *bhai jan*? It's quite late, high time to turn in. Shall I get your bed ready for you?"

"Please do."

"Are you really going to sleep without eating anything? Aren't you hungry?"

Although Irtazuddin was feeling hungry he said no. That was a lie, but if he admitted he was hungry it would mean some rice had to be prepared, and Shahed would be put on the spot. Rather than let his elder brother get on with it himself, he would insist on flapping about and cooking the rice for him. Surely it was better to tell a lie than let that happen. A lie? A white lie, but a lie nonetheless. Well intentioned lies were no less reprehensible than ill intentioned ones. Irtazuddin looked at his brother and said, "I was wrong to tell you I wasn't hungry, that was a lie. I do feel hungry. However I won't have anything to eat, I'm going to go to bed. Please get the bed ready for me, but don't put up the mosquito net."

"You won't get any sleep if I don't put the mosquito net up. There are a lot of mosquitoes around."

"Never mind if there are. I can never get to sleep inside a net, I feel suffocated."

Shahed made up a bed for his brother in the sitting room. He also hunted out a palm-leaf fan for him. Without a doubt Irtazuddin would switch off the ceiling fan before getting into bed, because he found it impossible to sleep in the draught from an electric fan; he always said electric fans gave him an unsettled feeling.

There really were a lot of mosquitoes. They were all around Irtazuddin, making that high-pitched whine of theirs. Goodness knows what they'd be like when he switched off the light. Perhaps he would be forced to wrap himself in a sheet to sleep, even in this heat. Mosquitoes were one of the reasons Irtazuddin disliked coming to Dhaka.

"Why are you waiting up?" he asked his brother. "There's no point. Go to bed."

Shahed was feeling like chatting for a while. He never normally went to bed before one thirty or two a.m., and it was now only half past twelve. In addition to that he was feeling depressed after his trip to his mother-in-law's place. It was unbelievable, Asmani had refused to come with him even when he'd told her about his elder brother's arrival. "Elder brother is here," he had pleaded abjectly, "Do come home, please do!" In reply Asmani had said, "Well, you can jolly well sit him on your lap and stuff yourself. There's no need for me to be there."

Shahed had never thought Asmani capable of saying anything like that. It had made him feel quite downhearted. Now he would have liked to enjoy a nice chat with his brother to get rid of his gloom, but it sounded as if Irtazuddin was in no mood for chatting.

"Have you come to Dhaka for any specific purpose, brother," he asked, "or just for a visit?"

"For a purpose. I came to see you and your family, that is a purpose, is it not?"

"Oh, yes."

"And I want to get hold of some good quality perfume. Mine has run out."

"I'll go and buy some for you."

"There will be no need for you to do that. You know nothing about the different qualities of essential oils; I shall do the buying myself. I also need to get a new flag for the school. The old one has got bleached from the sunlight."

"What kind of flag?" Shahed enquired in alarm.

"A national flag, of course!" said Irtazuddin in exasperation. "What other kind of flag could it be?"

"I don't think you ought to buy one, brother."

"Why not?"

"Because our country is going for independence, and there'll be a different national flag."

"Don't give me that nonsense. Our country already has its independence, so how can it go for more?"

"Brother," said Shahed gently, "you don't understand the situation."

"It's you lot who don't understand," said Irtazuddin, cutting him short. "You can't make a country independent just by shouting *'Joy Bangla'* a few times. Wait until the Pakistan army steps in, that'll be the end of *'Joy Bangla'*."

"Brother," Shahed started, "can I tell you something?"

"There's no need," replied Irtazuddin in irritation. "Go to bed now. We can talk in the morning. Please turn off the ceiling fan as you go."

"How long are you going to stay in Dhaka?"

"I shall depart tomorrow morning, *inshallah*."

"No, please stay another day."

"What would be the point in staying?"

Shahed did not reply. Irtazuddin had this way of countering one question with another, and as his counter-questions tended to come as a surprise it wasn't always easy to respond off the top of one's head.

Yawning, Irtazuddin said, "I would have stayed on, as I really wanted to see how much Runi has grown. But there's nothing to be done, school is in session. I can't neglect my school duties just to satisfy my own whims. School comes first, the rest comes after. A person has to operate like a compass, you see. A compass keeps to a fixed bearing, and so should a person. I keep my mental compass needle trained towards the school, and everything else follows from that."

Irtazuddin felt as if he was delivering a lecture in class. This was a constant problem: as soon as he started talking about something, a lecturing tone would creep in. This was one of the less desirable results of having been a teacher for so long; one treated everyone else as if they were a pupil.

"Shahed."

"Yes?"

"Do you have any puffed rice or anything like that in the house? I'm feeling slightly peckish."

Shahed got up. His face looked strained, for he was pretty sure there was no snack food in the house, and even if there was he was unlikely to find it. Certainly there was neither puffed rice nor rice flakes. Possibly there was some Bombay mix somewhere, but which of the countless tins and jars in the kitchen was it lurking in? Anyway you couldn't offer stale Bombay mix to someone who was feeling hungry.

He found a glass half full of milk under a saucer. The milk smelled vaguely sour – it was hard to tell whether or not it had gone off. Rather shamefacedly Shahed placed the glass of milk in front of his brother. "I couldn't find anything except this," he said in embarrassment.

Irtazuddin drank the milk in one draught. While doing so he realized it had gone off, but as Shahed would be hurt if he left any he drained the glass and said gratefully, "Thanks be to God. *Alhamdulillah*."

"Had that milk gone off?" asked Shahed.

"No."

Another lie. There was no virtue in hurting Shahed's feelings, but had it been right to resort to lying? No, it hadn't. If someone got hurt from hearing the truth, let them get hurt.

"The milk had gone a bit sour," said Irtazuddin, "but it was not unpleasant to drink."

Drinking the milk had reminded him of an interesting thing. In June last year he had witnessed a curious incident involving milk drinking at Santahar railway station. He had been on his way to Bogra, and he was having to wait four hours in Santahar for his connection. His train was due at five p.m. He had made himself comfortable in an easy chair in the station waiting room, and had dropped off to sleep. Suddenly he had woken up to find the waiting room filled with people. There was an air of excitement, as at an important public meeting. A man was sitting there who was clearly the centre of attention, and who looked familiar though Irtazuddin could not place him. He was a solidly built fellow with a round cap on his head, and his face was framed in a white beard. Somebody had come up and handed him a glass filled to the brim with milk, saying obsequiously, "This is milk from my own cow which I have brought for your reverence." The man, who had the look of an Islamic cleric, had retorted, "I don't really feel like having it; but as milk and honey were the two favourite drinks of our Prophet, here goes!" Saying which he had drained the glass in one gulp, and then exclaimed, "*Alhamdulillah*! That was excellent milk; from a black cow, I take it?"

"Yes, your reverence," replied the man who had brought it, bowing low in respect.

"I could tell as soon as I tasted the milk. Only black cows can produce such sweet milk."

And at that moment Irtazuddin had recognized the clerical gentleman: it was Moulana Bhashani°. He had seen many photos of him in the newspapers, but this was the first time he had seen him in the flesh.

Irtazuddin had risen to his feet at once and greeted him with a *salaam*. Moulana Bhashani had smiled at him and asked, "Did you have a good nap?" as if they had been old friends.

Humbly, Irtazuddin had replied, "Yes, sir."

"I'm sorry I disturbed your sleep; please don't take it the wrong way."

Then Irtazuddin had felt even more embarrassed. As there was no question of sitting lounging in an easy chair in the presence of such a famous person, he had remained standing. By that time the Moulana had changed the subject and was talking to a thin gentleman wearing a European style suit.

"Let me tell you what things have come to in this country. I passed through five different villages and I couldn't get change for a fifty rupee note anywhere –

that's the state we're in. Something has to be done about it. So do something. There must be no more dilly-dallying, enough time has already been wasted."

Moulana Bhashani had performed his late afternoon prayer in the waiting room in the company of a sizeable congregation which included Irtazuddin. As a result of joining this prayer meeting Irtazuddin had missed his train: for the Moulana had ended with a lengthy supplication lasting forty minutes, in the midst of which Irtazuddin's train had drawn out of the station. For a moment Irtazuddin had thought of tearing himself away from the prayers and catching his train, but in the event he hadn't done so. It was not right to leave while a prayer was being said, it would be a sign of discourtesy, and he had no wish to be rude to such a distinguished person. Missing a train wasn't such a big deal anyway – if you missed one you could catch the next – but it wasn't often that you came across a man like Moulana Bhashani.

Serving the stale milk seemed to have made Shahed quite miserable. Irtazuddin couldn't decide whether telling him the story about Moulana Bhashani would cheer him up or not.

"You might as well lie down now, brother," said Shahed.

Irtazuddin got into bed. "Turn off the fan, will you," he said.

"Why not leave it on, it's very hot."

"How many times must I tell you, I can't sleep when there's a draught from the fan."

Shahed switched off the fan.

Irtazuddin was tired out, and fell asleep straight away. He slept soundly the whole night through. He hadn't had such a restful sleep for a long time. When he woke up he saw to his surprise that a mosquito net had been strung up over him, and the ceiling fan was whirring at top speed. Shahed had seen to all that while he had been asleep, and it hadn't disturbed his sleep at all; in fact he had slept much better than usual. Perhaps he had been wrong all this time in his notions about mosquito nets and fans. He must reform his ideas. Making mistakes was human; the good thing was that one always had the opportunity to correct them.

2

Shahed's office was in Motijheel. It wasn't one of your streamlined modern offices, far from it, it was a positively shambolic one. Goods were stacked all over the place among the desks and chairs where the staff worked, despite the fact that there was a designated store room down on the ground floor. Offices don't normally have beds in them, but there was a wooden framed bedstead standing in this one; employees were often to be seen stretched out on the bed, and nobody thought anything of it. The building was a two storeyed one sandwiched between seven and eight storey blocks, and was dirty yellow in hue ("shit-coloured" in Shahed's words). It carried a disproportionately huge signboard bearing the legend "United Commercial". Some of the lettering on the signboard had flaked away, but nobody seemed bothered by that either.

It was an office with multiple functions: insurance, indenting, share dealing and more. The proprietor's name was Moin Arafi. He had formerly lived in Murshidabad District° in West Bengal. At Partition° he had crossed into East Pakistan bringing with him two hundred rupees, a silver hookah and an expensive shawl. He had sold the shawl and, to start with, entered the fruit trade. With great difficulty he had managed to hang onto his silver hookah. And now he smoked the hookah in his office. Moin Arafi had a theory that hookahs talked when you sucked them, and said he liked listening to his when he had nothing better to do. Nowadays Moin Arafi was not just a millionaire, but whatever the next grade is above that. He had taken up every business idea which had ever occurred to him, and money had flowed into his coffers like water.

Moin Arafi was sixty years old, a man of short, stocky build, light skinned, bald headed but with a dashing brown moustache. He treated his employees with great indulgence. Instead of calling for someone when he needed them, he would go and seek them out himself. He was always affable in manner, and was given to exclaiming in English, "Be happy, man! Be happy!"

He was known in the office as "Mr B.Happy", and everyone in the workforce genuinely liked him. Whenever there was a wedding anniversary, a child's birthday or a daughter's engagement party, Mr B.Happy would be invited to it, and whether or not he attended the function he would always send a present, and an expensive one at that.

Shahed was standing outside the office feeling exceedingly grumpy. It was nine o'clock, and the office wouldn't open until ten. He had come an hour too early. He could think of plenty of good reasons for arriving late at the office, but only one possible reason for getting there an hour early – sheer stupidity. Shahed wasn't actually stupid; he had done what he had done in order to show Asmani how cross he was. Still, if he hadn't made such a fine display of anger he would never have had to loiter outside the office an hour before opening time.

After spending four days at her parents' home Asmani had turned up this morning looking very cheerful and carrying a small tiffin carrier in one hand. Acting as if nothing at all had happened between them she had said to Shahed, "Hey, can you go and pay the rickshaw puller please, I don't have any change. And have you had your breakfast yet? Because I've brought some for you."

Without giving any reply Shahed had gone out to pay the rickshaw puller's fare. For a moment he had toyed with the idea of hiring the rickshaw for himself and going to the Dilbag Restaurant, where he could have parathas and *bundia* for breakfast and then carry straight on to the office. That would show her that he was annoyed. But he had realized he couldn't do that because he hadn't yet given

Runi her cuddle. It was four whole days since he had last seen his little daughter, and to him it seemed more like four years.

The newspaper had been delivered, and Shahed had gone back into the house with it in his hand. He had decided not to reply to any of Asmani's questions, but to sit there with his face buried in the paper. To his surprise he noticed that Asmani was busy tidying the house in a perfectly normal way. Even more surprising was Runi's behaviour: she was drawing a picture on a sheet of paper and not giving Shahed a single glance; it was as if she no longer recognized her own father.

"What did you do for meals these past few days?" Asmani had asked. "Did you do your own cooking, or did you eat out?"

"I ate out," Shahed had said in a dull voice.

"When did elder brother go?"

Shahed had been tempted to ask what difference that made to her, but he had suppressed the temptation and replied, "The day after he came."

"I'd written asking him to bring some dried mango paste when he came; did he bring it?"

Shahed had said nothing. It was perfectly clear that Asmani was saying all these things just to get back into his good books. It was just small talk, and there was no point in reciprocating.

"Shall I get your breakfast ready?" Asmani had asked. "I've got some rice-flour chapatis and pigeon curry."

"I don't eat pigeon meat."

"Why ever not?"

"It's not something I can explain. I don't eat it, and that's that."

"Well, would you have some chapatis with a different kind of meat?"

Shahed had glared at her sullenly. A suppressed smile was hovering on her face.

"I know you don't eat pigeon meat," Asmani had said. "It was mother who cooked a pigeon curry. But I've brought some leftover beef curry from the fridge. I'll just heat it up, and then you can have it."

Shahed had said nothing, but had gone on reading the newspaper with deep concentration. He was most upset about Runi. Where had she learned this trick of pretending not to know her father? She must have got it from her mother. Why was she so desperate to draw those squiggly pictures just now? And another thing, there was a bandage on her left arm; wasn't she going to tell him all about how she got hurt?

"Hello Mr *Rage* Kumar°!" Asmani had said. "Listen, if you think I'm going to say sorry you've got another think coming. I was perfectly within my rights losing patience with you and spending four days with my mother. However it was very wrong of me not to come and say hello to your elder brother. I'm prepared to beg his pardon for my transgression. But why should I beg pardon from you?"

"I'm not asking you to beg my pardon," Shahed had snapped. "Why are you going on like this?"

"If you can't speak to me in a normal fashion," Asmani had retorted, "I shall go back to my mother's place, I'm warning you."

"Go by all means, if you wish to."

"I've warmed up the meat, now do come along and have breakfast. All right, I admit it, I was naughty. Sorry. But I can't touch your feet in contrition just now. I'll do the foot touching stuff later on – tonight. Honestly I shall!"

After Asmani had said that, Shahed ought to have calmed down and gone to eat his breakfast. Rice flour chapatis and meat curry with a good gravy were things he really loved. Maybe it was Asmani's unconditional surrender that had suddenly made him feel even angrier than before. He had flung down the newspaper and stalked stiffly out of the room. The moment he had boarded the rickshaw his fury had subsided; but by then it had been too late to turn back. The rickshaw puller had started pedalling.

Shahed was standing there in front of his office. The office was now open, and if he wished he could go in and sit at his desk. Just next to the office was a kind of bamboo hut which functioned as a restaurant. The owner was a Bihari man, and every morning he used to cook large flimsy chapatis and a tasty chicken dish called *lotpoti*. It would be easy enough to send the office boy there to get a take-away meal. Shahed was quite hungry and his chest was hurting, but still he didn't feel like going into the office; he was feeling like going back home.

"How are you, young man?"

Shahed looked round in surprise. Mr B.Happy was standing right behind him. The fellow might be stout, but he trod very softly.

"What weighty assignment can have brought you to the office so early?"

"Good morning, sir! You're well, sir, I hope?"

"Of course I'm well! And how is your wee girl, the little baby?"

"Very well, sir."

"Be happy, young man! Be happy!"

So saying, Mr Arafi placed a hand on Shahed's shoulder. Shahed knew he would keep it there while they walked into the office together. It was hard to say how much of his manner was genuine friendliness and how much was put on. As a rule one could not expect kid glove treatment from a boss, and when one did receive a compliment one wondered whether there was something wrong somewhere.

"Mr Shahed."

"Yes, sir?"

"Business has gone quiet. But shouting *'Joy Bangla'* isn't going fill anybody's belly. Am I not right?"

One is expected to nod one's head in agreement at anything the boss may say. Shahed nodded his head.

"Be happy, young man, be happy!" said Moin Arafi, smiling broadly.

Shahed promised himself that one day, if a suitable opportunity arose, he would ask Mr B.Happy when he had started using that phrase. Who had been the first person he had said "be happy" to?

Another day had begun at the office, but in a rather desultory fashion. Quite a few members of staff hadn't turned up, and there was a feeling of incompleteness. In the old days this office had been very busy; all kinds of people had been running around bent on their various different tasks, the stores section on the ground floor had been a hive of activity, there had been altercations and scuffles. Now it seemed empty. There were no goods in the store room, and the office staff had nothing to do. Where previously the head clerk, Asgar Ali Dewan, had signed off a thousand vouchers, now he was only having fifteen or twenty to sign. Such work as he had was finished by midday, and then he was free to sit comfortably chewing betel leaf and discussing the future of the country. This was a subject dear to his heart. In his view God had printed over the country's prospects, in bold lettering, the word "CLOSED", just as a closed sign might be hung in front of a restaurant. He believed that the country had achieved nothing in the past, and would achieve nothing in the future. If anyone disagreed with him he would say sarcastically, "What was your name again? Abdul Goni, isn't that it? Well, now you can add the surname Infant. Your full name is now Abdul Goni Infant, because your intellectual capacity is at infant level. Got it?"

None of the others went near Mr Dewan. Why go out of one's way to be labelled an infant?

At around midday Mr Dewan had just seated himself comfortably with a quid of betel leaf and tobacco in his mouth. All of a sudden he beckoned to Shahed. "Come here a moment," he said, "there's something I want to tell you."

"I'm not in a mood to discuss the future of the nation," said Shahed.

"Come over here," repeated Mr Dewan irritably. "It's something quite different, but I can't say what it is until we can talk in privacy. It's an important matter."

Much against his will Shahed got up and went over. He sat facing Mr Dewan.

"Would you like some betel leaf?" offered Mr Dewan.

"I don't eat betel leaf," replied Shahed.

"All the more reason for having some. Try some and see what it's like."

"Just tell me what the important matter is."

"What's the rush?" asked Mr Dewan, masticating steadily. "There's no work at the moment, so there's no hurry. I've got a letter for you."

"What letter?"

"Yesterday, when you were absent, Mr Gourango was looking everywhere for you. He gave me a letter for you, with 'urgent' written on the envelope."

"Then let me have the letter, please."

"All right, all right, I'm going to give it to you! Why are you so impatient? Now, do you have any idea which way the country is going?"

"No."

"The national economy has been totally destroyed, and nobody has any clue. Our last hope is America and its PL480 wheat. If the wheat comes to an end so shall we."

"Oh, really," said Shahed.

Lowering his voice, Mr Dewan hissed, "Did you know our company is being sold?"

"No, I didn't know that."

"Mr B.Happy, the one you all regard as a model of perfection, is secretly selling everything off. He's going to run away to Karachi with the cash. His family have gone already, only he has stayed on. There'll be no wages next month. We'll have to stick our thumbs in sugar and suck them; or, if we happen to have diabetes, just suck our thumbs plain and simple."

"Who told you the company is being sold?" asked Shahed.

"Does anyone intentionally divulge secret information like that? I can just tell, by reading between the lines. But as for the boss' family going to Karachi, I know that for a fact. I purchased their PIA tickets."

"Is the boss living on his own, then?"

"I've no idea whether he's living on his own or not, but what I do know is that his family have done a flit. Mr B.Happy should from now on be known as Mr B.Sad."

"Please hand me the letter, I must go now," said Shahed, standing up.

"Don't you like listening to these things?" asked Mr Dewan. "The main problem with the truth is that people don't like hearing it, and similarly they don't like anybody who speaks the truth. People love hearing fiction, and they have great affection for anyone who tells lies. Anyway, if you don't want to chat with me that's that. Here, take it, here's Mr Gourango's letter."

Shahed did not have a particularly close relationship with Gourango. They had both joined the firm the same day, and by pure chance they had both been wearing yellowish coloured kaftans. "What a coincidence!" Gourango had said to Shahed, "we tally in every respect!"

An even closer connection had been discovered: each of them had a daughter as their first and only child, and while Shahed's was called Runi, Gourango's was called Runu.

As they sat drinking tea in the canteen after work that day, Gourango had referred to these coincidences and said, "It seems very clear to me that God is behind all this. We're going to find that events in the life of one of us will be matched by events in the life of the other. If I come to the office wearing a blue shirt, so will you. When a happy occasion takes place in my family something similar will happen in yours. If my grandmother dies, yours will pass away on the same day."

Shahed had laughed.

"Why do you laugh?" Gourango had asked.

"No, I just laughed, for no special reason," Shahed had said.

"I was talking about a serious subject," Gourango had said, offended, "so why did you make fun of it?"

"I'm sorry."

"No, really, please don't do things like that. I feel hurt."

And soon enough Shahed had discovered that it was Gourango's nature to feel hurt about the most trivial things. For example one day Gourango had turned up, sat down in front of Shahed's desk and said without further ado, "From today I'm going to call you *tui* instead of *apni*°, and you're to do the same with me." And he added in English, "This is final."

"But why...?" Shahed had asked in surprise.

Gourango's voice had filled with mortification. "Because," he had said, "we are friends. That is why. Have you ever heard of intimate friends addressing each other as *apni*?"

Shahed had said nothing.

"You're not in agreement?"

"We've known each other for less than a month," Shahed had replied, "wouldn't it look a bit odd if all of a sudden we started addressing each other in such intimate terms?"

"Look odd to whom?" Gourango had demanded.

"Oh, everyone," Shahed had answered.

"Very well then," Gourango had declared. "There's no need for you to use *tui* with me, and I shall not use it with you either. You have my word for it that I shan't talk to you at all unless it's absolutely necessary."

Gourango had gone back to his own desk. Soon afterwards Shahed had seen him saying something to another of the clerks and then changing desks with him. Gourango's old desk had been right in front of Shahed's, but the new one was much further away. Then after four or five days there he had moved back to his former location, and the same afternoon after closing time he had dragged Shahed to the canteen to stand him a cup of tea.

Shahed was quite tickled by some of Gourango's absurd infantile antics, though others he found more tiresome.

The most tiresome occasions were when Gourango invited him to his house for a meal. Invariably on those evenings Gourango would hit the bottle, and two shots of any spirit were enough to make him tipsy. After that there would be no knowing what he would say or do. One minute he would be roaring with laughter, the next he would be weeping or coming over to clutch Shahed's feet in abject homage. It was useless to talk of getting up and going home after the meal was over: Gourango would absolutely refuse to let him go. No, no, you must stay the night, he would say. Eventually it would reach the stage where Gourango's wife Nilima would come in and say to Shahed in a wretched tone, "Please, brother, do stay the night. If you go he'll make life hell for me, and start sobbing and smashing things." And, much against his will, Shahed would have to sleep over.

Shahed was sitting there with Gourango's letter in his hand. He hardly had the courage to open it, being in no doubt that it contained some kind of invitation.

This is what Gourango had written in formal old fashioned Bengali:

My dear buddy,

Two extremely significant events have occurred in my life. Exceedingly, immensely significant, so much so that it is not possible to mention them in a letter. Having come to the office and failed to find you here, I am returning to my dwelling in despair. Buddy, the moment you receive my letter, regardless of where and in what condition you may be, you must come to my house at once. If you do not come, I swear to God that I shall never speak to you again in my life. I have taken three days of earned leave and am encamped in my residence waiting for you.

Gourango

Impossible, thought Shahed, impossible to the power of ten. There could be no question of going there. He hadn't been able to talk to his own daughter for the past four days, and going to Gourango's house in Old Dhaka would mean not being able to return home at night. Another day would go by without his being able to spend time with his daughter.

Closing time at the office was five p.m., but it had hardly struck three before employees started to get up and go. Mr B.Happy had left the office at lunchtime; he was scheduled to go to Chittagong for some reason (something to do with clearance of goods from a ship in Chittagong port), and wouldn't be back for a couple of days. There was little point in Shahed's staying at his desk until five o'clock in an office empty of employees.

Shahed got up at around four o'clock. Mr Dewan was sitting there on his own. He never left his post before official closing time. "Why not stay on a bit longer," he suggested to Shahed. "Then we two colleagues can leave the office together."

"I've got things to do," replied Shahed.

"What Bengali citizen has anything to do these days?" sneered Mr Dewan. "That is, apart from shouting slogans at the top of their voice like a bullfrog in the rainy season – '*Joy Bangla! Joy Bangla!*' Do you know what slogan people should actually be shouting now? It should be '*Noy Bangla! Noy Bangla°!*' In other words, not Bengal but something else. Listen to me, I'm telling you, Mr Shahed, there's still time. If we wish to survive we need to change our whole culture. We must change our dress: there must be no more lungis and saris. We must change our eating habits: no fish, no rice. The Bengali language must be discarded, we must talk in some other language – maybe Urdu or Hindi or Panjabi. Do you follow me, or perhaps you don't get it?"

"I think it's you who need to get the true picture."

"How about a cup of tea? Come on, let me stand you a farewell cup of tea."

"I won't have any tea, thankyou."

"In that case there's no point in my holding you. You may go. *'Noy Bangla!'*.

On the way home Shahed bought a whole *seer* weight of *rasagolla*° from Moron Chand's sweetmeat shop°. *Rasagolla* were Asmani's favourite sweetmeat, and she had her own particular way of savouring them. First she would squeeze out the syrup and eat the ball plain; and then she would lap up all the syrup. There are childish traits in every adult's behaviour, and Asmani's method of consuming *rasagolla* had that childish element in it. Shahed's point in taking home Asmani's favourite type of sweetmeat was to convey to her, without words, the message "I'm sorry." The poor girl had gone to the trouble of heating up his food and putting it on the table for him this morning, and he had made a show of being offended, and had stalked out – that had been quite wrong of him.

A bird seller sometimes used to set up his pitch in front of the *Ittefaq*° office. He sold caged birds: parrots, munias, gallinules, doves. It would make a wonderful treat for Runi if he bought a bird and took it home for her. She would rush all over the house with the cage in her hand. Buying birds was a waste of money, for after a few days they would have to be set free; but right now it was a matter of giving pleasure to a daughter he hadn't spoken to for four days, so it would be justifiable to buy a few inexpensive munias. Shahed got a rickshaw and set out for the place by the *Ittefaq* office to find the bird man. He bought five munias for one and a half rupees, with a cage thrown in free.

Shahed got back home at five in the afternoon, with the sweetmeats in one hand and the bird cage in the other. He had an almost superstitious foreboding that he was going to arrive home only to find the house empty. The door would be padlocked and a note would be tucked behind the lock: "Gone away." Asmani would never let him go unpunished after he had rejected her breakfast and stormed out of the house that morning.

But there was no padlock on the door. Suddenly Shahed's heart was filled with joy and his humble abode seemed as precious as Rabindranath Tagore's° "No riches, no pomp, just a dear little nest." He felt it was worth surviving after all; being alive was reward enough in itself.

When she saw him Asmani asked in a perfectly normal tone, "Do you want your tea now, or after your bath?" It was Shahed's habit to have a wash down with hot water on his return from the office, and then take tea.

"I'll have a cup now, and another after I've had my bath," said Shahed.

"You haven't been buying birds again, have you," Asmani went on. "Who's going to look after them? Runi will get bored with them after a couple of days, and then what will happen?"

Instead of replying Shahed smiled a smile which was supposed to make it clear that there was now no unfinished business between the two of them.

"There's some hot water on the stove," said Asmani. "I'll pour it into the bucket for you."

"That's all right, I can do the pouring," said Shahed. "Where's Runi?"

"She isn't here," replied Asmani. "She's gone to my Mum's."

"Gone to your Mum's? What's all this about?"

"It isn't about anything. A little girl has gone to see her granny, it's as simple as that. My younger brother dropped in and she went off with him."

"I see," said Shahed.

He could hardly control his fury. It seemed crystal clear, Asmani was taking her revenge for what he had done that morning at breakfast. She had sent their daughter away to her mother's house. He ought to give her a stern rebuke, but he hadn't the stomach for it.

Asmani came along with his cup of tea and set it down in front of him.

"Why did you let Runi go there on her own?" he asked. "You could have gone with her."

"I *am* going to go," replied Asmani. "I was merely waiting until you came home. I'll be off any minute now."

"So you're going away too?"

"Yes."

"May I know why?"

"I don't feel like arguing about trivial things with you all the time, that's why. I'm going to have a few days of peace. I'm going to read books and listen to music. I'm going to relax."

"Very well," said Shahed.

"I've put the hot water in the bathroom," said Asmani. "You can have your bath now if you want to."

When he emerged after having his bath, Shahed realized Asmani was no longer in the house. She really had gone. Shahed went to his chair on the verandah and stayed sitting there until eight in the evening. Then he decided he would go over to Gourango's place; he could stay there overnight. He took the pot of *rasagolla* with him, and in the other hand the cage full of birds. He was feeling every bit as angry with his little daughter as he was with Asmani, and decided there was no point in giving the birds to Runi; he would give them to Gourango's daughter instead.

Gourango lived near Bangsal Road in Old Dhaka, in a side lane off a back street off another back street. The last bit was so narrow it looked as if a rickshaw couldn't get through it, yet rickshaws did go down there. No wider than a ribbon, the lane had a deep gutter on either side, and Shahed knew there would be dead cats and chicken entrails here and there in the gutter, and of course there would be an awful smell. He would ask himself why on earth he ever came to such a place. Anyone not used to walking along the lane would miss their footing and stumble into the open drain.

The building in which Gourango lived was a three-storeyed one. On the ground floor there was a shop selling cement and steel rod. Gourango lived on the first floor. On the top storey lived Gourango's father-in-law Haribhajan Saha. People of the Saha° sub-caste are usually sweet-tongued, but this gentleman was distrustful by nature and never spoke to anyone in a civil manner. The fashion for wearing the *dhoti* had gone out long ago in East Bengal, yet Haribhajan Saha still wore a *dhoti*. Relations between Gourango and his father-in-law were strained; they were hardly on speaking terms. When his wife was not present Gourango used to refer to his father-in-law as "that old bat". The building belonged to the old man, and Gourango was supposed to pay him rent of fifty rupees a month, but he never gave him a penny.

Shahed reached Gourango's place at nine o'clock and Nilima let him in. "Ah, so you've come at last!" she exclaimed in a relieved tone. "Your friend is going out of his mind with anxiety. There's no knowing what he might have done if you hadn't arrived. He's been brooding over his glass since early evening. I'm sure there are going to be ructions tonight."

The expression "pretty as a picture" could have been specially made for Nilima. Shahed thought he had never in his life seen any young woman as gorgeous as she was, and there was precious little chance of seeing the likes of her in the future. The first time he had set eyes on her he had been quite breathtaken. Since then he had seen her on numerous occasions, yet every time he was breathtaken all over again. Today there must be some kind of festival or celebration going on, for she was nicely got up. She had a tuberose stuck into her styled hair, and was wearing an expensive homespun sari, a brand new one she must have been wearing for the first time, for it gave off the scent of new cotton. What need does such a woman have of dressing up, Shahed thought to himself.

From inside came Gourango's unnaturally thick voice saying, "Nilu, is that Shahed who has just come?" Gourango's voice always got coarser when he started drinking.

Before Nilima had time to say anything Gourango pushed the door open and emerged from the room. "I told you Shahed would come," he said, looking at his wife. "Did I tell you, or didn't I?"

"Yes, yes, you told me."

"Then why," asked Gourango peevishly, "did you say he wouldn't?"

"Because it's so late," replied Nilima. "I didn't think he would come here so late at night."

"Of course he would come when it's late. Of course he would. He would even come at one o'clock in the morning. I asked him to come, so to talk of his not coming... Are you casting aspersions on my buddy?"

"What are you shouting for?" Nilima asked quietly.

"How could I not shout, when you're saying these odd things about my buddy! I will shout, of course I will! Do you think I'm scared because your father lives on the top floor? Gourango wouldn't touch that old bat with his ****!" The obscenity slipped effortlessly from Gourango's lips. Nilima, deeply shamed, looked at Shahed in embarrassment.

"Please do the best you can with your friend," Nilima said to him. "That stuff goes to his head, he can't handle it, but he will insist on drinking some every evening. It's a real pain!"

"What's that you've brought in that cage?" Gourango suddenly enquired in amazement. "Some birds?" After a few drinks he always started using the intimate form of address with Shahed, *tui*, which is what he did now.

"That's right," replied Shahed.

"Ask Nilima – I told her you would bring some birds today, you just ask her. It suddenly came to me in the evening. I mentioned it to Runu first of all, and then I told the wife. You don't believe me. Well, you just ask them. Ask Runu first of all, and then ask her mother. You don't believe me, I can tell from the way you're looking at me."

"Why should I disbelieve you?" protested Shahed. "I believe what you say."

"Even so, you should ask them. Go on, I insist, you've got to ask."

"Sorry, brother," said Nilima, "but please go ahead and ask, just so as to end this pantomime. He'll go on and on repeating the same stuff until you do. It's true, he did say that you'd bring some birds when you came. You can believe me. He's going to carry on making a fuss until you do believe that."

"Are you by any chance under the impression," asked Gourango, "that I'm drunk?"

"Yes," said Nilima.

"So you're accusing me of being drunk in front of my dear buddy?" complained Gourango in a pained voice. "And on this very special day too?"

"So what is this special occasion?" asked Shahed. "Is it your wedding anniversary?"

"No, nothing like that. No, it's just him making a lot of fuss about nothing."

Fixing his eyes on his wife Gourango said, "My buddy is going to stay with us overnight. You must get his room ready for him beforehand. He is used to having a sip of water every so often during the night, so you must provide what he needs, a jug of water and a glass."

"I know very well what is needed, if he does choose to stay," said Nilima.

"You know nothing whatever," retorted Gourango. "I'll tell you what you do know, and that's how to gabble. The queen of gabbling, that's who you are. That's the long and the short of it. Listen, you gabbler, you are not to remain in my presence any longer. The sight of you is making me angry. Go and get everything ready for my buddy to stay the night."

The reason for Gourango's inviting Shahed round became clear. Gourango's father-in-law had presented him with eighteen thousand rupees in cash.

"The old bat is entering his second childhood," explained Gourango in a low voice. "He's emigrating to India. The old codger doesn't have a grain of sense left in him. This country is going *Joy Bangla*, we Hindus are no longer going to be second class citizens, it'll be a case of *Proud son of the motherland On my native soil I stand*. Why are you emigrating, silly old twit? What are you going to do once you get to India? Tear out your grizzled ****, I suppose?"

"Well, now I know the first bit of good news," said Shahed. "What was the other bit?"

"Oh, the other bit was nothing," said Gourango.

"Well, let's hear it even if it's nothing."

"Nilu got through her radio audition successfully. Singing Tagore songs, you know. She got a Grade C."

"Oh! So she can sing, can she?" exclaimed Shahed in surprise. "I never had any idea she knew how to sing!"

"Huh, Tagore songs," growled Gourango in irritation, "it's hardly a question of knowing how. All you need in order to sing Tagore songs is to have a breathing defect and to put a nasal twang in your voice. Nilima has asthma and she's also good at talking through her nose."

"Could I hear some of her songs?"

"Don't you so much as utter the word 'song', I'm warning you. I simply cannot abide Nilima's panting way of singing. No, but what do you think of my sixth sense, tell me that? How accurately I predicted that you'd come here bearing a gift of birds. Wasn't my prediction amazingly accurate?"

"Indeed it was."

"I can predict all sorts of things. That old bat will have a fit and drop down dead when he reaches India, I can tell you that in advance. Mark my words."

Gourango took a long sip from his glass and fell asleep, just like that.

Shahed had to have his supper without Gourango. "I find it most embarrassing that you're having to eat on your own," said Nilima. "Runu isn't here, otherwise she could have eaten with you."

"Where is she then?"

"Upstairs with her granny. She isn't very well, she's got a temperature. I took those birds of yours up there and gave them to her, and she was delighted. Oh, there's something I want to tell you: my husband said nothing whatever about your bringing birds here. He's just been repeating whatever comes into his head, simply because he's had a drop too many. Listen, I want to ask you a favour: will you do it for me?"

"Of course," said Shahed.

"Your friend is so fond of you he would never refuse anything you asked. Would you ask him to lay off the bottle? I'm sure if you asked him he would give it up."

"Dear sister, I shall indeed ask him to do so."

At two o'clock in the morning Shahed was awakened by a confusion of noises. Gourango had woken up. Shortly afterwards he burst into Shahed's room dragging his wife behind him. "You wanted to hear her singing," he said in a sententious voice, "so here she is."

"The poor woman, she's been hard at work all day," said Shahed, "and now it's two o'clock in the morning. I'll come over and hear her singing some other time."

"What do you mean, some other time?" demanded Gourango. "You're going to hear her now. Wait till I fetch the *tabla* drums and harmonium."

"But who's going to play the *tabla*?" asked Shahed.

"I am," said Gourango. "Who did you think?"

Nilima sang. Shahed listened in amazement to her voice, which was that of a celestial chorister. It was as if someone far, far away was singing in wonderfully melodious tones:

> *The far bank rings with the peacock's cry,*
> *On this bank the cuckoo is silent - why?*

3

Police inspector Mobarak Hussain hadn't witnessed the dawn of a new day for a couple of years. He usually retired to bed at about one thirty in the morning; however he wasn't a good sleeper and he never fell asleep straight away. He would toss and turn, and it would often be three a.m. before he dozed off. A person who went to sleep at three in the morning could hardly expect to see the sunrise. But today he was up there on the roof, observing the dawn. The flat roof of his one-storeyed house in Sobhanbag was a pleasant place to be. Standing on the roof you could imagine you had been transported into the countryside, for there was greenery on all sides and it felt a bit like being in a forest. The sight of night fading away and day breaking over the trees was truly delightful, and enough to take anyone's breath away. Mobarak Hussain was now witnessing this sight, but it cannot be said that his breath was being taken away. He wasn't the kind of person whose heart could be much moved by anything he saw; and besides he was in a very gloomy frame of mind. He felt physically sick as well, and had a splitting headache. When one is in such a condition it is not easy for one's heart to dwell on the splendours of nature.

His wife had been in labour since early the previous evening. Her waters had broken at around one in the morning, since when she had been gritting her teeth in agony. The signs were not at all good, though Mobarak Hussain was not letting that worry him unduly. Women had an incredible tenacity of life, he thought, even more than the proverbial *koi* fish which goes on twitching even after it has been dismembered. They look as if they're done for, and yet they go on living. An experienced village midwife was with her, the one who had helped deliver her first three babies. To Mobarak Hussain's lasting regret those three had all been girls, but this time there was a chance it was going to be a boy. An amulet for his wife to wear had been obtained from the great Muslim shrine at Ajmer in India, and he himself had gone to the shrine of saint Shah Jalal in Sylhet to pray and distribute thanks-offerings. He hadn't had time to visit Shah Poran's shrine as well, and that had been a mistake. Shah Poran was Shah Jalal's nephew, and unless you prayed and paid your respects at both of their shrines the boon you wished for might not be granted – that's what people said.

The fact that his wife's labour pains were particularly severe was a good omen, for a boy baby gave rise to worse pains than a girl. Given the agonies Jamila was in, there was every reason to hope for good news. Still, one had to bear in mind that people didn't always get what they wanted.

Mobarak Hussain had been going through a bad time. He had previously been in the Intelligence Branch, but had suddenly been transferred from his plain clothes job to the uniformed police service. He would normally have been quite pleased. Being an inspector in plain clothes was a sorry business. You looked just like a Bengali teacher from some college or other, and when you passed through the crowd nobody gave you a second glance. The whole fun of being a policeman lay in the uniform. When you had your uniform on everyone would gaze at you respectfully the moment you appeared. Yet such was his bad luck, no sooner had he reverted to his khaki outfit than the trouble had begun. For there had been violent clashes pretty well every day since he had put the uniform back on. The Bengalis were an odd lot. If they trusted someone they would believe every single word he said. He might tell them their ears had been ripped off by a scavenging kite, and they wouldn't even bother to check whether it was true. Instead of passing their hands over the sides of their head, and finding their ears still happily attached to them right next to their sideboards, they would grab sticks and clubs, gather into a mob and race off in hot pursuit of the kite. Whereas if they didn't trust a person they refused to believe him even when he spoke the truth. The Information Minister Mr Shahabuddin had announced that Tagore songs were at odds with Islam and Pakistani tradition, and would therefore no longer be broadcast on national radio or television°, and what an infernal uproar that had caused. Everyone up in arms, demanding sackings and beatings and burnings and whatever else. A bloke had just made a statement, what was all the fuss about? And anyway what was so special about Tagore songs? A load of whining nonsense, that's what they were. There was nothing wrong in what the minister had said. Rabindranath Tagore had never written a single Islamic song, had he now? Could you find a single reference to the Prophet's holy mother in his songs? Not one. But the Muslim poet Nazrul Islam°, he did write quite a few Hindu-type songs. His *Shyama* songs, for instance. Rabindranath could perfectly well have written some Islamic songs if he'd wanted to. Anyone who knew how to compose songs could do Hindu ones or Muslim ones equally easily. So why hadn't he? He did grow a beard, and it was a good long one, measuring at least one and a half feet. And those caftans he used to wear, those were Muslim kind of caftans. If he'd only taken the trouble to write a couple of Islamic songs none of these problems would have arisen.

Public meetings, demonstrations, *lathi* charges, teargas – all for a few silly songs!

A Justice of the Supreme Court, Mr Hamidur Rahman, had made a passing remark, and that too had caused tremendous ructions. People didn't get to be Justices of the Supreme Court just by munching grass like a donkey; if they said something they did so after careful consideration. This gentleman had suggested using the Arabic script for writing Bengali. It wasn't as though that was a particularly bad idea. There were plenty of village folk who couldn't read or write Bengali, but knew how to read the Holy Quran. They would then be able to read Bengali too. What was so bad about that? It wouldn't lower the status of Bengali to write it in Arabic script, it would enhance it. Think of it, Bengali being written in the language of the Prophet, what a great honour! But even supposing for the sake of argument that it was a bad idea, what call could there be for making such a big fuss? What an extraordinary race of people they were, always preferring strife to harmony. They only felt at ease when disruption prevailed. They didn't approve of a strong leader like Ayub Khan°; no, they must give their votes to that senile hag Fatima Jinnah°. A woman in charge of the country, what an idea! Somewhere in the Quran or Hadith it said that women were not allowed to become rulers. But Moulana Bhashani had been running around persuading people to vote for Fatima Jinnah – him, a man versed in the Quran and Hadith, with the title of Moulana! What could have been gained by voting for her? More disruption throughout the country, that's what. What an impossible country it was, and now what an impossible leader.

Recently a new fashion had started – for 'points'. One day it was a six-point manifesto, another day an eleven-point demand sheet, next it would be a fourteen-point challenge. A nation which didn't have enough common sense to see that all these *points*° would simply lead to *disappointment*, well, its future was not a bright one.

In Mobarak Hussain's opinion it had been a foolish mistake of Ayub Khan's to drop the Agartala conspiracy case°. Ayub Khan was no fool, so why had he done such a foolish thing? That action of his had betrayed a certain weakness in him, and the Bengali people were apt to get excited the moment they smelt a whiff of weakness. So they were excited now, and Sheikh Mujibur Rahman had become their hero. Ayub Khan should have strung him up – if a dozen or so of the conspirators had been sent to the gallows everything would have gone quiet. For the Bengali people always bowed to the strong and baited the weak. As soon as they detected a hint of weakness they bared their claws. And the more they were roused the more dangerous it was for the police, for people had a deep hatred of khaki uniforms. There was nothing they enjoyed more than throwing things at the police. What a dire turn things had taken immediately after the death of Asaduzzaman°! People had started going mad right in front of your eyes. Mobarak himself had nearly lost his life. A little more and he would have been killed. As it was, he had been hit on the left elbow by a whole brick. It had made a dull cracking sound. At the time he hadn't realized that a bone had been broken, but that was hardly surprising considering what an agitated state he had been in. Although the fracture had healed, his arm hadn't gone back to normal. It was still painful at times of full moon and new moon, and it hadn't regained its strength: he was still unable to lift a full glass of water with that arm.

Mobarak Hussain came down from the roof looking very gloomy.

As yet no news had come from indoors. Somebody had been sent to fetch a female doctor. The lady from next door had come round; she was a woman who observed purdah scrupulously, but on this occasion she broke it in order to speak to Mobarak Hussain. The gist of her message was that the patient should be taken to hospital.

"Well, I'll see," Mobarak Hussain said. He was now feeling grumpier than ever. *Patient*, indeed! Here was a pregnant woman about to have a baby, a normal routine matter, so what was all this nonsense about hospitals?

At around eight in the morning Jamila's condition worsened. The ghastly grimacing and tetany intensified. She began calling feebly for her mother – a mother who had died many years ago, and sadly would not be able to come and sit by her daughter at her supreme moment of agony. Again and again she called: "Mamma! Oh, mamma!"

At one o'clock in the afternoon Jamila gave birth to a son and expired.

Although it is true that Mobarak Hussain was grieved by his wife's death, it is also true that considerable joy was mingled with his grief. After having had three daughters in succession, he now had a son. And the child was fair skinned, positively white in fact. He had a straight nose, not a broad flat tribal kind of nose like the girls.

Mobarak Hussain named his son Yahya. This was the name of one of the prophets. However that was not the true explanation for his choice of this particular name.

The baby was born on 25th March 1969, and that was the day on which General Yahya Khan came to power and promulgated martial law in Pakistan. From that moment everything went quiet. All the disruption and violence and killing stopped. There was no more clamouring on the lines of "rise up, Bengali nation" to be heard. The army had come out into the streets, and the timid Bengali public had so to speak retreated into its burrow. The police regained their power and prestige. No longer did people dare to say rude things each time they spotted a khaki uniform.

It was out of respect for the general called Yahya who had brought about these changes that Mobarak Hussain named his son by that same name. He then performed a naming ceremony for him at the shrine of Shah Jalal.

Mobarak Hussain had cut out from the newspaper and carefully preserved the letter written by Ayub Khan which had given rise to these remarkable developments.

Ayub Khan had written to General Yahya as follows.

President's House
24th March 1969

Dear General Yahya,

With deep regret I have been forced to recognize that the civil administration and normal agencies of control in this country have become inoperative. If the present alarming situation is allowed to get any worse it will become quite impossible to preserve the economic and social fabric of the country.

In these circumstances I can see no alternative but to step down from power. I have decided to hand over control to the Pakistan armed forces, as they are the only competent institution remaining in place at this juncture.

Ayub Khan

The belief that his son Yahya's birth had been a special blessing took root in Mobarak Hussain's mind. Every time anything good happened he put it down to the birth of his son. At around this time he had a dream in which he saw his deceased mother holding the baby Yahya in her arms and cuddling him. Then all of a sudden she had caught sight of him, Mobarak Hussain, and said to him in a voice tinged with annoyance, "Monu!" (that was the nickname she had always used for him) "Your days of insecurity are over. This child has come into the world as a herald of good luck for you. You must look after him carefully, you must take him to the shrine at Ajmer once every year, and from time to time you must give him venison to eat with his rice."

The following year, for the sake of his son's wellbeing, Mobarak Hussain married a middle aged woman named Safiya. This marriage was also a blessing for him.

Safiya was a substantially built woman. In Mobarak Hussain's eyes she had three outstanding virtues. The first was that she was a good cook. Every dish she made tasted delicious. Then she feared her husband as she feared death itself. In Mobarak Hussain's opinion this was one of the greatest virtues a woman could have: a family in which the wife did not fear and obey her husband could never be a happy one.

Safiya's third virtue was less an accomplishment than the result of an ingenuous nature. The most simple minded women are the ones who display this quality: namely, they see everything in their husbands' lives as their very own. They consider their husbands' children by a previous marriage as their own children. And this is what happened in Safiya's case. In no time at all Mobarak Hussain's three daughters became her own, and as for the boy, it was as if she herself had given birth to him just the other day.

One day at around noon Mobarak Hussain happened to return home unexpectedly. He went into the bedroom and there he found Safiya sitting on a mat chewing betel leaf, with one of his daughters resting her head in her lap, another leaning against her side and the third chattering and waving her arms. All three girls had betel leaf in their mouths.

As soon as they caught sight of their father the three girls ran away. Safiya suddenly felt scared, so much so that she let some of the betel leaf juice drip from her lips onto her sari. Mobarak Hussain was greatly displeased. People said that an aunt who doted on her nephews and nieces more than their own mother did must be a witch; in that case a stepmother who doted so much on her stepdaughters must be worse than a witch. And what was all this chewing of betel leaf? It was wrong for adults to share their addictions like betel chewing and smoking with children.

All that Mobarak Hussain said to his terror-stricken wife was, "Let's have less of this sitting around gossiping. I don't approve of it." Safiya hastily nodded, and some more *paan* juice drooled from her lips.

Mobarak Hussain's conviction that his son was a good luck talisman was further strengthened on 1st January 1970. That was the day on which Yahya Khan gave permission for political activities to be resumed, and on the very same day Mobarak Hussain was transferred from uniformed duty to the District Special Branch. No more khaki uniforms, plain clothes work from now on, and better still, answering directly to the central government. In times of unrest like these a khaki uniform was a dangerous thing to wear. The public had got the idea that anyone in khaki uniform was an enemy.

Two months after he had joined the intelligence branch, on 25th March, which was his son's first birthday, he was summoned to the divisional headquarters of the army intelligence corps. Colonel Shahrukh Khan wished to speak to him. The interview was to take place at seven in the evening, at a house in Sher Shah Suri Road in Mohammedpur.

Mobarak Hussain had made arrangements for a ceremony to be held at his house in honour of his son's birthday at five o'clock that afternoon, and had invited friends and relatives. Shalu Matbor the cook had been asked to come over from his shop in Old Dhaka and make *kacchi biryani* for the party. Now Mobarak Hussain was rather dismayed. There was no knowing how long the meeting might go on for. It was unfortunate indeed that he would have to miss the celebrations for his son's first birthday. Still, he had a feeling that this meeting boded well for him. Otherwise why would it have fallen on his son's birthday of all days?

He reached the house where he was to see Colonel Shahrukh at six p.m. It wasn't an office building but somebody's home. The occupant had a family, for sounds of children shouting and crying could be heard all the time. It was hard to believe that an important officer from the army intelligence corps could have called him for interview in a house like this. Mobarak Hussain had to wait a whole hour in what seemed to be a sitting room; though from the state of the room it didn't look as if anyone ever sat in it for relaxation. On one side there were a couple of dilapidated sofas, and opposite them were some cane chairs. The sofas had no covers on them, and the wooden frame of one of them was showing through the upholstery. The only form of decoration in the room was a glossy picture of the Kaaba in Mecca.

Mobarak Hussain was called for his interview at seven o'clock sharp. He started in surprise when he saw the colonel. Sitting there quietly was a pleasant faced youth who looked as if he was barely into his early twenties. One could imagine he was the victim of a painful love affair which had made him appear marginally older than he was.

The room in which the colonel was seated was quite large, but poorly lit. Even in that half light the colonel was wearing dark glasses, as if he was suffering from an eye infection. There was another person in the room besides the colonel. He was probably a Bengali, though he was much taller than the average Bengali man. He was sitting behind a large desk with a teacup in front of him, which he was using as an ashtray, and beside the teacup were two packets of K-2 cigarettes. The man was at least forty years old and had a rough kind of face; he had not shaved himself that morning so his chin was covered in stubble. Every now and then he would part his lips for no reason, and then his teeth showed, heavily discoloured as a result, perhaps, of his excessive smoking. His attention appeared to be wholly focussed on the teacup in front of him, and he hadn't given Mobarak Hussain so much as a glance. Mobarak Hussain couldn't tell whether or not the colonel had looked at him either, on account of the dark glasses he was wearing.

"Inspector Mobarak Hussain, sit down, please."

Mobarak Hussain sat down on the chair placed in front of the colonel's desk. He was feeling annoyed with himself for having forgotten to say "*Salaam alaikum*" when he entered the room. It might not be appropriate to say it now.

"How are you, inspector?" the colonel asked in English.

"Very well, sir," replied Mobarak Hussain in Bengali, and then immediately he thought, what have I done, the colonel surely doesn't understand Bengali, and in any case it's not as though I don't know any English, I could easily have said *I am fine, sir.*

After staying silent for a short while the colonel suddenly made Mobarak Hussain jump by asking him in perfect Bengali, with the correct pronunciation, "Inspector, are you for any reason afraid?"

Recovering from his shock Mobarak Hussain managed to reply. "No, sir!"

"Let's get straight down to business. Have you ever seen Sheikh Mujibur Rahman at close quarters?"

"No, sir."

"You haven't ever gone anywhere to see him? To pay your respects to him?"

"No, sir."

"Hundreds of people go to see him every day. They go and stand below the balcony of his house to listen to him speak, or just to catch a glimpse of him. Why haven't you gone there too?"

"Sir," replied Mobarak Hussain calmly, "I have never been posted at the Sheikh's residence."

"You would go there if you were posted there on duty?"

"Of course, sir."

The colonel leaned a little closer to Mobarak Hussain. "Does Sheikh Mujib want independence for East Pakistan, or does he wish to be the leader of an undivided Pakistan? What do you think?"

"I don't know, sir. Those are very weighty matters, and I'm only an ordinary police inspector. I'm a government servant."

"So if the reins of government fall into Sheikh Mujib's hands you'll be a servant of Sheikh Mujib?"

"Indeed, sir."

The colonel took a cigarette from his shirt pocket. Cigarettes normally come in packets, but the colonel's cigarettes were loose in his pocket – this was curious. While lighting his cigarette the colonel continued, "What is the thing you like best about your country?"

"Why do you say *your country*, sir? This is your own country too, sir," said Mobarak Hussain.

The ghost of a smile crossed the colonel's lips. Quickly suppressing it he replied in a grave voice, "I said that just to please you. Of course I know it's my own country. Be that as it may, kindly answer my question – what do you like best?"

"Real *monda* from Muktagacha," answered Mobarak Hussain quietly.

"*Monda*? What's that?"

"A type of sweetmeat made from curd cheese and steamed."

"So of all the things there are, your favourite is *monda* from Muktagacha!"

"Yes, sir."

"Very well. Now tell me this: do you think this country is going to be split up? Are we going to have two different countries with two different flags?"

"Pakistan will not be broken up, sir."

"What reason have you for saying that?"

"No reason, sir. It's just my heart which tells me it won't."

Taking another cigarette from his pocket and bringing it to his lips the colonel remarked, "That's what I think too. A man whose political guru was Huseyn Suhrawardy° would never wish to break up Pakistan. No, he will aim to become the leader of an undivided Pakistan. However Sheikh Mujib doesn't trust General Yahya, even though General Yahya has been acceding to all of his demands. After last November's cyclone and tidal bore Moulana Bhashani wanted to have the elections postponed, saying that elections were not appropriate in the midst of so much human suffering. Just to please Sheikh Mujib General Yahya refused to postpone them. I believe General Yahya wants only one thing: his line is, let things turn out as they may, let whoever wants to come to power, only at all costs Pakistan must be kept whole. Inspector Mobarak!"

"Yes, sir?"

"That's what you too hope for in your heart, is it not?"

"Yes, sir."

"I've sent for you because from now on you're going to be posted at Sheikh Mujibur Rahman's residence in Dhanmandi. You're going to worm your way into his household, you're going to make a place for yourself inside it. How you achieve that is up to you."

"And what will I have to do, sir?"

"Your job is to gain a foothold in that house, that's all there is to it."

"Nothing else?"

"No, nothing else. Every Wednesday evening you will report to Mr Zohar here in this house. You will have a little chat with him. No doubt you have realized who Mr Zohar is – this fellow who keeps chain smoking."

Mobarak Hussain looked over at Mr Zohar, then stood up from his chair and gave him a respectful *salaam*. Zohar did not respond, but continued staring at his teacup as before.

"Zohar is from Purnea District°," said the colonel. "He's a very close associate of mine, and he's a poet. You'd be impressed if you could hear his poetry being recited. You'll also be astonished to hear who his favourite poet is. His favourite poet is Tagore – your very own Rabindranath!"

Mobarak Hussain was not astonished, but he made a show of surprise. "Mr Zohar is a chain smoker," said the colonel. "Now tell me, Inspector Mobarak, how many cigarettes has he smoked since you entered the room?"

"Nine."

"Excellent, you have good powers of observation. You may go now."

"Am I to leave, sir?"

"Yes, you're to go."

"*Slamalekum*, sir."

"*Wa alaikum as-salaam*. Listen, inspector, I'm sorry I made you miss your son's birthday celebrations, please don't be offended. One has to make little sacrifices for the good of one's country."

Mobarak Hussain was not altogether taken aback. Of course they knew it was his son's birthday, there was nothing surprising about that; the intelligence service would never summon anyone without gathering some information about them. Presumably they also knew that he had named his son Yahya.

"Inspector!"

"Yes, sir?"

"Is there anything you wish to say?"

"No, sir."

"Let me give you one little tip. It's extremely easy to gain Sheikh Mujib's confidence. Right now he has unlimited confidence in every Bengali. He trusts all Bengalis; we distrust them all. He's making a mistake, and so are we. And just as he'll have to pay for his error, we shall have to pay for ours too. The only question is how much. All right, go now. Happy birthday to your son."

No. 32, Dhanmandi Residential Area had little in common with an ordinary private residence; the word *home* hardly fitted it. 'Home' conjures up images of drowsy noon, of sudden gusts of wind soothing the torrid air of late summer, of colourful saris hung out to dry on the railings. There was nothing like that here, just crowds of people as if it was market day in some village. All the time new cohorts of people were arriving while others were drifting away. Each lot of newcomers would be in a great state of excitement to start with, but after they had chanted their slogans a number of times their enthusiasm would start to wear off. Then they would look rather at a loss, for they were unsure what to do once they had finished their slogan shouting. Having marched all the way there with a band of followers you couldn't just suddenly melt away, you had to hang around for a while. Whoever was in charge of the group felt they would lose face if they couldn't wangle an audience with Sheikh Mujib before going away again.

A planet generally has some moons orbiting round it. Sheikh Mujib was a very large planet, and for that reason the number of satellites circulating around him was considerable. It was no easy matter to get past those satellites and approach the Sheikh himself, but one had to do the best one could.

Mobarak Hussain would be there from morning till night, watching all the goings-on. He enjoyed it. Sometimes at midday colossal cooking pots filled with food would appear: one day it might be a kind of meat broth called *teheri*, another day *khichuri* and meat. On those occasions an added excitement ran through the crowd, and that too would be fun to observe. The most entertaining thing of all was the learned talk of small-time politicians. Small leaders have their own small satellites, and it was to them that they would spout their learned talk.

"I cannot comprehend what the Moulana wants. The slogan of his party is 'Food first, vote later', but in fact to ensure the right to food we first need to vote. Observing the way he carries on one naturally gets the impression he's come to some kind of sinister understanding with Yahya. At the same time I really don't like the way the Communist Party is behaving. Mind you, it's quite tricky to say what the Communists may or may not do. I really must have a word with Sheikh Mujib about it."

The man who was intending to have a word with Sheikh Mujib was acting as if he was one of the Sheikh's chief advisors. In order to stoke up the enthusiasm of the party workers under them minor leaders of this kind would mastermind a bit of slogan shouting every so often. Each would try to ensure his group's slogans were different from everybody else's.

> *Beat up Yahya, brothers all, We shall have a free Bengal.*
> *Grab a soldier, or grab three, And we'll have them for our tea.*

The student leaders' attitude was the most remarkable of all. They made it seem as if it was they who were leading the entire popular movement. All right, they seemed to say, Sheikh Mujib was there too, and that was fine, but it wouldn't really matter if he dropped out of the picture, they would carry on and take the fight forwards. Gaining independence for the country wasn't such a big deal, it would be quite easy for them. Sheikh Mujib did nothing to discourage them from thinking like this; but then maybe he had no choice.

It was the morning of Mobarak Hussain's third day of attendance at the house in Dhanmandi. Sheikh Mujib had just said his dawn prayers and come down from the first floor of his house to the ground floor. He came straight up to Mobarak Hussain and asked in his husky voice, "Who are you?"

Without giving any reply Mobarak Hussain bent down and touched the Sheikh's feet in obeisance, and greeted him with a *salaam*.

"I often see you here. Who are you?"

"I'm from the Intelligence Branch, sir."

"So they've put you on duty at my house?"

"Yes, sir."

"Do you have a pistol on you?"

"Yes, sir."

"And what are your instructions?"

"To watch and see who comes and goes."

"Now you've told me all your secrets!" said Sheikh Mujib, laughing. "Aren't you supposed to keep your identity secret when you're in the intelligence branch?"

"Even though I'm here at the government's behest I'm working for you. I'm making sure nobody harms you."

"And why are you working for me?"

"Because you are the government."

Sheikh Mujib was greatly pleased by this statement. He put his hand on Mobarak Hussain's shoulder and asked, "What are you able to do for me?"

"I can do whatever you ask me to do. If you tell me to jump off the roof I shall do so."

"What's your name?"

"Mobarak Hussain, inspector of police."

"Where is your ancestral home?"

"In Kishoreganj."

"An excellent place, the homeland of the heroic Shokhina°. You have children?"

"Three girls and a boy. The girls' names are Moriam, Masuma and Mafruha, and the boy's name is Yahya."

"What are you telling me! Your boy is called Yahya?"

"My grandmother chose the name; she called him after the prophet Yahya."

"Here, come along with me."

"Where am I to go, sir?"

"I'm going to take you up onto the roof, and then I shall give the order for you to jump off it. Just to see whether you do know how to obey orders."

"All right, sir, let's go," said Mobarak Hussain placidly.

Sheikh Mujib led Mobarak Hussain upstairs to the first floor. There he said to his wife, "How about some breakfast for the two of us. See this lad, he's a new son of mine."

Sheikh Mujib's face was glowing with pleasure and satisfaction.

4

Today Irtazuddin Kashempuri was in a sad mood. After pacing up and down the verandah of Nilganj High School for a while he was now sitting in the teachers' common room. He was holding a newspaper which was two days out of date and had little more to tell him than what had happened in the capital city two days earlier. Nilganj was always two days behind Dhaka. Irtazuddin was trying to read the paper, but was unable to concentrate. It's difficult to concentrate on anything when you are upset. That morning the headmaster, Mr Monsur, had spoken to him in a way he was not at all prepared for. Mr Monsur was younger than he was, and being spoken to severely by a person younger than oneself was enough to put anyone in a bad frame of mind. Yet it wasn't really a question of relative age. There was a type of chilli which, though very hot, was quite small, and if you thought about it in that way the sharp words spoken by the headmaster should not have been impossible to stomach. But Irtazuddin could not stomach the words he had said, because it seemed to him that they were unjust.

The matter had been a trivial one. Last time he visited Dhaka Irtazuddin had brought back a large new flag for the school. It had cost twelve rupees, but though admittedly rather expensive it was made of silk and was three times the size of the old one. The green section was a good dark green, whereas in the old one that part had faded considerably. This morning he himself had hoisted the flag. The bright new cloth had caught the wind and flapped bravely, and the sight had been enough to stir the soul. If only the flagpole had been a bit taller and the flag a bit bigger, it would have been visible from a great distance, and people would have said proudly, "See that flag? That flag belongs to our own Nilganj High School." Village people loved to show their pride in small things like that.

Irtazuddin had stood staring at the flag in admiration for a few moments. It had made him think of a green parrot flying in the blue sky. Just as he was becoming dewy-eyed with emotion the school janitor Modhu had come up to him and told him the headmaster wanted to see him. With his heart still full of joy he had gone to the headmaster's study, fully intending to point out the glorious sight of the fluttering new flag to the headmaster.

Mr Monsur, the head teacher of Nilganj High School, had looked up and said to him in a flat tone, "Take a seat, will you, Moulana sahib." Then he had gone on with whatever he was writing in a preoccupied way, as if he was quite unaware that there was anyone at all sitting there in front of him.

Mr Monsur – M.A., B.T. (Gold Medal) – was a man of short stature and ferociously dark skin pigmentation. Behind his back the pupils in his school called him Mr Darkness. He was exceedingly strict. He had been headmaster of the school for nine years, and in all that time he had only once been observed to smile. That had been on 8th May 1963, when the annual Matric exam results had been published showing that a pupil of the school named Nepal Chandra Howladar had gained fourth place overall. There was a possibility that Mr Monsur might smile again if any other pupil of the school ever achieved a numbered position in the results league. However there was not much chance of that, as good quality pupils tended not to enrol in a village school of this kind.

Irtazuddin had gone on sitting there and the headmaster had gone on with his writing. It had seemed to Irtazuddin that the man looked even more serious than usual. Maybe he was not feeling very well, or maybe he had received bad news from his relatives. The headmaster often did receive upsetting news. His wife was mentally ill and lived at her father's village home, where she received various kinds of treatment. Either as a result of the treatment or else for purely natural reasons, from time to time she would become sane and the headmaster would bring her to Nilganj to live with him. At such times his face would brighten and he would look really contented. Even his dark skin would look less densely black. And almost every day he would take a walk along the banks of the river Sohagi with his wife. There was a banyan tree near their house, some of the dangling roots from which hung down into the river. Often the headmaster's wife could be seen sitting against the trunk of that tree, a timid looking woman with her face hidden inside the fold of her sari, whose manner suggested a newly married bride who had scarcely got to know her husband yet. She would be sitting there and the headmaster would be strolling nearby: it would be a charming sight. Then after a while the wife would go mad again and the headmaster, crestfallen, would once again take her away to her father's place. On his return to the school he would be in a very bad mood for some days, and find fault with everyone for no reason. Then he would return to normal. He would walk alone on the banks of the Sohagi river, or sit under the banyan tree on his own.

The headmaster had finished his scribbling and raised his eyes to look at Irtazuddin. In a low voice, almost a murmur, he had said, "I've just written a letter to my elder brother-in-law. My wife is not well, and they want to have her admitted to Pabna Mental Hospital."

"What's the matter with her?"

"Nothing new, just the old problem, though it appears it's worse this time. She went for my brother-in-law's wife with a metal fish-scraper, and would have slashed her with it. Now everyone's afraid, which is natural enough, so they have locked her into her room. Apparently she has been shouting and screaming a lot."

Irtazuddin had made no comment, but remained sitting there in silence. His spirits had sunk low. And at that point the headmaster had frowned and started his harangue.

"Mr Irtazuddin."

"Yes, headmaster?"

"I noticed you hoisting a new flag outside the school."

"Yes, I brought it from Dhaka. They charged me twelve rupees for it; it's made of silk. It's hard to get hold of a national flag nowadays, nobody seems keen to sell them any more."

"You have spent money on something entirely unnecessary. The school cannot afford to waste money like that. When you consider that I am not in a position even to pay the teachers their salaries..."

"But the national flag isn't something unnecessary," Irtazuddin had objected in a rather subdued tone of voice.

"We already had a flag."

"But the colour had faded."

"A faded flag is perfectly in order, for this country," the headmaster had said grimly. "Faded is exactly what it is."

"I don't get your meaning," Irtazuddin had said.

"There was a time when one cherished that flag as one's own," the headmaster had gone on in a serious tone, "but one no longer can. I suppose you have been following what is going on in this country; or maybe you don't keep abreast of the news?"

"I do keep abreast of the news."

"The signs are not good. The flag may change. That's why I consider you to have wasted twelve rupees from the funds of an already impecunious school."

"The flag may change?" Irtazuddin had repeated in astonishment.

"It will change. Not overnight, but change it will. That's what all the signs indicate. Do you know what Moulana Bhashani said in his recent speech at the Paltan recreation ground?"

"No."

"That's not surprising, as it wasn't reported in any of the papers. Not all the news gets into the papers; what should go in and what should be left out is something *they* decide."

"What did Moulana Bhashani say?"

"He said, 'Magnify the Lord, *Allahu Akbar*! Long live an independent East Pakistan!"

"No! This is incredible!"

"The flag will change. The crescent moon and star will go. The Moulana is a Sufi, he's in communion with the jinns. Through the jinns he gets to know future events in advance. The crescent moon and stars are not going to remain with us."

"If that really does happen," Irtazuddin had said pensively, "it won't be a good thing."

"Why not?"

"Because then we shall have to defer to the Hindus. How can it be good for Muslims to be enslaved to Hindus?"

"If we're fated to be enslaved to anybody then that's that, there's no escaping one's fate," the headmaster had replied wearily, "but what makes you think that just because this country became independent we would have to be enslaved to Hindus? What kind of a notion is that? If you're a man of the modern world it makes sense for you to think in a more sophisticated way. It's not as if we weren't enslaved to anyone already. We are. Do you know what proportion of civil servants in central government are Bengalis? Fewer than ten percent. Bengalis in the armed forces? It's best not to know. Can we go abroad without the approval of the West Pakistanis? No, we can't. Having won the elections, has Sheikh Mujibur Rahman been able to take his seat in the National Assembly? No, he hasn't. He's not being allowed to. And they never will let him, never. The talks going on now are nothing but hot air. So the time is approaching for us to pull down the flag and chuck it away."

"Shall I take the flag down, then?"

"Yes. For the time being let the old flag be flown, not the new one."

"Right, headmaster."

"And the money you paid for the flag will not be reimbursed to you from the school funds. You bought it without the approval of the purchase committee. You had no right to do that. Everything has to be done according to the rules. Rules cannot be sidestepped."

"No, indeed."

"Oh, and say a prayer for my wife, will you?"

"Certainly I will. God willing, I shall make a supplication for her after the midday prayers."

Irtazuddin, in low spirits, had then left the headmaster's study.

Phrases like "independent East Bengal" were certainly to be heard in people's conversation these days, he thought, but such talk was not to be taken seriously, and it was harmful stuff. Muslims had had to put up with a lot in the days of undivided India. And then Mr Jinnah, a hero of legendary proportions, had given the long-suffering Muslims their freedom. It would not be right to forget those events, it would be sheer ingratitude. No Muslim should forget how a Muslim used not even to be allowed to enter a Hindu's home – because the house would be polluted if he did. How a Muslim couldn't sit as a customer in a Hindu confectioner's shop to partake of his sweetmeats; instead he would have to stretch out his hands like a beggar, with the money for the sweets in them, and the sweets would be tossed into his outstretched hands. Many was the time he had had to endure this kind of humiliation. Had the people who were now chanting "independent Bengal" ever experienced this kind of belittlement? Well, Moulana Bhashani had, so why was he getting involved in the movement? How could a clever man like him fail to spot the devious Hindu plot behind it?

It was clear that India was engaged in a full-scale conspiracy with the aim of plunging the whole nation of Pakistan back into darkness. They, the Indians, were going about it in a very calculated way. For them it was nothing more or less than a bid to exact revenge for the loss they had sustained at Mr Jinnah's hands in his political game of chess. After all these years they had got their chance, and they were not going to let it slip from their grasp.

After the midday prayers Moulana Irtazuddin made a lengthy supplication to God for the cohesion and welfare of Pakistan. He had been supposed to put in a word for the headmaster's wife as well, but he quite forgot to do so. Realizing this with dismay once he had finished, he returned to his prayer mat to perform an extra set of prayers.

That same day at one p.m. President Yahya Khan went on air to announce that the inaugural session of the National Assembly was to be postponed. The date was 1st March 1971.

His speech was broadcast from Radio Pakistan Dacca as follows:

> *In the light of the stalemate between the two main parties representing East and West Pakistan I am obliged to defer the session of the National Assembly scheduled for 3rd March 1971. However I wish to make it clear that this postponement will not be for more than two or three weeks. During this period I shall make every endeavour to foster mutual understanding between the elected representatives of the two wings of our country.*

Night had fallen. After completing his dusk prayers Irtazuddin had turned to his cooking. The menu was simple: rice, *dal*, and potato *bharta*. He knew he had some best quality ghee in a jar, and he planned to stir two spoonfuls of it into the mash of boiled potato, raw onion and chillies. To a man whose stomach was grumbling as his was, the mixture was going to taste like ambrosia. The Prophet had often consumed nothing more than a couple of dates for supper: compared with that, this would be a feast.

But the potato *bharta* never got made. He had just three potatoes, and all three of them turned out to have gone rotten. On top of that he didn't have any chillies, either fresh or dried, and chillies were an essential ingredient for potato *bharta*.

"*Shukur alhamdulillah!*" exclaimed Irtazuddin. Thanks and praise be to God. One ought to be thankful to God in every conceivable circumstance, he thought, for God loved those of his servants who showed gratitude.

The water in the saucepan was boiling, and Irtazuddin was just on the point of tipping the lentils into the seething water when Modhu appeared and said, "The headmaster is calling you. You're to have supper with him tonight."

"What is there to eat?" asked Irtazuddin.

"*Mola* fish curry, *teki* fish relish, and *dal* made with mungo beans."

"Who did the cooking? You?"

"Yes, sir."

"*Shukur alhamdulillah!*" said Irtazuddin once again. Modhu kept house for the headmaster and did his cooking; he was an excellent cook. He used to make a thing out of fish scraps and a couple of marrow leaves which took your breath away when you tasted it. And anyone who hadn't tried his pumpkin *bharta* had yet to discover how delicious a *bharta* could be.

"Modhu!"

"Yes, sir?"

"This country's in a poor state, Modhu. Who knows what's going to happen."

"Well, let it happen!" said Modhu, his teeth flashing as he grinned. "*We can't negate what's in our fate!*"

Modhu looked unusually cheerful. He kept smiling broadly for no apparent reason.

"You haven't been smoking hash again, have you?" asked Irtazuddin with a frown.

"Maybe I 'ave and maybe I 'aven't," Modhu replied, sighing deeply.

"Isn't it possible for you to do without that stuff?"

"Oh, sure. I can do with it, and I can do without it."

Irtazuddin had let his lentils fall into the water. He scooped them out again and spread them out on a winnowing fan to dry. They could be aired and used again. It was not right to waste things, for God disliked those who caused wastage.

"Your honour, the weather ain't looking good. A storm could be brewing."

Irtazuddin felt mildly concerned. The hut he lived in was in a parlous state. Termites had got into all the main posts which held up the roof. The hut wouldn't be able to stand a fierce gust of wind in a storm. It needed rebuilding. He had planned to get the necessary work done before the onset of the rainy season, but it didn't look as if he was going to be able to do so, this time as before. Everything depended on God's disposition: if He wished the work to get done then it would get done, and if not then it wouldn't. Nothing was possible without His agreement. But in that case what point was there in a person trying?

Modhu was giggling.

"What's the matter?" asked Irtazuddin.

"Oh, nothing," replied Modhu. "I was just thinking of an old riddle. Shall I say it?"

"Very well."

Modhu recited:

> *Through rush and reeds the Cow proceeds,*
> *through mud Calf makes its way.*
> *The Cow was wed six months ago,*
> *Calf came but yesterday.*

"Tell me now, sir, what was it?"

"I don't know."

"'Tis really simple. Just needs a little thought."

"No, I can't think what."

"I'll tell you what it was then: a turtle's egg!"

"A turtle's egg," repeated Irtazuddin, "well, that's interesting."

"Will I ask you another?"

"I don't really want to listen to riddles, Modhu dear. Let's get moving."

Modhu was bursting with impatience. Riddles were something very dear to his heart. He had a reputation as a riddle solver throughout the local area, and his services were always in demand at weddings, where he would tease the bridegroom and his retinue with the most abstruse riddles he could think of.

It was true, the weather was looking ominous. Thick clouds covered the sky, split now and then by flashes of lightning. Each flash revealed clouds racing in from the west, and that was a bad thing. It meant a storm was on the way.

Irtazuddin was walking briskly. He wanted to reach the headmaster's house before the rain started. If he went round via the police station it would take longer, but the road was a good one, properly maintained by the local authority. On the other hand if he took a short cut through the fishermen's neighbourhood he could get to his destination much sooner, but there was one problem – the track would take him through an area of scrub where there were many snakes, and Irtazuddin had a great fear of snakes.

The first drops of rain were falling, and a cool wind had sprung up. It was cold enough to chill the bones. All round him the darkness was intense, but even in such darkness the metalled road seemed to be gleaming, and Irtazuddin felt he was walking along a river rather than a road. As he was passing the police station the light from a powerful torch dazzled him. It was a discourteous thing to shine a torch in someone's face, yet those people in the police station did it all the time. Still, one couldn't really blame them; they had to be able to see the faces of passers-by if they were to distinguish between saints and sinners.

"Slamalekum, your reverence!"

"Wa alaikum salaam."

"Can you recognize me? I'm Sadrul Amin, the O.C."

"I didn't recognize your voice, but now that you have told me I do recognize you."

"Please forgive me for the discourtesy of shining the torch in your face. Where are you heading?"

"I'm going to the headmaster's house; he has sent for me."

"Please give him my regards. He's a fine fellow."

"Right, I shall."

"Your reverence, I'm sure you've heard the news, Yahya has postponed the session of parliament. Now there's going to be trouble. Any officer posted in Dhaka is going to have a bad time. There'll be clashes with the public, and bloodshed. People's hackles rise as soon as they see a policeman. What's the matter, why are you so mad with us? (That's what I would like to ask them.) Aren't we people like you, who could easily be your father or brother? You live on rice and fish, and we police are no different, we eat rice and fish too. Your shit stinks no less or more than the shit of a policeman... Sorry, your reverence, I've been holding you up, please continue on your way. I can feel a few drops of rain falling. *As-salaamu alaikum.*"

"*Wa alaikum as-salaam.*"

Irtazuddin started walking again. Modhu had fallen back as soon as he had caught sight of the police officer standing in the road, but now he came up to Irtazuddin again.

"Sir," he said in a hushed voice, "you know our O.C., did you realize 'e's a very brave man?"

"No."

"Cor, such a nerve he 'as! Shall I tell you a story about 'im?"

"There's no need, thank you."

"Then you can answer this riddle of mine. Tell me, sir – *A musket of leather, a bullet of air* – what's that, do you think?"

"I've no idea. What?"

"I'll tell you sir, you see. It's a fart! The fart exploding is the bullet, and the leather musket, that's the arsehole!"

Irtazuddin stopped in his tracks, dumbfounded. What outrageous insolence, trotting out obscene talk of this kind in his presence! The fellow ought to be forced to do a hundred curtseys of contrition while pinching his own ears, to teach him never to say anything so rude again in his life.

The rain, after falling heavily for a while, had eased off, prompting Modhu to comment, "That's a bad sign, when heavy rain suddenly stops you can expect some calamity."

"Be quiet, will you," said Irtazuddin severely. "If you utter another single word, you shall feel the back of my hand."

"What 'ave I done wrong? I was just talking!"

"You've done plenty of wrong. Speak no more."

The headmaster was sitting on a wooden bench in his verandah, his form dimly picked out by the light from a hurricane lantern inside the house. The bench on the verandah was his favourite place to sit. From that vantage point he could see far and wide. In front there was a field of paddy, with the river to the south. In the rainy season the entire plain in front of the house would go under water, and when a wind blew the flood water would be swept by waves, just like the sea, and the sound of lapping water could be heard from the verandah. The headmaster was very fond of the scene.

"*As-salaamu alaikum!*" said Irtazuddin as he stepped up onto the verandah. "You sent for me?"

"I invited you to join me for the evening meal," replied the headmaster. "I get tired of eating on my own, day after day. And it's even worse when I'm feeling upset."

Modhu had brought some water for ablutions in a spouted pot, and Irtazuddin stood on a flat wooden bathing stool to wash his feet. Then he took his seat on the bench.

"I can't help thinking about my wife," said the headmaster. "In the end I wrote a letter to the elder of her brothers which I would like to read out to you."

"Please go ahead," said Irtazuddin.

Without hesitation the headmaster closed his eyes and proceeded to recite the letter by heart. He had the ability to retain in his mind any letter he had written, down to the last comma or full stop, for he was endowed with an exceptionally good memory.

To Abdur Rahman

Dear brother,

After reading of the current condition of your sister, my wife, I am quite overwhelmed with sadness. What a cruel test we are being subjected to! And where will this test end? The poor woman is suffering on her own account, and she is also causing suffering in others. It is not for me to suggest what steps should be taken in respect of her. Being so far away it is impossible for me to know the true position. You should do what you think best, that is all I can desire.

I am confident that you will not take any inappropriate decision regarding the sister whom you love so well.

I have no objection to her being admitted to Pabna Mental Hospital. I just pray to God that she may receive good and suitable treatment there.

Yours, etc.

Having completed his recitation of the letter the headmaster looked at Irtazuddin.

"Did you add any postscript?" asked Irtazuddin.

"No."

"And does what you said in the letter correspond to what you really think?"

"Of course."

"No," said Irtazuddin with a sigh, "that's not what you really think. You have reservations in your mind. That's why you have read the letter out to me, because you feel uncertain. What you want is for me to say yes, you have taken the right decision. You are looking to me for moral support."

The headmaster said nothing, but went on staring at Irtazuddin.

"There is one thing you can do," suggested Irtazuddin. "Have your wife sent here to you. If she's with you she may undergo a change. And if even then she doesn't improve, the two of us can take her to the hospital, and there we can discuss things with the doctors."

"You're saying I should fetch her here?"

"I am."

"Well then, why don't I do just that?"

The headmaster looked as if a great weight had been taken off his mind, and he was at last able to breathe easily again.

"I'm hungry," said Irtazuddin. "Tell him to serve the meal. The sky looks menacing, and I want to get back home as soon as possible. There's an ominous red over there in the west, and that's a sign that a storm is brewing."

Modhu appeared and said in a shamefaced mumble, "I can't serve the grub now. There'll be a bit of a delay."

"A delay? Why?" demanded the headmaster. "You had already done all the cooking."

Modhu offered no reply to the question but stood there scratching his head and looking uncomfortable. Eventually the truth came out. A dog had got at the food in the cooking pots and contaminated it. It was going to be necessary to do the cooking all over again. But even that was impossible at the moment, as the rice had run out and some more would have to be purchased from the market.

"What's this you're telling me!" exclaimed the headmaster in astonishment.

"There's this wretched dog as is driving me mad," said Modhu. "The only way to deal with 'im is going to be to poison 'im."

"Well, to tell the truth I'm not feeling very well," said the headmaster. "Earlier on I'd actually decided I'd skip the evening meal. I can just have a glass of cordial and go to bed. However we must give the poor Moulana something to eat, he's quite hungry. There are surely some rice flakes and molasses somewhere in the house?"

"I need boiled rice," said Irtazuddin. "The empty hole I'm feeling isn't going to be plugged by a few rice flakes with molasses. It's all right, I'll go home and cook some there."

"Take Modhu with you," said the headmaster. "He can do the cooking for you, and have a bite to eat himself before you send him back."

Irtazuddin set off with Modhu again. No sooner had they got onto the metalled road than a series of deafening thunderclaps rent the air.

A swishing sound was approaching from the thickets. "Ee, the storm's arriving!" cried Modhu in fear. "We'll 'ave cause to remember this day!"

The tempest hit them all of a sudden, and its first onslaught sent Modhu slithering off the road into a ditch.

Irtazuddin had to run over to the police station to take shelter. The storm went on raging well into the night, and the Moulana was obliged to take his evening meal inside the private quarters of the officer in charge. The O.C.'s wife served him most attentively, keeping her face well covered with the trailing end of her sari. She was heavily pregnant and took pains to try and conceal her contours.

The O.C. himself was not at home. When he had seen the storm approaching he had gone out, taking three constables with him. He was hoping to apprehend a certain robber called Harun Majhi, who was very likely to be found, on a stormy night like this, spending the hours of darkness in the company of his third wife. This lady's name was Rongila. She had once been a prostitute at a brothel in Gouripur. Harun Majhi had married her and built a house specially for her in Mindapur, a village about two miles away from Nilganj. The O.C. was aware that Harun Majhi occasionally dropped in to spend a night with her. With any luck the fellow would be there tonight.

The menu was good: beef curry, a *pabda* fish stew, fried bitter-gourd and a *bharta* made with aubergines.

"I enjoyed that meal very much, my dear," said Irtazuddin. "We can never be sure where the Almighty is going to arrange for our daily bread." After finishing the meal he held his hands out in the customary attitude of supplication and said a prayer: "O Lord, Most Forgiving and Merciful One, I give you thanks for the meal which I have just consumed with such relish. I pray to you that she who made such abundant provision for feeding me may be rewarded by enjoying victuals ten times as good in her house every day. Amen."

When he had finished his prayer Irtazuddin saw that the O.C.'s wife was wiping tears from her eyes. "Why are you weeping, my dear?" he asked in surprise.

"You said such a pretty prayer," said the woman, still dabbing her eyes with the end of her sari. "It made me feel weepy just to hear it."

When the storm was over Irtazuddin headed back to his house. When he reached the spot he froze in amazement. There was no sign of the house at all. The storm had carried it off. Irtazuddin did not utter a word, and it was Modhu who commented, "Sir, it's done for you good and proper!"

"Don't you let it upset you," added Modhu when Irtazuddin remained silent. "Here's a riddle, sir, let's see if you can solve it:
> See it you cannot, hear it you may,
> It comes in a rush and then flies away.

What d'you think it is, sir? It's really easy."

Irtazuddin gave no reply.

"I'll tell you," said Modhu cheerfully, "it's a hurricane! The hurricane comes rushing in and then flies away again. And yet you can't see it at all."

5

The name Kolimullah is hardly a suitable one for a modern poet. Poetry is all about playing with words, but there is nothing to play with in "Kolimullah". Your mouth opens wide when you pronounce it, and people can even see your tongue. Yet Kolimullah was a poet. At the particular moment we are talking about he was standing outside the offices of the daily newspaper *Dainik Pakistan*. He was twenty-five years old and a B.Com. student of Jagannath College. He had sat the Bachelor of Commerce exam twice already, but had not succeeded in passing it. Now he was making strenuous preparations for his third attempt. Kolimullah's father had cut off the supply of funds on hearing he had failed a second time, but this was not a major inconvenience. Kolimullah had two jobs as a private tutor, and took his meals at a restaurant near Kataban on a monthly contract basis. He slept at Iqbal Hall°. A third year honours history student from his home village named Raqib Ali, who was like an elder brother to him, was an intern of Iqbal Hall and let him sleep on the floor of his room. This system was well established in the university halls. As long as Brother Raqib had his bed to himself, any number of others were welcome to sleep on his floor. For if university students didn't look out for their homeless younger brethren, who would? The door was always open; even if one turned up at one o'clock in the morning it didn't cause any real problem.

There was only one problem, in fact – there was no peace and quiet for writing poems. Poem writing was something he had to do during his tuition lessons. People were generally quite happy if your lesson went on for two hours instead of just one, and you could put the additional time to good use. Kolimullah would give his pupil an essay to write, and at the same time compose his own poetry. He had decided that as soon as he had made his name as a poet he would publish an anthology entitled *Tuition Poems*. Every one of the poems would have been written while a tuition pupil of his was doing an assignment. Following the example of Rabindranath Tagore, at the bottom of each poem he would put the date and place of composition. For example at the foot of *Cloud Maiden at Noon* would come the dateline, *Montu's house in Jhigatola, 5th February 1971*.

The collection of poems would be published under a *nom de plume*. Kolimullah had been turning over a large number of possible *noms de plume* in his mind, though none of them had quite filled the bill. One that he rather liked was Shah Kolim°. It was fairly close to his real name, but putting "Shah" in front gave it a flavour of transcendental spirituality. Still, the name didn't sound modern; it suggested some kind of rustic bard, the kind who make up their ballads as they sing them, and slip in their own name at some point, like this:

> (refrain)
> *Shah Kolim doth say*
> *Thy downfall thou shalt meet*
> *On Judgment Day.*
>
> *Can father help? Or mother? Nay.*
> *Brother or Sister? Nay, o nay.*
> *Thy heart shall beat in a frightened way*
> *This is for sure, deny it not pray,*
> *Thy downfall thou shalt meet*
> *On Judgment Day.*

Apart from Shah Kolim one other name was on his list of favourites, Dhurjoti Das. It was a hard name, but modern. The words "Shah Kolim" made you think of a simple-minded bloke with long tangled hair, whereas "Dhurjoti Das" conjured up a very intelligent person with deep thoughtful eyes, wearing spectacles. But it was a Hindu name, and that was a bit of a problem. If one day he became famous the critics would have a go at him. "Why did you assume a Hindu *nom de plume*? Was it from a sense of inferiority? A feeling, perhaps, that a Muslim name was inadequate for a poet? Many of our poets have adopted *noms de plume*, indeed at one time our foremost poet Shamsur Rahman° used to write under an assumed name. He didn't see the necessity of borrowing a Hindu name, so why did you?"

Fierce sunshine was lacerating his scalp. Kolimullah was unable to make up his mind whether to enter the *Dainik Pakistan* office building or not. He wanted to hand his poem to Shamsur Rahman, the great poet, in person. He knew it was pointless to submit a poem by post. The people in newspaper offices never read what came in their mail; they didn't have time. They would chuck the envelope straight into the bin beside their desk.

He had thought hard and long about how he might address the great poet Shamsur Rahman. He had rehearsed it all in his mind, even though he realized that no amount of rehearsal was guaranteed to be of any use, as he had no way of knowing what the great poet would choose to talk about. It was possible that as soon as Kolimullah stepped into the room he would say, "Please go away for now. You can come back later. At the moment I'm too busy." But if Shamsur Rahman spoke nicely to him and, say, asked him whether he had read any of his poems, he would be on a safe wicket. Kolimullah had learned one of Shamsur Rahman's poems, *Asad's Shirt*, thoroughly by heart. He would recite it fluently and thus flatter the great poet. Great poets and writers were easily flattered.

Reciting the formula "*Ya Muqaddimu*" three times over, and taking care to put his right foot foremost, Kolimullah stepped inside the offices of the *Dainik Pakistan. Ya muqaddimu* means "O Thou Who Goeth Ahead". *Al-Muqaddimu*, The One Who Goes Ahead, is one of the ninety-nine holy names of Allah. Invoking God by this name three times and advancing with the right foot forward, Kolimullah knew, would guarantee success. He had failed to pronounce the holy name as he entered the examination hall before sitting his B.Com. exams, for he had been quite unable to recall it. Had he remembered it things would have turned out differently.

The poet Shamsur Rahman was sitting behind a huge ministerial desk. At his right side a tall, fair complexioned man whose appearance suggested a *zamindar*'s steward was talking at great length, wagging his head and waving his hands all the while. The poet was looking at him, but appeared not to be taking in all he was saying. Poets do not like listening to a lot of bullshit.

Kolimullah got the impression that the poet was pleased to see him. At least he was going to be able to escape from the steward's bullshit for a while.

Shamsur Rahman was sitting in the kind of pose the poet Sukanta° is commonly depicted in, with his elbow on the desk and his cheek resting on his fist. Glancing at Kolimullah he asked, "You've come to see me?"

"I've brought a poem for you, sir," replied Kolimullah. "I could have sent it in by post, but I have long entertained a desire to hand it to you in person."

Before the poet could say a word the man sitting next to him butted in. "Just leave it on the desk. Goodbye."

Fixing the steward fellow with his eye, Kolimullah thought to himself, Idiot, what are you butting in for? I wasn't talking to you. I have no need to put up with your crap. However out loud he said, "I came in order to hand the poem to Mr Rahman, not to leave it on the desk."

"Same thing," said the steward. "Mr Rahman will pick it up off the desk."

"I'm sorry, it is not the same thing," objected Kolimullah. "If we want to give someone a bouquet of flowers, we hand it to them, we don't just dump it on the corner of a table. The poem I have written may well be worthless, but to me it is just like a flower. I wish to place the flower in the poet's own hand."

Kolimullah was impressed by his own eloquence. It was true he had rehearsed this bit beforehand, but the fact that he had been able to fit it in so neatly was gratifying.

"What is your occupation?" asked Shamsur Rahman as he held out his hand to take the poem. "Are you a student?"

"Yes, sir, a student. I'm doing an M.Sc. in Physics at Dhaka University." His decision to tell this lie had also been taken in advance. It was something special to be writing poetry while studying a complex science subject. It was unlikely that Shamsur Rahman would go and make enquiries at the university.

"What's your name?"

"My name is Shah Kolim, sir."

"Is that an alias?

"No, sir, my real name. My family have the title Shah."

"Oh, I see."

Kolimullah was looking for an excuse to recite *Asad's Shirt*°, but no such excuse was forthcoming. He could hardly start glibly reciting the poem out of the blue. However the man who looked like a steward handed him his chance.

"You say you write poems," said the man, leering at Kolimullah. "Do you know anything about metric structure? You can't make a chariot without wheels, and you can't make a poem without rhythm. A poem has to roll. A chariot without wheels, that's prose. A chariot with wheels which can move along, that's poetry. Do you get the idea?"

"Thank you, sir, I'm doing my best to follow," replied Kolimullah out loud, with the utmost deference. But to himself he was thinking, Hold your tongue, silly old goat, I don't need any advice from the likes of you.

The steward hadn't yet got to the end of his lecture. "Before you write any poems at all," he went on, "you'll have to read a great deal of poetry. You'll have to find out what other poets are writing, what experiments they are undertaking with words and rhythm. All right, you've come to see the poet Shamsur Rahman; now tell me, have you ever read any of his poems?"

"Ah," thought Kolimullah, "as a reward for asking that question I am going to forgive you all your past sins, and a couple of future ones too." And without more ado he proceeded to roll *Asad's Shirt* off his tongue. His articulation was excellent, so was his manner of recital, yet Shamsur Rahman did not appear to be particularly charmed. Rather he looked as if any number of people had already turned up on previous occasions to recite poems to him from memory, and it was nothing new for him.

> *Red as a spray of scarlet oleander or*
> *a flaming cloud at sunset, Asad's shirt*
>   *flies in the azure air.*
> *Upon that lively shirt his sister once*
> *had sewn small buttons, silver stars,*
>   *with fine gold thread of love.*

> *His aged mother in the sun drenched yard*
> *gently had spread that shirt to dry.*
> *But now the shirt has left the tender shade*
> *of pomegranate bush, the intimate rays*
> *of sunshine in his mother's yard,*
> > *and in the main street of the metropolis*
> > *atop the smoke stacks of great factories*
> > *at every turn in the thronging avenues*
> *There it is, flying, flying ceaselessly.*

Shamsur Rahman did not let him finish, but cut in to say, "Take a seat. Would you like a cup of tea?"

"I won't have any tea, thank you, sir," replied Kolimullah, "but since you have invited me to sit down, I shall do so for a moment. For me it's a great privilege to be able to sit in your presence even for a short while."

Kolimullah took a seat. Ignoring him completely the steward fellow turned back towards the poet and resumed his hand waving and head wagging act, chattering away as if there was nobody else in the room but the two of them.

"Well now, Shamsur Rahman, listen to this next bit. I was coming back from Barisal by river steamer, with the Boss. We had been very busy all day, a meeting here, a meeting there, and so on. I had thought I'd get a good night's sleep on board the steamer, but no, it was not to be. As we were nearing Chandpur I woke up and couldn't get back to sleep. There was I, on the deck of the steamer, standing at the rail, with Chandpur town visible in the distance. The lights of the town were reflected on the water, and dawn was breaking. It was a captivating scene."

Oh, shut up, you old bore, thought Kolimullah. Captivating scene my hat. You couldn't even spell the word *captivating*.

"I was staring at the scene, lost in admiration, when suddenly I got a shock. Someone had placed their hand on my shoulder. I looked round and whom should I see but the Boss, with his pipe in his hand. The Boss greeted me by my name, and then said, 'What are you looking at, the beauty of Bangladesh?'"

What, the Boss put his hand on your shoulder and spoke to you? Kolimullah was thinking. You suppose you're the Boss's best friend or something? Put a sock in it.

"I told the Boss I had no idea he got up at dawn. He said, 'Do you think I'm going to let you lot enjoy the glory of our motherland in my absence? No way! Come along now, come and have tea in my room.' So I went into the Boss's cabin. He made the tea himself and handed it to me."

So he only gave you tea, sneered Kolimullah. Are you quite sure he didn't massage you from head to toe as well, and chafe your feet?

"So then the Boss and I had a serious discussion. I said to him, 'I'll tell you what you should do, you should rein in Moulana Bhashani, you know, reach an understanding with him.' The Boss said, 'You needn't worry about the Moulana. I know him well, and he knows me.'"

Ha, I see you're an even worse liar than I am, thought Kolimullah. So now you've turned into Sheikh Mujib's top policy advisor, have you?

Kolimullah got up from his seat. He couldn't bear to listen to any more of this bombast. Before leaving the room he bent to touch the feet of both the great poet and the steward in respect. The poet tried to resist, but the steward acted as though he was used to having at least fifty budding young poets paying homage to him every day.

The following week Shah Kolim's poem *Cloud Maiden at Noon* was published on the literature page of *Dainik Pakistan*. The week after that a verse drama of his came out in the *Dainik Purbadesh*. This had two characters, Subjugation, who was a blind young maiden, and Independence, an exceedingly handsome youth.

Soon after this Shah Kolim started letting his hair grow long and wild, and gave up shaving his chin. For the time being that is all we have to say about him, though he will reappear in due course.

6

It was Wednesday, Mobarak Hussain's day off. Even on his day off he used to put in a couple of hours' work, hanging around Sheikh Mujib's residence until ten or ten thirty a.m. From there he would head straight for Amin Bazar. After doing his weekly shop for groceries at the market there he would proceed to Moulvibazar, where a butcher called Quddus used to supply him with cuts of beef, of the best quality available. He would get back home before noon. Then it would be bath time for Yahya. Before he was given his bath Yahya would be rubbed all over with pure mustard oil. While being massaged with oil Yahya would laugh and wave his arms and legs in the air. When he was lowered into the basin full of water he would still be waving his arms and legs, but this time crying in protest. Mobarak Hussain loved to watch his little child laugh, and equally he loved to watch him cry.

This was the one day of the week when Mobarak Hussain had a midday nap. After waking from that he would start to get ready for his trip to Mohammedpur. Getting ready meant getting mentally prepared, for as soon as he knew it was time to make his way to Sher Shah Suri Road a strange kind of uneasiness would come over him. Indeed he couldn't even sleep peacefully during his Wednesday midday nap; instead he would have ugly, meaningless dreams. Once he dreamed he was sitting on Colonel Shahrukh Khan's lap. While the dream went on it seemed quite normal, as if sitting on a colonel's lap was a perfectly reasonable and appropriate thing to do. Another time he dreamed that he, Colonel Shahrukh and Mr Zohar were sitting down to dinner together. A whole roasted goat had been placed on the table, and the three of them were tearing bits off it. The trouble was that the goat was still alive. Whenever some meat was ripped from its body it would look round at the diners and mutter, "Careful, now!"

It seemed quite inconsequent to have these ugly, meaningless dreams, for Mr Zohar's conversations with him were in fact relaxed and normal in tenor. Sometimes Mr Zohar would even laugh and make jokes. When evening came he would offer Mobarak Hussain tea and kebabs, or sometimes an intensely flavoured ragout of cow's hooves called *paya*, which tasted absolutely delicious when served with thin, floppy *rumali chapati*.

In fact most of Mr Zohar's conversation would be about food. He would talk of the best things he had eaten, with details of where and when he had consumed them. He often used to mention a thing called sweet kebab. The meat would first be simmered in carrot juice, then the pieces of meat would be grilled on an open fire. Mr Zohar thought it unlikely that anything as good as that would be available in paradise itself.

In between the conversations about food, politics would also be discussed. This man's harangues on political topics were free from any element of uncertainty. His eyes would be shut while he spoke, and one felt he must be inwardly staring at a mental picture of the things he was talking about.

"You see, Inspector, whether a country becomes independent or not isn't something which depends on the people of that country, or on its revolutionary leaders. It depends on the great game of international politics. India wants East Pakistan to gain independence, as that suits its interests. It would teach a lesson to its arch enemy, Pakistan; it would break Pakistan's backbone. Then there's China, another of India's enemies, and hence a friend of Pakistan's. It's a major power: it gave India such a scare in 1960, India was shaking in its boots. China will never support the break-up of Pakistan. And since China is against it, America will be against it too, while the Soviet Union will stand by India. Taking all these things into account, it's a matter of whichever side of the balance weighs heavier... Do you follow me?"

"Yes sir, I get it."

"If Sheikh Mujib is a fool and declares independence without having made any prior arrangements, you'll see what happens. The army will put the rebellion down within a week. As long as India doesn't get involved, everything will be back to normal within two weeks. And then you'll see all the big revolutionary leaders queuing up to sing the Pakistan national anthem: *Pak sarzamin shadbad!* Human beings invariably bow down to superior strength. Nobody likes a weakling. Do you know why?"

"No, sir."

"Because most people *are* weak. They know they are weak, and they despise their own weakness. Consequently they despise weakness in others too. *Mankind abhors timidity because it is timid.* Now you tell me, Inspector, is Sheikh Mujib about to make that mistake? Is he going to declare independence? Will he take on the rôle of the proverbial Nidhiram, a warrior with no weapons?"

"Yes, sir, he will. He has no alternative. The people have made him their leader, and he has to give them their money's worth."

"Does he have any idea how many people in this country are going to lose their lives if he really does declare independence? In the streets of Dhaka alone the blood will be flowing knee deep. But let's leave all that nonsense. Whatever happens will happen. Tell me, how are you?"

"Very well, sir."

"Your wife and children are all right?"

"Yes, sir."

"There's no point in keeping them here in Dhaka. Send them away to some safer location."

"Which place will be safe, sir?"

"Now there's a good question: Which place will be safe? I know a poem about that. I can't remember all of it, my memory fails me. But the nub of it was this," and Zohar recited:

> *Reveal to me a safe retreat*
> *O God my Lord and Guide.*
> *O lead me to a safe place where*
> *From Cupid I may hide.*

From noon to half past twelve Mobarak Hussain was enjoying himself as he watched his son alternately laughing and crying. During this time the thought of Sher Shah Suri Road did not cross his mind. He was choosing to ignore the fact that today was the day he would have to go there, and today was the day the colonel would be present too. However he had already arranged for someone to deliver a pot of Muktagacha *monda* before the afternoon prayer time: he had resolved to take some *monda* with him for the colonel to taste.

The news that he could be found at home on Wednesdays seemed somehow to have leaked out, for lots of people used to come and see him on that particular day of the week. Most of them would turn up just about lunchtime. Today it was Moslem Uddin Sarkar who made an appearance: he was Mobarak Hussain's uncle, his mother's younger brother to be precise, and he used to dabble in small business ventures. He could never make a go of any of his schemes, and whenever he was short of cash he would come round to see his nephew and borrow money off him. Every time this happened Mobarak Hussain felt disgusted and exasperated, yet every time he stumped up, though the amount he gave was small.

Mobarak Hussain much preferred to eat his midday meal on his own. His idea was that there should be nobody else in the room at meal times; all the various items on the menu should be set out on the table within easy reach, and he should be free to consume his food at his own leisurely pace. The sound of him rinsing his hand at the conclusion of the meal should be a signal for someone – anybody handy – to enter the room bearing a little plate containing two wads of *paan,* complete with *zarda,* for him to chew.

But today there was no escape, he had to sit down for lunch with his uncle.

"Why are you looking at me in such a disgusted way, my dear?" asked Uncle Moslem Uddin Sarkar cheerfully, looking at his nephew. "I haven't come for a loan this time. In the present environment of civil unrest my business is doing well, I'm getting a good income."

"What kind of business are you doing now?"

"I'm dealing in salt and candles. And I'm about to go into kerosene too, it looks like taking off in a similar way. I'm just thanking my lucky stars. May these disturbances go on a bit longer, that's what I say. I shall be profoundly grateful to God if it carries on another couple of months. If you like I can take you on as a partner for the kerosene thing. Fifty-fifty split. What do you say, will you go into partnership?"

"No."

"Well, forget it. Let me tell you what I actually came about. Your eldest girl – how about getting her married? She'll be doing her Intermediate exams soon. Now's the time to arrange a match. I've found an excellent boy."

Mobarak Hussain was listening, but saying nothing. He wasn't at all in favour of talking while he was eating.

"The lad is really top notch. The good Lord himself would be offended if you let such a lad slip from your grasp. Such an opportunity is God-given."

"What does the boy do?" asked Mobarak Hussain.

"Nothing. But he's going to do great things in the future, God willing."

"What a brilliant marriage proposal!" growled Mobarak Hussain, giving his uncle a dark look. "Doesn't do anything, but will do great things in future!".

"The lad has no father or mother," went on Moslem Uddin Sarkar undeterred. "His mother died giving birth, his father died when the lad was eleven years old. This boy has acquired his education by dint of his own efforts, with some help from his friends and well wishers."

Mobarak Hussain said nothing. There was no point in opening his mouth. A marriage candidate who had no occupation and was furthermore an orphan – what was there to say?

"Do have a look at the lad."

"I see no need."

"Once you meet the boy and have a few words with him you'll love him. He's remarkably good-looking."

"I have no desire either to see or to talk to remarkably good-looking boys."

"I've asked him to come to your house this evening."

"Really. Why?"

"So he can sit down and have a cup of tea with you."

"Look, uncle," said Mobarak Hussain with considerable exasperation, "it isn't as if this was your kerosene business, where you can order a hundred tins of the stuff from a dealer at the drop of a hat. What do you mean by inviting this boy for tea without even consulting anybody beforehand?"

"It's not quite true that I didn't consult anybody. I've had a word with your wife. She agreed with the greatest pleasure."

"Well, you can tell the boy not to come after all. That's final."

"Calm down, now," said Moslem Uddin, "there's no need to be so cross. I shall go to him in person this afternoon and put him off. But it's a shame – an excellent boy slipping from your hands. Sometimes when a fellow is fishing with his rod and line a huge fish bites the hook, snaps the line and gets away, and then the angler is overcome with infinite regret. That's exactly the kind of disappointment I'm feeling. This one was a giant *kalbosh* fish. Do you know what a *kalbosh* is?"

Mobarak Hussain did not reply. He had finished his meal and washed his hands, and was now popping his betel wad into his mouth.

"The *kalbosh* is a cross between the *ruhi* and the *katla*. The father is a *ruhi* and the mother a *katla*. They're supremely tasty fish, but there's one problem – they can't breed. That's why there are so few of them. You only occasionally come across one."

"Uncle, I'm going to take a short nap. I shall put on the fan and have a lie down."

"I'll be on my way, then. Let me see if I can find the lad. He lives in Old Dhaka, in a maze of back streets, so it's difficult to find the place. He lives in a one room hut which he is renting. When I go into the hut it feels like walking into a tin trunk."

Mobarak Hussain started on his way to the bedroom.

"I haven't told you the most important thing about this boy yet. In works of fiction you read of kids who never in their life come second in any exam. He's like that. First class first in his BSc Honours Physics, first class first in his MSc, first in the Intermediate exam. He was second only in the Matric. He is not asking for anything, just eleven thousand rupees in cash, as he has some debts he needs to clear. Just imagine what the boy will achieve in future. He will join Dhaka University as a lecturer. He will get a Commonwealth Scholarship and go abroad with his wife to do a PhD. Shall I invite him to come for tea?"

Mobarak Hussain remained silent.

"Shall I tell him to come? Why not let him come? Just let him come, have tea and go away. Lots of people visit you here, and you give them tea and snacks. What's the harm?"

"I won't be at home this afternoon."

"Then I can ask him to come fairly late. He could have supper with us. May I invite him? The poor fellow eats out all the time, why not let him taste some home cooking and find out what real food tastes like?"

Mobarak Hussain gave neither a yes nor a no, but went to lie down. His eyelids were drooping and that was a bad sign. Invariably if he was too drowsy his sleep would unravel almost as soon as it had taken hold.

Today the colonel was looking even smarter than usual. He was wearing a short sleeved Hawaii shirt of patterned cloth, with a light green motif on a plain white background. On his head was a red sports cap, and as usual his eyes were hidden behind dark glasses. He looked just like a tourist who had arrived at some seaside resort for a holiday; one could imagine him parking his wife in the hotel before coming along to attend this important meeting. As soon as the meeting was over he would return to his wife, and they would join hands and take a stroll down to the beach together. As he was finding it hard to keep his mind focussed on the meeting he kept drumming his fingers on the desk.

"What's that you've got in your earthenware pot, Inspector?"

"*Monda* sweets from Muktagacha, sir. I brought them for you."

"Ah, that's the thing you said you liked best of all in your country, isn't it?"

"Yes, sir."

"Thank you. Now tell me, Inspector, how are you?"

"Well, sir."

"I've made enquiries, and I hear you are carrying out your duties in an exemplary fashion. I'm pleased with you." And he added in English, "You are a good Pakistani officer."

"Thank you, sir."

"I'm going to relieve you of that pistol you have with you."

"Sir," replied Mobarak Hussain in an anxious tone, "I am accountable for this pistol. If I hand it over to you I'll get into trouble."

"I have no wish to get you into trouble. All right, hand it in at your station tomorrow."

"Right, sir."

"These pistols you fellows are using are ancient. You might squeeze the trigger and the bullet wouldn't discharge properly. I'm going to give you a better pistol."

Mobarak Hussain could hear a rumbling in his stomach; his head was spinning, and the soles of his feet felt numb. He felt as if he was standing on a quicksand and gradually sinking in, and there was nobody nearby who would pull him out. Of course Mr Zohar was there, but as usual he had his head down and was dragging on a cigarette. Today Mobarak Hussain had failed to keep a tally of the number of cigarettes Mr Zohar had smoked, and if the colonel suddenly asked him he would be unable to give a reply. Then, no doubt, the colonel would be very angry.

"Inspector?"

"Yes, sir?"

"You've suddenly become very anxious. What's the matter?"

"No, sir, I'm not anxious."

"Yes you are. Your forehead is bathed in perspiration. Shall I tell you what's worrying you? You think I'm going to issue you with this new pistol and then give you the order to go up to Sheikh Mujib and fire at him point blank. I might tell you these were your special orders from high command. Isn't that what you're thinking?"

Mobarak Hussain glanced at Mr Zohar, who was trying not to smile. How many fags, how many fags had the gentleman consumed? If the colonel decided to ask for the number, he was going to get into hot water. O Allah, don't let him ask about the number of cigarettes this time!

"Inspector!"

"Yes, sir?"

"It is possible that we may indeed come up with a plan of that kind. Sheikh Mujib killed by an assassin. Goodbye the head of the movement, and consequently goodbye the movement itself. However, if such a plan is undertaken we shall not entrust the responsibility to yourself. You are a Bengali. We cannot trust any Bengali. We don't know what kind of a shot you are in any case; probably not a very good one. What we will need is a sharpshooter. Okay?"

"Yes, sir."

The colonel shook his head. He put his hand in his pocket and drew out a cigarette, which he placed between his lips but did not light. He drew air through the cigarette and pretended to puff out smoke, in a strange kind of charade.

"Inspector!"

"Yes, sir?"

"There's this fierce tiger sitting calmly there. You people are pestering it. You are poking it with sticks, you are pouring water over its coat. Over and over you are shouting in its ear, '*Joy Bangla! Joy Bangla!*' There is no doubt about it, the tiger is going to pounce. All right, now buzz off. Zohar, give him a pistol and six rounds of ammo. Many thanks for the sweetmeats."

When Mobarak Hussain returned home in the evening he had a fever. A fever plus a splitting head. He saw that Moslem Uddin had come back with that boy, whose name was Naimul. He looked like a sun-starved arum plant, pale and thin, and much too tall for his size. No doubt he had been nicknamed Mr Palm Tree at school. But Moriam was short in stature; she and this beanpole would not make a good-looking couple at all. The lad had an audacious expression on his face; he didn't lower his eyes even when you looked straight at him, but calmly stared back.

Mobarak Hussain sat down with them for the evening meal, but was unable to eat. His fever had got worse, and his stomach was churning. He abandoned his food and got up.

When Moslem Uddin asked his nephew whether he had taken to the lad, Mobarak Hussain replied, "No, I didn't like him at all. However you may go ahead and arrange the marriage. By all means get in touch with the boy's relatives and negotiate with them. But don't ask me to get involved. Just let me know when you've fixed the wedding date. I shall provide the necessary funds. How much cash did you say the child wanted?"

"Eleven thousand."

"I shall provide eleven thousand rupees, that's no problem at all."

7

Once you've read through a poem it stays in your mind for a while; maybe not the words, but at least the rhythm. It's like the rumbling of a train, which goes on reverberating in your head long after the train itself has sped away. That was just how it was when Shahed received a letter from his elder brother; it wouldn't stop ringing in his ears for quite some time.

Irtazuddin always wrote his letters on ruled paper. He couldn't use plain paper as he was never able to keep the lines of his writing straight enough. He wrote in large, clear characters, and the contents of his letters were equally transparent. The man had not the slightest trace of obscurity in him.

Shahed had read his brother's letter the previous day at around noon. He had gone through it once more before retiring to bed at night. Now it was noon again. Shahed was planning to go out and stay out all day, not returning home until after dark. At some point he would take the opportunity to post the reply he had written to his elder sibling.

This is what his elder brother had written:

Dear Shahed, Asmani and Runi,

(The letter was written to all three. Never since Shahed's marriage had this extraordinary man addressed a letter to Shahed alone, and since Runi had been born he had included her in the salutation too.)

> I am very much concerned for you. I live in a distant village and I cannot gauge what things are like in the city. I hear all sorts of things people are saying, but am unable to tell which reports are true and which are false. So I spend my time in anxiety. Each night I say a separate prayer to the Almighty for each of you, but even so I do not feel at ease. One proof of my unease is that I have disturbing dreams about you almost every night. In one dream I saw you racing along with my little Runi in your arms and Runi's dear mother beside you. A fearsome looking brute of a man with a spear in his hand was chasing you. It looked as if he would throw the spear at you any moment.
>
> Even though I am aware that dreams are nothing, just the spawn of one's mental tensions, nonetheless I cannot help worrying. Precedents exist for God Almighty giving us a warning through the medium of dreams.
>
> At all events, all of you must come here within three days of receiving this letter. This is my command to you.
>
> May God preserve you from all harm. Amen.
>
> Irtazuddin

Shahed's letter to his brother was extremely brief. He wrote:

Elder Brother, we are coming. We'll arrive within the week.

"Hey, where are you off to?" asked Asmani.

Shahed did not reply. He pretended not to have heard Asmani speak.

"Where on earth are you going, at the height of noon?" Asmani asked again.

Still Shahed said nothing. He had been refusing to talk to her for the past two days. He was trying to conduct a feud of silence, but his problem was that he was no good at keeping quiet for long periods, whereas Asmani was only too good at it. It was she who held the record, eighteen consecutive days without saying a word. The Guinness Book of Records did not take much interest in the Bengali national sport of marital sulking, otherwise it would surely have included a record of the maximum number of days a husband and wife had not spoken to each other. Shahed was convinced that Asmani's name would make it into the book.

For Asmani it was no great deal if they spent day after day living together without talking to each other. She seemed to manage quite happily without talking. It was much more of a problem for Shahed. If he wasn't able to say things to Asmani he would get a bloated feeling inside. After seven or eight hours he would think he was suffocating, and then would come the stage when he felt really sick. It was as if he was succumbing to a serious illness, one which prevented him from breathing freely.

Shahed hadn't spoken for forty-eight hours. He was past the suffocating stage and into the feeling sick one. Even so he had resolved not to utter a word until Asmani had begged his pardon. Asmani's manner suggested that she was now mentally prepared to say sorry, and was only held back by her pride. She had been unusually forthcoming, saying things which she didn't actually have to say, and she had been hovering around close to him.

It was Asmani who was chiefly responsible for the quarrel which had erupted two days earlier. Before retiring to bed Shahed had said, "Asmani, listen, why don't you go and stay with Elder Bro in Nilganj?"

"Why should I?" Asmani had retorted.

"The situation in Dhaka is not good, and the signs are ominous. Who knows what's going to happen, or when? What's the point in running risks?"

"And you would stay on in Dhaka?"

"Yes."

"You're saying you want to stay in Dhaka and I'm to go away? So Dhaka is dangerous for me but syrup balls for you?"

"Why are you talking to me like that?"

"Like what?"

"You are talking in a highly unseemly manner. I think a young lady who's got a Master's degree in English ought to know how to speak more delicately."

"What did I say that was indelicate? Syrup balls? If that's indelicate then what on earth is delicate? Sugar candy, is that any better? Cream buns?"

"Oh, please be quiet."

"No, I shan't be quiet. You just explain to me why Dhaka is bad for me but sugar candy for you."

"Oh, very well," Shahed had exclaimed in irritation, "stay here if you want to. You don't have to go anywhere."

"Listen," Asmani had said very seriously, "just tell me straight. Do you for any reason find my presence insufferable? You keep carrying on about my going away to Nilganj, as if it would be a huge relief to you if I did. What am I supposed to do if I go to Nilganj on my own? Have long conversations with your priestly brother about the Quran and the Hadiths?"

"I told you, there's no need for you to go."

"Then again, supposing I do have to go away, why Nilganj? There are plenty of other places I could go to."

"Asmani, you're making a mountain out of a molehill."

"Oh, so it's just me who makes mountains out of molehills, is it? What about you? You're claiming you never kick up a fuss unless the matter is of monumental importance? Tell me, didn't you fling your tea onto the floor, cup and all, the other day, just because there was a bit too much sugar in it?"

The matter might have rested there, but that was not to be. Asmani had taken her pillow and stood up.

"Where are you off to?" Shahed had asked.

"Never you mind. Lie down and have your beauty sleep. You're sure to get an excellent night's sleep without me beside you. Perhaps you'll have delightful dreams too, who knows."

Asmani had gone to lie down on the sofa in the sitting room. Shahed had named the sofa "the Divan of Discontent". Whenever there was an argument between the couple, one of them always went and slept on the sofa. Most often that one was Asmani.

So Asmani had gone to lie down on the sofa, and Shahed had stayed in bed. Runi was with him. However angry Asmani might be, she would never take Runi with her to the sofa and subject her to the depredations of the mosquitoes. Meanwhile inside his mosquito net Shahed had sat thinking. As far as he could see none of what had happened justified their sleeping apart; it was definitely an over-reaction. Asmani had been over-reacting a lot recently. The unsettled situation in the country was putting everyone under strain, and to some extent everyone was behaving a bit oddly, so Asmani could perhaps be excused on those grounds. But the next second Shahed was asking himself why, why should he always go out of his way to forgive her? Why should he be an ocean of indulgence while she was a mere puddle in comparison? It was then he had decided to see how long he could hold out without talking to her.

As he was putting his trousers on Shahed thought, maybe I could start talking again now. Either his waist had got narrower or the trouser waist had expanded for some bizarre reason, anyway it was not going to be possible for him to wear these trousers without a belt. He would never be able to find the belt himself, but if he asked Asmani she would track it down in an instant. Asmani had a supernatural ability to find things.

"Could you have a look for my belt?" asked Shahed without looking at Asmani.

"All right, I'll have a look. But tell me where you're going," Asmani replied.

"Oh, there's a little job I have to see to."

"Well, you can't go for your little job now, you must take Runi to the doctor's. She's been running a temperature for four days. So far you haven't even bothered to put a hand on her forehead to see how feverish she is."

"I'll take her this evening."

"No, not this evening, take her now."

"But where will I find a doctor at this time of day?"

"All right, wait until a doctor is available and take her then. But you mustn't go anywhere before that."

"Asmani, don't you think you're being a bit unreasonable?"

"If I'm unreasonable then I'm unreasonable, but I'm not letting you go."

Shahed, keeping a calm expression on his face, was tying his shoelaces. This simple task was one he never managed to get right. Somehow the laces would tangle themselves into a knot. This seemed to have happened on this occasion too.

"So you're going out anyway?" asked Asmani in an icy voice.

"Uh-huh."

"That's fine. Off you go. But you won't find me around when you get back."

"Where are you intending to go?"

"I shall go wherever I choose, there's no need for you to worry about that."

"I asked you to find my belt; please find it, will you."

"I'm sorry, I can't. You'll have to find it yourself. You've got eyes, you're not blind."

Shahed was in a glum mood as he stepped out of the house. Asmani was behaving in such a silly way. She had never been like that before; what was the matter with her? Or was it to do with him? Had he been doing something which got under Asmani's skin? Neither of them could really understand the other.

It would be evening before Shahed returned home, and doubtless when he got back he would find the door padlocked. Asmani would have gone off somewhere with Runi. And then he would have to set out in search of them. Asmani had quite a number of relatives in Dhaka besides her parents; she would go and stay with some relative whose address was unknown to Shahed. The situation in the country was horrendous, and at any moment the army might be deployed in the city, even the most ignorant people were well aware of that fact. The only person who was unaware was Asmani, and she wouldn't hesitate to leave the house and go off somewhere in a rickshaw. The very last thing one should do in these circumstances was to indulge in childish behaviour, yet Asmani had wilfully chosen this precise time for her infantile carryings-on. What a weird woman she was!

The moment he was in the street Shahed began to feel better. This was something he had noticed recently – he was starting to enjoy roaming the streets with no particular purpose in mind. What might be the reason? The city was preparing itself for some kind of crisis. Perhaps it was the pleasure of observing those preparations from close quarters? The pleasure of being a witness to all the excitement? The pleasure of seeing how everyone in the city was being drawn much closer together than usual?

Changes of this kind were to be expected before any big event. At the time of Eid-ul-Azha, the festival of sacrifice, strangers would come up to you as you led your newly purchased sacrificial beast along and ask gleefully, "How much did you pay for it?" And after hearing the price they would comment in delight, "Brother, you did well! *Mashallah*, that's a fine ox!"

It was just like that now. A fellow might be making his way to the shop to buy some groceries, and people he had never seen before would offer him advice – buy plenty of kerosene, there's going to be a shortage of it! Get kerosene, matches, candles!

If you went into a teashop to have tea, somebody would be sure to start asking you questions. "What do you make of the situation, brother? Is our country going to become independent, what do you think?" And a lengthy conversation about independence would ensue, with arguments for and against. People sitting at nearby tables would join in. Ultimately the discussion would end in unanimity. Everyone would be one hundred percent certain: yes, the country would become independent. Another round of tea would be drunk in celebration.

The city was waiting, waiting for independence. The experience of observing this at close quarters was a pleasurable one. Shahed felt so mellow, he went on wandering the streets until well after midday.

The sunshine was beating down and Shahed's body was damp with sweat. It would have been agreeable to go home and have a shower and a good scrub down, but Shahed didn't wish to return to the house. He wanted to show Asmani how angry he was. If he stayed away until midnight he could feel that the point had been made adequately.

Shahed hired a rickshaw to take him to Aga Masih Lane. That was where his dear friend Naimul lived, in a rented place with two rooms. It was a long time since he had been in touch with him. The problem with Naimul was that he would never initiate any contact with his friends; it was always they who had to go and seek him out.

The rickshaw puller, who was well past the first flush of youth, was pedalling hard, making the rickshaw fly along at breakneck speed.

"There's no great hurry, my friend," said Shahed, "Please go a bit slower."

But the rickshaw bowled along, and the rickshaw puller grinned as he said, "Sit tight, sir, I'm going to fly you there!"

"There's no need for flying," said Shahed. "You're going to have a crash, and then I'll be killed, and never have a chance to see our country independent!"

"So independence is coming, what d'you say, sir?"

"Definitely it's coming."

"Our Sheikh sahib is going to declare it today."

"Who says so?"

"Everyone knows."

The rickshaw puller slowed down. He seemed to enjoy discussing independence with his passenger.

"Once we're independent, poor blokes like me won't 'ave any more problems, will we, sir?"

"I should think not."

"Food and clothing, everything will be on the state, what d'you say, sir? Everything's going to be free."

Shahed made no reply. It seemed better not to encourage that particular concept of independence.

"Sheikh sahib is a real tiger, don't you agree, sir?"

"A tiger, yes, undoubtedly."

"Raised on good milk from a mother of good pedigree. What d'you say, sir?"

"Oh, definitely."

"The thing I really long for is to give our Sheikh sahib a ride in my rickshaw some day. I've been and prayed for it, one Thursday, at the shrine next the High Court. I wonder if my prayer will be answered."

"An honest prayer for an honest cause is always answered," said Shahed.

When he got down from the rickshaw in Aga Masih Lane Shahed made to pay the fare, but the rickshaw puller refused to take it.

"Why aren't you taking the money?" asked Shahed.

"Everything'll be free when we're independent," said the rickshaw puller. "Just pretend we're independent already!"

Shahed stared at the man. He must remember that face. If the country really did become independent he would have to seek him out.

The man's face was as blunt and hard as a rock. His hair was sticking up in tufts. He looked very much like a certain famous person, though Shahed couldn't think who it was.

"What are you looking at so hard?" asked the rickshaw puller, smiling.

He had no sooner spoken than Shahed remembered who the famous person had been. It was the American president George Washington.

The door of Naimul's hut was closed. As soon as Shahed rattled the chain Naimul said from inside, "The door's not locked. Give it a shove and it will open. Come on in!"

"How did you know it was me rattling the chain?" asked Shahed as he entered the room. "You used the intimate form of address, but it could have been someone quite different."

"I was making a rough estimate," said Naimul. "You turn up every seven or eight days, and today is the ninth day."

Naimul was lying on his bed, the upper part of his body bare, the lower half enveloped in a lungi. He had his nose in a substantial book, *The Works of Satinath Bhaduri*. The room was so small it only just fitted the bed and a table and chair. There was a clothes rack, but it had been stowed on the bed, at the head end, making the bed that much shorter. There wasn't enough room left for someone as tall as Naimul to sleep with his legs stretched out; he had to keep his legs bent while sleeping. However the ceiling of the room was quite high. At the end of a long rod which hung from this lofty ceiling was a fan, which was revolving steadily.

Without taking his eyes off the book Naimul said, "No talking, now. Go straight to the bathroom. There's water in the bucket, there's some soap and a towel, and there's a lungi too. Have a good bath, and after that we can start chatting."

"I can have a bath when I get home," protested Shahed.

"Do as I tell you. I feel uncomfortable myself, seeing your body bathed in sweat."

Shahed went into the bathroom. He started dousing himself with water and decided he had never appreciated a wash so much in all the thirty-one years of his life.

"Hey, you idiot," called Naimul, "are you enjoying your bath?"

"I am," said Shahed.

"There are two buckets full of water. Pour the first bucketful over yourself to cool yourself down. When you're nice and cool, rub yourself all over with soap. Take your time, soap yourself slowly and surely. And then rinse yourself with the second bucketful. Are you going to have lunch with me?"

"I won't say no."

"Then today I'm going to make you try this curry made with hilsa fish roes. Once you've tasted this fish roe dish, nothing else you ever eat anywhere will taste as good."

"Who's going to be making this roe thing?"

"Goni Miah, the cook. I've placed an order at the restaurant; the food will arrive by and by. Why are you sloshing the water in such a hurry? Pour it over yourself slowly, give yourself some relief."

Shahed went on dousing himself. He was feeling so good he was beginning to get drowsy. He felt like lying down on the cold floor of the bathroom and sleeping for a while. He would lie there snoozing while some kind person kept pouring water over him.

He heard Naimul's voice again.

"Shahed, I haven't told you yet. I'm getting married."

"No! Not really!"

"Why are you so surprised?" asked Naimul. "I never said I was going to remain a bachelor for the rest of my life."

"Have you seen the girl?"

"Yep. She's got a tribal type of face, like a Chakma."

"I don't believe it! So the bride has been selected and everything, yet the rest of us knew nothing about it?"

"It's me who's getting married, what need is there for you lot to know?"

"Has the wedding date been fixed?"

"Yes."

"When is it?"

"Today."

"You're joking!"

"Have I ever in all my life said anything in jest? Give me one instance."

"At what time will the wedding be?"

"At night. It's going to be a basic wedding in front of a marriage registrar. Are you willing? Yes, I'm willing. End of story."

Shahed had stopped dousing himself with water. Naimul was a very close friend of his, yet Naimul had not thought it necessary to let Shahed know he was getting married that very night. That was Naimul for you, he was always like that. Was he really like that, or was it in fact a kind of affectation? A way of announcing to everyone – Look at me, I am Naimul, I have never come second in any examination. I'm not like you, I'm something different.

"Shahed!"

"Yes?"

"The girl's name is Moriam. I've decided I'm going to call her Mori for short."

"Oh, great."

"My future father-in-law is a police officer. His name is Mobarak Hussain."

"You really are getting married today?"

"Yes. Today's a handy day to get married on. It's a very special day, the seventh of March, the day Sheikh Mujib is going to declare our independence. The time will come when this will be our National Day, a public holiday, so I shall never forget my wedding anniversary. By the way, are you intending to go and listen to Sheikh Mujib's speech?"

"Yes."

"Why, what's the point? It's going to be broadcast on the radio, why not listen to that? Cricket matches and speeches are better on radio."

Shahed emerged from the bathroom. "I enjoyed my bath," he remarked calmly, looking at Naimul.

"I knew you would," replied Naimul as he turned a page of the book he was holding in front of him.

"I'll be off now," said Shahed.

"Off?" said Naimul in surprise. "How do you mean?"

"I mean I'm going."

"Aren't you going to have lunch?"

"No."

"Are you offended, is that why you're going?"

"Why should I be offended? You haven't done anything to offend me."

"Well, like I'm getting married without having informed you. But I really don't hold with making a big palaver about personal affairs like weddings. You know what I'm like."

Shahed said nothing. He was heading for the door.

"Come before seven," said Naimul. "You must be part of the groom's contingent at the wedding. I'm going to call in on Professor Dhiren and ask him to come along too. I imagine he will agree if I ask him. What do you think?"

Shahed went out of the building without answering. He was feeling hurt and insulted. So Naimul was getting married without having let him know in advance? He was seething.

Shahed was making his way towards the racecourse. Sheikh Mujibur Rahman was to deliver a speech on the big open green there. It was vitally important to hear what he had to say. Of course it would possible to stay at home and listen to the speech on the radio, where it was to be broadcast. But you could never tell, Yahya Khan might suddenly interrupt the speech and bring his troops out into the streets. They had made their preparations for such a move. The Governor of East Pakistan had been changed: Lieutenant General Tikka Khan had been appointed as the new governor in place of Vice Admiral S.M. Ahsan. The very name Tikka Khan had an awesome ring to it. Yahya hadn't brought him in just for fun: he had another plan in mind, which might be put into effect any day. Who could say quite how horrendous that day would be, it might be a real Doomsday. Most of the people in East Pakistan were overlooking the doomsday part; they just imagined themselves suddenly living in an independent country. But independence wouldn't come that cheaply.

Torrents of people were flowing towards the racecourse. Nor were they coming quietly, they were shouting slogans as they moved along.

Bengali heroes, gun in hand, fight for freedom for our land!
Smash Bhutto's fat mug with your stave, to win the freedom that we crave!
Unheeded votes, or our own way? Our own way, our own way!
Our dear land gives us stamina – Padma, Meghna, Jamuna!

It seemed as though every single person in Dhaka had come along; there were hundreds of thousands of them. Whichever way you looked there was an unbroken sea of heads. Many people had brought children with them, and there were women too, saris covering their heads, looking all around them with wide eyes. A little girl perched on her father's shoulders was crying fitfully. Her hair was coiled on top of her head and tied with a red ribbon; she was rocking herself as she cried, and the red ribbon was bobbing; it was a charming sight. Shahed gazed admiringly at the bobbing ribbon, and wished he had brought Runi along. He could have sat her on his shoulders and let her witness this rare sight, this ocean of humanity. It was a great privilege to see this scene. Had so many people gathered in one place at any time in history, anywhere in the world?

Just before the speech began, two helicopters flew over. A wave of near panic swept through the crowd. Next to Shahed stood an elderly man with an umbrella which he was holding like a stave in an offensive posture, as if war was about to break out right now and he was going to join the fray, umbrella in hand. He turned to Shahed and said smiling, "'e's going to declare independence today, our Sheikh sahib!" Saying which he spat out the juice of the betel wad he was chewing. The juice landed on Shahed's trouser leg. The bright red stain on the white cloth looked just like blood. Shahed was about to say something rather cutting, but the speech had started and all around there was a tremendous hush as several hundred thousand people all held their breath at once. People wanted to hear every single word their great leader was going to say, without missing a syllable.

The speech went on. From time to time Sheikh Mujib would stop to take a breath, and then a great roar would rise, loud enough to shake the heavens: "*Joy Bangla! Joy Bangla!*"

The deep voice of Bangabandhu Sheikh Mujibur Rahman was floating through the air, and above him the helicopters were circling like pariah kites. Shahed was keeping an eye on the sky while listening to the speech. Suppose they did something this very day? Suppose those helicopters dropped a couple of bombs?

> *I have come before you today with a heavy heart. All of you know and understand that we have been doing our utmost. But sadly today the highways of Chittagong, Khulna, Rajshahi and Dhaka are covered in the blood of our brothers. The people of Bengal wish to stay alive, the people of Bengal wish to enjoy their rights. What crime have we committed? In the elections the people of East Bengal overwhelmingly gave their votes to me and to the Awami League. What we wish is to take our seats in the National Assembly, draw up a Constitution and make history for this country...*

The helicopters were being a nuisance. What did they want? The little girl had started to cry again; she was probably scared.

Shahed started considering whether or not he would go back to his friend's place when the speech was over. Today was Naimul's wedding day. Shahed could hardly think of staying away on such an occasion. He was cross with the fellow, but his anger must be suppressed for now. There would be time to demonstrate his annoyance later on... But what was this, why was he pondering all these things instead of listening to the speech? He must pay attention to every word the great leader uttered; the speech might contain cryptic instructions.

> *Soldiers, you are my brothers. If you stay in your barracks, nobody will reproach you. But don't try firing on us again. You won't be able to hold seventy million people down. Now that we have learned what dying means, nobody is going to be able to hold us down any more.*

Shahed was trying to follow the speech with full concentration, but it was no easy matter, concentrating so hard – from time to time everything would go blank. The human brain wasn't capable of such sustained effort, and sometimes it wanted a little break.

8

He went on rattling the door chain for some time, and finally the door opened. The man who opened it was bare-chested and wore a dhoti round his loins. His name was Dhirendranath Ray Choudhury. A former professor of Dhaka University, he was now living in retirement. He used to spend all his time reading books: he would start reading straight after breakfast, have a nap after lunch, resume his reading as soon as he woke up again and continue until he went to bed. He was enjoying his retirement to the full.

"Were you sleeping, sir?" asked Naimul as he bent down to touch the feet of this much loved figure in respect. "Have I disturbed your nap?"

Dhirendranath Ray Choudhury had in fact been asleep. But thinking this young student might be embarrassed if he said so he smiled and with effortless mendacity replied, "No, of course not! Why would I be taking a nap at this time of day?"

"Do you recognize me, sir?" asked Naimul.

"Why should I not recognize you? Of course I recognize you. Do come in. Tell me how you are, are you well?"

"Sir," said Naimul, "if you're still unable to recognize me I shan't come in. Every time I've been here so far, you haven't actually recognized me but merely pretended to know me."

"But I really do recognize you."

"In that case, what's my name?"

"Wait a second while I fetch my spectacles. Without glasses I can't make out anything that's out of range."

Smiling to himself, Naimul remained standing in the doorway. Dhirendranath Ray Choudhury went to his bedroom, put on his glasses, and returned to look at Naimul attentively for a while. "Your name is Shahed," he said eventually. "That's right, isn't it?"

"Fifty percent right, sir," said Naimul as he stepped into the flat.

"How can it be only fifty percent?" the professor asked, perplexed.

"My name is Naimul, and you said Shahed. Shahed is my mate. On three or four occasions I've had him with me when I came to visit you. And you've remembered his name, although he was never a student of yours, whereas I was a student directly under you."

"Well, how is Shahed?"

"He's well."

"Why didn't you bring him? You shouldn't have come on your own, you should have brought him along."

"Why ought I to have brought him, sir?" asked Naimul.

Dhirendranath Ray Choudhury surveyed his former student in confusion. Sometimes these students put a person well and truly on the spot

"Would you like tea, Naimul?"

"Yes, sir."

"All right, you go to the kitchen and put some water on to boil. Today I'm going to give you something highly unusual to eat with your tea: sesame seed toffee balls. How long are you going to stay?"

"About an hour. I'll have to go at seven."

"All right, that's no problem."

"I came to see you for a particular purpose, sir."

"And what's that?"

"I'm getting married, but I haven't got any responsible relatives in Dhaka. I want you to come along as my guardian."

"Of course, of course!"

Saying "of course" was a bad habit the professor had. He used to say "of course" even before he had finished listening to whatever was being proposed. At the university he had been nicknamed Professor Of Course.

"Sir, did you pay attention to what I was saying?" asked Naimul.

"Saying about what?"

"I was saying, I'm getting married and you are to be my guardian."

"Well, I *am* paying attention. And there's another thing – let me tell you the truth – now I really do recognize you. Even when you told me your name was Naimul I couldn't recall you, but now your way of speaking has jolted my memory. You got a Commonwealth Scholarship, didn't you?"

"Yes, sir. I got a place at Aberdeen University, solely on account of a letter you yourself had written to them."

"A letter? When did I do that?" asked Dhirendranath Ray Choudhury in surprise.

Naimul chatted with the professor while they drank tea. People usually sit face to face when they are chatting, but one of Dhirendranath Ray Choudhury's oddities was that he always made his students sit beside him, on his left side, when he was talking to them, and most often he would place his left hand on the student's back. It was Naimul's belief that the reason the professor could never recognize his students was that he never looked at their faces. However the moment he placed a hand on someone's back he could tell who it was.

"Sir, this is a special day I'm getting married on. You know what day it is?"

"A special day? What special day?"

"Today, it's the seventh of March."

"Why is the seventh of March a special day?"

"Please think a moment, sir, and tell me why it's special."

Dhirendranath Ray furrowed his brow and thought a moment. Then he looked at Naimul. "Seven is a prime number," he said. "March is three, and three is another prime number. That's why the day is special. Right?"

"No, sir. Today is the day Bangabandhu Sheikh Mujibur Rahman is going to declare independence. Possibly he has done so already."

"Declare independence? Not really? That's most interesting!"

Although the professor had said "most interesting" with a show of enthusiasm, Naimul knew he was not in the least bit interested. For this man even the most minor problem of physics was vastly more interesting than any worldly topic.

"Don't you ever give any thought to matters like politics and the state of the nation, sir?" asked Naimul.

"Who says I don't think about them? I do. I often do."

"No you don't, sir. The quantum theory takes up your entire universe, and you don't get to think of anything beyond that."

"Well, is there anything wrong in that?"

"There is, sir. You aren't something outside of our country and our politics. You exist within the system."

"Naimul," said Dhirendranath Ray Choudhury calmly, "there are counter arguments to your thesis. The world's work is apportioned. One type of people are made to fight, they are the warriors. Another kind go into politics because that's what they understand best. The economists are the ones who worry about the country's economy. I'm a quantum theory person and that's what I spend my time thinking about. You mentioned the system – let me say a few words about that. What is a system? It's the observable part of an experiment. Suppose I put a spoonful of sodium chloride in a glass of water. My system is then a salt solution in a glass. For the sake of argument let's say it's a closed system."

Dhirendranath Ray Choudhury continued his lecture with growing enthusiasm. Anyone seeing the way he was delivering it would have thought he was explaining some highly complex aspect of the quantum theory to a class full of students. Naimul glanced at his watch. There was enough time, the professor could be allowed to go on talking happily for a while longer. The man had no relatives around; they had all migrated either to India or to the United States, leaving him stuck in his tiny three-roomed house in Wari. His attitude was simple – what would be the point in abandoning home and motherland and moving somewhere else? Why should he go to India? He had been born in East Bengal, what question could there be of his leaving his homeland? Was he such a faithless son of the soil?

Dhirendranath Ray Choudhury brought out his famous Volkswagen car.
"Suppose we went by rickshaw, sir?" asked Naimul.
"Why should we go by rickshaw? It's your wedding day."
"Sir, it's scary, riding with you in your car. You drive in a world of your own, without looking at the road."
"Naimul," protested the professor, shocked, "you young fellows have got the wrong idea about me. I'm an extremely careful driver. I have never had a car accident to this day."
"But sir, if you haven't had an accident it's not because of your driving."
"Then what is it because of?"
"It's because you never go out in your car, you're always at home. I'm sure this is the first time in three months you are taking the car out."
"You're becoming very argumentative," grumbled Dhirendranath Ray Choudhury. "Arguing is not a good habit." He sounded quite put out.
The professor's annoyance was dispelled as soon as they got into the car, and he started talking with great animation about the Kaluza-Klein theory.
"Listen carefully to this, Naimul," he said. "Kaluza sent his paper to Einstein. Mark the date, 21st April, and also the year, 1919. In his paper Kaluza postulated a fifth dimension for the first time. Einstein had previously spoken of four dimensions. So here we have Kaluza proposing an extra dimension. Einstein said no, this paper is quite unacceptable."
"You're not watching the road, sir," said Naimul, "you're looking at me all the time while you're driving."
"It's all right, I'm driving perfectly well, just listen to what I'm telling you. Two years later, on 14th October 1921, Einstein changed his mind and accepted that paper of Kaluza's. I've got hold of the original paper, which is written in German. What I need now is someone who has a good knowledge of German. Are you in touch with anyone who knows German?"
Naimul was thinking how funny it all was. Here was this extraordinary man, quite out of touch with the real world, while the streets were filled with people, some of them chanting the most remarkable slogans.

Yahya, Bhutto, two bedfellows, hang them, hang them from the gallows.
Yahya we deride, we're going to have his hide.
Bengalis, take up arms! Death to all Yahya Khans!

But Dhirendranath Ray Choudhury was taking not the slightest notice of all this. His entire being was caught up in Kaluza's fifth dimension.

"Naimul!"

"Yes, sir?"

"The way you're getting married like this, without any retinue, it's quite odd."

"Not without any retinue, sir: you're coming along with me, and I've sent word to two relatives of mine, who will join in too. They're going straight to the bride's house."

"That makes a total of four people in the bridegroom's party. It would be preferable to have one more."

"Why would that be preferable, sir? Professor Kaluza postulated five dimensions in his theory, therefore there should be five people in my team, is that it?"

"You've got it right. You're an intelligent boy, I'm delighted to see how smart you are."

Dhirendranath Ray Choudhury was so delighted with the intelligence of his pupil that he let his car wander off the road into the drainage channel at the edge.

Even with a great deal of pulling and pushing they couldn't get the car's wheels out of the gutter.

"You're getting delayed," said the professor despondently to his student. "You must get a rickshaw and go on your way. If you'll give me the address, I'll catch up with you as soon as I can get the car lifted out."

"You don't mean I'm to go on my own, leaving you here?" objected Naimul.

"Of course. You must go on ahead. You are the bridegroom and everybody will be waiting for you. Everyone will be worried if you're late, particularly the bride. Go on, off with you. These are my orders, Naimul. Tell me the address, I'll memorize it."

Soon after Naimul had gone some people managed to heave the car back onto the road, and Dhirendranath Ray Choudhury drove on towards the address he thought the young man had given him. Naimul had told him the house was No 18, the area Sobhanbag, but the professor headed for Chamelibag instead. He spent the next few hours, until late at night, searching Chamelibag for a two storeyed No 18 with a yellow gate and two jackfruit trees in the front garden.

9

Moriam could hardly believe she was now married. A very strange feeling had come over her; her limbs were trembling and there was a palpitation in her chest. She had a raging thirst, yet after one sip of water the thirst vanished and she could drink no more, until after a while she would feel thirsty all over again. She put a hand to her forehead to see whether she was running a fever. You often felt peculiar when you had a temperature, she knew. But no, there was no sign of fever, her forehead was quite cool.

It was incredible, that tall thin young man sitting in the front room was her husband. Someone she had never seen before, never spoken to before, and yet, fifteen minutes ago, he had become the most intimate person in her life. Since seven minutes past eight o'clock this evening, thanks to that bizarre event called marriage, the two of them belonged exclusively to each other.

Moriam hadn't yet seen her husband properly, only rather vaguely from a distance. She was longing to see him close up. What were his eyes like? As long as he wasn't one of those people with cat's eyes! Those people with their strange grey irises, you couldn't look them in the eye when you talked to them, you felt you were talking to a cat and expected them to mew at any moment. Had he got joined-together eyebrows? Moriam greatly disliked people with joined-together eyebrows, but she knew the saying: what you most dislike is what you get. She was surely going to discover that this Naimul fellow had eyebrows which ran into each other. Ah well, never mind about the eyebrows, she would get whatever she was fated to get. Marriage was a matter of luck.

A moment ago her youngest sister, Mafruha, had come up to her and said, "Sis, your husband is very good looking." She had wanted to ask, "But has he got joined-up eyebrows? Pop back and check, will you please, darling?" – only she had felt too embarrassed to actually say that.

"Brother-in-law isn't going to stay here tonight," said Mafruha. "He's going away now."

Moriam's heart contracted. She hadn't even seen him properly yet, how could he go away? She doubted whether such a thing had ever happened before: for a groom to come, sit through the wedding ceremony and then vanish straight away. Moriam's spirits fell. However, putting on an air of indifference she replied, "If he's going, he's going. What does that matter to me? What time is he leaving?"

"His junior uncle is saying he's got to leave now, as he lives in Narayanganj and has a long way to go. But whether brother-in-law is planning to leave with him or not, I don't know. Brother-in-law hasn't said anything."

"Why do you keep saying 'brother-in-law'? It sounds awful. You don't even know him."

Moriam's words belied her real feelings, for the sound of her little sister saying *brother-in-law* was music to her ears. She said it in such a sweet, drawling way, "Bro-o-ther – in – Law".

"Tell me, Mafu," said Moriam (Mafu was her pet name for Mafruha), "how does this wedding sari look on me?"

"You look wonderful," said Mafruha.

"Run along now and see whether they're really leaving. If they go, who's going to eat all the nice things Mum has been cooking? And Masuma has been sitting watching the stove since early evening, she must be worn out."

Mafruha ran off to find out what was going on. Moriam stood in front of the mirror. She had done so several times before, and each time she had thought she looked pretty good. This time she thought she looked even better. Yet it was quite an ordinary kind of sari. *They* had brought it, the groom's people. It was green, but fortunately not a very bright green; for only village girls went about in garish green saris. This sari might be fairly ordinary, but Moriam had decided she would preserve it very carefully, and wear it every year on 7th March, her wedding anniversary. When her daughters grew up they would want to see her wedding dress. One of them might say, "Why is your wedding sari such a cheap one, Mum? It's a real Simple Susan village sari, anyone would look at it and think you were a field of rice."

And then Moriam would reply, "We got married in rather a hurry, and at the time our country was in a state of upheaval. Your Dad didn't have much money. He only had two kinsmen on his side, a distant cousin of his father's and his father's sister's husband, and when they suddenly turned up at our house that evening I didn't even know I was to get married."

"Didn't you have a proper wedding party then, Mum?"

"No."

"Didn't you have a turmeric ceremony before the wedding or anything?"

"No, there was nothing like that. When I was having a shower before putting on my sari my little sister – your junior Auntie – rubbed a load of turmeric paste onto my cheeks, but it had been pounded on a spice grinding block and there were some traces of dried chilli in it, which stung my eyes. Oh, it was agony! My eyes started weeping like mad, and everyone thought I was crying because I was getting married."

"Weren't you feeling like crying anyway?"

"No."

"But brides always cry on their wedding day. Why didn't you feel like crying?"

"I don't know. But everything was a bit strange at the time; there were public meetings and demonstrations taking place every day, the police were using firearms, there was a curfew and so on. It may have been because of that."

"Did you like Dad when you first saw him?"

"I liked him without even seeing him."

"But that doesn't make sense! How could you like him without even seeing him?"

"Get away with you now, child! I can't possibly explain so many ins and outs."

Moriam imagined her daughter refusing to go away even after this rebuke. Eyes wide with wonderment, she would want to hear all about her parents' wedding. And this was natural enough. Girls always love to listen to stories about their mothers' weddings.

There had only been two people on Naimul's side at the wedding: a distant cousin of his father's called Hafizuddin and his father's sister's husband, whose name was Hamidul Islam. Both of them lived in Narayanganj. As soon as the brief rite of union had been performed by the Kazi or marriage registrar, the two of them made it clear that they were keen to leave as soon as possible. Things were looking ominous. Sheikh Mujib's speech had not been broadcast on the radio after all, nor had any other programme been put on in its stead; the radio had gone silent altogether. It was possible the army had taken over the radio station; maybe they would be taking over the streets next. Better get back home as quickly as possible.

Moslem Uddin also wished to leave. He too thought it best to go home quickly, seeing as there was a possibility of trouble. He had to get to Jatrabari, which was on the way to Narayanganj, so he could tag along with the other two.

"If you can just hang on for about an hour," said Moslem Uddin, "the food will be ready. Moriam's mother is all on her own, and she's been hard pressed to get all the cooking done. I've been to check, and the pulao is already on the stove heating up." This was not true at all, for a servant had only just been sent to buy some more rice for the pulao. The *kalijira* rice which had been bought earlier on had been found to have a mouldy smell.

"Now that we're related by marriage," said Hafizuddin, "there will, *inshallah*, be many other occasions for eating together. But for today, please let us leave now. If you'll just call the bride's father, we'll take our leave from him straight away."

"Oh," said Moslem Uddin, "my nephew left the house a short while ago. He had to go to his office. You understand, I'm sure – if he's sent for he has to go straight away. The rules are very strict in a job like his."

"So our new *beai*, our new relative through Naimul's marriage, has gone away without saying goodbye to us, has he? Well, of course, we're pretty run-of-the-mill people, it must be said. We aren't important government office holders, we're just small businessmen."

Moslem Uddin had to do some fast talking in order to save the situation, though even then he had limited success. Both of the men continued to act as if they had been gravely insulted, and the insult had given them grounds for leaving without having eaten.

Mobarak Hussain was in fact still at home. He had called Moslem Uddin a short while before and said to him, "Look, the wedding is over now, and I can't stand any more of this fuss and palaver. Get them to leave, and tell the boy to go home too. We can fix a date later on for them to pick up their bride and take her away."

"I can hardly let them depart without eating anything," Moslem Uddin had said.

"Give them something to eat, then. But don't ask me to join in, I shan't take part. I'm not feeling too well myself, and Yahya is running a temperature. Having this wedding ordeal while there's illness in the house is more than I can stand."

The bridegroom's relatives had both departed, and Moslem Uddin had gone with them. The marriage registrar had already left earlier on, saying he had another wedding to perform. Now Naimul was sitting in the parlour alone. For a while Mafruha had been with him, but now she too had disappeared. She had been summoned to perform the task of stretching her father's hair, a job which filled her with apprehension: if she tugged too hard she would earn a sharp reprimand, but she would get equal blame if she didn't pull hard enough.

The middle daughter, Masuma, was in the kitchen. It was she who was doing all the cooking today. Safiya was sitting out on the kitchen verandah with Yahya in her lap, only occasionally popping back into the kitchen to tell Masuma what to do next. Yahya had a high fever and was crying a lot; he absolutely refused to leave his mother's arms.

"There's no need for you to come into the kitchen, Mum," said Masuma. "I can manage. Why don't you get some water and pour it on Babu's head."

"Pour water on him?"

"He's got such a high fever, surely you should cool him with water?"

"But supposing your father gets angry. The last time I doused him when he had a temperature your father was furious. He said it would make him catch cold and develop pneumonia."

"Well, do it in private so Father doesn't know you're doing it."

"Sit a bit further away from the stove, dear. Your sari might catch fire."

Masuma sat further back. All of a sudden it occurred to her that this stepmother of hers was even better than a real mother. She and her two sisters must have done something extremely virtuous to merit God's reward when He sent them such a good mother.

"Mum."

"Yes?"

"Is Brother-in-law sitting there all by himself?"

"Yes. Mafruha was with him for some time, but now he's alone."

"Oh, the poor fellow. It's not right for a man to have to sit all alone for so long, just when he's come and got married. Mum, I'll tell you what, why don't you send Sister to sit with him? She could chat with him."

"And supposing your father is angry?"

"But surely the poor lad needs to get to know Sister?"

"Wait till the cooking is done, then I'll send Moriam in with the food. Then your father won't be able to object."

"Brother-in-law looks like a prince, don't you think, Mum?"

"Yes. Moriam will like him."

"Oh, forget about Sis liking him, Mum. Even if you dragged the most notorious thug in from the street and married her to him, she'd love him with all her soul. She'd say in an adoring tone, 'All my life I'd always been hoping for a thug just like you.' Isn't that the truth, Mum?"

"I rather think it is."

"But I'm not like Sis. It's really hard to please me."

"Each one of you sisters has her own character – that's quite natural."

"And I won't have a pauper's wedding like this one. I'll have to have a sari from Benares, and enough jewellery to cover me all over. I don't hold with off-the-peg weddings like this."

"You need to reduce the heat on that stove, dear. The flames are too high."

"You know, Mum," said Masuma as she adjusted the fire, "Father hates all three of us sisters, he can't stand us. Why do you think that is?"

"Who says he can't stand you! He has very tender feelings for you all. Just he's a bit different from other people and it doesn't show."

"But if he had tender feelings..."

But Masuma couldn't finish her sentence. Babu had started waving his arms and legs and howling once again. Safiya went off with him to the bathroom, and there she quietly doused his head with water.

It was now ten o'clock at night.

It was time for Naimul to get his food. Moriam had entered the room carrying a tray. Her hands were trembling, and it looked as if they would suddenly give way and the bowl of *korma* would crash to the ground.

"Well, Moriam, how are you?" asked Naimul, looking at her.

Moriam felt a shiver of delight. What a lovely voice! And how affectionately he was asking her how she was! Moriam felt like saying, "I'm fine, and how about you?" She would use *tumi*, the familiar mode of address, right from the start. If you started off using *apni*, the polite form of 'you', that made it quite hard to change to *tumi* later on. A friend of hers, Joshi her name was, had got married and started by calling her husband *apni*, and now she was quite unable to change to *tumi*. Moriam didn't wish to make the same mistake; she would use *tumi* right from the beginning.

But there was nothing doing, no sound at all would come out of Moriam's mouth. There seemed to be a solid block in her throat.

"Your name," said Naimul, "is of such a kind that there's no way I can shorten it into a nickname. If I did shorten it I would have to call you Mori°, and I'm sure you wouldn't like that at all."

"You can call me anything you like," Moriam thought. "Whatever you call me, I'll love it."

"There's no need for you to serve me," said Naimul, "I can help myself. You needn't say anything, just take a seat and listen to me. There are some important things I need to tell you. But why are you staring at the floor? Look at me while you're listening. When you're being given important information you should look the other person in the eye."

How could she look him in the eye? She felt so funny now, she couldn't take in a word of what the fellow was saying.

"Listen, Moriam. I'm sure you think me a rapacious individual, because I've taken eleven thousand rupees off your father. I have some debts which absolutely must be paid off, that's three thousand rupees. I need the rest of the money to buy a ticket to America. I've won a teaching assistantship at the State University of Moorhead, North Dakota. They are going to pay me four hundred dollars a month, but won't pay for my ticket to go there. So I had to get hold of the money this way."

"When will you be going?" asked Moriam. The moment she had uttered the words she felt like giving herself a slap in the face. She had made Joshi's mistake and started using the polite *apni*.

"I've got my student visa," said Naimul, "so now I can go any time. I haven't told anybody about this, as I never like making a big deal out of things. Listen, Moriam, as soon as I'm in America I'll send back your father's money. I've told you all this so as to erase from your mind any idea that I'm a scoundrel."

The fellow stopped talking and continued looking at her. Normally if any man stared at her she felt uncomfortable, but now he was looking and she was really enjoying it! Ah, if only his skin could have been a shade lighter!

"Moriam!"

"Sir?"

"The cooking was excellent, and I greatly enjoyed my meal. Who did the cooking, your mother?"

"Yes."

"Well, I must leave now. It's very late."

Naimul was startled to see Moriam suddenly exit, as if there was some tremendously urgent duty she had to perform that very instant.

Safiya was sitting on the verandah. She had handed Yahya over to Masuma for her to hold. The whole day had been a great strain, and she herself was now feeling ready to collapse. Suddenly she was surprised by Moriam, who appeared in the verandah like a whirlwind and said in a low voice, "Mum, I won't let him go alone so late at night. I won't!"

Having arrived like a whirlwind Moriam had spoken her words like a whirlwind too, and Safiya couldn't catch what she was talking about.

"Mum," Moriam went on, "tell Father to make arrangements so he can stay here overnight. I really won't let him go alone. If he goes, I'm going to go with him."

Safiya finally caught on, and laughed.

"Why are you laughing, Mum?" asked Moriam in a tearful voice. "I didn't say anything funny. Fix something for him. I leave it to you how you do it."

But Safiya was unable to fix anything. After seeing off his son-in-law Mobarak Hussain came into the verandah to find his eldest daughter weeping bitterly.

"What's the matter?" he asked in tones of great exasperation. "What are you crying for? Don't you like the boy? I've done the best I can. Now wipe your eyes."

Moriam wiped her eyes.

"Off with you, now, go to bed. I'm warning you, don't let me see another teardrop."

Moriam gave her eyes another wipe and went to her bedroom.

10

Mobarak Hussain peered at the man intently. What was Mr Zohar doing here? At Sheikh Mujib's residence, so early in the morning? It was hardly daylight yet; according to his watch the time was five past six. Only people who were in the habit of performing the *fajr* prayer were normally up and about at that hour. Or perhaps he was mistaken, perhaps that man wasn't Mr Zohar at all, it was somebody else. His face looked the same, but it was nothing unusual to come across a person's double. Whenever Mobarak Hussain had seen Mr Zohar his face had been covered in stubble, whereas this man was clean shaven. Then again, Mr Zohar would undoubtedly have had a glowing cigarette in his fingers, but this man wasn't smoking. He had a pale ochre coloured shawl wrapped around him and both his arms were invisible under it, but he surely wouldn't have a lighted cigarette under his shawl. Who was he, anyway? Why was he wearing a shawl in such hot weather?

Even at this early hour there were many people around Sheikh Mujib's house. A gang of factory workers wearing read headbands had come from Tongi. They had arrived before the dawn prayer time and set up a rousing chant of *"Joy Bangla! Joy Bangla!"*. It seemed they had saved up all the vocal power at their disposal for a big shouting match outside Sheikh Mujib's residence. Alarmed by the din of their slogans, the neighbourhood crows had taken flight. Mobarak Hussain had gone up to their leader and said, "Sheikh Mujib is saying his prayers. Kindly keep silent for now."

"And who are you?" the leader had demanded irascibly. He had an exceedingly tough appearance, a mouth full of betel quid and a gold chain round his neck.

"I'm no-one in particular," Mobarak Hussain had replied.

The words 'I'm no-one in particular' have a magic of their own. A slight adjustment to the way they are spoken, and they take on an opposite meaning: I am somebody quite significant. That was the meaning Mobarak Hussain had given them.

"I'm the president of the Tongi Workers' League," the man had said as he spat out some red betel saliva. "My name is Ismail Miah. Sheikh Mujib knows me, he dined at my house once."

"Delighted to hear it," Mobarak Hussain had remarked.

Lowering his voice a little Ismail Miah had gone on, "Is there any chance of our getting fed here? None of us have had any breakfast yet."

"There isn't any provision for feeding."

"When will Sheikh Mujib come downstairs?"

"That's something only he can say, my friend."

"What are you here? What's your position?"

"I have no official position. As I told you, I'm nobody in particular."

There was Mr Zohar, strolling around close to the factory workers. He glanced at Mobarak Hussain a couple of times, but showed no sign of having recognized him. So could it be that this fellow was not Mr Zohar at all, just someone who looked like him?

Mobarak Hussain went closer. His suspicions had been right – the man was indeed Mr Zohar. Zohar looked at Mobarak Hussain and smiled, a smile of recognition and even of pleasure, as if he had bumped into the other by chance and was glad to see him.

"How are things, sir?" asked Mobarak Hussain.

"Fine," replied Zohar.

"Why have you come here?"

"Just to have a look. Has Sheikh Mujib passed any law to say that Bihari people are not allowed to come and look at him?"

"All this time I haven't seen you light a single cigarette."

"What, smoke in front of Sheikh Mujib's house! I could never do anything so disrespectful. Whatever else I may be, I'm not a rude person."

"Why are you wearing a shawl when it's so hot?"

Zohar was silent for a moment and then said, "The air was cool when I set out. But the case is not what you're thinking, I have nothing hidden under the shawl. Do you want me to take it off and show you?"

The two of them stared hard at each other, neither dropping his eyes. Then Mobarak Hussain said, "It's very hot, so it would be best to remove your shawl."

The hint of a smile appeared in the corners of Zohar's mouth, though the smile died before it had blossomed. Zohar was evidently amused by Mobarak Hussain's words.

"And if I don't take it off I'll have to go away from here?"

"That's it."

"Then I'll be off. But I feel like a cup of tea. Is there a tea stall anywhere nearby?"

"There is."

"Come along then, let's go and have tea together. Addictive pleasures should never be enjoyed alone. Drinking tea is an addiction, wouldn't you say?"

"Let's go."

The two of them emerged from House No. 32 and crossed Mirpur Road. On the far side was a barber's shop, which caught the eye of every passer-by as it had an amusing sign hanging outside it:

> THE ROAD WHERE SHEIKH MUJIB DOTH STOP
> IS ALSO WHERE I HAVE MY SHOP!

The barber's shop hadn't yet opened, but the tea stall had. A boy aged about ten was rolling out parathas ready for frying. He had a pathetic, orphaned look and big round eyes.

Entering the teashop Zohar took off the shawl, folded it lengthwise and draped it over one shoulder. Then he looked at Mobarak Hussain and smiled. "Now do you believe there was nothing hidden under my shawl?" he asked quietly.

Mobarak Hussain nodded.

"If you still have doubts you can frisk me."

"There's no need."

"Why don't we take our tea and sit out on the roadside with it? Do you have any objection?"

"No, no objection."

They stood together on the pavement. Zohar had lit a cigarette, which was probably why he now looked more cheerful.

"Inspector."

"Yes sir?"

"You remember I once set out my reasons why I thought East Pakistan would never become independent?"

"Yes, I do remember."

"Did you think my arguments were valid?"

"I did."

"But now I realize my reasoning was at fault. If Sheikh Mujib so desires, this country will indeed become independent. Do you know how I have worked that out?"

"No."

"It was seeing your reactions that made me realize. It is unthinkable that any Bengali would do anything to harm Sheikh Mujib. Forget about actually harming him, no Bengali can even entertain the idea of going against him. If that is the case, what alternative is there to independence? It amazes me to think that a person could reach such a position in so short a time."

Mobarak Hussain said nothing. Though not a habitual tea-drinker, he was quite enjoying this early morning cup.

"Inspector."

"Sir?"

"Even now I don't think anything that has happened yet needs to worry the authorities in Pakistan. Sheikh Mujib is a leader from a middle class background, a bourgeois figure. Leaders of that sort don't in the first instance think along lines of armed conflict; they prefer less disruptive solutions. Take for example India's Jawaharlal Nehru or Mahatma Gandhi. They achieved the independence of their country by going to jail, by conducting a non-cooperation movement. They were both bourgeois leaders, and they didn't approve of armed conflict as a first resort. Nor will your Sheikh Mujib. Do you follow what I'm saying?"

"I'm trying to, but I'm rather slow witted. I can't grasp things that easily."

"I believe your Sheikh Mujib is another one with Gandhi-type ideas in his head. He thinks of running a non-cooperation movement, being sent to jail and winning independence that way. He will be content even if full independence proves not to be possible for the time being. He'd settle for a confederation, a kind of united states. Those earlier leaders knew very well that such a fate would befall Pakistan. When Muhammad Ali Jinnah realized there were going to be two separate bits of Pakistan he was disappointed enough to say, 'What good is a worm-eaten Pakistan to me?'"*

"People change," remarked Mobarak Hussain.

"Of course they do," Zohar replied promptly. "Circumstances change them. Like the notorious robber who turned into a holy man. A great *sadhu* can turn into a murderer. That's precisely the problem. You seemed to enjoy that cup of tea quite a lot; would you care for another?"

"I would."

"Don't you want to go and listen to the speech?"

"What speech?"

"Moulana Bhashani is to give a speech at the Paltan ground today. I reckon it will be a very significant one, which will be worth listening to."

"I never listen to speeches," said Mobarak Hussain. "I can't abide them. Anyway, I'm on duty at Sheikh Mujib's place. I can't forsake my post."

"And for whom are you actually performing that duty, may I ask?" said Zohar as he tossed away his second cigarette and lit a third.

Mobarak Hussain was unable to answer.

"You don't know what to say," remarked Zohar quietly, "because you yourself don't know what the answer is. But I know. The entire Bengali nation is currently on duty for one single person, and that person is Sheikh Mujib. If only I was a Bengali instead of a Bihari I should relish the situation."

---

* see *Ardhek Jivan (Half a Life)* by Sunil Gangapadhyay – **Author**

Mobarak Hussain was standing near the gate of House No. 32. There was even more of a scrimmage than usual. People were arriving all the time, and the road outside was like a river bed with a current of humans flowing along it. There were waves in the flow, just as in a real river, now more people, now fewer. Mobarak Hussain enjoyed watching this strong, swift torrent of humanity. The idea suddenly struck him that he ought to bring his three daughters here to see the sight; they might think it was fun. They seldom got out of the house and never saw anything like this. It was not far from home; he should bring them some day.

"Hello, what are you up to? How are things?"

Mobarak Hussain jumped. Sheikh Mujib was making his way out, attended by his retinue. Several cars were waiting in the road outside, and he was about to climb into one of them, but had stopped short on catching sight of Mobarak Hussain. He was smiling.

"I'm fine, sir!"

"Are your three daughters all right? What were their names, now – Moriam, Masuma and Mafruha, isn't that it?"

"Yes, sir, you've got it."

"Moulana Bhashani is giving a speech at the Paltan ground today, aren't you going to go and listen? It's no good only attending to me, you should hear what others have to say too."

Sheikh Mujib went on his way, and Mobarak Hussain was left staring after him. That man had remembered the names of his three daughters, having only ever heard them once! To say that he had an astonishing memory would be an understatement.

Mobarak Hussain was not in the least bit interested in hearing Moulana Bhashani's speech, yet he went to attend it. Even more remarkable, he took two of his daughters along. He had wanted to take all three, but the eldest was nowhere to be found; it seemed she had slipped out of the house and gone somewhere without telling anyone. Mobarak Hussain made a mental note that such wanton behaviour must be punished, would be punished in due course. True, the eldest daughter was married now, but what of that? She still lived with him, and as long as she continued to remain at home she must obey the rules of the house.

Masuma and Mafruha were both stiff with fright. It was no pleasure for them to go places with their father, but nor did they dare refuse. They emerged from the house feeling downcast and not a little apprehensive. Their father hadn't told them where he was taking them, and they didn't have the courage to ask him.

Mobarak Hussain chartered a rickshaw, and made the youngest daughter sit on his lap. Mafruha looked as if she was ready to die with shame; she felt like crying, and only with a great effort could she hold back her tears.

"We've still got some time," said Mobarak Hussain, "would you like an ice cream?"

"No, thanks," mumbled both girls.

"Why ever not? Come on, let me get you some ice cream."

Mobarak Hussain went into a Baby Ice Cream shop and bought ices for his daughters. They both set to, licking their cones with gusto, and the sight was a pleasing one.

"Sheikh Mujib knows the names of all three of you," remarked Mobarak Hussain as he lit a cigarette. "He was asking me about you this very day. He asked how you all were."

"How come he knows anything about us?" asked Masuma timidly.

"Oh, that's a long story," replied Mobarak Hussain. "There's no need for you to hear that. Hurry up now, finish off your ices, the speech has started already."

"What speech?" Masuma asked in surprise.

But Mobarak Hussain gave no reply. It irked him to have lengthy conversations with his daughters.

The Moulana addressed the sea of people on the Paltan ground as follows.

> Thirteen years ago, at the Kagmari conference, I said 'goodbye, let's go our separate ways'. For although the late Shaheed Suhrawardy was a man of keen intelligence, he was unable to agree with what I had proposed that day. I had realized that if the two sections remained together, then, just as the two sections of someone's heart can be destroyed by the germs of a fatal disease like consumption, so would the two parts of Pakistan both be damaged. That was why I said, 'You lot can draw up your own constitution, and let us draw up our own. In the words of the Holy Quran, lakum dīnukum wa liya dīn – let you have your religion and let me have mine.' And now Sheikh Mujibur Rahman has found his way home. I congratulate seventy million Bengalis for having at long last accepted what I, an old man, said thirteen years ago. *

At the time Moulana Bhashani was giving his speech Moriam was in Old Dhaka, searching for a particular address in Aga Masih Lane. Her efforts to find it were unavailing, and she was feeling terrified. She had never before gone anywhere on her own, let alone sought out an address in an unfamiliar area. She was looking for Naimul's house. Since his departure after the wedding Naimul had been out of touch. The rest of the family were useless, they didn't even attempt to find out how he was. But these were bad times, and one never knew what might happen to anyone.

Moriam had resolved to go and fetch him that very day. Never mind what any of her family members might say. Even if her father drew his pistol and shot at her, she wasn't going to leave her man on his own any longer.

The poor fellow lived alone and took his meals in a restaurant. Why should he have to eat in restaurants? How could he hope to remain in good health if he went on eating restaurant food day after day? And if he fell ill it was she, Moriam, who would have to look after him; for who else would do it?

Just before dusk she was finally led to the house by a thuggish looking young man with a moustache. Speaking in the Dhaka city dialect he said, "Mista Naimul lives in this gully. Call 'im – 'e'll shout back."

Moriam was convinced she had fallen into a trap. How could Naimul possibly live in such a slum? This thug must have purposely led her astray. Next minute he would shove her into the hut and shut the door on her. Trembling, Moriam rattled the door chain. She was watching the thug out of the corner of her eye; he was still there, standing in the lane, gazing at her.

After she had rattled the door chain twice Naimul's solemn voice could be heard saying, "Come in, Moriam, the door isn't locked."

---

* *Documents of the Bangladesh War of Liberation: Volume Two*, Ministry of Information, Government of the People's Republic of Bangladesh.

How could he know who was at the door just from hearing the chain rattle a couple of times? Moriam never did get to the bottom of that mystery, for Naimul would never tell her.

11

"Listen a moment," said Asmani as she set down the cup full of tea, "you're going to have to make a trip to the shop."

As was her habit, Asmani had had a bath as soon as she got up in the morning. She had put on a clean sari and painted a vermilion spot on her forehead; very likely she had added a light dusting of antimony around her eyes as well; anyway, she was looking gorgeous.

"Hey, why aren't you answering?" she continued.

Shahed frowned and took a sip of tea. He had two newspapers in front of him, the *Dainik Pakistan* and the *Ittefaq*. He hadn't yet unfolded the *Dainik Pakistan*. The pages of both newspapers were full of red hot news. Listening to his wife's chatter and going to the shop were low priorities right now; his immediate concern was to go through the papers, and he could think about other things later on.

"Drink up your tea quickly, now," urged Asmani, sitting down beside Shahed.

Asmani seemed more cheerful than usual today, though it was hard to say why.

Shahed sipped his tea. It wasn't quite sweet enough, but he couldn't be bothered even to ask for another spoonful of sugar, as if asking for sugar would be a waste of precious time. A great picture had been printed on the front page of the *Dainik Pakistan*. Black flag flying, Sheikh Mujibur Rahman was on his way to the President's House for a meeting with the President. The paper would undoubtedly carry a detailed report on what had been said at the meeting.

"Don't even touch those newspapers now. Once you start reading them you'll be glued to them for at least an hour. You must finish your tea and pop along to the shop, that's far more urgent than any meeting between Sheikh Mujib and Yahya."

"Oh, really?"

"Yes, indeed. Let Sheikh Mujib worry about his country, I have to worry about my own household and its food supply."

"Isn't the country yours too?"

"For me household comes first, country second."

Scathing words came to Shahed's lips, but he controlled himself. It was no good getting bitter so early in the day. He concentrated on scanning the paper.

Asmani stretched out an arm and plucked both the newspapers from him. Shahed felt the blood rush to his head, but he mastered his anger and lit a cigarette. He didn't wish to start a quarrel just now; there would be plenty of time for that later. The important thing at this juncture was to get the two newspapers back, using some clever stratagem so that Asmani wouldn't realize what was happening. At this moment he was desperately keen to peruse the papers, but he knew that wives tended to view anything their husbands were particularly keen on with disapproval.

Asmani put a hand on Shahed's back. "As well as going to the shop," she said, "you'll need to make a trip to the market. We have nothing left, you'll have to get rice and other groceries. Everybody else has been buying foodstuffs and stocking up their larders; it's only us who have no supplies."

"Let me just have a look at the papers," said Shahed, trying not to sound too keen.

"Not now," said Asmani. "You can't have your papers yet. You must go to the shop, and then the market; and after that you can have your papers back. They aren't going to fly away."

"Nor will the shop fly away, or the market for that matter," argued Shahed, suppressing his irritation.

"Oh all right," said Asmani, "I'll be very kind and let you off going to the market until later. But you must go to the shop. You simply have to get a size two exercise book for Runi. She insists on drawing some pictures now, before she has her breakfast. So far she's refused to eat anything. She's become so stubborn, that little girl of yours! I'm pretty sure it's from you she's inherited her stubbornness. If she wants to do something, then that's it. So, you've finished your tea, haven't you? You'd better get going. The child got up at seven o'clock this morning, and it's ten now. She hasn't had a bite to eat."

Shahed didn't argue. He stood up and pulled on his shirt.

"I feel bad myself about stopping you from reading your papers," said Asmani, "but anyway, when you get back from the shop you'll find a steaming cup of tea with the papers neatly folded beside it .Oh, and by the way, you must get the kind of exercise book which has an elephant on the front cover. It will be no use buying any other kind. You've no idea what a little miss your daughter has turned into. Make sure you remember the elephant on the cover."

"I shall."

"Why are you making that face like a disgruntled owl? You look just like President Yahya. Overwhelmed with all the problems of Pakistan, grumpy and weary. I've noticed your moods are always at their worst in the early morning. Hey, General Yahya! Your Excellency! Will you be going to the office today?"

"No."

"That's a good thing. In that case you can shave Runi's head today. A girl's hair will never grow really thick unless she's had her head shaved several times in childhood. So please buy a razor blade, and a bottle of Dettol in case she gets cut."

"And what else do you want? Tell me the whole lot in one go."

"There's nothing else. Well, if tenderness was on sale in the shops I'd ask you to buy a few pounds of that. I notice you've been dreadfully lacking in it recently. Oh, and there's no tea left, get some tea. Sugar, too. If you don't get those two things you'll have to drink tea with neither tea leaves nor sugar in it."

"Now just think whether there's anything else you've forgotten. I'm not going to start to-ing and fro-ing between home and shop like a weaver's shuttle."

"Nothing else. You know, when you're really cross your face does look a bit like Yahya Khan's. I'm not joking, honest. That place where you men grow moustaches, it's unusually large in your face just as in Yahya's. Oh, but what *do* you call that moustachey area?"

"I don't know."

"But that's crazy, you don't even know the name of the bit where you males go to so much trouble cultivating your moustaches!"

"Why are you babbling away like this?" growled Shahed. "You're giving me a headache."

Within ten minutes or so Shahed returned with exercise books, tea, sugar and razor blades.

"But I told you to get an Elephant Brand exercise book! Your daughter is going to burst into tears when she sees this one."

"There weren't any Elephant Brand ones."

"How come? There must have been, only it was you who forgot to ask for one. You took whatever the shopkeeper gave you and slunk home with that. Go back and change it – please."

"I'm not going to go and change it," said Shahed as he took off his shirt. "You can give the child the one I brought. You're spoiling her by indulging her all the time. The rule in life is that you can't always have what you want, yet your daughter has somehow acquired the idea that if she wants a thing she'll automatically get it. If she wants an Elephant Brand exercise book, she must have an Elephant Brand one, if she demands Tiger Brand she must have a Tiger Brand one. What is all this?"

"Why are you talking to me like that, with great staring eyes?"

"I've had wide open eyes since birth, that's why. But why are *you* looking at *me* with narrowed eyes? What have I done wrong, that I deserve to be squinted at so narrowly?"

"Well, what are you going to do when the child starts crying her head off?"

"You should explain things to her. If you explain the situation to her she won't cry her head off. Children can follow logic. It's adults who are the problem. Adults who are unwilling to follow logic."

"Then kindly go and explain to her yourself, using your celebrated logic."

Shahed sat down with his newspapers. After glowering at her husband for a while Asmani went to see Runi. Almost immediately Runi's ear-splitting cries began to be heard, such lusty yells it seemed they would bring the house down. It was impossible to ignore the wailing and concentrate on the papers. Shahed's mood was rapidly deteriorating. He felt like going and giving his daughter a slap on the cheek, but that was not an option, for if he did that Asmani would scowl and sulk all day, and come the evening he would find she had decamped with Runi to her mother's place.

"Come here, Runi darling," Shahed called. "I want to talk to you."

Runi appeared immediately.

"Why are you crying, Runi sweetheart?"

"I want to draw some pictures, Daddy."

"Excellent, that's a really good idea. Please go ahead and draw some. You know I bought an exercise book for you. In fact I was supposed to get just one, but I got two."

"But I need a book with an elephant on it. I can't draw in a book like this, this book is rubbish!"

"There weren't any of the Elephant Brand books in the shop, that's why I couldn't buy one. I'll get one next time I go out."

"No! I need it now!"

"It's not possible for people to have exactly what they want all the time, darling."

"Yes it is!"

"No, it isn't."

"It is!"

"Don't be like that, Runi. If you talk like that it makes Daddy really angry. Before you know where you are Daddy might land a big smack on your cheek."

"You can't!"

"Look, you're making me very cross, Runi dear. Be a good little girl now, trot off and draw your pictures and let Daddy read his paper."

"No, you can't!"

Runi grabbed the newspaper, and before Shahed could say anything she started ripping it up. Her face was grim, though it looked as if she was deriving a certain satisfaction from tearing the paper to bits. Excess of grief turns a heart to stone, as the proverb goes. This was the case with Shahed as he watched his daughter shred his newspaper. The instant the first great wave of shock had passed he gave her a slap on the cheek, and Runi started crying again, filling the house with her yells. Asmani came rushing in, picked up the child and stalked off with her. Shahed felt desolated. He supposed he could, if he really felt like it, pick up the bits of torn newspaper and read them like that, but he didn't want to. He longed to give his daughter another slap; it seemed to him the first one hadn't been quite sharp enough.

Runi's wailing had stopped. If the slap had been too hard she surely wouldn't have stopped crying so soon. Shahed felt like getting out of the house and going somewhere far away for a while. Maybe he would go to the market – there was in fact a real need to stock up on rice, pulses, oil, salt and so on. Everyone else had been buying those things, why hadn't he? And he could buy a few cartons of cigarettes, for in wartime cigarettes were the hardest thing of all to come by.

Asmani entered the room carrying Runi on her hip. "Look," she said in an anxious tone, "take a look at this, she has blood coming out of her mouth. Open your mouth wide, Runi darling. Go *a-a-h*."

Runi opened her mouth wide. It was a fact, her mouth was full of blood. "What have you done, what have you done to the child?" asked Asmani, mortified.

"She's cut her cheek somehow," replied Shahed rather uncertainly. "There's no need to get so upset. Let me have a look, let me hold her for a moment."

"No, I won't let you hold my little girl. How can you have the gall even to ask to hold her?"

Asmani burst into floods of tears. Runi was stretching her arms out ready to be carried by her father. Small children have this ability to forgive the person who has wronged them in a very short space of time.

"Let me just see where the cut is," said Shahed. "If necessary I'll take her to a doctor."

"You don't have to do anything of the sort. I'm warning you, don't try to pick up my little girl, don't so much as touch her."

"Why are you making such a hullabaloo, when your child isn't crying at all? And look, the bleeding has stopped. There's no more blood coming out."

Still crying. and with Runi still in her arms, Asmani went back to the other room. Shahed was now so miserable he almost felt like weeping himself. How pleasantly the day had begun, and now what a mess it was in. There was no point in his sitting morosely at home; the best idea was to go out for a while. Perhaps he might go to the office. If he did some shopping on his way back from the office Asmani might be slightly less angry with him. And he must buy a whole pile of exercise books with elephants on the cover for Runi, yes, and a kite, for she had talked about having a kite some time ago.

Shahed did not have a good time at the office. The place was half empty; hardly any of the staff had come in to work.

Rustom, the office messenger or peon, was quietly dozing on his stool. For a moment his eyes opened, he registered Shahed's presence and drew himself up as if he was going to stand, but then his eyes closed again and he fell back into his torpor.

The United Insurance Company. Once it used to be thronged with people, and now the only things buzzing around it were a few flies. It was the same in every firm which was owned by non-Bengalis. The boss was staying away from the office and the office had been taken over by the flies.

"Why have you come in today?" enquired the cashier Nibaron. "There's a strong rumour that the army is going to be deployed in town today. The discussions between Sheikh Mujib and Yahya have fallen through. Everyone is at home getting themselves prepared. So what are you doing here in the office?"

"Well, you're here in the office yourself," remarked Shahed.

"There isn't anything for me to do at home. I've already sent my family away to our village. So I came to the office, to spin yarns with you and anyone else."

"Fine, do carry on and start spinning."

Nibaron proceeded to relate all manner of interesting tales. Some of the stories had a ghostly element. The day Nibaron's uncle had been cremated a man who looked exactly like the uncle had been observed sitting on the bed in his bedroom. The man was entirely naked apart from the sacred Brahmin thread draped across his shoulder. But none of these stories appealed to Shahed.

"You look worried," said Nibaron, leaning closer. "Why don't you send your wife to your village home, then you can be like me, with no more cares in the world than a spinning top. I can spin here and there just as I please."

"I must be going," said Shahed.

"Stay a bit longer, let's chat. Would you like tea? Shall I call for some?"

"No, I don't want any tea, thankyou."

"Why not? Do have a cup of tea. Be happy!"

"How long are you going to stay in the office?" asked Shahed as he stood up to go.

"I'm actually living in the office," replied Nibaron cheerfully. "I've moved in with my pillow and all my bedding. An office is the safest place to be, these days."

It was about one o'clock when Shahed left the office building.

The city seemed to be preparing itself for some kind of special occasion. Barricades were being set up in the streets. In front of Shahed's eyes a few thousand men came pushing an ancient bus before them, and then tipped it onto its side in the middle of the road. One wondered whose bus it was they had got hold of. Had Sheikh Mujib issued an order for the streets to be barricaded? Such a thing was hardly conceivable unless ordered by him. Offices were opening and closing under his instructions, banks too.

On 23rd March, Pakistan's Republic Day, there hadn't been a Pakistan flag to be seen. Only three had been visible: one at the President's House where Yahya was staying, one at the Governor's House and one at the airport. The Bangladesh flag was being flown at the British Deputy High Commission and the Soviet Consulate. The legations of China, Iran, Indonesia and Nepal had initially put up the Pakistan flag, but in response to popular pressure had then lowered it and replaced it with the Bangladesh one. There had been no such confusion at the American Embassy, for they did not put up any kind of flag at all. Most amazing of all, the East Pakistan Rifles, at their headquarters in Jessore, had chosen to fly the Bangladesh flag.*

Today at the end of the day's television transmission the Pakistan national anthem *Pak sarzamin shadbad* was played as usual, but the fluttering Pakistan flag was not shown.

The indications were not reassuring, they were distinctly ominous. It was unthinkable that the Pakistan Army would stand by and watch all these things happening without taking any action. There was no doubt that terrible events were about to unfold; the only question was when.

Shahed didn't feel like going home yet. But what else could he do? What else? He might visit Naimul's house and spend a bit of time there. He knew that his friend's wedding had taken place, but he hadn't seen him since then. It

---

* *Bangladesher Tarikh (Annals of Bangladesh)*, Muhammad Habibur Rahman; *Ekattorer Dosh Mash (Ten Months in 1971)*, Rabindranath Trivedi.

occurred to him he should tell the girl who had married Naimul how lucky she was. Accordingly he decided that if he found Naimul at home he would get him to take him to his bride's parents' home, and there he, Shahed, would say to Naimul's wife, "Dear sister-in-law, you have no idea what an outstanding fellow you have acquired as your husband. But I do know. Naimul will get cross with you about all sorts of trivial matters, he will give you plenty of hassle, but you must always forgive him straight away: for this fellow is a genuine diamond, in whom there is no trace of impurity. If you wish I can give you a written guarantee."

Naimul was not at home. The door was padlocked, and there was a message written on a scrap of paper tucked into the padlock.

TO WHOM IT MAY CONCERN
I have become a temporary member of my father-in-law's household.
My new address is No. 18 Sobhanbag (First Floor), Mirpur Road.
Kindly do not visit me except in case of the utmost necessity.

Shahed read the note and smiled. He decided he would somehow pacify Asmani, and then take her along to visit Naimul at the father-in-law's home that evening.

Shahed got back home at around two p.m. He hadn't done any of the intended shopping for groceries, as he had forgotten to ask Asmani for a list of the things that were needed, but he had bought six Elephant Brand exercise books, a box of colouring pencils and a placatory sari for Asmani. The sari was, of course, sky blue (or *asmani* in Bengali), and it was made of Rajshahi silk. Asmani's resentment would surely soften considerably as soon as she was presented with the sari, and when she read the note attached to it her anger would be dissipated altogether. The note said, "Don't be like that, please, darling!"

The house was locked up. This did not surprise Shahed unduly, indeed he had feared he might return to find that something like this had happened. Asmani would have locked up the house and, in high dudgeon, made her way to her mother's place in Kolabagan.

But Asmani wasn't in Kolabagan. Her mother was quite upset.

"The whole city is in such a terrible state," she said to Shahed, "why did Asmani go out at all? And why do the two of you keep having silly rows with each other? I'm really annoyed with my daughter, but I'm equally annoyed with you. Go quickly now and find out where she's got to. Dear son-in-law, you've made me extremely uneasy. The city is in a frightful state and now you tell me this..."

Shahed searched all over the place for his wife and daughter, but could find no trace of them. He had left the sari at Asmani's mother's house, and that bothered him too: how embarrassing it would be if his mother-in-law happened to read that little note. It was getting very late, though as he had no watch he couldn't be sure quite how late it was. There was hardly anybody abroad in the streets, and there were no rickshaws either. The roads were so well blocked at various intervals by barricades, there was no question of rickshaws moving around as usual.

While Shahed was pacing the streets the army was deployed in the city. It was the night of 25th March 1971.

Tracer bullets flying across the sky. An aurora lighting the heavens. Patterns of light, as if dozens of glowing lanterns from a carnival were glimmering off and on. Fire spewing from the mouths of machine guns, like sparks from party sparklers. Explosions like erupting fireworks. It was a festival, a new kind of festival. A festival of slaughter and destruction. Nobody had been prepared for this particular jamboree. The sleeping population of Dhaka woke up in terror: what was happening, what was going on?

Everyone in fact knew what was happening, but nobody understood any of the details. Heavy military trucks and jeeps were trundling unhindered through the streets of the city. But hadn't all the thoroughfares been barricaded? How could they have removed all the obstacles so quickly? There were strange noises in the road. Had they sent out tanks, was it tanks which made those odd sounds as they moved along? And what was that continuous droning sound? Then there was another noise, even more peculiar, like *whoosh, wheee*!

Fear and curiosity are close companions. People in the grip of terror can be quite inquisitive at the same time. Here they were, standing at their windows, clutching the bars as they strained to see what was going on outside. Some had even come out onto their verandahs. Humans succumb to a grim kind of fascination when confronted by horrific scenes of death and destruction; after a while their senses are numbed and their brains start functioning erratically, and then they may do things which have no logical explanation.

And indeed odd behaviour of that kind started to take place. Humble, unassuming men of the harassed father-of-large-family type started screeching *"Joy Bangla, Joy Bangla!"* at the top of their voices. Such men, probably, had never once demonstrated in the streets during the long months of unrest, never chanted a single slogan; no, they had gone to their office every day and then done a bit of shopping before trotting home, carrying their little gunny bag with a gourd and the tail of a hilsa fish sticking out of it. How had they suddenly been transformed?

Soon after, the wailing and shouting of terrified people began to be heard. By then there were fewer tracer bullets lighting the sky, for they were no longer needed. The whole city of Dhaka was aglow: fires had started all over the place, and coils of black smoke were rising into the air. Earlier on gunfire had been crackling all over the city, but now it was limited to specific areas. The telephone network was out of order. The streets were not merely empty of humans, for the first time in history they were empty of dogs too. Nobody had any way of knowing what was happening or where. What had become of Sheikh Mujibur Rahman? The whole country had been under his control, hanging on his every gesture, so why was he silent now? Before his final meeting with Yahya he had told reporters that he was hoping for the best but prepared for the worst; then what had become of his preparations? Or had war broken out? Nobody could say.

A detachment of the army entered the university campus. With them they had a list of university lecturers. No longer human, they had assumed the rôle of the angel of death. They had come, in human garb, to harvest souls.

"Who lives in this house? The provost of Jagannath Hall? A Hindu, an accursed infidel? What's his name? Jyotirmoy Guha-Thakurta?" *

---

* *Ekattorer Sriti (Memories of 1971)*, Basanti Guha-Thakurta.

While his men surrounded the building an army lieutenant pushed into the house. Professor Jyotirmoy Guha-Thakurta, dumbfounded, stared at him in incomprehension.

"Are you the professor?" the lieutenant asked in Urdu.

"Yes," replied the professor in English.

"I'm going to take you away."

"Why?"

The lieutenant was in a hurry, and without replying to the question he started pulling the professor out of the house. The professor's wife Basanti Guha-Thakurta and his much-loved daughter Dola could not understand what was going on. They assumed the soldiers were taking the professor away for questioning; that was surely the worst that might happen. But he mustn't be taken away with nothing on his feet. Basanti Guha-Thakurta darted back indoors to fetch some sandals for him to wear. In the brief space of time before she returned the soldiers had dragged Jyotirmoy Guha-Thakurta outside and shot him.

Beside their house lay the corpse of Dr Moniruzzaman, face up. Another three bodies lay a short distance away. One was still faintly murmuring, "Water, water!"

Gone was the absent minded professor of philosophy Dr G.C. Dev. Before he had been shot he had spoken almost cheerfully. "Yes, I'm a Hindu. Everyone in this house is a Hindu." [*]

Maybe he believed that no persecution of the Hindu minority would ever take place, or maybe something quite unrelated was passing through his mind.

Professor Fazlur Rahman of the Soil Science department, Dr Anudvaipayan Bhattacharya, professor of Applied Physics, Dr Moniruzzaman, head of the Statistics department, Geography professor Muhammad Abdul Muqtadir, Professor Sharafat Ali of the Mathematics department, Professor M.R. Khan Khadim of the Physics department, and colleagues Muhammad Sadiq and Dr Muhammad Sadat Ali, lecturers in the Education and Research Institute, all of them now lay dead.

Soldiers poured into Iqbal Hall and Jagannath Hall. They were resolved not to let a single student escape with his life. *We've put up with your 'Joy Bangla' long enough. We're not going to stand for it any longer.*

At the two women's colleges of the university, Rokeya Hall and Shamsunnahar Hall, the girl students stared in horror and alarm as soldiers broke down the gates and entered their compound. They were too terrified even to shout for help, but stood and watched as a Pakistan army platoon marched towards them.

Army personnel set fire to the *Daily Ittefaq* office. The offices of *The People, Ganabangla* and *Sangbad* newspapers were all ablaze. Shahid Saber, a poet of meditative cast, had made the *Sangbad* office his home and used to sleep there at night; now, roasted alive, he perished in the flames.

The military operation which the Pakistan army had set in motion at one o'clock that morning was dubbed Operation Searchlight.[♦]

The operation was led by Brigadier Abrar of the 57th Brigade. In overall command was Major General Rao Farman Ali, whose brief was to bring Dhaka

---

[*] *Ostorage Sriti Shomujjol, Bangabandhu, Tar Poribar o Ami (Bright Memories at Sunset, Sheikh Mujib, His Family and I),* Mominul Haque Khoka.

[♦] *Witness to Surrender,* Siddiq Salik.

city to heel. The task of getting the rest of the province under control lay with Major General Khadem.

It was Brigadier Abrar who had sent a joint force consisting of the 18th Panjab, 22nd Baluch and 32nd Panjab regiments to ravage the university campus.

He despatched the 31st Panjab regiment to Rajarbag, the location of the Dhaka city police headquarters, to teach a lesson to the thousand or so police officers there.

The 18th Panjab was to inculcate some discipline among the treasonous folk of Old Dhaka.

The task given to another Baluch regiment was to cool down the hotheads in the East Pakistan Rifles, in the Pilkhana area of the city.

The 13th Frontier regiment was not given any particular brief; it was to remain on standby in the city cantonment as a reserve force.

The 43rd Light Bombers had been sent to take care of the airport at Tejgaon.

And a platoon of commandos were sent to No. 32 Dhanmandi, to arrest Sheikh Mujib.

At one in the morning the jubilant voice of the commander of the 57th Brigade, Major Zafar, came on air over the wireless system: "Big bird in the cage... Others not in their nests... Over."

Sheikh Mujib was brought to the cantonment in an army jeep. Major Zafar enquired whether General Tikka wished to check and see the captive with his own eyes. "I don't want to see his face," Tikka replied.

At 9 p.m. on 25th March, in the staff office of the commander of Dhaka zone, Major General Farman Ali, General Tikka had laughed as he explained to the officers charged with responsibility for the Dhaka operation, "We must create such a reign of terror in Dhaka city that the milk in the breasts of nursing mothers will turn to curds. East Bengal is like a small creature which is misbehaving, and Dhaka is its head. All we need do is smash its head to a pulp. I shall lift the curfew on the morning of 27th March, for, *inshallah*, the whole country will be back to normal by then."

With great affability General Tikka had poured tea for everyone with his own hands, and gone on, "As Shakespeare put it in *Hamlet*, I have to be cruel only to be kind. My cruelty will be a demonstration of mercy, mercy for the Bengali people. When a surgeon amputates a limb affected by gangrene he does it for the patient's own good, even if the patient doesn't realize the fact. If we don't save the ailing patient of Bengal, who will?"

At the end of the meeting the general had made a joke about the intelligence of Panjabi soldiers which made everybody crease with laughter. Laughing in front of a superior officer is a grave impertinence, but nobody could help themself, the joke was too good.

A short while after Operation Searchlight had begun, Bhutto met General Tikka Khan at the Governor's House. Bhutto seemed tense and excited, and was keen to know what was going on and what stage the operation had reached, but General Tikka Khan paid scant heed to him. There was no way he was going to discuss the details of a military operation with a civilian. Huffing and puffing, Bhutto asked if he could accompany a military convoy that night, in order to see for himself what the situation was like in Dhaka city. With a smile the general said no. "Why not?" demanded Bhutto, stamping his foot. The general simply replied, "Because I say so."

"I wish to speak to President Yahya," Bhutto spluttered.

"President Yahya has left Dhaka and right now is on his way to West Pakistan," said Tikka.

"Then why wasn't I informed?" asked Bhutto, stamping his foot again. "I could have gone with him."

"You were left behind so that you could observe East Pakistan when it has been pacified. Would you care for some coffee, Mr Bhutto, as the prime minister in waiting of an undivided Pakistan?"

Being referred to as a prime minister in waiting soothed Bhutto considerably.

An eyewitness account written by *Daily Telegraph* reporter Simon Dring was the first report posted from Dhaka to be published abroad. One section of his lengthy article reads as follows:

City Lies Silent

Shortly before dawn most firing had stopped, and as the sun came up an eerie silence settled over the city, deserted and completely dead except for the noise of the crows and an occasional convoy of troops or two or three tanks rumbling by, mopping up.

At noon, again without warning, columns of troops poured into the old section of the city, where more than one million live in a sprawling maze of narrow, winding streets. For the next eleven hours they devastated the 'old town', as it is called.

The lead unit was followed by soldiers carrying cans of gasoline. Those who tried to escape were shot. Those who stayed were burned alive.

Shahed was trapped in a house belonging to people he did not know at all. On that fatal night of 25th March he had done the only thing he could think of and darted into a back lane in Bijoynagar, the area where he happened to be. He had climbed over the gate of a one storeyed property and started hammering on the front door with all his might. A small girl had pulled aside the curtain and peeped at him through the window. "Who is it?" she had asked timidly.

"You don't know me, darling," Shahed had replied, "but please let me in."

Nobody opened the door. The sound of vehicles could be heard in the street.

"Let me in, sweetie," Shahed had repeated.

The little girl's mother had then opened the door. Like her daughter she was scared; her face had gone quite pale and she was trembling.

"What's going on out there?" she had asked.

"The army has taken over the city," Shahed had replied. "You'd better close all your windows and put out all the lights. You shouldn't have left those lights on."

From inside the house had come the croaking voice of an old man. "What did you open the door for, daughter-in-law? Who's that you're talking to?"

Shahed had had no opportunity to reply to the old man's question, for before he could speak a mortar shell had landed close by, followed by a second which seemed even closer. The whole house had rocked, and all the framed pictures hanging on the sitting room wall had fallen to the floor. A droning sound was audible. The electricity supply had gone off and the house had been plunged into darkness. Terrified, the old man had started wailing like a small child: "Oh, daughter-in-law! Oh, whatever is going on? And who are you talking to?"

The little girl had started screaming and crying. The darkness was frightening her even more than the noise of firing.

"Stay where you are, darling," Shahed had said to her. "Don't move. The floor is covered with splinters of broken glass."

A crisis draws people together. Paleolithic men used to form gangs whenever they knew dangerous predators were around, and perhaps those ancient instincts are still preserved in modern man. In the horrors of that night people came much closer to each other.

Shahed had been with this family for only three hours, and already he had begun to feel like a family member. He had started treating the woman, who was the wife of a Dacca College English teacher named Sanaullah, as if she was his younger sister, and addressing the old man, Sanaullah's father, as uncle. And Sanaullah's little daughter had attached herself to him with no hesitation. She was called Kongkon, but she was unable to pronounce her own name properly and if you asked her for it she would say "Kokon". She was about five years old, and by that age she should have been able to say "ng", so evidently she was slightly retarded in her speech. Although Shahed was a total stranger, here he was now in the family's bedroom, sitting on the big wooden framed bed along with everyone else.

Shahed hadn't yet found out Kongkon's mother's name. Her father-in-law called her Manu, but that could hardly be her real name; more likely it was an abbreviation which the old man used out of affection. It was clear from the way the old gentleman spoke to his daughter-in-law that he was extremely fond of her, though he scolded her continuously. His scoldings seemed not to upset Kongkon's mother at all, she was obviously quite used to being regularly ticked off by her father-in-law.

A hurricane lantern had been lit. Kongkon had fallen asleep, but the other three were sitting staring at the lantern. When surrounded by darkness humans love gazing at a source of light, as long as it isn't an electric lamp which hurts the eyes.

"Brother," said Kongkon's mother, looking at Shahed, "have you had anything to eat?"

"No," replied Shahed. "But I don't wish to eat anything now. In these circumstances the question of eating doesn't arise at all."

"We haven't got much in the way of food. But I can heat up some rice and fry an egg for you."

"I'm not hungry."

"Daughter-in-law," the old man exclaimed indignantly, "I'm disgusted at the way you are talking and behaving. Shall I give you some rice, shall I give you an egg, what kind of chatter is that? You heard him say he hasn't eaten; so cook the rice, fry the egg and serve it to him. If the lady of the house won't observe the rules of hospitality then who will? The man in the moon?"

"No, uncle, I'm really not at all hungry," protested Shahed in embarrassment.

"You just pipe down, son. With all this shooting going on one doesn't notice whether one's hungry or not. All of a sudden you may realize your stomach is aching for food. Daughter-in-law, you can take the hurricane lamp and go and put the rice on to boil. Put an extra handful in, I'm going to have some too."

Kongkon's mother took the lantern and went off to the kitchen.

"Where is Kongkon's father?" asked Shahed.

"Oh, don't ask me about the silly fool," growled the old gentleman. "If you so much as mention his name the blood will rush to my head. The idiot has gone to

Barisal. I told him the country was in a dangerous state and there was no sense in going anywhere, but still he went."

"He had some urgent business there?"

"Oh, incredibly urgent. He had to attend a friend's wedding. The fool, how could he think his friend's wedding was more important than the safety of his own family? Didn't his wife, his daughter, his old father count for anything to him? My daughter-in-law is little more than a child, and I am almost incapacitated. And he chose to sample tasty wedding dishes while we were here being shot at. The irresponsible ape! I told him the battery in our transistor radio had run down, and asked him to get a new one before he left. All right, Dad, he says. And did he buy one before setting off? Not likely! His lordship forgot. His lordship forgets everything except his friends' weddings. Huh! Much may he enjoy the wedding feast!"

The old fellow suddenly went quiet. There was a noise of firing coming from very close by. Shouts and cries could be heard. "Put out the lantern," said the old man in terror, "put that lantern out!"

Kongkon had woken in alarm and started to cry. "Shahed," exclaimed the grandfather, "you must make her stop crying. If the soldiers hear her crying they're sure to come this way. Put your hand over her mouth."

It was three twenty-five in the morning.

The firing had stopped for a while, but now it started up again in all earnest. The doors and windows of Moriam's room were tightly closed; a lighted candle was on the table, and Naimul was sitting in the candlelight eating a meal. He was eating with relish, but the pleasure Moriam derived from watching him eat was even greater. The only thing that pained her was the fact that when Naimul had asked for some raw green chillies to go with his meal she had been unable to supply any, as there wasn't a single one in the house. In future, she vowed, she would make sure there were always plenty of green chillies, as Naimul liked some with every meal.

"Are you enjoying the food?" asked Moriam.

Naimul said nothing but nodded in the affirmative. Moriam loved the way he nodded: most people gave just two nods of the head to mean "yes," but this special man of hers gave three. She decided from now on she too would give three nods whenever she had any nodding to do. She would follow her husband's lead in all things. Naimul suddenly stopped eating and turned to Moriam.

"You know where the best chicken pulao in all Dhaka can be found, Mori,?"

"No, I don't know."

"At Saini the Wrestler's shop in old Dhaka. I shall take you there one day so that you can taste it."

"Oh, when?" asked Moriam in a wistful tone.

Naimul glanced at his wife and grinned. What a lovely grin he had! How prettily his lips curved when he smiled! She felt like reaching out and touching his lips. She had never done anything of the sort before, but one day she would try it. And then if she saw it didn't bother Naimul, she would do it regularly, she would feel his lips with her fingers every time he smiled.

Gunfire could be heard outside. Moriam's parents' house was on a main road, and tanks were moving along it with a heavy grinding sound. Yet here they were, with this candle in front of them, having a nice cosy chat as if they were the only two people in the world.

"Mori!"

"Mm?"

"Who cooked this chicken pulao I'm eating?"

"Mum."

"It's excellent. You must learn how to make it."

"I shall learn tomorrow."

Naimul had finished his meal and was rinsing his fingers over his empty plate. Moriam longed to wash his hands for him, but she still felt shy in his presence and couldn't carry out any of the things she wanted to do. She must get over her shyness.

"Mori!"

"Yes?"

"You've got a deranged *koel* cuckoo living round here. It's calling incessantly, at night as well as by day. I can hear it now."

"I expect it's calling because it's scared. After all, shots are being fired."

"If it was a question of being scared, you'd expect the crows to make a clamour too. But not a single crow is cawing."

"That's true."

"Which bird has the most beautiful voice, tell me?"

"I don't know. Which one?"

"The *chokh-gelo* bird, the one which goes 'ko-kelo, ko-kelo'. Have you ever heard a *chokh-gelo* bird calling?"

"Yes, I have."

"Do you know what they call that bird in Hindi?"

"No."

"They call it *piu-kaha*."

"Oh, I've heard of *piu-kaha*, but I never realized it was the same as the *chokh-gelo* bird."

"And do you know what it's called in English?"

"No."

"In English it's the brain fever bird."

"What an ugly name!"

"Yes, it certainly sounds awful. Mori, aren't you feeling rather hot?"

"I am, actually."

"I can suggest something to make you fell a bit cooler."

"What?"

"You could take off your sari."

Moriam went scarlet with embarrassment.

"Now why ever should you feel embarrassed in front of me?" asked Naimul.

Moriam looked away as she said, "Then put the candle out first."

"No," said Naimul, "that's not allowed. The candle shall continue to burn. Bodies look different in different kinds of light. They look a certain way under an electric bulb, another way in candlelight, and quite different again in the light of a flaming torch. Right now I want to see what a naked Moriam looks like by candlelight."

"No, no, I couldn't! You must put the candle out first!"

Naimul did not extinguish the candle. Moriam's whole body was tingling. Every cell in it had got the message – something horrendously pleasurable was soon to take place.

"Please put out the candle," pleaded Moriam in a tearful voice. "Please!"

"No!" said Naimul, and he smiled. And then Moriam realized it was just as well he hadn't put the candle out – had he done so she wouldn't have been able to see that bewitching grin. She stretched out her hand to finger Naimul's lips.

13

At eight a.m. on the morning of 26th March a 1961 model Chevrolet, with an armed escort mounted in a jeep in front and a lorry behind, drew up in front of the Hotel Intercontinental. This convoy was to take Zulfiqar Ali Bhutto and his companions to the airport.

Bhutto looked scared. To all the reporters' questions he gave the same answer: "I have no comment to make."

When he landed in West Pakistan he announced cheerfully, "By the grace of God, Pakistan has been saved." *

---

* from a report by Sidney Sondberg.
Sidney Sondberg was the reporter on whom the character of the hero in Ronald Joffe's Oscar winning film *The Killing Fields* was based. - **Author**

Documents of the Bangladesh War of Independence
Information Ministry
Government of the People's Republic of Bangladesh
Volume 8, Page 50

Pardeshi
daughter of Choton Dom
Sweeper°, Government Veterinary Hospital
Dhaka

On the morning of 27th March 1971, after the horrific massacre carried out in the capital city Dhaka by the soldiers of the Pakistan Army, Mr Idris, an administrative officer under the then Chairman of Dhaka Municipality Major Salamat Ali Khan Shur, together with a few other officers, arrived at the gate of the Veterinary Hospital in a municipality truck and started bawling "Pardeshi! Pardeshi!" In fear and trembling I came out of my quarters. Mr Idris kept furiously shouting, in an extremely rough manner, "All you sweepers come out here! If you want to save your skins all of you must immediately go and collect the corpses which are piled up in various parts of Dhaka city, take them to the Dhalpur garbage depôt and deposit them there. Failing that, none of you shall be spared, you will all be killed." The following sweepers were already sitting in the truck: (1) Bharat, (2) Ladu, (3) Kishan.

As I could see no way of disregarding these orders, I climbed into the truck and sat there. When about eighteen of us sweepers and other menial workers had been collected in the truck and brought to the municipality office, we were split into three groups of six, each with two sweeper inspectors to supervise, put into three trucks and sent to Banglabazar, Mitford Hospital and the University respectively. I was in the Mitford truck. At about nine o'clock our truck parked outside the Mitford Hospital mortuary. We got down from the truck and entered the mortuary, where we beheld the gruesome corpses of about one hundred young Bengali men, their chests and backs peppered with machine gun bullets. As instructed by my supervisor I went into the mortuary, seized each corpse by the heels, dragged it out and handed it over to the other sweepers standing there so that they could load it onto the truck. I noticed that the chest or back of every corpse was riddled with machine gun bullets. After I had removed all those bodies I turned to another corpse which had been laid on a long table and covered with a sheet. I raised the sheet and saw the naked body of a pretty girl aged about sixteen. The breasts and genitals of the body had been mutilated, some flesh around the posterior had been hacked away and the breasts had been heavily bruised. Seeing this, and the long black hair which reached down to waist level and the eyes which were large and innocent like those of a deer, I simply could not hold back my tears and I started weeping. Under a barrage of abusive and threatening yells from my supervisor I carried this comely, blameless cadaver with the utmost care and respect, and hoisted it on board the lorry. When we had loaded all the bodies from the Mitford mortuary onto the truck we drove them to the Dhalpur garbage depôt, where we tipped them into a huge pit. I observed many other sweepers and menials offloading corpses which they had collected from various parts of Dhaka city and discharging them into the same vast pit. I noticed that most of the bodies were not clothed, indeed none of the corpses of girls and young women which were being thrown into the pit had any clothing on them at all. I observed that their pure bodies had been mutilated and their genitalia and buttocks grotesquely butchered. At about two p.m. we were taken by municipality truck to the Kali temple in Ramna green. There the truck was stationed outside the temple door, two of us were left standing in the truck while the other four of us were sent inside the temple building. We observed that the whole place had been burned to cinders. I extracted forty-one incinerated corpses from various parts of the temple where they had been lying in disarray. These corpses too we took to the Dhalpur garbage depôt, where we cast them into the pit. I was feeling utterly revolted from dragging human bodies around and inhaling the stench of decomposing human flesh. The following day I did not go out on body collection duty, for I was in no fit state to do so; I was unable to face any food the whole day long, feeling too full of disgust to touch anything. The morning after that, on 29th March, when I reported to the municipality office again, I was sent with a number of other sweepers to collect corpses from Shakhari Bazar. Fires were still burning in front of the Judge Court, and as Pakistan army soldiers were on patrol we were unable to enter Shakhari Bazar with our truck from that end. We had to make a detour via Patuatuli, past the police outpost there, to enter Shakhari Bazar from the west. When our truck had made its way into Shakhari Bazar we got out and proceeded to enter every building in the street. There we saw so many corpses – gruesome decomposing corpses of grown men and women, young people, old people, school children, teenagers, babies. Their idols had been dashed to the ground. I observed that most of the female copses were completely naked. Some of them had had their breasts cut off. Some had sticks rammed into their vaginas. I saw many badly burned bodies. Panjabi soldiers were dancing around like demons firing shots from their rifles. Bihari people were going from house to house looting valuable items including gold and jewellery and making off with them. With gunfire going on all the time around us, in fear of our lives, we collected two truck loads of bodies, but after that we did not dare to enter Shakhari Bazar any more that day. On the morning of 30th March my team were instructed to collect corpses from Millbarrack. I went with a municipality truck to Millbarrack quay and saw innumerable bodies scattered on the quayside, many of them bound together with rope. Undoing the ropes we removed all the separate bodies, of which there were ten or fifteen in each group. They were all well built young men and youths. They were all blindfolded and had their hands tied tightly together behind their backs. I saw that their faces were darkened, they had been burned and disfigured by acid. When close to them I smelt an unbearable chemical smell. Some of the groups of bodies had their chests and backs riddled with machine gun bullets. Many bodies had been viciously battered with batons or bayonets, some had their heads smashed in and their brains oozing out, others had vital organs spilling out of chest wounds. I saw the horribly mutilated naked corpses of six pretty young women at the riverside. Each corpse had its eyes blindfolded and its hands and feet tied tightly together. The bodies were riddled with bullets, their faces, breasts and genitalia were bloody and repulsively mutilated. We collected seventy corpses and dumped them all at the Dhalpur garbage depôt, making two separate trips with the truck. After that I was ordered to collect bodies from Sadarghat, Shyambazar and Badamtali quays. I recovered decomposing bodies from the riverside at all the said locations, and disposed of them at Dhalpur garbage depôt. On the morning of the same day as I collected corpses from the Kali temple, I also picked up some bodies from the staff quarters behind Rokeya Hall at Dhaka University, and a body from a professor's house west of Rokeya Hall. From inside the staff quarters behind Rokeya Hall I got a total of nine bodies, including male individuals and children, and at the professor's house I recovered, from the foot of the stairway, the body of a professor wrapped in a quilt.

signed,
Pardeshi
21/3/74

Documents of the Bangladesh War of Independence
Information Ministry
Government of the People's Republic of Bangladesh
Volume 8, Page 44

Chunnu Dom
Dhaka Municipality
Railway Sweepers' Colony
Block 223, Railgate No. 3
Phulbaria, Dhaka

On the morning of 28th March 1971 our municipality inspector of sweepers, Mr Idris, called me and took me to Dhaka Municipality to do corpse collection. From there he first took me in a truck, along with Bodlu Dom, Ranjit Lal Bahadur, Ganesh Dom and Kanai, and put us down at the entrance to the Court at Shakhari Bazar. The aforementioned five of us observed that in the road next to the southernmost entrance to the Judge Court, which leads into Shakhari Bazar, the gutters on both sides of the road were strewn with numerous decomposing bodies of young men and women, grown women and men, teenagers and children. We saw that many of the corpses had become bloated and grotesque. Houses on either side of Shakhari Bazar were in flames. I saw many half incinerated bodies lying around. Nearby, on both sides, I saw Panjabi soldiers on patrol. I saw people and household goods smouldering in every building. I entered one building and brought out the burned bodies of twelve young men as well as a young woman and a child. We recovered corpses of young men and women, teenagers, children, infants and old people from every house in Shakhari Bazar. I saw Biharis filled with riotous zeal pillaging items from a great number of corpses while the Panjabi soldiers stood guard. I saw Bihari people removing valuable goods from every building and making off with them – doors and windows, gold and jewellery, all kinds of things. While removing corpses I entered one building and found a helpless old woman, who was terrified and kept calling out for water. I was too scared to give her any water, indeed I got the wind up and made a quick exit. I would have liked to bring her some water, but as armed Panjabi soldiers were on patrol I wasn't able to come to her aid. On 28th March 1971 we removed three truckloads of bodies from Shakhari Bazar, one hundred bodies at a time, dumping a total of three hundred bodies at Dhalpur garbage depôt. On 29th March, starting from the morning, we recovered bodies from the mortuary at Mitford Hospital and from both sides of the access road, from the Siva temple at the university, from the Kali temple on Ramna green, from Rokeya Hall, Muslim Hall and Dacca Hall. On that day our truck went first to the driveway of Mitford Hospital. The aforementioned five of us got down in the driveway and saw the decomposing, bloated and disfigured corpse of a young Bengali man. As the body's tissues were breaking down we had to attach a metal hook to it and raise it into the truck that way. Our inspector Pancham was with us. Then we went into the mortuary and saw the piled up corpses of innumerable young men and women, children, infants and old people. Bodlu Dom and I dragged corpses out of the mortuary by their feet and assembled them by the truck, while Ganesh, Ranjit (Lal Bahadur) and Kanai attached the hook to each decomposing body and hoisted it into the truck. I noticed that every corpse was bullet riddled. Some of the female bodies had had their breasts cut off, their genitals mutilated and the flesh of their backsides cut away. Seeing the female corpses I got the impression that their breasts had been violently ripped off before they had been killed, and steel rods or gun barrels had been thrust into their vaginas. It looked as if the genitalia and buttocks of these young women had been slashed with sharp knives and then burned with acid. I noticed that all the girls had their hair tied up. We loaded one hundred corpses at a time, drove them away and dumped them at Dhalpur garbage depôt.

On 30th March 1971 Daksina Dom was detailed to assist us aforementioned five sweepers. That day our truck went to Satmasjid. While I was recovering bodies of Bengali people from in front of the Seven Domed Mosque there were numerous Bihari men standing all around, laughing and joking at the reversal of the Bengalis' fortunes. We picked up the bodies of eight young Bengali men from outside the mosque, some of which were lying face down, and all of their backs were riddled with bullet wounds. While recovering these bloated, decomposing corpses I noticed some were dressed in lungis, some in cotton pyjamas, and others in Hawaii shirts and expensive Tetron trousers. We recovered twelve bodies from the river, all of which were blindfolded and had their hands tied behind their backs. The twelve corpses on the riverbank were all bullet-ridden. These bodies looked as if they were those of well to do upper class young Bengali men. We took all the bodies we had found at Satmasjid and dumped them at the Dhalpur garbage depôt. On returning from there we went with our truck to Minto Road to collect more corpses. We recovered two bloated, decomposing bodies dressed in Western style trousers from the roadside in Minto Road. While we were on our way to Dhalpur we picked up the freshly shot body of an elderly beggar from in front of the Dacca Stadium mosque. His begging bowl, tin canister and walking stick were lying on the ground beside him. From outside the Siva temple in the university area we recovered the bodies of two pretty young women and three young men, all covered in wounds. We got a partially burned girl's body from Rokeya Hall, a decomposing corpse from the entrance of Muslim Hall and four students' bodies from inside Dacca Hall. On the following day, 31st March, we recovered three decomposed bodies from a watercourse in Bashabo. As I was ill that day I was unable to go and collect any further bodies.

thumbprint
Chunnu Dom
7/4/74

15

The dawn following a night of horror normally comes with an element of expectation, a hint of possible happiness. Whatever else daylight may bring, it brings hope. Birds start singing, and their song is like an omen of peace and wellbeing. Even the monotonous "kaa, kaa" chant of the house crows at first light sounds auspicious, for they, too, are spreading the good news – the light has returned.

The ghastly night of 25th March was over, a new day had begun, birds were singing their hymns – and yet no glimmer of hope was there. It was as though after one long dark night had been traversed another long night was beginning: instead of night being followed by day, night was being followed by night.

Shahed was sitting on a chair in Mr Sobahan's bedroom, in this household of total strangers over which the elderly Mr Sobahan presided. He hadn't shut his eyes for an instant the whole night through, and now his eyelids were smarting. From time to time he would try to give them some relief by closing them, but then almost immediately he would open them again, feeling that this was hardly the time for sitting with one's eyes shut.

Mr Sobahan had spread his prayer mat over his bed and was saying his prayers. He had slept for a while during the last part of the night, and had had a disturbing dream. His son had been on a river launch, on his way back from Barisal to Dhaka, and his friend and the latter's newly wed wife had been with him, together with a number of relatives. They were sitting in a cabin with all the doors and windows closed, singing and chatting merrily. Suddenly the hull of the launch had cracked open and water had started gushing in. The boat had gradually started to sink. The other passengers were rushing all over the place, desperate to escape; some of them had jumped into the river and were trying to swim to safety. A few country boats with their sails up were visible in the background, coming to the rescue. But Mr Sobahan's son Shalu was unaware of all this. He was now busy playing cards. The newly wed bride was among the card players, and everyone was having a great time. None of them realized the launch was sinking, they were too wrapped up in their enjoyment. In his sleep Mr Sobahan had yelled at his son, "Hey, you clown, you idiot, open the door at once, take a look at what's going on! You congenital idiot, you can play cards some other time, now open that door! Open that door!"

At that point Shahed had given him a little nudge to wake him up. Even then all the old man could say to Shahed, in a voice still heavy with sleep, was, "Has he opened it? Has he opened the door?"

Since having that nightmare Mr Sobahan had been filled with anxiety on account of his son. He had made a vow to sacrifice a chicken on his behalf, and also to perform one hundred extra *rakat* of prayer. He had been busy doing these extra prayer cycles ever since completing his basic dawn prayer. It was now eight o'clock and he had only got through forty. To start with he had been doing the prayers from a standing position, but then he got intense arthritic pains in his knee which prevented him from performing all the actions. Now, kneeling on his bed, he couldn't even get his head to bow low enough, because of pain in his lower back. He had placed a couple of pillows at the end of his prayer mat, and was just managing to touch them with his head during the prostrations.

Kongkon was finding her grandfather's strange new style of prayer most amusing. She giggled each time Mr Sobahan touched the pillows with his head, and she drew Shahed's attention to the funny spectacle by pointing at it. Overnight she had become very friendly with Shahed, whom she now called

"Babu." Why she had chosen the name Babu was anybody's guess; often there is no accounting for children's notions.

Kongkon had been made to sleep on the floor, for fear of stray bullets, and the floor had been cold. As a result Kongkon now had a sore throat. Her tonsils were inflamed. Monowara, her mother, had tried to get her to gargle with warm water, but without success. The child swallowed the water as soon as it was in her mouth.

Shahed was finding it impossible to stay sitting still for any length of time. He was spending much of his time pacing up and down; however there was little space in the house for movement. He could go from Mr Sobahan's room to the sitting room, from there to the verandah, then from the verandah to the sitting room and back to Mr Sobahan's room. To and fro, like a weaver's shuttle. It was a bit scary to go onto the verandah, as it was within sight of the street. If any soldiers passed on the road they would be able to see a person moving about on the verandah, and who knows, they might even shoot at him.

"Why do you keep walking about?" asked Kongkon.

Shahed did not reply. What answer could he give? He didn't know why himself.

"Do you like walking, Babu, is that why you keep walking about?" asked Kongkon.

"Yes."

"Why do you like walking?"

"I don't know."

"Why don't you know?"

"Stop bothering him, Kongkon," came Monowara's voice from the kitchen.

"Why mustn't I bother him?" asked Kongkon.

She had started the question game. Just like Runi. Once she had started asking questions she would never stop. She would go on and on till she did your head in. Once he had had to smack her to stop her, when she was taking the inquisition too far. Runi also had trouble with her tonsils and got sore throats. The merest suggestion of cold would giver her a sore throat, and she wouldn't be able to swallow anything. She would wail sadly to her mother, "Stop it from hurting, stop it from hurting."

Shahed had no wish to dwell on thoughts of Runi or her mother just now. Yet he kept thinking of them. Where were they, at this most terrible of times? How were they? He could imagine that Asmani would have stayed awake all night, but would Runi have slept? She must have been terrified by all the sounds of gunfire. Runi always got a fever when she was afraid, and that was a problem; for when she had a temperature she insisted on nestling in her father's arms, not her mother's. If she got a fever now, Asmani would be in trouble.

Shahed had stopped strolling around and was installed in a cane chair in the sitting room. The transistor radio wasn't working, since there were no batteries, so there was no way of telling what was going on outside. The one storey bungalow he was in did not abut on any of the neighbouring houses, and there was no easy way of communicating with the neighbours. There was another one storeyed dwelling on the north side, at no great distance, and if you stood in the verandah and shouted any occupant of that house should be able to hear. But there were no people in the house, it was locked up and empty.

Shahed's eyes had begun smarting again, and his left eye was weeping. He closed both eyes. Then Monowara appeared at his side, holding a cup of tea.

"Have some tea, brother."

Shahed reached out and took the cup.

"I've got some *khichuri* on the boil," said Monowara. "That will have to be our breakfast for today. I haven't got any wheat flour in the house at all."

"How are you off for groceries?" asked Shahed. "Rice, lentils, kerosene, that kind of thing?"

"There's enough for one or two days," answered Monowara. "He said he would do the shopping when he returned. Only of course now we don't know where he is."

"As soon as the curfew is lifted I'll go out and get some things for you before I leave," said Shahed. "They're sure to lift the curfew, even if only for a short time. The problem is, how do we know when or for how long they are going to lift it? We really do need a radio."

"*Bhai*," said Monowara, "do you happen to be a smoker? Because Kongkon's Dad left his packet of cigarettes behind, and if you care to smoke I can pass the packet on to you."

"Oh yes, please, I'd be glad to have a cigarette."

Monowara produced the packet from the folds of her sari; she had come with the cigarettes ready, and matches too, in anticipation.

"Thankyou, *bhabi*," said Shahed gratefully. "You cannot possibly imagine how delighted I am to get my hands on this packet of fags."

"You mustn't keep worrying yourself," said Monowara. "Your daughter and wife are fine. You'll be seeing them as soon as the curfew is lifted."

"How do you know that?" asked Shahed.

"My heart tells me so. Last night when I was doing my nocturnal prayers, I prayed not only for Kongkon's Dad but also for your wife and your daughter. The moment I'd finished saying my prayers I was overcome by a feeling of peace, and I realized that God had heard my appeal. I can always tell when Allah has accepted a prayer of mine."

Tears came to Shahed's eyes. And as he wiped them away in Monowara's presence – in the presence of this young woman who was a complete stranger to him – he felt no embarrassment at all.

Runi had been retching and vomiting this morning. She had already been sick twice during the night when the noise of gunfire had frightened her. Now it was nearly eleven o'clock and she hadn't eaten a thing so far, though the girl really ought to have something in her stomach if she was going to keep throwing up. Why was she vomiting anyway? Asmani was holding her daughter's head with both her hands, and her hands were trembling with alarm. The child's body was abnormally cold, and what did that signify? If she had a fever she ought to be hot, not cold. Surely something awful wasn't on the way! When a child was incubating some ghastly illness it was often impossible to get any warning of it in advance. The kid would go around laughing and playing as usual, and then all of a sudden he or she would collapse, and then there wouldn't even be time to get them to a doctor. Supposing something like that was happening now? If it was, how could she get Runi to a doctor?

There was a curfew over the city, and they weren't saying anything about lifting it. The only items being broadcast on the radio were Islamic psalms and songs of praise, punctuated every now and then by a solemn announcement in broken Bengali – "*If any individual is observed in the streets he shall be shot on sight.*"

"How do you feel now, darling?" asked Asmani.

"All right," replied Runi.

"Do you think you're going to get sick any more?"

"No."
"Come along, then, let's wash your face."
"No."
"Don't you want to have your face washed? You can wash your face and rinse out your mouth."
"I don't want to rinse my mouth."
Although she had said she wouldn't, Runi did rinse out her mouth, and Asmani washed her face for her.
"Do you feel all right now, darling?"
"Yes. Where's Daddy?"
"Your Daddy is there, your Daddy is fine."
"Where is he?"
"At home. Where else would he be?"
"I want to go to Daddy," said Runi, putting on a determined expression.
"It's no good just saying you want to, darling. It isn't possible. There's a curfew out there, and if the soldiers see anybody in the streets they're going to shoot them."
"I want to go to Daddy."
"As soon as the curfew is lifted we'll go and see Daddy, don't worry."
"I want to go now."
"Don't be obstinate, darling. This isn't the right time for being unreasonable."
"I want to go to Daddy! I want to! I want to! I'm going to go!"
Asmani gave her daughter a smack. Runi didn't cry, but stayed standing there defiantly. The child was getting more and more disobedient as time went on. Fancy having to smack her at such a tender age! And the poor mite was ill, and had no meat on her, and her arms and legs were quite cold; Asmani began to feel really bad. What should she do now? Maybe she should just pick the child up and cuddle her? But no, not even that was an option, for Runi would resist and hold herself rigidly. It would take a long time for her anger to subside.
"Listen, Runi darling, be a good girl now," said Asmani.
"I won't!" said Runi. "I want to go to Daddy! I'm going to go!"
Asmani left her daughter in the bathroom and returned to the sitting room, so discouraged and remorseful that she was on the verge of tears. What a dreadful situation she had got herself into! When she'd left home in a huff she had come and taken refuge here at Kumkum's house. Kumkum had been her best friend throughout her school and college days. Whenever she felt like walking out on Shahed and going to stay somewhere else, it was here she would come. Kumkum's mother treated her exactly as if she was her real daughter. This was her second day here, and she had been receiving the very best of care and attention. They had provided a separate room for her and Runi to sleep in. Kumkum's mother would speak to her reassuringly almost a hundred times a day: "Don't worry at all, dear daughter, just keep calling on God to have mercy. As soon as the curfew is lifted we'll find Shahed, and then all of us will go away into the countryside."
Kumkum's family had already packed their bags, and all they were waiting for was for the curfew to be lifted. This made Asmani feel very awkward. Even worse, Kumkum wasn't there, she was at her husband's parents' home in Comilla. So there was nobody for Asmani to chat to or confide in. There was in fact Kumkum's father, Mr Motaleb, and he was a non-stop talker, but Asmani didn't like listening to him. Flecks of spittle kept flying out of the good man's mouth as he talked, and she couldn't stand the sight of that; it gave her the creeps.

Mr Motaleb was sitting in the sitting room. He had a smile on his face, as if he was pleased about something. Some people are at their best during periods of adversity, and greatly enjoy talking about the bad times; maybe he was one of those people.

"Have you heard the latest news, my dear?" he asked in a cheerful voice when he saw Asmani.

"No, *chacha*, I haven't," replied Asmani flatly.

"They've beaten the Bengali nation to a pulp. The situation now could be described as a sorry mess."

"I see," said Asmani.

"The Bengali race is finished, you may as well accept it. Within five years you'll see everyone is speaking Urdu. It'll all be *ham karenge, tum karenge*."

"I see," said Asmani again. She no longer cared about any of these things. If Sheikh Mujib had been arrested, so be it, if the Bengali people started speaking Urdu, so be it too. What she needed was her husband; apart from that, nothing mattered. She made a mental vow: never again in her life would she leave Shahed and go off in a huff. Not even after a furious row, not even if Shahed spat at her.

"Asmani!"

"Yes?"

"There's a strong rumour that the army will go for a second offensive, on an even more massive scale." Mr Motaleb's speech was peppered with English jargon. "What happened last night was a mere patter on the *tabla* drums, the real music hasn't started yet. But anyway their main targets are the big towns. For the time being they're not going to attack the villages. Only when they've totally destroyed the towns will they move on into the countryside. Therefore we all need to go away to our village homes."

"I see," said Asmani yet again, without following what he was saying. She really couldn't understand why this old man seemed to be taking so much pleasure in discussing such ghastly things.

"If we're unable to trace Shahed, we'll have to go ahead without him. The situation we're in now is one of *ya nafsi* –'watch it Jack, save your back!' Do you get what I mean? It's every man for himself."

"I see."

"So be prepared. We're going to go sailing in a dinghy along the Buriganga river. The rivers are still quite safe for travelling. Those West Pakistanis are scared of water, you see."

A sound of retching came from the bathroom. Runi was getting sick again. Asmani rushed to rejoin her – she had quite forgotten how she had abandoned Runi in the bathroom after losing patience with her earlier on.

The curfew was lifted on the following day, Saturday 27th March, for a period of three hours starting at 9 a.m.

The streets filled with crowds of people. After an earthquake all the people come rushing out of their houses though their attention remains focussed on their hearth and home, and the situation was just like that now. People had come out into the street yet they longed for nothing more than to get back indoors again. Every face bore the signs of stress and fatigue caused by lack of sleep, as nobody had slept a wink for the past two nights. They wondered whether there were any other instances of a man-made catastrophe preventing all the inhabitants of a city from sleeping for two whole nights.

Shahed got hold of a rickshaw. The curfew had only been temporarily lifted for the space of three hours, so he had no time to lose. It had taken him quite a while to extricate himself from the house where Kongkon and her family lived. Old Mr Sobahan had been very reluctant to let him go, and Kongkon herself had clung to his hand to stop him leaving. She had been on the verge of tears as she begged him, "Please stay here, Babu, please stay!"

The rickshaw puller was an elderly one, and he was having difficulty in keeping going. Furthermore, unlike most older people whose curiosity has diminished with age, he was showing a keen interest in his surroundings and kept stopping to look around in astonishment. *Goodness, there was a whole slum colony here a couple of days ago, and now there's nothing, only a few blackened stumps...* Shahed felt like telling the rickshaw puller that this was no time for gawping with amazement, it was rather a time for keeping one's head low and going off in search of one's nearest and dearest. But he didn't say anything. It was the rickshaw puller who spoke up.

"They've killed the students at Iqbal Hall, the lot of 'em."

It sounded altogether unlikely. But at a time like this it was impossible to gauge what was believable and what wasn't. Maybe they really had killed students. Yet even if they'd killed every last person in Dhaka, what could one do about it anyway?

"You say they've killed all the students at Iqbal Hall?"

"Uh-uh."

"Did you see for yourself?"

"Yup. I did."

"And what else have you seen?"

"Doom. The wrath of God. The Day of Judgment, that's what I've seen."

The wrath of God, that it was indeed. And where would it end?

There was an army jeep parked in front of Dacca College, with an army officer and two privates standing beside it. The officer was smiling and saying something, and the two soldiers, although standing to attention, were listening to him eagerly. Shahed lowered his head to avoid the possibility of coming into eye contact with any of them. He was smoking, and that made him anxious. Suppose they were offended by seeing him with a lighted cigarette in his hand? Should he chuck the cigarette away? For some reason his mouth was filling with saliva, but he certainly wouldn't dare to spit it out; they might interpret that action in the wrong way. Just let them carry on with their conversation, he thought, and let us go by with our heads down.

The first place where Shahed went to look for Asmani was his parents-in-law's house. The building was locked and empty. A man from the house next door explained to him that the entire household had piled into a car and driven off about half an hour earlier, though he couldn't say which individuals had been in the car or why they had gone away. He seemed ill at ease talking to Shahed, and he kept frowning. Shahed realized it was pointless wasting any more time in conversation with the man, yet he didn't feel like moving on, his limbs seemed to have turned to stone. He hardly had the energy to walk on and find another rickshaw. Where should he go next? To his own house? Yes, that's where he should have gone in the first place, for surely Asmani would have sent someone there to look for him. Indeed, in all probability that was where Asmani's mother had been heading in her car. Shahed looked at his watch. Of the three hours for which the curfew had been lifted, one hour had passed already, and only two were left. He had to get back to his own safe haven within that period, there was no room for delay. Why was the time going by so rapidly?

A few shops had opened, and people were feverishly buying things. There were crowds at the open market: everyone needed to stock up on basic foodstuffs, especially as nobody could say how long the curfews might last. With so many people bustling around doing their shopping the city looked almost normal.

Again it was the rickshaw puller who started the conversation. "They've killed Sheikh Mujib," he said.

"Don't say so!" exclaimed Shahed. "It can't be true?"

"Yes, it's the truth. It's because he's dead that things are like this. If he'd been around everything would have been quite different."

Shahed lit a cigarette. It was the last one in the packet; he would have to buy some more. He would get the rickshaw puller to stop while he bought a few packets from a roadside shop somewhere. The sunshine was intense and glaring, and he felt quite dizzy. Should he put up the hood of the rickshaw? Better not, for putting up the hood would suggest that he was trying to hide something. Shahed looked at the sky. It was a deep blue, bluer than it had been for a long time, and the sight of it convinced Shahed that Asmani had returned home and was anxiously waiting for him. Runi was playing happily, and as soon as she caught sight of her Daddy she was going to come running up to him and throw herself into his arms. And she would rub her head against his cheek. Every child has peculiar behaviour patterns of his or her own, and one of Runi's was rubbing her head against her father's cheek. It was hard to say how or why such a habit had developed; no doubt a psychiatrist would be able to explain it.

In a passing rickshaw a man was sitting beside a woman who was almost certainly his wife. He was cradling her in his arms, and she was sobbing audibly. The man was embarrassed by her crying, and he was looking around him with glances of despair. Asmani would weep in the same way if he didn't get back to her in time.

Shahed's house was locked up. Asmani hadn't returned.

What now? Should he stay here or go back to Kongkon's house? When he had left Kongkon's family he had promised he would return, so he ought to do so. They had no rice or groceries in store and he really must buy some for them, as well as some antibiotics for Kongkon, whose tonsils had swollen up – she was so much like Runi in that respect. Gargling had had no effect, antibiotics were needed, and he could remember the name of the right one – Orsine K. But would there be any pharmacies open?

Shahed started walking. He wasn't sure how much time he had, but he knew that if he glanced at his watch he would be convinced the amount of time remaining wasn't enough. There were still plenty of people moving around, and that meant the curfew hadn't resumed yet. He spotted a pharmacy which was open. It too was thronged with customers. Shahed bought his Orsine K syrup, and was struck by the way the shopkeeper served him and took payment just as if everything was as it always had been; as if nothing was wrong at all.

He couldn't see any rickshaws. He walked on, trying to find one, and when he had got as far as the railway crossing he noticed three soldiers in a group. One of them had an unusual kind of uniform; it was black. He had never before seen a soldier in a black uniform. One of the soldiers was beckoning to him. Was he really signalling to him to come nearer? Or were Shahed's eyes deceiving him?

No, the soldier wasn't beckoning him. So what should he do now? Smile politely at the soldiers? No, probably not. A smile might be misinterpreted. He should just move away from the spot as quickly as possible. But not too quickly, or the soldiers would wonder why he was in such a hurry to get away, and conclude that he was a miscreant.

When Mr Sobahan saw Shahed he almost screamed with joy. He turned towards the kitchen and called to his daughter-in-law, "Quick, *bou-ma*, come here! Shahed has come back!"

Kongkon was lying down in her mother's bedroom. Mr Sobahan went to alert her, too, and called to her excitedly, "What are you lying there for? Get up, Shahed has come, your Babu has come!"

Seeing Mr Sobahan now, it was clear that he felt relieved of all his worst fears. Someone had come, he need no longer worry, the responsibility had now passed out of his hands for the long days and nights ahead.

Monowara was astonished to see all the supplies Shahed had brought. He hadn't forgotten anything. Rice, pulses, cooking oil, kerosene, wheat flour, batteries, everything was there. Most remarkable of all, he had brought some medicine for Kongkon.

"*Bhai*, you are a most efficient person," said Monowara.

"People always act differently in a crisis," replied Shahed. "I've never been the least bit efficient up to now."

"Nobody in the world could be more inefficient than Kongkon's father," said Monowara. "Let me tell you a little tale. Once I was suffering from a dreadful headache. My head was splitting, it was that bad. I asked my husband to go and get some aspirin tablets from the pharmacy. Two hours later he came back home with every kind of purchase you could think of – fish and meat from the market, vegetables, guavas, bananas – just no aspirins. He'd forgotten that little item. I can tell you, it's hard living with such an absent minded person."

"But it can be amusing too, living with someone absent minded."

"You're right," said Monowara, "there can be some fun in it too. You know what happened once, before Kongkon had been born, it was. We were supposed to go and attend a wedding that evening, and he ..."

Monowara abruptly stopped her narrative. She had remembered that the person she was addressing was a complete stranger, with whom reminiscences of a highly personal nature ought not to be shared.

"Aren't you going to finish the story, *bhabi*?"

"I'll tell you the rest some other time. Listen, I haven't yet asked you the most important thing – did you find out where your wife is?"

"No," replied Shahed. "I went to her mother's house and it was all locked up. The neighbours couldn't tell me anything."

"Don't you worry, brother," said Monowara. "They're safe and sound."

"But how do you know?"

"I know it in my heart. What my heart tells me is always right."

Mr Sobahan, meanwhile, had fitted the new batteries into the transistor radio and switched it on. With the volume turned low, he was following the transmissions. A number of martial law edicts were being broadcast, and he was listening attentively to each of them. A non-native was reading the announcements in a distorted kind of Bengali – for example, he was saying *sumoy* instead of *shomoy* for "time", *gozob* instead of *gujob* for "rumour". *Do nod pay any heed to roamers.* Mr Sobahan wondered whether they had killed off all the Bengali employees in the radio station, so there were none left who could read out the announcements.

When the martial law announcements were over some instrumental music was broadcast, and after that there was a programme on health matters. The subject was chicken pox. Mr Sobahan absorbed the information about chicken pox with equal attentiveness. The fact that antibiotics were ineffective against chicken pox suddenly assumed great significance for him. He now looked nothing like the Mr Sobahan of the previous night; here now was a man who was more or less at ease, proud to be engaged in the serious business of holding a transistor radio to his ear, keen to pass on to others all the information he was gleaning from it

"Good news," he told Shahed, "tomorrow the curfew will be lifted again, for two hours. Two hours may seem like a short time, but it isn't really, it's a lot. You can do all sorts of things in two hours. Please remember to get a few more batteries tomorrow."

Moving on to the subject of what to cook for the evening meal, Mr Sobahan said to Monowara, "*Bou-ma*, you should make some *khichuri*. It's customary to eat *khichuri* at happy moments in the rainy season, but it can also be eaten in times of danger and adversity. Why not do a light *khichuri* with curried eggs."

It was ten o'clock at night by the time they had finished eating their *khichuri* and curried eggs, and shortly after that the noise of furious gunfire erupted. It was coming from somewhere to the north. Now they were back in the same situation as the previous night. From time to time the sound of heavy military vehicles could be heard in the street, and in addition to the racket of gunfire they could hear a deep *boom! boom!* coming from somewhere. Mr Sobahan could not make out what the noise was.

"What's making that booming noise?" he asked Shahed anxiously.

"I don't know, uncle," said Shahed.

"Are they firing cannons? Why would they be firing cannons?"

At around midnight other noises started coming from the west, this time much closer to hand. Bullets screamed above them; it sounded as if they were grazing the rooftops.

"Lie down on the floor, everyone," ordered Mr Sobahan in a quaking voice. "We must all stay together in one room. At times of mortal danger distinctions of kinship and sex cease to signify. Shahed, you must lie down with us."

They all lay down on the floor of the sitting room. Kongkon, who was beside Shahed, lay with one leg across him. Runi never slept like that, she would always curl up into a little cocoon. And she would put her thumb in her mouth and suck it in her sleep – a very bad habit.

Mr Sobahan was thoroughly frightened. Fear had made him start stammering.

"Everyone call on God for all you're worth," he said. "We must use the formula our great spiritual guide Abdul Qadir Jilani° always used. Concentrate and say, *la ilaha illallah*."

"I'm scared," said Kongkon, "turn on the light."

"We can't turn on any lights," said Mr Sobahan.

The noise of gunfire was coming closer, and people could be heard shouting and screaming. Mr Sobahan went on chanting deliberately, in a loud voice, "*la ilaha illallah, la ilaha illallah*."

16

There were only two hours of grace between curfews.

And there were so many things Shahed needed to do in those two hours. By hook or by crook he had to find out where Asmani was. But he was confident that he would manage to do so this time. Doubtless Asmani was trying to find him just as he was trying to find her. The first time the curfew had been lifted it had happened unexpectedly. Asmani and whoever was with her would have suddenly got the news that the curfew would be suspended for a couple of hours, but they wouldn't have had time to organize anything. But today's gap in the curfew had been announced well in advance, so Asmani would surely have made some kind of plan. Shahed decided he would first go to his mother-in-law's place. If he drew a blank at that address he would move on to his own house and wait there. But he was sure he would find something out today, for he had had an auspicious dream last night which could only mean that he was going to see Asmani. He had dreamed that he was sitting in the verandah of his house, crying his eyes out, and then his elder brother Irtazuddin had appeared in the verandah and said in a tone of annoyance, "What are you crying for, silly?" "I can't find Asmani," he had sobbed. "But how do you expect to find her if you sit at home blubbing like that?" Irtazuddin had said. "Come along now, come with me." And they had gone out into the road, which was crowded with people. And there among the crowds was Asmani, sitting on a handcart, beautifully got up. She had all her jewellery on, she had a sandalwood paste mark on her forehead, and she was wearing what looked like her wedding sari. Shahed had tried to rush over to the cart, but the crowds had got in his way. Anyway, Asmani had seen him and was smiling at him.

The dreams you have in the early morning are the ones which come true. This dream would surely turn out to be right. Shahed walked ahead briskly. The roads were indeed crowded with people just as the one in his dream had been; it was as if everybody in the city had come out into the streets at once. There were rickshaws around, too, though not very many of them. Every time he spotted one which was empty Shahed made a dash for it. "Can you take me to Kolabagan?" Every rickshaw puller he asked took an inordinately long time to make a decision. Instead of saying no straight away they would contemplate deeply, glance to left and right, spit on the tarmac, wipe their brow with a cloth, and then finally mumble, "Nope, I'm not going there." It was just a waste of time trying to get hold of a rickshaw; precious seconds were ticking away, and there was no justification for wasting any of them.

When he reached the road junction beside the Science Laboratory Shahed was finally able to hire a rickshaw, but it was hardly worth having. Although the rickshaw puller was in the prime of life he was no good at pedalling, and Shahed could have got along faster on foot.

"Can you go a bit faster, brother?" Shahed coaxed him.

The rickshaw puller craned his head round and had a look at Shahed. Then he went on, even slower than before. Shahed felt like jumping down and continuing on foot.

As they were nearing Kolabagan Shahed saw an incongruous sight, a horse-drawn carriage decorated with friezes of coloured paper, over which the Pakistan flag was flying. Inside the carriage was a girl of about twelve or thirteen with reddish hair, dressed in a full gypsy skirt, and there were four young lads with her. They were all eating *paan* and looking very cheerful. Evidently they were on their way to a party of some kind; clearly not a wedding, but some similar kind of event. They were Biharis, and Biharis love celebrations of all sorts. The awful tragedy of these days had not affected them; they were in a world apart.

Shahed found nobody at his parents-in-law's house. The tea stall opposite the house had opened for business; but the owner of the stall knew nothing about the family's whereabouts. Shahed made enquiries at several neighbouring houses, but nobody had any information; one person did tell him that the occupants of the empty house had driven off in a black car, however he wasn't at all clear when that had been.

Shahed arrived at his own house half an hour before the curfew was due to end. As he opened the gate and started to make his way in he suddenly felt short of breath, and his head began to spin; he was sure he was about to collapse. There was no padlock on the front door; someone was inside the house. Asmani must have come back. Although the front door had been unlocked the windows and side door were still closed; but that was only natural, for at times like these nobody would want their doors and windows to be open. Thoughts flashed through Shahed's mind: would there be enough rice and other groceries in the house? Probably yes, because Asmani was such a competent housewife. Maybe there wasn't enough kerosene, though. If not, he would have to go out and get some this very minute. There was still half an hour to go, and he'd noticed that the big shop near the crossroads was open. Kerosene, tea, sugar... Asmani liked to have frequent cups of tea, strong with plenty of sugar. Shahed wondered whether to dash off and do the shopping before making an appearance in the house, or whether to go in immediately and say to Asmani, I'm here, there's no need to worry. For Asmani would surely be in a state of great anxiety, not having found him at home. There was one snag about saying hello straight away, and that was Runi: the moment she saw him she would rush up to him and throw herself into his arms, and once he had picked her up it would be impossible to put her down again. If any shopping was to be done, he would have to do it while carrying Runi in his arms.

The front door was bolted on the inside. Shahed shoved it and banged on it for what seemed like a long time, until at last a timid male voice came from the other side of the door.

"Who's there?"

"It's me, Shahed," said Shahed. "Open the door."

The door was opened, and to his astonishment Shahed saw Gourango standing in the doorway. Gourango with his face covered in stubble and his eyes all yellow: he looked as if he had been suffering from a serious illness of some kind.

"Where have *you* suddenly sprung from?" asked Shahed.

Gourango made no reply, and Shahed repeated his question. Gourango was staring at him as if he couldn't comprehend what he was saying.

"Is there anyone else here?"

"No," replied Gourango.

"So how did you get inside?" asked Shahed.

"I broke the padlock," mumbled Gourango. "My dear buddy, there's absolutely nowhere else I can go. If you kick me out the army will slaughter me."

"Who said anything about kicking you out?" asked Shahed.

Gourango was silent. He was staring fixedly at Shahed's face.

"Where are your wife and daughter?"

"Oh, they're all right," muttered Gourango.

"But where are they?"

"With my father-in-law. But I want to stay with you."

"I don't understand," said Shahed. "Why do you want to be with me?"

"Buddy," said Gourango in the same muted voice, "I want to stay with you. I've got money. All the money my father-in-law gave me, I've got it on me. You can take it and spend it as you wish. Just let me stay here."

"Tell me the truth," said Shahed in alarm, "where are your wife and child, where are they really?"

"I've told you, they're fine. Both of them, they're fine. My daughter had a bit of a fever, but I expect it's gone down by now. I haven't been too well myself. I came here to have a rest. My head keeps spinning all the time. Oh, buddy, I'm quite hungry as well. Please give me something to eat. Don't worry about money, I've got plenty. Buddy, I really must lie down now. Please call me when the food's ready."

Gourango slept like a log until the evening. Shahed tried several times to wake him, without success. Not long after night had fallen Gourango woke up of his own accord.

"How do you feel now?" Shahed asked. "Has the dizziness stopped?"

"I'm fine," said Gourango. "The soldiers killed my little girl – that's why I'm feeling a bit depressed."

"And your wife? Where is she?"

"They took her away. I don't know if she's still alive. If they have killed her then it's for the best – best for her, best for everyone. My father-in-law is dead too. Buddy, please keep it to yourself, all this I'm telling you. If the soldiers find out I've been saying bad things about them they'll be cross, and they'll take me away too. It's not the soldiers' fault, they have to obey orders. They were just doing what they'd been ordered to do, don't you agree?"

"Where were you when they took your wife away?"

"Crouching behind the door. They turned everything upside down searching the house, but they never looked behind the door. It's all part of God's little game. Buddy, remember to keep all this a secret, don't let any of it slip out. If any of it comes to the attention of the army people there'll be big trouble for you as well as me."

"I've made some *dal* and boiled rice," said Shahed, "come and eat."

"I will," said Gourango, "I'm very hungry. I feel like some hilsa fish steamed in mustard. Boiling hot rice and hilsa fish *paturi*..."

No sooner had he finished speaking than Gourango lay back and fell asleep again. Shahed remained sitting beside him. The poor man was weeping as he slept. Shahed had never before realized how terrible it could feel to watch a person crying in their sleep.

The night was wearing on. The electricity supply had gone off in the early evening, however it wasn't totally dark in the house as Shahed had lit two candles which he had set side by side on the table. He had found the candles on a shelf in the kitchen. Asmani had stuck up a list of what was where on the kitchen door, for use on the frequent occasions when she went to stay at her parents' house. As he read through the list now Shahed felt tears coming to his eyes.

> Rice, lentils, puffed rice - in tins, Runi's room, under bed.
> Laundry soap, candles, matches - on kitchen shelf, extreme left.
> Spices, salt - on kitchen shelf, right end. Each spice jar labelled.
> Tea, sugar - on top of meat safe.
> Onions, garlic, ginger - in creel beside meat safe.
> Mustard oil - next to stove.
> Love - with me, wherever I happen to be.

It was just like Asmani to add something funny to a purely factual note. So when making a list of household items she had unexpectedly slipped in that bit about love – "*with me, wherever I happen to be.*"

She had done a similarly funny thing on their wedding night. Their nuptial bed had been arranged in a large room on the first floor of Asmani's parents' house in Kolabagan, and had been beautifully decorated with flowers. As soon as he had stepped into the room Shahed had been struck by how pretty Asmani looked. He had seen her several times before that, but had never thought her so very gorgeous. As he sat down on the edge of the bed Shahed had said, "It's awfully hot today, don't you think?" He had intended his opening words on this occasion to be "How are you, Asmani," but in the event something completely different had come to his lips. "It's awfully hot," he had said, as if his chief concern was the state of the weather.

Asmani had looked up on hearing Shahed's words, and replied quietly but clearly, "Actually one can expect it to be hottish in the hot season. Hot in the summer, colder in winter. God is unlikely to alter the seasons on your account."

Shahed had been dumbfounded. What was she playing at, rattling off a whole lecture like that? Had the tension of the wedding and the great heat affected her brain?

"Why are you goggling at me like that?" Asmani had continued. She was calling him *apni* in a very formal way. "I get really annoyed when men stare at me. Watch what you're doing or I shall gouge your eyes out."

Shahed had jumped to his feet in alarm, and then Asmani had burst out laughing. "Sorry," she had said, "Please don't take offence." She was now using the more affectionate *tumi* to address him. "I was joking. I made a bet with two of my cousins – one hundred rupees if I dared to scare you on our wedding night. Right now they're watching us through the window. What are you standing for, do sit down."

Shahed had sat down, but he was still feeling ill at ease. He was afraid this beautiful creature was about to play some other weird trick on him.

"Are you angry?" Asmani had asked.

"N-no," Shahed had replied shakily.

"I frightened you on our wedding night," said Asmani, "that was really naughty of me. And you know what that means – you're going to be scared of me for the rest of your life."

Shahed had gone out to sit on the verandah. Rain had started to fall and there was a cool breeze helping to dissipate the stifling heat. Every now and then a strangled sound came from Gourango indoors, a throttled groan as if someone was standing with their foot on his neck so that he couldn't give voice to the screams welling up inside him. Shahed was quite surprised at himself – he was hardly affected by Gourango's horrific ordeal, as if it was purely Gourango's problem and nothing to do with him. Did people change at times of great peril, so that only their own welfare and their own tribulations mattered to them? Had everyone in the country begun to change like that? Could even Runi be changing?

Shahed didn't want to think about Asmani. Whenever he thought about her he felt a strange feeling inside, a sort of uncomfortable lump in the chest. Where on earth was Asmani? What was she doing? She had always been a great one for reading novels late at night and suddenly being moved to tears, and sobbing loudly. Once he had been woken by the sound of Asmani crying, and he had sat up in alarm.

"What's the matter?" he had gasped.

"Nothing's the matter," Asmani had replied in a tearful voice, "You can go back to sleep. I was just crying over this novel."

"What novel is it?"

"One of Tarasangkar's°. It's called *Bipasha*."

"And what do you find worth weeping about in any book?"

"Oh, it's just the way I am. I never cry about the sad things that happen to me, but instead I cry over the misfortunes of characters in novels."

"You're just a bit barmy."

"I know I am. You should marry someone with a perfectly sound brain, and live happily ever after with her. I shall watch from a distance and enjoy the spectacle."

"What on earth are you on about now?" Shahed had asked in annoyance.

"I'm perfectly serious. I shall come along myself and set the two of you up in your new household. Won't you marry her? Go on! Please, please!"

"Turn off the light, now, and come to bed."

"No, I don't want to go to bed. I'm going to read the book all over again."

"What, now?"

"Yes, now. You get one kind of pleasure from reading a book without knowing what the end is going to be, but there's a different charm in reading it when you *do* know what's going to happen. But if the light is going to bother you I can go and read in the other room."

"Oh, do whatever you want."

The rain was getting heavier, and there was a bit of a breeze, too. The wind was making the boughs of the alstonia tree dance. Seen from the verandah the tree looked somehow rather ghostly. This same tree had once given Asmani a great fright. She had woken up in the middle of the night, got a tumbler of water and gone out to sit in the verandah. Shortly afterwards there had been a loud scream, and Shahed had woken up and rushed out to find Asmani sitting there trembling, with the shattered tumbler at her feet.

"What's the matter?" Shahed had asked.

"The tree was beckoning to me," Asmani had stammered.

"It was just the wind moving the branches," Shahed had said, "and that made you think the tree was beckoning."

"I'm not a little child," Asmani had said through her tears, "I know what I saw."

Asmani had been deeply shocked and that very night she had developed a fever.

But no, he mustn't keep thinking about Asmani. She was sure to be quite safe and sound. She must be with her parents, and nobody could ever feel more secure than when they were with their parents. Maybe he hadn't found her today, but he would certainly see her tomorrow. Tomorrow as soon as the curfew was lifted he would go to Sector Ten in Mirpur, where an aunt of Asmani's lived. She would surely be able to tell him something. If she couldn't give him any direct lead he would get the addresses of other relatives from her.

On the way to Mirpur he would also have to call in on Mr Sobahan's family. Without any doubt they had really been expecting to see him today. And he would have to arrange for them to move to some safer location.

But what about Gourango? Was he likely to go and live with any relatives he might have, or would he want to stay here? It would be no great problem to let him stay here; he could stay as long as he liked. It would be even less of a problem if and when Asmani turned up. Asmani was an exceptionally competent girl when she was in the right frame of mind; nursing Gourango in his terrible pain would be something she could take in her stride.

"Buddy! Buddy!"

Gourango was calling him, in a hoarse voice. Shahed went inside. Gourango was sitting on the bed with his mouth open, panting hard. He seemed to be having trouble with his breathing.

"I've cooked some rice and *dal*," Shahed said. "Would you like to eat?"

"Yes," replied Gourango promptly.

"Get down from the bed and onto your feet. It's all right, I'm holding you."

Shahed kept a grip on Gourango as he helped him off the bed.

"I need to have a bath, my friend," said Gourango "I haven't had a bath for the last three days."

"There's some water in the bathroom," said Shahed, "and the soap is there. Or shall I get some hot water for you?"

"Please do. But listen, my dear buddy, I want to stay here, I don't want to go anywhere else."

"That's all right, there's no problem. You can stay here."

"I've got an uncle in Agargaon, he's a wireless officer or something like that, but I don't want to go to his place."

"You can stay as long as you want."

"Buddy, I've got a pain in my chest, I can't breathe properly."

"Have a bath with hot water, that'll make you feel better."

"All right," said Gourango in a tiny voice. "Listen, my dearest buddy, my limbs seem to have gone stiff, I can't flex them properly. See, I can't bend my fingers."

Gourango held his hand up for Shahed to see. His fingers were bending as normal.

"You see, buddy, my fingers won't bend."

"They'll soon be all right again," said Shahed.

"When will they?" asked Gourango.

"Let's see what a new day brings," suggested Shahed.

"Ah," said Gourango.

Another dawn, another day. In the past it had been hard to distinguish one dawn from the next, but now one could feel the difference; each new day had its own character.

The curfew had been lifted and people were filling the streets. Shahed had set forth, and Gourango had come with him. Gourango was running a fever and not feeling at all well, yet he absolutely refused to stay at home. He said he would die of sheer terror if he was left alone in the house. But he felt no less unsafe in the streets, and every few minutes he would say to Shahed, "Let's go home, buddy. I'm scared, let's go back." Shahed found this highly irritating. There was no question whatever of going back home. Today, without fail, he had to find out where Asmani was. First of all he would have to go to Mirpur, Sector Ten, where her aunt's house was. He didn't know the house number, but as he had been there a couple of times before he thought he should be able to recognize the building. However, before going to Mirpur he really must go and see how Mr Sobahan and his family were. There was no doubt about it, they'd be anxiously waiting for him. He hadn't been to see them yesterday, and the elderly gentleman would certainly be consumed with worry on his account.

The front door of Mr Sobahan's house was locked; a very large padlock was dangling from the door chain. It looked as though the family had cleared out yesterday and gone to some safer location. People didn't feel secure anywhere in Dhaka these days, and many kept moving from one house to another. Even though there was that padlock on the door, Shahed spent a few minutes rattling the door chain and listening; for another ploy which people were adopting was to stick a padlock on their front door and go on living quietly inside. The idea was that if the army happened to call they would see the padlock and assume that the house was empty.

"Come on, buddy," whimpered Gourango. "Let's go home. There's no-one here."

"I've got to go to Mirpur," said Shahed.

"I'm scared," said Gourango.

"If you're too scared you can go back to the house, but I really must go to Mirpur. Somehow or other I just have to find out where Asmani has got to."

"I can't stay in the house by myself, dear buddy. I would die of fright. I'm not a brave person at all."

Shahed did not reply. He had no time to waste on talk. What he needed now was to find a scooter taxi, or failing that a well-built muscular rickshaw puller who could get him to Mirpur fairly quickly. There was so little time: the curfew was due to resume at twelve o'clock.

They got out of the rickshaw where Sector Ten began; from here on it would be a matter of searching for the right house. Shahed had a vague recollection that there was a hibiscus bush growing by the gate in front of the building, and that the house had a name, some kind of English name beginning with S.

"Watch out, buddy, soldiers," hissed Gourango. "To our right, beside the tea stall. Oh goodness, they're looking at us."

Shahed stopped still. The teashop had a name, *Rahmania Tea Stall*. A group of five soldiers were standing outside it. One of them was slurping tea from a saucer, and the rest were standing there looking grim. There were no other people nearby, only the owner of the teashop in his white vest, sitting there with his head bowed. He hardly looked like a living being; from a distance one had the impression of a painted cardboard cutout of a tea stall owner which somebody had placed there.

"He's beckoning to us," said Gourango in a low voice, "what are we to do?"

It was the soldier drinking tea from a saucer who was signalling to them. He had a smile on his face.

"What shall we do?" murmured Gourango. "Shall I run away?"

"You stay standing there just as you are now," said Shahed. "Whatever you do, don't even think of running. I'll go over and see what they want."

"Oh no, buddy, don't go."

Shahed moved towards the soldiers, whereupon two of them raised their rifles and trained them on him. Shahed couldn't see why they had to do that. Maybe it was standard procedure, and they had been told to aim their rifles at any Bengali who approached them, as a warning. But why were they calling him over in any case? The one with the tea had stopped drinking and was staring at him. He still had a smile on his face, which was a hopeful sign. Or was it really a smile? Some people had expressions like that, which meant that even when they were furious they still looked as if they were smiling. Suddenly a gunshot rang out extremely close by. Shahed goggled. Had they shot at him? Probably not, for if he'd been shot he would surely have felt some pain, and his shirt would have gone all sticky with blood. Neither of those things had happened.

Gourango was gaping. He switched his gaze from Shahed to the soldiers. The soldier with the tea, who had now finished drinking, gestured to Gourango to go away. Gourango started walking off.

Shahed was still advancing towards the group of soldiers. The fact that he was able to walk meant that he hadn't in fact been shot. People can't usually walk when they've had a bullet through them. He stopped short when he was still a few yards from the group.

"*Tera nam kya*? What's your name?"

They were asking him his name. What on earth did they want with his name, what difference could it make whether he was called Shahed or Fakhruddin or anything else? He told them his name. The soldier who had been having tea poured the dregs from his teacup onto the ground and muttered something, while Shahed stared at him unblinkingly.

"*Kan pakaro*! Grab hold of your ears!"

What was this? Why was the soldier telling him to hold his ears, a sign of contrition? What had he done wrong? Shahed took hold of his ears with his hands. The soldier motioned for him to do the squats, alternately crouching and standing, another belittling form of punishment. Shahed started doing the squats. The soldiers must have found this amusing, for now all of them were smiling.

17

Moriam knew very well that the country was going through a terrible time, when anything might happen at any moment, but even so she couldn't help having secret feelings of joy. She was disgusted with herself for being so complacent, she rated herself lower than the meanest cockroach in her bathroom, yet what could she do? Was she supposed to deliberately suppress her happiness and go around with a forced look of tragedy on her face?

Her joyful feelings were largely the result of what Naimul had said. As soon as the curfew had been lifted Naimul had told her he was going to pop out and have a look around to see the lie of the land.

"I won't let you go," Moriam had said straight away. "You mustn't."

"Very well," Naimul had said. "I shan't go out without your permission."

How lovely! "I shan't go without your permission." It was enough to make a girl cry.

"What would you like for lunch?" Moriam had asked then. "I'm going to do the cooking today, Mum is not feeling well."

"Whatever you cook, I'll relish it. But..."

"But what?"

"But rather than you going off and doing all that cooking, it would be far better if you would just sit down here, in front of me. At times of adversity one longs just to keep gazing at one's nearest and dearest. For we're facing bad times now."

Naimul's words had made tears come to Moriam's eyes. Even if these were bad times for everyone else in Bengal they were good times for her, she felt. No kind of adversity would be allowed to come between the two of them.

Naimul had started turning the knobs of the transistor radio. There was no impatience or frenzy in his movements; despite all the turmoil outside, the fellow was adjusting the controls as calmly and deliberately as if he was tuning in to some programme of songs and music.

"Listen, do you really want to go out?" Moriam had asked.

"I do, actually, but today I'm giving priority to what *you* want. If you say yes, then it'll be yes, and if you say no, it'll be no."

"Ah well, in that case you must go. But only for one hour!"

"Thankyou!"

"I shall be waiting on my prayer mat for the entire time you're away."

"I'll come back as quick as possible."

"While you're out there you must keep reciting the *Yunus* prayer°. Do you know it? If not, I can write it out on a piece of paper for you."

"There's no need, I do know it."

"And mind you come back pronto."

"It's nine twenty-five now," Naimul had said. "I'll definitely be back by ten twenty-five."

"No, say *inshallah* – *deo volente*, God willing. How can you talk of the future without saying *inshallah*?"

"*Inshallah*. Have hot water ready on the stove; as soon as I get back I want to have some lemon tea."

Now Moriam was kneeling on her prayer mat, ready to perform some cycles of voluntary (*nafl*) prayer including all the short Quran verses that she knew, each of which she intended to recite three times over. The minute Naimul had left the house Moriam had known she had made a terrible mistake and should never have let him go. As she prayed she kept interrupting her recitations to make a direct appeal – *Allah, please keep him safe, Allah, please keep him safe*. But not once did she spare a thought for her father, of whom there had been no news since the night of 25th March. Maybe Moriam thought there was no cause for concern, as it was nothing unusual for a police officer to be away on duty for days on end.

Safiya's face was taut with fear and anxiety, but it was something entirely different which was causing her discomfiture. On that night of 25th March she had made a terrible discovery – Babu was stone deaf. Yahya was by now generally known by the nickname Babu, and it was only Mobarak Hussain who persisted in calling him Yahya. Yes, he was quite unaffected by all the sounds of gunfire and exploding mortars. Though wide awake, he never winced or jumped at any of the noises. And then an awful suspicion crossed Safiya's mind – maybe he couldn't see either. She held a brightly coloured ribbon close to his eyes, but he didn't reach out for it. She shook a rattle in his face, and without taking any notice of it he turned in a different direction and beamed. Safiya couldn't imagine how she was going to break this awful news to her husband. Would he be able to bear it? And supposing he asked why it had taken her so long to become aware of the problem, what would she say then? A sinister thought flashed through Safiya's mind: she would go up onto the rooftop with Babu in her arms and jump off the roof with him. It was hard enough for babies who could see and hear to survive in this troubled land; how would this little one manage? And how was she going to deal with the feelings of fury which would overcome his father when he found out?

Naimul had said he would return by ten twenty-five, and at precisely ten twenty-five he came through the door. Moriam was still on her prayer mat.

"Where's my lemon tea, Mori?" asked Naimul.

Moriam was mortified. Naimul had kept his word, he had returned at exactly twenty-five minutes past ten, but she had failed to keep her side of the bargain. She hadn't even put any water to heat on the stove.

"Never mind," said Naimul, "don't get up, I don't need any tea."

"What did you see?" asked Moriam.

"I saw what they wanted me to see," replied Naimul.

"How do you mean, what they wanted you to see?" asked Moriam.

"It was simply to show us what they're capable of that they lifted the curfew for three hours. They wanted us to observe what they'd done, and obediently turn into jellyfish."

"I don't get it, what do you mean?"

Naimul smiled. He had such an amazing smile, Moriam felt little shivers of delight every time she beheld it.

"Wait, let me fetch you your tea," she said.

"I don't want any tea, thanks," said Naimul. "Just sit down and listen. Let me tell you an amusing thing I saw."

"Surely there can't have been anything particularly amusing to see?"

"You know the Shahid Minar°, the monument to the Bengali language martyrs, they've smashed it into tiny pieces and hung a sign over the ruins saying *Mosque, place reserved for prayer*." *

---

* *Ostorage Sriti Shomujjol (Bright Memories at Sunset)*, Mominul Haque Khoka.

Naimul was smiling, but this time it was a different kind of smile, and the chuckle that went with it sounded hollow and grim.

"Listen, Moriam, I'm going to tell you something extremely important, so please listen carefully. The real war with the Pakistani army is about to begin. They have no idea what a horrendous war it's going to be. And I'm going to join in."

"What? What did you say?" stuttered Moriam aghast.

"I'm going to go to war," repeated Naimul as he lit a cigarette. "I've no idea yet how I'm going to do it or where I'm likely to get any weapons from, though I do know that something is sure to be arranged."

"You're going to war? You're going to fight?"

"Yes. But there's no need for you to be frightened, I'm not going to be killed. I'm pretty intelligent, you know, and I shall be extremely careful. Intelligent people always make sure they survive themselves before trying to help anyone else, and I shall do the same."

"You're going to leave me and go away?" Moriam stammered.

Naimul took a long pull at his cigarette. "Yes," he said, "and I shall see you again – in a free, independent Bangladesh!"

"Are you going to go right now?" Moriam's words were like a cry of mortal agony.

"No," replied Naimul. "Today I'll be here with you. I'll set off tomorrow, as soon as the curfew is lifted, that will be farewell time. Today is for us, just the two of us."

And Naimul sang, in English,

She was a child and I was a child in this kingdom by the sea,
But we loved with a love that was more than love, I and my Annabel Lee.

Moriam was sobbing uncontrollably. While his wife sat weeping Naimul gazed at her with a tender smile on his face.

As they twiddled the knobs of their radio sets on the night of Saturday 27th March 1971 many people in East Pakistan chanced upon a remarkable broadcast. At 8 p.m. someone called Major Zia° announced that he had seized authority as head of state and went on, "I hereby declare the independence of Bangladesh." He appealed to his citizens to join in an all-out war against Pakistan.[*]

It was as if a high voltage electric shock had suddenly galvanized the Bengali people. Inspired by this broadcast announcement the nation's sagging backbone drew itself erect, its eyes recovered their sparkle. It was incredible, how the voice of a previously unknown individual could unleash such a strong spirit of defiance.

When he heard the announcement the subdivisional police officer of Pirojpur Subdivision went wild with joy and started whooping like an excited child, "The war has begun! We have embarked on our war! Now there is nothing to fear!" And he flung open the police armoury and handed out two hundred rifles to local people as a first step in the preparations for battle. On 5th May he was shot in cold blood by the Pakistan army. Thirty-two years later his eldest son embarked on a novel about the war entitled *Josna o Jononir Golpo*.

---

[*] *Ekattorer Ronangon (Theatre of War 1971)*, Shamsul Huda Choudhuri.
Ekattorer Dosh Mash (Ten Months in 1971), Rabindranath Trivedi.
Amar Ekattor (My 1971), Anisuzzaman.

Much confusion has arisen surrounding the declaration of independence broadcast by Major Zia from Kalurghat radio station. How many times did he read out that declaration? And on what date was the other statement read out, to the effect that Sheikh Mujibur Rahman was the undisputed leader of Bangladesh and that the declaration of independence had been issued on his behalf? How many times was that statement read out? It is with regard to these questions that confusion exists. Certain documents point to a declaration of independence having been issued by Bangabandhu himself, before Ziaur Rahman had read out his one. For example, the chairman of Chittagong District Awami League, Mr Abdul Hannan, reportedly broadcast a Bengali translation of a declaration of independence by Bangabandhu at 2 pm on 26th March, and at 7:40 pm this Bengali translation was broadcast a second time, read out by the Vice Principal of Hathazari College, Mr Abul Kashem Shondip.

In his own diary Major Zia wrote about the declaration of independence as follows: "On 27th March sporadic clashes were taking place all over the city. At 6:30 pm I went to the radio station. Searching for a scrap of paper I found an exercise book, on one of whose pages I quickly scribbled down the first declaration of the War of Independence. In that first announcement I also wrote that I had assumed responsibility as temporary head of the Bangladesh government... Shortly afterwards I went on air and broadcast the declaration. On 28th March the declaration was broadcast from Kalurghat radio station at fifteen minute intervals, starting in the morning. On 30th March the second announcement was broadcast with the agreement of the political leaders."

There should be no room for confusion in the history of our war of independence. In this matter we really must rise above party politics and personal opinion. As the Sanskrit scholars said: satyen dharyate prthvi, satyen tapate ravi, satyen vati vayushcha, sarvang satyen pratisthitam – *Truth keeps the world in place, truth makes the sun shine, truth makes the wind blow, everything is founded on truth.* – **Author**

18

Today Foyzur Rahman, the police chief for Pirojpur Subdivision, was in a very good mood. He felt slightly guilty for being so inappropriately cheerful, for the country had been plunged into terrible uncertainty and bad times had begun. Nobody in their right mind should have been cheerful in these circumstances; was there perhaps something wrong with his brain?

The idea that he might be out of his right mind worried him for a while, and induced him to fervently recite the chapter of the Quran known as *Al-Rahman*. In this surah one particular line is repeated again and again: "so which of the favours of your Lord are you going to deny?" Ah, what a beautiful line that was!

He was still kneeling on his prayer mat, having completed his dawn prayers. He didn't feel like standing up and going away. Saying his dawn prayers was not something he did regularly; as he often didn't get to bed until late at night it was hard for him to wake up in time. But today he had woken early after having the most beautiful dream. In the dream he had been walking along in a huge procession of people escorting a bridegroom to his bride's home on their wedding day. There had been musicians marching alongside, playing their various musical instruments. In the dream it wasn't quite clear who was getting married to whom, but he knew someone very dear to him was involved. He had a feeling the bride was his elder daughter Shefu, but in that case how could he, the bride's father, be in the bridegroom's procession? It didn't add up, so what was really going on? It was the effort of trying to puzzle this out which had woken him up. Glancing at the clock on the table he had seen the time: four twenty-five in the morning. The *adhan* for the dawn prayer would be given in a few minutes' time. He had quietly slipped out of bed, performed his ablutions and stood waiting for the prayer call, and as he waited it had suddenly struck him what a fortunate fellow he was. He had his wife and children around him and could want no more. God had been extremely kind to him.

He performed two cycles of optional prayer by way of thanksgiving, accompanied by these humble words: "O Merciful One, you have been excessively kind to me, and I thank you for it. Our country is facing bad times. I had none of my children near me; three were in Dhaka and one in Comilla. You have brought them back to me safe and sound. O Allah, I give thanks to you."

He would have liked to remain sitting on the prayer mat a while longer, but his dearly beloved pet deer Ira had sprung up onto the verandah and started pestering him. She was poking him with her horns, grabbing his shirt from behind with her teeth, tugging at him and generally trying to get his attention, so he had little choice, he would have to have a word with her. For he often used to talk quietly to the deer when nobody else was around. Anyone overhearing one of his conversations with her would have thought he must be talking to one of his own six children.

"What are you up to, my pet? You think it's a grand idea to rip my shirt to bits, don't you? And why are you making that hissing sound? Do you think you're a snake, hissing like that? Now just lie down quietly beside me. Stretch out your neck and let me give you a tickle. No, don't you dare lick me, or I'll have to do my ablutions all over again."

After having his conversation with the deer he picked up a weeding spud and went down into the garden to do some weeding. Ira accompanied him. He had planted a variety of winter crops in the vegetable plot and invested quite a lot of effort in caring for them, but the results had been disappointing, nothing but a few tomatoes and ladies' fingers. He plucked a couple of tomatoes and offered them to Ira, but she didn't touch them; she seemed to be in the mood for a game, and was prancing about playfully.

Dawn had broken. One by one the other members of the household were waking and getting up. Foyzur Rahman watched his eldest son Bacchu pacing from end to end of the verandah as he brushed his teeth. That was Bacchu's peculiar habit, to keep walking all the time. Maybe he was thinking deeply about something. That son of his and Prince Charles of England had been born on the same day and at the very same hour, which was surely a good omen. He would have to keep comparing the course of Prince Charles' life with that of his son.

His son was no longer visible, having ducked out of sight as soon as he noticed his father watching him. Foyzur Rahman gave a little sigh. For some unknown reason all his children were inordinately scared of him. He had never managed to build up a normal, easygoing relationship with any of them. According to the Sanskrit proverb, *śoṛash varśetu putra mitra bodacaret* – at the age of sixteen a son may be called a friend – but his son had not become his friend. It would be better if he had, as father and son could then have held little meetings to discuss the situation in the country. His son would have told him what was going on in Dhaka and he would have reported what was happening in Pirojpur. For plenty of things were taking place even in this small provincial town, and if momentous events were to happen they might happen here as easily as anywhere else. There were about ten million rupees in the government treasury here, guarded by a detail of fifteen police from the Armed Battalion. The officers who made up this armed guard would come from Barisal, be on duty here for one month, and then return to Barisal once the next batch had arrived to take over. This was the system which had been operating for many years, but of course it might break down. Once law and order went out of the window everything would start breaking down – and the treasury would surely be pillaged.

The senior government representative in Pirojpur Subdivision was the Subdivisional Officer or S.D.O., a member of the Civil Service of Pakistan. The current occupant of the post was Mr Muhibullah, who was a native of Sindh Province in West Pakistan. This placed Foyzur Rahman in an awkward position. Supposing hundreds of angry citizens surrounded the S.D.O.'s bungalow and demanded that this West Pakistani fellow be handed over to them, what should he do then? Should he get his police constables to defend the S.D.O., or should he stand by and watch as the crowd seized the helpless Mr Muhibullah and dragged him away? What rôle should he play? And would his men obey his orders anyway? When a state began to break up it was the police force which became the first casualty. The chain of authority was broken, orders were no longer obeyed, and once a police force had lost its discipline it was no longer any kind of force at all.

Not only that, there existed another irritant peculiar to this part of the country, and that was the Naxal gang. A group of youths was in the habit of roaming around local village areas committing armed robberies under the banner of the Naxal revolutionary movement. The leader of the gang was a young fellow called Fozlu. He had been keeping himself and his henchmen well out of sight, but now, scenting a change in the wind, he was beginning to break cover, and had recently been seen walking around in public with a distinctive swaggering gait. Foyzur Rahman had received a tip-off that Fozlu had his eyes on the treasury.

Suddenly overcome by a sensation of queasiness, Foyzur Rahman abandoned his weeding. The uneasy feeling seemed to be growing in direct proportion to the advance of daylight: it was a problem he had been experiencing recently, an uncomfortable sensation which came over him progressively as the day wore on. It was at its worst around sunset, after which it faded away again. Was it some kind of physical disease, or a mental condition? He really ought to raise the subject with Dr Siraj, the civil surgeon from the government hospital. Dr Siraj normally dropped in every day, but Foyzur Rahman never remembered to bring up the topic of his queasy symptoms while he was there.

He was a real gentleman, this Dr Siraj, and very straightforward. You only had to converse with him for a short while to experience a great wave of optimism; you began to wonder why anything had ever been worrying you. He was stout, his movements were ponderous and so was his voice. He always spoke in lowered tones, but with such clear articulation that every word stuck in your memory.

"My dear S.D.P.O.," he would say, "listen, do you realize what position people like yourself and I are in, people like us who are posted in out of the way places, virtually as remote as the Andaman Islands? You could say that they are on God's privileged list. Let me explain. The Pakistan army is going to carry out all its murder and mayhem in the larger population centres. At the moment they have their hands full trying to bring the big cities to heel. After that they'll turn their attention to district level, and only after that to subdivisional towns. But by then the whole game will be over."

"How do you mean, the game will be over?"

"The outcome will have been reached, whatever that may be. Either we'll be Pakistan or we'll be Bangladesh. Or maybe something in between, that's another possibility. Some kind of loose federation. Or something on the American model, a United States of Pakistan, with Bangladesh as one of its states, Punjab as another, then Sindh, Baluchistan ... do you get the idea?"

"I'm trying to."

"It's not as if the Pakistanis will be able to get very far with their genocidal activities. The United Nations Organization exists, does it not? Not to mention all the major powers. When Podgorny from Russia gives Yahya a rap on the knuckles, Yahya will get the runs, he'll be so scared. And no doctor will be able to cure his diarrhoea – the only remedy will be to put a cork on the bottle. But even supposing nobody from outside disciplines Yahya, how is he going to wage war from a thousand miles away? Is it that easy? It waging war as simple as playing conkers in a playground?"

"I must say I don't see any such easy solution as you are suggesting."

"You think the matter is more complicated?"

"I do."

"You are a practising Muslim, don't you believe what the Quran says?"

"What do you mean, of course I believe what the Holy Quran says!"

"Allah says, in surah *Bani Israil* of the Holy Quran, 'I have hung your fates around your necks like garlands.' In other words, what's going to happen to us has been decided in advance. What point is there in worrying about what has already been fixed?"

"No point, indeed. Whatever is supposed happen will happen. But even so, we shouldn't just sit there quietly with our hands in our laps."

"Well, what are you going to do then?"

"Prepare to face the danger."

"How? The army is going to come along with machine guns and rocket launchers, and you're going to face them with hundred year old .303 rifles? They've been trained to fight battles, while you've been trained to run after thieves and scoundrels. Forget it, empty your head of all such ideas. But please tell your wife to prepare a nice cup of tea, and we can chat over that. Just don't raise your blood pressure by worrying unnecessarily; take life easy."

Foyzur Rahman washed his hands in a bucket which was always kept in the garden. Ira was jostling him from behind. Realising she probably wanted a drink, he held the bucket out for her at head level. She put her nose into the bucket and sucked up some water. It was interesting, he thought: cows, sheep, goats and their kind drew up water like a siphon, while dogs and other carnivores lapped it up with their tongues. What was the reason for that? Maybe he should ask his eldest son, who always had his nose stuck in a book and would probably know the answer to the conundrum. Discussing random topics like this might also be a way of making their relationship more easy and less formal. He noticed his son standing there with a cup of tea in his hand, facing the sun with his eyes closed and taking occasional sips of tea without opening his eyes or changing position. What was he up to? He cleared his throat to catch the young man's attention. His son started in alarm and looked towards him; he had a glazed look in his eyes as if he was afraid. But what was there to be afraid of?

"What are you doing, son?" he asked.

"Nothing"

"Why were you facing the sun with your eyes shut?"

Bacchu didn't answer; he was casting nervous glances all round, as if seeking a way to escape from his father's presence. But Foyzur Rahman felt like carrying on the conversation.

"I've heard there's a man in Swarupkathi who has dealings with jinns," he said. "He can make the jinns manifest themselves, right there in people's homes. These jinns can speak, and put their hands on people's heads and say prayers for them. I was wondering whether to have this fellow brought here, so as to see for myself what it's all about. What do you think, should I send for him?"

"Oh, yes, get him to come here," cried Bacchu eagerly. "When can you do it?"

"I suppose I could have him brought here today, if I want. Let me see what I can do."

Foyzur Rahman could see his son's eyes gleaming with enthusiasm and excitement: clearly Bacchu was delighted with the idea. He decided to try the first topic again.

"Why were you facing the sun with your eyes shut?" he asked.

He had a feeling Bacchu would answer this time, now that he had been softened up a little. The feeling proved to be correct, and he listened with great interest as the young man started to speak. He sounded rather like a teacher lecturing a class full of students. Maybe the lad was destined to end up as a teacher?

"The rays of the sun create vitamin D inside the body. If you face the sun with your eyes closed vitamin D will be formed inside your eyes. You mustn't keep your eyes open, as the sun's rays include ultra-violet waves which would damage the retina."

"Ultraviolet? What's that?"

"Light with a very short wavelength and high energy level."

"I've seen Brahmins in Hindu villages who gaze at the sun and recite some kind of incantation after bathing in the pond."

"They're reciting the *suryamantra*, the sun mantra. It's a way of worshipping the sun. I know that mantra."

"You know the *suryamantra*?" gasped Foyzur Rahman, staring at his son in astonishment.

"Yes: *ang jabākusum shangkāsang kāsyapeyang mahā dyuting. dvantāring sarva pāpaganang pranata hosami dibākaram.*"

"How come you've learned the sun mantra by heart?" asked Foyzur Rahman, much surprised. "You belong to a Muslim family, after all."

Bacchu was deeply embarrassed, and Foyzur Rahman was tickled by the sight of his embarrassment. Anyway, today's little conversation had been longer than any previous one. Another time he must ask his son why it was he had taken the trouble to learn that mantra.

After having breakfast Foyzur Rahman went and changed into his police uniform. He hadn't put on uniform for the past two days, but today he had a special reason for wearing it. The reason was, however, a secret one, and he had said nothing about it to anyone.

His office was situated inside his own home: it was one of the rooms in the official S.D.P.O. bungalow he occupied. It was still just as it had been in olden times. A gigantic manually operated curtain-fan hung from the ceiling, and it had its own professional fan-puller named Rashid, who was on the official pay-roll. As soon as Foyzur Rahman took his seat Rashid would start pulling his rope to make the fan swing slowly to and fro. He had been told not to bother, as there was an electric fan on the desk, but he always persisted in pulling for a while in accordance with regulations. Foyzur Rahman's children were all fascinated by the fan. Once he had discovered his second daughter Shikhu swinging on its rope. It was amazing to think that a hand-pulled ceiling fan from the period of the British Raj could still be in use in Pirojpur in this day and age.

"Rashid!"

"Yes, sir?"

"How are things going, all over?"

"Fine, sir. It's '*Joy Bangla*' everywhere."

"Nothing more than '*Joy Bangla*'?"

Rashid was silent. Of course there was more than just '*Joy Bangla*' going on, but he wasn't going to mention those activities just now. All in good time. Rashid sometimes supplied Foyzur Rahman with valuable intelligence.

"Is the boat ready at its moorings?"

"Yes, sir."

"You must go and put some bedding in the cabin, and make it nice and comfy. Put some pitchers of water in the boat too. If my children have to go away anywhere in the boat, you're to go with them."

"Yes, sir."

A subdivisional police chief used to get an official boat with his job, a sizeable boat with its own crew, who were all on the government payroll too. Foyzur Rahman's children were always longing to go for a joyride in the boat, but he never let them. Today he was breaking his usual rule.

Foyzur Rahman glanced at the clock. It said 10:25 am. He was waiting for it to strike eleven, but the time was passing very slowly. There were plenty of files sitting on his desk, but he had no heart to look at them now. He could use the time to make out a T.A. invoice, for none had been submitted the previous month; however there seemed no point in making out a bill in these circumstances, for where was any payment going to come from? He opened a drawer in his desk and pulled out a thick two hundred-page scribbling book with a hard cover. For quite some time now he had been trying his hand at writing a play for radio. The play was entitled *So Many Stars in the Sky*, and there was a story behind the title. One evening his youngest son Shaheen had been sitting outside in the yard, and suddenly he had looked up into space and called out in delight, "There are so many stars in the sky!" Foyzur Rahman had been deeply struck by the way his infant son had constructed this sentence in perfect Bengali, and had immediately decided he would write a novel based on it.

The fact that he was now writing a radio drama rather than a novel also had a story behind it. Mr Baharul Haque, Assistant Programme Producer at Radio Pakistan Dacca, was a native of Pirojpur, and Foyzur Rahman had got to know him socially. Mr Haque had told him that if he could write a play of suitable quality he, Mr Haque, would do his best to have it broadcast.

Foyzur Rahman sat working on his radio drama with deep concentration until half past eleven. He deleted some of the scenes he had written previously. The new scene he now created was so moving, tears came to his eyes as he finished writing it. He wiped away the tears and stood up, while Rashid watched in amazement. Quite a few things about this new S.D.P.O. puzzled Rashid; for example the good man would often sit down to write something or other, and then tears would start rolling down his cheeks. There must be some secret behind it all, and he was very curious to know what it was. Still, it was no use being curious, he was just a humble fan-puller, and how could he possibly fathom what was going on inside the mind of a chief of police?

Mr Muhibullah, the S.D.O., was sitting in a cane chair on the verandah of his bungalow. He frowned as he observed Foyzur Rahman coming towards him. There could be only one reason for the Subdivisional Police Officer's coming to see him – some problem to do with law and order. There were bound to be problems, but he no longer had any power to solve them. He was mildly surprised to note that the S.D.P.O. was in full uniform.

Foyzur Rahman saluted the S.D.O., and Mr Muhibullah got up from his chair and asked quietly, "Is anything wrong?"

"Sir," said Foyzur Rahman, "you've got to get away from Pirojpur."

Muhibullah remained silent.

"Sir, I have a river launch ready for you at Wheelerhat. That launch will take you as far as Barisal, where you should be safe. You should try to proceed from Barisal to Dhaka, and thence to your own country."

"They could easily kill me on the way to Barisal."

"Fifteen men from the Armed Police Battalion will be on the launch, having finished treasury duty. I have instructed them to take care of your personal safety."

"Are they likely to obey your orders?"

"Yes, sir, they will obey."

"And when am I to leave?"

"Now."

"Take a seat here while I get ready. There's just one little question I'd like to ask you if I may; you can think it over before you reply."

"Yes, sir, what is the question?"

"Which way do your loyalties lie, with Pakistan or with the insurgents?"

"Definitely with the insurgents."

"Then why are you helping me to escape? No, never mind, you don't have to answer that one."

Foyzur Rahman saw the S.D.O. off at Wheelerhat launch terminal. As he was about to board the boat Muhibullah suddenly stopped in his tracks and turned to him.

"You are a brother. You are the brother I never had," he said.

It was now nine in the evening. Foyzur Rahman had just received a message to the effect that Muhibullah had reached Barisal safely, and was expecting to travel onwards from Barisal to Dhaka the same night, on board the river steamer the Rocket.

The streets of Pirojpur were thronged with people parading as if for battle. The slogan they were chanting was "We too are ready to stand up against Yahya." They were pronouncing the word for "against" in the manner peculiar to Barisal District, *bruddhe* instead of *biruddhe*, and it sounded quite funny. The leader of the demonstration was a young National Awami Party activist, Ali Hayder Khan, who was a good friend of Foyzur Rahman's. He often dropped in at the S.D.P.O.'s bungalow for tea of an evening before starting one of his rallies. When he continued on his way to the demonstration he would take Foyzur Rahman's two older sons along with him, and they would join in the chanting with great enthusiasm, Barisal accent and all. "We too are ready to stand up against Yahya!" They would have their father's personal .22 rifle with them, sharing the one weapon between the two of them. When he saw his sons parading with the rifle Foyzur Rahman felt mixed emotions, pride and apprehension at the same time.

But today the S.D.P.O.'s sons were not joining in the demonstrations, because there was to be a jinn summoning session at their house and they were brimming with excitement.

The man who was going to summon the jinns was called Kofiluddi. He was a strongly built fellow in the prime of life. His features were lost in a jungle of beard, his eyes had a glazed look, and he was dressed in a lungi and a dark green *kurta*.

Kofiluddi made everyone assemble in one room, where a prayer mat was laid out on the floor. He explained that he was going to kneel on the mat and recite various surahs, the *al-Jinn* surah in particular, and thus cause a jinn to become physically present. Once the jinn was present no disrespectful talk would be allowed; if any questions were to be put to the jinn, this must be done in an extremely polite way. Everyone would be able to feel the jinn's presence but they would not be able to see him, as the room would be in darkness. No lights of any sort would be allowed.

Everyone had performed their ritual ablutions beforehand. Now they were all sitting there in the darkened room, waiting. It was so dark nobody could even see a hand in front of their face. Kofiluddi was reciting his surahs with full concentration in a deep voice, using his own peculiar style of recitation. Suddenly there was a *flop* sound in the centre of the room, as if someone had jumped down from the ceiling and landed on the floor, and then there were more plopping sounds as if someone was moving around on frog-like feet. Kofiluddi was still doing his recitations. At that point the jinn's voice was heard saying, "*As-salaamu alaikum*. I have come."

The effect was terrifying. The only outsider in the room was Kofiluddi, and there was no way anyone else could have slipped in to play the rôle of jinn. Yet everyone could hear both Kofiluddi reciting and the jinn speaking at one and the same time. Furthermore the *flip-flop, flip-flop* of someone walking from one side of the room to the other could be heard quite distinctly. From time to time a sharp *whish* like the hiss of a snake was also audible.

The police chief's second son Zafar Iqbal overcame his fear sufficiently to speak. "Where do you live?" he asked.

"I live in the town of Kohqaf," replied the jinn.

"Will Bangladesh become independent?"

"Never."

"Why not?"

"All of us jinns are united in praying for Pakistan. *Pakistan Zindabad!*"

The jinn gave replies to a few further questions. Then he placed his hands on each person's head to give them his blessing, and explained that he couldn't stay much longer as today the jinns were getting together to say a special prayer for the preservation of Pakistan, and it was time for him to go and join in the prayer ceremony.

Foyzur Rahman and his wife were fully convinced that a jinn really had come to their house, and Kofiluddi received a handsome gratuity before he was allowed to go on his way. Neither of them had ever before seen a jinn summoned to earth in this remarkable fashion, and if it hadn't been for his prediction that Bangladesh would never achieve independence they would have been totally satisfied.

"Of course Bangladesh will become independent," said Zafar Iqbal. "No jinn came down at all. I tape recorded the whole proceedings, and if a jinn really had come he would have noticed that I was doing so, and got angry. It was nothing but a lot of trickery by Kofiluddi."

Foyzur Rahman was delighted to observe how bold his second son had been, making a tape recording of the jinn's utterances on the sly. He would never have thought of that himself. But an even bigger surprise was awaiting him. His eldest son played the tape through, listening carefully to all of the dialogue, and came up with strong evidence that no jinn had appeared. At one point in the supposed jinn's discourse he had pronounced the word *prothom* in an entirely local Barisal style, *porthom*. If the jinn had come from the town of Kohqaf, his son reasoned, then why would he say *prothom* with a Barisal accent?

So there was no need to feel gloomy about the jinn's prediction that Bangladesh would not become independent; the jinn was none other than Kofiluddi himself.

Foyzur Rahman retired to bed that night feeling extremely pleased with the intrepidity and intelligence his sons had shown. A man with sons like that, he thought, had no need to worry, they would be equal to any challenge. He had already lain down to sleep when, on a sudden impulse, he got up again, performed ablutions and prepared to perform the *tahajjud* or late night prayers.

No sooner had he stood on his prayer mat to start the prayers than there was a sound at the front door. Someone was rattling the chain in great urgency; he could guess from the way they were rattling that something dreadful had happened. Nobody would knock on the door of the subdivisional police officer's bungalow in the middle of the night like that unless something pretty ghastly had taken place.

What should he do, complete his prayers or go and see who was at the door? By rights he ought to finish his prayers first, but whoever was at the door was in no mood for waiting, they were rattling the chain incessantly. Aroused by the noise, Foyzur Rahman's wife Ayesha and elder daughter Sufia had both woken up and risen from their beds in alarm.

Foyzur Rahman stepped off his prayer mat, reflecting that everyone was going through exceptionally bad times and it was impossible to tell what might happen at any minute, therefore he should first of all go and find out what was going on.

It was the officer in charge of Pirojpur town police station who was at the door, and he was accompanied by his second officer.

"Sir, you must come to the police station," said the O.C. very quietly the moment Foyzur Rahman had opened the door.

"Why, what's happened?"

"They're going to transmit an urgent message by wireless, and they want to speak to you."

"Who? Who is giving this urgent message?"

"They didn't say. Army high command, I think. However it could possibly be police headquarters."

Foyzur Rahman swiftly changed from his lungi into trousers, and put on a shirt.

"Where are you going?" his wife asked him anxiously.

"To the police station."

"What for?"

"I'll tell you later."

"You should take one of the boys with you. Shall I wake them?"

"No need to wake anyone. And don't feel frightened, there's no reason. Nothing has happened which should frighten you."

The wireless message was from police headquarters in Dhaka; it was a statement by the Inspector General which was being broadcast. A non-Bengali wireless operator made the announcement. "All districts in the province are under army control. Military operations at subdivision and thana levels will commence shortly. All sections of the police force are hereby instructed to cooperate fully with the military authorities. They are to maintain law and order and carry out all orders from the army in the interests of national security."

Foyzur Rahman received the message.

"What are we to do, sir?" asked the O.C. He was looking grey with worry and had beads of sweat on his face.

"The police force has always stood shoulder to shoulder with the ordinary citizen," said Foyzur Rahman. "We shall continue to do so now. We shall stand alongside the people of our country."

"But what about those who don't wish to do so?"

"That's for them to say, not me."

"Aren't you going to give any orders?"

"No. The chain of command in the police force has broken down. In these circumstances orders no longer count for anything."

"If anyone in the police force wishes to retire to their native village, are they to go?"

"Yes, let them go."

Foyzur Rahman was walking back to his quarters. There were no street lights at all in the town, and no lamps were burning in people's houses, but the moon was up and he had no difficulty in seeing his way by moonlight. It suddenly struck him that a moonlit town was even more beautiful than a moonlit village.

He stopped walking and stood still for a few minutes glorying in the moonlight. When he started walking again he noticed someone following him at a distance. Whenever he paused that person paused, and when he continued walking that person also continued walking. What was going on?

"Who's that over there? Who are you?"

The person who was following him came to a halt.

"Come here!" commanded Foyzur Rahman in his sternest police voice.

The person advanced timidly, head bowed. When he came close and stood still Foyzur Rahman recognized him: it was Rashid the fan-puller.

Foyzur Rahman resumed his walk, and Rashid followed with his head down. This was Rashid's custom, to follow his master wherever he went, without exception, however late the hour.

Suddenly Foyzur Rahman remembered that strange dream of his, when he was walking along in the bridegroom's procession. Rashid had been just behind him then too: the one who faithfully followed him in real life had followed him even in his dreams.

"Rashid!"

"Yes, sir?"

"Are you married?"

"No, sir."

The two of them walked along in brilliant moonshine. Then it occurred to Foyzur Rahman – in that dream, too, there had been a moon in the sky. The bridegroom's retinue had been anointing themselves with silver moonlight as they marched along.

19

Today General Tikka Khan had put on a light ghee coloured kaftan to go with his smart leggings, and he was wearing Afghani slippers on his feet. He had tried tying an embroidered Kashmiri cummerbund round his kaftan, but taken it off again as its red, yellow and bright green colour scheme seemed too bold. He had applied a dab of scent to his ear lobes, using a perfume called *mishkat-e-anbar*. A cousin of his used to send him this perfume from Saudi Arabia; on the whole he didn't like its powerful smell, but today he was finding it quite agreeable. He had managed to get himself into a relatively chipper mood, which he was going to have to keep up for the next hour or two.

For today was his birthday. In honour of the occasion two cakes had been brought from the Hotel Intercontinental. The cakes had been made to order and each one had *Zinda Pakistan* written on it in Urdu. They were to be cut up and eaten at two separate events in the evening. His guests at the first event would be selected intellectuals from Dhaka city, including university professors, poets and writers, artists and people from the film industry. They had been asked to arrive at 7 p.m. Transport would be provided to collect them and take them back home again after the party.

When the party was being planned Tikka Khan's aide-de-camp Ismat Khan had said he thought none of the invitees would turn up.

"Everybody who is invited will come," Tikka Khan had said. "Nobody will be missing."

"Sir," Ismat Ali had insisted, "I really don't think any of them will come."

"Do you want to bet?" Tikka Khan had asked. "Come on, let me have a little wager with you."

"If we do lay a bet, you're going to be the one who loses," the A.D.C. had said, "because I'm always very lucky with my betting. Whenever I bet on something I win."

"All right, let's see. If you win you'll get a big fruit basket. But you won't win; do you want to know why?"

"Please tell me."

"Because intellectuals are cowards. As Shakespeare put it, 'Cowards die many times before their deaths'. They're dead already, all of them, and dead people have no will power. Do you get me?"

"I think so."

"They're ready to lick the floor in order to stay alive. There may be one or two exceptions, as every rule has its exceptions. By the way, what do you think of this perfume I've put on?"

"Rather strong."

"Not faint like a watercolour but vivid like a bold oil painting. Right?"

"Yes, sir."

"Watercolours won't do in wartime, everything has to be in oils. If you look at it like that, this perfume is quite appropriate."

"Yes, sir."

The guests arrived on time. They were apprehensive. A nervous tension was apparent in the way they stood, the way they sat, the way they did everything. Even the way they breathed suggested that they were too fearful to fill their lungs properly. They all sat stiffly with straight backs. Frightened humans always keep their spine rigid; that way their nerves remain taut.

"I'm really delighted," said General Tikka, "because you have taken the trouble to heed my invitation and come here. Now, I know some of you but not all. If you will kindly introduce yourselves one by one, I shall be greatly honoured. No, don't stand up, do remain seated while you speak, please do."

"I am Dr ---, professor of English language and literature, Dhaka University."

"Thank you, sir, thank you for coming."

"I am Dr ---, associate professor, history department, Dhaka University."

"Thank you, sir, thank you for coming."

"I am ---. I am a poet."

"I am honoured to meet a poet."

It took some time for the introductions to be completed, as General Tikka stopped in front of each of his guests and stayed standing there for a few moments with a polite smile on his face. He shook hands with some of them, even embraced one. When the introductions were over the general gave an elegant speech, all of it in English.

> "I feel greatly honoured to think that such a talented and erudite group of people as yourselves have responded to the invitation of a mere soldier like me and turned up here today. Today is a special day for me. On this day, in an obscure, remote village in the Panjab, I first saw the light of day. It is hardly fitting for a soldier to indulge in the absurd childishness of celebrating a birthday, but I am doing it as an excuse to have you all here with me.
>
> As I am sure you will recognize, we have crushed the miscreants with all their evil machinations. Behind the miscreants stands the treacherous Awami League. But one evildoer will always help another, and it is evil Hindustan which is helping the Awami League. We are now preparing to teach pernicious Hindustan a lesson. The Awami League has already been chastised, and the chief devil is now back in his cage. Later, at our own convenience, we shall let the devil out of his cage, and we have some interesting plans regarding him.
>
> A branch of the Hindustani radio corporation Akash Bani has recently been broadcasting under the title of Free Bengal Radio and announcing that Sheikh Mujib is leading a movement in support of the rebels. I hope that by the end of my speech there will be no remaining confusion in your minds regarding this subject. In tomorrow's papers there should be a picture of Sheikh Mujib sitting in Karachi airport.
>
> I have nearly reached the end of my speech. Very shortly the cake will be cut, and then you will have a cup of tea with me. I also have a little present for each of you, namely a fruit basket. In English there is an expression, 'say it with flowers', but I have slightly altered this and am going to 'say it with fruit'.
>
> You must all do your best for Pakistan. Don't let yourselves be influenced by the things the traitors say. The country is now on a war footing, and in wartime we have to make tough decisions. Please do not do anything which might oblige us to resort to drastic measures."

The cake was cut. It had a large green candle at one corner. "I'm going to make a wish," said General Tikka, closing his eyes and blowing out the candle. "My wish," he explained, "was for peace and friendship. Come on, let's eat the cake," and he personally handed a slice of cake to each guest. The special guests were beguiled by the general's civility.

For the next half hour the general chatted about this and that. He told the story of how he had killed a wild sow with a javelin in the Rann of Kutch. When one of the guests expressed surprise that wild boar could be found in a desert area like the Rann of Kutch the general instantly whipped out a photo album and displayed a picture of himself with the sow.

He also spoke about the art of war.

"The world's top military strategist was Alexander the Great," he told the history professor. "Did you know that the name of Alexander the Great can be found in the Holy Quran?"

"I didn't know that, sir," replied the professor in surprise.

"Yes, Alexander the Great is mentioned in our sacred Book. In it he is referred to as *dhul qarnain*."

Everyone present was fascinated and amazed by what the general was saying, and also impressed by the breadth of his knowledge. They forgot for a moment that he was a truly redoubtable figure, widely known as the Butcher of Baluchistan. The general saw them all off in person.

Then began the second get-together, a meeting with senior police officers. The Inspector General was not present, but there were three Deputy Inspectors General and two Assistant Inspectors General. All but one of them were Bengalis. The army general cut the second cake for them, and went through all the same words and actions he had used with the first group. Nothing was omitted; he even repeated the story of his hunting exploit in the Rann of Kutch. This time, it is true, nobody queried the existence of wild swine in the desert, but nevertheless the general showed the photograph of himself standing, spear in hand, beside the dead body of the wild sow.

The speech the general addressed to the police officers was succinct.

> "I always prefer to be brief when talking business, so please listen carefully. I expect 95% loyalty from Bengali police. They may reserve the other five percent for their Bengali brethren if they wish, that does not bother me. A fair number of police officers are coming over from West Pakistan to assist you in your work. There will also be a paramilitary force supporting you. Is there anything anyone wishes to say?"

"We have nothing to say, sir," said the A.I.G. of the Special Branch.

"How can you claim to speak for everyone?" asked the general tersely. "You may state that you personally have nothing to say, but how do you know none of the others wants to say anything?"

The A.I.G's face went pale.

"Answer me separately, each one of you," said General Tikka.

Each officer replied that he had nothing to say.

"My discussion with you is now over," said the general "You may go. I have these orders for you – you are to get the police force back under control and operative within twenty-four hours. The intelligence section of the army is keeping a very close eye on the police – I have warned you. There is a basket of fruit for each of you; please take it. Good day, officers."

The general went to the army officers' mess for dinner. It had been announced that he would dine with all the top brass of the armed forces. Elaborate arrangements had been made for the meal. A navy cook called Abdul Khaleq had been specially commissioned to do the cooking for this evening's feast – he had an almost legendary reputation for his 'Saffron Chicken' dish. This special item had been duly prepared, and a Bihari man had been brought from the Mirpur area to make beef kebabs. The kebab man was grilling his meat on an open fire outside the mess, and anyone who wanted kebabs had to come to him with their plate, so he could serve them sizzling hot from the fire.

Some chairs and tables were set up in the open area outside the mess, and many of the officers had taken their seats there.

In addition to this excellent food, drinks had also been laid on: Australian red wine, Russian vodka, Black Label whisky, various beers. Vodka was the most in demand. Particular drinks fit particular occasions, and on this occasion vodka seemed to be the thing; everyone was ignoring the expensive Black Label whisky and going for the vodka. Only General Tikka had a glass of red wine in his hand. He had finished his first glass and was now on his second. It was a pleasant evening, the oppressive heat having been relieved by a cool breeze. One sensed that rain had been falling somewhere further away.

The general frowned when the thought of rain crossed his mind. Rain was not a good thing at all. The arrival of the monsoon meant transport problems for the army. What a strange land this was – all rivers, irrigation channels, floodlands – water, water, water. He had heard that a vast area in the Sylhet region became totally submerged once the rains started. When a breeze blew over the flooded area it made waves just like the waves of the sea. It wasn't the army's job to control such areas, it should be something for the navy to deal with. The general drained his glass in one draught and filled it again. This wasn't the right way to drink wine, he knew; wine should be tasted in sips, hardly wetting the lips. Vodka, whisky and suchlike were like wild drumbeats and hearty clapping, while wine was the gentle music of a flute.

Brigadier Shams suddenly sprang to his feet and raised his glass of vodka. "Cheers to the general on his birthday!" he cried. Everyone who had been sitting stood up, and one toast followed another.

"Let us toast Pakistan."

"Let us toast the great people of Pakistan."

"Let us toast fallen soldiers."

Usually army officers' parties quickly take off and go with a swing. But in spite of all the elaborate preparations today's party was falling flat. Maybe the basic problem was the absence of any catalyst. The fair wives of the army officers are normally present at such gatherings and act as a catalyst; they know how to rise to an occasion and get a party going. Today's party was devoid of women.

Everyone looked at Colonel Jamshed and called on him to perform some of his tricks. Normally he carried various props for conjuring tricks around with him, coins, string and scissors, a pack of cards, ping-pong balls, but it transpired that he hadn't brought any of these things with him today. So he borrowed a one rupee coin from someone and did a few vanishing tricks with it. He closed his fist over the coin, and when he opened his fist again the coin had disappeared. He concealed the coin in his right hand, and then produced it from his left.

Even Colonel Jamshed's conjuring show was falling flat. The best thing now would be to end the party. If you let an unsuccessful party drag on too long it can give rise to various problems. General Tikka announced the conclusion of the event, and delivered a short closing speech in Urdu.

"The Pakistan army is one of the best armies in the world. It has been entrusted with a sacred duty, that of defending the motherland, and it is going to discharge that duty in such a way that it shall be inscribed in letters of gold in the history of our nation. We are going to make the ignorant people of East Pakistan learn their lesson. Our method of teaching them this lesson will be sterner than anything they can possibly imagine. We are in a state of war, and it is said that in wartime the human virtues of kindness, sympathy and mercy have to be buried in a pit three cubits deep. We shall bury them in a pit seven cubits deep. Humane feelings are to be reserved for humans, not for opportunistic, Hindu-worshipping perverts like the East Pakistanis.

I shall end my address by extending my congratulations to all of you in advance, and by quoting the words of tank brigade commander General Rommel, known as the Desert Fox. When embarking on his campaign in Egypt General Rommel said, 'The moment you show mercy to the enemy you will cease to be a soldier. Suppose you are pointing your bayonet at an enemy soldier's chest. Suddenly you glimpse his anguished face and feel sorry for him. You hesitate and lower your bayonet. The enemy soldier will then happily do the job in your stead, and plunge his bayonet into your heart.'"

Leaving the army mess, the general headed back to his quarters. He made his driver move aside and took over the steering wheel himself. It gave him a fine feeling to drive the vehicle through the streets. Dhaka city was back to normal. That was excellent. The news of this return to normality must be disseminated via the press, radio and television. Foreign journalists must be summoned, to see for themselves how clear the city was.

The Dhaka newspapers had been coming out as two-page broadsheets, which was not good enough. Newspapers should look like newspapers. He would have to speak to Major Siddiq Salik about it; it was a matter for the Inter-Services Public Relations Officer.

20

A prose article by Shah Kolim appeared in the literature section of the *Dainik Pakistan*. It was entitled *Pakistan of the Pure Soul*. Since 25th March he had started writing under a new name, Golam Kalandar, and he had slightly altered his appearance too. His hair and beard were longer than before. As the armed forces regard long, unkempt hair with suspicion he had taken to wearing a colourful embroidered cap on his head whenever he went out in the street, and he also wore sunglasses. These sunglasses had been presented to him by a Pakistani officer called Major Siddiq Salik°, who was in charge of the Press Corps and sometimes dropped in at the newspaper's offices. An excellent understanding had grown up between Kolimullah and the major. Kolimullah could sometimes be observed taking a lift in the major's jeep, and on one particular occasion he was invited for lunch at the army officers' mess.

After consuming his lunch Kolimullah had assured the major that he was ready to give the last drop of his blood for the sake of Pakistan. He had gone on to declare that the night Pakistan had been delivered from ruin he had performed twenty cycles of prostrations and offered special prayers to Allah. There had been some loss of life, he admitted, some innocent people had met their deaths; but that was bound to happen, there was no way it could have been avoided. Whenever any great act was undertaken there would inevitably be a few ugly side effects, but one had to concentrate one's attention on the grand act itself.

Major Siddiq Salik had issued Kolimullah with a pass which was proving very useful. When a curfew was on he could move in the streets, showing his pass when required.

Kolimullah had rented a three-roomed house in the Mirpur area. In fact he could hardly be said to have rented it; he was living in it for free. The owner had gone away to his village home telling Kolimullah he need not pay any rent. "Just stay here and look after the house," he had said. "It cost me a great deal of effort to acquire it, and I don't want to lose it. This house, it represents the life savings of a poor man. And I've heard that Biharis are moving in and taking over people's empty homes."

"No problem," Kolimullah had said, using an Urdu expression – bits of Urdu vocabulary had begun to creep into his speech – "nobody will be able to take over the house. No Bihari is a match for me. Besides, I'll put up a sign in Urdu saying 'This is the house of a Muslim', with a black star. The star symbol is the main thing, any Bihari or any soldier seeing it will instantly understand that this is *saccha mukam* – the home of a true believer." How smart his little touches of Urdu sounded.

In this Mirpur house Kolimullah's days were passing rather well. He had engaged a cook called Bacchu Miah, who was seventeen or eighteen years old and came from Ruwail in Netrakona. When Kolimullah had interviewed him for the job he had said he knew all the main types of cuisine, local, *Mughlai* style and English, and even a bit of Chinese, as he had worked for a while in a Chinese restaurant.

In the event it turned out that he had no knowledge of any kind of cookery. Every dish he produced looked like special diet for an invalid, and tasted like it too. The most commendable thing about Bacchu Miah was that he himself, on tasting one of his creations, would be the first to condemn it. "Lord 'ave mercy on us! What's the matter with this curry! I dunno if you'll be able to stomach it, brother. I must've got lousy turmeric, that's why it's like this. I'll 'ave to get some new turmeric."

But even after a fresh supply of turmeric had been purchased the curries neither looked nor tasted any better.

Kolimullah had to put up with Bacchu Miah because he couldn't find anyone else. It had become difficult to get hold of new servants in Dhaka, for the city was half empty. None of the people who had fled around 27th-28th March had returned, in fact people were still leaving the metropolis in dribs and drabs. Radio Pakistan, of course, maintained that the city was back to normal, and that the schools, colleges and universities were about to re-open; banks were operating normally, government offices were functioning.

It was announced that those people who had been led astray by evildoers and absconded from their posts would be excused for their temporary absence if they now returned to their places of work.

But people didn't seem to trust the radio any more; instead they trusted rumour. There was no end to the rumours of various kinds which were circulating, and Bacchu Miah was an expert in collecting them. Not a shred of gossip could be passed around without Bacchu Miah getting hold of it. One day he disappeared early in the morning, was missing all day and didn't return until eight in the evening. On his return he was grinning all over.

"Brother!" he said, "d'you know what's 'appened? I'll give yer two millets. Two millets to guess."

"Get out," said Kolimullah. "I'm not going to employ you any longer."

"Never mind," said Bacchu Miah, not in the least perturbed. "If you won't, you won't. Whatever shall be shall be. But come on, guess what's 'appened! I give yer one millet!" He was well able to pronounce the letter N, but always said "millet" instead of "minute".

"Oh, stop it, do stop your chatter."

"Brother! Tikka is finished. Fin-isssshed!"

"Who's finished?"

"Tikka. General Tikka. Got four bullets in 'im, didn' 'e, went down like a light. Blood all over the place. Army's all in a tizzy, they ain't got no leader no more."

"Who told you this?"

"Everyone in the city knows. If I'm telling a lie I'm a bastard, my dad ain't my real dad. You can switch on *Shadhin Bangla* and listen to what they say."

The news was broadcast on *Shadhin Bangla* (Free Bengal) radio that evening. "General Tikka Killed. According to an unconfirmed report, East Pakistan Martial Law Administrator General Tikka Khan has been assassinated by the liberation army. Great unrest in Dhaka city. Army on red alert."

"What do you say now, brother?" asked Bacchu Miah. "I'm a poor fella, now that the news 'as gone stale you believe it. Funny thing God did when 'e made the poor. No-one believes a poor fella when 'e brings fresh news, they only believe 'im after it's gone stale. Two rupees, now, if you please."

"What do you want two rupees for?"

"Need to get rice and ghee. Today I'm gonna make chicken pulao. Learned 'ow to make it from Mona the chef. Just wait till you taste it. 'E was an expert and 'e was mighty fond of me."

While Kolimullah was tasting the highly unsavoury chicken pulao prepared by Mona the chef's favourite pupil, a speech by General Tikka was broadcast on radio and television. The general was making a personal appearance in order to announce some new martial law regulations. On TV he could be seen smiling as he spoke, as if pronouncing martial edicts was something which gave him a great deal of pleasure.

"What do you make of that, then?" said Kolimullah, looking at Bacchu Miah.

"Brother," Bacchu Miah explained, "that ain't the real Tikka, it's a lookalike. They must 'ave got 'old of 'im to encourage the soldiers. The real one is finished. That's most likely a brother of 'is. Brothers look alike. If I'm telling a lie my dad ain't my dad, I'm a bastard. What was the chicken pulao like?"

"You tell me, what was it like?"

"Awful. That ghee weren't no good. Dalda brand, adulterated. Mona the chef, my old teacher, 'e would never have cooked chicken pulao using dodgy ghee. Not if you paid 'im a million rupees."

"Oh, put a sock in it."

"All right, I'm not saying any more."

"You have absolutely no knowledge of cookery."

"What are you saying, brother? I was Mona the chef's chosen assistant. 'E loved me more than 'is own son. Only now it's wartime, I can't concentrate on me cooking, that's why it don't always come out right."

"What war are you talking about?"

"Hey, come off it, brother! Outside of Dhaka it's going on all the time – wham! boom! pow! crump! The Bengal Regiment is pinning 'em down, Major Zia's got the Pakistan army between 'is teeth. 'E's gripping like a turtle, won't let go even if you kill 'im!"

"Pish tush, you moron! Nothing is happening at all. The only war going on is the one on *Shadhin Bangla* radio, and that's an imaginary one."

"Imaginary?" repeated Bacchu Miah in a wounded tone.

"Listen," said Kolimullah as he lit his pipe. Having acquired this pipe from the major, he took great pleasure in reclining in an easy chair during his leisure hours and lighting it up. "Listen while I explain. This war is taking place on the radio. No ammunition is necessary, just a loud voice. *Shadhin Bangla* radio isn't real, and none of the news on it is real."

"No, don't say that!"

"They announce that Sheikh Mujib is there with the freedom fighters, giving them their orders, and then we see a photo in the newspapers showing him in Karachi airport. They report that Begum Sufia Kamal° and Dr Nilima Ibrahim° have been killed, and then we see their picture in the papers: by God's grace both of them alive and well. Then we hear that Tikka Khan has been killed. And do you still really think that he has?"

"Of course! Brother, that Tikka you think you saw, God is my witness, that's just a lookalike. The real one is done for. If my words are untrue let lightning strike me."

"Just go away, will you."

Kolimullah was enjoying his present existence. Accommodation was no problem at all. Not only did he have the place in Mirpur, there was another property he could use as well. The owner of the house in Jhigatola where Kolimullah used to give private tuition was about to go away into the country, and he too had asked Kolimullah to look after his dwelling, and had given him a key. This house in Jhigatola was a large one, and it was full of things. Kolimullah had decided he would move into it at some stage. It wasn't a good idea to stay too long in one place, one started putting down roots. For someone who wrote prose it hardly mattered if they put down roots, but for poets it was a problem. Poets should not have roots. Like their lines of poetry they should always keep flowing.

Quite apart from that, Kolimullah loved rummaging through the personal possessions in other people's homes. In the house he was currently occupying he had had great fun opening a padlocked trunk which had been stowed under the bed in the main bedroom. It contained all sorts of little items; letters, pictures. A series of letters written to a girl called Nayla turned out to be highly pornographic. It was her husband who had written them. Kolimullah had never read such obscene material before, and he added the letters to his own private collection. There was also some money in the trunk, two hundred and twenty-one rupees in a sealed Horlicks jar. Why had they left money behind? There was no telling. Kolimullah kept the money, Horlicks jar and all, and from time to time used bits of it for his expenses. It gave him quite a pleasant feeling to do so.

Kolimullah was walking in the torrid heat of noon. His route took him past the High Court; and he was on his way to the *Dainik Pakistan* office with another new prose composition in his pocket. It was entitled *The Great Poet Iqbal*.

21st April was Iqbal Day, and the article was to be published on that date. Contributions for special days like that were always in demand. This article too was to appear under the name of Golam Kalandar. Golam Kalandar was building up quite a good reputation, though it would be even better if he could get some articles published in English language newspapers as well. Kolimullah was not at all good at English, and found things like active and passive, and the different tenses, very hard to deal with.

Kolimullah was enjoying his walk. The roads were almost empty. The few people out and about were walking silently, their eyes fixed on the road.

Previously rickshaw pullers had gone around tinkling their bells all the time even when there was no need to do so, but now there was no tinkling to be heard. Most of the rickshaws were empty; there were so few customers. Previously people had tramped the streets without any particular purpose, but now nobody was venturing forth unless they absolutely had to.

Walls and buildings were spotless, with no sign of any graffiti. The political slogans which had been daubed on them before had been erased by order of the martial law authorities. No longer was it possible for slogan writers to come out and do their work at dead of night: there was a curfew from 9 p.m. to 5 a.m., and anyone seen in the streets would be shot on sight.

Kolimullah lit a cigarette. All right, smoking while walking was bad for the health, but so was too much fussing about healthy lifestyles. There should be moderation in all things. Take for example the High Court judge, Justice B.A. Siddiqui. He had been such a high principled man, he had previously refused to swear in General Tikka as Governor of East Pakistan, and for that he had even been celebrated in popular slogans like *'Joy Bangla! Joy Siddiqui!'* But now he had changed his tune, and graciously conducted General Tikka's swearing-in ceremony. * *'Bol Hari, Hari bol'*, as the Hindus say, bowing to their deity. My wares are for sale, stop me and buy one.

Dhaka was under control now. There was no problem with Dhaka. Whenever rebel gunfire was heard, a helicopter would come along and drop a couple of bombs. Bomber planes were ready too. All those Bengalis who imagined they were going to win independence for their country using spades and pickaxes had failed to reckon with celestial chastisement. Now they had been shut up. No more grousing, everybody must sit down now and learn how to write Bengali in Arabic script. A committee of experts set up by Yahya had recommended just that –

---

* Not only General Tikka's, for he also swore in the Quisling Governor Malik and his cabinet. – **Author**

Bengali was to be written in the Arabic script. What fun! *Ba* plus *zabr* 'ba', then *nun*, then *lam* plus *zabr* 'la'... 'ba-n-la'! Wasn't that brilliant?

Arriving at the *Dainik Pakistan* offices, Kolimullah found himself face to face with the Procession for Peace°. The Procession for Peace was using a lorry to move around; it had to visit a number of different localities in the city, far too much to cover on foot. Kolimullah surveyed the peace envoys with great interest. It would be a good thing to get to know them; their help might be needed in times of peril. He couldn't recognize all of them, but there were Khan-e-Sabur, Khwaja Khayruddin, Ghulam Azam°, Benazir Ahmed. Suppose Bangladesh ever became independent, thought Kolimullah – it was quite impossible, but just suppose – then what would become of these guys? These doves of peace, would they go on cooing in the same conciliatory way then?

An almost perceptible wave of alarm swept through the Dainik Pakistan office when Kolimullah made his appearance. The doorkeeper jumped up from his stool to give a salute. Just outside the office door a man from the printing section accosted Kolimullah.

"Kolim *bhai*, how are you, brother? I didn't see you yesterday, were you poorly? How about a cup of tea now, in our section?"

The reason for all the attention showered on Kolimullah was his familiarity with the major. Those who are close to the sun reflect some of its brilliance themselves. Kolimullah handed in his article on Iqbal the poet and sat down to a cup of tea. The tea in newspaper offices is generally good, and as soon as one has finished the first cup one feels ready for another.

"Oh, Kolim *bhai*, how are you?"

It seemed the cashier had entered the room for some purpose, then caught sight of Kolimullah and become a little flustered. Fear was written in his eyes. Kolimullah suddenly felt deeply gratified – this was great, someone was looking at him in awe! He had spent most of his own life in awe of others; now the tables were turned, and people were scared of him.

"You're all right, are you?" asked Kolimullah, sipping his tea.

"Yes, brother, thanks to your prayers."

"Prayers? You think I have time to pray for other people's welfare?"

"You're quite right, no time for praying, more a matter of saving one's skin."

"Why, what do you mean? Saving one's skin from what?"

With malicious glee Kolimullah observed that the fellow had gone ashen faced. He had said the wrong thing by mistake, and was now terrified.

"There's something I want to talk to you about," he said in a cold voice. "In private."

"Of course, of course."

"Just go back to your room, I'll be with you as soon as I've finished my tea."

"Of course. Certainly."

"Make sure there's no-one else around."

"Right. Right."

"Your name is Helal, isn't it?"

"Yes. Yes, it is."

"Well, wait there for me, I'm on my way."

Mr Helal slunk back to his room on leaden feet. The poor man's heart was in his boots. That particular illness was now in season – the hearts in boots syndrome.

Kolimullah finished his tea and got another cup. The longer he took before going over to see Mr Helal the better; let the silly fellow die of anxiety while waiting. He had suffered enough tension in his own life, now it was the turn of these creeps to have a taste of it.

"How are you, Mr Helal?"
"I'm fine."
"Your face looks haggard, I don't think you're well at all. Aren't you sleeping well?"
"Oh yes, I'm sleeping all right. Kolim *bhai*, can I offer you tea?"
"No thanks, I've just had two cups."
"Would you like anything else? I can get them to fetch something."
"No, I won't have anything. Listen, Mr Shamsur Rahman, our poet, hasn't been coming in to the office recently. What's going on? Has he gone off to join in the fighting?"
"Oh, no. No."
"Then where is he?"
"I really don't know."
"Is he somewhere in Dhaka city?"
"No."
"So where is he?"
"I've no idea at all where he is."
"But you know he isn't in Dhaka city, so how can you say you have no idea where he is? Where is his village home? You must give me the address. I'll go and see him, I'll find out what kind of things he's been writing recently."
"I really don't have any knowledge of his whereabouts."
"Well, acquire that knowledge and pass it on to me."
Mr Helal was sitting there tongue-tied; beads of perspiration were glistening on his forehead.
"Get them to bring me a nice wad of *paan* with spiced tobacco in it, will you," said Kolimullah. "My mouth feels too sweet after that tea."
"Of course, of course."
"Now, let me have some paper and a pen, and find me a quiet room where I can work. Make sure nobody disturbs me. Only if the major comes, let me know."
"Certainly, certainly."
"Don't bother to fix any lunch for me, I'm supposed to be lunching at the mess with the major." This was a complete and utter lie. Kolimullah was particularly fond of telling little lies of this sort.

Kolimullah was reclining in an easy chair. A fan was revolving overhead. He was busy trying to compose a poem, the first line of which had suddenly come to him. It wasn't a bad line at all: *Snow white, a lonesome egret cleaves the mournful sky of East Bengal.*

He deleted the word 'mournful'. *Mournful sky* sounded far too much like Jibonananda°. In place of 'mournful' he put 'clouded'. But that didn't sound good. People were forever writing about *clouded sky*, and had hacked the phrase to death. He crossed out 'clouded' and substituted 'silvered'. The next few lines flowed quickly from his pen.

> *Snow white, a lonesome egret cleaves the silvered sky of East Bengal.*
> *Long years, long years ago his mate had died.*
> *Year out his mate's deep sighs waft through his plumes.*
> *He cannot soar, his mate's grief weighs him down,*
> *Weary he feels, seeking a haven safe to spread his wings.*

Now he was in full poetry writing mode. The next few lines were queueing up to be written one after another, in fact they were jostling each other quite impatiently. At that point Mr Helal stuck his head round the door.

"The major has come, and he's asking for you."

If he were to abandon his composition and spring to his feet immediately it would look as if he, too, was scared to death of the military. That would never do. Kolimullah made a gesture which seemed to say, I'm busy writing, I can't be disturbed now, come back later.

Mr Helal saw the gesture but insisted, "He's asking for you."

Kolimullah got up in a manner which suggested that he was much put out at having to break off in the middle of his writing.

"Hello, poet!" cried the major in English as soon as he saw him.

Kolimullah shrank with feigned modesty and embarrassment.

"What were you up to?" asked the major. This time he spoke in Urdu, addressing Kolimullah in the familiar form. Kolimullah had by now picked up enough Urdu to carry on a conversation.

"I was writing a poem about Pakistan, sir."

"Good. Excellent. A poet in action."

"Are you unwell, sir?"

"Why, do I look unwell?"

"Yes, sir." Nothing about the major's appearance suggested that there was anything wrong with his health, but Kolimullah resorted to subterfuges of this kind when he wanted to create an impression that he was deeply concerned about another person's wellbeing.

"Physically I'm fine, even if I'm slightly ill at ease mentally. Of course it's normal to be ill at ease when a war is going on."

"What war, sir? People can't wage a real war with sticks and stones. Can I offer you some tea, sir?"

"No tea, thankyou. Now, do you want to earn a bit of extra income? I have a little job for you."

"Sir, other people may expect money when they do you a favour, but how could I possibly accept any payment from you?"

"Well, you can do the work and get paid for it. It's a job that will benefit the country. It's all about fighting the enemy."

Kolimullah went cold all over. What was the man suggesting? That he should take part in the war? Once during his childhood he had dented another boy's head with a marble fired from a catapult, but that was as near to armed combat as he had ever been. He had seen a rifle from a distance but had never yet touched one. He thought of saying, "Sir, I can do pretty much anything, but not join in the fighting. I'm a member of the Shah clan, and we are not allowed to kill people." But in the end he didn't say that. It wasn't as if he had to trot off to war with a rifle on his shoulder the moment the major asked him to. Time was on his side.

"Sir," he said, "I shall do whatever you tell me. I have no idea about fighting, and I've never even touched a gun, but if you tell me to do so I shall take up a rifle and face the foe. God and the Prophet be with us."

"Warfare isn't only a matter of firing bullets from a rifle," said the major. "There are many ways of waging a war. For example, all this running about visiting newspaper offices and radio and television stations which I'm doing, that's a form of warfare too. I'm going to give you the address of a certain person; I've spoken to him about you, and he will give you a job to do."

"*Alhamdulillah* – God be praised! Write down the address, I'll go and see him today. What is his name?"

"His name is Zohar, and he's from Purnea District. He's a highly cultivated gentleman. He writes poetry, the same as you do."

"Not really? Oh, sir, please write a letter of introduction for me, I'll take it and go and see him."

"No letter will be necessary. Just tell him your name, that will suffice."

"Shall I refer to you, sir? Say that you sent me?"

"There'll be no need."

The major rose from his seat, ready to move on.

"Sir, please do have a cup of tea before you go," pleaded Kolimullah. "I haven't had any myself today, I was just waiting, in the hope of having tea with you."

The major sat down again, and Kolimullah rushed off to get the tea.

When he saw Mr Zohar Kolimullah felt disappointed. He had thought Zohar must be an extremely important person, whose importance would be manifest in the way he behaved and spoke, and whose appearance would match his importance. First impressions mattered.

In reality Mr Zohar was clearly getting on in years, and though his hair hadn't actually gone grey yet his face was covered with a whitish stubble of beard. There were dark bags under his eyes, and the eyes themselves, bloodshot like those of a dope addict, were sunk deep in their sockets. The man was wearing a shawl even in the intense heat of summer, and the shawl was not altogether clean. He was sitting with his feet up, and could easily have been mistaken for a kebab shop assistant. His face looked as singed as one of his kebabs.

"Major Siddiq sent me to see you," said Kolimullah.

"I see," said Mr Zohar in perfect Bengali, without looking at him.

Kolimullah was unsure what to do next. Should he draw up that wooden chair and sit down opposite Mr Zohar, or ought he to remain standing? The room was small and the shutters were closed. There was only one spare chair, and it was some distance away. If there was to be a tête-à-tête the two participants should surely sit face to face, not in opposite corners of the room. But maybe Mr Zohar did not go in for tête-à-têtes. There was a heavy fug of cigarette smoke in the room. Kolimullah was a smoker himself, but this overpowering smell made him want to throw up.

"The major told me you were a poet," remarked Kolimullah, "so I was very keen to see you with my own eyes."

"There's a light switch on your right," said Zohar. "Turn it on to brighten the gloom, then you can observe me properly."

You fathead, thought Kolimullah, who do you think you are, Tikka Khan himself?

How fortunate it is that one person cannot hear what another is thinking. "Sir," said Kolimullah as he switched on the light, "shall I get that chair and sit in front of you?"

"If you wish to," said Zohar.

"I happen to be a poet myself, sir. I compose these little scraps of poetry, don't you know. Recently I've been trying some prose writing too."

"Why not. *In the realm of hunger all the world is prosaic*, so what about the world in the realm of war?"

For a moment Kolimullah was lost for words. So this Bihari kebab vendor was familiar with the works of the poet Sukanta – how extraordinary! True, the major had mentioned that he was a cultured person. But as Kolimullah pulled the empty chair over and prepared to sit down in front of Mr Zohar the latter said, "Come back some other time, I'm not feeling well today."

"Right, sir," replied Kolimullah at once. "When should I come?"

"You can come any day. I'm usually here in this room. Nowadays I'm confined to my hole, I'm an animal in its burrow."

"Then I'll be off, sir. *Slamalekum*."

"*Wa alaikum as-salaam*. Do you have a pen and paper on you?"

"Oh yes, sir," exclaimed Kolimullah eagerly, "I always have a pen and paper handy."

"Then write down this address."

Kolimullah wrote down the address.

"That's the home address of a police inspector named Mobarak Hussain."

"Am I to go and see him, sir?"

"That will hardly be possible, as he was killed on the night of 25th March. But you are to contact his family. Very likely they are unaware that the inspector is dead."

"Shall I convey the news of his death to them?"

"You needn't tell them anything, just find out how the family members are and whether they are facing any kind of problems. I would like to do something for them. That inspector was a very honest man. In this age of corruption and insincerity it's hard to find a genuinely straightforward individual. Whenever I see an honest fellow it gives me a boost."

"Should I mention you, sir, when I talk to them?"

"There's no need at all to mention me... Kolimullah?"

"Yes, sir?"

"What kind of person are you yourself? Straight or crooked?"

"Crooked, sir."

"Fine, it's crooked people we need, actually. You may go now."

"Yes, sir. *Slamalekum*."

Without returning his *salaam*, Zohar lit another cigarette.

You bastard, you kebab seller! thought Kolimullah.

"Oho, what's going on in your mind, poet?"

Kolimullah was startled out of his wits. Was this bastard actually capable of reading people's minds? It wasn't out of the question, there were so many types of people in this world.

"Nothing, sir, it was just a line of poetry which came to mind. I was turning it this way and that in my head."

"Don't fiddle with it too much or it may break."

"Yes, sir."

"Now take your leave. Clear out!"

"Yes, sir."

21

The normal rule is for the *shefali* or coral jasmine bush to flower in the months of Ashwin and Kartik (October), the *kadamba* tree at the time of the full moon in Asharh (June-July), and the *shimul* tree in the heat of Chaitra (March-April). But here was the *shefali* shrub in front of Moriam's house, bursting into flower in the month of Chaitra, that is to say in April. One of its branches had reached the first floor verandah, and it was covered in white blossom. Had the plant gone crazy? If a human being can go mad, why shouldn't a plant? Plants are living things too, after all.

When Moriam told Masuma the news about the *shefali* flowering in April, Masuma said, "So what?"

"Come and have a look," urged Moriam.

"Sis, I'm honestly not that keen on looking at flowers," said Masuma.

When Moriam brought the news to Safiya, Safiya said, "Oh, really?" – but she was clearly not at all interested.

"Come along, Mum, let me show you!" said Moriam.

"I'll have a look later," said Safiya. "Let me finish what I'm doing first." But she wasn't actually doing anything, other than sitting beside Babu with her eyelids drooping.

Moriam went back to the verandah to have another look at the inflorescence. The branch was out of reach, otherwise she would have picked some of the flowers. You could obtain a nice yellow dye from the tube of the jasmine-like flower, she knew, and if you used the dye to colour a rice pudding it gave it a delicious floral scent.

After gazing at the flowers a while longer Moriam went to her room. She was desperate to pass the news on to a certain person, only she didn't know where that person was. She didn't even know how to contact him, though that hadn't stopped her from writing to him almost every day, until her writing pad was full of unsent letters. Some day, surely, she would be able to get those letters to him. Moriam closed her door. It bothered her when people barged into her room while she was in the middle of writing a letter. Letter writing time was private, and she didn't want anyone else around her at that time.

Moriam always got into difficulties at the very beginning of her letters. How should she address him? She wasn't satisfied with any of the salutations she could think of. She was strongly tempted to call Naimul 'Nai' for short. If he could call her Mori, why shouldn't she call him Nai? The problem was, when you wrote 'Dear Nai' it sounded distinctly odd. *Nai* means 'is not' or 'does not exist' in Bengali, so it sounded as if you were writing to someone who didn't exist.

This is what Moriam wrote.

> Hey,
> How are you? You'll never guess what's happened. Flowers have appeared on the *shefali* tree in front of our house. It's incredible, because *shefali* trees never flower in April. I think the tree has gone crazy. If people can go crazy why shouldn't trees? Plants do have feelings of their own, the scientist Jagadish Bose discovered that fact.
> You know, I've gone crazy as well. I can't sleep a wink at night. I sit up awake all night long. I can't get to sleep until after the dawn prayers. When I hear the *adhan*, instead of saying my prayers I fall asleep. I don't wake up again until ten or ten thirty. Then after my midday meal I have another sleep. I get up at dusk. Or rather I am told to get up. Because

sleeping at dusk is bad, it's unlucky. Apparently no wild creatures sleep at dusk, they move about restlessly at that point. But is that really true? You tell me.

Now I'm going to give you some important news. News number one - there is still no trace of Father. Nobody knows where he is. The worst effects of Father not being at home are being felt by Mother. She doesn't know how to make ends meet. Father never gave her any reserves of money, and the money she had in hand has all been spent. As Father had stocked up on rice, pulses, oil and things beforehand we were able to manage for a while, but now the stocks are at an end. Every time Mother sees one of us three girls she goes "What am I to do now?"

Father has money in the bank, but we can't get at it. Anyway, don't you worry about all that. Because we do have relatives in Dhaka, and one or other of them is sure to come over some time to see how we are. And Grandfather is sure to send someone from the village to check out how we are getting on. You know my great uncle from Jatrabari, that uncle of my father's who came to our wedding? He must be in difficulties himself. If only he would come and see us all our problems would be solved.

Mother and us three sisters all have bits of jewellery we can sell if necessary. So don't you worry in the slightest. The owner of the house opposite ours has taken his whole family away into the countryside. He has left his brother-in-law behind to guard the house. This fellow's name is Ratan, but we call him Heron Bhai because he looks just like a heron. Mother has decided she'll get him to sell some of our jewellery for us. We sisters don't like Heron Bhai coming to our house. He has an evil look about him. And he has Bihari friends. He often goes to their house and hangs out with them. He even wears a coloured neckerchief like a Bihari.

You know, we all live in mortal fear of the Biharis. There's a curfew from nine at night until five in the morning, and it seems the Biharis break into people's houses during that time. They choose houses which have young girls living in them. It's so scary!

At night we all sleep in the same room. Mother keeps a kitchen bill-hook ready beside her. I ask you, what could Mother do with her bill-hook if a whole gang of them broke in?

Anyhow, you mustn't worry about all those things. We have decided we'll go to our village home as soon as we get hold of someone we know and trust who can take us. If we can get to the village we won't have to live in fear any more.

Keep well, and look after your health. There's no need for you to do any reckless feats of daring. Let other people demonstrate how brave they are, but please don't do it yourself.

Now let me give you quite a different bit of news. Mother thinks I'm going to have a baby. She says my features have taken on a maternal look. Things are not really as she imagines they are, but I pretend she's right. See how mischievous I am?

That's all for today. I'll write again tomorrow. Listen to this, before you retire to bed you must recite the Ayatul Kursi and clap your hands three times. Then no evil or danger can take place within the radius covered by the sound of your clapping. We do it every night.

Your Mori

When she had finished writing her letter Moriam went out onto the verandah once more. She felt she must have another look at the unseasonal blossom. If she could pick one or two of the flowers, she could daub her letter with some of the yellow dye from the base of the petals. From her vantage point she could see Heron Bhai, and he was looking in her direction. He had three of his cronies with him, all of them with lips red from chewing betel leaf, and wearing kerchiefs round their necks. They too were looking up at the verandah. One of them suddenly started clapping, seeing which the other two followed his lead and joined in. Heron Bhai was the only one who wasn't clapping. Moriam hastened to leave the verandah and take refuge indoors.

"What's the matter?" asked Safiya.

"Nothing," said Moriam, "I'm just feeling a bit scared."

"What are you scared of?"

"While I was on the verandah I could see Heron Bhai hanging out with a couple of his pals, and they were staring at me. That kind of staring is no good. Mum, let's go away to our village home."

"But how? Who's going to accompany us?"

"We could go on our own, wearing burqas. We'd just board the train, and get off at the other end."

Safiya made no reply. The baby was crying and she busied herself attending to him. She was extremely fond of her three step-daughters; they were good girls, intelligent yet very simple-minded, entirely free of guile and duplicity. Even so, there was one aspect of their behaviour which rather shocked her: they seemed quite unconcerned about the fact that their father was missing. They were acting as if he was simply out of town on a tour of duty and would be back in a few days' time. Surely as daughters they should show some feeling for their father? For a person to go missing in times as bad as these was a very serious matter – didn't they realize that? All right, let's say he was a bad person, a real heel, who behaved uncouthly with all and sundry, was always carping and finding fault, always in a foul mood; even so, he was their father.

One of them had just got married, her head was full of her husband and nothing else meant anything to her: forget about her, let her stay in her little world of coral jasmine flowers. But what about the other two? They hadn't got married, they weren't committed to exclusive soul mates of their own, so shouldn't they be at least moderately worried about their father? Yet they actually seemed to be somewhat relieved that he was not at home, as if now they were free to do as they pleased. Last night Masuma had come rushing in to say, "Mum, they're doing a smashing play on Akash Bani radio, don't you want to listen?"

Safiya had been aghast. What was the girl saying, was this the right time to sit listening to plays on the radio?

"The play is based on a novel by Achinta Kumar Sen-Gupta," Masuma had continued excitedly. "The title of the novel is *The First Kadamba Flower*."

"You girls can listen to it, darling," Safiya had said. "I've got to attend to Babu."

"But Babu is fast asleep, Mum!" Masuma had objected.

"I don't really like listening to plays," Safiya had said. "You listen." And she had sat there beside Babu, her face grim. Nobody called the baby Yahya any more – the name Babu seemed to have stuck.

Babu had been sleeping quietly, and there she had sat, gazing at him in his sleep. After a while he will wake up, she had thought, but even then his world will remain a dark one. He will stretch out his arms and grope for the person who loves him, his only friend in the world. And who is she? A woman called Safiya to whom he is not even related. Safiya was by now convinced that Babu could neither see nor hear – but she hadn't said a word about this to her step-daughters, though she would have been hard put to explain why this was.

Safiya was sure her step-daughters didn't realize what a ghastly upheaval was going on in the outside world. Instead they were carrying on their own lives almost unconcerned. More, they were deriving a certain enjoyment from the circumstances. When they all slept in the same room at night they thought it was great fun. The three girls would lie down side by side, chattering quietly and sometimes subsiding into giggles. When they started giggling one of them would say, "Hush, don't laugh so loud, the soldiers will hear!", and that would make them giggle even louder.

One night the youngest had said, "Sis, why do soldiers abduct girls?"

"To pet them," Masuma had replied. "If they catch you and take you away, you'll see how they…"

And Masuma had burst out laughing before she had finished her sentence. Masuma was laughing, so was Moriam, and in the midst of it all Mafruha had asked in surprise, "What's so funny?" Then all three of them had giggled louder than ever.

Safiya's heart skipped a beat as she listened to the girls laughing. In times of happiness laughter conjured up yet more happiness, but in times of adversity it invited greater misfortune. In a house where someone had just passed away, if anyone laughed before the body had been buried it meant another member of the same household was going to die: this was a tried and tested rule.

So while the girls laughed Safiya had palpitations and felt suffocated. She was aware of something the girls couldn't sense – that truly horrific times lay ahead. As she envisaged all the horror Safiya couldn't sleep at night, but lay tossing and turning until the early hours. When her eyes finally closed she had ghastly dreams; ghastly and also filthy. So filthy were her dreams that she shuddered with revulsion even after waking up, as if she had actually been defiled. She often saw her late father in her dreams. He had come home and was fussing about as though he was in a great hurry to get moving. He would burst into the bedroom and cry, "Hey, Khuki, do hurry up and get ready, we've got to catch the launch." In real life he had always called Safiya 'Safi', and it was a mystery why he called her 'Khuki' in her dreams. "Why are you in such a hurry, father?" Safiya would say. "We can't up sticks and leave just like that. I've got children and a husband, I'm a married woman."

"Oh, stuff all that," her father would say, shaking his head, "I don't want to hear about husbands and children, the launch is about to cast off. Come along, Khuki, come quickly." And he would grab Safiya's hand and start pulling her away. At that point Safiya would wake up.

Safiya saw this same dream quite frequently, though it wasn't always a launch they were catching; sometimes it was a train or a rowing boat or a bus. However the basic theme never changed.

Being dragged away in a dream by a person who had died was a bad omen. If you had a dream like that the rule was to make a charitable donation to try and ransom your life; you should also call a *moulana*, say a prayer of repentance and prepare yourself for death. Safiya had done none of these things, but she was trying to complete a set of recitations – the holy *Yunus* prayer, one hundred and forty thousand times over.

Safiya knew that when the prophet Yunus, alias Jonas, had been inside the whale's stomach he had despaired of life and given himself over to repeating the invocation *la ilaha illa anta subhanaka inni kuntu minaz zalimin*, 'There is no deity but You, may your name be magnified, and I am one of those who have gone astray.' The effect of this recitation had been to make the whale regurgitate Yunus, thus saving his life. Since then the invocation had been called 'the *Yunus* prayer', and anyone who got into a predicament comparable to being swallowed by a whale could ransom their life by reciting it.

Safiya felt she was now in the whale's stomach; not only she herself, but the entire country. Everyone in the country should now be reciting the *Yunus* prayer.

Around the time of the *asr* prayer, not long before sunset on a Friday afternoon, somebody started vigorously rattling the chain of the front door. Moriam took fright and rushed to join her stepmother. Masuma, meanwhile, had been reading a novel. Naimul had brought dozens of works of fiction into the house with him, and these were now in Masuma's possession; she was going through them one by one. When the commotion at the door began she was in the middle of a novel by Banaphul called *Jangam*. Roused by the insistent rattle she flung the book down and ran to her stepmother's room.

Safiya hustled the three girls into one room and locked the door from the outside. Then, with Babu in her arms, she went to answer the door. If soldiers were there they might take pity when they saw she was carrying an infant.

"Who is it?" asked Safiya in a shaky voice.

"There's no need to be afraid," said a voice from outside. "Please open the door."

"Who are you?"

"You won't know me even if I tell you my name. I'm Shah Kolim."

"What do you want?" asked Safiya.

"Open the door first, then I'll explain. I've already told you there's no need for you to be scared. I'm not a Bihari, I'm a Bengali. I'm not one of the military either. If I'd been a Bihari or a soldier I could easily have smashed the door down and made my own way in by now."

Safiya opened the door and let the man called Shah Kolim into the house.

"I've had a great deal of bother tracing your house," complained Shah Kolim. "The address I had was incorrect. I've been tramping around since one o'clock, and now it must be at least four. I could do with a glass of water, please. Are you living on your own here?"

"Yes, I'm on my own."

"No you're not, you have three daughters as well as this baby. Why are you fibbing to me? You're afraid, are you? There's no need to be afraid. Now, how about that water."

Safiya went and got a glass of water. After talking to the man for a while she decided it was true, she didn't have anything to fear from him.

"I've come to find out how you are," said the man. "I need to know whether you're facing any particular problems."

"But who are you?" asked Safiya.

"I've already told you," replied Shah Kolim. "My name is Shah Kolim. I write poetry. My poems are published in various newspapers and magazines. A certain gentleman has sent me to see you. He's a friend of your husband's, someone who wishes him well. He's sent me to find out whether you're in any kind of difficulties. So tell me – are there any problems?"

"Do you know where my husband is?" asked Safiya eagerly.

"Sorry, I don't know," said Shah Kolim.

"Is he alive?"

"I know nothing about his situation."

"Does his friend know? Could I go and see him?"

"His friend doesn't have any information either. He sent me to get news from you, though I see now that you know no more than he does. But I've been talking too much, and my throat has gone dry. A cup of tea would do me no end of good. Would you be able to fix some?"

While tea was being served Shah Kolim met Moriam and Masuma. He was struck by Masuma's appearance. A very pretty girl, with a slightly flattened nose which set off her beauty even more. She could speak well too, and had a way of bobbing her head at certain points, and fluttering her eyes in an attractive way.

"You actually look like a real poet," said Masuma.

"And a real poet is what I am," replied Shah Kolim.

"What do you do when the moon is in the sky?" asked Masuma. "Do you stare at the moon with your mouth open?"

"I gaze at the moonlight. If you stare at the moon you can't see the moonlight. Poets never stare at the moon, they always admire the moonlight."

"Well, when will it be full moon? Let me see if you know. If you get the answer right I'll be convinced you really are a poet who keeps track of the moon's phases, but if you don't, then you're just a P.P."

"What do you mean, a P.P.?" asked Shah Kolim in some surprise.

"P.P." said Masuma. "It means pseudo poet."

"I see."

"Are you offended by what I said?"

"No."

"You ought to be offended. Why aren't you?"

"You are such an extraordinary girl, it's hard for a P.P. to be offended by you."

Shah Kolim stayed on until 8 p.m. He recited his own poem *Cloud Maiden at Noon* with a great deal of feeling. Twice during the recitation, it is true, Masuma burst out giggling, and that should have been enough to raise his hackles as a poet; but far from getting angry he reflected that he had never heard such a sweet sounding, musical laugh before. And a line of poetry came to him:

A laugh like a ripple unfolding on sonorous Drupadi stream

He wasn't sure about 'Drupadi', but it fitted in neatly, and ended in 'di' just like 'nodi', the word for stream. The two words rhymed beautifully.

Shah Kolim decided he would personally take charge of conducting the helpless members of this family to their village home. These days leaving the city and going to the country was no problem. Rickshaws and handcarts were operating normally in the city, and outside of the city area there were boats, lorries and buses to travel on. There might be checkpoints here and there, but nothing to worry about.

22

Asgar Ali and his son Moznu Miah were out in the virtually empty streets of Dhaka city with their handcart. Moznu Miah was nine or ten years old, bare-chested and clad in a pair of dark grey trousers; he had a prayer cap on his head. A prayer cap was a desirable adjunct, to make it clear that he was a Muslim. For some reason Moznu was feeling very glum, but by contrast Asgar Ali appeared quite cheerful. He was forty years old, strong and well built. There was something wrong with his left leg which made him drag his foot, though this did not hamper his work as a cart puller. Since 25th March he had been letting his beard grow, for people said that the army wouldn't harass any man who had a beard and could recite the declaration of faith like a pucca Muslim; they would just clout him a couple of times and then let him go. As this word had got round many Hindu men had started growing beards too, and putting on Muslim caps when they went out into the street, and even tucking a wad of cotton wool with Middle Eastern perfume on it into their ear just like a Muslim. Of course by now the army had got wise to such tricks and it was no longer enough to have a beard and a cap; you had to remove your lungi and show whether you'd been circumcised or not.

Asgar Ali was worried for his son, who hadn't yet been circumcised. It troubled him to think of the awkward situation which might arise if they were stopped by soldiers. Neither of them was able to recite all four *kalima* from memory. Asgar Ali knew just the first one, the *kalima tayyib* or basic declaration of faith – *la ilaha illallah, muhammadur rasulullah*, 'There is no deity but God, and Muhammad is the envoy of God.' Would knowing just one *kalima* be enough? He had been trying to teach Moznu this particular *kalima* for quite some time, but the boy still hadn't got it by heart. It was quite possible that the army people might let Asgar Ali himself go when they saw he knew one declaration of faith and was circumcised, but still they might arrest Moznu and take him away. Protest would be useless. If you argued with soldiers they shot you. They would drag the boy away in front of his eyes, and he would be unable to say a thing. He wouldn't even be able to cry. Soldiers went mad if they saw anyone crying. They got furious if they saw you smile, and equally furious if they saw you weep. Strange people they were indeed.

"Are ya feelin' unwell, son?" asked Asgar Ali, turning towards his child. "If ya feelin' poorly get on the cart, I'll push ya."

"I'm a'right," said Moznu.

"Ya 'ungry?"

"Nah."

"If ya 'ungry tell me. Tonight we'll 'ave parathas an' meat. Or rather, it's up to God wot we 'ave. If God says so we'll 'ave parathas, otherwise we'll 'ave tap water."

Moznu remained silent. He was walking along with his head bowed.

"Ya frettin' about ya mum?" asked Asgar.

"Yeah," said Moznu instantly.

Now Asgar knew what the matter was: the lad was missing his mother. He hadn't seen her for ages, and in the mean time war had broken out, and they had no idea what had become of her.

"I told ya, we'll go see 'er soon. There's too many checkpoints at the moment. 'Em soldiers are grabbin' people left an' right. They find anythin' not quite as it should be, and wham-bam! An' it's you I'm most worried about, son. Ya ain't bin circumcised, and ya can't say yer *kalima*. Well, 'ave ya got it by 'eart now?"

"Nah."

"Come on, let me 'elp ya. Starts, *la ilaha* – then wot?"

"Dunno."

Asgar noticed that his son was wiping his eyes. That was a bad sign. He was crying for his mother. But he wasn't so very young any more, if he went on blubbing for his mum like a baby he'd never get anywhere. He needed to make a living, he should be figuring out how to scrape a few rupees together. Going "Mum, mum!" all the time, well, that might get him a mother's sympathy, but not a full stomach. What counted for most in this world? Your mother? Your father? No! Your daily bread. Your rice. *Anna*, the Hindu people called it. Blessed victuals.

"Ya 'ungry, son?"

"Nah."

"Would ya like some *khechuri*?" Asgar Ali pronounced *khichuri* an odd way. He was very fond of that particular dish. You could get a plate of it for half a rupee, though that wasn't really enough to fill the stomach.

Even the mention of *khichuri* produced no change in the boy's expression. He kept staring at the ground as he trudged along, never once raising his eyes.

"Ah well then," said Asgar, "I'll take ya there Thursday. Best day, Thursday. Auspicious. Friday's the holy day, but Thursday is special. Ya can stay there with ya mum for a few days. Let me see if I can get ya circumcised before then. Depends if I can find a surgeon barber. Can't be sure where anyone is, in war time."

Moznu's face lit up. "I'm 'ungry," he said.

"Wot ya like, *khechuri*?"

"Boiled rice an' egg curry."

Asgar let out a little sigh. There was no hope for the kid. He would rather have egg curry than something really good for him, he was throwing away a golden opportunity to eat *khechuri*. He would surely go on to miss all the best openings in life.

"Try *khechuri*."

"I like egg curry."

"Ah right then, egg curry if ya must."

Asgar changed direction with his handcart. He was feeling quite pleased with himself, for he had been earning good money the past few days. Plenty of people were migrating out of Dhaka, taking their possessions with them. Some wanted to go to the railway station at Komlapur, others to the bus terminus, and they had any amount of baggage with them. When they hired Asgar and his cart the amount they paid was pure profit, for Asgar was no longer paying any fees to the owner of the cart. Nothing had been seen or heard of the owner since 25th March, and it seemed likely he had come to a sticky end. On the night of 25th March the handcart had been in Asgar's possession. He was feeling unwell, his foot was swollen, so he had decided to keep the cart at his place overnight and go and explain things to the owner in the morning. But then the hostilities had broken out, it had seemed like doomsday to Asgar, and it wasn't until two days later, when things had quietened down a bit, that he had gone to call on the owner of the cart.

The owner used to live in a couple of huts he had set up for himself in the Katabon area. When Asgar had reached the place he had seen no huts, nothing at all. The whole area had been cleared of buildings. While he was gaping in amazement a bearded man of Bihari appearance had come up and asked him who he was looking for.

"I'm lookin' for the 'andcart gaffer, Mr Idris. He 'ad an 'ouse made of corrugated iron. There were two little mango saplings in front, about waist 'igh."

"Corrugated iron huts, thatched huts – they're gone," the bearded man had said. "Mango trees, jujube trees – all gone. The people who lived here, gone too. I advise you to go back home and say your prayers to the Almighty."

Even in those dire circumstances Asgar had reflected that whatever God did, He did it for a good purpose. Along with all the horror He had provided certain benefits. Like, for example, making Asgar the effective owner of the handcart. He would no longer have to stump up three rupees a day for the use of it. If ever he fell ill he could spread a blanket on the cart and go to sleep on it without torturing himself trying to think how he was going to afford the daily fee. Indeed he could hire the cart out to someone else, for now he was to all intents and purposes the owner of it. Wasn't there a saying, 'a beggar today, a prince tomorrow' – it was perfectly true, and now it applied to him.

God's mercy was boundless, for here Asgar was, making good money in wartime. It was not a good idea to stray out of Dhaka city just now, but he would have to do so for the sake of his son. The boy couldn't stop worrying about his mother. God hadn't yet granted him the wit to realize that life was far from simple. Asgar Ali did sometimes try to bring the truth home to him and give him useful advice. He rather enjoyed offering advice to his son. After listening to it the boy would nod gravely and say "Yeah." It was a pleasure to hear him, the way he said "Yeah." Advice was very necessary if one was to stay alive during troubled times. Asgar used to offer advice on various subjects, religion, God's justice, the rewards of patience, everything. However these days most of his advice related to the occupation army.

"Listen, son, if ya see a soldier never look 'im in the face. Keep yer 'ead down an' carry on walkin', like as if ya ain't seen 'im. Got it?"

"Yeah."

"S'pose the soldier tells ya to stop, 'e says *halt*. Ya mus'n't run away. If ya run ya done for. Bang! Bullet in ya spine. Got it?"

"Yeah."

"An' never smile at a soldier, an' never blub in front of a soldier. Soldiers can't stand anyone smilin' or blubbin'. Got it?"

"Yeah."

"Whenever ya get a chance, say *Pakistan Zindabad*. Try sayin' *Joy Bangla*, an' pow! pow! Stuffed full o' bullets ya be. Got it?"

"Yeah."

"Some of 'em soldiers, they wear black shirts. Black brigade, they're called. 'Em lot are real devils. If ya see a black shirt from way off, duck in an alleyway quick as quick, don't even peep at 'im. Got it?"

"Yeah."

"Each time ya go out, keep sayin' *Allahu, Allahu*. God 'as ninety-nine names, but the best one is *Allahu*. It's like, the best thing ya can eat is *khechuri*, an' the best name for callin' God is *Allahu*. Keep sayin' *Allahu* to ya self an' ya'll be safe. Got it?"

"Yeah."

Asgar Ali was heading for a food stall in Nilkhet. There were several simple restaurants round there which served really good food. You could ask for second or even third helpings of gravy, no bother. A bowl of *dal* would cost you two annas, and when you finished what was in the bowl you could have a bit more without extra charge.

Asgar had got as far as the Balaka Cinema when suddenly he went cold all over. Five or six blackshirts were standing there, and beside them was a truck with a canvas hood over it. There were more soldiers in the back of the truck, but they were ordinary ones, not blackshirts.

"Don't look at 'em, son," said Asgar in a low voice. "Don't look t'wards the cinema. Keep going *Allahu, Allahu*. An' put ya cap straight, it's leanin' to one side."

Asgar Ali glanced back at his son, and was dismayed by what he saw. Far from putting his cap straight the boy was goggling at the soldiers with wide eyes. Asgar dared not make any admonitory gesture, as the soldiers would see him and realize he was communicating by signs. Signs and gestures were something soldiers could not abide.

"Hey, you there, carter! Stop!"

Asgar felt as if the sky had caved in. This was more than a setback, it was total disaster. There was absolutely no hope of escape – unless the Prophet himself intervened. Asgar Ali closed his eyes and fervently recited the surah *Fatiha* in his head. It was the only surah he knew by heart.

"What's your name?"

As soon as he took a proper look at the person who had spoken Asgar Ali realized he wasn't a soldier at all, but a Bengali man, apparently someone a bit out of the ordinary. He had a team of other people with him, holding cameras and other pieces of equipment. This fellow who had asked him his name was wearing a brightly coloured shirt and had a yellow cap on his head. It was no mean achievement to be gadding about in a garish shirt and flamboyant cap during a period of military rule; not many people could have got away with it.

"My name's Asgar, sir," Asgar Ali replied humbly. "Lad's name is Moznu. We're simple folk, we ain't done nothin'."

"Why are you so nervous?" asked the man with the cap. "There's nothing to be afraid of. We would like to make a recording of a few things you say. It's for a television programme. You know what television is?"

"Yes, sir."

"We're doing a series of interviews with people from various strata of society. You just need to say that the situation in Dhaka is normal, and there are no problems. All right?"

"Yes, sir."

"You mustn't say anything negative. Just stick to positive things – the city is tranquil, there are no problems of any kind, the shops are open, business is going on as usual – that sort of thing. OK?"

"Yes, sir."

One man came and held a camera in front of Asgar's face, another was holding up a thing like an umbrella. The man with the cap stood right next to Asgar Ali with a microphone in his hand, almost touching him. He was wearing an expansive smile on his face.

"And now we are going to speak to a labouring man from the city of Dhaka, one who earns his living by the sweat of his brow. He and his son have been working in the city for many years as handcart operators. Well, my friend, may I know your name?"

"My name is Asgar. Son's name is Moznu."

"Are you encountering any problems as you ply your cart in Dhaka city these days?"

"Oh, no, sir."

"What are things like in the city?"

"Great. *Mashallah*, God's will be done. Everythin's fine."

"As you look around you, what do you feel, do you feel there are any particular problems affecting the city?"

"No, sir."

"Are you happy with the present situation in the city? Are you earning enough?"

"Oh, yes, sir. *Pakistan Zindabad.*"

"Thank you very much, brother Asgar Ali."

Asgar wiped the sweat from his brow. By the infinite mercy of the Deity, he had escaped from danger by a hair's breadth. That man with the cap was a good sort. He had pulled a packet of cigarettes from his pocket and offered Asgar one. And that wasn't all – he had given him five rupees too. Asgar had imagined total disaster, and now he realized he had been in luck. How hard it was to tell whether God was going dump you in the fire or whisk you out of danger and give you a reward. Who would have guessed he might earn something not by hard labour but simply by saying a few words! Even in this day and age, five rupees was quite a lot of money.

When it came to the point Moznu changed his mind and chose beef curry instead of egg.

"'Ave as much as ya want," said Asgar cheerfully. "Eat whatever ya want. Then again, there's more to it than that."

"What?" asked Moznu.

"*Rijek*," explained Asgar. "Fate. It's God as decides when we're to eat an' wot we're to eat. 'E's already planned wot ya gonna 'ave, see. If ya 'ave egg curry, it means God 'as put ya down for egg curry, an' if ya have beef *bhuna*, God 'as put ya down for beef. That's wot's in your *rijek*."

"An' s'pose I 'ave both?"

"Then ya can take it to mean that the Almighty 'as ordained that 'is much beloved servant Moznu Miah is gonna 'ave egg curry an' beef curry, both. Why, d'ya wanna 'ave both?"

"Yeah."

"Garn then, 'ave both. No matter. It's wot God desires. 'Ain't nothin' I can do about it. I'm just a tool of 'is. Whole world is jus' a workshop full of 'is tools."

Asgar was pleased to see how well Moznu was eating, wolfing his food down with great relish. He was savouring his rice mixed with meat curry, leaving the egg to one side. From time to time he would pick the egg up and have a look at it, then put it back on the edge of his plate, as if he hadn't the heart to sink his teeth into it. Poor kid! During the crackdown, from the night of the 25th March right through the whole of 26th March, he had had nothing to eat, and that was more than twenty-four hours. Both of them, father and son, had been hiding in a pit, a huge pit on a building site in Motijheel. During all that time Moznu had never once said he was feeling hungry. He was such a well behaved boy.

"Meat curry taste nice?" asked Asgar.

"Mmm."

"'Ave the egg, go on."

"Not yet. I'll 'ave it later."

"You hankerin' for yer mum?"

"Yeah."

"If ya really hankerin'," said Asgar Ali darkly, "maybe somethin' can 'appen. I mean, maybe we can go now. We finish our meal, we get on a bus, off we go. We get there before dark. Buses are running again these days."

Moznu was staring hard at his father. His eyes were glistening, as though he might burst into tears of joy at any moment. Asgar Ali had finished his meal and was contentedly smoking the cigarette which the man in the cap had given him. He had also asked the servant boy in the restaurant to fetch him a wad of *paan* with spiced tobacco in it. Yes, he had made up his mind: they would go to the village today. His son was looking at him in such happy expectation, it would be wrong to destroy his happiness. The joy of a child is a precious thing.

There was a military check post at Tongi bridge where all the passengers in each bus were made to disembark, after which they would be interrogated and have their luggage checked by soldiers. Asgar Ali's bus drew up at the checkpoint. There were thirty-eight passengers on the bus. Six of these were singled out and led away. For absolutely no reason whatsoever they were made to line up on the bank of the Turag river, and there they were shot in cold blood. Their corpses fell into the river and slowly floated away. One of these six hapless people was Asgar Ali. Right up to the moment of death he had no notion he was about to be shot; instead he was looking at Moznu, who was clutching a packet containing a green sari they'd purchased for his mother. The only thing on Asgar Ali's mind was that the soldiers might confiscate the sari.

On the local news programme *In Town Today* which was shown on television at nine o'clock that night, a number of interviews with Dhaka residents of different social strata were shown. Among those interviewed were a government officer, a businessman, a housewife, and as a representative of the labouring class there was Asgar Ali himself. The housewife was beaming as she confirmed that the situation in Dhaka city had much improved. During the troubles the price of beef had gone up to two rupees a *seer*, and now even top quality beef was only one and a half rupees. The price of onions and salt had gone down too.

Asgar Ali was the last person to be shown. The reporter had asked him whether he was satisfied with the present situation in the city.

"Oh, yes, sir," Asgar Ali had replied. "*Pakistan Zindabad!*"

"*Pakistan Zindabad!*" cried Gourango in unison with Asgar Ali.

Gourango was lying stretched out on the bed with a warm rug over him. He was watching television, goggle eyed. He had taken to watching TV from the moment transmission started in the afternoon to the moment it ended late at night. The final item would always be the Pakistan national anthem, *Pak sarzamin shadbad*, and Gourango would join in and hum the tune. At that moment he would look quite happy. He never spoke to Shahed. If Shahed asked him a question he would give no reply. But he talked to himself, mumbling indistinctly. When Shahed asked him what he was talking about he would give a reproachful look, as if Shahed had uttered some outrageous remark which had wounded him to the core. Another problem with Gourango was that whenever he went to the bathroom he left the door wide open. Apparently if the door was shut he felt terrified.

Shahed realized that Gourango was suffering from some kind of acute mental illness. He ought to be seen by a doctor, but at present there was scant hope of finding the right one, the whole city was in such a state of disruption. It was anybody's guess how long things would go on like this. There was a pharmacy not far away where a doctor sometimes held a surgery, and Shahed had gone to consult him.

"This country's gone mad," said the doctor, "and everyone in it is suffering from mental illness. There's no cure. I'm going to prescribe a tranquilizer. Get him to take it regularly, it will keep him in a drowsy state."

Gourango was given a dose of the drug every evening. It didn't send him to sleep, but after taking it he was able to talk in a more or less normal manner. The things he said were still very muddled, but the tone of his speech was quite conventional.

"Buddy, I've decided to become a Muslim. A real Muslim. Being a Hindu is too much of a hassle, I can't stand it any longer. Though I'll have to go on celebrating Durga Puja. After all, it only comes once a year. I can do the devotions in secret. Will that be a problem?"

There is no point in trying to answer questions of that kind, and Shahed remained silent. This didn't bother Gourango at all; he went on with his ramblings.

"Listen, buddy, what's the safest place in East Bengal at this moment? Do you know?"

"No."

"The safest place is a Hindu property in Old Dhaka. The kind of house the army attacked, where they killed all the occupants. You know, like my own house. The soldiers are never going to attack those same buildings a second time. Do you get it?"

"I see."

"I've decided I'll go and live in my own house. It would be a mistake to lose possession of it. That's the plan I've thought up, don't you think it's a good one?"

"Mm."

"Why don't you come with me? Us two brothers, we'll live there together."

"Go to sleep, now. It's very late."

"Just because it's late in the night that doesn't mean I'm going to sleep. You know very well, buddy, I don't sleep at night, I sleep in the daytime. I've found a new name for myself, Gourango the owl. Isn't that a brilliant name?"

"Mm."

"When I turn into a Muslim I'll have to change my name. What name should I choose? Come on, buddy, think of a name which matches yours."

"I'll give it some thought."

"No, not 'will', think about it now."

"Oh, give us a break, for goodness' sake! I've got so many things on my mind, I'm in no mood for being pestered."

"So I pester you, do I? I suppose I annoy you?"

Shahed said nothing, but he was indeed feeling considerably annoyed.

"Do I annoy you? Tell me, do I?" cried Gourango, raising his voice.

"You do."

"Well, I won't much longer. I'm leaving tomorrow morning."

"Where will you go?"

"That's something for me to decide. You never did like me, I knew all along. Wait till it's morning, as soon as rickshaws appear on the streets I shall take my leave."

"But you're not well. This is no time for doing crazy things."

"So what is it a time for? Annoying people? *A time for annoyance*! Let me think now, what should my new name be, Gourango Birokto Das? G.B. Das for short."

"Put a lid on it, please, like a good fellow."

"No, buddy, I shan't put a lid on it. I shall continue to annoy you. Whatever annoying remains to be done, I shall do it tonight. Tomorrow I'll be gone."

The following morning, very early, Gourango did indeed leave Shahed's place. He said nothing to Shahed, who was still asleep, but left a note by his pillow. The note was brief.

>Buddy, I've gone.
>Take care.
>Gourango Annoyance Das

23

My name is Gourango Birokto Das. Now I am in my own house. How agreeable! I live in my own house, I can eat and drink as I please. Yes! Clap, clap, clap!

Gourango believed he was happy. Very happy. His house was intact, his possessions were still there. Groping behind the bookshelf he had found a half bottle of Old Smuggler, full, and with its seal unbroken – an entire half bottle of rum! And rum was something which didn't spoil with keeping, the longer you had it the better it tasted. To make sure it was all right he took several swigs straight from the bottle. It tasted fine. Not just fine, the taste had matured, it was terrific. Gourango reflected that though such a marvellous drink had been created with the name of rum, or Ram, nothing similar had been developed in the name of Ram's brother Laksman°. If there had been a Laksman spirit he could have sat down together with both of the legendary brothers, and taken alternate sips – a sip of rum, a sip of the other – what bliss!

The front door was closed, so were all the shutters. Even though it was daytime it was dark indoors, and that was not such a bad thing. Darkness had its own special appeal. Human beings were remarkable creatures, he thought; they knew how to make themselves happy when they chose to do so. So here was he, Gourango, being happy. He was sitting on the living room carpet with his legs splayed out, imagining that everything was as it used to be. Nilima had gone upstairs to see her father, taking Runu with her. Doubtless some sort of tiff had taken place between her and Gourango, and she had gone upstairs in a huff to sulk in the old man's room.

That was what women were like. They stored grievances in their heads. Men were never like that: when they quarrelled they would get the whole thing over in one go, and then five or ten minutes later they would have forgotten all about it. But women never forgot. Five or ten years later they would still have the quarrel in mind.

Gourango took a few more swigs from the rum bottle. It would be pointless to save the rest, now that it was almost empty. Besides, there was nothing to eat for lunch, and with this stuff in his stomach he wouldn't feel so hungry.

Mosquitoes were whining around the room, but they were benign mosquitoes, they weren't biting him. In daytime mosquitoes didn't bite, thought Gourango. They only bit in the night, but then they stung you all right. Oh, what an inspired piece of poetry! *In daytime mosquitoes don't bite, they only bite in the night, but then they sting you all right.*

How amusing it would be to recite that snippet of verse to Runu, for she liked poetry. The little girl was with her grandfather right now. And that old man's name was ... Haribhajan Saha. Now, students, analyse the compound word *Haribhajan. Hari* – a name of God. *Bhajan* – devotional song or worship. *Haribhajan* – one who sings hymns to God as a form of worship. Go on, then, you old dotard, you can jolly well carry on singing your hymns to God, your business in this world is over and done with.

The mosquitoes had now started biting Gourango. They were driving him mad. Was there any frankincense in the house? Mosquitoes always avoid incense smoke. There certainly must be some frankincense around, for Nilima, being such a dutiful, religious-minded woman, used to burn it in front of a picture of the god Siva every evening. She would stand for a while with her bowed head touching the icon, and pray. What was it she used to say in her prayer? "*Hé Devadideva Mahadeva* – O Siva, greatest of all the gods, please make my home and family happy and prosperous." But all that incense smoke she had offered

Siva had been in vain. The soldiers had come and destroyed her home and family. They had finished everyone off, leaving just one person alive so that the mosquitoes could make a feast of him. Gourango took a long swig from the bottle and thought, *Go on, mosquitoes, have your fill, drink all the Hindu blood you will.*

Gourango was beginning to feel depressed. His thoughts had started moving in the wrong direction. If a person thought sad thoughts when they were drunk, their sadness would increase tenfold, yet if they thought happy thoughts their happiness would merely be doubled. That was very unfair. If one's pain was to be increased by a factor of ten, one's joy ought also to be enhanced in the same proportion. Gourango made himself think of happier things. He imagined Runu was sitting behind him leaning her back against his. This was something Runu often used to do; she would sit with her back against his, playing with her dolls in a little world of her own and chattering to herself. Gourango would be unable to see her face. This was how he imagined things to be now.

"What are you doing, Runu dear?"

Gourango fancied that Runu had answered in her small voice, but her words were unclear and he couldn't make out what she had said.

"Would you like to listen to a story, darling?"

"Yes."

"What kind of story would you like?"

"One about mosquitoes."

Gourango jumped in alarm: he had clearly heard someone say "about mosquitoes". The word "mosquitoes" had been pronounced in a slow, distinct way, just the way Runu always spoke. Should he turn round and check to see whether Runu really was sitting there behind him with her back against his? Better not, he thought, better just get on with the story, the story about mosquitoes.

"Listen then, darling. Long, long ago there were no mosquitoes in the world at all. This is the story of how they came into existence. The fishermen had to go out fishing all night long, but they got very sleepy. Often they fell asleep when they were meant to be catching fish. One day they said to the goddess Sitala, "O goddess, please do something to stop us from falling asleep at night." The goddess said, "So be it," and she scraped some dirt from her left hand and gave it to the fishermen saying, "Take this dirt and throw it into a pond near your home. That will do the trick, you won't fall asleep at night any more." They did as she had told them and threw the dirt into a pond. And then thousands and thousands of mosquitoes rose whining out of the pond, and what do you think happened then? The fishermen went out fishing, and they were unable to fall asleep because the mosquitoes kept biting them all night long."

Gourango poured the remaining rum down his throat. His head was spinning now, and he was feeling queer. Was he about to throw up? If he was, he was; there was nothing he could do about it. There was a tap on the door. Startled, Gourango looked round. How amazing, Nilima was standing in the doorway. It must be an illusion, he had had too much rum.

"How are you, Nilima?" mumbled Gourango.

Nilima gave no reply, but backed away a few inches on the other side of the doorway. Now he could no longer see her face, but he could see the border of her sari. He could make out the free end of the sari stirring in a breath of air. Suddenly he was convinced that what he was seeing now was reality, and the events which had taken place previously were an illusion.

"I was away for a few days," he explained, flustered. "I was at Shahed's place. Shahed is all right."

Nilima still said nothing.

"Are you cross with me?" asked Gourango. "Times are bad, and it's not right to get cross at such a time. I'll tell you what, pack a few things into a bag, and I'll take you and Runu over the border. We'll go to Agartala. Lots of people are going there, there'll be no problem."

"Hey!"

Who had said "hey"? Nilima? So it wasn't a dream, everything that was happening was real. Definitely real. He could even smell Nilima's hair. She used a hair oil called Gandharaj or something like that, which you could smell from miles away. Gandharaj, scent imperial, the name was quite fitting.

"Who said that? Nilima, is it you?"

"Yes."

"Why are you keeping your distance? Come closer."

"Do you realize where you're sitting?" asked Nilima.

"Where I'm sitting?" repeated Gourango in confusion.

"Take a look."

Gourango looked. He hadn't sat down on the sofa; he was sitting on the floor with his back against the sofa and his legs stretched out in front of him.

"I'm sitting on the floor," said Gourango. ""It's a bit dusty."

"Look properly. Can't you see the dark stain?"

"Yes, I can. What kind of stain is that?"

"You don't know what made that stain?"

"No."

"When it has dried, blood makes a dark stain. Didn't you know?"

Gourango studied the dark patch in horror. He was shivering all over, and a dull pain was filling his chest. He didn't feel at all well.

"Water," he murmured. "I want some water."

Nilima disappeared from the doorway. Maybe she had gone to fetch some water. While waiting for it Gourango got sick. The dark stains were covered over with vomit. So much the better. Yes, that was preferable.

The room was defiled. No matter, Gourango thought, he wasn't going to stay here, he was going to flee with his daughter and his wife, cross the border with them and go to Agartala. It would be better if they could go to Calcutta, as he had relatives there, whereas he knew nobody in Agartala. Never mind, he had masses of cash with him. Uh-oh, no, that was wrong, he didn't have the money with him, he'd left it with Shahed. Leaving money in Shahed's care was as good as putting it in the bank, in fact better, because banks had closing days while Shahed was available all the time. There was only one problem, Shahed spent much of the day roaming the streets. You could never tell, the army might shoot him dead any moment.

"Nilima! Nilima!" called Gourango softly.

Nilima's voice seemed to come from afar. "What is it?"

"Have you got Acharya Bhabatosh's address anywhere?"

"Mm."

"We'll need it. Before setting off for the border we'll get three protective charms from the venerable master Bhabatosh – one for you, one for Runu and one for me. With protective amulets round our necks we'll be in no danger."

"Mm."

"In one way it's lucky the soldiers killed your father. If he'd been with us it would have been difficult to get over the border. The old fellow wouldn't have been able to walk far enough. So don't be too miserable about your father's demise. He was getting on in years and he died, that's all. The only awkward thing is that he died an unnatural death, so his spirit is unsettled. We shall have to perform the customary oblations for him. I'll see to everything, don't you worry."

"Right."

"Please bring me some water. I want to rinse my mouth."

Gourango had the impression Nilima was standing in the doorway. She was not moving, and her face was blurred. Was he just seeing things under the influence of alcohol? In despair Gourango started calling for his daughter: "Runu! Runu! Oh, Runu!"

When he had got over his intoxication Gourango's behaviour returned to normal. He had a refreshing shower, and then cooked a *khichuri* of rice and lentils. It was from Shahed that he had learned how to make *khichuri*. Before that he had never realized how easy cookery was. If he had known, he would have picked up a few recipes from Nilima. It would have been so useful if he could have learned how to make that steamed hilsa fish *paturi*.

Gourango ate what he had cooked with considerable relish. He felt a pang of regret because Shahed wasn't there with him; Shahed would have enjoyed this *khichuri*. Gourango had had the clever idea of adding a tablespoon of ghee to the mixture. The hotness of dried red chillies combined with the butteriness of ghee produced a delectable taste. If Shahed had been there they could have chatted away happily as they ate. He would have said to Shahed, "Buddy, what do you make of the *khichuri*? Even better than yours, don't you think?"

"Yes, it's wonderful," Shahed would surely have said.

"Well, tell me, who has played the most important rôle in making this *khichuri* a success? I'll bet you ten rupees you can't guess. Maybe you think your contribution was the most important one, but that's not so."

"Then whose contribution was so important?"

"Nilima's. It's only because she stored everything in such perfect order that this tasty dish could be prepared. Everything I needed was there – rice, pulses, spices, oil, ghee. Everything set out as neatly as items on display in a museum."

"I've always noticed that your wife is a very orderly person," Shahed would have said.

"You can talk about orderly," Gourango would have said, "but Nilima is more than that. How many kinds of pulses do you reckon there are in the house? I'll give you ten rupees if you can guess correctly."

"I can't guess."

"Four kinds. Lentils, black gram, mungo beans and chickpeas. How about honey? She has two kinds, wild Sundarbans honey and the bottled medicinal variety. Would you care for some honey now? Finish off your *khichuri* and have a spoonful. That'll serve as a dessert."

After finishing his meal Gourango went to bed and had a long sleep. He didn't get up until after dark. Without turning on any lights he switched on the TV and watched that for a while. Some ordinances issued by the martial law administrator were being proclaimed. Gourango tried hard to remember all the instructions. He would have to obey them in full, for whatever country one lived in, one had to obey the laws of that country.

When he had done with watching television he sat down with his transistor radio. It was always fun to twiddle the knobs on a radio, he thought. One minute you got Radio Peking: *chao mao kau*. Then you got the news in Bengali. Then it was something else, which went *ching ming ping*. After turning the knob for a while he tuned into an Indian station, Akash Bani Shiliguri. They were announcing that an independent Bangla Desh Government had just been set up A decree of independence had been promulgated from Vaidyanathtala in Meherpur District. The interim president and head of state was Syed Nazrul Islam, the prime minister was Tajuddin Ahmed, the head of the armed forces was Colonel M.A.G. Osmani. The date was 10th April 1971.

The following day Gourango became totally insane. He could be seen wandering around in the streets accosting everybody he bumped into. He would lower his voice and say, "Tell me the name of the interim president of Bangladesh. I'll give you one minute. If you can answer within the minute you'll receive a prize. You can't do it? Right, I'll set you an easier question. What's my daughter's name? You can have three guesses. You'll pass the test if you can get it in three."

24

Shahed was beginning to look like a madman. There were grey pockets under his eyes, which had become discoloured, and his chin was covered in a week's growth of stubble. There was a button missing on the shirt he was wearing, creating a gap through which his stomach showed. Even the way he walked had a deranged air about it, and when he spoke he stumbled on his words. It was 10th April and still he had no clue as to Asmani's whereabouts. He was now following a regular daily routine. As soon as he got up in the morning he would go to Kolabagan to see whether his mother-in-law had returned, or whether anyone had left any message. Then he would go to his office. Although the office was open there was virtually no-one around and no work to do. Mr B.Happy had disappeared without trace; possibly he had gone away to West Pakistan. After sitting in his own room in the office for a while, and having a few cups of tea, Shahed would go out again and wander in the streets until two in the afternoon. He kept thinking he could hear Runi yelling for him: "Daddy! Daddy!"

But nobody was really calling. At two o'clock he would slip into a roadside diner for lunch. Immediately he would have an intuition that Asmani had arrived back home, and had started tidying up and cleaning the house in her usual way. He could see Runi repeatedly going out onto the verandah and hear Asmani scolding her sharply, saying, "I'm warning you, you are not to go on that verandah, it's too dangerous these days." Runi's face would fall each time she was ticked off, but she would manage not to cry.

Once thoughts like this had entered his head he would no longer feel like eating. He would get up without finishing his meal, wash his hands and leave, impatient to return home without a moment's delay. He would get back to the house only to see the padlock still on the door. There was no sign of Gourango either; Shahed wondered what had become of him.

Shahed was sitting listlessly in the office, with his feet up. He had a cup of tea in front of him, but after taking one sip he had set down the cup and not felt like drinking any more, though the tea itself was quite good. He hadn't had a wink of sleep all night. At one point he had dropped off for a while, but then he had had the most frightful dream. There was a huge army truck full of little children, all of them crying and wailing. Among all the other children had been Runi. She wasn't weeping out loud but she kept wiping her eyes on the sleeve of her frock. A soldier was aiming a machine gun at the children, leering as he did so. This nightmare had made Shahed wake up in a flurry, and after that he hadn't been able to get back to sleep.

Now he was feeling drowsy, and he was tempted to have a nap in his office chair. Then Mushtaq, the office peon, came with the newspaper and placed it on the desk. Mushtaq was a native of Bihar. He could speak excellent Bengali, and had always used it previously, but now he had taken to speaking in Urdu. Mushtaq had a blue patterned kerchief round his neck. Shahed had noticed that for some reason the Biharis were all wearing coloured kerchiefs round their necks these days. Maybe they had worn them before too, only he had never taken any notice. Now such things caught one's eye, because the Biharis were a focus of attention. They had become separate and distinct, and they had sided with the army. They seemed to relish the awful predicament the Bengalis were in. Maybe they thought the army would finish off the entire Bengali population and turn the country into a Bihari domain specially for them.

Shahed had started to nod off, but he flinched and sat up on hearing Mushtaq's little cough. Mushtaq had some perfume on him which gave off a nauseating smell, and he had lined his eyes with antimony. Mind you, he had often used antimony in the past as well; it was a thing Biharis were rather keen on.

"Did you want to say something, Mushtaq?" asked Shahed.

Mushtaq smiled, flashing his teeth.

"How's the situation in the country, what's your opinion?"

"*Bahut accha*," replied Mushtaq in Urdu. "Very good."

"Have the army quietened everything down?" Shahed continued to speak in Bengali, while Mushtaq responded in Urdu.

"The trouble-makers have all been dealt with, by the grace of God," said Mushtaq.

"The old trouble-makers may have been dealt with, but new ones may appear, who knows?"

"Nothing more will happen. India will keep silent, because China is on our side."

"You can go now, Mushtaq," said Shahed, yawning. "I'm going to have a nap."

"Aren't you feeling well?"

Shahed did not reply. He was sickened by the smell of Mushtaq's cheap perfume. That kind of perfume was made to be poured on cadavers before burial, not to be worn by the living.

Mushtaq left the room. Probably he had been eager to chat about the current situation in the country. Just like the Bengalis, Biharis love gossiping.

Shahed picked up the newspaper. *Dainik Pakistan* was now coming out with only two pages in it, and there was virtually nothing in the way of news. Through force of habit he glanced over the paragraphs.

> Five distinguished intellectuals have welcomed the army's campaign. They have thanked General Yahya Khan for taking steps appropriate to the circumstances. They have called on the public to be constantly on their guard against those elements who do not believe in an undivided Pakistan. ...

PRICE OF RICE STABLE IN OPEN MARKET

An illustrated report. One picture showed a beaming merchant weighing rice on a pair of scales. Judging by his cheerful face he had never been more pleased with the business of rice trading than he was now.

FOUR DIE AS BUS PLUNGES INTO DITCH IN SWITZERLAND

There was a detailed report, together with a photo of the bus being lifted by a crane.

Shahed scowled. How was it that a newspaper in a country where thousands of people were being viciously slaughtered every day was printing pictures of a bus in a ditch in Switzerland? Four people had died, but even if four hundred had died it made no sense to print such things. He felt like crumpling up the newspaper and chucking it in the bin. But what good would that do?

"Are you there, brother Shahed?"

It was Mr Dewan. He pushed the door open and came in. His mouth was filled with a wadge of *paan*, and he had a cigarette in his hand. He seemed to be deriving a great deal of enjoyment from puffing at his cigarette, and his face was cheerful.

"Are you feeling ill, Shahed?"

"Not at all."

"You've been letting your beard grow, you look like a wandering ascetic. Have you got any news of your wife?"

"No."

"Have you made enquiries at your village home?"

"No."

"Most of the people who have fled from Dhaka have ended up in their village homes. Whereabouts is your father-in-law's village?"

"In the lowlands of Mymensingh District. It's very remote, and Asmani would never try to get there on her own."

"A starving tiger will even eat rice plants. When they're running for their lives Bengali people are capable of covering great distances."

"She wouldn't go anywhere without me. I strongly suspect she is still in Dhaka, or somewhere close to Dhaka."

Mr Dewan pulled up a chair and sat down. Shahed was surprised to note the light-hearted way he started swinging his leg.

"Shahed *bhai*!"

"Yes?"

"If you had listened to me then, you wouldn't be in such a fix now."

"Listened to what?"

"Don't you remember? The day after Sheikh Mujib's big speech on 7th March – what I said to you then? *The situation is very grave*, I said, *send your family into the country*."

"Did you say that?"

"Most certainly I did. There isn't a soul in the office I didn't make that suggestion to. But they say *a poor man's words bear no fruit until they're withered*. What I said then is old and withered now – and the value of my words has been borne out. Nothing came of my words while they were still fresh. You'll never believe me when I tell you that my own wife was dead against going away into the country. She argued, she screamed at me, she wept. I almost had to use brute force to get her onto the river bus. But I did get her to go, and consequently I'm free of worry now. If I hadn't put her on the river launch that day I'd be in the same quandary as you are now. Shahed *bhai*..."

"Yes?"

"Why don't you come along with me, this very day, I'll take you somewhere."

"Where?"

"There's this very religious man everyone calls Bhai Pagla. He's a saintly type. I can take you to see him."

"But what would be the use of my seeing him?"

"I told you, he's a saintly type. These people have supernatural powers. He'd be able to close his eyes and tell you where your wife is at this moment."

Shahed said nothing.

"There are always crowds of people thronging around the great man," Mr Dewan went on enthusiastically. "It's not easy to speak to him in private. But I have connections, I can fix it. How about it, are you willing to go?"

"No."

"There's nothing to be lost. Those people are highly religious, you know, real mystics."

"I'm not willing to consult spiritualists and dervishes."

"Other people are ready to gobble up shit when in trouble, but all you have to do is go and visit this seer. Pakistan army personnel go to see him, even some top-ranking officers visit him regularly."

"I've already said no. Please don't keep insisting."

Despite having said he would never do so, Shahed did in the end go to consult Bhai Pagla. Mr Dewan had been as good as his word and arranged for him to see the holy man in private. Bhai Pagla was in his inner sanctum, sitting cross-legged on a carpet in the centre of the small chamber. He had a salver piled with quids of *paan* in front of him.

The holy man was busily chewing betel leaf. There was a spittoon to hand, which was shiny and looked as if it was made of silver; every so often he would lean over and expel a jet of betel juice into it. In his right hand he was holding a set of prayer beads, a *tasbih*, with particularly large segments, and it was circulating steadily as his fingers worked rapidly from bead to bead – this didn't stop even when the holy man was talking, so somehow he must have discovered a technique of holding a conversation and mentally chanting the glory of God at one and the same time. Holy Bhai Pagla was not very old; he had a full but wispy beard which was stirred by the slightest movement of air, and his voice was unusually sweet.

"You have no news of the whereabouts of your wife and daughter?"

"None."

"What is your wife's age?"

"Twenty-two, twenty-three maybe." Shahed could not see why it was necessary for the man to know how old she was.

"What does she look like?"

What had that got to do with it? But Shahed replied, "Oh, not bad."

"Tell me her name."

"Asmani."

"No, her proper name."

"Nushrat Jahan."

Bhai Pagla closed his eyes, and remained sitting there with his eyes closed for five or six minutes. The *tasbih* in his right hand was working furiously. At length he opened his eyes and said, "It's all right, she is alive and well."

"She is well?"

"Yes. Your daughter is well too. *Mashallah*, God's will be done."

"Where are they?"

"Not in Dhaka city, some distance away. They left Dhaka by boat."

Hold your tongue, you fraud, thought Shahed to himself. Every single person who has fled from Dhaka has done so by boat, along the river. They're hardly likely to have flown, are they, you pompous humbug.

"They're in a two-storeyed building," said Bhai Pagla, "and there's a garden in front, with hibiscus flowers in it."

That's quite enough from you, thought Shahed, save your breath.

"You will not see them for a long time."

"Is that so?"

"Yes. Your wife is expecting. You are going to have another daughter."

"I'm delighted to hear that. Well, I'll take my leave now, your reverence."

Bhai Pagla stuck out his foot so that Shahed could touch it and perform an obeisance, but Shahed did not bend down. The fellow's self-importance was giving him a headache.

While on his way back from seeing the reverend Bhai Pagla, Shahed fell into the hands of the military. It happened in a peculiarly undramatic way. He had said goodbye to Mr Dewan and then gone over to a roadside stall to buy some cigarettes. He had just purchased a packet of Scissors brand when a man came up to him. The man was a Bengali.

"What's your name?" asked the man quietly.

"What do you want with my name?" retorted Shahed.

"Just come along with me," said the man in a low voice.

"What for?"

"It's something important, very important."

Shahed crossed the road alongside the man. He hadn't noticed until then that there was an army vehicle standing there.

There was no alternative, he had to get into the jeep.

Pakistan army personnel carriers were not like ordinary jeeps, they had a rather longer wheelbase, and there was no upholstery to sit on, just bare metal seating. This particular vehicle had probably just been repainted, as it smelled strongly and nauseatingly of fresh paint. Shahed was shoved roughly into the back of the truck, and would have slipped and fallen in the pitch darkness if someone hadn't caught hold of him and guided him to a seat. Shahed thanked this person mentally in Bengali. The English expression "thankyou" is suitable for using out loud, but the Bengali *dhonnobad* is always best said silently in one's mind.

Although nothing was visible in the darkness Shahed could tell that the vehicle was full of ordinary folk like himself, and that these people were all terrified. Frightened people give off a particular odour which, though faint, is foetid and cloying. The smell of fear numbs people's nerves.

The vehicle started moving. The popular idea that army vehicles race along at high speed is mistaken. This personnel carrier moved very slowly. Its suspension was poor, and it kept bouncing wildly, so that Shahed's head banged into one of the metal rods supporting the roof canvas. "Sit tight and hold onto this bar as firmly as you can," said the man sitting next to Shahed. He had an extraordinarily soothing voice. In the dark he guided Shahed's hand to the bar he had mentioned. Some voices are so pleasant, if you hear them once you are keen to hear them again, and this man's voice was like that. In order to hear it again Shahed addressed him.

"Where are we going?"

"I don't know," said the man. "We've just got onto Mirpur Road."

"Why have they taken us into custody?" asked Shahed

The man made no reply. The vehicle started bucking furiously again, but as Shahed was gripping the bar firmly he avoided getting hurt. The lurching was so violent it could have sent him flying.

Why were the army snatching people off the street and taking them away? What purpose did they have in mind? Shahed couldn't figure out any possible reason they could have for seizing him. He wasn't a political leader, or even a party activist. He wasn't a writer or a poet or a singer. He was a nobody. No-one outside his family circles even knew him. So how could the army people have singled him out? Had these last few days of anguish, discomfort and worry made him look wild and fierce? Might anyone looking at him imagine he was capable of committing acts of violence? Shahed was quite incapable of doing anything at all violent. He was an ordinary person, and ordinary people never do anything out of the ordinary. They get average results in their exams, secure an undistinguished job, marry a run of the mill girl and lead an unremarkable life, and that was exactly the case with Shahed. His whole existence was circumscribed, he led an uncomplicated and very limited life.

The vehicle performed another hectic waltz and then came to a halt. Nobody moved, all was still. What was going on? Had they reached their destination? If so, the soldiers would make everyone get out, but there was no sign of anyone preparing to offload. Shahed drew a cigarette and matches out of his pocket, but didn't light up. Just sitting there with the cigarette in his hand was satisfying enough. The vehicle had stopped in a dark place, and as no light was filtering into the rear compartment he couldn't see the faces of any of his fellow passengers. It would have been a relief to be able to see their faces; at a time of great danger the sight of a human face gives one courage.

"What's going on?" whispered Shahed.

"They're picking up more people," said the man sitting beside Shahed.

"Who do they pick up?"

"Whatever people they happen to find."

"But why?"

"I don't know, brother, I simply have no idea. Go ahead, you can smoke your cigarette, nothing's stopping you. At the stage we've reached now nothing matters any more."

"Would you like one?"

"I don't smoke."

Shahed lit his cigarette, and for a brief second, by the light of the match flame, he could see the faces of his fellow travellers. He got a sudden shock – everyone was staring attentively at him. Why were they looking at him, what had he done? Had he done something dreadful? Or worse, was something dreadful about to happen to him? After taking a puff of his cigarette Shahed got over his initial shock. The mystery of why everyone had been staring had a simple explanation: he had lit a match in the darkness, and they had been staring at the match, not at him. So there was no need to be scared. Shahed noticed that he was in fact feeling slightly less afraid. Was that because of nicotine from the cigarette going into his system? Did nicotine give people courage? He remembered a film he had seen about the second World War; he couldn't recall the name of the film, but it was a Russian one, and in it a Russian colonel was about to be put to death by a Nazi firing squad. They had tied his hands behind his back and made him stand facing a wall. The colonel had twisted his head round and said, "Might I have one last cigarette?" His request was granted. Since his hands were tied, a German soldier had to light the cigarette for him and put it in his mouth. With the glowing cigarette between his lips the colonel had said thankyou to the soldier, and then started puffing it with great satisfaction. He had had a faint smile on his lips as if he found the whole incident rather amusing.

Do things really happen the way they are presented in films? If the soldiers led Shahed away ready to shoot him, would he be able to say, "Might I have a cigarette?" Supposing they did give him a cigarette, would he be able to keep it between his lips, at one side of his mouth, and smile calmly while smoking it like that colonel? Would any particular memories spring to his mind just as he was about to die? Shahed didn't have any very outstanding memories; all his memories were of a humdrum sort. Dramatic events did sometimes occur in the lives of ordinary people, but nothing dramatic had happened to him. The way he had just been arrested and taken away by soldiers was the most dramatic thing that had taken place in his life till now. If he came out of it alive he would be able to yarn about it to Runi's children when he was an old man: *Listen, grandchildren. It was a dark night in 1971. Your mother was only six years old at the time, and I didn't have any idea where she was. I was almost crazy with worry. I went to see a holy man called Bhai Pagla, and on the way back...*

The vehicle started moving again. No additional people had been picked up. Extraordinary though it seemed, Shahed was beginning to feel sleepy. His eyes were drooping, and he kept nodding off with his head resting on the next man's shoulder. He felt ashamed – why was he falling asleep when faced with such a colossal danger? He ought to be praying non-stop. If nothing else he should recite the *Ayatul Kursi*° and blow the words towards his chest three times. But he didn't know the whole *ayat* by heart. Still, there were other things to recite. That formula the prophet Jonah° had recited in the whale's stomach, thanks to which he had been delivered, *la ilaha illa anta subhanaka inni kuntu minaz zalimin*. Shahed was now so drowsy he couldn't recite the words correctly; instead he fell into a profound and refreshing sleep. His head was leaning on the shoulder of the man beside him, and this gentleman made no objection; indeed he stuck his shoulder out so that his poor exhausted neighbour could sleep in comfort.

Lieutenant-Colonel Jamshed°, known to his contemporaries as Jash, was an officer in the intelligence corps. He was a jocular type who was constantly cracking jokes; such was his wit that he could even make people without any discernible sense of humour burst out laughing. But he wasn't only a fountain of wit. Among his other accomplishments he was also a good conjuror. If he got hold of a pack of cards he could hold an audience spellbound with it for half an hour. He excelled at sleight of hand, and for him it was child's play to produce a bright new coin from nowhere and then make it disappear again. Colonel Jash was a bachelor. The reason he gave for not having married was that he loved travelling around in trains, taking a window seat and staring at the passing scenery. If he got married he would have to let his wife take the window seat, and thus be deprived of his greatest enjoyment. So he preferred to stay single.

This ebullient Colonel Jash had been in the intelligence corps from the very beginning of his army career, and he loved his job. Intelligence work often involved elements of mystery, amusement and surprise, so it was no wonder a magician would be drawn to it.

The inter services intelligence corps normally restricts its operations to within the armed forces, but Colonel Jash had extended his remit and was working with civilians too. The job was simple enough, detaining various kinds of people from various points in the city and hauling them in, then chatting to them for a while. He quite enjoyed chatting to people who were out of their wits with terror. Most of the unfortunate people Colonel Jash called in for his little chats were duly sent on to the death squads. On this matter Colonel Jash's conscience was perfectly clear. We are in a state of war, his reasoning went, and in the early stages of a war it is necessary to instil terror in the mind of the enemy. Terror, despair and uncertainty – creating all three of these sensations amounted to a preliminary victory. The enemy's morale had to be crushed; once his morale had been sapped he would never be able to rise again.

Lots of people who were brought in disappeared without trace. Their relatives were unable to find anything out about them and were left in a state of utmost uncertainty. They would talk to others about their predicament and spread the news; horrendous rumours would pass rapidly from mouth to mouth. And this was the exactly kind of thing that was needed in wartime.

Colonel Jash was wearing a light ghee coloured Hawaii shirt, and he had a cigar between his fingers. He never smoked cigars, or even cigarettes; tobacco smoke gave him a headache. But when he was questioning detainees he liked to have a cigar in his hand. Keeping it alight was a problem – he had to draw on it from time to time – but he enjoyed the act. There was something particularly dramatic about examining prisoners while holding a cigar. Colonel Jash's room was a small one. The furniture was sparse: a small desk, behind which was the revolving chair he himself sat on, while in front was a chair with arms where the person being questioned had to sit. There was a ceiling fan, one which ran on DC electricity and produced more noise than ventilation. The colonel could have had a superior type of fan installed in its place had he so wished, but he had chosen not to. He liked the way the repetitive grinding noise of the fan tended to accentuate people's fear. His revolving chair also made a noise when it turned, a grating noise which he likewise approved of. Suppose there was some terrified person sitting in front of him in fear of their life. He would take a bit of time relighting his extinct cigar and then suddenly spin round in his chair and glare at his victim – the grating noise would make the petrified individual turn blue with shock. A delightful scenario.

Shahed was sitting in the chair facing Colonel Jash, reduced to a jelly. To begin with he had rested his arms on the arms of the chair, but then it had struck him that such a posture might appear disrespectful, and he had put his hands in his lap. He was in urgent need of the toilet; his bladder was bursting.

The colonel swivelled his chair round and regarded Shahed. "*Ap ka tarif?*" he asked quietly in courteous Urdu. "What is your distinguished appellation?"

Shahed couldn't understand the question. What did *tarif* mean? If only he had known a bit more Urdu, then he could have got himself out of this tight spot. He ought to have learned Urdu at school, he should have chosen Urdu instead of Arabic in Class VI. He had chosen Arabic in the hopes of getting higher marks, but the gamble hadn't paid off. In the exams he had to take in order to move up from Class VIII to Class IX he had achieved pass marks in every other subject, but got only thirty-two percent in Arabic.

The colonel leaned forwards slightly as he repeated, "Sir, *ap ka nam*?"

A shiver went through Shahed. Why had the fellow addressed him as "sir"? Was he being funny? But he had a perfectly straight face. Perhaps he was just being polite.

"My name is Shahed," replied Shahed in English.

"Don't you speak Urdu?"

"No, sir."

The colonel picked up the pack of cards which lay on the table. This was a little game of his. After asking the person's name he would shuffle the cards for a while and then draw one out. A red card meant the death penalty, a black card meant let the fellow go. There was a fifty-fifty chance of survival, it was a matter of testing the person's luck. Whenever he played this game of chance he felt rather like God. The colonel picked a card – it was red. The four of diamonds. This young man was out of luck.

"Are you married?"

"Yes, sir."

Seeing as the fellow was married, let him have a second chance. The colonel drew another card. Red again, the two of hearts. Amazing! Really unlucky, this chap. Very.

"Do you have children?"

"Yes, sir. One daughter."

Oh, all right. One more chance, for the daughter's sake. But if it's red again, that's the end of it. The colonel shuffled the cards again. The probability was that a black card would come up this time; three red cards in succession was unlikely.

But it was red for the third time running. The queen of diamonds. The colonel smiled cheerfully and said, "OK sir, you can leave."

His head reeling, Shahed left the room. Colonel Jash placed a red cross next to his name.

Was it possible, could human beings be sentenced to death for no reason at all? Was death such a small thing, such a simple, easy thing? Instead of being weak with terror Shahed was merely shocked and incomprehending. Normal people didn't even rip a leaf off a plant without some reason, he reflected. Think of those long, thread-like processions of ants which can be seen on the ground in the rainy season – people took care to step over them, because they had no wish to crush and kill even so insignificant a creature as an ant. So why were this lot slaughtering so many human beings without rhyme or reason? There must be something wrong somewhere, but what? Who was at fault? Surely not him? Fair enough, they might take everyone to a field, line them up, make a note of their names and addresses and let them go, or at the very worst, subject them to some form of punishment – but kill them? That was going too far.

A man with a long beard, who was dressed in some kind of flowing gown, came up to Shahed and said, "Recite the *kalima*. The declaration of faith."

So this man must be an army chaplain, who was getting everyone to recite the *kalima* before they died. There were nine of them standing there including Shahed, and he was the middle one in line. Were they going to take them away one by one to shoot them individually, or would they shoot them all at once? Who was going to give the order to fire, would it be that young officer with three stars on his shoulder flash? He must be a captain. He was looking very cheerful; nobody glancing at his face would ever guess what a gruesome incident was about to take place.

A kind of earthen platform could be seen, and around it a number of soldiers with rifles were waiting at stand-easy. That earthen platform was doubtless the place of execution. There wasn't any pit or ditch nearby, so where were they going to dump the dead bodies? If there had been a river handy they would have tossed them into it, but there was no river and no hole in the ground. Could the whole thing simply be a trick? They might just be putting the wind up people for the hell of it. They'd think it was fun to scare people to death, great fun.

"Excuse me, brother," said Shahed to the man standing next to him, "what time do you have on your watch?"

The man stared at Shahed in an uncanny way and said nothing

"Sorry, but what time is it?" asked Shahed again. "I haven't got a watch on me, so if you'd be kind enough to tell me..."

"Five past four."

"Thankyou."

The man was still staring at Shahed. "Do you have any idea why they've brought us out here?" Shahed asked.

"Of course."

"Why have they?"

"Can't you stop jabbering, you know very well why they've brought us here. Just say your prayers."

The man had hardly finished speaking when the first four in line were led away to the earthen mound. The place where Shahed was standing was in darkness; the only light reaching it came from a yellow painted verandah nearby. But the mud platform was well lit; three bamboo poles had been erected beside it, and the electric bulbs mounted on them were glaring brilliantly. Shahed watched with intense fascination as the four men were marched away. The whole thing felt like a dream. The men were walking with a swaying gait like puppets in a puppet show, not the way real people ever walk.

The four men's hands were being tied behind their backs. One of them was reciting the *kalima tayyib* out loud, *la ilaha illallah, muhammadur rasulullah*. What's going on, Shahed thought, why are they tying those men's hands behind their backs? What are they going to do to them? Are they really going to kill them? And then are they going to come for us? But what have we done wrong? There must be some mistake somewhere, which will come to light any moment now.

In a moment all would become clear. Everything he'd seen had been a frightful dream. He would wake up and find things back to normal; he would be lying in bed with Asmani, and Runi would be between them, curled up and fast asleep. One of her legs would be sticking into Shahed; but if he tried to move it she would wake up, and then it would be impossible to get her back to sleep again. He would have to walk up and down on the verandah with her in his arms until his legs ached. And just when he thought she had fallen asleep so he could put her back in bed, she would lay her head on his shoulder and say, "Tell me a story, Daddy," and then he would immediately have to start a story-telling session.

"Attention!"

There was a clacking noise. Shahed started shivering. His perception of the scene in front of him had become hazy, but now it sharpened up again. There were the four men, they were being made to stand with their backs to the soldiers, so their bound wrists were visible. Quite a number of soldiers were aiming their rifles at them. How many, should he count them? No, what was the point. Think of something else. Maybe dawn was going to break soon. Were there any stars in the sky, why not look up and see? Yes, there was Orion with the three stars in his belt.

"Fire!"

There was a loud report. The men who had been standing there were no longer upright.

Not a shriek, not a gasp: for a moment the universe was perfectly still. Then a low groaning sound could be heard. Amidst the groans a dying man called weakly, "Farida! Farida!" Who might she be, this Farida – his beloved wife, or perhaps his precious first-born daughter?

Shahed's world caved in; he staggered and fell to the ground. Almost at once he could feel Asmani gathering him up and laying him down on a bed. She poured water over his head and ran her fingers through his hair: it was a wonderful feeling. His eyes were heavy and he fell into a deep and relaxing slumber; it was as though every cell in his body had gone torpid and sunk into unconsciousness. Then Runi came and started stroking him with her small hands, but her hands were surprisingly cold, as if she had been playing with water. Dimly he could hear Asmani saying, "What's the matter, why are you in such a state?" With a great effort he tried to explain. "I'm having a nightmare, Asmani, a really terrible nightmare. Hold me in your arms, you mustn't leave me for an instant." In a firm voice Asmani replied, "No, I shall never leave you."

Whether it was because he had fainted or for some quite different reason, Shahed was not killed. His survival would remain a big mystery, which he himself was never able to fathom however hard he tried. He woke to find himself lying on a wooden framed cot. He was the only person lying on the cot, but there were a number of other people sitting on it

Before he could decide whether he was really there or simply imagining things, he lost consciousness again, or maybe he just fell asleep. He continued to have the impression that Asmani was stroking him all the time.

Once he had had severe chicken pox and his whole body had been in agony.

"Come here, let me reduce the pain for you," Asmani had said.

"You always have to be funny, don't you," Shahed had retorted in annoyance. "How can you possibly reduce pain?"

"I shall stroke you lovingly, that will make you much more comfortable."

And amazing though it seemed, as soon as Asmani had started stroking him the torment had been much reduced.

Even while in the realms of unconsciousness Shahed was distinctly aware of Asmani steadily running her hands over his body.

Shahed was released at midday on Tuesday 13th April. An army major pointed at him and said "Clear out!" It took Shahed some time to realize that this "clear out" meant that he was free to go. Even after he had climbed into a rickshaw he went on thinking, this is just a dream, as soon as the rickshaw starts moving the dream will be shattered. The rickshaw got under way, but the dream went on. Then Shahed thought, the moment the rickshaw puller opens his mouth and says something the dream will be at an end. But the rickshaw puller kept silent and the dream went on. It was Shahed who spoke first.

"How are things in our country?" he asked.

The rickshaw puller turned round to look back at Shahed, but said nothing.

"Where are you from?" asked Shahed.

"Faridpur. Jaynagar village."

"Right. Well, my village home is in Kendua in Mymensingh District. I was in military detention but have just been released."

Again the rickshaw puller craned his head round to stare at Shahed, but said not a word. There was no hint of interest, curiosity, surprise or anything else in his eyes; they were the eyes of a zombie.

Shahed got back to his house at about two p.m. The house was empty, there was no sign of Gourango, and the front door was unlocked, for he had left without fastening the padlock. Shahed slept solidly from two until six in the evening. He got up and sat for a while in the verandah, then went back inside the house to write a letter.

Asmani,

I don't know where you and Runi are. I have been worrying a lot about you for some time, but now I have stopped worrying. I am sending this letter to Brother so that you'll get it if and when you get in touch with him.

> Asmani, I think the people of this country are going to start a war against the Pakistan army. I wish to be among the first of the freedom fighters, that's why I'm ceasing to worry about you, and as from today I am starting to look for some way of being useful.
>
> I shall see you again, not in an enslaved country but in a liberated one. But if we don't meet again, if I am killed, you mustn't grieve for me. Please explain everything to Runi. She may not understand yet, but one day she will understand.
>
> I've just been through a terrible time. While that was going on I could sense that you were near me. I know that wherever I am you will be right beside me.
>
> Lots of love for you and for Runi.

Just as he was preparing to date the letter after writing it Shahed got a little shock. It was 13th April, their wedding day. At the time he had been rather anxious in case the thirteenth was an unlucky day to get married on. Hearing this his elder brother Irtazuddin had scolded him and said, every single day that God has created is an auspicious one.

25

Tuesday 13th April 1971

The prime minister of China, Chou En Lai, announced that the People's Republic of China was committed to defending Pakistan from external aggression in order to preserve its integrity. He said the Chinese government would offer Pakistan its full cooperation to help it maintain its sovereignty.

That same day, just after the midday prayer, Khwaja Khayruddin and the leader of the Jamaat-e-Islami° Ghulam Azam led a Peace Committee procession starting from Baitul Mukarram mosque. The Jamaat leader Ghulam Azam also led a prayer for the victory of the Pakistan army and called on the faithful to stand up and confront the enemies of Islam and Pakistan.*

---

* Source: *Dainik Pakistan, Dainik Purbadesh* newspapers.

26

The homestead where Asmani and Runi were staying was called Darogabari. It was an impressive property deep inside the village, comprising a two storeyed brick built house with a mango orchard behind it, and on the south side a pond with a flight of stone steps leading down to the water. The water in this pond was as deep and limpid as a crow's eye. There were two cherry trees covered in white cherry blossom standing side by side near the bathing steps – foreign trees one would not expect to see in a village – and a variety of hibiscus bushes filling quite a large area in front of the house. Bhai Pagla's clairvoyance had been accurate as far as hibiscus plants were concerned.

Mr Motaleb's father Sarfaraz Miah had been an inspector of police during the period of British rule. He had built the house after taking his retirement. Former police officers from the British era tended to take on the manners and appearance of a *zamindar* or traditional landowner as they got older, and this had been the case with him. That was why he had erected such a grand building in the heart of such an obscure village.

Sarfaraz Miah was still alive. The venerable gentleman was nearly ninety years old; he was very emaciated and walked with a stoop, but he could still see and hear quite well. Mentally he was slightly deranged. At the slightest provocation he would start calling for his shotgun; on occasion he would actually go to his bedroom and bring out the old double-barrelled fowling piece. "I'm going to shoot all the bastards dead!" he would cry furiously, and then he would point the gun at the sky and fire into thin air. The moment the noise of the shot reached his ears he would come to his senses and start behaving normally again. He would look mildly embarrassed at having put on such a display of manic over-excitement.

Runi had been feeling unsettled and frightened ever since coming to the house, and small wonder. The head of the household was a madman who spent all his time looking after his hibiscus bushes and talking to them, and occasionally appeared brandishing a shotgun: he was hardly the kind of person any small child could feel comfortable with. Runi was going through a grim nightmare from which Asmani, with the best will in the world, was unable to rescue her.

Runi's very first encounter with Sarfaraz Miah had been a terrifying one. At first she had liked this new home with so much open space all round and such pretty hibiscus flowers: those bushes seemed to have blossomed in little bursts of scarlet flame. Runi had run around gathering the flowers in the lap of her frock; she had been so happy she almost felt like crying. Just then a stern voice had come from behind her.

"Oy, you! Little girl! What are you up to, picking those flowers? Who told you you could pick flowers? Who does this degenerate child belong to, anyhow?"

Startled, Runi had spun round. Behind her was a very old man who looked rather like a monkey. His eyes were smouldering. There was something peculiar about the way he was standing, all bent and crooked.

"Why are you picking those flowers?" the old man had asked again. All the flowers Runi had gathered in her frock fell to the ground.

"Don't move!" the old man had commanded in his stern voice. "I warn you, don't move, stay standing just where you are. There'll be trouble if you move an inch."

Runi had remained standing where she was. She couldn't have moved even if she had wanted to, for all the muscles in her body had seized up in her terror and consternation. She had watched with huge eyes as the old man went galumping away, for all the world like a monkey, and disappeared into the house. This had given her a chance to escape; but if she was to run to her mother she'd have to go through the very door the old man had just vanished through, and that was out of the question. Otherwise she might have run down to the steps by the pond, but Mummy had told her she was never to go near the water. So she had stayed put. The old man had reappeared out of the house and come galumping towards her again, but this time with a double-barrelled shotgun in his hands.

"I'm warning you, don't move! I'm going to shoot you for picking my flowers!"

Runi had reckoned that the old man wouldn't really shoot her, and felt sure that there were no bullets in the gun. She had thought it might even be a toy gun, for grownups sometimes tried to scare children with toy weapons. Her father had once pointed a pistol at her and shot her with it. There had been a loud snap, and at the same time a small flame had come out of the muzzle of the gun. It had actually been a cigarette lighter. The gun the old man was holding was surely something of that kind.

"Say your prayers, little girl. This is your day of judgment."

Runi had tried to scream for her mother, but no sound would come out of her mouth.

Sarfaraz Miah had aimed at the sky in his usual fashion and fired into vacancy. Runi had fainted and collapsed on top of her collection of hibiscus flowers. Then there had been a great hullabaloo throughout the homestead.

Runi had regained consciousness almost immediately, but her temperature had shot up. As there was no thermometer in the house there had been no way of telling how high it had gone. Asmani had sat silently at Runi's bedside. She couldn't be bothered even to touch Runi and gauge her temperature; she was thinking how pointless her own life had become. She felt like going away into a quiet corner all on her own, and weeping. The house was vast and had plenty of quiet corners in it, and there was no need to worry about Runi, somebody was dousing her with water and a doctor had been sent for, so it wasn't essential to sit with her, but nevertheless Asmani had remained sitting there. The doctor had come, he had given Runi some medicine, Runi's fever had abated and she had started smiling in her normal way. Only Asmani herself had been unable to get back to normal. She had stayed awake all night thinking gloomy thoughts.

Suppose Kumkum's mother suddenly said something like, "All right, it's been quite a long time now, why don't you go and stay somewhere else for a change?" For the good lady was no longer treating her with the same friendliness as she had at the beginning. In fact Asmani had overheard her one day saying to a servant girl, "I can't find my own daughter, yet here I am having to take care of someone else's."

And it was a fact. Asmani was just a friend of Kumkum's, she was no relation of theirs, so why should they bother to support her?

Every day now Asmani used to consider taking Runi and setting off for Dhaka on her own. Was such a thing really so unthinkable? Surely other people were heading for Dhaka too?

There was just one problem, she had no money. That is, she had precisely fifteen rupees in her handbag. But she had four gold bracelets on her wrist, which could doubtless be sold, and Runi was wearing a necklace made out of one *tola* of gold, which could likewise be traded for cash. The current price of pure gold was two hundred rupees per *tola*. Even allowing for a reduced rate on account of impurity, she should be able to get two hundred and fifty or three hundred rupees for the bracelets and chain together. It always felt awkward to be without cash. Now Asmani was feeling ill at ease all the time.

Why had her well ordered life suddenly been upset like this? Her fate had got tangled up with that of a strange family, things were not at all as they should be. She had no idea where Shahed was, or even if he was still alive. And where was her mother, was she at their village home? How could she find out? Everything was in such a mess; would it ever get sorted out again? It was a fact of life that once things were in a mess they tended to get worse and worse.

Asmani stayed up late at night to write a number of letters: to Shahed, to her mother, to Shahed's elder brother in Nilganj, to her uncle in Chittagong. In each letter she gave her present address and explained how it was she had ended up in a remote village in Munshiganj. She didn't know whether the postal service would ever become operative again, but she wanted to make sure that if and when it did resume her close relatives would find out where she was.

Would the situation in the country get any better, and if so, when? How much longer would she have to go on living with strangers in a strange place? Asmani simply didn't know. And it wasn't just her; nobody in the country knew anything.

Terrible news was being broadcast on the BBC. It seemed civil war was raging all over the country. So how long did a civil war last, six months, a year, seven years? How long would the civil war in East Pakistan go on? If it carried on for seven years, would she have to spend all of that time cooped up in this Darogabari in Munshiganj, with the old madman terrifying her little daughter whenever he felt like it, and calling the precious child a degenerate?

Asmani made two copies of her letter to Shahed, one to go to their home address and the other to go to his office. Shahed would surely call in at the office at some point, and the letter would be waiting for him whenever he did. Asmani's letters to Shahed had no salutation at the beginning of them. She had written many letters to him before they had been married, and none of them had contained any salutation. How was she supposed to address him: Dearest, My Darling, O Precious One, or simply Shahed – she didn't feel comfortable using any of these. She knew of no Bengali word which could express the affection she felt in her heart.

Asmani tried to adopt as normal and casual a tone as possible in her letter, as if she had come to this village in Munshiganj on a picnic outing, was having a great time, and would be returning home as soon as the picnic was over. She wrote as follows:

> No doubt you are anxiously looking for us. There's no need to be anxious, we are quite well, very well in fact. I'm not in the least worried about our own situation, but I am very worried about you.
>
> I hope you aren't annoyed because we came here without telling anybody. Please don't be cross. There's no point in getting cross anyway, as from this distance I can't possibly do anything to soothe you. It's useless being angry if nobody else can see your anger, don't you agree?
>
> Oh, I haven't yet told you where we are. We're actually quite close to Dhaka. The area is called Munshiganj. From Munshiganj river-launch station you have to go ten miles inland. The village is called Sadarganj, and the homestead where we're staying has its own name too, it's called Darogabari. The gentleman who built the house was formerly a police inspector, a *daroga*, and his name is Sarfaraz

Miah. He is still alive, but his brain has gone a bit addled. He sometimes comes out with a gun and fires a blank shot into the air. He did this the day after we came here. Since then all the cartridges for the gun have been hidden from him. They talked of hiding the gun too, but decided not to in the end, because they thought if he couldn't find his gun he might go even crazier.

Now let me tell you how it happened that we ended up here. When I walked out on you that day I went to my friend Kumkum's house. Their house is in Gandaria. Kumkum's father, Mr Motaleb, is particularly fond of me. Her mother also treats me exactly as if I was her daughter. After those horrible things which happened on 25th March their family got very alarmed. Everyone in the neighbourhood was fleeing from Dhaka, and they wanted to get out too. But then I didn't know where you were. You had locked up our house and gone off - how was I to know where you'd gone? Our house was locked and empty, and so was my Mum's.

So there was nothing else I could do, so I came here with Uncle Motaleb and his family. Sarfaraz Miah, the owner of Darogabari, is Uncle Motaleb's father.

Anyway, there's a fellow called Moznu living at Uncle Motaleb's house in Gandaria, and he is supposed to be going out and looking for you every day. I guess he's probably found you by now, in which case you know where we are and how we are.

Runi is missing you a lot. But apart from that she is well. Mentally upset, it's true, but physically well. Considering what we've been through staying physically well is quite an achievement, don't you think?

Keep well, you. Lots and lots of affection,
Asmani

Asmani had felt like writing "lots and lots of kisses" rather than "lots and lots of affection", but she hadn't dared to do so. Somebody else might open the letter and read it, and it would be extremely embarrassing if they saw that bit about kisses.

The moment Asmani had finished her letter it struck her that she'd missed out the most important thing, though she wasn't sure what exactly that thing was. So she started a second letter. This time there was a salutation, and her eyes filled with tears even as she wrote it. This is what she wrote:

Oh, Mr Babu!

Where are you, where are you, where are you? I'm dying. If I don't get to see you I shall die, I really shall. Do you realize I don't think of anyone else any more, I don't even think about Mum or Dad, let alone my brothers or sisters, I just think about you, only you! There's a beautiful pond in this property, with a set of paved steps going down into the water. Often late at night I make sure Runi's asleep and then steal away to the pond and sit on the steps. And then I just think of you. I don't care whether the country gets independence, I don't care about anything else, I only want you. Why did things happen this way? Why did I get separated from you? When I see you again I shall never leave your side, I shall never run away from you

again. I can't stand it any longer. Come here and hug me. When will you come, when, when?
 Your Asmani

For some time now Asmani had been trying hard to help Runi get over her fear of Sarfaraz Miah so that she wouldn't have to cower indoors all day and night, but could go out into the garden and run around and play. Any girl who had been raised in the overcrowded backstreets of a city would normally be delighted to find herself in the fresh open environment of a village; but not Runi. She wasn't even willing to go downstairs from the first floor to the ground floor. Sometimes she would venture onto the verandah and peep timorously at Sarfaraz Miah, then dash back inside, quaking with fear.

At her age, Asmani thought, once a phobia had been established it was very hard to get rid of it. Like a plant, fear put down roots in the mind, and those roots went on growing. What was needed was to weed out the fear, roots and all, but Asmani had no idea how that could be done. Would it do any good if Sarfaraz Miah were to call Runi to him and speak a few affectionate words to her? Asmani was far from sure, but still she went to have a chat with the old man. Sarfaraz Miah responded in quite a normal manner.

He was busy loosening the earth under one of the hibiscus bushes with a trowel. As soon as Asmani appeared in front of him he spoke to her.

"And how are you, my daughter?"

"Very well, thank you, sir."

"You are actually the equivalent of a granddaughter to me, yet I called you daughter; please don't be offended. It is, I think, permissible to address any girl as daughter. Don't be offended, my dear, please don't."

"Oh no, sir, I'm not offended."

"Remember, this is your own home, never forget that. I've noticed you often go and sit on the bathing steps at the pond. Do you like those steps?"

"Yes, very much."

"I'm very pleased to hear it. I took a lot of trouble setting up this homestead. I had the pond dug, I had the steps put in, I created this garden. Yet there's no-one around to appreciate these things, I live here all on my own. Thank God the war has begun; because of that, you people have come here. Am I not right?"

"Yes, sir."

"Your little girl got a big fright that day. I'm most embarrassed about that. You see, from time to time something comes over me – my brain seems to stop working. A sort of fire starts burning inside my head. These things come with old age. Old age is a miserable thing."

"If you could call my daughter over and say some nice things to her, I'd be grateful."

"I shall, dear daughter, I shall. All in good time. There's a time for everything, you know. Mangoes ripen in the month of Jyaistha, not in Kartik; do you get what I'm saying?"

"May I go now?" asked Asmani.

"Very well, you may go," said Sarfaraz Miah without looking up. "But there's one thing I want to say to you. Be prepared. These are bad times for us all. I saw it all in a dream, for I get lots of important information from my dreams. Our country is going to go up in flames, dear child, in flames, I'm telling you. You're going to have to take your daughter in your arms and wander through the countryside. And mark you, these things I'm telling you aren't just an old madman's ravings, they're facts obtained from dreams."

Asmani stood there in astonishment. What was he saying? There was no need to take a deranged person's words too seriously, yet this was somehow unsettling.

"There's something else as well, my dear," said the old man as he straightened up. "You haven't got your husband with you. You are good looking. You are young. A girl's worst enemies are her good looks and her young age. You are taking refuge with strangers. In these circumstances danger may be lurking. Be on your guard."

It was impossible for Asmani to ignore what the old fellow had said, for he had correctly diagnosed a problem of an altogether different sort, one which she was unable to mention to anyone else let alone seek advice about. It was the way Mr Motaleb, her friend Kumkum's father, was behaving; she found it offensive. Under the guise of giving her consolation he would often lay his hand on her back. Asmani was a friend of his daughter's, so of course he had a right to pat her on the back, but Asmani knew the way he did so was not right. A woman can easily sense the difference between a benevolent touch and a salacious one.

One day Asmani had gone down to the pond to bathe when suddenly Mr Motaleb had appeared with his bathing towel in hand, obviously intending to get into the pond himself. Immediately Asmani had prepared to make herself scarce, but Mr Motaleb had told her so stay where she was.

"Don't go away, my dear, don't go away. The steps are rather slippery, and I'll need to hold onto you as I go down them."

Saying which he had come close to Asmani and taken her hand. When he let go again his hand suddenly flew to Asmani's breast and fingered her. He made it look as if the movement was accidental.

Asmani had moved away at once, but her limbs were trembling and her head was reeling; she felt she was going to lose her balance and fall into the pond.

"The water's rather cool, I see," Mr Motaleb had remarked in a perfectly normal tone. "Don't you find it cool?"

Asmani hadn't answered. She was longing to get away, but her legs were still trembling too much to walk.

"Have you heard what the army have been doing?" Mr Motaleb had gone on. "They've been all the way to Chowk Bazar, targeting Hindu properties. They capture all the girls, and guess what they do them. They remove all their clothes, leaving them naked, then they stuff them all into one room. They don't even bother to close the door – as the girls have no clothes on they daren't run away. The soldiers carry out their operations by day, and at night they have fun with the girls. A frightful business."

While Asmani was walking away Mr Motaleb had shouted after her.

"Where are you off to? Hang on just five minutes. I'll finish bathing and then we can go back together. At my age I shouldn't be left on my own when bathing; you never know, I might suddenly have a stroke or something. If I have a stroke and collapse in the water, will you be able to pull me out?"

What was Asmani to do now? Go to Kumkum's mother and say, Auntie, your husband has just been groping my breasts?

Asmani was feeling quite unwell. The moment she entered the house she got sick, and her head was spinning so badly she had to sit down. She was by now almost certain that Uncle Motaleb wasn't the only cause of her sudden queasiness; no, inside her a new little life was beginning to take shape. She had

had her suspicions a while ago, when they were leaving Dhaka; now there really was no doubt.

Asmani stayed sitting there. She couldn't summon the strength to stand.

27

Never before in his long life had Irtazuddin suffered the misfortune of not being able to get up in time for the dawn prayer. Everybody has a clock inside them which ticks silently away, keeping the time for them and reminding them of whatever they need to be reminded of, but Irtazuddin's clock must have developed a fault. He had not woken in time for the dawn prayer, and when he did wake up it was broad daylight and his feet were bathed in sunshine. His shame and remorse knew no bounds: it was unthinkable, he was going to start his day without having performed the prescribed devotions at dawn.

He had gone to bed very late the night before, maybe that was why he had overslept. But no, that was no justification at all. It was no good coming up with one excuse after another to try and gloss over a mistake, it was much better to admit the mistake frankly. Despondently Irtazuddin performed his ablutions and said his prayers. Even though he was doing the dawn prayer later than the prescribed time, he reflected, it would still count in full as normal; and this was because the Prophet himself had once overslept and failed to perform his dawn prayer at the correct hour, following which a special dispensation had been introduced in his honour allowing that particular prayer to be performed at any point before noon without being counted as out of time. What a remarkable man he was, our Prophet, mused Irtazuddin as he stood there on his prayer mat: each and every thing he had done and said was still remembered with such reverence and such affection.

As a way of punishing himself Irtazuddin went without breakfast. He set off for the school at exactly nine thirty. It would take him fifteen minutes to get to the school, and he would still have another fifteen minutes in hand until lessons started at ten. At the moment, though, no classes were being held, as no pupils were coming to school. There hadn't been any official announcement regarding whether or not schools were to remain open. In practice only a few of the teachers were coming in. These ones would turn up, chat for a while in the common room and then go home again.

The subject of their conversation was always the same – the state of the country. Almost all the teachers present would take part in the discussion with apparent glee. They quickly reached unanimity regarding the Pakistan army – it was a fearsome beast. For some strange reason they enjoyed extolling its courage and heroism.

"Have you heard, they've been clamping down really hard. Every place they've been to, they've turned it into a graveyard."

"All that song and dance about fire and revolution, they've put an end to it just like that. Only those who've actually felt the wrath of the Pakistan army know what it's capable of."

"They've got some crack troops in reserve, ones which they normally keep chained up in the darkness. They're really awesome, literally Angels of Death. They let them loose only when necessary, and when they do, that's it, nothing can stop them. They haven't let them out yet, though they will when it comes to fighting against India. Until then they don't need to."

"Mercy is something they don't go in for. Their approach is more like, grab your plank and hammer your nails in. Once they've got hold of a plank they won't let go of it until they've whammed a few nails in."

"They're coming our way, hammering nails as they go. With their hammer and nails they're going to bash the Bengalis into shape. The Bengalis imagined they were going to play snakes and ladders with the lion, but the lion isn't one for playing snakes and ladders."

After discussing matters military the teachers would proceed to have tea and *jhal muri* – pop-rice mixed with salt, mustard oil and green chilli. In former days they would have started vying for possession of the newspaper, but as no newspapers were reaching the village any more this stage in the proceedings was currently in abeyance. Saghir Uddin the maths teacher usually played a round of two of chess with the English teacher, Kalipad babu. Mr Kalipad was an astute chess player, so Mr Saghir invariably lost and made a bit of a fuss following his defeat. That was the present routine in the school, and it varied very little. The only disquieting element in this tranquil existence was the looming threat posed by the advance of the Pakistan army, but even this was discussed cheerfully by the teachers. They got a slight thrill from it; an unpleasant thrill, but that hardly seemed to matter.

"When do you think the army will get as far as Nilganj?"

"It won't be long. They're nearly here. They've already entered Mymensingh and they can push on to Nilganj any day. And they're not going to give any advance notice of their coming. All of a sudden you'll hear them. Armageddon in Nilganj, machine guns going *ta-ta-ta-ta-ta*."

"Rather alarming, don't you think?"

"Distinctly alarming. These fellows are just like Azrael, the angel of death. They'll shoot sooner than talk. And if you happen to be a Hindu, you've had it."

"How can they tell a Hindu from a Muslim?"

"They make you strip and check if you're circumcised. And they test you on the four declarations of faith, the *kalima*. If you get the *kalima* even slightly wrong you're shot."

"I don't even know all four of the *kalima* myself!"

"You'd better learn them by heart. You should do so without delay. There won't be any time for learning them once the army arrives. You'd share the same fate as the A.D.C. of Mymensingh."

"Why, what happened to him?"

"They asked him to say the four declarations of faith. He got the first one right, the *kalima tayyib*, but he got mixed up on the *kalima shahāda*. Then they asked him to recite the correct formula of intention for the *witr* prayer. He couldn't do that, and straight away they took him to the bank of a river and shot him, bang! bang!"

"What, they ask about the *niyya* for the *witr* prayer too?"

"They ask about everything. The Pakistan army is very hot on religious details."

"That's ominous."

"It's ominous all right, it's a hazard of gigantic proportions. In fact you could more or less compare it with doomsday."

Yet nobody seemed unduly concerned by the prospect of doomsday. It was a beautiful sunny day in the village of Nilganj, with an April sky of brilliant blue. People were working in the fields, and it seemed there was nothing at all to worry about. There was trouble in the cities, but then there always was. The alarming things which went on in urban areas didn't affect the countryside. Emperors came and went, that was the way of the world, but as long as the change of regime didn't affect life in the village all was well. It could normally be taken for granted that the village wouldn't be affected. Great political upheavals started in the cities and ended in the cities, they didn't overflow into the countryside.

When Irtazuddin arrived at the school he found that almost all the teachers were absent. A strong rumour was going round to the effect that the army had started spreading outwards from Mymensingh. A large detachment was said to have gone to Haluaghat, and it might come on to Nilganj any time. The headmaster was in school, for he always attended daily from ten till five regardless of whether or not any pupils were present. Mr Saghir and Mr Kalipad were also there.

Mr Saghir was playing a good game of chess today, and Mr Kalipad wasn't making much progress. His queen was hemmed in, and it looked as if he had no alternative but to sacrifice her. The maths teacher's face was wreathed in smiles; he could hardly contain his jubilation. When he saw Irtazuddin he hailed him cheerfully.

"Have you heard? The army are approaching Nilganj."

"Is that so?" asked Irtazuddin.

"Go and see the headmaster, he's got all the latest news."

"Have the army made any announcement about their coming?"

"No, of course not. Do you expect them to give formal notice of their arrival? They'll appear quite unexpectedly. And check mate the king with a straight rook. Ha-ha!"

"What are you laughing about? The army are on their way, is that anything to be happy about?"

"It makes no difference to us, we're neither with the hares nor with the hounds. The sooner the situation calms down the better. Then we can go on teaching our pupils and drawing our salaries – what more do we want?"

Irtazuddin set off for the headmaster's office while Mr Saghir bent over his chessboard. He could take the queen if he wished, but he preferred not to. Let her stay as she was, in check. He could have her later, for there was no way she could escape. He moved one of his bishops without much premeditation: since his opponent's queen was in check there was no need to think too deeply.

Mr Monsur the headmaster had his head down and was busy writing something. He looked up when Irtazuddin came in.

"What's wrong?" asked Irtazuddin.

Mr Monsur made no reply. He was always loath to discuss his personal affairs; it went against the grain. The truth was that for the past three nights he hadn't had a wink of sleep. His wife had come back to live with him again, and normally her mental state improved when she was with him; but this time was an exception. At the moment she couldn't even recognize him as her husband. When she saw him entering the bedroom one night she had started shrieking.

"Who are you? What are you doing in my room? Watch your step, I'm warning you!"

"Ashiya, it's me, can't you recognize me? It's me. Me."

"Stop it, don't you dare go 'me-me-me' like that! I'm warning you!"

The headmaster was having to sleep in another room, and Ashiya had to be kept under lock and key. If she was allowed out she would go wandering by the riverside on her own.

"I hear the army are coming this way," said Irtazuddin.

"They're going to come, no doubt about it," said the headmaster as he laid his pen down.

"What's the point in their coming to out of the way places like this?"

"They have to do it if they want to gain full control of the country. The only question is when they will arrive. They've already seized control of the towns, now it's just a matter of fanning out. They're not meeting any resistance, therefore the wider deployment is likely to take place very soon."

"Will there be any resistance in future?"

"Certainly there will. Who knows, maybe it's already started. The days ahead are full of horrors, Mr Irtaz. Nobody realizes that, but I can see it all."

"How is your wife?"

"Not well. It was a mistake to bring her here, I think she was better off staying with her parents and brothers. It was a wrong decision of mine to bring her here."

"It's very hard for humans to judge which of their actions are wrong and which are right. Often it's impossible to know. Only God can tell what is wrong and what is right."

"That's the big advantage you true believers have," remarked Mr Monsur with a deep sigh, "you can entrust all responsibility for everything to God and lead your own lives unconcerned. Even if some major crisis comes along people like you can accept it as the will of God and carry on acting normally."

"Isn't that a good thing?"

"No, it isn't. Man has been provided with a conscience, he is endowed with the power of thought, he has inherited the highly subtle skill of logic as his birthright. If after all that he accepts everything as God's will and shrugs off responsibility, how can that be right?"

"God has told us to be long-suffering."

"Well, that's great, just keep suffering as long as you can. Have you had any news of your younger brother? Shahed, that's his name isn't it?"

"You're in rather low spirits today," observed Irtazuddin.

Mr Monsur made no comment. When a person's spirits are high they long to share their happiness with those they love, but when they're feeling low they have no desire to beat their drum and go around telling everyone.

"Reverend!"

"Yes, headmaster?"

"Have you ever heard of a man called Confucius?"

"No, indeed."

"A renowned Chinese philosopher. He used to speak of the Five Relationships. They were five specially significant types of bond. Would you like to know what these Five Relationships were?"

Irtazuddin had started to get restless. It was prayer time. The time slot for the prayer was limited. If the headmaster launched into an analysis of the Five Relationships the limit might be passed. Also, the wife of the officer in charge at the local police station had sent word that she urgently needed to see him and he would have to go over there as well, though he had no idea what the urgent business could be.

"Listen, Moulana sahib, these are the Five Relationships: the one between a ruler and his subject; the one between a husband and his wife; the one between a father and his son; the one between an elder brother and a younger brother; and the one between two friends. See?"

"I see. But I don't understand why you suddenly brought up the matter of relationships."

"Because not a single one applies to me. As a subject I have no relationship with the rulers of Pakistan. I have no relationship with my wife. I don't have a son with whom to have a paternal relationship. And I have no brothers and no friends."

"What, no friends at all?" asked Irtazuddin gently.

"Oh, yes, I have," the headmaster quickly conceded, "I have you. I wasn't thinking of you. One always overlooks the people one is nearest to."

"It's prayer time," said Irtazuddin as he rose to his feet. "May I go now?"

As soon as a Muslim stands on the prayer mat ready to pray he is supposed to clear all wordly thoughts from his mind. Usually Irtazuddin managed to do that, but this time he failed. Thoughts of the Chinese philosopher named Confucius kept floating through his mind. Even as he was reciting the opening surah, the *Fatiha*, it struck him that Confucius had got it wrong, he had missed out the two most important relationships of all: the relationship between mother and son, and that between mother and daughter. Had he missed out these two intentionally, or as a result of an oversight? Perhaps he hadn't had a good relationship with his own mother.

Irtazuddin made a mistake in the prayer ritual and had to start all over again. This time it was the police inspector's wife who came drifting into his thoughts. He knew her name but couldn't recall it just now.

When a man was at his prayers it was as though he was standing face to face with God. And if, while facing God, he then strained to recall some woman's name, well, that was not merely gross impertinence, it was something even worse. Irtazuddin tried desperately not to search for the name, but it was no use. It was in the back of his mind – that name, that name, it was the name of some kind of fruit. What fruit? Grape? Pomegranate? There was a K in it. He could think of one fruit beginning with K, but nobody would name their child after it: Kola. It meant banana. No, no! Then what *was* her name?

Meanwhile Mr Saghir had started making a big fuss. He had lost the game even though he had taken Mr Kalipad's queen. It had been a mistake to take the queen at all. She had been placed there as a bait, and like a fool he had taken the bait and then got into difficulties.

"Pure trickery, that's what it was," roared Mr Saghir. "Tricking people isn't chess."

"In what way was I tricking you?"

"You pretend you don't know? You Hindus are a deceitful lot. It's no bad thing that the army are catching all the Hindu men, trimming their willies and turning them into Muslims. They should cut off yours as well."

"What on earth are you on about?"

"I'm stating a simple truth. Don't ever play tricky games with me again. Do you understand? If you want to play with me, play straight."

"But it's not me who wants to play, it's you who force me to do so."

"I force you to play?"

"Most certainly."

"I see you're not just a trickster, you're a first class liar as well!"

"Me, a liar?"

"Oh, put a sock in it!"

"Why are you raising your voice like that?"

"I said stop it. Silence, you *malaun*°!"

When Irtazuddin finished his prayers and returned to the common room he saw that the two men had resolved their differences and sat down to another game of chess. Maybe Confucius had been right, the relationship of friend to friend was an important one. Just as having a brother or a sister was a matter of good fortune, so was having a real friend.

The O.C.'s wife° took Irtazuddin by surprise when she ducked down to touch his feet as a sign of profound respect. Irtazuddin was quite upset by this submissive gesture. At that very moment the young woman's name came to his mind: she was called Komola°.

"My dear," said Irtazuddin, "bowing low to give a *salaam* is not correct. A human being should never bow in front of any entity except God. This is what God himself has ordained."

"That kind of rule is all right for learned gentlemen like yourself," replied Komola shyly, "not for very ordinary people like me. I had a dream, and that's why I asked you to come, to discuss the dream I had."

"But I'm not qualified to analyse dreams. Still, do tell me all about yours. At what time did you have it?"

"In the early hours, before dawn. I'd just had the dream and woken up when I heard a cock crow. In the dream I saw a huge open area covered with reeds and their tall white plumes of flower. I ran hither and thither in delight. After some time I stopped running around and sat down to rest. Then I noticed that there were hundreds of grass seeds caught in the fabric of my sari. I was surprised, and wondered how I'd picked up so many grass seeds in an area of reed beds. I started picking the grass spikes out of the cloth, but every time I pulled one out a spot of blood appeared in its place. Soon my whole sari was covered in blood. That's what I saw in my dream. Ever since then I've been feeling rather uneasy."

"You shouldn't feel uneasy just because of a dream," said Irtazuddin. "Expectant mothers always tend to be nervous, and that often causes unpleasant nightmares."

"Is there nothing more to it than that?"

"God sometimes sends people warnings through their dreams. However He sends his messages in coded form, and it's hard to draw the correct conclusions from them. I'm afraid I don't have sufficient knowledge for that, I'm rather a literal minded fellow."

"Uncle, you must come and have supper with us this evening."

"Let's leave it for another time, dear niece."

"No, you must eat with us today. Today's a special day for me."

"What kind of special day? Is it your wedding anniversary?"

Komola hung her head and made no reply, but smiled.

"I'll definitely come to supper then," said Irtazuddin.

28

The date was 14ᵗʰ April 1971, a Wednesday.

The officer in charge of Nilganj police station, Sadrul Amin, was sitting on a cane stool outside his quarters. He was feeling exceedingly hungry, but he couldn't ask his wife when dinner would be ready because she was confined to bed. She had been racked by labour pains since morning and was not at all in good shape. It was her first pregnancy so it was bound to be difficult, but if Sadrul Amin had realized it would be this bad he would have taken her to her parents' home for the delivery. They could have seen to everything, fetching doctors and herbalists and doing whatever else was needed. Then when the time came he would have received a telegram: "A BOY CONGRATULATIONS". He would have bought some celebratory sweetmeats and gone to his parents-in-law's place in triumph. But instead of that he had been a fool and kept his wife at home with him. Now he was totally out of his depth. There was a properly qualified doctor available in Nandina and he had sent a constable there to fetch him, but the doctor hadn't yet come and there was no sign of the constable either. Sadrul Amin suspected that instead of going to Nandina the constable had headed for his own village home. Nowadays orders were no longer orders, everyone was doing just as they pleased. There should have been ten constables, one second officer and one sergeant at the station, but now there were only four men in all. Nor were they performing any duties; they were spending their days and nights snoozing contentedly. Instead of springing to their feet and giving a salute the moment they caught sight of the O.C., now they merely turned over in bed and yawned.

Three armed robbers, Harun Majhi and two of his associates, had been held in the police cell for the past two weeks, and that created another problem for Sadrul Amin – what to do with them. In normal times he would have received the Pakistan Police medal for having apprehended such a notorious dacoit as Harun Majhi, but in the present circumstances all he was receiving was a lot of grief. He was unable to pass the prisoners on to headquarters, and instead was having to feed them with meals from his own kitchen. The most convenient thing would be to release Harun Majhi and then decamp with his wife to her parents' home. He could come back when the situation returned to normal. At the moment it was impossible to tell what was going on – the country was neither Pakistan nor Bangladesh.

Human beings couldn't go on living in this way. Only the wild beasts in the jungle could live entirely without law and order. They managed to do without police stations or courts; but human beings needed these things.

The O.C.'s living quarters were within the police compound. Village women would never venture inside the compound; they regarded the whole police station with a mixture of fear and suspicion. But Sadrul Amin was fortunate in that two women were now there attending to his wife in her confinement. One was the Haji's wife, the other was a village midwife everyone called Shoti. Shoti was the local expert and could be relied on. The Haji's wife was an elderly woman, and older women were also reliable; they could draw on long experience to solve any problems which might arise.

Sadrul Amin was none too optimistic. He had had an ominous feeling since morning, as if something dreadful was going to happen. Could that dreadful thing be his wife's death? The moment such thoughts came to his mind he felt utterly drained and his throat went dry. When people are worried they feel hungrier than usual, and Sadrul Amin was now suffering from hunger as much as anything else.

Of course there were snack foods in the house, puffed rice, rice flakes, jaggery and so on, and if he wanted he could get someone to fetch something of that kind, but he couldn't bring himself to do so. It wouldn't be right to sit down to a bowl of puffed rice and molasses while his wife was in such a critical condition.

He would have liked to go and sit with his wife for a while. No doubt the poor girl was feeling really frightened. Normally when a woman was giving birth to her first child she would have her mother and various aunts hovering around her, but Komola had none of her relatives near. If she knew her husband was sitting beside her holding her hand she would have more confidence. But it wasn't possible, local custom was strict – no men were allowed into the room where delivery was to take place. Only when the woman was able to take her newborn baby and move to another room could her husband or other male relatives join her. At one stage Sadrul Amin thought, bother the rules, I'll go and sit by her anyhow. He had been most embarrassed the night before, when he'd seen the festive meal of pulao and *korma* his wife had prepared. He had asked her what it was all about, and she had smiled and said nothing. Only when Irtazuddin had arrived as an invited guest had the truth come out: it was their wedding anniversary. It had been so bad of him to forget the date.

Sadrul Amin lit a cigarette. Smoking on an empty stomach made his whole body squirm, and he felt he was going to get sick. Then the Haji's wife came from the confinement room. She was a *haji* herself, as she and her husband had performed the *hajj* pilgrimage together, and to prove it she always went around in a burqa. But though she covered her face she was quite modern in outlook and did not mind speaking to unrelated males. She was not like most other women in Nilganj who, on catching sight of a strange man, would prepare to flee for their lives or else freeze into lifeless stumps.

"Things aren't going well," said the Haji's wife in a grim tone, looking Sadrul Amin in the eye. "You should call on God to assist. And you should send someone to see the Moulana in Kolosh-hati and get some *utar*. We'll need to wash the navel with *utar*."

"What's *utar*?"

"Holy water, water that's had a prayer said over it. *Utar* from the Moulana in Kolosh-hati is our last resort. So send a policeman there quickly."

"Right."

Sadrul Amin set off across the compound towards the office. The sky had clouded over and drops of rain were falling. Everything that was going on today seemed half-hearted and inadequate. If it was going to rain it should do so in buckets, and the sky should be really black.

A clanking noise came from the lock-up. Harun Majhi had seen Sadrul Amin coming.

"I'm 'ungry, mister O.C.," he called, baring his gleaming white teeth in a smile. "Aren't you gonna feed us? Yesterday we 'ad nice pulao and korma, today it looks like water only."

"Quiet, you!"

"But I'm 'ungry. If ya wanna 'ang me ya can 'ang me, but if ya starve me to death that ain't justice, it ain't."

"Silence, you wretch!"

Harun Majhi laughed. His skin was jet black, his face amiable, even endearing. Seeing him nobody would guess that he had committed up to a dozen murders in cold blood.

"We're having problems at home," said Sadrul Amin. "No cooking has been done today."

"So we gotta starve? Can't ya rustle up some puffed rice or something?"

Yes, why not rustle up a snack, that was a good idea. Sadrul Amin would have a bite to eat himself. He must also send someone for the *utar*, but looking around he couldn't see any of his constables. How times had changed! Before there had always been someone on sentry duty twenty-four hours a day, and the hours had been sounded on a gong; in fact the village people had relied on the police station gong for telling the time. But now there was none of that. Sadrul Amin stepped up onto the verandah of the police station. Looking out, he suddenly saw that two jeeps and three trucks were approaching. They were moving slowly. The road surface was very uneven, so there was no way they could go any faster. Sadrul Amin's heart started beating wildly. The army had arrived. *Ya gafurur rahim!* Oh, merciful God, the army!

The convoy was being led by Colonel Mushtaq of the Panjab Regiment. He had been heading for Bhairab, but had just received orders not to proceed. Instead he was to halt in Nilganj. No reasons had been given; the wireless message had been a very brief one. Perhaps there had been some trouble on the road ahead. A certain amount of trouble was being created here and there, but it was insignificant. For example a few over-zealous youths might aim their .303 rifles at the convoy and fire a few shots: a ridiculous exercise, of course, though sometimes the consequences of such foolish capers could be unfortunate. Up to now the colonel's unit had not suffered any damage. There were reports that the Bengali section of the army had revolted, but so far nothing about their having gone into battle. They had no ammunition, though of course they could soon solve that problem, as India was right there beside them. India had been waiting since 1947 for a chance to teach Pakistan a lesson, and this was their opportunity. The ignorant Bengalis didn't realize what India actually wanted, which was to take over East Pakistan. Anyway, India wouldn't get any chance to do that; it would be duly chastised, and at the same time the pesky Bengalis would also be taught a lesson.

Colonel Mushtaq's jeep shuddered violently and came to a halt. With a disgusted look he craned to look at the vehicle's wheels from his window. Evidently a tyre had been punctured, and that meant a ten minute delay. Ten minutes is a long time for a convoy on the move; in that space of time some major mishap could occur. At the moment there was no guerrilla activity in the countryside. If there had been he would have made his men get out of their vehicles and stay on the alert, but there was no need for such caution now. This was an unmade road in a poor area, and there were paddy fields on either side, there was nothing to fear. The colonel got down from the jeep and stood watching the men change the wheel. He was sweating in the heat. If they had to spend the night in Nilganj he would make sure he got a shower.

He had been going around in the same khaki uniform for three days, and all the sweating was making him look emaciated. It was a sordid business. He had last week's *Newsweek* with him but hadn't yet had time to read it; maybe he'd be able to do so tonight. It was taking those men a long time to change the wheel. There was too much sloppiness going on; in wartime things like that ought to be fixed in a matter of seconds. Colonel Mushtaq frowned with annoyance but said nothing.

The O.C. of Nilganj police station saluted the colonel. Behind him three constables were standing in the present arms position.

"*Sab thik hay?*" asked the colonel in Urdu. "Is everything all right?"

"Yes, sir," replied Sadrul Amin in English.
"Very good. What's your name?"
"Sadrul Amin."
"An excellent name!"

The colonel smiled. Sadrul Amin seemed to have lost both the blood in his veins and the hungry feeling in his stomach, and even the sight of the colonel's smile did nothing to dispel his discomfiture. His heart was still beating wildly.

The colonel held out his hand and Sadrul Amin shook it.

"Why are you afraid? Don't be frightened," said the colonel solemnly.

That was at three o'clock in the afternoon. Two hours later the scene had changed.

Sadrul Amin was led to the bank of the Sohagi river and shot dead. He was not the only one; besides him there were five Hindu men and two students from Ananda Mohan College, who were Muslims.

In the seconds before he died Sadrul Amin was anxiously wondering whether the man he'd sent to fetch the holy water had come back yet.

Some people have profound philosophical thoughts when they are about to die, but Sadrul Amin could only think of holy water. He had rather enjoyed running that quaint village word for it over his tongue – *utar*.

Nilganj police station was full of life and bustle. Soldiers had been put on sentry duty at the gate. Two pressurized vapour lamps had been hung up outside the main building and countless insects were buzzing around them, attracted by the brilliant light and having a rare time.

Behind the station was a brick-lined well with a raised rim, next to which the colonel's tent had been set up. Colonel Mushtaq Ahmed was sitting on a chair outside the tent with his feet propped up on a stool, and was trying to overcome his weariness. He hadn't yet had a chance to take off the clothes he'd been stuck in for three days, but intended to do so shortly. A bucket of cold water drawn from the well had been placed ready for him to bathe with, but before having his bath he wanted to make sure that adequate food and accommodation had been arranged for his troops. Proper accommodation for all the soldiers was not vital but food was, as the whole company had had virtually nothing to eat all day.

Mushtaq Ahmed was reasonably satisfied with the feeding arrangements that had been made. In villages there weren't any shops so it was difficult to get hold of all that was needed, but here sufficient supplies had been obtained. Two goats had been slaughtered and the cooking had begun. It wasn't going to be possible to make chapatis, so the menu would be meat curry with rice. A Bengali-type meal, since they were on the Bengalis' home ground. To hungry men any kind of food would seem palatable.

Mushtaq Ahmed lit a cigar and sat staring up at the sky. It was clear and hundreds of stars were twinkling. There, he could see the seven sisters; it was never possible to see them so clearly from the city. Those seven stars lay close to the horizon, so you needed a wide open space to view them properly. The police compound was very open, with scarcely any vegetation inside a two hundred yard radius. This was an important point in the present circumstances. Every police station needed to be outside the range of a .303 rifle, in case any desperado tried shooting at it from behind the cover of trees and bushes.

Somebody had brought a full mug of coffee and set it beside Mushtaq Ahmed. In fact it was Farid Uddin who had brought it, the second officer of Nilganj police station, who had now been made interim O.C. Farid Uddin remained standing to attention in front of the colonel. He couldn't very well go away, yet he could hardly endure standing there, and his knees were shaking. It felt like being face to face with death itself.

"Do you have something on your mind?" asked Mushtaq Ahmed, sipping his coffee.

"Yes, sir," replied Farid Uddin, without having understood the question.

"Speak up, then."

Farid Uddin went on standing there mutely just as before. The colonel gestured to him to go away, but Farid Uddin failed to understand the gesture too. To tell the truth he was not in his right mind. He was still struggling to comprehend how anyone could put so many people to death in such a casual way. They had led them to the riverside and made them line up on the bank. Before anyone realized what was going on an officer, stifling a yawn, had given the order to fire. The burst of gunfire had been like a brief piece of music. Even then Farid Uddin had not taken in the fact that people were being killed. The whole scene had been like a dream. Surely it must have been a dream, such ghastly things never happen in real life. In real life nobody yawns while giving the order to fire. And he hadn't just imagined that detail about yawning, he had been right next to the officer who gave the order, a tall beanpole of a man with a thin moustache and a blotch of leucopathy on his lower lip. Farid Uddin knew that for the rest of his days he would have endless nightmares with this frightful man in them.

Again the colonel signed to Farid Uddin to go away. The coffee was good, and he wished to enjoy it on his own. He needed it to suppress his hunger too, for the evening meal wouldn't be ready until much later.

A short time later Farid Uddin, sweating uncomfortably, was back in the office. He was occupying the O.C.'s chair. No soldiers were present, only two police constables sitting ashen-faced on the long bench. In the chair opposite Farid Uddin sat Harun Majhi, looking very pleased with himself. The colonel had ordered the release of all the occupants of the police cells.

All the orders now were verbal, nothing was being put down in writing. This would surely cause problems in the future. At some point an entry would have to be put in the general diary: *By oral command issued by Colonel Mushtaq Ahmed all persons detained in the police cells were released. Among those released was the notorious dacoit Harun Majhi.*

The incident at the riverside also needed to be recorded, but how should he describe it? He had been present at the time, and at some stage someone might ask why, given that this event had taken place in the presence of a police officer, the latter had raised no objections. Responsibility for maintaining law and order rested with the local police. They might say to him, Farid Uddin, why did you not enter a charge against the army under Section 324 of the Criminal Justice Code? Section 324 clearly states that 'causing deliberate harm by lethal weapon or other lethal means' is an offence. Or indeed a charge could have been entered under Section 148, 'affray involving the use of dangerous weapons'.

"Mister O.C.!"

Farid Uddin jumped. Harun Majhi was sitting there with his hand stretched out and a big smile on his face.

"What's the matter?" asked Farid Uddin.

"Give us a fag or something, Mister O.C., sir. I could do with a smoke."

Farid Uddin didn't argue; he handed Harun Majhi a cigarette. He felt like smoking one himself, yet somehow didn't quite dare to do so.

"Situation's pretty grave, Mister O.C., sir."

"Mm."

"One word of command, eight men dead. Voice of doom. What ya say, sir?"

"Mm."

"That's the Paki army for you. They like to settle the score with a bullet. Pay on the spot, cash down, no credit."

"Do stop your chatter, Harun."

"What'd our old O.C. sahib do when 'e was about to die?" persisted Harun Majhi, lowering his voice. "Did 'e cry?"

"I don't know."

"'Ow come? You was there with 'im."

"No, I wasn't."

"Eh? When they gave orders to grab some 'indus and bring 'em in – I thought it was you as nabbed 'em?"

"Harun," said Farid Uddin sharply, "the situation is serious. The less you speak the better for everyone. They've let you out – why not go home and get back to your robbery. Cut out the talking."

"These military guys, are they gonna stay 'ere?"

"I've no idea."

"The old O.C., 'is wife was gonna 'ave a baby, d'ya know what 'appened about that? Did she 'ave 'er baby?"

"I've no idea."

"O.C. sent a chap to get some *utar* water – did 'e get any? Surely ya know?"

"Just shut up, will you, Harun."

"A'right, sir, if that's what ya want, I'll shut me gob. Just gimme another fag."

Silently Farid Uddin passed him another cigarette. Harun Majhi lit it from the stub of his first one, which was still glowing.

"That old O.C. of ours," Harun went on, "Mister Sadrul I mean, 'e was a very brave man, 'e was. 'E 'ad the guts of a tiger."

Farid Uddin made no comment. His head had suddenly started splitting, and he could hardly hold it up. He'd never felt like this before; what was going on?

"Mister O.C., sir, d'y' know how Mister Sadrul caught me? Let me tell ya. It's a good story."

"I don't care for stories. Just pipe down."

"I'd gone to me wife's brother's place. I'd 'eard they'd 'ad another son. I took a proper look at the baby and gave 'em a nice crisp 'undred rupee note for luck. Wife's brother says, Brother-in-law, he says, why not stay 'ere tonight, 'ave pot luck with us, go on. So in the end I agree. During the night, in the wee hours, police come and surround the place. I 'ad me gun with me, it was in me bag, and it was loaded. There's me whippin' it outa the bag when the O.C. comes in through the door. I'm gonna shoot you, Mister O.C., I says. Go on then, 'e says, you can shoot me. 'Ain't easy to talk like that when yer standing in front of a gun, I can tell ya. Needs guts. Guts of a tiger. O.C. 'ad the guts of a tiger."

"That's enough, Harun. One more word and I'll shove you back in the lockup."

"Not possible," objected Harun with a broad grin. "I been freed by the military, you ain't got the power. Maybe if Mister Sadrul Amin 'ad been around... 'E 'ad the guts of a tiger, and you, you 'ave the guts of a civet, I'd say. Ha ha! Sorry, Mister O.C., sir, please don't take offence. A true word can cause no offence, as they say."

The cooking was done, and the food was being doled out to the men. The colonel was bathing next to the well: he was sitting completely naked on a low stool while two batmen poured buckets of ice cold water from the well over his head. He was deriving the greatest satisfaction from his bath; all the tiredness had slipped from his body and he felt exhilarated. Right now a few beers would have added to his sense of wellbeing, but he had none with him. He did have a bottle of vodka and one of good French wine. The wine was being reserved for a special occasion: 11th May, his wedding anniversary. Rozina had promised him that by hook or by crook she would get to *Bangal Mulk* for that day. They had been together for every one of their anniversaries throughout the thirteen years they had been married, and this time was to be no exception. He had no idea how Rozina was going to get to *Bangal Mulk* in wartime, but maybe she would manage, for she had no lack of intelligence or determination. Even more to the point, she was the niece of Lieutenant General Gul Hassan Khan, and there is a lot that a general can do.

While the colonel was still having his bath a message came on the wireless – Colonel Mushtaq was to set off for Durgapur with his troops immediately. When he heard this the colonel swore under his breath. The bastards! But it was not clear who he was referring to.

The company set off for Durgapur at 3 am. At the same time the wife of the late police Officer in Command Sadrul Amin gave birth to a boy. The baby had powerful lungs, and his cries brought the police compound to life: "Waaa! Waaa!" The colonel could hear these cries as he got into his jeep and he realized that a baby had just been born. The crying of a newborn baby is supposed to be a good omen, so he felt optimistic about the journey ahead and looked pleased as he took his seat in the vehicle.

Rain had fallen steadily all morning. Around noon it had eased off for a while, then in the afternoon the sky had darkened and more rain had come. Asmani was watching it come down. Standing in the verandah at Darogabari she had an extensive view. The sight of falling rain in a wide open arena was quite impressive. A grey veil seemed to be drifting down from the heavens, sometimes getting swirled and distorted by the breeze. It was wonderful. One never saw rain like this in the city. From the first floor Asmani could see Runi getting wet; she had stolen downstairs and out into the garden, and was trying to pick some jasmine flowers. If Sarfaraz Miah saw her she would receive a severe scolding, and then, more worryingly, she would get a fever again. Her temperature had only recently got back to normal. Asmani knew she should give her daughter a little lecture, but she didn't feel up to it. When disciplining a child both parents needed to be involved: one could do the ticking-off while the other soothed and comforted. But who would do the soothing bit now? Thinking of Shahed almost made tears come to Asmani's eyes, but she pulled herself together, telling herself that this was not the right time to be weepy. Better to go on watching the rain. Now, that image of the rain falling like a veil, how come no author had ever used it? Did writers always live in cities? When she next saw Shahed she would raise the subject of rain and veils with him. Where was he now, she wondered, and was it raining there too, and if so, was he watching it fall? She doubted that he would be watching it, for Shahed wasn't the least bit poetic by nature. On rainy days what he really liked to do was to wrap himself up in a quilt and have a good sleep. When he woke up again he would raise his head from the pillow and say something like, "How about a spot of *khichuri* for lunch, darling? *Khichuri* with fried aubergines, that would be perfect." He was funny in his choice of foods. The things that went best with *khichuri* were hilsa fish or meat *bhuna*; fried aubergines with *khichuri* was a weird combination.

From somewhere inside the house Mr Motaleb was calling. "Asmani! Where has she got to? Asmani!"

Asmani didn't feel like leaving the verandah. There was Runi, out in the rain, stealing flowers and casting furtive glances around her, and Asmani was relishing the sight. Her little daughter was getting quite rebellious. Asmani wouldn't often get such opportunities as this to observe the child's latest acts of naughtiness from a secret vantage point. And apart from that Asmani could guess all too easily why Mr Motaleb was calling for her: he wanted to have a little chat. While talking to her he would stare at her intently. He would pretend to offer sympathy and lay his hand on her back. What a disgusting character he was. His filthy nature was becoming clearer and clearer as the days went by. The things he talked about were odd too. He was forever going on about the army, and he often told the same story two or three times over, detailed descriptions of ghastly things soldiers had done. This type of conversation was pointless, and Asmani felt she couldn't stand hearing another word about the army.

"Asmani! Asmani!"

"Yes, uncle! I'm coming!"

Even after saying she was on her way Asmani stayed standing there for some moments. Every minute she delayed seeing Mr Motaleb was worth while. It would mean one less minute of torture.

When she got there Asmani realized Mr Motaleb hadn't just called her for a chat after all. Something was going on. The entire household had assembled in Sarfaraz Miah's bedroom. Sarfaraz Miah himself was reclining in an easy chair, smoking a hookah with a long stem; he appeared to be enjoying his smoke. A large cup of tea had been placed on the arm of his chair. Mr Motaleb's face was grey, he seemed upset and was having trouble articulating his words. All the other members of the household were gathered there, and all of them looked equally grave; only Mr Sarfaraz was his normal self. He stopped puffing at the hookah, picked up his cup of tea and calmly started sipping it. After each sip he extended the tip of his tongue and waggled it; evidently the tea was rather hot.

Asmani couldn't imagine why this meeting had been called, but she didn't like to ask, so she stood there in silence.

"What's your opinion, father?" Mr Motaleb was saying to Sarfaraz Miah.

"We shouldn't take too much notice of rumours," replied Mr Sarfaraz, sipping his tea. "It's an unlikely story, soldiers going from house to house seizing the girls and making off with them. You shouldn't listen to hearsay. The Pakistan army is one of the most prestigious in the world. Boys from respectable families go into it. They're world famous for their gentlemanly behaviour. How can you forget all that?"

"What you say is quite true, father," said Mr Motaleb. "I hadn't thought of it that way."

"There's another thing," said Mr Sarfaraz. "This is Darogabari. Darogabari has a certain prestige. The army know how to show respect where respect is due, that's something they are trained to understand."

"You're quite right," said Mr Motaleb. "Let's forget about evacuating for the time being."

"Definitely forget it. Where would you go, now, with all this rain? We can't just go and move in with anyone we feel like."

"That's an excellent point," agreed Mr Motaleb promptly, "in this rainy weather how can we expect anyone to take the whole crowd of us in?"

"Never trust rumours," said Mr Sarfaraz, draining his teacup. "Trust God instead. Close the gates, say the *Ayatul Kursi* and sit tight. God willing, no ill will befall us."

"And if the army really did come and see that the occupants of Darogabari had fled, they would suspect something wasn't quite right about us," added Mr Motaleb.

"There *is* something not right," retorted Mr Sarfaraz. "You yourself are the thing which isn't quite right. Now quit all this faffing about. I can't stand so much fuss of a morning. Go and have your meeting somewhere else."

The person who had delivered the warning about the army's intentions was a man called Quddus. He was a simple man, dressed in a vest and lungi. He was squatting on the ground with his head bowed. Gentlefolk tend to treat such simple people's words with scepticism at the best of times.

"It's all right, Quddus," said Mr Motaleb. "You can go now. We'll send for you if and when we consider it appropriate."

Quddus did not move from where he was.

"You'll never get time to send for me," he said firmly. "Listen while I tell you, you gotta leave now. Those army fellas are waiting for the rain to stop. Soon as the rain eases off they're gonna come out in swarms. And the first place they're gonna visit is Darogabari."

"How can you be so sure?" asked Mr Motaleb. "Surely the army haven't been discussing their plans with you?"

"Let's say they have," said Quddus with a shrug. "You must do what I say, there's no time to lose. Time is limited."

"Why should they come to Darogabari first?"

"They've got Mozid Miah with them. He's got a long-standing grudge against you folk in Darogabari."

"He may have a grudge," said Mr Motaleb, "but the army hasn't."

"I'm begging you on bended knee, take heed of what I say."

"Right, Quddus," said Mr Motaleb, "you pop along now. We're going to stay put. It's not a good idea to run away from the house, the army might get suspicious. Soldiers are always very suspicious-minded in wartime."

"Uncle! Please don't ignore what I said!"

"I have listened carefully to all that you had to say. Now it's up to us to make up our own minds and take our own decisions. We can't rely solely on your judgment."

Quddus got up and went away.

"I don't like this," said Jaheda. "Why not do as he suggests?"

"If we're going to keep listening to rumours we're done for. I've got a better idea, you should get some food ready for the soldiers. Chicken *korma* and parathas. They love parathas and meat."

Jaheda went off to prepare the parathas and meat.

The rain eased off shortly before sunset. And lo and behold, a file of soldiers appeared at Darogabari just as dusk was gathering. With them was Mozid, the homeopathic doctor whom Quddus had mentioned. Sarfaraz Miah, dressed in a *kurta*, came out of the house and Dr Mozid darted forwards to touch his feet in respect.

"What's all this about, Mozid?" asked Sarfaraz.

"They want to ask you a couple of questions."

"And why are you accompanying them?"

"They didn't know how to get here, they asked me to show them the way. I couldn't say no, seeing as the army had requested it. These fellows aren't the kind who take no for an answer."

"So you're leading them around? Marvellous."

The leader of the troop was a young captain. Very courteously Sarfaraz Miah invited him to take a seat. But the captain had no use for courtesy.

"Awami League, are you?" he demanded roughly in Urdu.

Sarfaraz Miah was outraged. Here he was, a gentleman ninety years old, and this slip of a boy was addressing him as *tum*, the familiar form for 'you' in Urdu. However he suppressed his annoyance and replied humbly in Urdu, "No sir, Muslim League."

"Are you a Muslim?"

"Yes, sir."

"Where's your beard?"

At this point Sarfaraz Miah made a foolish mistake. Speaking in perfect Urdu, he reminded the captain that he himself was a Muslim who had no beard. How could a beardless Muslim take another to task for not being bearded?

It was unlikely that an army officer would swallow such insolence calmly. At a signal from the captain one of the soldiers came up and gave Sarfaraz Miah a kick with his boot. Sarfaraz Miah collapsed and rolled off the verandah onto a flowerbed. No sound came from his lips.

There were three other males in the household apart from Mr Sarfaraz and Mr Motaleb, but they had been hiding. At this point they came out into the open. The soldiers apprehended all the men except Sarfaraz Miah and led them away.

They were shot the same evening. Mr Sarfaraz died in the early hours of the following day, after vomiting blood all night long.

30

"Where are we going, Mummy?" asked Runi.

Asmani did not know how to answer her daughter's question, as she herself had no idea where they were heading for. They had boarded the boat in the mid morning. It was quite a sizeable country boat with a sail, though the sail was not in use at the moment as the two boatmen were poling the boat along. They were following an irrigation channel of no great breadth, which was still only partly filled with water. In addition to the entire female side of the Darogabari family there were two male passengers on board. One was the Quddus who had been pleading with Mr Motaleb the day before. Today he was looking quite smart: he was wearing a *kurta* and a pair of *paijama*, and had a blue skullcap on his head. He was chewing *paan* in quite a relaxed manner. His lips were bright red from the juice and from time to time he wiped them with the sleeve of his *kurta*, which was getting covered with red smears. The other man was a stranger, a Hindu gentleman called Keshob babu. Even in the heat of the day he was wearing a heavy shawl. He was lying face down on the deck of the boat. This gentleman was a minor functionary, a *peshkar*, at Mymensingh Judge Court, who had fled to his village home with his two daughters when the situation had begun to look dangerous. When the army had approached the village he had sent the daughters away to his aunt's home in Ichapur, and now he was on his way to find out how they were. Keshob babu was elderly and in poor health. He suffered from asthma, and had been overtaken by an attack of it soon after boarding the boat. He was tossing and turning, trying to get air into his lungs but feeling stifled. Asmani had no idea who he was or where he was hoping to get to along with the rest of them. She seemed to have lost interest in such matters. As far as she was concerned the boat could go wherever it pleased, it made no difference to her.

The open end of the boat's awning had a sari stretched over it to prevent strangers from seeing the women inside. Asmani was peeping out through a gap in the screen, while the women inside wept and keened in subdued tones. Their keening sounded quite surreal, and came in intermittent waves. For a while they would all be quiet, and then they would all start wailing in unison again.

Asmani just sat there quietly. She was slightly embarrassed by the fact that she wasn't crying too, and indeed wasn't even feeling like crying. Why was that? She was virtually a member of the family by now, and she had witnessed those horrendous events with her own eyes, so why wasn't she ready to weep and wail?

Runi was sitting on the deck, trying to reach the water with her fingers. The way she was leaning over the gunwales she might easily fall into the canal. Asmani knew she should say a few words of reprimand, yet she couldn't be bothered. If the child fell in, she fell in.

"Where are we going, Mummy?" Runi asked again.

"I don't know," replied Asmani peevishly.

"Why don't you know?"

Asmani remained silent.

"Tell me, Mummy, where are we going?"

"We're heading for Ichapur." It was Quddus who gave this answer.

"Why are we going to Ichapur?"

"Runi, will you kindly keep quiet," said Asmani.

"Why should I keep quiet?"

Asmani said nothing, and Quddus took over. "We're going there to escape from the soldiers, sweetheart."

"Are the soldiers killing every single person?"

"Almost, yes."
"Aren't there any soldiers in Ichapur?"
"No."
"Why not?"
"Our country is huge, isn't it, they can't get everywhere."
"Is our country huge?"
"Goodness, yes, huge is the word for it."
"Why is that old man going like that?"
"He's sick. Got asthma."
"Is he going to die?"
"Heavens no, sweetheart, don't say that. Dying ain't that easy. Dying's quite a business."

Asmani glanced at Quddus. How could he say that dying wasn't easy? He'd only just seen for himself how easy death had become. They had taken away three men, three healthy men with nothing wrong with them, then in the early morning news had come that Mr Motaleb's body was lying on the riverbank and the corpses of the other two had floated away down river. Mr Motaleb's body had not been brought home. Who was going to fetch it when everyone's first thought was to save their own skin and most people were busy trying to escape? Mr Motaleb's wife Jaheda Khanam had been even more fearful than the rest. Quddus had gone to her and said, Missus, why don't we go together and collect the body. If you're with me the soldiers won't do anything, they'll see it's a woman who's come to collect her husband's dead body. They may be bad, but they're human, and they'll let us get away with that. But Jaheda had refused to go.

On board the boat now Quddus was behaving as if nothing had happened. He wasn't shedding any tears, he had asked a woman he didn't know for some *paan*, and now he was chewing the *paan* with evident enjoyment. Occasionally he was sticking his head out from under the awning to spit surplus juice into the water. In his lap he had a pillow which he wasn't letting anyone borrow; hidden inside it were his money and gold ornaments.

Asmani was looking lazily at the scenery. How beautiful it all was! Nature was quite indifferent to the woes and sufferings of mankind, and always carried on doing its own thing. The canal water was remarkably clear and sparkling. At this time of year the water in rivers was usually clouded; it didn't start to become clear until about the end of August, so why was the canal water so limpid? From time to time parties of egrets flew by – the sight of white egrets flying across a blue sky was really splendid. If the country ever got back to normal and she found Shahed again, the two of them must come for a boat trip along this very same canal. Would she, would she ever see Shahed again?

Keshob babu had sat up. His eyes were reddened and discharge had gathered in the corners of them; the sight was not pleasant.

"Feeling any better?" Quddus asked him.
"Slightly better," replied Keshob babu, "but my eyes are giving me trouble."
"Junctivitis, I 'spect. A lot of it going around at the moment."
"How much longer will it take to get to Ichapur?"
"About two hours, maybe."

Runi was staring steadily at Keshob babu.

"Shouldn't look at the eyes of someone who's got junctivitis, sweetheart," said Quddus. "If you do you'll catch it yerself."
"Why?" asked Runi.
"I wouldn't know," said Quddus off-handedly. "It's just one of God's rules."

God's rule or not, Runi continued to stare. She hadn't seen a red-eyed man before.

"We need to tune in to the news," said Keshob babu.

"Tune in, then, if you want to," said Quddus, "you've got your *tansistor*."

"But the ladies are grieving, is it right to turn on the transistor radio now?"

"'Tis up to you."

Keshob babu tuned in to Radio Pakistan Dacca. The news was that the situation in East Pakistan was entirely normal. A team of foreign reporters had toured the province and reported that law and order had been restored in full by the army. All kinds of business activities were being carried on as usual. Staff attendance in offices was at normal levels. Anyone who had not yet reported for duty was urged to do so without delay. The Foreign Ministry of the People's Republic of China had announced that anything going on in East Pakistan was an internal matter which concerned only the Pakistan authorities, and no intervention from outside was justifiable. A shipload of rice despatched from West Pakistan in order to stabilize the price of rice in East Pakistan had berthed in Chittagong and unloading had commenced.

"Well, everything's just fine in our country," said Quddus.

"Hmm," said Keshob babu. He looked worried.

The boat reached Ichapur at around two p.m. The quayside area was deserted. Normally the moorings would be alive with numerous boats and their crews, sculls for hire, freight dinghies and so on, but now everything was dead. Even the little tea stall was closed.

"I got a peculiar feeling," said Quddus. "What's going on, I wonder?"

It didn't take long for them to discover what was going on. An army platoon had descended on Ichapur early that morning and set up camp in Ichapur police station. Then all hell had been let loose. The soldiers had brought drums of kerosene with them, and they had started setting fire to all the Hindu-owned properties they could find. It was a good day for burning down houses, as there was no wind and the weather was fine.

None of the party on the boat disembarked except for Keshob babu. With a tragic look on his face he turned to Runi and said, "Please say a prayer for me, darling."

Runi was perplexed. Why had he picked on her, when there were so many adults around? In any case, she didn't know how to say prayers for people.

The boat cast off, and the boatmen started poling away for all they were worth, eager to get away from the area as fast as possible.

An old man squatting on the bank hissed a warning: "Get away, quick! Quick!"

"Where are we going to go now?" asked Asmani.

Quddus took some *paan* out of a small tin and stuffed it in his mouth. With a complete lack of interest he replied, "I don't know."

"How far is Singdha from here?" asked Jaheda.

"Not at all far," said Quddus, spitting into the river.

"Then let's go to Singdha. That's where my father-in-law's sister lives."

"Right," said Quddus.

"Listen, Asmani," said Jaheda, turning to face her, "you're not coming to Singdha with us. It's since you started tagging along that so many unpleasant things have happened to us. In any case I can't suddenly turn up in Singdha with such a huge crowd of people in tow."

"Oh! But where am I to go, then?" asked Asmani, flabbergasted.

Jaheda made no reply. She turned away and settled herself among her cushions. She had just put a fresh wad of *paan* in her mouth, and her mouth was full of leaf, nut and juice.

"Why doesn't she want us to go with her?" asked Runi.

Asmani said nothing. There was nothing she could say.

"Where will we go now, Mummy?" asked Runi.

"I don't know," replied Asmani with the same indifference as Quddus had shown.

Jaheda was lying back with her head resting on her pillow and her eyes closed. She looked as if she was asleep, except that her jaws were still busy chewing *paan*. For a moment Asmani thought of saying to her, "Auntie, I'm not well, I'm expecting a baby, please don't abandon me like this." But then she thought, what's the use. She herself was feeling sleepy, and if she'd had a pillow of her own she would have laid her head down on it and had a nap. Like that she could have whiled some time away in untroubled sleep.

31

The children of Subdivisional Police Officer Foyzur Rahman and his wife Ayesha Begum were on board a country boat.

Ayesha Begum was fasting. This was a voluntary fast which she was undertaking for the sake of her husband's wellbeing. Dusk was falling and it was time to break the fast, but she had nothing to break it with, not even a cupful of water.

She and her children had been hiding at the home of a well-to-do family in the village of Babla in Durgapur Union. Conscious that Ayesha Begum was the wife of the local S.D.P.O., the members of the host family had treated their guests with the greatest kindness and consideration. But all of a sudden their host, Khosru Miah[*], had come to Ayesha Begum and told her that he could no longer offer her and her children shelter in his home, and that they would have to go elsewhere.

"But where can I go?" Ayesha Begum had asked in dismay.

"It's up to you to decide where you're going to go," Khosru Miah had said. "I've arranged a boat to take you. You must board it now."

"But I don't know this area at all. Where shall I go, with all my children? Particularly with two daughters approaching maturity?"

"You're wasting precious time. I've asked you to get on board the boat, kindly do so at once. We've heard news that the army have killed your husband and are looking for your sons. If we let you stay here we'll be doomed, all of us."

"At least let us stay the night. Please. We'll leave tomorrow morning and go wherever we can."

"Quite impossible. Now get on board that boat."

"Have a little mercy. We're in a position of great danger."

"Everyone's in great danger. This is no time for talking about mercy."

Khosru Miah had already given orders for the family's belongings to be loaded onto the boat. Taking her youngest daughter's hand Ayesha Begum had climbed on board, weeping as she went.

"Where do you want to go?" the boatman had asked.

"I don't know," Ayesha Begum had replied.

Night had fallen. The boat was snaking its way along the tortuous waterways of Barisal. A short while ago Ayesha Begum had dipped her hand into the river and broken her fast with river water. The boatman was feeling very uncomfortable as nobody would tell him which way to go. From time to time he would try to get an answer out of them.

"Come on, out with it now. Where do you want to get to?"

"Nowhere," replied the S.D.P.O.'s eldest son. "We want to keep wandering about in this boat."

"But that's not on," complained the boatman.

"Oh yes it is," retorted the eldest son. "It's spot on."

The boatman was eyeing him nervously, as he had a gun in his hand. Not only him, the second son was holding one too.

The S.D.P.O. had always had a special fondness for small arms. He possessed his own private pistol as well as his official one. And he also had two .22 rifles.

---

[*] Khosru Miah is a pseudonym. As my mother forgave this gentleman for all his heartless cruelty I too have forgiven him. – **Author**

Now, faced with the greatest danger in their lives, the S.D.P.O.'s children found themselves armed with these weapons. Barisal District was a notorious area for robbers and pirates, and it was only to be expected that news of a helpless family adrift on a boat would soon reach the miscreants.

As the boat rounded a wide bend in the river a young man came into sight, racing along towards them. He looked about twenty-one or twenty-two years old and was wearing a prayer cap on his head. He held up a hand, signalling for the boat to stop. The boatman drew up to the bank and the young man explained what he wanted.

"I go to the house where you were staying to teach their children the Quran. When I heard you were being thrown out of the house I felt very bad about it. Would you like to stay in my house? My house is a small one and I live there alone."

"We'd love to stay with you," said Ayesha Begum immediately.

"How do you know this fellow won't invite dacoits to rob us in the dead of night, or even hand us over to the army?" objected her eldest son.

"Since the lad has offered us shelter, we should trust God and accept his offer."

Ayesha Begum and her family reached the house, which was tucked away amid dense vegetation, at about ten o'clock at night. Ayesha Begum still didn't know for certain whether her husband really had been killed. Rumours were circulating, but nobody had definite news. She sat up all night with her two daughters reading the Quran while her two sons stood guard, their rifles loaded.

At dawn the fan-puller Rashid appeared. His eyes were red and his face looked gaunt.

"Tell me what's happened to your master," said Ayesha Begum the moment she saw him. "Where is he?"

Rashid remained silent.

"Is he alive?"

"Yes, ma'am," said Rashid. He was fibbing, for he knew everything that had happened, but he couldn't bear to convey the bad news to the family.

"If he's alive, then where is he?" asked Ayesha Begum.

"On the run. Listen, ma'am, there's no point in worrying about him now, we've got to think about you lot. I had to search hard to find you, but find you I did, and now I ain't going to let you stay here, I'm going to take you somewhere else. I'm going to take you to a saintly man in Gowarekha. I've already spoken to him. You'll be quite safe there."

"When are you going to take us there?"

"Now. I've fixed a boat. Don't be scared, ma'am, you've got me with you. I'll defend you with me life, I won't let nothing happen to you, I won't. Swear by the Prophet, swear to God."

So Rashid took the refugee family to Gowarekha, to the home of a certain Moulana. After installing them there he returned to Pirojpur with the intention of recovering a number of useful items from the S.D.P.O.'s quarters and bringing them to Ayesha Begum.

Rashid was arrested just as he was entering Pirojpur. He was taken to the police station, where he was to be interrogated in order to establish where the members of the S.D.P.O.'s family currently were. The officer at the head of army command in Pirojpur, Colonel Atiq (who was a well-known football player and one time member of the Pakistan national football team) was particularly keen to trace three of the S.D.P.O.'s children who had been university students and were said to have undergone training as freedom fighters in Pirojpur.

Colonel Atiq was being assisted by the O.C., the officer in charge of Pirojpur police station. Maybe it was simply in order to save his own life that this gentleman was cooperating with the army. The following exchange took place:

"Where are the S.D.P.O.'s family?"

"I don't know, sir."

"Of course you know. I've received intelligence that you know. You don't just know where they are, you are actually taking care of them."

"I know, sir, but I'm not telling."

"You know what the army are like. If you don't tell, they'll do awful things to you."

"I'm not saying a thing, sir."

"Come off it, you might as well save your own skin, for goodness' sake! At times like these it's every man for himself. Where are they, tell me?"

"Never. I'm never going to say."

That same evening Rashid was led away to Wheelerhat launch terminal and shot.

32

21st April 1971

The daughter of Huseyn Shaheed Suhrawardy°, Begum Akhtar Sulaiman, commented in the course of a press conference in Karachi that the Pakistan government had had no alternative to launching a military operation in East Pakistan. She said that when, in early March, there had been speculation that Sheikh Mujibur Rahman might be about to proclaim the independence of East Pakistan, she had gone to Dhaka and, calling on the memory of her late father, begged Sheikh Mujibur Rahman to refrain from any such disastrous action.*

---

* *Ekattorer Dosh Mash (Ten Months in 1971)*, Rabindranath Trivedi.

33

26th May 1971

The Pakistan government admitted that thirty thousand members of the police force, fourteen thousand members of the regular armed forces and four thousand members of the East Pakistan Rifles had defected.*

---

* Source: *Dainik Pakistan* newspaper.

34

2nd June 1971

The Governor of East Pakistan, Lieutenant General Tikka Khan, promulgated the Razakar° Ordinance 1971.

> "The task of the *razakar* militia shall be to assist the Pakistan army. They shall be provided with weapons. Their main functions will be seeking out guerrilla fighters, informing the army of any persons harbouring guerrilla fighters, and guarding railway lines and bridges."

In a joint statement eighty-three lecturers of Rajshahi University confirmed that they were receiving very courteous and sympathetic treatment from the Pakistan army. They stated that there neither had been nor was now any public support for the secessionist movement in the province.

In the words of a joint statement issued on behalf of the staff of Mymensingh Agriculture University, "We strongly condemn any attempt to split our dear motherland of Pakistan. We are saddened and shocked by the unilateral declaration of independence issued by certain political extremists."

The majority of lecturers at Dhaka University have reported for work. They have issued a statement to the effect that they are encountering no obstacles in the performance of their duties.*

---

* Our intellectuals used to be very fond of issuing statements. They still are. – **Author**

3rd June 1971

United Nations Secretary General U Thant stated that what was going on in East Bengal was the most tragic event in the history of mankind.

Speaking from Vatican City Pope John Paul requested world leaders to restore peace to East Pakistan.*

---

* What is remarkable is that no leader of any Muslim country opened his mouth in protest. However in West Pakistan the poet Fayez Ahmed Fayez, a winner of the Lenin prize, wrote an article in *Dawn* newspaper protesting against the inhumanity of the Pakistan army. He also wrote a poem dedicated to the Bangladeshi freedom fighters entitled *Paon se lahu ko dho dalo* (*Wash the blood from your feet*). – **Author**

36

11th June 1971

Governor Tikka Khan announced a general amnesty for all Bengali miscreants. A plan for a reception camp for returning refugees was also mentioned. In one announcement it was stated that any loyal Pakistani could return to the country without fear of reprisal.

The Governor gave orders for the opening of a reception centre for the benefit of returnees.

37

The poet Shamsur Rahman was sitting in an inner room in half darkness. The house where he was staying was in the village of Paratoli in Narsingdi Subdivision of Dhaka District. It was made of mud and it had windows, very small barred windows rather like the ones at the booking office counter in a railway station, for village people do not like their windows to be too large. Such apertures let in precious little light or air, and are windows in name only.

The poet was seated close to the window, on a basketwork stool made of cane. This cane stool was the most comfortable thing in the house to sit on, though it had one drawback, there was no back rest to lean against, so one had to remember to sit bolt upright all the time. In the present circumstances it was best to sit upright and alert in any case. He was gazing at two aubergine plants growing in the courtyard. Some remarkable aubergines were growing on them, of the same pure white as a duck's egg, a variety he had never seen before. It looked as if the plants were growing eggs instead of fruit. As a city dweller who had come to live in the country he found many details of village life quite fascinating. Whenever something new caught his eye the words of Robert Frost came to mind:

> *Heaven gives its glimpses only to those*
> *Not in position to look too close.*

"*Kobi sahib*! Mister Poet! Are you there?"

Were his ears deceiving him, or was someone calling for him? Hadn't he heard that rather effeminate male voice somewhere before? He was living here incognito, and nobody here knew him as 'Mister Poet'. So was it an outsider? Shamsur Rahman was alarmed. In bad times like these being sought out by unknown visitors meant trouble.

The poet was wearing a bright green lungi but was bare from the waist up. His pale torso almost glowed in the darkness. He stood up to receive the visitor just as he was, without a shirt on. City manners were out of place in a village setting, and as for delicacy, that was one of the first things to go to the wall in wartime.

"Do you recognize me, *Kobi sahib*? I'm Shah Kolim, your disciple."

"Disciple? Am I supposed to be some kind of guru?"

"You are my guru, without any doubt."

Kolimullah bent down to touch Shamsur Rahman's feet in obeisance, and although the poet recoiled swiftly he was unable to elude the obsequious fingers.

"Oh, how wonderful it is to see you!" gushed Kolimullah with a beaming smile. "It feels rather like meeting Livingstone."

"What do you mean?"

"Oh, Livingstone had got lost in the jungles of the Amazon, and the National Geographic commissioned someone to go and look for him. After a lot of bother this person found out where he was. He came upon this white man in the midst of a group of black people, stepped forward and said, 'Dr Livingstone, I presume?'"

The poet continued to stare at Kolimullah, taking in none of the latter's long-winded narrative. The problem was that he couldn't recognize the fellow. Maybe it was because of his beard. These days any number of men were altering their appearance by letting their beards grow. This man was bearded, had applied antimony to his eyes, and was wearing a prayer cap. The clothes he was wearing were new.

"Your skin is the same colour as Livingstone's, and one could almost say you were lost in the jungles of the Amazon too. Sir, I don't think you have recognized me. I met you in the *Dainik Pakistan* office. I recited one of your poems to you by heart, *Asad's Shirt*. Now maybe you remember?"

Shamsur Rahman nodded blankly as if he had remembered. In fact he recalled nothing.

"I'd been hoping to meet you, but never imagined I'd find you like this."

"And how did you find me?"

"Oh, it's a long story. I can sit down and tell you the whole tale if you wish. Couldn't we go inside and sit down?"

"Yes, of course," said Shamsur Rahman in embarrassment. So far he had been keeping this Shah Kolim fellow on his feet in the verandah while he himself stood in the doorway clutching the door. Anyone observing the scene would have got the impression he was deliberately blocking the entrance to prevent Shah Kolim from entering.

"Would you like tea?" he asked.

"Could you manage that?" asked Shah Kolim as he sat down on the mat which covered the bedstead in the reception room.

"Yes, indeed. I can give you tea sweetened with molasses."

"Oh, excellent! I haven't had tea with molasses for ages. Yes, I'd love tea. What a privilege to sit down to tea with you, a great privilege."

The poet went out of the room to give orders for tea to be prepared, and to put on a shirt. He didn't feel he could go on sitting bare-chested any longer in the presence of this individual. Nor did it seem likely that the man would take his leave soon after having his tea. He looked very much the type who would dig in for a long stay.

Kolimullah gave a little "Aah!" of satisfaction as he sipped the molasses tea.

"This tea is excellent. The scent of molasses has blended perfectly with the flavour of the tea. It's too good to justify having only one cupful. I really must have another cup of it."

"Certainly," said Shamsur Rahman without enthusiasm. "However I'm rather busy, so I won't be able to give you a great deal of my time."

"You don't need to give me any time at all, sir. Do please get on with your work, I'll be fine on my own. I'll be enjoying that tea. I'd like to just spend a few precious moments in the house of a poet, then I'll be on my way."

"How did you know I was here?"

"It's quite an involved story, sir. I'm accompanying a family to their village home as their chaperone. They're the family of a police inspector – his wife, three daughters and one son. When we reached your village the inspector's daughter Masuma suddenly fell ill. She started bleeding from the nose. Each time she holds a handkerchief to her nose it rapidly gets soaked in blood. They have relatives in this village, and we're stopping with them at the moment. As soon as we've had Masuma checked by a doctor we'll carry on. We're heading for Faridpur – that's where Masuma's family's ancestral home is."

"I see."

"We haven't found a qualified doctor. There had been a Hindu one called Hori babu, but he's fled to India with his whole family for fear of being targeted by the army. In a way it's a good thing the Hindus are leaving. *Monkeys belong in the forest, Hindus in Hindustan*, as they say."

"How on earth can you say such a thing?"

"Oh, those were just random thoughts, please don't take any of it seriously. But I haven't yet told you the main thing, which is how I found out where you were. One of Masuma's uncles happened to mention that you were in the village, and that you were in hiding. But sir, this is not at all a good place for you to hide."

"Why not?"

"Because if anyone wants to find you they can do so blindfolded. For the simple reason that you've come to the most obvious place, your own native village. You know which is the best possible place to flee to, sir?"

"No."

"The best place is Hindustan. All the suspects are crossing over the border into India."

"How do you mean, suspects?"

"The anti-Pakistan brigade."

"So which side do you happen to be on?"

"Listen, sir, this beard, this eye-black, it's all put on. I've adopted this attire in order to look like a Pakistani. It's the only way to survive – by changing your feathers. Please don't be misled by my outward appearance, sir."

The poet sighed. He couldn't think what to say. It was impossible to tell when this person was telling the truth and when he was lying through his teeth.

"Do you enjoy living in the country?" asked Kolimullah.

The poet inclined his head slightly. It wasn't clear whether this meant he did enjoy life in the village, or the contrary.

"You should go back to the city, sir."

"Why?"

"The city's crammed with people and anyone can live anonymously there. It's impossible to remain anonymous in a village. Just see how easily I rooted you out today."

"Hmm."

"Go back to your job in the newspaper office and start working as normal. Nobody is going to harass you. You can think and do as you please, you can write your poems. You have nothing to fear from the army."

"How can you say there's nothing to fear?"

"The army won't trouble a respected poet like yourself. They're keen to show the outside world that Dhaka is back to normal. Please take my advice, sir, come back to Dhaka."

"And what would you gain from that?"

"You would be safe, you would be writing what you wanted – that's a big enough gain for me. You won't be safe in your village. They're setting up all sorts of things like Peace Committees° and Al-Badar brigades°. Who knows when some of them may seize you and take you away. That's what's worrying me. If local militias grab you you'll simply disappear. If the army arrested you at least you could be traced."

"Have you finished your tea?"

"Yes."

"Can I offer you another cup?"

"No thanks, it's all right. I sense you're a little annoyed with me. Please don't be annoyed. I write poems myself, so I know what it's like being you."

"I'm not annoyed."

"Aren't you writing any poems? Have you written any since the army crackdown?"

"Yes."

"Would I be able to read one of the poems? I would love to read any poem written after the crackdown."

"Why?"

"People say poets are the soul of a nation. I really believe it's true. Genuine poets are the soul of the nation. Not me, I'm second class as a poet and second class as a national soul too. But you're different. Anyone who read one of your recent poems would be able to feel the pulse of the nation."

"You really want to read one?"

"Yes, sir."

"I wrote a pair of poems a short while back. They are like twin daughters to me."

"Oh please, sir, bring your poetry manuscript book and let me read them. And if it's not too much trouble, another cup of that molasses tea."

The poet rose to his feet. There was an uncertainty in his manner as he left the room, as if he was debating whether or not it was right to let this stranger hear poems so dear to his heart.

Kolimullah was left sitting alone for quite a few minutes. He doubted whether it could take the poet such a long time to fetch his poetry book; perhaps he was going to bring it and the tea at the same time. Kolimullah was feeling hungry, and he knew molasses tea wasn't going to still the pangs of hunger, on the contrary, it would aggravate them. This was a problem with village life – people never offered any snacks with their tea, not even biscuits or Bombay mix. In some households they might serve a few slices of ripe papaya; alas, these village simpletons didn't realize that ripe papaya didn't go at all well with tea.

The poet returned, carrying the tea things himself. There was one cup of tea, with two balls of sticky-sweet pop-rice on a separate saucer.

"I don't feel like reciting poetry today," he admitted as he set the tea and rice balls down in front of Kolimullah.

"That's quite all right," exclaimed Kolimullah, biting into the first ball of pop-rice. "If you don't feel like it, let's leave it. The poet has the final word."

One of the poems Shamsur Rahman had written at his village home was entitled *Independence*.

Independence, you
  are an indelible poem by Rabindranath Tagore, an irreducible hymn.
Independence, you
  are Nazrul Islam, a giant among men,
  your mane of tangled hair quaking with creative zeal –
Independence, you
  are the glorious congregation at the Shahid Minar,
  shrine of the language martyrs of the 21st February,
Independence, you
  are the fiery-hot demonstration, gay with banners, loud with rallying cries.
Independence, you
  are the smile of a peasant in his field of corn.
Independence, you
  are the untrammeled swimming of a village lass
  in a lotus pool at the torrid hour of noon.
Independence, you
  are the knotted biceps of a labouring lad
  his supple fluent arm bronzed by the sun.

> *Independence, you*
> *are the spark in the eyes of a freedom fighter*
> *in the depths of a vast gloom.*
> *Independence, you*
> *are fine-honed words in the incendiary speech*
> *of a gifted young student under a shady wayside tree.*
> *Independence, you*
> *are tempestuous debate in every tea-stall, on every village green.*
> *Independence, you*
> *are the crazy gales of dark spring storms which knit the horizon.*
> *Independence, you*
> *are the heart of the mighty Meghna in flood.*
> *Independence, you*
> *are the noble lawn of a father's velvet prayer mat.*
> *Independence, you*
> *are the tremulous shake of a mother's white sari spread in the yard.*
> *Independence, you*
> *are the stains of henna on the soft palm of a sister's hand.*
> *Independence, you*
> *are a colourful placard as bright as a star in the hand of a friend.*
> *Independence, you*
> *are a housewife's raven hair let loose*
> *untamed and wild in the morning breeze.*
> *Independence, you*
> *are the pretty coat worn by a boy,*
> *the play of sunlight on a girl's cherub cheek.*
> *Independence, you*
> *are a garden cottage, a cuckoo's call,*
> *and the quivering of leaves in an ancient banyan tree.*
> *Such is the desire of writing verse for me.*

Dusk had nearly fallen.

Kolimullah was on his way back. If he walked all the way to the village bazaar he would be able to get a rickshaw-van, but travelling along unmade cart tracks in a rickshaw-van was an uncomfortable business. All the bumping and jerking made one's heart, lungs and liver collide into each other. Better to walk than put up with that. Kolimullah had no trouble with walking: he was fit and healthy and capable of walking for hours on end. There was only one bad thing about it – when walking he never got any inspiration for his poetry. If he had been riding in a rickshaw on a smooth road surface right now, he would very soon have had a poem forming in his head. Most of his poems came to him while he was travelling in rickshaws.

And today, Kolimullah reflected, he really needed to compose a poem. It was urgent. For today a good marriage opportunity had appeared in his sights. Weddings had been in season since the crackdown. The parents of unmarried nubile girls had been falling over themselves to get them married off, as if somehow marriage was the solution to all their problems, as if it was only single girls who were in danger and not married women. What the fools failed to realize was that as far as the army was concerned it mattered not at all whether a woman was single, married or widowed: the only thing they noticed was her sex.

If he really did get married to Masuma the event could be counted as a true blessing from God. She was such an excellent young girl. Only one thing, she was a bit too smart. A wife was a companion for life, so it was no good if she was too dull witted, but it was also not desirable for her to be too clever. *A conch-worker's saw cuts both ways*, as the saying went.

A line of poetry did come to Kolimullah's mind as he walked along. 'No comrade was there at my side.' Not bad, but it had only eight syllables, ti-tum ti-tum ti-tum ti-tum. There should be sixteen syllables for a full line. 'No comrade was there at my side to feel that grief I could not hide.' There, sixteen syllables, with the two halves rhyming nicely.

A bit later – as a result, no doubt, of haggling over the fare with the driver of the rickshaw-van – Kolimullah found he had lost the entire line of poetry. The vehicle was trundling along and he was sitting fairly comfortably on the flat boards behind the rickshaw puller. The road was relatively even and the van was not jolting. The circumstances were favourable, dusk was falling, an agreeable breeze was wafting overhead: perfect conditions for composing poetry in one's mind. Yet Kolimullah's mind was a complete blank. It would be so useful if he could make up a full poem. If, some day in the future, he became a famous poet he would be able to talk about it in his interviews. "Behind this particular poem lies a story. Let me tell you the tale. It was 1971, a time of terrible suffering. The celebrated poet Shamsur Rahman had fled to his village home, and I suddenly had a compelling urge to see him. Taking my life in my hands I travelled from Dhaka to his village. But one cannot arrive empty-handed at the home of a great poet, so sitting in the back of a rickshaw-van I wrote this poem. The poem was in my pocket as I approached my goal. Just then dusk was falling. In the words of that favourite poet of yours, Rabindranath, *tinted with evening's ruddy glow, a day in early spring...*"

The rickshaw-van jolted violently. Kolimullah just managed to save himself from falling off. This was not the right time to compose poetry, he decided. He should keep his eyes and ears wide open while sitting on the van. A poet with broken limbs was hardly an attractive proposition. And today there was every possibility of his getting married, but it would be difficult for a wedding to go ahead if the bridegroom was not in one piece.

The rickshaw puller carried on pedalling. It dawned on Kolimullah that he had missed a great chance. Having been closeted with the great poet for several hours, he could very easily have said to him at some point, "*Kobi sahib*, tonight I'm to get married, so I'm going to ask you for a little favour." The poet would have been taken aback. "What kind of favour?" Kolimullah would have said, "If you could write a couple of lines by way of a blessing for me and my wife, it would be a small matter for you but it would mean a great deal to us." The poet would surely have consented to write something; for he was an unassuming man, and unassuming people always find it difficult to say no.

Kolimullah himself was by no means an unassuming person, but he knew very well how to act the part of one.

"There's something I want to say to you," said Masuma's mother. "I won't beat about the bush. Times are very bad, nobody's keen to have an unmarried nubile daughter on their hands. I've had a talk with Masuma, and she likes you. We know very little about you, but you seem to be a good sort. Would you think of marrying Masuma?"

"Madam," said Kolimullah in his humblest manner, "ever since I first met you I have regarded you as my mother. The way you look, the way you talk, everything reminds me of my own dear mother. I'm not saying this for the first time, I've said it to you before. I shall do whatever you tell me to do, as you are my mother."

"Marriage now would not mean a full wedding, just the basic rite of union in front of a cleric. The full ceremony will take place when circumstances return to normal. God willing by that time my husband will also be with us."

"Mother, I shall do whatever you say."

"What I want is for the marriage to be consecrated before we go on to Faridpur. Do you have any objection to that?"

"Please address me simply as *tumi*, mother. And I've already said, I'll do whatever you tell me to do."

Kolimullah got married that very night. The group was supposed to resume their journey to Faridpur the following day, but Kolimullah persuaded everyone that they should return to Dhaka instead. Now that he was going to be with them all the time, it would be better to stay in the city. There would be more security there, and besides, they needed to find out where Masuma's father was. He might turn up at the house any day. Nobody knew where Moriam's husband was either; if he wanted to make contact he would surely do so at their Dhaka address.

Everyone accepted Kolimullah's reasoning as unassailable. They returned to Dhaka by river launch. Masuma stuck close to her husband throughout the journey. All the females in the group were wearing burqas, but Masuma was the one who periodically lifted her veil.

"I want to look at you all the time," she whispered once, "but from inside a burqa I can't see you properly. What am I to do, eh?"

38

The sub-editor of the newspaper *the Daily People*, Nirmalendu Goon, was in hiding in Barhatta village in Mymensingh District. He had not had any great difficulty in fleeing from Dhaka. With his long black beard he looked like a young Sufi. The day he left Dhaka he started by taking a stroll in the city. He approached the area of the Shahid Minar and inspected it from a distance. He knew that the late Professor G.C. Dev's flat was nearby, and although he had never known the philosopher something drew him to the place and he stood and gazed for a while at the empty apartment. He walked a bit further and observed Iqbal Hall from afar°.

Walking on, he approached the High Court compound and saw something unusual. The army had set up two long tables in the road, making a kind of temporary bureau for the reception of surrendered weapons. Numerous announcements had been made on radio and television ordering all civilians in possession of weapons to hand them in at their nearest police station. However in practice many police stations were deserted, all their Bengali staff having absconded, and maybe that was why this army reception facility had been set up.

Quite a number of Dhaka citizens were handing in weapons. None of them looked at the soldiers as they did so; they kept their eyes lowered and stared at the ground as if they were deeply ashamed of their crime, the crime of possessing firearms.

One of the soldiers came up to Nirmalendu Goon and asked him roughly what he wanted.

"I'm watching the people hand in their guns," said Nirmalendu Goon politely.

"You're standing here just to watch that?"

"Yes, sir."

"Get away from here. Scram!"

The soldier made a gesture as if he was waving a bothersome fly to oblivion. Nirmalendu Goon went on his way. He walked, and he walked, and he walked. From Dhaka he walked all the way to Mymensingh. From Mymensingh he walked to Netrakona. From Netrakona he walked to Barhatta, and there he walked into his own ancestral home. It was there, sitting alone in the dead of night, that he wrote a short poem entitled *Firearms*.

> *A scrum at the police post, the city's terrorist suspects*
> *Are handing in their arms. By army orders, timid folk*
> *As if honouring a pledge made at a holy shrine*
> *Set down their shotguns, rifles, pistols, cartridges*
> *On the counter, a gangster's kit neatly arrayed.*
>
> *But I alone have flouted martial law,*
> *Weak rebel that I am, who slunk demurely home*
> *Concealing a weapon of fire more lethal than all,*
> *My very heart. Which I did not hand in.*

39

Irtazuddin Kashempuri was feeling very cheerful. It was normal for him to feel uplifted at the dawn prayer hour; at that time a special kind of joy would invariably infuse his soul. He himself never knew why this was; maybe it was just the pleasure of starting a new day. Not only human beings: animals, birds and plants were all starting their own new day, and there was a delight in being part of the general revival. But today there was an element of sadness mingled with Irtazuddin's joy. From his bedroom came the sound of a small baby crying, not continuously but in little bursts which ended as suddenly as they began. It was a very long time since a baby's cries had been heard in his house. While kneeling on his prayer mat Irtazuddin reflected that there was a touch of holiness in the crying of a baby; whenever he heard the sound his heart was moved.

The baby had not yet been named. It was Sadrul Amin's child. Sadrul Amin had never had a chance to see the baby's face, he hadn't even survived long enough to hear the news of its birth. That must be about the saddest thing that could happen to a father, thought Irtazuddin. Still, no doubt God had some purpose behind it all.

Irtazuddin had made Komola come and stay in his house with her baby for the time being. When conditions were better he intended to take them to Khulna. Komola's mother lived in Bagherhat in Khulna District, and going there would give Irtazuddin the opportunity to visit the famous shrine and mosque of Khan Jahan Ali.

Today Irtazuddin spent much more time than usual on his prayer mat. There was a reason. He had recently been doing a *khatm-e-Yunus*°, a long cycle of prayer recitations, and today he had reached the final instalment. After completing the prescribed dawn prayer he had gone on to do a series of personal prayers and supplications. When he had finished all that he felt a great inner peace.

For some days now he had been feeling unsettled, he had been sleeping badly at night, he had had various unpleasant dreams. These nightmares made no sense at all, but one had been particularly vivid. Shahed had come to Nilganj. He was on his own and looked emaciated and elderly. His collar bones were sticking out, his lips were pale, his hair had gone white.

"Why are you like that?" Irtazuddin had asked. "Your hair has gone white, you look old, what's happened?"

Shahed had mumbled some reply which Irtazuddin could not catch. Irtazuddin noticed to his horror that Shahed was scratching his head all the time. His hair was teeming with lice and the lice kept dropping from his head and falling to the ground.

"Why are you on your own?" Irtazuddin had asked. "Where have you left your wife and child?"

Again Shahed had mumbled indistinct words.

"Why are you mumbling?" Irtazuddin had said. "Speak clearly and say whatever you want to say. Try clearing your throat. I see your head is full of lice, don't you take baths any more?"

"Elder brother, I'm in a terrible predicament," Shahed had said, starting to cry. And then Irtazuddin had woken up.

That night Irtazuddin had been unable to sleep any more, and he had sat down and written a letter to Shahed.

Shahed,

My blessings for you. We are quite well. I am worried because I haven't had any news from you. I sent you two separate telegrams from Phulpur telegraph office, but have received no reply to either. I have also written a letter to you, but have not had any reply.

The situation in Nilganj is now satisfactory. Earlier a half mad army officer made a halt in Nilganj for a matter of hours. He had several people killed for no reason whatsoever. One of them was the O.C. of Nilganj police station, Mr Sadrul Amin. By the infinite grace of God that officer stayed only for a very short time. At present a small detachment of soldiers has set up camp at Nilganj police station. Their commanding officer is a captain named Muhammad Basit. He is a very civil and honest man. Most important of all he is religious minded. Last Friday he joined in the congregational prayers with everyone else. After the sermon he gave a speech in English. I was much pleased by the content of his speech. He said we had gone through a lot of trouble and suffering in order to free ourselves from the yoke of British rule. Now a new conspiracy had been hatched and we should all be on our guard against this new conspiracy. All Muslims are brothers. Brothers should stand shoulder to shoulder. If one brother makes a mistake the other brother will set him right again.

There is a good relationship between the captain and the local Hindus. He often sends for Kalipad babu, one of our teachers, to play chess with him. Kalipad babu is also impressed by the captain's civility. At the captain's behest a local peace committee has been set up. I am the president of the committee. At present peace reigns in Nilganj.

The widow and infant child of Mr Sadrul Amin are currently staying with me. I am going to take them to Khulna and then travel by the Rocket river steamer service to Dhaka, where I shall collect you and bring you here. I am much unsettled, worrying about you.

Irtazuddin had gone out early in the morning to post the letter, only to find that the post office was closed. The postmaster had gone away without telling anyone, leaving the office door padlocked. The only other place where the letter could be posted was Phulpur. Irtazuddin was not in good shape – when he walked his knees ached and his ankles got swollen – but nevertheless he had walked all the way to Phulpur to post the letter himself. He could have got someone else to do it, but he never delegated his personal duties to other people. The Prophet had always done his own chores himself, and throughout his life Irtazuddin had been intent on following the Prophet's example. There was no way he was going to depart from his principles merely on the pretext that he was getting old. So he had gone to Phulpur; and there he had sent off a telegram as well as posting the letter.

Once again the telegram had brought no response. Probably the postal system all over the country had ceased to function. Irtazuddin had felt very uncomfortable. In order to relieve his frustration he had decided to perform an *istikhara*, an appeal for revelation of the right course of action. To do an *istikhara* you had to recite a certain particular prayer formula and then go to sleep with your mind purified and clear. The answer to your query was then supposed to come to you in a dream. However the dream might not be very explicit. God replied to the questions of his subjects in the form of metaphors, and interpreting metaphors was invariably tricky.

Anyway, Irtazuddin had performed his *istikhara* and gone to bed. He had dreamed, and what he had seen in his dream was Runi eating something from a large dish. He had asked her what she was eating and she had said she wasn't going to tell him. He had asked if he could try a bit of the food and Runi had said she wouldn't give him any.

So what had been the meaning of that dream? Runi had been eating, and that meant she was alive and well. She had been eating from a large dish, which also boded well. If she had been picking food from a small saucer it would have meant she was hungry. But he had seen Runi on her own without any sign of either parent; had that been significant? Could Shahed and Asmani be in some kind of trouble? He had asked Runi for a sample of the food and she had refused to give him any. Did that contain a further message? Surely it did, yet he had no idea what.

It was after that dream that he had started the *khatm-e-Yunus*, which he had just completed today. Now he felt much better; something inside him said that there was no longer any cause for fear.

As Irtazuddin was rising from his prayer mat Komola emerged from the bedroom.

"How are you, my daughter?" asked Irtazuddin.

"I'm all right," said Komola.

"Has your son's temperature gone down?"

"It has."

"*Alhamdulillah*."

"Uncle, I want to tell you something. It's quite important," said Komola.

"Go ahead and tell me," replied Irtazuddin.

"I don't want to go to Khulna. I have nobody really close to me living there. Mother is no longer alive. I have a step-brother but we're not on good terms. If I go to Khulna with my baby I'll find myself in a perilous situation."

"The only one who may put us in peril is God, and the only one who can deliver us from peril is also God. Dear daughter, you may stay in this house as long as you wish, there's no problem at all."

"You are so very kind, uncle. Can I make you a cup of tea? Go on, have some tea."

"Very well, you can make tea. While that's going on I shall sit here with your little son in my lap. There's a surah in the Quran called *Al-Rahman*. I shall recite that and puff it over his head. God willing your son will grow up to be a good person."

After having his tea Irtazuddin went out for a walk. This was no morning constitutional undergone purely for health reasons; the fact was that walking down to the river after his early morning prayers was a source of sheer pleasure for Irtazuddin. This year the water level in the Sohagi river was rising rapidly. The surface of the river was swelling and trembling, and each day it looked different. Watching it change was one of the simple pleasures in life.

Today Irtazuddin observed that the water had risen even higher. Were there going to be floods? Nilganj stood on relatively high ground and didn't easily go under water, but it was supposed to flood once every seven years. Maybe this was the seventh year?

"Moulana *sab*, your rev'rence, 'ow is yerself today?"

Irtazuddin started and looked round. Nibaron was standing there with a big smile on his face. This character was a real merry-andrew; even at the worst of times he kept smiling broadly. It was a remarkable virtue. He was short in stature, he had very dark brown skin and a cascade of wavy hair reaching down to his shoulders. With his simple open face he could be the life and soul of any musical session, conjuring up the right mood in an instant. And he had the most soulful singing voice in the whole district.

"Where have you suddenly sprung from, Nibaron?"

Nibaron smiled, came forward and touched Irtazuddin's feet in respect. The way he performed this little *pranama* was eccentric: after bowing down and touching the feet he brought his fingers to his tongue as if to taste them.

"Folk like me, we're birds of the jungle, no telling where we'll flit. I been roaming around, and here I am now."

"But times are bad, are you sure it's a good idea to roam around so much?"

"Arr, you're right there indeed. But I can't abide staying put. Folk say clear out, go to India. But why should I? This is my homeland – ain't it?"

"Of course it is."

"Me own homeland, everyone knows me. Wherever I go, folk say hi, come and sit down. Who'd know me in India?"

"You're quite right."

Nibaron started humming and then sang:

> *The bird lives in his forest, sipping the honeycomb.*
> *How can he leave the forest, abandoning his home?*
> *A great fire grips the forest, the flames are red and grim.*
> *And now that bird, you tell me, what shall become of him?*

"You made that up just now, standing here?"

"Yes, sir, I did."

"Not bad. And what are you doing, all alone on the river bank?"

"I been feeling glum. So I think, let me go and sit by the river. River water flows, flowing water sweeps troubles away."

"Come with me, Nibaron. Come and have breakfast."

"No thankyou, sir," replied Nibaron politely. "I come to get me mood right, let me see if I can get jolly."

"Why are you feeling so depressed?"

Again Nibaron crooned.

> *In the sky the vulture wheels, his shadow scours the ground.*
> *Watching while men and women die, my horror is profound.*

Irtazuddin was tempted to spend some more time with Nibaron, but decided he ought not to do so. Nibaron had come to the river to be alone, and should be allowed his solitude. Irtazuddin returned home and Nibaron went on loitering on his own. Around midday some soldiers came to the riverside and took Nibaron away. Their captain had heard about him and was keen to hear him sing.

Captain Muhammad Basit derived considerable pleasure from listening to Nibaron singing one of his songs, and his only regret was that he didn't have a tape recorder with him. If only he'd had one he could have made a recording of the song.

"Sing the same song again," the captain told Nibaron. "Tell me, what sort of song is it?"

"We call it a song of *mortal separation*. Real separation. A parting as breaks the 'eart."

The captain didn't know Bengali, so Mr Saghir, the maths teacher from Nilganj High School, was interpreting for him. Quite a friendship had grown up between the captain and Saghir Uddin, and Mr Saghir, like Kalipad babu, often came over to play chess with the army officer. The captain was not particularly good at chess, but Saghir Uddin would deliberately make false moves so as to let him win. He knew that losing at chess was enough to put anyone in a foul mood and, wise man that he was, he was unwilling to risk letting an army officer's mood turn foul.

Nibaron sang,

> *Dear bird, reclining on the wall, why art thou dozing when I call?*

Which Saghir Uddin translated thus:

> *Oh my lying bird, I am calling you, why are you not responding?*

Captain Basit treated Nibaron to a cup of coffee, and even had a little chat with him using Saghir Uddin as interpreter.

"You're a Hindu?"

"Yes, sir, a Hindu I am. Please pardon me."

"Being a Hindu isn't a crime, so there's nothing which needs pardoning. Of course there are good and bad Hindus just as there are good and bad Muslims."

"I'm very pleased to 'ear you say that, sir."

"And I was very pleased to hear you sing. I'm going to write a letter of recommendation for you. If you ever get into trouble show the letter and you'll be safe."

"Sir, yer too kind."

"This is not about kindness. I'm merely acknowledging merit."

"Only a man with kindness in 'im can ever acknowledge merit."

Captain Muhammad Basit wrote out a letter of recommendation and handed it to Nibaron. He also presented him with the pen he had used to write it. Nibaron touched the captain's feet in his idiosyncratic manner, which tickled the captain even more. He thought how nice it would be to take a photograph of Nibaron's gesture which he could show people back home.

Harun Majhi was squatting in Irtazuddin's yard, smoking a bidi. With him was his long standing accomplice Kala Miah. A casual observer might be fooled into thinking Kala Miah was a puny weed, but he had the lightning reactions of a cobra. He too was puffing at a bidi. He was sitting with his back to Harun Majhi, as he was not so uncouth as to smoke in front of his mentor. Irtazuddin was not at home; he had gone to Shekherhat to buy some palm sugar for Komola's baby. The baby kept coughing and palm sugar was supposed to relieve coughs.

When Irtazuddin returned he was surprised to see the pair of them squatting there. Harun Majhi and Kala Miah instantly threw away their bidis and rose to their feet.

"What's all this?" asked Irtazuddin.

"I want to ask ya a favour," said Harun Majhi in a subdued tone.

"What kind of favour?"

"I brought a gold chain for O.C.'s little son. I want to put it on 'is neck."

"Some chain you've stolen, I presume? How could you give him such a thing?"

Harun Majhi scratched his head in embarrassment. It was perfectly true, the chain was the fruit of a robbery. He didn't normally hang on to his stolen goods, but this piece had been lying around for some reason.

"Now stop sitting in my yard," said Irtazuddin. "Go home."

"It's not like we got any 'ome to go to. Can't yer bring out Mr O.C.'s babe for a minute and let us see if 'e looks like 'is dad? 'Is dad was a brave fella, had the guts of a tiger, 'e did. When I think 'ow them lot killed 'im I start shakin' with anger. It's great that you've taken 'is wife and kid into your 'ouse to look after 'em. You'll go to 'eaven for that."

"Thank you, I can do without your assessment of my chances of going to heaven."

"Please do bring O.C.'s little kid out for a sec. I'll squint at 'im from a distance, just to see if 'e looks like 'is dad."

Irtazuddin came out of the house with the baby in his arms. Harun Majhi eagerly stretched out his hands. Irtazuddin had strong reservations about handing the baby over to a ruthless highwayman, but the dacoit was holding out his arms in such an appealing way he could hardly refuse. Irtazuddin put the infant in Harun Majhi's grasp.

"What's 'is name then, Moulana *sab*?"

"He hasn't been given a name yet."

"Oh look, look, see 'ow 'e's blinkin' at me!" exclaimed Harun Majhi in delight. "'Ello little one, what ya lookin' at, eh? Your dad arrested me, did ya know that? A very brave gentleman 'e was. You gotta be brave like 'im when you grow up. You ain't gonna turn into a cow with no 'orns, are ya?"

"That's quite enough," said Irtazuddin. "Give him back to me now and I'll return him to his mother. A small baby should never be separated from its mother for any length of time."

Harun Majhi handed the infant back, touched Irtazuddin's feet in respect and went on his way. As Irtazuddin was lifting the baby into Komola's arms he noticed the gold chain gleaming on its neck. He was most annoyed.

Two soldiers were standing outside a homestead in Nilganj called Fokirbari. They were out on patrol and had been invited by the people at Fokirbari to refresh themselves with *dab* or green coconut. They had finished the liquid from the half-ripened nuts and were tasting the thin lining of tender white coconut flesh with great relish. A few locals were watching them nervously from a respectful distance. The second son of the Fokirbari household was now cutting up some more green coconuts; this time the precious liquid was being thrown away and the immature coconut flesh was being scraped out and put on a plate ready for eating.

Well hidden among the rice plants in the neighbouring paddy field, Harun Majhi and Kala Miah were watching this scene of coconut eating.

"Would ya be able to get 'em two with a spear?" whispered Harun Majhi.

"One of 'em, yeah," said Kala.

"One for you, one for me," suggested Harun Majhi.

"Forget it," said Kala Miah.

"Right, forget it," agreed Harun Majhi straight away. "Anyway we don't 'ave any spears."

Harun Miah was edging along a path between two rice plots, keeping his head low. Suddenly he changed his mind. They had no spears with them, it was true, but getting hold of a couple of spears would be no problem. When they had finished guzzling coconuts the soldiers would carry on walking in the direction of

Nilganj High School, doubtless in a relaxed frame of mind. On the way they would have to pass through a bamboo thicket. Then it would be a simple matter to strike from behind with spears. The soldiers had a couple of decent rifles on them which they would take over, and these would come in useful for robbery jobs. At the moment Harun Majhi's armoury was empty, he had no weapons except a machete. He didn't actually know how these army rifles worked, but that was something that could be learned. Guns were all more or less the same, you pressed the trigger and off went the bullet.

"Kala Miah!"

"Mm?"

"Come on, let's get 'old of some spears."

Kala Miah gave his boss a long, unblinking look. "Let's get going," he said.

At three in the afternoon Captain Basit was roused from his nap to be given the news that village people had killed two of his soldiers using simple spears.

By six in the evening one third of the homesteads in Nilganj had been set on fire and thirty-eight people had been shot dead. Among those killed was the singer Nibaron. Captain Basit's letter of recommendation was in his hand, but not even that could save him.

At eleven o'clock at night Captain Basit got a shock when he heard bullets being fired at Nilganj High School from somewhere in the jungle to the south. He had had no idea that those Bengali dogs could be as bold as that. Little did he know! He wasn't reckoning with the insane courage of a Harun Majhi. The latter was firing out of the wilderness in order to work out how an army rifle worked. He had his own plans in mind, and he was going to use the rifle to shoot from close quarters. Dacoits do not generally shoot from a distance, they fire their guns at very close range.

Six o'clock in the morning. Heavy rain had begun to fall. From time to time lightning was flashing, and its brilliance would momentarily pick out Harun Majhi and his accomplice Kala Miah making their way towards Nilganj High School.

"'Ow about a little fag, boss?" Kala Miah was asking.

"And 'ow yer gonna light a fag in all this rain?" countered Harun Majhi.

"S'pose yer gotta point there," admitted Kala Miah despondently.

Harun Majhi was not in the least afraid, yet a shiver ran down his spine. Somehow he had the feeling that he and Kala Miah were not alone, there was a third person with them. He was there beside them, Sadrul Amin, the former officer in charge of Nilganj police station. Harun Majhi knew his mind was playing tricks, as it often did, but he couldn't get away from that intimation of the O.C.'s presence. Maybe he should mention it to Kala Miah. No, that might not be such a good idea, for in spite of his outstanding courage Kala Miah was terrified of ghosts.

40

Undated letter from Captain Muhammad Basit in Nilganj to his mother in West Pakistan.

Respected and beloved Mother,

Salaams. Mother, I have received the letter you sent via Major Safdar Jamil. I got it in good time. I also got the sultanas and pine nuts which you sent. Many many thanks.

I am well. There is no need for you to worry about me. We have brought the unruly Bengali people under control. A few lackeys of India try to make trouble here and there, but by the infinite grace of Allah those dogs too are tucking their tails between their legs and running away. The day is not far off when we shall have sent every one of those dogs from East Pakistan to Hell.

At the moment I am posted to a place called Nilganj. I am getting on reasonably well here. I have established peace and order in the area. I have lost one or two men in the process, but naturally the losses on the other side have been many times greater.

Customarily we think of the Bengalis as being timid. This notion is incorrect. Last Thursday in the dead of night a party of just two Bengali men suddenly stole into our camp with the intention of killing me. They did not succeed in killing me but they did cause a certain amount of damage.

You needn't worry, the following day by noon we had arranged reinforcements, and we are now being far more cautious than before.

Now, Mother, what I'm going to write next is important. You know General Begh quite well, indeed I believe he is some kind of relative of ours. Please get him to approach our Commander in Chief General Gul Hassan and ask him to have me transferred back to West Pakistan. You mustn't think it's because I'm scared that I want to go back home. I am not scared at all. The main reason I want to be transferred is that my health is breaking down here.

This is a dreadful country. On dry land there are snakes, and in water there are things which are even worse, creatures called leeches. The main item in these leeches' diet is human blood.

You can face an enemy with a rifle, but it's impossible to face these snakes and leeches.

So, Mother, by whatever means you can, get me transferred to Western Command. Maybe Senior Auntie (Father's elder brother's wife) can help in this matter. Please give my salaam to Senior Auntie, and my affectionate greetings to little sister Rehnuma. Has her wedding date been fixed yet?

Please pray for me, Mother. Recently I have been feeling below par, both mentally and physically.

Your affectionate younger son

Captain Muhammad Basit

Documents of the Bangladesh War of Independence
Information Ministry
Government of the People's Republic of Bangladesh
Volume 8

Jotindronath Mondol
Village: Shoshid
Post Office: Moushani
Thana: Shorupkathi
District: Barisal

On 17th Baisakh a gunboat of the Pakistan army, travelling via Jhalkathi along the Katakhali river, approached Shoshid marketplace. On arrival they moored the gunboat alongside the marketplace and disembarked into the village. The moment the Pakistan army soldiers entered the village the local residents, men and women alike, fled for their lives in all directions. Having entered the village the soldiers first looted the more valuable articles, then set fire to nine houses and destroyed them. That day they shot two men. One died instantly and the other was seriously injured.

On 26th Baisakh the Pakistan army came to our village again, accompanied by some *razakar* vigilantes. In a gunboat and speedboat they penetrated into the interior along narrow irrigation channels. They looted the clothing stores of Motilal Debnath (Banerjee) and Hiralal Debnath and loaded the goods onto the speedboat to take them away. They stole 12,000 rupees in cash from Motilal Debnath, attacked him with bayonets and finally shot him most cruelly. That day eighteen people from our village were shot or bayoneted to death. There was a man named Jiten, the brutal Pakistan army soldiers tied him tightly to a coconut palm, piled straw at his feet and set light to the straw. When his whole body was enveloped in flames and he was yelling terribly the barbarous soldiers shot at him, blasting half of his head away.

All this happened in front of his wife. The army soldiers had seized her and brought her there and they brutally killed her husband in front of her. The soldiers also seized a young widow called Khiroda Shundori and stabbed her all over with their bayonets until she died. Another woman had run and hid in scrubland nearby with her little boy and girl. A soldier aimed his rifle at them and killed all three of them with a single bullet.

That day every house in our village except four were set on fire and destroyed.

On 5th Jyaistha the Pakistan army once again came from Jhalkathi to Shoshid marketplace in a gunboat, and they set up camp in the marketplace. That same day soldiers killed two people from our village. One of them was the secretary of the local school, Kali Kanta Mondol. The Pakistan army soldiers had looted the school library and smashed everything up. There was some relief wheat for the students being stored in the library, and the soldiers poured petrol on it and set fire to it. It was while trying to put out the flames of the burning wheat that the secretary got shot.

On this occasion the Pakistan army remained encamped in Shoshid marketplace for ten days. During this time they raped a considerable number of women. They raped many women in our village alone. They would go into the village by night, brutally molest the womenfolk and bring a few girls back to their camp. Each girl would be serially raped by a number of soldiers acting like wild animals. Once they took an eleven year old girl to their camp and subjected her to prolonged brutal abuse. This girl was found alive when the army went away, and she was rescued. For three months she was unable even to walk.

During the same period the Pakistani soldiers also viciously and inhumanly abused a young woman who was eight months pregnant, as a result of which the girl died when giving birth and her baby died too.

On 25th Shrabon the Pakistan army, assisted by collaborators, proceeded from Jhalkathi to Shongkor Dhobol village with a gunboat. They seized Asmot Ali and Rohini Mistri and came on to Shoshid village. There they shot and killed a lad called Sunil Sarkar. Heavy rain started to fall, and the Pakistani soldiers took shelter in the house of Rohini Kumar Mondol. They got hold of a harmonium, tablas and drums, played music and sang songs, and feasted on bananas. When the rain stopped and they got up to go they shot the head of household, Rohini Kumar Mondol, and killed him. Of the two men they had brought with them as captives, they released one for a ransom and shot the other in Shoshid marketplace. They beat him severely and verbally abused him before killing him. They warned the one they released that everyone must say '*Joy Pakistan*' instead of '*Joy Bangla*'.

During the period of conflict they set fire to Ashathkati, Jinhar, Madra, Purbojolabari, Moushani, Juluhar, Ata, Jamua, Joushar, Gonopotikathi, Aramkathi and other villages in Shorupkathi Thana area. They brutally slaughtered many people. They hacked two men of Madra village to death with axes, because they had voiced objections when the Pakistani soldiers were about to rape a young girl. They raped a very large number of women during the period. In Shorupkathi alone the Pakistani soldiers raped more than one thousand women.

In all the Pakistan army killed about two to three hundred people in our thana. After independence 156 human skulls were recovered from a pond behind the school at Atghor Kuriana.

When they had gained control of Shorupkathi the Pakistan army set up camps at Shorupkathi, Kuriana, Shoshid, Baukathi, Jolabari and conducted their operations from there. In the area under the Jolabari camp there were thirty-three villages inhabited solely by Hindus, and these the Pakistan army razed to the ground.

signed,
Jotindranath Mondol

Aleya Begum
Village: Bagheria
Post Office: Shonagazi
District: Noakhali

The Pakistan army established camps at Shonagazi and Motiganj and then, assisted by informants and *razakar* thugs, proceeded to attack neighbouring villages. They would suddenly enter a village, loot money and valuables and subject the womenfolk to atrocious abuse. For fear of persecution almost all the young men and women of the area left their homes; some fled to India and others sought refuge with relatives in distant villages.

When the Pakistan army occupied Shonagazi in June I left my husband's home and fled to a distant village. In August I gave birth to a baby. Two months after this I was unwell, so I left my parents' home and sought refuge at my husband's home in Bagheria. I was in a very weak condition and I was having to take medicine prescribed by a doctor.

In October/November there was a big increase in the intensity of the oppression being committed by the Pakistan army, collaborators, *razakar* vigilantes and the Al-Badar and Al-Shams brigades. Whenever we heard that Pakistani soldiers were entering the village we would slip out of the village and go to hide in another village. Then on 15th November the Pakistan army plus supporting militias attacked my husband's home. The Pakistani soldiers seized me, grabbed my baby and threw it to the ground, and started cruelly maltreating me. Their violence made me lose consciousness. Four or five of the brutes abused me mercilessly, ill as I was, and then went away leaving me lying unconscious. Later my husband and other relatives got a doctor and managed to resuscitate me.

signed,
Aleya Begum

Dr Abdul Latif
Village: Siramishi
Thana: Biswanath
District: Sylhet

At 9 o'clock on the morning of Tuesday 31st August about fifteen Pakistani soldiers and a similar number of *razakar* militiamen entered Siramishi marketplace. No Pakistan army personnel had been there previously. The commander of the *razakar* squad was a school teacher. He ordered all the employees of the post office and tehsil office to go to Siramishi High School. There a Peace Committee was set up. Innocent members of the public came to the school full of anxiety. After a few minutes' discussion the Pakistani soldiers made the local Siramishi people sit on one side and the government employees and outsiders on the other. After a while these two groups of us were led away separately to different places. I had been working in the village as a doctor for about seven years and the group I was in consisted of outsiders and government employees, 26 people in all. We were taken to the head teacher's office in the school. Our hands were bound tightly. We were told we would be taken to the neighbouring thana, Jagannathpur, and released there. We were led out and taken away by boat. Meanwhile the other group of 37 people from Siramishi village and market also had their hands tied and were taken to a different village. Our group of 26 were taken by boat to Kochrakeli village, and there we were made to stand in a row in shallow water at the edge of a pond. Our hands were tightly bound behind our backs. The Pakistani soldiers and *razakar* militia then shot at us from two directions. I received bullets in my arms and legs and plunged into the pond. With great difficulty I got to the far bank and hid among vegetation. After staying there a while I returned to the first side, wounded as I was, and came close to the fallen. I examined each of them carefully and confirmed that they had all achieved martyrdom, killed by the bullets of those vile barbarians. Meanwhile the 37 local Siramishi men had been taken to an open field and shot in a similar manner. Though wounded I managed to reach a different village, where I took refuge. The names of those whose lives had been taken are given below: Abdul Barik (member of the Union Council), Abdul Latif, Sundar Miah, the Tehsildar (local tax collector) and two of his sons, the Postmaster of Siramishi Bazar post office, the Head Teacher of Siramishi High School, a teacher of Siramishi Primary School, Nazir Ahmed, Ekhlas Miah, Mazid Ullah, Dobir Miah, Rushmot Ullah, Tayyub Ali, Mosadder Ali and others. The Pakistan army and its camp followers were not content with having slaughtered 63 innocent people on 31st August. On 1st September they set fire to Siramishi bazar and Siramishi village, and heinously violated many women.

signed,
Abdul Latif

Musammat Chanubhan
Village: Phulbaria
Thana: Brahmanbaria
District: Comilla

I am an unmarried woman, fatherless and destitute. The only other member of my family unit is my widowed mother. I have no brothers or sisters.

When the Bangladesh independence movement began the Pakistan army set up a camp in Pattan Union. Towards the end of June the repressive activities of the Pakistan army and *razakar* militia increased in both severity and cruelty. Local *razakar* activists looted a great deal of property in our village and elsewhere in the union. At dead of night on 17th July Banu Miah, Shona Miah and Chand Miah came to my home, seized me and took me to the Pakistan army camp. The Pakistani soldiers danced in delight when they saw me, and all my tears failed to arouse the slightest hint of compassion in them. When the *razakar* thugs had seized me I had pleaded with them and fallen at their feet in supplication, but the more I wept in front of them the more cruelly they went on abusing me.

The inhuman devils of Pakistani soldiers kept me in their camp and in their bunkers for five days, and although I was very weak they kept brutally assaulting me and pressing me to tell them anything I knew about the freedom fighters. When I said I knew nothing about the liberation army they got angry and beat me. Throughout those five days they would not even allow me to take a bath.

In return for capturing me the *razakar* thugs received a lot of liquor from the fiendish Pakistani devils, and were also given permission to plunder the local villages for loot. I frequently lost consciousness as a result of the abuse I received from the soldiers. When I regained consciousness I could still see and feel them mistreating my debilitated body. To this day I feel horror whenever I think of it.

After the *razakar* militia had seized me in the night of 17th July my mother went to the liberation army commander in Keshobpur village, Nazir Ahmed, on 18th July and gave him the grim news that I had been captured and taken to the Pakistani camp. Late in the night of 21st July the commander, with a large number of freedom fighters, attacked the Pakistan army camp and bunkers at Phulbaria. Taken by surprise, the Pakistani soldiers and the *razakar* militiamen surrendered. At the time of the attack they had all been busy molesting me. The freedom fighters arrested fourteen soldiers and three *razakar* men, and took them and me over the border to Tripura state in India. In front of me they buried the *razakar* and army devils alive. After our country had achieved independence I returned from Tripura to my own home in Phulbaria.

signed,
Mst. Chanubhan

42

It was 10 o'clock at night and the rain was sluicing down.

Naimul was at the homestead of Mr Talebur Rahman, assistant headmaster of Atitbari School. He was in the inner courtyard. Rainwater was pouring off one end of the corrugated iron roof in torrents, and Naimul was taking a shower in this cascade. The water was ice cold and Naimul was shivering, but he was determined not to retreat before finishing his bath.

Mr Taleb was waiting in the verandah, holding a muslin drying cloth and a freshly laundered lungi. Beside him stood his eldest daughter, Chapa, who was in Class IX at school. She was holding a hurricane lantern. Mr Taleb's wife Amena Begum had also been watching the scene of Naimul's ablutions, but now she had gone to the kitchen to see about some supper. There was nothing ready cooked; she would have to rustle something up pretty quickly. Egg curry, fried aubergine, *dal* made with black gram. There were chickens in the coop and it would have been nice to be able to offer some chicken curry, but as there is a prohibition on slaughtering during the hours of darkness that was out of the question.

The fellow having a shower was no ordinary young man, he was a freedom fighter. Mr Taleb and his family had heard on *Shadhin Bangla* radio that people called freedom fighters were beginning to wage war, but this was the first time they had actually clapped eyes on one of them. How handsome he looked! One got the impression he was from a well off family. Now he was tramping around the countryside.

"Do you need soap?" asked Mr Taleb. "There's some in the house if you want it."

"No need for soap," replied Naimul.

"Isn't that rainwater rather cold?"

"It's very cold indeed."

"Then don't stay under it for too long. You'd better come in now."

"Just a minute," said Naimul.

"Shall I order tea for you?" asked Mr Taleb. "We can do tea, tea with molasses at least; we've got everything that's needed. There'll be a bit of a delay until food's ready, so why not have tea as soon as you've finished your shower, it'll do you good."

"Yes, please, I'd like some."

Chapa rushed off to tell her mother to make tea. It pained her to take her eyes off the stranger even for a few seconds. A freedom fighter had come to their house, a freedom fighter with a gun – it was incredible. She wanted to listen carefully to every word the man said.

"If you don't mind my asking," said Mr Taleb, "where are the other members of your unit?"

"There are no others. I'm a unit of my own. Possibly you'll recognize the name if I tell you. My unit is called the Hasuinya Group."

Mr Taleb exchanged a look of amazement with his daughter. Everyone in the area had heard about the highly daring exploits of the Hasuinya Group. Was this man the Hasuinya?

"Don't you think the name's good?" asked Naimul. "*Hasun* means broom, and the *hasunia* or 'hasuinya' group is going to sweep the army out of our country."

Chapa giggled. The way the man talked seemed so funny! Abruptly she stifled her laughter, for Hasuinya of the Hasuinya Group was staring at her in surprise. Embarrassed, she slipped away to the kitchen to fetch the tea. She must

235

tell her mother that the stranger having a shower was none other than the famous Hasuinya.

Hearing Chapa giggle had made Naimul lose his composure for a moment, for she had sounded just like Moriam. There was no similarity in appearance between Moriam and the girl with the hurricane lantern, but their way of laughing was almost identical.

Amena Begum had nearly finished the cooking. All that remained to be done was the black gram *dal*. The little beans were on the boil, but they were taking a long time to soften. She was just as keen as her husband and daughter to observe the unusual visitor at close quarters, but it was simply not possible. She dared not leave the kitchen in case the beans stuck to the pan and burned. There was little enough to eat as it was, and if one of the items was ruined the poor fellow would go hungry. Those freedom fighters were always out roaming the countryside and probably never got a chance to eat a decent meal.

Naimul was sipping his tea with enjoyment. He and the schoolmaster were both puffing cigarettes. The teacher didn't normally smoke: but this was a very special evening, one which would never come again, and he felt he ought to have a cigarette just to underline how special it was.

"Please tell me some things while you're drinking your tea," said Mr Taleb. "I'd love to hear what you have to say."

"What kind of things do you want to hear?" asked Naimul.

"Tell us about the war. How you fight, that sort of thing."

"I hate talking about war. Shall I tell you something quite different?"

"Oh yes, please do!" said Chapa with great enthusiasm.

Naimul racked his brains for a funny story, but couldn't think of one. If he could amuse the young girl and make her giggle he would be able to hear Moriam's laughter once again. He turned to Chapa and started narrating what came to mind.

"Listen to this, Chapa. There was once a biologist, and he carried out a clever experiment. What he did was this. He took two different species of fish and put them in the same aquarium. The fish of one species were big; the other lot were tiny. The big fish could eat the little fish and considered them as food. The biologist had placed a glass screen in the middle of the aquarium, with the big fish on one side and the little fish on the other. What do you think happened? Every time a big fish spotted a little fish and darted towards it with its mouth open ready to swallow it, it bumped into this invisible barrier and stubbed its nose. It could never get at the little fish to eat it. This went on for days and weeks. Eventually a day came when the big fish seemed to realize that, for whatever reason, it wasn't possible for them to eat little fish, and they stopped trying to do so. And then, guess what, the biologist removed the glass partition so that the two species of fish were swimming in the same space. But even then the big fish didn't eat the little ones. The little ones swam right past their mouths and still they didn't try to catch them."

"Goodness!" exclaimed Chapa. "Is that really true?"

"Yes, it really happened. You see, the glass partition was no longer there in the aquarium, but it had stuck inside the big fishes' heads."

"But how could a glass partition get inside a fish's head?" asked Chapa.

Naimul was astonished. Chapa had asked exactly the same question as Moriam had – how could a glass partition get inside the head of a fish? So it wasn't just Chapa's laughter which resembled Moriam's, their thought processes were the same too.

From the other side of the door came Amena Begum's voice. "Your supper's ready, shall I bring it in?"

"Please do," said Naimul. "I'm very hungry."

"When you've eaten you must have a good sleep," said Mr Taleb. "I've prepared a bed for you. You won't have to worry, I'm not going to go to bed, I'll stay up all night on guard."

"And I'll stay awake as well," said Chapa.

"There's no need for anyone to stay awake," replied Naimul. "I shall sleep soundly anyway. I'm not in the least afraid of anything happening."

Naimul had his meal, surrounded by the Taleb family. Amena Begum felt bad. The young fellow was downing his food so hungrily; if only she had been able to offer him some more substantial items to eat.

"How far is Chandrapur from here?" asked Naimul, turning to Mr Taleb.

"It's quite a long way from here," replied Mr Taleb. "You want to get to Chandrapur, do you? Who will you be seeing there?"

Naimul gave no answer. Such information could not be divulged.

The rice platter was rapidly emptying. Amena's heart sank. Was even the amount of boiled rice she had made insufficient?

The *pir* or holy man of Chandrapur was called Surma Baba by his attendants and followers, because *surma* – antimony or eye-black – was the only thing he ever wore. Day and night he stayed cooped up in a darkened room with only one door, the doorway being veiled by a thick hessian curtain. Nobody except a *khadim* or attendant was allowed inside. Only if a devotee was very persistent indeed would the holy man consent to see him, and permission to enter be granted to the devotee. Before entering the presence of Surma Baba the devotee had to apply antimony to his own eyes. An attendant would be sitting at the entrance with a stibium pot, and would expect a placatory gift in exchange for applying eye-black to the visitor.

Today there was a crowd at the holy man's sanctuary in Chandrapur. For one thing it was Thursday. On Thursdays there was always a programme of ecstatic chanting of God's name lasting all through the night. The chanting would stop at dawn, and then a sacrificial meal would be shared among all present. The food handed out for this *shinni* would be something on the lines of beef, goat or chicken curry and a *khichuri* of rice and lentils. Thanks to Surma Baba's blessing the fare was always delicious, and anyone who had ever sampled it would remember it for the rest of their life.

But there was another circumstance which was making this particular day different. At the holy man's express invitation a Pakistan army major was to come from Dharmapasha. Since he would only be staying till sunset the cooking of the *shinni* had been brought forward. As a special honour to the major the meal was going to be distributed at late afternoon prayer time. Before that a prayer would be said for Pakistan. The *pir* had called on all his followers to take part in this prayer session, and many of them had turned up.

In the major's honour Surma Baba had wound an ochre coloured shawl round his waist to make a kind of skirt. He had also made a personal visit to the kitchen to inspect the cooking, something he never normally did.

Naimul was sitting outside Surma Baba's cell. He was wearing a shawl and his face was hidden in a jungle of beard. He had shown a keen interest in getting an audience with the holy man. There was little hope of being given one on such a busy day, but after he had primed one of Surma Baba's attendants with two packets of Capstan cigarettes and ten rupees in cash the attendant had told him he would try to arrange something. So Naimul was now waiting patiently. He had told the attendant that he had brought a little gift for Surma Baba, and that the attendant himself could expect a further tip when the interview was over.

Even in the heat Naimul was wrapped in his dark shawl, which was almost like a blanket. His eyes were reddened and he was coughing from time to time. The thing affecting his eyes was conjunctivitis, which had been dubbed the *Joy Bangla* sickness, as everyone was catching it this year. Usually it didn't persist for more than a week, but in Naimul's case it seemed to have become permanent; at least, it had been going on for twelve days without respite. It wasn't particularly troublesome, though it meant he couldn't stand looking at bright sunlight without his eyes smarting.

Naimul hadn't had anything to eat since morning, and it was now midday. The smell of the cooking was making his stomach rumble. He could tell from the aroma that the *shinni* truly was going to be delicious.

It was Naimul's turn; he was called to the door of the holy man's cell.

"Tell the Baba your problem very briefly," the attendant told him. "Don't go into long explanations, he understands everything anyway. Now, let me put the *surma* on your eyes. That will cost one rupee."

"Can't I do without the antimony?" asked Naimul. "I've got an eye infection."

"Nobody can see the Baba unless they have *surma* round their eyes," snapped the attendant in irritation. "When the major comes he's going to have to put it on too. Even if Tikka Khan comes to see him the same rule will apply."

"All right, put it on then. Be gentle."

Surma Baba had taken off his shawl. It was hot in the room and he was sweating; with an impatient look on his face he was using the shawl to wipe the sweat away. On a low stool in front of him was a brass beaker containing water. A fan lay nearby. The holy man kept fanning himself rapidly for a few seconds and then taking a sip of water. Naimul had never seen anyone wield a fan so rapidly.

"What do you want?" Surma Baba asked Naimul in an irritable tone, using the most demeaning form of address. "What is it you want?"

"I've brought an offering for you," said Naimul humbly. "I wanted to hand it to you in person."

"Is it goods, or money?"

"Money."

"How much?"

"A good amount."

The look of irritation vanished from Surma Baba's face. He almost smiled as he said, "The amount is of no importance to me. For me one rupee has the same value as a thousand rupees. All the money I get goes to help the poor and needy. That is a form of worship; it has a special name, *haqqul ibada*. Put your money in that donation box under the stool. Then say whatever it is you want to say and be off with you quickly. The major will arrive soon."

"Did you invite the major to come, your reverence?"

"Of course I did. Would he come otherwise?"

"Your reverence, if you don't mind, if it's not an impertinence – might I ask you a question?"

"What question?"

"I've heard that the army have been killing a lot of people, and that they've been carrying young girls away and taking them to their camps. And you invite these people to visit you. Doesn't it seem a little odd?"

"Odd?" retorted Surma Baba sharply. "Don't you know the rules of war against infidels? The property of infidels is fair booty, which we are permitted to take. And the daughters of infidels are classed as infidel property."

"But this war isn't against infidels, it's being waged against the people of this country."

"Wait a moment, what are you getting at? Tell me clearly. Who are you?"

"My real name is Naimul, but you wouldn't know me by that name. I have another name you might recognize – Hasuinya. Now do you know me?"

Even in the semi-darkness of the room Naimul could see that Surma Baba's face had turned ashen. Naimul threw off his black shawl, revealing the sten gun.

"Listen, Surma Baba, you are not going to shout, you are not going to make a sound. Stay sitting exactly as you are. I have come to assassinate the major. There are four others with me, waiting outside. You have heard of the Hasuinya Group?"

"Yes, son, I have."

"My team is called the Hasuinya Group."

"*Ya ghafurur rahim*! Merciful God! What are you saying!"

"You're scared?"

"Yes sir!"

"Don't sit there all naked like that, put some clothes on."

Surma Baba quickly wrapped the shawl round himself, while Naimul put his own shawl back on. The man had already been sufficiently intimidated.

"Oh, sonny, you won't do anything to me, will you?" stammered Surma Baba in a shaky voice.

"If you help me kill the major I won't do you any harm, but if you don't cooperate I shall certainly slaughter you. I'm going to remain right here with you, and when the major comes in to see you I'm going to shoot him."

"Oh, my son, what are you saying!"

"What have you got to be scared of? You're a distinguished *pir*, a man of religion. The moment you die you'll go straight to heaven. You'll have seventy houris massaging your feet."

"Listen, I beg you, forgive me if I've done anything to offend you!"

"I think you know what the Hasuinya Group are like. Forgiveness is not part of their repertoire. It's gone on leave; maybe when this country gains independence it will make a comeback."

One of the attendants pulled the hessian curtain aside and peered in.

"Oy you!" he snapped gruffly at Naimul. "Come out of there! No-one's allowed to stay with the Baba that long."

"We'll need more time," said Naimul. "I haven't got to the main point yet. Surma Baba, tell your *khadim* I'll need more time."

"He needs more time," said Surma Baba as if reciting an incantation. "You may go."

The attendant let the curtain drop and went away. The room was in darkness again.

"Don't any female devotees ever come to see you, Surma Baba?" asked Naimul.

"They do."

"And do you sit there naked when they're present?"

"There's too much heat in my body, son, that's why I can't bear to have any clothes on. Oh, my dear son, please forgive me this once. If you forgive me I promise I'll become a supporter of '*Joy Bangla*'."

Naimul lit a cigarette. "Have a smoke," he said, holding out the packet for Surma Baba. Surma Baba took a cigarette. It took him a long time to light it with a match, as his hands were trembling.

"People say you commune with jinns. Is that true?"

"Yes, son, it's true."

"And you have a number of tame jinns who obey you. How many do you have?"

"Three. There used to be four, but one died, and now there are only three."

"Why don't you call them and get them to save you from your predicament? How could anyone with three jinns under his control get so scared, I wonder? What's the matter, have you lost control of your bladder?"

"I haven't yet, but I do need to go to the toilet, son, I badly need a piss."

"You'll have to do it here. I'm not going to let you go anywhere."

There was a whishing sound. Surma Baba was urinating.

In the late afternoon news came that the major was not going to make it after all. However he had asked for a portion of the *shinni* to be sent to him, and a constable from Dharmapasha police station had just arrived by boat to collect the sanctified victuals.

"So our little plan can't be carried out," said Naimul, getting up to go. "In that case may I take my leave?"

"All right, son," said Surma Baba, hugely relieved, "that's fine, you may go."

"Why not take off your shawl and be naked again," said Naimul calmly. "You are known as the naked ascetic, let me kill you in your unclothed state."

Surma Baba was staring blankly at Naimul as if unable to take in what he was saying.

"What are you waiting for?" chided Naimul. "Take it off."

Naimul shot him with his sten gun at point blank range, feeling no qualms. Only one thing bothered him – his appetite had been ruined.

Dharmapasha police station offered a one thousand rupee reward for anyone who could hand over Naimul of the Hasuinya Group, either dead or alive. The reward was announced by the president of the peace committee. This gentleman spent his nights at the police station, for he felt unsafe in his own home. He met his death on the second day after the announcement of the reward. He was assassinated at noon, outside a teashop in the bazaar, and the assailant was Naimul himself.

"How are you, Mr President?" Naimul had said to him. "You recognize me, I suppose? I'm Hasuinya."

The committee president had been chewing *paan* with spiced tobacco. Juice trickled from his lips.

"You know how many girls are being held captive at the police station?" Naimul had continued.

"No girls are being held at the station," the president had stuttered.

"Tell me the truth," Naimul had insisted. "I warn you, there's a sten gun under my shawl and it's pointing at you."

"I d-don't know how many girls there are."

"I suppose you have no daughters of your own – or do you?"

"I don't understand what you're getting at."

"You'll understand all right, once you've got a bullet in you. It's an amazing thing, the moment a bullet enters the body the mind becomes perfectly clear. A bullet acts like a pill for clearing the head."

At this point in the conversation the president had tried to make a run for it, but he had stumbled and fallen. Then and there he had been shot.

For a while people were fleeing hither and thither within the country, like duckweed circulating on the surface of a pond. Dhaka people were leaving the city and heading for the countryside. People from one village were leaving it to take refuge in another. People from Rajshahi felt that any district other than Rajshahi would be safe to go to. Everyone seemed to be abandoning one place in favour of another, always in search of a safe haven.

Around the middle of June, when the *razakar* militia had become properly organized, the exodus began: people started leaving the country to go abroad. Thousands of refugees began to drift over the border. Their idea was, if they could only get outside the territorial limits of their own country they would have a chance of survival. But what a painful odyssey they faced!

The family of Foyzur Rahman was one of those preparing for the odyssey. They intended to cross over the border and head for Calcutta. There was only one way to do it – by river, passing through the Sundarbans. Many people were using this route; and many were having their journey cut short when they fell into the hands of river pirates.

The Pakistan military authorities were also aware of this escape route. Pakistani gunboats regularly patrolled the main rivers, and as soon as they saw a boat laden with passengers they would train their guns on it.

Ayesha Begum was not willing to travel through the Sundarbans with her children in these circumstances. Her main concern was for her two elder sons. The situation was such that the army, in league with *razakar* vigilantes, might at any moment surround the place where they were staying and carry off the two young men. So she had a long talk with the head of the family in whose house they had been taking refuge, and made a plan to send her two sons away to a place of safety. But let us hear the tale in the words of Ayesha Begum's eldest son.

We were in a backward village fifteen or sixteen miles from Pirojpur, a small village next to a river. I cannot remember the name of the river; maybe it was the Boleshwar or the Rupsha. The river was attractive, and the village even more beautiful. It was as if someone had carefully decorated the landscape with coconut palms and areca nut palms. It was the middle of the rainy season and the river was in spate. On moonlit nights silvery light would twinkle down like falling blossoms and some of it would catch in the trees. Altogether it was like a scene from a fairy tale. I was living in this dreamlike setting with my mother and siblings; but none of us had any dreams in our minds.

Mother kept weeping. There was a rumour going around that the Pakistan army had killed my father. Not only that, they were searching for me and my younger brother Zafar Iqbal. We were both university students. Both of us had been seen going around armed with guns. We had thought we could hold the soldiers back with .22 rifles, but in reality this had not been possible. A Pakistan army gunboat had landed at Wheelerhat without encountering any resistance. A detachment of soldiers had marched from there into Pirojpur town, and that was the beginning of an orgy of destruction and slaughter.

By this time we were on the run. We were turned out of the place where we first sought refuge. Nobody wanted to take us in, as we were dangerous people with a price on our heads. In the end we were given shelter by a Moulana at Gowarekha. This man was a devout follower of the holy man of Shorshina, and a loyal Pakistani. He used to pray for Pakistan at every prayer time, asking that it should remain united. And yet he offered us shelter, and was wholehearted in his defence of us. Time and again he used to reassure Mother in his booming voice: "There's nothing to fear, I won't let the army get at your sons. You can rely on God above, and me on earth. If they want to shoot your sons they'll have to shoot me first."

Mother wasn't altogether reassured, for the army had started a campaign in that area, burning one village after another and slaughtering people indiscriminately. And it was the Moulana himself who used to bring news of these massacres; he used to make us all gather together and then describe the latest atrocities to us with apparent relish.

"Today in Kaukhali they made twenty people line up and then they swept them with brush fire. Everyone died."

"Today they strung two men up on a date palm and told them to say '*Joy Bangla*'. Then they shot them, bang! bang!"

"Today they chopped the Hindu pharmacist's head off with one stroke of the axe."

A glow of enthusiasm could be detected in the Moulana's face as he described these atrocities. I simply couldn't make the man out. He was a genuinely good hearted person, and it wasn't only us he was sheltering; he had taken in some young Hindu men as well

In those days there was no way a Hindu could turn. As soon as the army heard that someone was a Hindu that was it, there would be no further discussion, he would be shot. Hindu families had deserted their homes and gone to hide in the jungle with their small children. As it was the rainy season the jungle was full of snakes, rain was falling all day and night, the whole situation was too awful to describe. They couldn't even run away and cross the border into India, for the escape route led through the Sundarbans where army gunboats were patrolling all the waterways. The liberation army was not yet strong enough to offer refugees any help.

We were stuck in an exquisitely beautiful village in our own homeland. We wanted to flee and go abroad, but death was prowling all around. So there we were, in acute distress and terror, passing one long day, one endless night after another.

Then one day the Moulana of Gowarekha came to see Mother. His face was grave.

"We've got to get your two sons away from here," he said. "We can't afford to wait."

"Why?" asked Mother in surprise.

"I've decided the situation is too dangerous."

"Why?"

"They're grabbing all the young men and killing them off."

"So where do you intend to send them?"

"I'm going to send them somewhere where the army won't detect them."

"Is there any such place?"

"Certainly there is. I'll put them in the holy man's Quranic school in Shorshina. They can stay in the school hostel. If necessary I'll get them enrolled in the school - they can be in the sixth grade."

"I entrust my sons to your care," said Mother. "Do what you think best."

Each of us brothers dressed up in a cotton *panjabi* and lungi, and stuck a round prayer cap made of woven cane on our head. Then we set off for Shorshina. We had to go by boat. The journey was not going to be without risk, for army gunboats were on patrol. We were in fear and tension all the way, and it felt as if our journey would never come to an end. The moment we heard the throb of a motor we had to quickly steer the boat into a backwater and wait till the coast was clear. From time to time the Moulana would say something like "don't look to the right, boys," and we would avoid looking to the right as there would be a decomposing corpse floating there.

The hermitage of the Pir or holy man of Shorshina was beautiful. The compound was situated next to a river and was immaculately maintained. There was a large and spacious hostel for the students. Altogether it was an impressive mission in a very out of the way place. No wonder it was famous, and successive presidents of Pakistan had come to visit it and spend time in it.

We arrived in Shorshina in the afternoon, tired and hungry. Some madrasah students gave us a mash of shredded chapatis, milk and sugar to eat, and we devoured it eagerly. As the army had been leaving the madrasah in peace the students were perfectly happy. We heard that the Pir of Shorshina had a direct telephone link with Pirojpur, and that the captain phoned him three or four times a day and asked for his blessing before starting any operation. The students were delighted to hear that we two brothers had come to get enrolled in the madrasah. However we did not reveal our true identity to them.

Our Moulana took us to see the Pir just before sundown. The holy many was talking to the people standing around him, and we didn't dare to go close. We could hear the Moulana speaking to him in a low voice, and the holy man getting angry, but we couldn't catch all they were saying. Most of the time the Pir was replying in Urdu. There was some talk about my father. The Pir said, "I know that man, he's a great traitor. The captain has talked to me about him. Go away, now, be off with you."

The Moulana said something else in a low voice, evidently about us two brothers, which made the Pir flare up and cry furiously, "No, no! Why did you bring them here?"

So the Moulana took us back to his village. He didn't disclose any details of what had been said. We set off on our journey back by boat, praying that it would soon be totally dark, for the army gunboats did not venture out in darkness. We were sitting on the exposed deck of the boat; the river was swollen by the tide, the sky was overcast and light rain was falling. Suddenly the boatman said, "Look!" We looked. Two corpses were drifting by in the water. There was nothing extraordinary about that; it was a very commonplace event, for countless dead bodies were floating down the rivers every day; the vultures would doze while perching on them, having become tired of eating human flesh. But there were no vultures on the bodies we saw now. I stared at them transfixed, unable to look away. There was the corpse of a young man in his thirties wearing a green shirt, and clinging to his neck was the body of a little girl aged about seven. She had a set of red glass bangles on her wrists. Probably she had wrapped her arms round her father's neck, trusting in his protection, moments before death overtook them both.

We now live in an independent country, Bangladesh. The greatest and most prestigious medal this country has to offer is the Independence Medal. The military hero Ataul Gani Osmani°, the rebel poet Kazi Nazrul Islam°, the intellectual Munier Chowdhury°, the philanthropist Ranada Prasad Saha°, the artist Zainul Abedin° are recipients of the medal.

It is 1980, nine years after the liberation war. On Victory Day I hear an announcement on radio and television - the Independence Medal has been awarded to none other than Moulana Abu Zafar Muhammad Saleh, the Pir of Shorshina.

Words cannot express my dismay.

44

It was Shahed's last night in Dhaka city.

He had decided to leave for Comilla at dawn. Asmani's father's ancestral home was in the Chouddogram area of Comilla District. Shahed had never been there before, but that was no great problem, he would be able to find the place. Asmani's grandfather had been an influential figure in his village community. As he had once been a trader in Rangoon his homestead was generally known as Rangoon Bari. Even if Shahed couldn't remember Asmani's grandfather's name he remembered about Rangoon Bari, and he reckoned he should be able to locate the homestead and then hopefully find Asmani and the rest of them there.

Agartala, in the Indian principality of Tripura, is not far from Comilla. It was quite possible that the family had packed their bags and gone over the border to Agartala. If that was the case Shahed would go there himself, and search all the refugee camps. A whole family group couldn't disappear without trace.

But it was also possible that Asmani and her relatives would turn up at the house after Shahed had left, maybe the very same afternoon or evening, so Shahed had made sure they would find out where he was. He had stuck a note to the mirror in the bathroom, as follows:

> Asmani,
> If you read this letter you will realize that I'm out of danger. I have left Dhaka to go and search for you. Don't worry about me. Great danger does not recur repeatedly, so assume I am all right. Wait for me in this house. I have left rice, lentils, flour and oil for you in the kitchen. Look carefully in the lentil tin.
>
> Shahed

He underlined 'lentil tin'. There was some money hidden under the lentils in the tin. Asmani might arrive without any cash on her, and she would need money.

By this time Shahed had none of his own money left; he was using Gourango's. There had been no further sign of Gourango. Shahed had gone to Old Dhaka one day to look for him, not without great trepidation, but had found Gourango's house padlocked. He had shoved a note under the door. If Gourango had seen the note he would surely have come to see Shahed, so it was fairly evident he had not found it.

Shahed's boss Mr B.Happy had been very helpful in connection with his plan to go to Comilla. There had never previously been any system of identity cards at the office, but now the boss had had cards printed and photos attached, and had issued one to every employee. In Shahed's case he had also provided a special pass signed by an army colonel, which read: 'The bearer Shahed Uddin is a loyal Pakistani. He should be subjected to no harassment.'

Mr B.Happy did something which seemed incredible to Shahed. Non-Bengali he might be, but he had ushered Shahed into his private office, closed the door and announced in a low voice that he had decided to become a freedom fighter. "I'm rather too old for going to war, but still I'm trying. I haven't managed to get in contact with them yet, but I shall do."

"But why do you want to fight?" Shahed had asked.

"Why shouldn't I?" Mr B.Happy had replied. "You tell me. I came to this country penniless. I engaged in business here and improved my fortune. Now I have a house, a car, money in the bank. This country has given me so much; isn't it right that I should give something in return?"

"And your family? Do they know about your plans?"

"They do. They have gone away to West Pakistan, they have a rather different outlook. Each person has their own ideas."

"Will our country become independent, what do you think, sir?" Shahed had asked.

"It will. The days of the Pakistanis are numbered. They are molesting womenfolk, and that is something God does not like at all. Anyway, off you go now. Go and find your wife and daughter. That letter I procured for you, keep it as carefully as if it was a sacred amulet. It will get you out of any danger. Be happy, man, be happy."

Before a person could get out of Dhaka they had to pass through a number of checkpoints: the *razakar* militia checkpoint, the West Pakistani police checkpoint, and finally the army checkpoint. At each stage they had to show their 'dandy card', their identity card. After that had been checked their baggage was gone through. Someone might even come and feel their neck to see whether it was hard or not. A hardened neck meant a fugitive policeman or EPR rifleman – habitual bearing of arms toughens a man's neck muscles.

The most humiliating part of the examination was the circumcision test. Each man had to lower his trousers to show whether or not he had been circumcised. The West Pakistani policemen particularly enjoyed this part of the checking and cracked endless jokes as they went about it. They practically staggered and fell into each other's arms with laughter.

Shahed had to undergo this test and pull down his trousers and underpants. The officer doing the check was holding a thick pencil, red at one end, blue the other, and used it to poke Shahed's anatomy. He seemed to take pleasure in doing it.

"Say your name." The interrogation took place in Urdu.

"Shahed."

"Where are you going?"

"Chouddogram, Comilla."

"Why are you going there?"

"My father is ill. I want to see him."

To give substance to the story that he was going to visit his ailing father Shahed was carrying a bag of grapes and apples, which he held out for inspection. He was one of the lucky ones, and was allowed back onto the bus without having had to produce the colonel's letter. Several others were not allowed through; instead they were being detained and interrogated. Eventually they might be released, but then again, they might not. There was always that uncertainty. These were times of endless uncertainty.

Shahed and his fellow travellers were checked again as they queued to board the ferry for the Meghna river crossing. This time the army was doing the checking. Even the women wearing burqas had to lift their veils and show their faces, for the military wanted to make sure the people inside really were female. The soldier who had the task of checking the women was quite civil; he reassured each of them saying, "Don't be afraid, dear, you're my sister!"

On the ferry Shahed had one of the oddest experiences in his life. He had bought a portion of *jhal muri*, oiled and spiced pop-rice, in a paper cone. He hadn't eaten all day, his stomach was rumbling and he thought the pop-rice might stave off the pangs of hunger. Just as he was about to toss a handful of *muri* into his mouth a little girl of about Runi's age, who looked like a vagrant, suddenly came and threw herself at his legs, making him drop his paper cone.

Shahed was on the point of pushing the little girl away and reprimanding her when he stopped dead. This child was no stranger, he knew her well: it was Kongkon, the one who couldn't pronounce her own name properly and called herself 'Kokon'.

"Oh, it's you! So where have you sprung from all of a sudden? Where's your Mum? And where's your Grandad?"

The little girl made no reply, but stayed clinging to Shahed with her cheek against his leg.

"Kongkon! Answer me! Who did you come here with?"

Still Kongkon said nothing. A small crowd started to gather round the two of them.

The mystery of who had brought Kongkon so far was soon solved. It was a man called Ramzan, a painter and decorator from Badda in the northern suburbs of Dhaka. It was obvious that he was hugely relieved to have found Shahed, and he poured out his whole story. After the crackdown he and his wife's younger brother had gone on the run, crossing the Buriganga river to get away from Dhaka. They weren't the only ones, thousands were fleeing the same way. Then the air force had started dropping bombs, and everyone had scattered to take cover as best they could. When things had quietened down a bit Ramzan had found he had this little girl with him. She was hanging onto his shirt and nothing would induce her to let go.

"Yer see, brother, it's like this, the little lass can't explain nothing. She knows the names of her Mum and Dad, but what use is that, I ask yer? What I needed to know was the address. I'm a painter by trade, yer see, and I'm out of work, never know when I'll get my next square meal. How am I going to look after a kid?"

"Where are you heading for now?" asked Shahed.

"To me wife's elder brother's place, he married a girl from Maijdi and he's got a shop there. I'd decided to take the lass there and leave her with him. Now the good Lord has let me meet you, and a big weight is off me mind. What relation of yours is she, brother?"

"I'm her uncle."

"*Alhamdulillah*! Now yer can be together, see – uncle and niece."

Kongkon was still gripping Shahed's leg tightly. She wasn't looking up, and her small body kept shivering. Shahed laid a hand on her back.

"It's all right, Kongkon," he said, "don't be afraid. I'll take you back to your parents. Eh, Kongkon? How about it?"

"Mm."

"Are you hungry? Do you want something to eat, a banana? Let me get some bananas and you can eat one."

"Mm."

Shahed bought some bananas and was just about to hand one to Kongkon when he realized she had fallen asleep. Her body felt hot, she had a fever. Still asleep, she got sick all over Shahed's trouser leg.

I met Kongkon in New York. A partner of the publishing firm Muktodhara, named Bishwajit, had taken me to visit a book fair. Many American Bengalis were enjoying themselves at the event. Food stalls had been set up, a video drama was being shown on a large screen, there were even booths selling saris and jewellery. Altogether quite a festive atmosphere had been created. And then a very pretty young woman in her early thirties came up to me and touched my feet in true Bengali traditional style as she uttered a respectful word of greeting. Surprised, I took a step back.

"Should I call you uncle or should I call you sir?" she asked.

"You may call me whatever you like," I replied.

"Then I'll call you uncle. If I said sir it would feel as if you were my teacher and were about to tick me off. I must say you do have a stern look about you."

I liked the way the young woman expressed herself so articulately.

"I'm proposing to take you to my flat," she went on. "You're a writer and I want to tell you a very interesting story."

"I never write stories I've heard from anyone else," I objected.

"You'll want to write my story once you've heard it," she said. "I'm ready to bet you one thousand dollars that you will."

After finishing at the book fair I let Kongkon take me to her flat. It was a typical New York apartment, small but neat. The whole setup was in fact a model of elegance and beauty. Kongkon was married to an American man who worked in a construction company and they had one child, a son named Robin or Robby for short. Robby had gone out with his father to see the film Lion King.

"They'll be back in a while," said Kongkon, "then we'll all have dinner together."

"So I have to stay on until dinner time?"

"You certainly do. But you needn't worry, dinner time doesn't mean ten o'clock at night like in Bangladesh. Here dinner is eaten in the early evening. Now please sit comfortably with your feet up like you normally do, and I'll tell you my story."

"How do you know I usually sit with my feet up?"

"I saw you doing it at the book fair. Do you think it's only you writers who are gifted with powers of observation? What about us readers?"

I sat on a comfortable sofa with my feet up and Kongkon began her tale.

"Of course I was a very young child then and I can't remember everything clearly, much of it is reduced to hazy impressions. But certain memories stand out very clearly. For example I can remember Uncle Shahed bathing me, it was in a market place or somewhere like that. He was pouring water over me out of a kettle, and the water was quite warm. He was alternately pouring the water and rubbing me over with soap. The soap had a lemony fragrance, I remember that very distinctly. That memory is so much part of me that even now I only like using lemon scented soaps.

Uncle Shahed bought me a new frock and some new shoes. He also got a cheap plastic doll for me. I still have it, I'll show it to you later. We stayed one night in a hotel, and I can't begin to describe how peacefully I slept with Uncle's arms round me. I have a plan to go and look for that hotel if ever I visit Bangladesh, and stay another night in it."

"You think you'll be able to trace the hotel?"

"Of course. The hotel is in a place called Daudkandi. The walls and roof of the building are made of corrugated steel sheeting, and you can see a river from it. I remember every detail about it."

"So carry on with your story."

"I remember Uncle Shahed walking for miles and miles with me on his shoulders. That's when we were heading for the border. We were going to leave East Pakistan and make for Agartala. Every now and then Uncle Shahed would get tired and set me down. 'Will you be able to walk for a bit?' he would ask me. 'Yes,' I would say. But I could never walk far, and soon Uncle would pick me up and put me on his shoulders again. Far from having a hard time, I was actually enjoying myself. There were lots of other people walking the same way alongside us. There was an old woman whose son was carrying her along in his arms."

"You even remember that old woman?"

"Yes, because Uncle Shahed said to me, 'Look, that man is carrying his mother in his arms, and I'm carrying my mother on my shoulders – isn't that funny?' He called me mother instead of niece, you see."

"And then what happened?"

"We reached Agartala in the early evening. From there you could get to various refugee camps by lorry. When we got into the lorry Uncle Shahed said, 'Listen, darling, there are lots of different camps, and we're going to look for your Mum in every one of them. It's not all that likely we'll find her, but if we don't you mustn't worry. You've got me with you, and somehow or other I'll make sure you are reunited with your Mum in the end. All right?' And I said 'All right.'

I started running a fever while we were travelling in the lorry. Uncle wrapped me up in a shawl and folded me in his arms, and I felt as if it was my mother who was hugging me tight. And guess what happened. We found my mother and grandfather in the very first refugee camp we came to."

"No! You don't say so!"

"Yes. But I have no recollection of us finding them. All I can remember is Mum, Grandad and Uncle Shahed crying their hearts out. I thought Uncle Shahed looked very funny when he was crying, and I kept my eyes fixed on him."

Kongkon was moved to tears. First she wept silently, then after a few moments she covered her face with both her hands and started sobbing loudly. Just then the doorbell rang – it was probably her husband returning from the cinema with their son. Kongkon made no move to open the door but tried desperately to control her weeping.

Watching the grief-stricken young woman I was suddenly struck by the realization that it was not Kongkon sitting there weeping. It was Bangladesh, my motherland herself.

45

The place where Shahed was putting up in Agartala was called the Nirala Hotel. It was a long low one-storeyed building with a corrugated iron roof which looked rather like a school. From its windows you could see hills and distant forests of *sal* trees. Though the room was as cramped as a rabbit hutch it got plenty of light and air. The food at the hotel was good too; they did a dish consisting of pigeon-pea pottage mixed with vegetables which was extremely tasty. The proprietor of the hotel was Mr Misra.

"All the people from East Pakistan call me Misri Babu," he told Shahed when they met for the first time, "and you should do so too. I'm actually of East Bengali origin myself. My mother was from Nobinagar in Comilla District."

"Well, how are you, brother?" Shahed asked.

"I'm fine," said Misri Babu cheerfully, "but it upsets me to see the pain and suffering you people are going through."

"Your hotel is nice," said Shahed. "It's neat and clean."

"Water supply is a problem," said Misri Babu. "There are too many people in town now, and the municipal water supply is insufficient. Please try to pardon us, I'm afraid you won't be able to have a bath every day. Though there is a lad called Fotu who will always fetch a couple of bucketfuls for you if you offer him a rupee."

Shahed had now been staying at the hotel four days. Every day he spent an extra rupee for his two buckets of water. Before going to sleep he would ladle the water over himself and have a good long bath, and after that he would sleep soundly. When he woke in the morning he would reflect that it was a long time since he had had such a good sleep, without any fear of being woken and seized by the Pakistan army in the middle of the night, or having his throat slit by Bihari marauders while still slumbering. Sometimes he felt he wasn't living in the real world any more, but savouring the peace of heaven.

It seemed extraordinary that he had managed to hand Kongkon back to her mother. How could such an improbable thing have come to pass? Was there really some kind of being watching over everyone, causing lost children to be returned to their parents by its own inscrutable methods? After 25th March Shahed had begun to lose any such belief, but now his faith was returning.

Since delivering Kongkon Shahed had been feeling very relaxed, as if his duties were now over and he could take things easy. Now was his chance to discover the Agartala he had heard so much about at the time of the Agartala conspiracy case°, to explore it as a tourist. No doubt there were plenty of things to see. This was the first time Shahed had ever been abroad. He had never even thought of going to another country, as he had never possessed a passport. And here he was now, having reached foreign soil without any travel documents at all.

He had searched high and low for Asmani and Runi on his first couple of days here. He had looked in every one of the refugee camps, he had consulted the lost persons bureau, he had scanned the guest lists of all the hotels: there was no sign of Asmani anywhere in Agartala. Even then you could never tell, maybe one morning he would be sipping tea from one of those clay cups at a roadside tea stall when a little girl would come trotting up and fling her arms round his legs. He would be thrown off his balance, the clay cup would fall and smash to pieces on the ground. Irritated, he would be just about to give the little girl a good talking to when she would open her mouth and say, "Daddy! Daddy! It's me!" If such a thing could happen with Kongkon, why shouldn't it happen with Runi too?

One evening Shahed went to the cinema and saw a film. The film was *Sagarika*, starring Uttam and Suchitra, and Shahed enjoyed it. When he left the cinema after the show he had a feeling that everything was all right: he was fine, Asmani and Runi were fine, and one day he would take Asmani to see the film for herself. Yes, he certainly would.

Shahed hadn't been back to the camp where Kongkon and her mother and grandfather were. He knew he ought to drop in every day and see how they were, but for some reason he couldn't bear to do so. Once he went almost as far as the camp gate, only to turn back. He wasn't sure why he had this aversion. Maybe it was because in his heart he knew that every time he saw Kongkon he would be reminded of his own Runi.

Another day he got details from Misri Babu and went off to see Nirmahal, the palace of the maharajahs of Tripura. The palace was reflected in its lake, and behind it were groves of ironwood trees with their pretty flowers called *nagkeshar* or 'serpent's tresses'. What a delightful scene! At once Shahed made a plan to bring Asmani to Agartala once Bangladesh had become independent. They could stay in the Nirala Hotel, and one evening they would go to see Nirmahal, and then they would wander in the *sal* forests and dally in the *nagkeshar* plantations. How did that song go?

> *Nagkeshar flowers swinging, swaying, falling,*
> *Dance little girl for me,*
> *O dance little girl for me.*

Then one day Shahed went to visit the guerrilla fighters in their camp. This was in a place called Melaghor, located somewhere between Kasba in East Pakistan and Bhelunia in Tripura. The officer in charge was Major Khaled Mosharraf°, the commander of No. 2 Sector. The camp was hidden in dense forest and suffered from an acute shortage of water – the one kind of shortage which cannot be shrugged off lightly. In it hundreds of lads and young men were being offered training. Shahed made friends with one of them called Iftekhar, a second year honours physics student from Dhaka University.[*]

"How are you, brother?" asked Shahed.
"I'm all right," said Iftekhar.
"Has your training begun?"
"Not yet. Registration is still going on."
"What's the food like?"
"We have two meals a day. The evening one is the better of the two."
"Why is it better?"
"Because we eat it in the dark," explained Iftekhar smiling.
"I don't get you," said Shahed.
"There are lots of little grubs in the rice, but at night we can't see them so we don't mind." And Iftekhar laughed heartily.

---

[*] In due course Iftekhar became a member of the intrepid Crack Platoon and infiltrated Dhaka city where the platoon harassed the Pakistan army so much that the very word 'Mukti' or 'freedom fighter' instilled terror in their minds. When making house to house searches the first question the Pakistani soldiers would ask was "Where are the Mukti?" Another member of the platoon was Rumi, the valiant son of Begum Jahanara Imam°, the 'Mother of Martyrs'. Rumi was caught by the Pakistan army on 29th August, tortured and killed. He was a true national hero of Bangladesh. – **Author**

Shahed was impressed by the young lad's irrepressible good humour, and he said, "Brother, if you have no objection I'd love to invite you for a meal at my hotel. Couldn't you get an exeat and come into town one day?"

"Nope," replied Iftekhar, "but you may offer me a cigarette if you like. I usedn't to smoke, but now I've started the habit."

Shahed felt hugely embarrassed, for he had no cigarettes on him. "I'll bring you some tomorrow," he promised. "Several packets."

"There's no need."

"Yes, there is a need," retorted Shahed. "You could do with them. I'll be coming here tomorrow in any case, because I'm going to join you. Tell me, which one is the recruiting officer? And what does one need to qualify as a freedom fighter? Courage, presumably. That's something I lack entirely."

"Me too," said Iftekhar.

It was late at night when Shahed got back into town. The journey was quite a long one, and he had been riding in the back of a truck on bumpy unmade roads. On the way he had got soaked with rain several times over – mountain rain which stopped as suddenly as it started. Shahed had felt a fever coming on even as he travelled.

He couldn't eat anything before going to bed; his temperature was rising rapidly. He felt cold with only one blanket, and called the hotel boy to fetch him another. Misri Babu came round to see him and gave him a couple of tablets. In a feverish sleep Shahed dreamed of Asmani. She was at their house in Dhaka, sitting in the bedroom. Runi had a temperature and Asmani was giving her a cold compress. She was talking to Runi in a voice full of exasperation: "Just see how silly your Daddy is. We've come back to Dhaka and he's still sitting tight in Agartala. Has he lost his marbles altogether?"

"Don't be cross with Daddy, Mummy," Runi was saying.

"How can I not be cross with him?" protested Asmani. "Here I am, all on my own. How am I supposed to get you to a doctor? Or who's going to fetch one for me?"

"Daddy will fetch one," said Runi. "Daddy's coming."

Shahed woke up from the dream. The following morning, very early, he set off for Dhaka nursing a temperature of 102° Fahrenheit.

46

30th July 1971

"In the afternoon daughter-in-law and I went to the hospital to see Hasina's baby son°. The army guard there behaved atrociously. Yesterday Hasina's mother had gone to see her and the baby for a brief ten minute visit, and now from today they have imposed a new rule: nobody is allowed to go in and see them at all. Such inhuman treatment. Even criminals in jail are allowed visitors at times. I wonder how many more awful things God will make us witness. Still no letter from Choton. No news of anybody. I have to entrust them to God's care. God is merciful." *

---

* *Freedom Fight, Triumph of Freedom, the Diaries of Begum Sufia Kamal.*°
Hasina: Sheikh Hasina, daughter of Sheikh Mujib and future Prime Minister of Bangladesh. The baby was Sajeeb Wazed (Joy).

8th August 1971

Interview with the President of Pakistan, General Yahya Khan, by journalist Ralph Shaw, published in the *Sunday Times*.

The president said, "Sheikh Mujibur Rahman is alive and well in Pakistan's top level jail. However beyond that I cannot give any promise as to what his future holds.

He will be tried in accordance with the law. That does not mean I'm about to have him shot tomorrow, and he might of course die of natural causes. He is being held in the best jail in Pakistan. He does not have to perform forced labour. He has his own small cell with a bed, a fan and a hot water supply. He is also under the care of a doctor.

Sheikh Mujib had been losing weight as a result of being restricted to a West Pakistani diet. However Bengali food is now being provided and his weight has gone up again.

He tells a good dozen yarns every day, and he cracks jokes."

48

The scene was a special cell in the government jail in Lyallpur (now known as Faisalabad). In it a very special prisoner was being held in conditions of maximum security. Armed guards stood on duty outside it round the clock, and the prisoner's every move was being observed. What was he doing now? Was he walking up and down inside the cell as he regularly did, or was he standing by the window trying to see the sky outside?

This prisoner only did three things. He read the Quran, he peered out of the window at the sky and he paced up and down. Sometimes one or other of the guards would give him a greeting and he would return their *salaam*. Anything like that had to be reported to the jailor immediately, and every single detail of the prisoner's daily life had to be sent on to President Yahya Khan himself.

Nobody in the outside world knew where the prisoner was or how he was passing his days, for great secrecy was being maintained. Various rumours were circulating in both Pakistani and foreign newspapers, but the Pakistan government was neither confirming nor denying what they said; on the subject of Sheikh Mujibur Rahman it chose to remain silent.

One of the rumours was strong enough to have appeared in the *Statesman* in Calcutta. According to this rumour Sheikh Mujib was on hunger strike. He had started his fast in June, and had announced that he wouldn't break it until he was allowed to see his wife and his youngest son Russell. And he was spending all his time writing. He wrote day and night, page after page, though nobody could say exactly what he was writing about.

There was even a rumour that Sheikh Mujib had become insane and spent his days and nights spouting meaningless speeches or mumbling incomprehensibly.

Sheikh Mujibur Rahman was going through a period of great uncertainty. The riddle which concerned him most was whether he would be preserved alive or put to death. He often pondered this subject as he puffed quietly away at his pipe (he had been allowed a supply of tobacco as his one and only luxury in jail). If the Pakistan army won the battle for East Bengal he would surely be executed; but if they lost, what then? There would still be a high probability of his being done away with, if only from a keen desire to exact revenge. And if he was sentenced to death what method would they use to kill him: would he be hanged, or sent to a firing squad? Would he never again see the sweet face of his son Russell? His elder daughter had been expecting a baby, would he never know if a grandchild had been born?

Whenever he thought of his own family he felt slightly ashamed. What was he doing, forgetting the bigger picture and worrying only about his nearest and dearest! He was the guardian of a nation's dreams and aspirations, everyone in the country was pinning their hopes on him – how could he sit here speculating about his own demise?

Occasionally he would drift into a kind of stupor, and he would hear that cry so dear to his heart, '*Joy Bangla!*' From some secret corner of his heart a voice would say, "Don't despair, you shall hear that happy chant again one day!" In his own words, "Call it intuition, telepathy, sixth sense or what you will. Maybe it was a kind of divine inspiration. All I know is that my heart was telling me – yes, we shall achieve victory."

On 3rd August 1971, in a televised speech addressed to the nation, President Yahya announced that Sheikh Mujib would be put on trial, charged with high treason.

Arrangements for the trial were quickly put in place. The hearings were to start on 9th August. The chief judge was to be a brigadier of the Pakistan army, and sitting with him on the tribunal would be two colonels, a wing commander, a naval commander and, as the only civilian, a district sessional judge

Sheikh Mujib entered a plea of not guilty, and refused counsel. The trial began. Each day Sheikh Mujib was conducted to the court room under heavy guard in the morning, and brought back to his cell at five in the afternoon.

The court room was in a red brick building within Lyallpur jail. In order to reach the court the prisoner had to pass through four heavy iron gates and go down a long narrow corridor. Uniformed commandos carrying sub-machine guns stood on guard.

President Yahya always appeared slightly inebriated, as if well steeped in his favourite drink, Black Dog whisky. Even at top level meetings his speech would be slurred, though he seemed quite untroubled by this.

Today, however, he was sober. He was quickly trying to clear the stack of files on his desk. He was in a hurry, for the Chinese ambassador was coming to see him at President House. He had already cajoled ten million dollars of aid money from China, and now he was negotiating for a shipload of arms which was to include some light tanks of Chinese manufacture. Thus today's meeting with the Chinese ambassador was of the greatest importance.

While the president was busily engaged his door opened and in came Zulfiqar Ali Bhutto. The president glanced briefly at him and growled, "Say what you've come to say, I'm going to carry on with my work while I hear you. I'm extremely busy this morning."

"Are you intending to give Sheikh Mujib the death sentence?" asked Zulfiqar Ali.

"Of course," replied the president without looking up from his papers.

"For God's sake don't do that!"

"Why not?"

"He's too big a figure for you to put him to death."

"You think I'm not strong enough to kill him?"

"If you put him to death the whole world is going to jump on us, the Americans in particular. The Americans will let you get away with slaughtering as many Bengalis as you wish, but Sheikh Mujib? No way."

"My good fellow, do you suppose I don't know what the Americans are thinking? I am in constant communication with them. Nixon isn't at all bothered about what happens to Sheikh Mujib. I know Nixon well, I keep closely in touch with him. But I can't talk any more now, the Chinese ambassador is on his way here. No, you may be assured that I will string Sheikh Mujib up on the gallows. He's going to pay for all the trouble he's given me. Now goodbye." *

---

* Sources: 1. *Bangabandhu Sheikh Mujib: A Leader with a Difference*, Obaidul Haq.
   2. *Sheikh Mujib's Life in a Pakistani Jail*, Ahmed Salim, translated by Mofidul Haq.
   3. *The Decline and Fall of Sheikh Mujib*, Raihan International, Tehran, 1st August 1971.

Source: *Dainik Bangla*
Date: 4th January 1972
Title: *How Begum Mujib Passed the Days of the Liberation War*

Begum Mujib Remembers her Days of Misery

Following the familiar route by daylight on the first day of the Bengali New Year I made my way to that fortress-like building on Road No.18. Begum Sheikh Mujib was sitting in the reception room. She welcomed me with a smile. I made a reference to the house and at once she laughed and said, "At least it's somewhere to take refuge. For one and a half months after the crackdown of 25th March I didn't even have that, I was fleeing from one place to the next, and in that period of time I moved house at least fifteen times."

Begum Mujib was laughing, yet I could see her eyes cloud over with an indefinable sadness even as she did so.

It was that ghastly night of 25th March. Sheikh Mujib was lying in bed in his darkened bedroom listening to the cries of agony emanating from a Dhaka racked by bombs and explosions. At times he sat up in alarm.

At one point a piece of shrapnel burst into the room, ripping through the window shutter and grazing the leg of his youngest son Russell. Sheikh Mujib groped in the darkness and retrieved the fragment of shell case. That same terrible night the barbarians came to the house and seized him and led him away. Begum Mujib and her two younger sons were left there on their own.

On 26th March there was a curfew lasting all day. The noise of guns firing was still going on. An eerie sense of mortal danger pervaded the silent dwelling. "Outside huge mortars were pointing their nozzles at my house as they trained their sights on Dhanmandi Girls' School. I was too scared even to close the windows." At midday, while the curfew was still on, Begum Mujib's eldest son Kamal managed to reach home after a risky passage dodging from house to house.

Night fell, the blackest of nights. Listening to Yahya Khan's menacing radio announcement, delivered in a horribly deliberate manner, Begum Mujib understood the serious nature of her plight. Without losing any time she took her second and third sons and climbed over the garden wall to seek refuge with the neighbour, a doctor. Meanwhile her eldest son Kamal, together with Mr Mohiuddin, jumped over another wall and fled in a different direction. From eleven o'clock onwards the sound of mortar detonations became almost deafening, and from then until five o'clock the next morning, in the intervals between periods of fitful sleep on that ghastly night of 26th March, Begum Mujib listened to her family home being shelled. To this day she does not dare to imagine what would have happened if she and her sons had not fled promptly enough that evening.

On the morning of 27th March she moved on with her two sons to take refuge somewhere else, and for the next month and a half she was continuously fleeing from house to house. Finally the Pakistan army traced her to a house in Moghbazar and made her move to the present building on Road No.18.

When she cast her mind back to the events immediately preceding her move to Road No.18, Begum Mujib's face clouded over. "At that time I was staying at a house in Moghbazar. My elder daughter Hasina was pregnant. She and her husband, my own husband's younger brother and his wife, my daughter Rehana and son Russell were all there with me. Suddenly one day Pakistani soldiers came and surrounded the house. An officer told me I had to move to a different place where I would be under army control. I didn't know what to expect. Anyway, I was suddenly filled with the courage of desperation and indignantly told the officer that I wouldn't move an inch unless he could show me his orders in writing. He replied in an arrogant manner, saying that if I didn't come quietly with his men they would have to use force. I had no choice but to submit, however I told him that if I was to move everyone in my household must come with me too. The soldiers discussed this briefly among themselves and then agreed, and they transported us all to this house in Road No.18."

When I asked Begum Mujib about her first hours in the house at Road No.18 she laughed. The house had been full of rubbish and there wasn't so much as a reed mat to sit on, let alone any chairs or sofas. To start with the whole family had had to squat huddled together on a single strip of floor about four feet wide, next to a window.

The sight of her pregnant daughter having to put up with conditions like these distressed Begum Mujib greatly. She couldn't say anything, but just looked around helplessly hoping for some kind of relief. Maybe God took pity on her, for one of the officers on guard duty at the house, a Pathan, noticed her distress and got a sweeper to clean out the house. He also saw to it that some chairs and a blanket were provided.

This Pathan officer was something of an exception among the generally heartless Pakistani soldiers guarding the family in their prison.

Many memories of pain and hardship from her days of imprisonment in that building in Dhanmandi are indelibly inscribed on Begum Mujib's heart; however there is also the much happier memory of the moment when, in that same house, she held her beloved first grandchild in her arms for the first time.

An Interview with Begum Mujib

Noon on a December day. I sat in the lounge on the first floor of Bangabandhu's house in Road No.32, Dhanmandi, talking to Begum Mujib. She described painful and terrifying moments in her life as a prisoner last year.

"Soon after 26th March my eldest son Kamal went over the border into India. Hasina was pregnant, but despite her physical weakness she was my greatest support in those days.

On 12th May we were taken to that one-storeyed prison of a house on Road No.18. I had to survive under the eyes of a Pakistan military guard. Among the soldiers on guard duty there were two members of the Civil Armed Force in civilian dress. They effectively controlled the army guard.

I remember a particular incident which took place when Jamal and Rehana had been squabbling in my bedroom. Jamal was finding it very difficult to adjust to life as a prisoner, and he had become rather hot tempered and excitable.

That day the two of them were having a rather more acrimonious row than usual, when all of a sudden one of the Civil Armed Force officers burst into the room. His eyes inflamed with anger he spoke roughly to Jamal. 'These days you're getting too big for your boots. If you carry on making a disturbance like this we're going to take you away to an army camp, string you up by your heels and give you a good whipping. We shall also take steps to ensure that you will never again be able to enjoy the sight of a human face.' The officer was shouting and ranting. At first I stood there stunned, but after a while I recovered myself and asked him to leave the room. The officer gave all of us a dirty look and stalked out of the house."

After the officer had left Begum Mujib decided on her course of action. That very day she wrote to all the relevant authorities from the president downwards complaining about the officer's foul behaviour.

"However from then on Jamal seemed to become ever more unsettled. He kept trying to find a way of escaping. On 27th July Hasina gave birth to her baby at Dhaka Medical College Hospital. It was my first grandchild; however none of us were given permission to go and see him. Confined to the house that day I was in agonies, chafing with frustration. I wept as I prayed to merciful God.

On 5th August Jamal ran away. He had been preparing for this for some days. He used to tell me that if he did manage to escape I was to wait three or four hours before letting the guards know. When he disappeared I knew he must have got away. I felt very uneasy, for I was aware that if he was captured that would be the end of him; but there was also the consolation of knowing that if he did manage to stay at large he would have a much better time of it. The search for him didn't begin until lunchtime, about 2 p.m. Then everyone started looking high and low, saying 'Wherever can Jamal have got to?' I acted the part of a mother frantically searching for a lost son.

I straight away sent a letter to the authorities accusing them of having kidnapped my son and demanding his return. This put them on the spot, for I had earlier written to them asking them to be especially vigilant in case of kidnap attempts. The colonel who came to enquire into the matter was clearly alarmed at the thought that Jamal had actually been abducted by members of the armed forces. He gave me a few assurances and took his leave. After that the level of security in which we were held was further increased.

Towards the end of August I received a letter from Jamal. At that time my mother-in-law was seriously ill in hospital and I had been given permission to visit her there for two hours each day. Young men used to slip over from India and come to the hospital posing as visitors. Under the eyes of the Pakistani guards I would place my hands on a young fellow's head as if blessing him, and pretend to be urging him to get on with his studies like a good boy. While this was going on a letter would secretly change hands. Then I would personally see the young visitor out of the hospital. I was horrified to think of the risk such youngsters were running; but there was absolutely nothing I could do about it, except call on God to protect them.

That's how my days were spent. I kept my household going on the few savings I possessed. There was so much tension, suffering and want, real life was in abeyance. In that kingdom of death we just survived from moment to moment, amidst fear and uncertainty.

Relatives and friends were scattered all over the place, and I had no way of knowing how they were faring. I didn't worry too much about my husband, as I knew that God alone had the power to save him.

I knew all that, yet still my blood used sometimes to run cold. What an awful situation my dear children were in, and how uncertain was our life in this cramped prison!

As November drew to an end I began to realize that something significant was going to happen in December. In our incarceration we were cut off from the outside world, but we did have a transistor radio. We had heard that Bangabandhu would be put to death the moment India gave official recognition to Bangladesh, so we were looking forward with mixed feelings to Indira Gandhi's historic speech which was to be delivered in Calcutta on 3rd December. Indira made her speech, and I was transfixed; somehow I couldn't tear myself away from the radio. Later that night, after the end of the news on Akash Bani, the presenter suddenly informed listeners that an important announcement was to be broadcast shortly. Tired though we were at the end of the day, all of us huddled round the radio to listen. Time passed, and no announcement. One by one the children went off to bed. I lay down with the radio next to my ear, waiting for the announcement to be made, but in the end I fell asleep too. I was woken by the harsh racket of anti-aircraft gunfire, and guessed that war must have broken out.

On 6th December India officially recognized Bangladesh as an independent state. This news gave me a very strange feeling and threw my whole being into confusion. The children started crying for their father. I tried to comfort them, but joy at the recognition of

Bangladesh mixed with terror that my dear husband would be put to death had totally benumbed me."

Each day in December brought new horrors. On 18th December, when all the units of the Pakistan army were being removed (following their defeat by the Indian army), it was only the two Civil Armed Force officers who were withdrawn from Begum Mujib's house.

"As soon as they were gone the ordinary soldiers in the guard became restless. At first they expected they would be taken away too. But by noon, when shouts of '*Joy Bangla*' were filling the air all round, they had begun to get the wind up.

There was a clothes line made of wire outside the house. That night a jangling noise from the wire made us all wake up. I was confronted by a pair of bloodshot eyes: the sergeant of the guard, Riaz, was standing in our verandah. 'Call Khoka,' he ordered in a stern voice. 'Khoka is asleep,' I replied calmly. 'If you have anything to say, tell me.' He gave me a hard look, then said, 'You just be careful.'

At nine in the morning Major Tara Singh of the Indian army came to the house. He looked just like a civilian, but before approaching he had positioned a platoon of soldiers at the ready all round the compound. He had nothing but a walkie-talkie radio in his hands as he stood outside the gate talking to the Pakistani guards. At first they refused to surrender, then they asked if they could have two hours' time before handing themselves in. When the major started walking away from the gate after hearing their request my children immediately started screaming from inside the house: 'Don't go away, major! You mustn't go! If you give them time they're going to kill us!' And indeed they would have slaughtered us all if given the chance. However the major did not give them time, but came through the gate into the compound.

The Pakistani soldiers then came trembling out of their bunker and surrendered." *

---

* *Documents of the Bangladesh War of Independence*, Volume 8, Page 635, Information Ministry, Government of the People's Republic of Bangladesh.

50

Nilganj congregational mosque, built by Haji Motlub Miah, was the most attractive of the few permanent brick-built edifices in the area. Haji Motlub Miah had turned his mind to matters of religion late in life. He had declared that the best form of worship was *haqqul ibada* or practical ministry, in other words doing things for the benefit of others. As one example of this he had embarked on the building of this mosque. His age was then almost seventy and he was suffering from a number of ailments and disabilities. The day the construction work began he had a dream in which he saw a man looking like a Sufi saint, dressed in a long white *kurta* and wearing a turban on his head. This holy man had a crooked staff in his hand, and raising it he poked the Haji on the chest saying, "Motlub Miah, you had reached the end of your earthly span, but then you embarked on a meritorious task. So now you shall not die until that noble task is completed. Make sure you do the work properly." Then the saint had disappeared and Motlub Miah had woken up. He had found a dark bruise on his chest where the saint had tapped him with his staff.

Haji Motlub Miah had therefore been filled with enthusiasm as he got on with the building of the mosque. There was no need to hurry, he could take his time and do the work to a high standard. Whatever happened, the job must take as much time as possible. First a cement floor was laid, then the cement floor was replaced with a mosaic one. Originally there was to have been a single minaret, then he decided to have four instead. That would take time, but let it take as long as it liked! Let the building of the mosque never be completely finished, let there always be another door or window still to come – such was the Haji's wily plan. However his plan came to nothing, for he died just after one minaret had been constructed. The first ceremony to take place in the mosque was his own *janaza* or funeral service.

Nowadays Haji Motlub Miah's mosque was known as the One Minaret Mosque. At the festival of Eid people would come from far and wide to say their prayers there. Even at regular Friday prayers there would always be a good turnout of worshippers.

Ever since the Pakistan army camp had been set up in Nilganj attendance at Friday prayers had increased still further. Mats had to be spread outside for the overflow of the congregation. Captain Muhammad Basit used to attend the Friday service with one or two army colleagues, and after the prayers were over members of the congregation could be observed milling around the captain and lining up to shake his hand. This might seem surprising, but it was a fact. A few of the faithful even went so far as to embrace him.

Moulana Irtazuddin was the man who always led the Friday prayers. He would be wearing a carefully ironed tunic and a spotlessly white turban. He lined his eyes with antimony on Fridays, and dabbed perfume on his ear lobes. The Prophet had been fond of pleasant smells, so it was right that every Muslim should use perfume in respectful imitation of his ways.

The Friday prayers were scheduled to start at 1 p.m., but sometimes the congregation was kept waiting – waiting, that is, for the captain to arrive. The muezzin, Munshi Fazlul Haq, would be standing in the verandah of the mosque looking out for him. From where he stood the police compound was clearly visible. When the captain emerged from the compound wearing his flowing *kurta* Munshi Fazlul Haq would get quite excited.

On Fridays Irtazuddin would always be at the mosque by noon. At that time the mosque would be empty, not even the muezzin would be there. The members of the congregation would turn up one by one and Irtazuddin would take pleasure in meeting them. Some of them looked as if they were in a great hurry; they were unable to relax, they kept fidgeting and cracking their fingers and looking at their watches. Others seemed to have come against their will, and the expression on their faces was that of a fish out of water. A few really keen mosque-goers would come from considerable distances, eager to receive religious guidance. They would always arrive early, and Irtazuddin would enjoy talking to them about the Quran and the Prophetic traditions. There were so many complex issues in Islam, so much tricky detail, and Irtazuddin relished any chance to discuss such things.

But the present time was not like normal times. Now it was wartime. In wartime people don't adhere to normal patterns of behaviour. On Fridays people were coming to the mosque in fear and trembling, and nobody was in the mood for listening to anything.

Irtazuddin was kneeling on his prayer mat with his head bowed. He had a *tasbih* in his right hand, a set of ninety-nine prayer beads which he was fingering one by one. For each bead he had to mentally recite one of the ninety-nine names of God.

Ya Rahmānu – O Merciful One!
Ya Sādiqu – O Truthful One!
Ya Quddūsu – O Holy One!
Ya Mumītu – O Bringer of Death!

After reciting *Ya Mumītu* Irtazuddin ground to a halt. The next few names of Allah had slipped from his mind, but that one kept going round and round in his head: *Ya Mumītu, Ya Mumītu!* O Bringer of Death!

Outside the mosque, under a *kadamba* tree on the south side of the open yard, squatted four Hindu men. One of them was Poresh, the owner of a sweetmeat shop, and he was wearing a *dhuti*, the looped loincloth traditionally used by Hindu males. He had dared to show up in a *dhuti* in such dangerous times only because he and the others were to be converted to Islam straight after the noon prayers. Once they had become Muslims they would be wearing *panjabi* and lungi, so this was the last chance to put on a *dhuti*. Two of the four men were members of the scheduled castes, at the bottom of the Hindu caste system. Although *sudra* people are generally said to be very courageous, these two were cringing with apprehension.

The captain had said he was very interested in seeing Hindus being converted to Islam, and it was he who had selected Muslim names for these four: Abdur Rahman, Abdul Qader, Abdul Haq and Abdus Saleh. He had wanted to present each of them with a copy of the Quran, but it had transpired that Nilganj's one and only bookshop had not a single Quran in stock. The captain had been quite annoyed.

The captain had also given orders for the four converts to be circumcised in accordance with custom. The Muslim barber had been sent for, and he was ready to perform the operation using a sharpened splinter of bamboo. It was the captain's view that a circumcision was an enjoyable event worth recording, so although he had no camera of his own he had got hold of one for the purpose.

The call to prayer was given at a quarter to one. As soon as the *adhan* had been called Irtazuddin came out of the mosque and went over to the *kadamba* tree. The four men squatting under the tree shifted their positions anxiously. Only one of them dared to look up at him; the others kept staring at the ground.

"Are you feeling all right?" Irtazuddin asked them.

Three of the men nodded, the fourth looked away.

"Is it only you yourselves who are planning to be converted?" asked Irtazuddin. "Won't the other members of your families become Muslims too?"

"Everyone will be converted," replied Poresh, "us first and then the rest later."

"I don't know what your religion says about such things," said Irtazuddin, "but in our religion preserving one's own life is considered a solemn duty. If you think you can save your lives by becoming Muslims then by all means do so. You have a right to survive."

Mukul Saha covered his eyes with a corner of his *dhuti* and started sobbing. Looking at him Irtazuddin went on, "There is a well known verse in the glorious Quran which says, *lakum dīnukum wa liya dīn* – your religion for you, my religion for me. In Islam there is no coercion regarding other religions."

Irtazuddin was about to say more, but at that moment the muezzin Munshi Fazlul Haq came rushing up to him.

"The captain has just left the police compound. There are six others with him today. That makes seven of them including him."

"I'm not going to lead the prayers. As from today you are to act as imam."

"What – what are you talking about?"

"I had been intending to address the congregation before the service and give them a full explanation of why I'm no longer willing to be the imam at Friday prayers, but I shan't now. I'm going home."

"You won't even join in as one of the congregation?"

"No."

"But, but ... what is all this?"

"I've thought it all out very carefully. From now on I shall not take part in the Friday prayers, for the simple reason that in a country under despotic rule congregational prayers are against tradition. So long as the noble Prophet was in Mecca and Mecca was ruled by the Quraish, he never said any congregational prayers. It was after he had moved to Medina that the surah called *Jumu'a* was revealed. That was the surah which contained instructions for performing the Friday noon prayer in congregation. Only then did he start *juma* prayers."

"Please don't be crazy. The captain is almost here."

"I don't care if he is. I'm going."

When he had got back to his house Moulana Irtazuddin performed the noon prayer. After finishing the prescribed ritual he made his own private supplication. "O merciful and forgiving one, if I have made any mistake please pardon me. I am deficient in both wits and knowledge. The decision I have taken was informed by the modicum of intellect and information which I possess. If I was in error please show forgiveness. I appeal to your boundless mercy."

Tears came to his eyes as he begged for forgiveness, and he wept for a while. He never normally felt like crying when he was saying his prayers, and indeed it was a long time since he had shed any tears at all. When he had ended his supplications he remained kneeling on the prayer mat. He didn't get up to change his clothes, as he knew the captain would send for him and ask him a number of questions. He had a fairly clear idea of what he was going to say to the captain, and he knew the captain wouldn't be at all pleased with what he heard. And he knew that if he incurred the captain's wrath he might well become the next person to be lined up on the river bank.

He was not afraid of death. God had already ordained when and how he would die, for the life and fate of every mortal was immutably recorded on a divine tablet called Lauh-e-Mahfuz. There was no point in being afraid of the death which God had arranged for him.

Komola, the late police inspector's wife, popped in and out of the room several times. She was too awed by the sight of Irtazuddin kneeling on his prayer mat with his eyes closed to say anything, until finally she plucked up courage and asked him what the matter was.

"I'm feeling a little preoccupied," said Irtazuddin, "that's all."

"Do you want to have your meal now, uncle?"

"No, I won't eat anything just now. Listen, my dear, and please mark my words carefully. If anything happens to me you must go and see the headmaster. He is a very honest man, and he will do whatever needs to be done."

"Why are you saying such things?" asked Komola in alarm.

"As I said, I'm feeling a bit worried, and worried people say all sorts of things."

"Can I make you a cup of tea, at least, uncle?"

"No, my dear, I don't want anything. Though I wouldn't mind a glass of water. Of all the things to eat and drink in this world, water is the best; it's one of the most sacred provisions God has made for us. Every time you bring a glass full of water to your lips you should give abundant thanks to the Lord – that's the advice I would give you."

Captain Muhammad Basit sent for Irtazuddin shortly before *asr*, the late afternoon prayer time. The acting O.C. of the police station came with two constables to escort him to the police compound. The O.C. totally avoided looking Irtazuddin in the eye, as if for some reason he felt unequal to the task of facing him.

Before setting off for the police compound Irtazuddin performed his ritual ablutions. Then he picked up Komola's son and stroked him, remembering how fond the Prophet had been of children and how he had sometimes referred to them as the flowers of heaven. To follow the Prophet's example and make much of children was a virtue, yet somehow Irtazuddin was unable to practise it. The only child he really felt drawn to was Shahed's daughter Runi. Doubtless this indicated a weakness in his character. Still, he was beginning to feel an affection for this son of Komola's. When he picked him up he always made a grab for Irtazuddin's beard, and then it would be hard to make him let go: if forced to release his grip he would start crying.

Captain Basit had a cup of coffee in front of him, black coffee with no sugar. From time to time he took a sip of it and grimaced at its bitter taste. Irtazuddin was seated on a chair facing him. A cup of coffee had been supplied for him as well, but he had not touched it.

Captain Basit lit a cigarette. He blew out a long stream of smoke and made a dismissive gesture with his hand. The sergeant major and two privates who had been in the room walked out onto the verandah, though they continued to follow what was going on inside. The captain leaned forward slightly.

"I hear you have refused to lead the Friday prayers if I am in the congregation," he said. "Apparently you said something to the effect that the prayers would be null and void if such an evil person as myself was taking part."

Irtazuddin explained calmly why he had decided not to lead the Friday prayers. Captain Basit's face hardened.

"You say that there is no place for congregational prayer in a subjugated land. Are you then saying that East Pakistan has been subjugated?"

"Yes, sir, I am."
"Do you realize what you are saying?"
"I do."
"Do you know what kind of punishment will be meted out to you for having said it?"
"No."
"There is only one form of punishment for all enemies of the state. You are one of the Muktis. You are in league with the insurgents."
"In doing what I have done I have acted purely in accordance with my own judgment and conscience."
"You don't want Pakistan to endure? You want to become a boot-licking dog, a lackey of Hindustan?"
"Good sir, all I want is to be a genuine Muslim. The duty of a true Muslim is to oppose tyrannical rule."
Captain Basit discarded his cigarette and lit a new one. "Moulana," he said, "you've taken leave of your senses."
Irtazuddin remained silent. Captain Basit took a sip of his cold coffee and made a face.
"I know a good remedy for madness," he went on, "and I'm going to cure your folly so thoroughly that for the rest of your life you'll do nothing but count your prayer beads and go 'Pakistan, Pakistan' all the time."
Irtazuddin let out a little sigh.
"Don't sit there in dumb silence, Moulana. Speak up, say something!"
"I have said all that I had to say, captain."
"You have nothing more to add?"
"No, sir."
"Well, do you know how I'm going to punish you? You're going to be stripped naked and then paraded round the entire village. And I'm not joking. I always punish traitors with the greatest severity."
"If the Lord has included such humiliation in my fate then I shall have to undergo it," said Irtazuddin. "God said in surah *Bani Israil* of the Holy Quran, 'I have hung every man's fate around his neck like a garland.' My fate is inscribed on my brow. And your fate is likewise awaiting you."
"Are you trying to scare me?"
"God is the one entitled to inspire fear, not me."
Captain Basit stood up from his chair and tapped his desk, whereupon the sergeant major and his two underlings promptly entered the room.
"Tell the O.C. to strip this traitor naked and haul him round the village. You lot are to go with them."
And Moulana Irtazuddin, that most honourable man, so profoundly respected by everyone in Nilganj, was paraded around the village stark naked. First he was taken to Nilganj High School, then he was led to the village market place where a small incident took place. A tailor darted out of his shop with a sheet which he wrapped round Irtazuddin and held in place for him. It happened so quickly the soldiers were unable to stop him in time.
At dusk, just after the *maghrib* prayer, both Irtazuddin and the tailor were led to the banks of the Sohagi river and shot. In the moments before he died Irtazuddin made his very last supplication to God in a loud and confident voice.

"Lord, please have mercy on the one who threw away his life in order to save me from embarrassment. For him please open the gates of your infinite beneficence." *

---

* The tailor, though wounded, lived to tell the tale. It was from him that I heard this true story, which took place in the Netrakona area. – **Author**

51

The headmaster of Nilganj High School, Mr Monsur, was in his bedroom sitting on the edge of his bed. His head was bowed. In front of him sat his wife Ashiya, her head covered over with the loose end of her sari. Remarkably she was now perfectly sane; no trace of her mental illness was visible.

It was around midday and heavy rain was falling. The rain had started the night before. Mr Monsur was unable to recall any previous occasion when Nilganj had had such heavy rainfall. He gave a little sigh.

"Ashiya," he said, looking at his wife, "Ashiya, if you will give your consent, there's something I would like to do."

"What kind of thing?" asked Ashiya in a small voice.

"I'd be glad if you'd bare your head first," said Mr Monsur. "I want to look into your face while I'm talking to you."

Ashiya slipped her sari back off her head.

"My very good friend Irtazuddin Kashempuri always used to say that God would never forgive any man who acted in such a way as to cause distress to his wife," Mr Monsur began. "That's why I require your permission before doing the thing I wish to do."

"What kind of thing is it?" asked Ashiya again.

"Yesterday evening the soldiers took Irtazuddin Kashempuri to the riverbank and shot him," said Mr Monsur, "and they imposed a curfew in the area. The moulana's dead body is still lying there on the bank of the river, and nobody is daring to go anywhere near it. I wish to recover his body and arrange a proper burial for him."

"Will you be able to do that on your own?" asked Ashiya.

"Why shouldn't I be able? Anyway, I'll have to do it."

"Let me go with you."

"You? You want to come too?" asked Mr Monsur in surprise.

"Yes, I do. Suppose you get shot by the army, in that case I want to die with you. There would be no point in my surviving without you."

The inhabitants of Nilganj were treated to the bizarre spectacle of the headmaster, assisted by a woman with her head tightly covered, straining to remove the massive body of the late Moulana Irtazuddin in torrential rain. They were having great difficulty in shifting him. Quite a few people saw this scene, yet not one of them came forward to help.

Suddenly a man could be seen braving the rain to go over and lend a hand.

"Stand aside, mother," this man said in Urdu, "let me do some pulling for you."

"Who are you?" asked Mr Monsur.

"I'm a private from the Baluch Regiment and my name is Aslam Khan." *

---

* The funeral service or *namaz-e-janaza* for Irtazuddin Kashempuri was held after the liberation of Bangladesh had taken place. On the occasion described here he was buried without any ceremony, for no cleric could be found to conduct the service. – **Author**

52

Asmani was looking at Runi in despair. It was shocking to see how naughty the girl had become. She had been moaning all morning and now it was midday. Her problem? She wanted some *sandesh* to eat, a kind of sweetened milk fudge. Asmani had no idea how the thought of *sandesh* could have got into the dear child's mind. Surely she hadn't seen anyone eating such a thing, here in a refugee camp? Yet it was not impossible. By now Runi had learned how to go wandering all over the place on her own. She would slip away without telling her mother and go exploring. One moment she would be at Asmani's side, the next moment she was nowhere to be seen. On one occasion she had gone missing for hours on end in the middle of the day. Asmani had got really worried, and had been on the point of reporting Runi's disappearance to the camp wardens when suddenly there she was, prancing along happily with a bun in her hand. When questioned she wouldn't say where she'd got the bun from. Asmani suspected she must have cadged it off somebody. The child had picked up the habit of begging, and didn't hesitate to accept things from strangers.

But of course she couldn't really blame Runi. They were all beggars now, people who had fled their own motherland and gone to live as parasites in somebody else's country. Twice a day they had to line up with their plates to be fed. The shame of it! And there was no knowing when it would end, this shameful and embarrassing situation – maybe they would have to spend the rest of their lives in refugee camps. Asmani was weary of thinking about such things. At the moment her main concern was to keep Runi near her, to prevent her from getting lost. If she were to get lost it might be impossible for Asmani to find her. And then, after being passed from hand to hand Runi would eventually end up in a red light area, and she would forget that she had ever been a member of a normal family.

How rapidly the child was changing! One day Asmani had overheard her using dirty words to another child, "I'll boot you up the backside" or something rather more colourful. Asmani had run out and grabbed Runi by the arm.

"Darling, what language, how can you!" she had said, almost in tears.

"He swore first," Runi had retorted defensively.

"He may have, but does that mean you have to swear too?"

"Yes."

"You do realize that was a very dirty word you used?"

"Not really, I know some much worse ones."

Asmani didn't know how she was going to keep her daughter in check, she felt quite out of her depth. The whole environment was so unhealthy. Theft was rife inside the refugee camp. One refugee would steal an article of clothing from another, then the thief would be caught red-handed, a fight would break out, camp wardens would be alerted and rush to the scene. The wardens would use strong language themselves: "Look at you! I thought you'd come here to save your skins, not to go around stealing things. You people only know three kinds of work – shitting, pissing and stealing!"

Sometimes representatives of the Bangladesh government in exile would come visiting. They wore tragic expressions on their faces, as if their hearts were breaking at the sight of the harsh conditions the refugees were enduring. And they made flowery speeches. "We are Bengalis. We may be battered, we may be destroyed, but never shall we bow our heads. Be patient. Our valiant freedom fighters are waging war. Victory is within our grasp."

They would announce ambitious plans. A school would be opened for the refugee children so that their education could continue unhindered. A drama would be staged with refugees as its heroes, something on the theme of patriotism, to demonstrate to the world that even in such circumstances the beacon of Bengali culture was undimmed.

Foreigners often came along to take photographs. Some of them would be armed with movie cameras and accompanied by masses of paraphernalia. What really made their day was if one of the refugees happened to die during their visit: then they would film carefully constructed shots of the dead body and views of all the grieving relatives.

These foreigners frequently brought little presents with them, such as toilet soap or sweets for the children. A frightful commotion would ensue as everyone rushed forward at once to grab some of the booty. Runi would be among those who threw themselves into the fray. Once she emerged from the scrimmage with a bar of toilet soap which she bore proudly home to her mother – it was as if she had won a great victory on the battlefield.

Also among the visitors to the camp were senior officials of the West Bengal government. The provincial president himself came on one occasion and delivered an excellent speech, at the end of which he put his hands together in front of his face and said, "All we have been able to offer you is shelter. We would like to have offered you more, but we are not in a position to do so. For this I beg your pardon."

Every so often word would go round that Indira Gandhi might be planning to visit the camp. Then everything had to be put in order. Camp wardens would burst into tents waving their batons and shouting, "Come on, tidy up all your bedding! Anybody caught relieving themselves in here is going to be in big trouble!"

There was a dispensary in the camp with a red cross sign outside it. It opened every day. A couple of doctors would be on duty, and they would carefully examine the patients and write prescriptions for them, but then be unable to issue any medicines as there were none in stock. From time to time a consignment of donated drugs would arrive, but these would be used up almost immediately.

The Red Cross kept a list of expectant mothers, and Asmani was on the list. For that reason she received a tin of protein biscuits every week. It was Runi who benefited: she kept nibbling away at the tasteless biscuits and wouldn't let her mother come near the tin. But Asmani was happy with this. Her maternal instinct told her that Runi was growing and needed extra food, which she herself had no means of providing.

Runi had been whining for *sandesh* all morning. How on earth was Asmani expected to get any for her? She had parted with the last of her money yesterday; now she didn't possess a single penny. Yet she felt so sorry for Runi, if she had had one last rupee she would gladly have spent it to get some *sandesh* for her.

"Aren't you going to get me some *sandesh*?"

"Oh, I will," said Asmani.

"When? I want it now. Now!"

"Do stop crying, Runi."

"I *shall* cry," retorted Runi grimacing. "I'm going to scream! I'm going to pinch you!"

"Right, let's get out of here. You can do your screaming and pinching out of doors, we're not going to have it in here."

"No, I want to scream here! I won't go outside!"

Asmani hustled her daughter out of the shed, she almost dragged her out, and then she gave the child a resounding slap on the cheek. Runi was taken by surprise and stood staring. Her mother had never done anything like this to her before.

"You hit me, Mummy!" complained Runi.

"I'm going to wallop you to bits," said Asmani, and slapped Runi's cheek again with all her strength.

"*Slamalekum*, sister-in-law!"

Asmani spun round and saw a strange man standing there. His face, bronzed and sunburnt, was lost in a wilderness of beard, wild straggling hair covered his scalp.

"Do you recognize me, sister-in-law? It's hardly likely that you would. I can hardly recognize myself these days. Is Shahed here in this camp?"

"No, he isn't here. It's just me and my daughter."

"Where is Shahed, then?"

"I don't know. I don't even know whether he's alive or dead. You're Naimul, right?"

"Spot on! Yes, I'm Naimul."

"Are you a freedom fighter?"

"Yes. Your daughter's name is Runi, isn't that it? So why is Runi getting thrashed?"

"She wants some *sandesh*," explained Asmani calmly. "You wouldn't be in a position to buy her some, would you, by any chance?"

"Yes, I can do that," said Naimul, "but not just now. I'll bring some in the evening."

Asmani watched as the man strode away on his long legs. She could tell from the way he walked away that he was not likely to return. These were troubled times, and in troubled times people often didn't keep their word.

Runi had stopped crying, and she made no more fuss about *sandesh*.

Naimul had said he'd come at dusk, but he didn't appear. Asmani thought maybe he had been detained somewhere and would turn up later in the night. But still he didn't come.

"Mummy, shall I go to bed now?" asked Runi. "I don't think he's coming."

"Yes, go to bed," said Asmani. "When we get back home and meet up with your Daddy you can have all the *sandesh* you want."

"When will we go home, Mummy?"

"I don't know."

Asmani's eyes were misting over. She couldn't bring herself to look at Runi. Her slap had left a mark on Runi's cheek; that area had gone red and swollen up.

"Mummy," said Runi, "I don't think I want any *sandesh* after all."

"Well, whatever you feel like eating, your Daddy will get it for you."

It was probably the sight of her mother weeping which made Runi start to cry. She clutched the free end of Asmani's sari, hid her face in it and moaned between sobs, "Do you think Daddy remembers us, Mummy?"

That night Runi had a fever; her temperature shot up quite high. Asmani sat up the whole night with Runi's head in her lap.

It was early morning when Naimul returned.

"Sorry, sister-in-law," he said shamefacedly, "it took me longer than expected to get organized. And I forgot to buy that *sandesh* for your daughter; I haven't brought anything at all. Now you must get ready. Gather all your things."

"Where are we going?" asked Asmani in astonishment.

"To Barasat. To my aunt's house. She's settled over here, you see. I spoke to her yesterday and arranged everything, it'll be no problem. I can't just leave you here in the camp."

"What are you saying, brother?" gasped Asmani.

"Please don't waste any more time talking, dear sister-in-law. I've got a jeep with me, and I've had a word with the camp authorities. My aunt and her husband are really nice people, and they'll look after you just as if you were their own daughter. You do need looking after, in your present state."

"You're seriously telling me to move?"

"Most certainly. Listen, sister-in-law, you mustn't feel the slightest hesitation or compunction about this. Let me tell you a little story to help you overcome any reservations. Please follow it carefully. When I was studying at university I was in truly dire financial straits. Forget about buying textbooks, I didn't even have any money for food. When he heard about this Shahed's elder brother, the Moulana, started sending me a remittance of money every month. He made me promise never to tell Shahed, and I never did. But now I'm telling you. Oh, but I'm such a brute, I never even let Brother Moulana know when I got married! Have you any idea how he is these days, sister?"

"No, *bhai*, I don't. I don't know anything about anyone."

The ramshackle jeep was hurtling along the road, raising clouds of dust as it went. Naimul was in the seat next to the driver and Runi was sitting on his lap. Runi's fever had abated the moment they had boarded the jeep, and now she was chattering away. Naimul found her really amusing. Runi would tell him a story and Naimul would laugh and exclaim, "This kid is a brilliant story-teller! Shahed hardly knows how to speak at all, so where did his daughter get her eloquence from?"

Naimul made the driver stop outside a shop they were passing.

"Come along, it's time for a refreshment break," he said to Runi. "Time for *sandesh*. Let me see how many *sandesh* you are able to eat. Us two are going to have a competition to see who can eat the most!"

They reached Barasat in the early evening. There it was, as pretty as a painting: a single storeyed cottage shaded by trees and creepers. No sooner had the jeep pulled up at the gate than an old woman came hurrying out. She embraced Asmani with both arms and said, "Come, my dear, come along in. We've been expecting you since lunchtime. Dear me, but your face is looking quite haggard. You've been having a hard time, haven't you?"

Then an old man came clomping out of the house on wooden sandals. He was bare chested.

"Let me see our daughter from East Bengal," he said very pleasantly. "Let me see her face. Oh my goodness, but she's got rather a dark complexion! We're all light-skinned in this house, you know. I'm afraid we can't start admitting dark girls to our fair household. No, we can't accept her, I'm afraid!" And he chuckled merrily.

At last, after what seemed like years, Asmani felt at home once more. She felt she had known this old couple for ever.

What a strange thing war is. It tears people apart – and it brings people very, very close together.

53

Naimul was sitting on an elevated mound from where he had a wide view over the plain. The world around him was baking in harsh sunshine, but he was sitting in the shade of an alstonia tree whose large leaves made an awning over his head. There were a lot of these *chatim* trees in the locality; it was unlikely that anyone had planted them on purpose, so they must have seeded themselves. In the area where he had been last week there were any number of *shimul* trees, the ones also known as silk-cotton trees. Every few yards you would come across one. *Shimul* trees were not so good for sheltering under, as their trunks were studded with sharp protuberances and you couldn't lean back against them. *Chatim* trees on the other hand were fine for leaning against, but they were silent trees – their leaves were too large to whisper in the breeze.

Naimul was wearing a green lungi; however it had not been sewn together to make a tube in the normal way. Under the lungi he was wearing shorts. Shorts were the garment of choice for freedom fighters, but they couldn't let people see they were wearing them, as that would immediately give the game away. Hence the unsewn lungi – when the time for action came it could be whipped off in an instant. The upper half of Naimul's body was clad in a black T-shirt with a dirty cotton shawl draped over it. The shawl was necessary, even in such heat, to conceal the sten gun slung over his shoulder. It was not Naimul's ideal choice of weapon, a sten gun, as its range was only fifty yards and seldom could a guerrilla fighter get within fifty yards of his enemy.

Naimul was leaning back with his legs stretched out in front of him. At his feet was a man in his early thirties named Rofik, who was squatting on the ground like a frog and looked as if he might leap away at any moment. Even his eyes were like frogs' eyes, large and protuberant, ready to spring out of their sockets at the slightest provocation.

Rofik was a great talker. He had been chattering non-stop ever since he had come to say hello to Naimul. He showed little interest in what Naimul said; it was his own chatter which was keeping him occupied.

"You're a guerrilla commander then, sir, eh?"

"Mm," murmured Naimul, yawning. Keeping one's identity secret was one of the first rules in a guerrilla's training, but Naimul felt it was hardly worth arguing.

"And you come to blow up the bridge at Shombhuganj? In that case there's something you oughta know."

"What do you mean?"

"Three other groups already tried. They got pulverized. Them lot put their machine guns on them, filled them all full of bullet holes."

"Do you know what a machine gun is?"

"Come off it, sir, how couldn't I? These days little babes in arms can recognize a machine gun when they see one. They know what a mortar is. They know what a *pikaywan* is."

"A 'P.K. One', what's that?"

Rofik looked at Naimul with glistening eyes. Whoa, that fellow claimed to be a guerrilla commander yet he didn't know what a *pikaywan* was! Or maybe he was having him on? Rofik hated being made a fool of.

"Where's your weapon then, sir?"

"I've got one, don't worry."

"Where'd you hide it?"

"Why do you want to know? You're going to run off and inform the peace committee?"

"Nah, what are you suggesting, sir!"

"Isn't there a peace committee in this area?"

"Ha, t'would be odd if there wasn't. Yeah, of course there is. Previous chairman got killed by the freedom fighters, now there's a new chairman. You want to bump him off? I know where he lives, I can take you there."

"How about a cup of tea, could you get me that?"

"Where'd I find any tea in the middle of these fields?"

"Well, that's a good point."

"Come on, sir, let's go to the chairman's house and you can have tea there. He's got tea and biscuits and everything. Hey, if he hears you're a guerrilla commander he'll wet his pants! Such a scaredy-cat he is."

"What's the chairman's name?"

"Hashem the Chairman. Two wives he's got. He got one of them from the lowlands, a right beauty she is. But she's a bit loose, everyone knows that."

Naimul yawned again. He always yawned repeatedly when he was stressed, though he wasn't sure why this was. Humans yawned when their oxygen supply was too low: did that mean his body ran short of oxygen whenever the tension rose? And would that be because the brain used a great deal of oxygen when under stress?

The main reason why Naimul was feeling tense was that the other members of his team hadn't yet turned up. They had been due to arrive early yesterday morning along with a load of PEK 1 plastic explosive complete with fuse, cordex and detonator. They were going to need a minimum of twenty-five kilograms of explosive; it would be impossible to fracture the main span of the bridge with less than that. It was now midday. The team were going to arrive by boat – it was still safe to travel that way as the army had yet to deploy any gunboats or launches on the local rivers, and were restricted to moving around on land. This was mainly because the water levels were low, and only small skiffs and dugout canoes could be used, craft much too humble for military purposes.

Had the team run into trouble somewhere, Naimul wondered. In the present situation dangers were apt to crop up suddenly without any prior warning.

"What's your name, Commander *sab*?" asked Rofik, leaning towards him.

"My name is Naimul."

"You been sitting in this spot all morning. Some special reason, is there?"

"No," replied Naimul with yet another yawn. "I'm just sitting where it's nice and shady." But the shade was not the real reason for his being here. The boat was heading for this exact landmark, his men would stop and disembark as soon as they saw the *chatim* tree. There was also the fact that a long stretch of the local road was visible from here, and any movement of Pakistani troops on the road could be observed.

"Sunshine's really hot," remarked Rofik. "Let's have one of your fags, Commander *sab*, I'll have a little drag and see what it's like. The commander who was here before you, he gave me a whole packet of fags. He was a real lion heart."

Naimul gave him a cigarette. Rofik took it and puffed away happily, expertly exhaling the smoke through his mouth and nostrils. Naimul decided this frog-like fellow had probably been hoping for a smoke all along, and now that he'd got his wish he would go waddling off, meet up with some cronies and have a good chin-wag about the guerrilla commander he'd met. It struck Naimul that he had come across a wonderful variety of odd characters in the course of the war; if he'd been a writer he could have spent the remainder of his life writing about them.

"Which militia d'you belong to, Commander *sab*? Mujib brigades?"

"So you know about the Mujib brigades too, do you?" exclaimed Naimul.

"Why shouldn't I? Each militia's got its own style. Mujib brigades have the best training, and they've got good weapons. But they don't get on with the other fighters."

"Which ones are best?"

"All of them's good, as long as they're slogging the Pak army. Wouldn't you say so, Commander *sab*?"

"Mm."

"Bashing them peace committee jokers is good too. But them peace guys are our own countrymen, you got to remember that. What you say, sir?"

Naimul lit a cigarette for himself. Cigarettes were numbered and there was no sense in finishing them up too quickly, but seeing Rofik puffing away had made him want one too.

"Know how the old peace chairman was done in? Shall I tell you?"

"No thanks."

"When they dragged him out and tied him to the mango tree he was wetting his pants to bits. He was blubbing away enough to melt a heart of steel. If I'd been a freedom fighter I'd have let him go. I'd have said, 'Here's your punishment, you dog, you're going to have to lick up all that shit you just done.' That'd be a better punishment than killing him, wouldn't you say, Commander *sab*? Ain't easy, licking up shit. Even your own."

Naimul made no reply, nor was any needed. Rofik was the kind of talker who doesn't wait for a response before carrying on to his next topic.

"New chairman's had it too," went on Rofik, extracting a final long puff from his cigarette. "Whenever freedom fighters pass through they bump off the peace committee lot, even if that's the only thing they manage to do."

"Don't they do anything else?"

"Nah."

"Don't they manage to kill any government soldiers?"

"To tell the honest truth, sir, no they don't. Them Pak army fellows ain't turtle doves you can knock off with a kid's catapult. No, they're tough old boots. They're Azrael, they're the angel of death himself. They don't know the meaning of the word fear."

"Have you ever seen any Pakistani soldiers?"

"I should think I have! Yeah, once they got me to carry a big box of ammo on my head for them. I was working in the fields, I was, and along they come and call me and Fazlu – Fazlu from Pubpara that is – and stick these great cases full of bullets on our heads. And Gawd, were they heavy! My shoulders were aching for the next couple of days. Can I have another fag, please, Commander *sab*?"

"Sorry, I can't give you any more."

"Well, I'll be going then. I did enjoy having a chat with you."

"You're not going anywhere. Sit down again right there where you were. Since you like chatting you can go ahead and chat, but don't imagine you're going to get away."

Rofik stared at Naimul in surprise. It was hard to get the hang of these freedom fighters. Up to now the commander had been talking in such a friendly, relaxed way, but now suddenly his voice had turned sharp and he had a fierce look in his eyes.

"But there's a little job I need to attend to, Commander *sab*."

"Forget that, you've got to stay sitting here. If I let you wander off you're going to inform everyone in the entire district that guerrilla fighters are in the area, and I can't afford to let that happen. Plus, I need you."

"What do you need me for?"

"You can show me the chairman's house, I don't know where he lives. And you can give me some other bits of information. Is Shombhuganj bridge guarded by the Pakistan army?"

"How would I know? It's not as if I ever go over the bridge. It's a railway bridge after all, not one for pedestrians."

"Where do the *razakar* fellows hang out?"

"In the police compound."

"How many of them are there?"

"Look, I never been and counted them. It ain't my job to keep a tally of them *razakar* blokes." Rofik had begun fidgeting restlessly.

"Stop fidgeting!" said Naimul sharply.

"What, I ain't even allowed to move? That ain't fair."

Naimul raised his shawl just enough to reveal the Chinese sten gun hanging over his shoulder. Rofik stopped fidgeting and froze. His eyes started out of their sockets. You couldn't trust the army people an inch, but nor could you trust these freedom fighters. There was no knowing what they might do at any moment.

"What's the name of the commander of the *razakar* unit?" asked Naimul.

"Zainal."

"I presume you know where Zainal lives. Do you?"

"Yes, sir."

"Doesn't he pop back home to see his wife sometimes? He surely doesn't stay in the police compound twenty-four hours a day."

"You going to shoot brother Zainal?"

"I'm not sure. I may do."

"Zainal goes to have tea at Sulu's tea stall every afternoon. He don't go alone, he always has a couple of others with him. And they have guns with them."

"That's no matter."

"Where you going to shoot him? At the tea stall, or will you take him away somewhere?"

"Let's see what can be done."

"Commander *sab*, I'm bursting, I desperately need a slash. Let me go down to the field and have a piss. I can squat on the path there."

"You can urinate here," said Naimul with a yawn. "There's no need for you to go down to the field."

"You want me to piss in front of you?"

"You can turn your back and do it in the opposite direction. But don't move away."

"Commander *sab*, I'm a *Joy Bangla* supporter, you know."

"But that's precisely why I'm keeping you here. *Joy Bangla* people are what I need."

"How long are you going to stay sitting here?"

"I've no idea," replied Naimul, lighting another cigarette.

"Don't smoke all of it," begged Rofik, "let me have a couple of puffs too. Those Indian fags have a specially nice taste."

Naimul handed him a whole cigarette.

"Is it going to be tonight, the fighting?"

"Mm."

"Where are your men?"

"There aren't many in my team. Just the two of us."

"So who's the other one?"

"You. I'm going to teach you how to throw a grenade. Are you up to it?"

The lighted cigarette fell from Rofik's lips. This is a real nut case I've got mixed up with, he thought.

"I'm sure you know what a grenade is. You know the names of all the different kinds of weapon, so you could hardly not know a grenade. It's like an iron ball."

"Oh, I know about grenades. There's two kinds. The best one is called an *enegra* grenade and you have to fit it on a rifle barrel to fire it."

"But I'm not going to give you that kind. The kind I'll give you has a pin which you have to pull out with your teeth, and then you have to chuck it at your target."

"That won't work, my teeth are no good," gibbered Rofik. "Tooth decay. Look!" And he bared his teeth to show Naimul.

"Those teeth will be good enough," said Naimul calmly.

The afternoon went by, and still there was no sign of Naimul's team. Nor was there any way of finding out what had gone wrong. He couldn't make up his mind whether to wait for them or withdraw.

Had his men been apprehended? The probability of that happening was low, yet it wasn't altogether out of the question. A month ago the entire team of a leader called Kader had been captured at Johukandi in Sherpur. A special dinner party had been their undoing. The owner of the house where they had sought shelter was so delighted to realize they were freedom fighters that he had arranged a banquet in their honour that evening. A goat was slaughtered and pulao was prepared. It took a long time for the goat meat to be cooked, long enough for disaster to strike: sure enough, the army came and surrounded the homestead. And now when the rules of guerrilla warfare were being expounded at the training camp one of the jokes which always came up was, whatever you do, don't be like Kader the Goat.

Kader had been a very courageous fighter, but one small mistake had earned him the nickname of Kader the Goat, whereupon all his bravery had been forgotten. People tend to remember others not for their best qualities but for their faults. Thus while Kader should have gone down in history as Kader the Great he ended up Kader the Goat.

"Commander *sab*!"

"Mm?"

"Feel my forehead a moment."

"What for?"

"I got a fever. Need to curl up under a warm blanket. Have pity on me, I'm not well."

"Mm," said Naimul again.

"Shall I trot along, then, Commander *sab*?"

"You can forget all about trotting along," said Naimul. "I'm going to send you over to where the *razakar* unit have their outpost, near the bridge."

"I wouldn't go anywhere near, not if you gave me a million rupees. Forget it."

"Why should I?"

"Bridge is guarded by them black soldiers. Death itself."

"What, the militia with black uniforms?"

"I don't know if they're militia or what, but I do know they're death. One look at them, one look at their shadow even, and you're a dead man."

"On your feet now," said Naimul standing up.

"Where are we going?"

"We're going to have a look at those black soldiers' shadows."

"But have you seen the sky? Rain's coming."

Naimul looked up at the sky. Thick dark clouds had gathered. This boded well, for the Pakistani soldiers weren't used to the torrential rains of Bengal, and they would retreat under cover. They doubtless thought the booming sound was cannons being fired, and each peal of thunder would make them quake with fear. If only his team were here, they would be able to fix that bridge in the rain. One of the team members, Nasim, was an expert at handling plastic explosives. He was a little stumpy fellow who didn't seem to know how to walk in the normal way, but always hopped and jumped along. The others had given him the nickname of Mister Spring. Then there was Sunnot Miah, only he couldn't stand being called by that name and insisted on being called 'Sunnot of Gournodi' instead. Naimul hadn't yet found out why he had chosen this particular appellation. He was a lad who knew no fear, and after each operation he would complain bitterly. "I was hoping to achieve martyrdom, but no luck this time. Awful shame! Let's see if I can do better next time." He could wriggle along the ground like a snake while carrying a bag full of grenades, keeping much lower than a normal person crawling. When he had got really close to the enemy he would leap up and sling his grenades, muttering to himself, "Go, little bird, go where you're meant to!" Most of his little birds did land where they were meant to. Sunnot had a powerful delivery: a grenade projected from a grenade thrower can travel up to fifty yards, but he could send one forty yards using just his wrist and arm.

At around dusk the rain started pouring down in torrents. And then Naimul's team arrived in their boat, soaked to the skin. Rofik was overjoyed; his face lit up in a huge smile.

"There, sir, now you've got your men. Now you can dismiss me. I'll light a fag and saunter back home, puffing as I go, and then jump into bed."

"Stay where you are," ordered Naimul, "and don't move. You've talked enough already, don't let me hear another word from you."

The team members were hungry, tired and weary.

"When the operation's over we'll sit down to a slap-up meal," Naimul told them, "but we're not going to have anything to eat beforehand. I've got everything ready, and we're going to have this guide with us. His name is Rofik."

"No, no, forget it, Commander *sab*," gasped Rofik promptly. "I ain't going with you. I only recently got married, I got a brand new wife at home."

"New wife, old wife, it makes no difference, you're coming along with us. Now, everyone listen, this is my plan of action. The whole scheme is somewhat unusual, so pay attention. The plan is not subject to alteration. I never go in for long discussions, because arguments don't lead to good decisions. Right. The bridge is guarded by a detail of *razakar* irregulars, six or seven in number. Sometimes they have two militiamen with them, but there are none today. We're going to give them a tip-off that the bridge is due to be blown up early next morning. They ought to believe this since it is in fact true, we are going to blow it up in the course of this night.

When they get the news either the whole lot of them will trot off to the police compound to inform the army people, or else some of them will go to the compound and the rest will stay guarding the bridge. The ones who stay at the bridge are very likely to desert their post after a while, but if they do stay put they'll keep firing wild in the dark to steady their nerves.

At the same time we shall also tip off the army people in the police compound, telling them the bridge is about to be attacked. This message will go via the peace committee chairman. The army will send a detachment of soldiers to defend the bridge. There is only one route they can use to get there, the District Board road. Now, our team will divide into three sections. One section will ambush the soldiers on the road, one section will go to the bridge and one section will besiege the police compound. For the attack on the police compound we shall make use of Energa grenades. Our sub machine-gun will be at the bridge. I shall shortly decide who is to be in each section, but first, does anyone have anything to say?"

Rofik was the first to speak, but his comment was brief. "Oh Gawd!"

"We really need have something to eat, if only a handful of puffed rice," Mister Spring chipped in simultaneously.

The rain storm stopped as suddenly as it had begun. At around 9 p.m. a gap in the clouds revealed the moon. It was eight days old, and though it wasn't brilliant it provided a certain amount of illumination.

"Moonlight among clouds is a bad thing," said Sunnot of Gournodi. "Ghosts show up in this kind of moonlight. I'm not scared of regular soldiers, but ghosts do freak me out."

Just as Mr Hashem, the peace committee chairman, was about to go to sleep a dog started barking in the courtyard of his homestead. At the same time he thought he heard a number of people moving about.

"Who's there?" called Mr Hashem in a trembling voice.

"It's me, Rofik. Rofik from Uttarpara."

"What do you want?"

"Would you come out here a minute, please. The *mukti* commander is here."

As Mr Hashem emerged from the substantial building several other doors opened too. Women could be heard weeping. Among the women was a singularly pretty one, who was no doubt Mr Hashem's new wife from the lowlands.

Chairman Hashem was wearing a short-sleeved shirt and a lungi and had a torch in his hand. He was aware that the knot of his lungi was coming loose, so to avoid the risk of the garment dropping to his feet he was gripping it with one hand, while the other hand held the torch.

"Who are you all?" he asked apprehensively.

"We're freedom fighters," replied Naimul. "Are you keeping well?"

"Quite well, yes," said Chairman Hashem in a strangled voice, "quite well."

"Are you afraid, by any chance?" asked Naimul.

By way of answer Chairman Hashem started coughing. The weeping in the women's quarters grew louder. An elderly woman came hurrying out and grasped the chairman's hand; she was probably his mother. "Please listen to me a moment, sons," she pleaded between her sobs.

"There's no need for you to be scared," Naimul reassured her. "I never kill Bengali people. You can stop crying."

The women all stopped crying at once.

"My lads have come to blow up the railway bridge," explained Naimul. "When they've finished the job they're going to come back here for a feast."

"Right," said Chairman Hashem. "Yes, yes, of course. Of course they can have a feast."

"You're to prepare boiled rice and a good hot chicken curry."

"How about I make some pulao for you, sonnies?" asked the old woman.

"You may indeed; it's a long time since we had pulao."

"Come inside and sit down," said Chairman Hashem. "Have some tea, I can ask them to make tea for you."

"We won't have any tea, thankyou," said Naimul. "We're going over to the bridge now. But I have a little job for you."

"What job?"

"You must go to the police compound and inform the army officer that freedom fighters have got into the village and are about to blow up the bridge. Feel free, just tell them the truth. You can even tell them we're going to come back to your house for pulao and chicken curry after demolishing the bridge, it won't matter."

"My son ain't going nowhere," objected the old lady. "I can see what you're doing, it's a trick to get him out of the house. Listen, son, just tell me how much money you want, I'll give it you. There's jewellery in the safe too, have it if you want."

"Granny," said Naimul, "if you want your son to survive unscathed you'll have to do as I tell you. I can't stand arguments, I really can't."

"Auntie," urged Rofik, "our Commander *sab* is a man of his word. If you don't do as he says there'll be big trouble."

Naimul looked at Rofik. "Now, you go to the bridge and tell the *razakar* sentries that it's about to be blown up. One of our team will follow you and watch from a distance to see if you do the job properly. If he suspects any funny business he will shoot. Got it?"

Rofik's jaw dropped and his eyes bulged a little further out of his head.

In guerrilla warfare things seldom go according to plan. Decisions have to be revised on the spur of the moment. Often it is not even possible to change strategy: once a medium sized team has been split into sections there is no chance for them to get together again for a new briefing.

Remarkably, however, Naimul's plan worked just as intended. As soon as the *razakar* men received the news that the bridge was about to be attacked they threw down their .303 rifles and fled.

A small band of eight men sallied forth from the police compound, only to turn round and go back in again.

The grenade thrower Naimul used worked perfectly. One missile went ten or twelve yards from the gun and didn't explode, but two consecutive Energa grenades burst right through the wall.

Naimul was able to re-deploy the group waiting in ambush at the roadside in time for them to join the siege of the police compound.

Normally even the smallest units of the Pakistan army had light machine guns with them, but no machine gun fire issued from the compound. Either something had gone wrong with their LMG, or they didn't have a gunner.

The rain had started again, and peals of thunder could be heard at intervals. A thunderbolt struck a palm tree in the police compound with a tremendous crash. The soldiers doubtless thought they were under fire from a mortar gun. They stopped firing their rifles and held up a white cloth tied to a bamboo pole to signal their surrender.

Naimul's team also ceased firing. Calmly but loudly Naimul called out, "Hello, come out of there. We have stopped firing." A mere five soldiers emerged from the compound, hands in the air. Behind them came three West Pakistani policemen and the Bengali O.C. Naimul stepped up onto the verandah of the police station.

"Are you in good health, police inspector?" he asked the Bengali policeman.

"Y-yes, sir," replied the O.C. in discomfort.

"So many members of the police force have joined the fight for our independence, and here you are, working for the enemy. That's not very good. Anyway, listen to me now. You can tie up those soldiers for me."

"Yes, sir."

"Why are there so few of them? Shouldn't there be more?"

"There were more, but the day before yesterday HQ sent an urgent message recalling some of them."

"You have wireless here?"

"Yes, sir."

"Has any message been sent to say that the compound has been attacked?"

"No, sir."

"Why not?"

"There's no operator, sir."

"When you've tied up the soldiers you're to go to the bridge, taking them with you. You can help us blow up the bridge."

"Yes, sir."

Turning to the army captain Naimul said quietly in English, "You have surrendered, and I am now responsible for looking after you in accordance with the Geneva conventions. The problem is, we are a guerrilla unit and we operate all over the countryside. There's no way I can drag you everywhere with us; it would be impossible even if I wanted to. Not only that, many members of our liberation army have been captured by your people and in every case they have been sent before the firing squads. Why should I deal any differently with you?"

The team of freedom fighters arrived at Chairman Hashem's homestead for their meal just before dawn, to the chairman's considerable surprise. When they had sat down to eat the commander of the team very politely asked his hostess if she could spare him a few green chillies to go with his rice. Yet Hashem had heard that this polite, well behaved young man had only a short while ago lined up five Pakistani soldiers and three policemen on the bridge and shot them, letting their bodies drop into the river.

Rofik had run away the moment the firing had begun, but he reappeared at the scene of the feast and quite unobtrusively made himself useful by helping to serve out the food. Then when he got a suitable chance he spoke to Naimul.

"Sir, I'm going to stick with you for the rest of my life. I ain't going to leave your side. I know I ran away cause I was scared, but I swear I won't do it again."

And Rofik kept his word. He served in Naimul's team until he met his death during the Kachpur operation. He became quite an expert at using a sub-machine gun. In the Kachpur operation it was only because he continued firing his SMG after receiving bullet wounds himself, and went on shooting until he died, that Naimul and the others were able to escape.

Another fighter, Private Hamidur Rahman, showed similar heroism. During the attack on the Dholoi border outpost he enabled his platoon to beat a retreat by keeping up a continuous hail of covering fire until he succumbed to his wounds. By sacrificing his life he saved a whole platoon.

Private Hamidur Rahman has been posthumously awarded the Bir Shrestha medal°, but Rofik's name doesn't even appear on the official list of freedom fighters.

54

He was wearing dark glasses and a spotless white T-shirt, and was sitting bolt upright. The watch on his left wrist, whose strap was slightly too loose, kept slipping up and down whenever he moved his arm, but although this irritated him nobody observing him could have detected his irritation, for it is the eyes which betray human emotions and this man usually chose to keep his well hidden behind his dark glasses. A certain mystery surrounded him.

Ziaur Rahman° was his name. He was sitting outside his tent on a folding chair made of wood. The location was beautiful, rolling hills covered with forest in all directions, with no sign of human habitation. This place was called Teldhala, and it was some ten miles distant from the small town of Tura in the kingdom of Meghalaya. Major Zia studied the dense jungle for a while and then glanced up at the sky. Clouds were scudding over; they weren't rain clouds, but in this part of the world you never could tell, torrential rain might start pouring down any time.

It was in this beautiful forest setting, almost like paradise, that the First, Third and Eighth Battalions of the East Bengal Regiment had been brought together to form a crack infantry brigade known as Z Force – the Z being derived from Ziaur Rahman's first name.

Major Ziaur Rahman, officer in command of Z Force, was feeling a little peeved, having received reports that the commander in chief of the Bangladesh Army, General Osmani, was displeased with him. In General Osmani's opinion the East Bengal Regiment's recent attack on Kamalpur border outpost, ordered by Major Zia, had been over-ambitious. The attack had led to the deaths of three members of the regiment, with sixty-six injured. The commander of Delta Company, Salahuddin, had been killed while Hafizuddin, the commander of Bravo Company, had been seriously injured; in other words two companies had lost their commanding officers.

It was General Osmani's opinion that as the liberation army was short of both manpower and weapons it was not sensible to engage in reckless exploits incurring heavy losses.

Major Zia's argument was that he was the one in the field actually waging the war, and it was up to him to decide what to do and when. The commander in chief, who was based at the headquarters of the Bangladesh Government, was unaware of the situation on the ground.

Major Zia aired this opinion frankly at a meeting he had with Major K.M. Shafiullah, leader of S Force, and Major Khaled Mosharraf, leader of K Force. He argued that in a guerrilla type war such as the present one there was no need for any commander in chief; all that was needed was a command council. Furthermore it had been a mistake to bring an old officer out of retirement to take overall command of the army. Needless to say General Osmani was not very pleased when Major Zia's views were later relayed to him.

Major Zia spent some time inside his tent, then came out again and sat in the same place as before. He was now holding a letter. It was a short note he had written, in English, to Major General Jamshed of the Pakistan Army, who was now commander of the 36th Division in Dhaka. General Jamshed had been Major Zia's commanding officer when Zia was serving in the Punjab Regiment.

Major Zia had written as follows:

> Dear General Jamshed,
>
> My wife Khaleda is under your custody. If you do not treat her with respect I shall kill you some day.
>
> Major Zia

The letter was handed to Major Shafayet, who arranged for it to be posted in Dhaka. Curiously enough, the letter did reach Major General Jamshed.[*]

---

[*] *Rokte Bheja Ekattor (1971, A Year Bathed in Blood)*, Major (Retd) Hafiz Uddin Ahmed.

55

Source: *Dainik Bangla*
Date: 2nd January 1972
Title: *How the Pakistan Army Tormented Major Zia's Family*

While Major Zia was Organizing Fierce Resistance Barbarous Pakistan Military Victimized his Family

by Manzur Ahmed

While the hero of the Bangladesh liberation war, Major (now Colonel) Zia was mobilizing fierce resistance to the Pakistani army of occupation and causing them much harassment, the brutal Khan military pounced mercilessly on his family and relatives as a mean way of relieving their frustration. Among others Colonel Zia's brother-in-law Mr Mozammel Haque, Senior Co-ordination Officer of the Industrial Development Board, did not escape the effects of their malicious thirst for revenge.

After Chittagong city had been taken over by the enemy and Begum Khaleda Zia, disguised in a burqa, had fled from the city and travelled by river steamer to Narayanganj, it was Mr Mozammel Haque, her sister's husband, who met her there and brought her to Dhaka. The date was 16th May. A curfew was in force all over Dhaka, and a curfew had also been imposed in Narayanganj from dusk onwards. Despite all this he had come out in his car, having stuck a Red Cross label on it, and sped to the Narayanganj steamer terminal.

Some ten days after Begum Zia had been brought to Dhaka, about 26th May, all officers of the Industrial Development Board bearing the name Haque were summoned by the Pakistan military and asked whether they were anyhow related to Colonel Zia. Mr Mozammel Haque realized that danger was looming. On that occasion he did not reveal his connection to Colonel Zia, but on a pretext of illness went home early and immediately tried to make arrangements for Begum Zia to move away from his house.

Unable to find any other suitable haven, on 28th May he took her to the house of an uncle of his in Dhanmandi where she stayed for a few days. Then on 3rd June she was taken to the quarters of the Assistant Director of the Geological Survey, Mr Mujibur Rahman. A few days later she moved to the house of Mr S.K. Abdullah, Deputy Director of the Geological Survey.

On 13th June Pakistan army soldiers raided Mr Mozammel Haque's residence. The unit which carried out this operation was led by one Colonel Khan. Colonel Khan asked questions about Begum Zia, declaring that she had been seen at Mr Haque's residence. When he failed to extract any information from Mr Haque he grilled Mr Haque's ten year old son Don. Don replied flatly that he had not seen Begum Zia, his mother's sister, for three years.

Having failed to get any information the Pakistani soldiers searched Mr Haque's house. They left without having found anything connected with Begum Zia, but before leaving they warned Mr Haque he would be hauled off to the cantonment if he refused to disclose the truth.

From then on Mr Haque was aware of being followed. Wherever he went a shadow would be tracing his steps. He therefore took leave from his office, giving the pretext that his mother was ill, and started making plans to flee Dhaka with his whole family.

In accordance with these plans on 1st July the family slipped out of a rear entrance and boarded two auto-rickshaws, leaving Mr Haque's car in its garage as a decoy. Their plan was to go first to Begum Zia's uncle's house in Dhanmandi and stay there a few days. However they had got no further than the Science Laboratory when one of the auto-rickshaws broke down. This led to their making an unplanned stop at a close friend's house in nearby Green Road, and there a surprise lay in store for them. As soon as Mr Haque set foot in the house his friend's wife told him they had received a letter with his name on it from Colonel Zia, and had been seeking a chance to forward it to him for the past few days.

Mr Haque was surprised, and could not understand why a letter from Colonel Zia to himself had been delivered to this friend's house. He asked to see the letter and his friend's son produced it. He then sent the young man off with it to see Mr Mujibur Rahman at the Geological Survey and ask him to check with Begum Zia whether it was genuinely written in Colonel Zia's handwriting.

As it was now getting dark Mr Haque asked whether he and his family could stay at the friend's house overnight. However their hosts suggested that they should go somewhere safer, and the friend's son drove them over to a small house in Sutrapur, where they spent the night in a rather cramped room.

Next morning they found that the house had been surrounded by Pakistani soldiers. About ten armed men were standing in front of the building. In charge of the platoon were two captains, Captain Sajjad and Captain Arif. They entered the house and started interrogating the family about Colonel Zia and Begum Zia. Mr and Mrs Haque denied that they had any connection with them, but Captain Sajjad brought out a group photo showing them posing alongside Begum Zia, and they were obliged to admit they were related. However they insisted they did not know where either Colonel Zia or Begum Zia were.

At about 5 p.m. Mr and Mrs Haque were made to board a military vehicle and taken to the crossroads at Malibag. The vehicle parked in front of Mouchak Market and the couple were kept sitting in it until dark. There they were told that Begum Zia had been arrested. After that they were driven around the Second Capital area and then back to the house in Sutrapur, where they were set down. They made their way back to Mr Haque's friend's house in Green Road by night, and from there they returned to their own house in Khilgaon.

It should be mentioned that on the same day the Pakistan army seized Begum Zia and Mr S.K. Abdullah at Mr Abdullah's residence in

Siddheswari, and also took Mr Mujibur Rahman into custody. Then on 5th July when Mr Mozammel Haque went back to work Captain Sajjad came to his office, arrested him and took him away to the army cantonment.

He was kept waiting outside the Field Investigation Unit (FIU) office at the cantonment until ten o'clock at night, at which point he was transferred to a cell in School Road.

Before he was put in his cell his watch and rings were removed and his wallet was taken off him. Although he hadn't eaten all day he was not offered any food.

Next morning he was offered nothing more than a cup of lukewarm tea and then taken to Captain Sajjad's office. There Captain Sajjad asked him what he had been planning. Mr Haque said he had not been planning anything. Captain Sajjad called him a liar and threatened him with electric shock treatment as a punishment. After failing to extract any information Captain Sajjad ordered him to be subjected to a spell of 1000W radiation.

Accordingly that night Mr Haque was made to lie on his back in his cell with two dazzling five hundred watt bulbs suspended a couple of feet above him. He had to endure this intense discomfort for about four hours on end.

Next day he was hauled back in front of Captain Sajjad, and the latter once again asked him about the plans he had, what had he discussed with Sheikh Mujib, whether he had intended to go to India and so on. Mr Haque denied all knowledge, whereupon Captain Sajjad struck him violently on the neck. Then he ordered another twenty-four hours of 1000W radiation.

At one p.m. Mr Haque was taken to his cell and the lamps were turned on. After a few hours he started screaming in agony. Again and again he shouted, "Why don't you kill me outright? Stop torturing me like this!"

A Pathan N.C.O. came and stood outside the cell door while he was screaming. Evidently this soldier could not bear watching Mr Haque's agony; it doubtless pained him to witness the suffering one human being had chosen to inflict on another. So he called the guard and ordered him to turn the lamps off. He instructed him to switch them back on if he heard a jeep arriving, but extinguish them again once the jeep had gone away.

Captain Sajjad continued to interrogate Mr Haque for several more days, and subjected him to a different kind of torture. Mr Haque was forced to write one statement after another, each of which would be torn up in front of his eyes. When one statement had been ripped up he would be asked to write it out again; then the new copy would be torn up in its turn, and he would have to write yet another. In the end he was so tired and demoralized he lost the ability to write. He had nearly lost his sight too, as a result of exposure to thousand watt illumination. He could hardly tell the difference between night and day.

On the afternoon of 26th July he was taken to the Inter Services Screening Centre (ISSC). One hundred and ten prisoners were incarcerated in one small room. At five in the afternoon he was brought out and put to work filling some large steel drums with water for the camp kitchens. One other person was assigned to the same job: it was Mr S.K. Abdullah of the Geological Survey. Together they had to fill a large bucket with water from a tap, carry it almost a quarter of a mile and tip it into one of the three drums. At night everyone was made to line up and food was doled out to them one by one. It was rice and dal, the first hot meal Mr Haque had eaten since his arrest.

Next morning his hair was cut off and his scalp shaved, and many other inmates received the same treatment.

Mr Haque was detained in various rooms within that camp for several days, then on 6th August he was moved to the Field Investigation Centre (FIC). The officer in charge of the centre was one Major Faruqui, and there was a Sergeant Major Niyazi whose job was to supervise the torture of prisoners. Faruqui once again interrogated Mr Haque and told him to write out a statement. This exercise turned out to be the same form of torture as before: for three days on end he had to repeatedly write out the same statement, watch it being torn up in front of him and write it all over again.

On 9th August he was transferred to the Second Capital, where he was held in various cells for nearly one and a half months. On 21st September he was removed to Dhaka Central Jail, from which he was finally released on 30th September.

In the interim *razakar* thugs had raided his house three times and looted most of its contents. Later, on 13th December, they even stole his car.*

---

* *Documents of the Bangladesh War of Independence*, Volume 8, Page 476, Information Ministry, Government of the People's Republic of Bangladesh.

56

The house in Naya Paltan in which Kolimullah was now living with his wife and in-laws was called Hena Villa. It was a two storeyed building containing a total of eight rooms, two of which faced south. He and his wife Masuma were living in one of the south-facing rooms, while his mother-in-law was occupying the other along with her eldest daughter Moriam, youngest daughter Mafruha and infant son Yahya. Moriam had been allotted a separate bedroom, but she wasn't living in it; she said she was scared to be in a room on her own. In front of the house there was a small area of grass with flower beds containing native flowering plants. On one side of the building there was a grove of sweet-blossomed *hasnahena* bushes. Then there was a large rear garden with two *kamranga* trees, one of which had a marble surround to it. Kolimullah went and sat there every day with pen and paper at the ready. He loved nothing more than to lean back against the trunk of the *kamranga* tree and look up at its fretted leaves, toy with new lines of verse, ponder why it was that life seemed so blissful. His cup of happiness would have been altogether full if only he could have created some fresh poetry. Since he had got married poems hadn't been coming to him any more, he hadn't composed a single one. Nothing but a single line which had occurred to him one day:

Flushed with desire, the carambola flower

And that had been it. No second line had come along. However the first line had lodged itself securely in his head. Kolimullah was convinced that unless he could get the first line out of his mind nothing further would appear, so now he was concentrating his efforts on trying to expunge that first line from his brain. Clearly it wasn't going to be an easy matter. That single line kept going round and round in his head like a gramophone record with the needle stuck. Being a poet was a real trial; ordinary people had no idea how painful it was.

Kolimullah's wife was delighted with their new home.

"Whose house is this, in actual fact?" Masuma had asked.

"Yours," Kolimullah had replied.

"How can it be mine?" Masuma had objected. "If it was mine it would be called Masuma Villa, but it isn't, it's called Hena Villa."

"Wait till the new plaque is installed," Kolimullah had replied, yawning, "then you'll see. I've placed the order. The name of the house is to be in black letters on white marble. It should have been ready by now, but there's a shortage of craftsmen so it's been delayed."

"What name have you ordered? Masuma Villa?"

"No, Cloud Maiden. That's the name I've chosen for the house."

"Cloud Maiden? Who's that?"

"You. I wrote my poem *Cloud Maiden at Noon* with you in mind, have you forgotten that? You're so forgetful, how are you ever going to run a household, I wonder."

"Tell me the truth, who does own the house?"

"It belonged to a Hindu lawyer who has fled to India. I've arranged a transfer of ownership."

"How did you manage that?"

"Oh, I have contacts."

"But when this country becomes independent it won't be yours any more."

"Who said this country's going to be independent?" Kolimullah had retorted gruffly.

"What? Won't it become independent, then?"

"Never. To achieve independence by letting off fireworks would take at the very least a hundred and fifty years. Bengalis aren't like that – do you know what they're like? They're a nation of sparks. They sparkle with enthusiasm about any new thing, then after a while the spark goes out, just like that. Do you know the verse Rabindranath wrote about sparks?"

"No."

"He wrote:

> *The spark sprouted wings for an instant of flight,*
> *He died as he flew, but felt no less delight.*

"You know so many poems! It's amazing!" said Masuma, filled with admiration. The more she saw of her husband the more she admired him. She often wondered how it was possible for anyone to be at once so knowledgeable and so good. It was lucky war had broken out in their country, she thought; that was what had led to her suddenly, unexpectedly getting married to such a remarkable person. If it hadn't been wartime, and if her father had been around, no doubt some qualified doctor or engineer would have been selected as a marriage partner for her. Nobody would have thought of looking for a poet.

Not only did Masuma passionately and sincerely believe everything her husband said, she considered it her duty to quote his words to other people too. For this reason Moriam had given her the nickname "His Master's Voice", but far from being annoyed by the label Masuma was quite proud of it.

Each evening after dinner Kolimullah gathered the family together and sat down to watch the television news. When the news programme was over he would expound his own thoughts about the situation in the country. Masuma hugely enjoyed this time. While he talked she kept thinking what a marvel it was for any man to be able to speak so eloquently. And his manners were so delicate! Even though he was in his wife's presence he never looked at her while he was speaking; instead he politely addressed all his comments to his mother-in-law. And how touching was his way of calling her 'Mother'! Most men affected a falsely intimate 'Mum' when speaking to their wife's mother, but not he, he always went 'Mother'. Masuma was convinced that nobody except a poet could possibly use the term 'Mother' for their mother-in-law in such a charming fashion.

"Listen carefully to what I'm going to say, Mother. It's one of our failings as a nation that we never listen carefully with our brains, we listen only with our ears. We make a great fuss about the past but don't pause to consider what the future is going to bring. We are incapable of analysing a situation. But today I'm going to offer you a little analysis of my own. Just see what you think of it.

Who is the main figure behind the campaign of squibs and bangers which masquerades as a liberation war? Sheikh Mujibur Rahman. Where is he? In jail. What lies in store for him? The hangman's rope. Therefore the topic of Sheikh Mujibur Rahman is closed. That topic ends in a full stop. Not a comma, not a semi-colon; no, a full stop.

So who else is left? The elected representatives belonging to the Awami League. What are they doing? Deserting their party one by one and going over to Yahya's side. Another of them did so today, Sirajul Islam Choudhury, MP for Chittagong. You saw that on the television news just now – you did notice that bit, didn't you? Last week it was two Awami League MP's from Bogra who joined the pro Pakistan camp. None of these people are fools, they can tell which way the wind blows. They know when to support which party.

The ones who fled to India during the initial offensive now find themselves in an awkward position. They can't cross over to Yahya's side even if they wish to. They're awaiting their opportunity. They expect to be back.

They're hoping that India will fight for Bangladesh, but that hope is rooted in ... I won't say rooted in sand, I must really say rooted in shit. Sorry, Mother, I used a bad word, please pardon my rudeness. Indira Gandhi isn't a peasant girl, she's a sophisticated woman. If India started a war with Pakistan hundreds of Chinese soldiers would immediately pour into India via Ladakh. In no time they'd penetrate as far as Meghalaya. And then what situation would Indira find herself in? She'd have to say, I don't need your charity, but will you kindly bring that dog of yours under control. And that's not all. America is sitting there ready to pounce. President Nixon may be half asleep, but even so he has sent a signal to India. The message is: Indira, for some time you've been rather too close to our long standing enemy Russia and so far we've said nothing, but now our patience is at an end.

Do you realize what America is like, Mother? America isn't just a tiger, it's a tiger and a half, it's a super-tiger. Tigers spring onto their prey and seize it by the neck, but super-tigers don't even bother to jump, they can just swing their tail and thump their victim with it, and that's it, end of story."

"What's going to happen to the people who've been fighting for independence?" asked Moriam fearfully.

"Big sister," said Kolimullah turning towards her, "I don't feel inclined to give an honest answer to your question, seeing as Brother has gone to join the fight. Who knows what he's going through, in all the wind and rain and mud. Still, I should speak the truth. They're going to be disillusioned, indeed many of them have been already. They're going to throw away their weapons and try to slip back to their own homes. The ones who had originally been proper soldiers will be court martialed, but I don't know what will happen to the ones who were never in the regular army. They may be punished, or a general amnesty may be declared.

Well, that's the end of today's discussion. You should go to bed now, Mother, you haven't been getting enough sleep, you need a lot more. And don't let things worry you. Worry won't fill anyone's belly. *'Tis work that earns our daily bread.*"

The old saying 'work earns our daily bread' fitted well with Kolimullah's present lifestyle. These days he was very busy, supplying odd things to the army. Some of the things were very odd indeed. Once he had to procure a whole ton of coconut oil for them. What could they want with a ton of coconut oil? Were they intending to oil the wheels of their tanks with it? He could have enquired and found out, but he hadn't bothered, there was no point in being too inquisitive. His job was to deliver the goods. Supplying goods to the army meant one thing: money. Payment in cash.

Apart from his income as an army supplier he was getting other money from an entirely new source. True, it was an immoral source, but in a wartime economy right and wrong were like twin brothers which were almost impossible to tell apart. Honest, dishonest? They both looked just the same.

This new scheme for making money consisted in offering to obtain news from detention centres. The relatives of missing persons were desperate for information. They didn't mind how much money they had to spend, if necessary they would sell all their jewellery, sell their home even, as long as they could find out the one thing they wanted to know – whether their loved one was alive or not.

Quite a few people had gone into this business of information brokering. It was a way of making money without even getting off your backside. No risks were involved. Considering how many Biharis were doing it why shouldn't he? In fact it was a good thing that he was in the business; that way some money stayed in Bengali hands instead of going to the Biharis.

Admittedly he did have a Bihari business partner, Moznu Sheikh, to whom he had to give half of his earnings. Sadly it was impossible for him to keep the whole lot himself. It would have been better if he could have traded all on his own, but that was out of the question, as in this line of business people would only trust Biharis. Nowadays no Bengali would normally trust a Bihari in any circumstance, yet this information racket was an exception.

This is how the business worked. Someone would come along and say his brother had been seized by the army, and he needed to know whether he was in a detention centre or not. Then he might want to send a message to him, or try to arrange for his release.

Kolimullah would first of all try to make an accurate assessment of how much money the person had at his disposal. There was one kind of procedure for people with little money, and another for those with plenty. With anyone appearing to have an average level of wealth Kolimullah might start by holding an interview along these lines:

"When did they arrest your brother?"

"On Monday."

"Give me the date. 'Monday' is not enough."

"The eighteenth."

"Write down your brother's full name and date of birth on a sheet of paper and hand it in to me. Have you brought a photograph?"

"No."

"But that's ridiculous, why haven't you brought one?"

"I'll go and fetch one right now. There may not be a separate portrait, but I do have a group photo."

"What use is a group photo going to be, I ask you? You must find a separate passport photo. But don't bring it today, I'm busy. Come back tomorrow at about the same time."

"Right. Will it be possible to get any information?"

"My dear fellow, I can hardly tell you that. You do realize the complexities of the situation, don't you? I'll do my best, that's all I can assure you."

"How much should I pay you?"

"Oh, forget about that for the time being. First let me see if I can get any leads. Come back tomorrow with the photograph, and if you wish to send any kind of message to your brother jot it down in the form of a letter. But be very careful not to mention your brother's name in it, nor should you sign your own name. If the letter happened to be seized there would be dreadful problems."

"Shouldn't I give you a down payment, brother?"

"Hey, you must have more money than you know what to do with! Just go home now, and say a few prayers to the Lord. You'll have a chance to fork out some of your money later on."

The client would go home fully satisfied, feeling fairly confident that Kolimullah's agency was an honest one.

For the next couple of weeks the client would be led by the nose. First he would be told that the brother was almost certainly alive.

Next time it would be fully certain that he was alive, but the army would be severely maltreating him. Some money would be paid to try and stop the maltreatment.

Next time the news would be that Brother was starving. They were giving him only one dry chapati per day. A further payment might mean he would get his proper rations, though this could not be guaranteed.

Finally a large sum of money would be charged for bribing the army people to release the fellow and then bringing him home. It would be stressed from the outset that there was only a thirty percent chance of success. "With luck your brother will be released; otherwise all your money will have gone for nothing. Think it over, see whether you wish to take this risk or not. If you ask for my advice I shall say you shouldn't risk it. These days they often accept money on the understanding that they'll release a prisoner, but then they omit to do so. They are utterly unscrupulous people."

Even after this warning had been given the clients would invariably pay up. Then they felt at least they had made an effort, however small the chance of success might be.

Once he had said his carefully chosen words Kolimullah had absolutely nothing further to do. It was a case of sitting back and letting the money roll in. It often struck Kolimullah that wartime was really a test of one's intelligence. Anyone who had any wits at all could prosper from the war, whereas for a blockhead it spelt disaster. Kolimullah was sometimes amazed at his own ingenuity.

Kolimullah was still keeping in touch with Mr Zohar. However these days Mr Zohar was a great deal busier then before; there were always lots of people with him in his room, and seldom did Kolimullah manage to have a word with him. Kolimullah got the impression that the purpose for which he had originally been called to see Mr Zohar was no longer an issue, which was why he was not being summoned any more; however it was far from clear what that purpose had actually been. If they no longer needed him they ought to tell him so and let him go, but they weren't doing that either. However busy Mr Zohar was he always gave Kolimullah a knowing look and a nod, which in itself was quite something. Mr Zohar had considerable power, and a mere glance from such an influential person was worth a lot.

It looked as if Mr Zohar's health had got even worse. He had been wrapping himself in a shawl all along, but now he also wore a long sleeved pullover under the shawl. It was a mystery how anyone could stand wearing both a shawl and a pullover in such sweltering heat. And he kept coughing all the time, a chesty cough like that of a person with TB. It was hard to tell, but conceivably the man was actually dying of tuberculosis.

Just when Kolimullah had convinced himself that Mr Zohar was never going to send for him again and that there would be no more tête-à-tête meetings, he received a message telling him to come and see him. This time there was nobody else around; Mr Zohar was on his own. He was sitting in his usual position with his legs up, and he was coughing.

"How are you, poet?"

"Oh, all right, sir, by your blessing," replied Kolimullah, as if crushed by his own humility.

"Making good money?"

Kolimullah was slightly taken aback. How could Mr Zohar know anything about his little business? No, the fellow was probably shooting in the dark. Those people were adepts at shrewd guesswork.

"Make what you can as quickly as you can," advised Mr Zohar between coughs. "This opportunity may not last much longer."

"Are you feeling unwell, sir?" enquired Kolimullah in order to change the subject.

"Yes, I'm ill. Personally I suspect I have lung cancer, that's why I'm not going to see a doctor. I trust you're well?"

"Yes, sir, I am."

"So you've married one of Mobarak Hussain's daughters?"

This time Kolimullah reeled with shock. There was no way Mr Zohar should have known about that. How on earth had he found out?

"Yes, sir," he said, trying to conceal his astonishment. "A helpless family, I felt very bad. Nobody to take the rôle of guardian. Considering the whole situation I decided to take on that big responsibility. I had you in mind also, sir."

"Me? How is that?"

"You said you'd like to do something for the family."

"Kolimullah!"

"Yes, sir?"

"You're pretty smart, but I happen to be a good deal smarter than you. I can tell straight away when a person says something simply to humour me, and I really cannot stand it."

"Please forgive me, sir, if I've done anything wrong."

"Now, have you heard about the new Al-Badar brigades° which are being set up?"

"No, sir."

"Well, I want you to go into the Al-Badar. We need a few bright people in there."

"Whatever you say, sir."

"Have you read the Holy Quran?"

"I'm a Muslim," exclaimed Kolimullah, pretending to be shocked, "how could I not have read the Holy Quran, sir!"

"In the Holy Quran," Mr Zohar continued quietly, suppressing his cough, "God says this: '*I create man in the highest form, but when he is altered I bring him down to the lowest level.*'"

"Ah, what a splendid verse!" gushed Kolimullah.

"You were a poet," said Mr Zohar, leaning towards him, "and a poet is the highest form of mankind. I want to see how much you alter, when it comes to alteration."

"Are you annoyed with me for any reason, sir?"

"No, not annoyed. Can one poet ever be annoyed with another? By the way, there's a verse about poets in the Holy Quran – do you know it?"

"No, sir."

"Find it, and have it in mind next time you come. Then we'll discuss it."

"Right, sir."

As he was leaving Mr Zohar's room Kolimullah thought, your days are numbered, old man. People always get a bit religious minded as they approach death, that's why you've started quoting bits of scripture. Huh!.

But despite entertaining such defiant thoughts he did join the Al-Badar the next day.

57

Kolimullah's cook Bacchu Miah had changed his spots and turned into a Bihari. He didn't have to go to any great lengths to achieve the transformation – he had to crop his hair short, buy a pair of sunglasses and a gaudy neckerchief, and get hold of a folding knife to keep in his pocket.

Every day he used to spend some time wandering around Dhaka city with his mouth full of *paan* and a cigarette in his fingers. A strong smell of perfume would emanate from his body.

People would glance at him fearfully, and Bacchu Miah enjoyed that. He only had to park himself in front of a cigarette stall for the owner to get all flustered and desperate to do just about anything to please him. Bacchu Miah would clear his throat with a sort of belch he had recently learned. The belching sound scared people too, and that was another thing he found highly amusing. Then he would eject some red *paan* spittle through pursed lips. Biharis spit out their paan juice in a different way from Bengalis; they make a special show of it, and Bacchu Miah had mastered the art.

"You a genuine Pakistani?" Bacchu Miah would ask the stallholder in Urdu, once the latter had been reduced to a nervous wreck. He would make his voice very harsh.

The stallholder would nod his head emphatically.

"Bring out some cigarettes," Bacchu Miah would go on, spitting a second time, and speaking in an even deeper voice.

The stallholder would instantly whip out a whole packet of cigarettes and offer it to him. Usually they were Capstan cigarettes which were worth ten paisa a piece, no joking matter.

"Roll up a *paan*. Double *zarda*, not too much lime."

The stallholder would swiftly set to and start preparing the wad of *paan*. However sheer terror would make his hands shake. Bacchu would then start to feel sorry for him.

"Wot you so scared for, brother?" he would say in Bengali, speaking more softly. "I ain't no Bihari, I'm a Bengali. Just I'm acting Bihari-like."

But even that wouldn't dispel the stallholder's fear. His eyes would betray deep suspicion. Probably this was all some new kind of trick.

"Don't be scared, bro. I swear, I'm a Bengali. Me name's Bacchu Miah. I ain't just a Bengali, either, I'm a *mukti*!" The last words in a hushed voice.

The stallholder's eyes would grow huge.

"In the daytime I dress up like a Bihari, you see, I go around like this. Pick up information about the Pak army. At night it's boom! boom! That's us bombing. Don't you 'ear our bombs going off at night?"

"Oh yes, I do."

"D'you 'ear anything last night? Try and remember."

"I did."

"'Ow may times, eh? I tell you, three times. Twice in early evening, once at eleven o'clock. I was in that operation at eleven o'clock. Wasn't in the earlier one. Three Pak soldiers killed in the eleven o'clock operation."

By this time the stallholder would have started trusting Bacchu Miah. The fear would have vanished from his eyes and his face would have lit up.

"Have a cup of tea, brother!" the stallholder would say gaily.

"Wot, you got stuff for making tea in your stall?"

"No, but I'll send for some."

"Oh, aw right then. But first lemme pay for the fags. We're *mukti*, we are, we ain't allowed to take stuff off folks by bullying 'em."

"Heavens!" the stallholder would protest, almost shrieking. "You expect me to charge you for them cigarettes? I'm not such a bastard!"

Bacchu Miah took great pleasure in masquerading as a freedom fighter. He really felt he was one.

"How are your operations going, brother?"

"Don't you 'ear the bombs at night?"

"Course I do. Sometimes hear them in daytime too."

"Day and night, it's all the same, as far as we're concerned. You'll 'ear 'em all the time. Some new guys are coming to join our team. New ones keep coming every day."

"*Alhamdulillah!*"

"The army bods are shitting in their pants. Know what I mean?"

"Of course I do."

"D'you listen to *Chorompotro*?"

"I should think so! Can't get by without listening. *Chorompotro* and the sound of the bombs in Dhaka, those are the two things we can't go to bed without, me and my family."

Bacchu Miah was becoming bolder and bolder as the days went on. He started going out of his way to greet any Pakistan army soldiers he came across. The soldiers tended to trust Biharis. Bacchu Miah would hold out his packet of cigarettes to them and say in Urdu, "*Bhai, halot kya?* – How are you, brother?" He used to have whole conversations with them.

"You should finish off all the *mukti*," he would say to them in a grave voice, squirting out his red *paan* spittle. "Finish off the Bengalis, all of 'em!"

His Urdu was deficient, but that didn't matter, many Biharis couldn't speak Urdu properly either. Biharis could be identified by the way they spoke in a mixture of Bengali and Urdu, and Bacchu Miah could parrot the same mixture.

Bacchu would return home before dark and cook himself a pottage of rice and lentils. He didn't have to bother his head as to whether the dish would be palatable or not, as he was the only person there. He could chew his rice and lentils raw for all it mattered. That was the great thing about being on your own. He was still living in Kolimullah's house, and sometimes he would wonder what had become of his employer. Kolimullah had given him ten rupees for his expenses and then vanished without trace. Could he have been killed? These days losing one's life was an unremarkable matter. You could die if you ventured out of your house, and you could die if you stayed put. The angel of death was working overtime in Dhaka.

When he had finished his meal Bacchu Miah would go to bed and lie with his ear glued to the radio. He didn't want to miss a single item in the *Shadhin Bangla* broadcast, and above all he had to listen to *Chorompotro*. While this serial drama about freedom fighters was going on he would imitate one of the heroes repeating his catch phrase, "Go on, let 'em have it!"

As he listened he thought to himself, ah, if only I could be a freedom fighter, I could go and let 'em have it! Then the Pak army would find out what fighting really meant, and what the Bengalis were really like!

One day, it was a Friday, there was a rattle at the door. An ominous kind of rattle, which possibly meant trouble. No Bengali person would ever agitate the latch so violently: these days Bengalis tended to knock very timidly at front doors. Maybe it was a Pakistani soldier!

Recently the bastards had started carrying out house to house searches. They would grab all the young men and haul them away – and those young fellas would never return. It had become really risky to be a juvenile male. Calling on the great saint Abdul Qader Jilani to assist him, Bacchu Miah went and opened the door. To his amazement Kolimullah was standing there. He was sporting a beard, had a prayer cap on his head and was wearing a freshly ironed *kurta*.

"Still around, are you?" exclaimed Kolimullah. "You didn't run away, then."

"How could I do a runner?" retorted Bacchu Miah, touching Kolimullah's toes in respect. "You never left no money for me to live on. I been surviving without food. Where were you?"

"So you've been selling my stuff, have you?" said Kolimullah after casting a swift appraising glance over the property. "The house seems short of furniture."

"You can check it all if you want."

"Go and make some tea, I could do with a cup. Oh, and have you been sleeping on my bed, by any chance? It looks very much like it."

Bacchu Miah chose not to reply and went off to make the tea. What Kolimullah had said was perfectly true.

Previously he had slept on the floor, but nowadays he was using his employer's bed. Well, in a wartime economy all things were equal, teak and mango wood cost just the same. So why shouldn't he sleep in a proper bed?

Kolimullah calmed down as he sipped his tea. The main thing was that Bacchu Miah hadn't deserted the house. He had been guilty of theft, no doubt, but it was only natural that he would filch the odd thing.

"And where were you, sir?"

"Oh, I got married," said Kolimullah. "That kept me rather busy."

"Got married?" repeated Bacchu Miah in astonishment.

"Yup."

"So where's the mistress?"

"She's around. I've arranged another house for her."

"What's she called?"

"What do you need to know *that* for? Gracious, such impertinence!"

"Won't I get to meet 'er?"

"Well, well, you're such an important guy she's got to be introduced to you, is that it? Listen, you're to carry on staying here just as you are. You can guard the house. Got it?"

"I got it."

"I'll drop in to see you from time to time. And I'll give you money for your expenses. The selling of furniture has got to stop."

Bacchu Miah had brought a cup of tea for himself too. As a sign of courtesy he turned away to avoid his employer's eye each time he took a sip from it. He was glad his boss had got married; it was dismal working in a household where there were no womenfolk.

"When'll we get independence, d'you think, sir?"

"We already have independence, how can we possibly have it twice over? Enough of that nonsensical talk."

"Right, sir, enough it is."

"You're a domestic servant. You must behave like one. Your job is to do the cooking, have you got that?"

"Okay, I've got it. Though these days I 'ardly get time to cook rice even. Have to carry out me duties."

"What duties?" asked Kolimullah sharply.

"I'm a *mukti* now, sir," said Bacchu Miah in a flat tone.

"A what?"

"A *mukti*."

Kolimullah was staring at him in horror. The sight of his boss staring in horror like that tickled Bacchu hugely. No, he wasn't just a servant any more, some bloke who did the cooking. He was a *mukti* – and that was quite something.

"You've become a freedom fighter?"

"Yes sir. I sleep in the daytime, go on operations at night. We got an operation planned for this very night. Pray for us, sir. Can I get you another cup of tea?"

Kolimullah said neither yes nor no, so Bacchu Miah went away to make more tea. He was delighted to see that his employer had believed him implicitly. This was only possible thanks to the 'wartime economy': for in wartime every lie was accepted as true, that was one of the funny things about it.

"Sir," said Bacchu Miah as he handed Kolimullah his fresh cup of tea, "please pray for us, we got a big operation on tonight. God knows if I'll get back in one piece. Doubt it, somehow."

"Where is this operation?"

"Can't tell you, sir. That's orders."

"Bacchu Miah!"

"Yes, sir?"

"I warn you, don't play the goat with me. You expect me to believe you became a freedom fighter in the short time I was away?"

"Suppose you're right," admitted Bacchu Miah after a pause. "Still, I am going to join up and be a *mukti*. Been talking to them about it."

"Stow it, will you!"

"Right, sir, I'll say no more. You going to 'ave a bath, sir? Will I hot up some water?"

"No."

"Shall I rub you down with oil? You'll feel good. It's nice to have a bath after 'aving oil rubbed in. Can I?"

"Go ahead, then," said Kolimullah rather haughtily.

Soon Kolimullah closed his eyes in bliss. He had suddenly realized Bacchu Miah's massaging skills were quite impressive. In fact it wouldn't be a bad idea to drop in at this house every now and then for a dose of his treatment. Massage improved the circulation, it was good for the body. And a healthy body meant a happy disposition.

"Bacchu Miah!"

"Yes, sir?"

"Where did you learn such an excellent massaging technique?"

"You know Mona Miah the chef, me old teacher? I used to rub 'im down a lot, that's 'ow I learned."

"Well, you're not really cut out for waging war, you're certainly not cut out for cooking, your true vocation is that of a masseur. Do you hear me?"

"Yes, sir."

"Would you like to hear a bit of Panjabi poetry on the subject of war? I heard Mr Zohar recite it and jotted it down. Listen – '*Suleh kitiya fateh zi batabe kamar jang ti mul na kaseye ni.*' It means, 'If peace can bring victory, do not go to war.' Isn't it a nice bit of verse?"

"Ain't no way for us except goin' to war," observed Bacchu as he massaged Kolimullah's shoulders. "Them Panjabis won't go away unless we fight 'em. Devilish lot they are."

"Pipe down, boy."

"Okay, sir."

"The Bengalis aren't a warfaring nation. Understand?"

"I get it. Still, I'd really love to go to war. If I could knock off one single Panjabi I'd think my life 'ad been worth while."

"That's quite enough, stop your chatter now."

"Yes, sir."

So relaxing was the massage that Kolimullah had started drifting off to sleep. Taking advantage of this situation Bacchu Miah opened his heart and went on talking.

"Sir, even if I ain't ever gonna be a fighter, if only I could watch when an operation's going on. See, the *mukti* on one side, Pakistan on the other, shooting at each other. Pakistan get wiped out, all of 'em, they ain't equal to our *mukti* boys, couldn't even lick their arse. Ah, if only I could see it 'appen. Well, let's see what God 'as in store. If it's in me fate I'll get to see it. What d'you say, sir? Sir? You asleep?"

When he was absolutely certain Kolimullah was asleep Bacchu Miah slipped his hand into Kolimullah's pocket and drew out a ten rupee note. In the 'wartime economy' theft was no longer counted as a crime.

Maybe the Almighty, the Merciful One, grants everyone their wishes in the end, and maybe that's what happened in Bacchu Miah's case. Anyway, he was granted the opportunity to see a sizeable operation carried out by freedom fighters. Kitted out as a Bihari, he was hob-nobbing with a number of West Pakistani policemen, some soldiers of the black-uniformed brigade and a second lieutenant of the Pakistan army near the crossroads known as 'Pak Motors' when he saw a black Toyota car drive up close to them and screech to a halt. One window of the car was rolled down and a dense hail of gunfire issued from it. A hand grenade was also thrown from inside the vehicle.

The car then sped off as rapidly as it had arrived. Bacchu Miah died having just witnessed one of the more daring exploits carried out by the guerrilla fighters of Dhaka city. Not many people are filled with delight at the moment of their death. Bacchu Miah was.

58

Kohinoor Mansion is an apartment complex in the Park Circus area of Calcutta. One of the most important figures of East Pakistan, Moulana Abdul Hamid Khan Bhashani°, was staying at a medium sized flat in this block. His companion there was Saiful Islam, a loyal follower, who had been in the Muzaffar section of the political party Bhashani had founded, the National Awami Party. Saiful Islam's job was to disseminate Moulana Bhashani's press releases, make copies of his letters to heads of state, deal with postage and so on.

The Moulana was leading a somewhat lonely existence in exile. He was not part of the mainstream independence movement. Having spent most of his long life tirelessly fighting the establishment he at last seemed to be getting a little weary.

He had written a letter to Indira Gandhi in his own hand. In it he had said, *'My eldest son died in a rustic setting. For this reason my elderly wife wishes our final resting place to be in some tranquil village too...'* * The letter struck a sad and solemn note, as if the Moulana could hear a bell tolling for him somewhere in the distance.

Moulana Bhashani was now sitting in the lounge of his flat. He was wearing an unsewn lungi topped by a spotlessly white tunic. From his right hand hung a string of prayer beads which he was counting steadily through as he mentally recited the ninety-nine names of the deity. He was gazing calmly into space. The prime minister of the Bangladesh government in exile, Tajuddin Ahmed°, had just arrived for a private talk with him. The prime minister touched the Moulana's feet respectfully and gave him a *salaam*.

"How are you, your reverence?" asked Tajuddin obsequiously.

"I'm very well," replied the Moulana. "I'm having a great time, sitting here killing flies. There are a lot of flies around here."

"You're not facing problems with your feeding arrangements, are you?"

"Forget about my feeding arrangements," retorted the Moulana, interrupting the count of his prayer beads. "If you've got anything important to say, please go ahead and say it."

"I'm having quite a few problems myself, your reverence."

"Nobody's without their problems. However I can see what your difficulty is. The gale does more damage to the big trees than the little ones, and you're a big tree now."

"But I never had any desire to be one."

"Yes, I suppose that's perfectly true."

"I've come to you to seek your advice."

"About what?"

Tajuddin was silent. For several minutes the *tasbih* circulated rapidly in the Moulana's hand, bead after bead. Finally the Moulana stopped counting and spoke.

"Always act according to your own judgment," he said quietly. "That's what I advise. You'll find there's a roaring trade in adulterated advice during wartime. If you ask for advice the stuff you'll get will be contaminated. Look at me, throughout my life I've always relied on my own judgment. Oh, by the way, are you hungry? Would you like anything to eat?"

Tajuddin shook his head silently.

---

* *Shadhinata Bhashani Bharat* (*Independence, Bhashani and India*), Saiful Islam.

"I'm getting old," remarked the Moulana with a deep sigh. "I've lost all my physical strength. I'm still strong in mind, but not in body. If I had any physical strength I'd ask you to make me a guerrilla commander and send me away to my own village to fight."

"A great deal of fighting can be done without weapons."

"But in the end weapons are necessary. I notice in the papers that the French writer André Malraux wants to take up arms and join the freedom fighters in Bangladesh, even at his age. I found that piece of news so touching, tears came to my eyes, and I said a heartfelt prayer for him. I'm going to write and thank him. Please see that the letter gets sent to him."

"Yes, sir, I shall. Do you have any further instructions for me?"

"There's one thing. Whether you call it an instruction or a request or a suggestion."

"What is it?"

"Make sure I'm sent back to the rural hinterland of Bangladesh once it's independent. My time is near, and I would like to die in my own village."

The Moulana closed his eyes and started fingering his prayer beads again. When the prime minister made to get up and go he gestured to him to sit down again.

"Bring your head close to mine," he said calmly, opening his eyes again, "I'm going to breathe a little prayer into your ear. And by the way, you're not going away until you've had something to eat. How about some toasted rice? I'll tell them to make some. Torrefied rice tossed with oil and chillies – real Bangladeshi village food."

The prime minister leaned his head closer, his eyes closed. The Moulana placed both hands on his head and mumbled a prayer over him.

59

Letter of a Freedom Fighter to his Mother Sent from the Bangladesh Hospital in Meghalaya

786 °

Virtuous and Respected Mother,

This letter brings you thousands of *salaams* from me. I also offer thousands of *salaams* at the blessed feet of Grandmother and Grandfather. And *salaams* or blessings, according to their respective status, to each and everyone at home.

Next let me inform you that I am well. The report of my death which you received was incorrect. A mortar shell hit both my legs, and I have been given appropriate treatment. I am now in hospital, and God willing I am getting better. Many distinguished persons have come to visit me. My name has been included in the list of wounded freedom fighters, and that is very good news indeed. It means once our country is liberated I shall receive a pension for life.

Now I have to give you some very bad news. Brother Gafur from Shubhopur and Enayet from Mishakandi (you won't know Enayet, he's a very brave freedom fighter and a devout Muslim, he never missed any of the daily prayers even while in action) have been captured by the army. We don't know what their fate has been, we still haven't received any news. When I was wounded and had fallen on the battlefield at Birampur Gafur picked me up and ran more than three miles with me on his back. He then dropped me at the camp and went back to join in the fighting. Then he was caught by the army. Such is the irony of fate. I cannot help weeping every time I think of dear brother Gafur.

Mother, I must now give you another rather bad piece of news. You must seek strength in God and not weep too much. Whatever God causes to happen, it is always for the best - you must remember that. The doctors have decided to cut off my legs from the knees downwards. They say there is no other way to save my life. You must keep this a secret from Grandmother. She is old, and the news would cause her too much pain. You never know what effect it might have on her.

Mother, two nights ago I saw Father in a dream. He was sitting beside my bed and he was wearing a long white *kurta*. He put his hand on my head and stroked me lovingly. I had a chat about small family matters with him. Unfortunately I cannot remember what was said. It was a great pleasure to dream of Father after such a long time.

I am well, Mother, so you mustn't worry about me.

Your beloved son
Abdul Goni

P.S. The date for the operation hasn't been fixed yet.

60

This autobiographical account was written by Captain Dr Sitara Begum, holder of the *Bir Pratik* medal of honour, who worked at the Bangladesh Hospital.

It was 1961 and I was a student of Holy Cross College. I used to be involved in a lot of sporting activities. After qualifying as a doctor and doing a six month internship I enlisted in the Pakistan Army in June or July 1970. The reason for this was that my elder brother was already in the army. Up till the time the liberation war started I had the rank of lieutenant. Towards the end of 1971 General Osmani promoted me to captain. My elder brother Haider was actively involved in the liberation war, and my younger brother A.T.M. Safdar (Jitu) was also engaged in supplying messages and secret intelligence to the liberation army.

In October 1970, when I was stationed in Comilla, my elder brother Major Haider was transferred from a posting in Cherat, Rawalpindi, West Pakistan to a posting in East Pakistan with the 3rd Commando Battalion. It was during Ramadan - as far as I can remember the date was 5th February - when my brother and I went on leave to [our family home in] Kishoreganj. I had one month's leave and my elder brother had two weeks' leave. But my brother returned to Comilla after one month [*sic*], before his leave had been consumed. That was when the general unrest caused by the political crisis began.

In the first or second week of March I returned to Dhaka. At that time my elder brother was stationed in the cantonment. He used to come and see me secretly at the house of an aunt and uncle of ours. As instructed by him, when my leave was finished I reported back for duty and then returned to our house in Kishoreganj. However when there was an air raid on Kishoreganj station we fled from the house. The parents-in-law of a maternal uncle of ours lived in a place three miles from our home, and that's where we went. After staying there for a week we returned to Kishoreganj. Captain Nasser and my elder brother Haider came down there while preparing to blow up two bridges in Mymensingh. At around this time two or three telegrams came from my headquarters in Comilla cantonment putting pressure on me to report for duty. My father replied to them with the message "She is sick".

After I had been in Kishoreganj a week, and just two days before the occupation forces burst into the town, we fled to my mother's maternal grandparents' home in Hossainpur, about ten or twelve miles to the north. While there we used to get bits of news about my elder brother. There was a rumour that he had gone to Agartala and was training freedom fighters, but we did not believe this. At that time notices were put up in Kishoreganj saying that there would be a ten thousand rupee reward for anyone who could facilitate the capture of my elder brother and my father. Towards the end of July my elder brother, having heard reports that the Pakistan army had killed our parents, sent a member of the liberation army to where we were in order to find out whether there was any truth in them.

At the end of July we spent eight or ten days at a stretch travelling by country boat, via the camp at Gojdiya in Kishoreganj subdivision, to Meghalaya. We spent a week at Tekerhat in Sylhet. My elder brother somehow found out that we were there. Then we travelled by lorry to Shillong [in Assam]. As Father had fallen ill during the journey we stayed in Shillong for four or five days. Then we passed through Gouhati and in the first week of August we reached Meghalaya. Two or three weeks later I joined the Bangladesh Hospital there.

I was allocated to No.2 Sector. The Bangladesh Hospital in Meghalaya was constructed of bamboo and had about four hundred beds in it. Three or four final year students of Dhaka Medical College were serving there. From England had come Dr Mobin, Dr Zafrullah, Dr Kiran Sarkar Debnath, Dr Faruk Mahmood, Dr Nazimuddin and Dr Morshed. These were the most noteworthy ones. There were a dozen or so volunteers who had been in the army, though none of them with a rank higher than sergeant major. No Indian doctors worked with us on a regular basis. However we had to go to Agartala and Udaypur for medicines, and the District Commissioner of Udaypur, Mr Banerjee, the Director of the Education Board in Agartala, Dr Chatterjee, and also Dr Majumdar and Dr Chakrabarty all afforded us a great deal of assistance and cooperation.

Our operating theatre was a hut whose walls and floor were lined with a kind of plastic sheeting. During the time I was there only two patients died of diarrhoea or dysentery.

Many soldiers of the Indian Army also came there for treatment. I sometimes used to go and visit the Indian Army Hospital in Agartala.

We also received a great deal of help from the Indian Army. The majority of our patients suffered from malaria.

Once an Indian Army truck went off the road into a ditch and overturned. It was packed with soldiers. The wounded ones were brought to our hospital in our own ambulance for treatment. General Rob's helicopter was hit by bullets, and he also received treatment at our hospital.

Even when I was working at the hospital I was unable to meet up with my elder brother Haider. He was exceedingly busy almost all the time. I saw him just occasionally. Our parents rented a mud hut not far from the Meghalaya camp and passed their days there, sitting and sleeping on plastic bags spread on the floor. Big brother hardly managed to see them either.*

---

* *Muktijuddha: Detlain Agartala* (*Liberation War: Dateline Agartala*), Harun Habib.

61

It was noon on 16th August, at the end of Shrabon month in the rainy season, when Naimul got right into Dhaka city. He managed it without any great difficulty. He had made his way on foot through various villages in the Narsingdi area. If he had tried to get in by bus, train or river launch he would have run into difficulties at the checkposts, where he would have been asked to show his *dandy* (identity) card and subjected to interrogation. People were being detained on the merest suspicion, and a curiously sunburnt young man of urban middle class appearance like himself would have been arrested on sight. No questions, the lockup.

Even wandering through villages was not without its hazards. The network of local *razakar* vigilantes was by now well established. They were always on the lookout, ready for any chance to loot and plunder. The peace committees were on their toes too. Any unfamiliar face in a village was immediately spotted. "What's your name? Your business here?"

Naimul was carrying some papers to establish an identity. He had a letter issued by a peace committee chairman, Haji Asmatullah. Typewritten and stamped with the official rubber stamp of a peace committee, it read as follows:

> **In the Name of God, the Merciful, the Beneficent**
> The bearer, Farhad Khan, a resident of Sirajganj, is a loyal subject of Pakistan. You are requested to afford him every kind of assistance and cooperation at all times.

Naimul only had to show the letter once. When he was coming into the outskirts of Dhaka a *razakar* commander took it and turned it over in his hands with a serious expression on his face. From the way he was looking at the piece of paper it was evident that he was unable to read.

"Tell me your name and background."

"My details are there, in the letter," said Naimul.

"I know they're written there, but I want to you tell me!" retorted the commander testily. "Your mouth isn't locked, is it? If it is, let me know, and I'll open it with my key. I do have a key for opening mouths, you know."

"My name is Farhad Khan."

"Where are you heading for?"

"Dhaka."

"What for?"

"My wife is in Dhaka and I want to see her."

"What's your wife's name?"

"Moriam," replied Naimul quite truthfully.

"Stand there with your arms raised, you're going to be body-searched."

Naimul stood with his arms up. A different man came up and frisked him, thumping him in the process. Naimul had the impression the two of them were enjoying their job, and he knew exactly why. If you're carrying a rifle people shrink with fear at the sight of you, and it's quite gratifying to observe their alarm.

"What's the situation like in Dhaka, do you know?" asked Naimul.

"Fine," replied the commander.

"Any *mukti* in the city?"

"Might be one or two. None in our area."

"Still, be on your guard. Even if there are none now they may suddenly arrive."

"That's enough of your gossip," snapped the commander irritably. "Get moving, go wherever you're going. You can give us a little tip to buy *paan*."

Naimul gave him a ten rupee note which the commander nonchalantly pocketed.

In the month of Shrabon the sky is supposed to be cloudy and the sun should not be shining, or if it shines it should only do so hazily: that is the normal rule. This day, however, was an exception. There was bright sunshine and the city was sweltering under a pall of its own fiercely shimmering perspiration.

After weeks of trudging along bumpy cart tracks and over muddy fields Naimul found the smooth asphalt of the city streets a delight to walk on. The roads were clear, walls were free of graffiti, there were no crowds of people or traffic. Pakistan flags flew from every building and even rickshaws had little paper flags fluttering on them.

Naimul was heading for Shantinagar where there was a hotel he knew, Hotel Zindabahar. He had previously lived in one of its rooms, No. 18 it was, for a matter of months, so he knew the hotel staff and it would probably be quite safe for him to book in there now. First he would take a room, No.18 if possible. Then he would win over the room boy with a one rupee tip and get him to fetch two bucketfuls of hot water. Using the hot water he would have a luxurious bath, scrubbing himself so thoroughly he would use up an entire bar of soap; for it was a long time since he had had a proper bath, and his body was crying out for one.

After having his bath he would order a meal. That hotel did a curried hilsa fish roe dish and a kind of thick soup based on the head of a carp, both of which were beyond compare. He would get them to bring the food to his room, and there he would feast palatially. To round off the meal he would have a wad of *paan* with sweet spices in it. Then a cigarette. And then he would lie down for a quiet post-prandial nap.

Only then, when he had finished his nap, would he set out to look for Moriam and the others. He was almost resigned to the fact that he wouldn't find them, for it was very unlikely they would have remained in Dhaka, they would have moved to somewhere safer. Dhaka could hardly be described as safe: the city's present uncluttered, disciplined atmosphere belied its real state.

Dhaka was now uncannily empty of pariah dogs and house crows. The lack of dogs had a straightforward explanation: the occupation soldiers, who evidently loathed dogs, kept shooting them on sight. But what about the crows? Surely the soldiers weren't shooting them?

Naimul kept an eye out for crows as he marched along.

'Kaa! kaa!' goes the crow,
'Dhaka city's dead, you know!'

Nice rhyme, thought Naimul.

But it wasn't long until he spotted a dog. There it was, a fairly healthy looking ochre coloured pie dog lying on the pavement in a sprawling, somehow melancholy pose.

"How are things, old fellow?" asked Naimul. The dog scrambled to its feet at once.

Those were the first words Naimul had uttered since entering Dhaka. If he'd been in the habit of keeping a diary he could have made a nice note of it.

> *Entered Dhaka noon of 16th August. The very first words I spoke were, 'How are things, old fellow?' The question was addressed to a dog. This dog had an ochre coloured coat and he limped when he walked. He accompanied me for quite a long way. He only held back when I crossed over the road at Shantinagar crossroads, and even then he went on looking at me as if to say he would willingly come after me if I would just give him a sign. I might actually have called him, but I didn't, and that was because I had noticed a barber's shop nearby and immediately thought about getting a haircut. I then entered the barber's shop.*

Barbers everywhere invariably chat to their customers while they do their job, but the one who cut Naimul's hair uttered not a single word, he just snipped away silently. Naimul felt pleasantly at ease. It was the first time it had ever occurred to him that having a haircut could be an agreeable experience. He was starting to feel sleepy. It wasn't at all a good idea to fall asleep in a barber's chair, but he was having a struggle to stay awake.

"What's your name?" he asked, stifling a yawn.

"Tayyab," replied the barber quietly.

"It's your shop?"

"No, the boss owns it."

"You the only employee?"

"Yes."

"D'you get a lot of custom?"

"Fair amount."

"Do the army people come for a cut?"

Tayyab gave no reply. Probably he was under orders never to make any kind of comment relating to the army.

"Are there any *mukti* in town?"

The barber paused in his snipping for a moment before going on. He did not reply to the question.

"You live in the city, surely you notice *mukti* goings-on? I'd expect you to."

"Oh, there are some goings-on. You a *mukti*?"

"Uh-huh," said Naimul quite calmly.

"I could tell by looking at ya."

"How so?"

"A fellow can tell. Shall I massage ya scalp?"

"All right. But give me a shave first."

The scalp massage was so relaxing, Naimul really did fall asleep. Nor was it a five minute nap, he slept long and deep. Tayyab made no effort to wake him, but instead sat in the next chair with a rolled up newspaper in his hand. There were a lot of flies buzzing around, and every time they tried to settle on his sleeping customer's face he chased them off with his newspaper.

It was mid afternoon when Naimul woke up. The sunshine had gone and the sky had clouded over. In the month of Shrabon clouds mean rain, and if it rained that would spell trouble for Naimul. He had come to Dhaka without any change of clothes.

Tayyab was watching him. His face was expressionless.

"I must have fallen asleep," exclaimed Naimul in irritation. "Why didn't you wake me?"

Tayyab did not speak.

"How much do I owe you? A haircut, a shave, and a head massage, how much does all that come to?"

"Nothing," said Tayyab. "You don't owe me nothing."

"How do you mean, nothing?"

Again Tayyab declined to reply.

"It's getting late," said Naimul. "Come on, brother, out with it – how much?"

"Ye're a *mukti*," said Tayyab in his blank, emotionless way, "and I don't take money off *mukti* people. No use trying to force me to, either. Ya won't be able to."

Drops of rain were beginning to fall as Naimul stepped out into the street. He couldn't get a room at the hotel. The hotel was under different ownership and even had a new name; it was now the Pakistan Hotel.

"We aren't allowed to accommodate guests," the new owner told Naimul sternly. "We have our restaurant, you can have a meal. But no room."

"Army orders?"

"Yes. And they sometimes check. They give us no peace."

"Is there any other hotel nearby?"

"Have a look. See if you can find one."

Naimul tried two other hotels. At one they told him he could have a room if he was part of a family including children, but not if he was a single person.

"I just need somewhere to stay overnight," Naimul told the proprietor. "Please see what you can do."

"Find some relative who can put you up," suggested the proprietor wearily. "That's your only possibility. No hotel will take you. Don't you have anyone in Dhaka?"

Wasting no more time Naimul set out to see whether he could find the family. One never knew, he might get a pleasant surprise. He might find that Moriam was indeed in Dhaka, and in the very same house. He would rattle the door for a few minutes and eventually he would hear the anxious voice of Moriam's mother coming from inside: "Who is it?"

That lady would never, never let any of her daughters answer the door. She would always go to the door herself, and even after the visitor outside had said who they were she would ask one more time: "Who is it?"

So after Naimul had rattled the handle for a while it was she who would ask from the other side of the door, in a voice muffled by fear, "Who's there?"

Naimul would lower his voice to say, "It's me, mother. Me, Naimul. Open the door! And don't tell anyone I've come, I want to give them a surprise."

She would open the door, and then, no doubt, she would be unable to control herself and start screaming, "Moriam! Just see who's here!" And then what would happen? Moriam would come hastily down the stairs, lose her footing and sprain her ankle. That girl, she had a real talent for stumbling on stairs. It was almost unthinkable that she would get the bottom of the stairs without twisting her ankle on the way.

And then when she saw him what would Moriam do? She would take a great leap at him, bowl him over and bring both of them crashing to the ground. It was a real possibility, Moriam was that kind of girl. In the excitement of the moment she wouldn't stop to think who was watching. Her mother would be standing there, her sisters would be standing there, never mind, she absolutely *had* to jump onto her husband. Forget what Mum and them think, she would tell herself, it doesn't matter a hoot... just wait, when the darling fellow goes upstairs I'm going to seize his hand and squeeze it, and if he's embarrassed and tries to pull his hand away it will do no good, I'll just hold all the tighter...

The front door of Moriam's family home was sealed. Not just one, but two very large padlocks were guarding it. Naimul lifted one of the padlocks and stood there contemplating it for a while, though he would have been at a loss to explain why he did so.

The curfew would start at 9 p.m. Previously 11 p.m. had been the cut-off time, but about a week ago this had been brought forward two hours. Naimul would have to find somewhere to stay before then. He had hardly any contacts in Dhaka city, but he started making his way to Aga Masih Lane, where he had lived for quite a long period. The landlord of the place where he used to live would surely not turn him away.

But Aga Masih Lane was closed. Something must have happened, as the army had cordoned off the whole area and soldiers were conducting house to house searches.

He could always go to Komlapur railway station and spend the night sprawled on a bench. No, the railway station was not safe, the army was guarding it carefully, and a man without any luggage loitering on its precincts would immediately arouse suspicion.

It was already past eight o'clock. Just one hour remained until the curfew was called. As a last resort Naimul set out to try and locate Shahed's house. He had been there a few times before, but was not sure he would be able to find it in the dark. Somehow the city had changed since 25th March; it was no longer its old self and places were hard to recognize. Naimul told himself that if he didn't find Shahed at home he would stuff Asmani's letter through the door, and then at least he would have discharged one obligation. Then he would knock on any likely door and say to the people, I've got nowhere to stay, please let me sleep here just for tonight, as soon as the curfew is lifted in the morning I'll be off.

Naimul had now begun to think it had been a mistake to come into Dhaka at all. It had been a sudden caprice, really. The idea of having a break had taken root in his mind. A break – a chance to eat some proper food, have a decent sleep in a proper bed, have a good bath in warm water using plenty of soap; and if luck permitted, see Moriam too.

But in practice nothing had gone according to plan. One thing, he had had a haircut. But he hadn't yet managed to have a bath, or eat, and there seemed to be absolutely no prospect of sleeping in a comfortable bed either. If anyone did take him in he'd have to bed down on a sofa in their living room; it was unlikely they'd give up their own bed for his sake.

Naimul found Shahed's house about five minutes before the curfew was due to start. A lamp was glowing inside the house. The doors and windows were tightly shut, but a glimmer of light was escaping through the cracks. Somebody was at home, even if it wasn't Shahed. Meanwhile the rain was coming down heavily. Naimul rushed forward and sprang onto the verandah.

"Shahed, are you there?" he shouted.

The door opened before he had time to shout again. Shahed was standing there, his eyes wide with astonishment

"I trust you've got plenty of toilet soap?" Those were the first words Naimul addressed to Shahed. "I've got to have a really good bath, with soap. What are you staring at me like that for? Don't you recognize me?"

Shahed made no reply, but went on staring. There was nothing in his gaze, neither surprise nor joy.

"The way you've let your beard grow," remarked Naimul as they went indoors, "you look one hundred percent like a Moulana. Anyone would take you for a qualified cleric straight from Deoband. You've even got a prayer cap on your head, do you wear it all the time?"

The perfumed smoke of an incense stick was coming from the bedroom. The burning joss stick was next to a prayer mat spread out on the floor.

"What's going on?" asked Naimul. "Why the incense sticks?"

"I've been doing a *khatm-e-Yunus* – reciting the *Yunus* prayer one hundred and twenty-five thousand times over."

"Have you finished it?"

"Yes. I got to the end during the *maghrib* prayer session this evening. I don't know what's happened to Asmani and Runi, that's why I've been doing this penance."

"Well, now that you've done it you may get the news you're waiting for. You can never tell, it's a strange world. But please heat up some water for me, I want to have my bath. Where do you take your meals these days?"

"I cook at home."

"Cook something now, I'm dying of hunger. What can you do? I feel like having some *khichuri*, would you be able to manage that?"

"Yup."

"Have you got any eggs?"

"Yes."

"Then cook *khichuri* and eggs. Oh and I warn you, I eat more than I used to. Three times as much. So make plenty. You've got lemons and green chillies?"

"No."

"Well, you surely have some pickles, I know Asmani loves her pickles."

"Yes, there's some pickled stuff."

"Good. The only thing I can think about now is food, food. I keep remembering all the delicious things I've ever eaten."

Shahed set to and started cooking on the kerosene stove while Naimul went into the bathroom, leaving the door wide open. From where Shahed was standing in the kitchen everything inside the bathroom was clearly visible, but Shahed carefully avoided looking that way as Naimul had shed all his clothes and was having his bath stark naked. Shahed could tell Naimul was enjoying himself, but it was a mystery to him how anyone could be so blissfully happy in these times of gore and suffering.

"You've joined the freedom fighters, is that right?" asked Shahed.

"Yes."

"How's the war going?"

"Well."

"Lots of guerrillas have infiltrated Dhaka city now."

"Why haven't you enlisted?" asked Naimul. "There you are, a Deobandi cleric with a long beard, just sitting tight."

"I couldn't join up because I didn't know what had happened to Asmani and Runi."

"If you find out where they are will you join up then?"

"Yes."

"That's a delicious smell coming from the *khichuri*. What have you put in it?"

"Mixed spices – *garam masala*."

"How many eggs have you boiled?"

"Three. One for me, two for you."

"Do four of them. I'm going to eat three."

"Right. Have you come to Dhaka in order to fight here?"

"No, I've just come for a break. I felt like seeing Mori, though I haven't managed to."

"Mori? Who's that?"

"My wife. Mori's a pet name I use. It's short for Moriam."

"Everything about you is totally daft," exclaimed Shahed in disgust. "Whoever heard of anyone calling anyone else 'Mori' as a pet name?"

"Each person has his own style of showing affection. What do you call Asmani?"

"I call her Jep."

"Jep? What on earth does Jep mean?"

"It doesn't have any meaning."

"I'm sure it does mean something, only you don't want to say. Well, don't tell me if you don't want to. I'll get the truth off her. Next time I see sister-in-law I'm going to call her 'Jep Bhabi', just you wait."

Tears sprang to Shahed's eyes. The moment Naimul had said the words 'Jep Bhabi' a beautiful image had flashed into his mind. The four of them, Shahed, Naimul, Asmani and Runi, had gone on an outing somewhere. It was a really beautiful location with hills in the background. They were all feeling slightly chilly. And Naimul was busily teasing Asmani; he kept saying 'Jep Bhabi! Jep Bhabi!' to her.

"Finished the cooking?" called Naimul from the bathroom.

"Just a little bit left to do."

"Tell me when you're done, then I'll come out of here and sit down to eat straight away. I'm going to carry on sloshing water over myself until then."

"But you may catch cold."

"You know how some watches are waterproof, well, us *mukti* are coldproof. Sun and rain have no effect on us. I'd love to have some of Asmani's roast duck right now. Once I ate an entire duck she had cooked, all on my own, and she called me a duck-eating ogre. Do you remember?"

"I do."

When he sat down to eat Naimul started toying aimlessly with his *khichuri*.

"I can't understand it," he said plaintively, looking at Shahed. "I'm not hungry any more. All I want to do is go to sleep. Could you keep my share of the *khichuri* and put it on one side? I'll eat it when I wake up."

"You haven't eaten anything," objected Shahed.

"Somehow my hunger has turned into sleepiness. If I don't lie down now I'll die."

Naimul abandoned his meal and stood up.

"Oh, I've brought a present for you," he added. "I should have given it to you right at the start, but delayed doing so intentionally."

"What kind of present?" asked Shahed in surprise.

"A letter."

"A letter from whom?"

"Show me where I'm to sleep first. And listen, mind you don't disturb me once I've dropped off. You're not to wake me even if the Pakistan army bursts through the door. The letter is in my trouser pocket. You can take it out and read it."

As Shahed started reading the letter an earthquake seemed to rock his world; the house swayed, a roaring noise filled his ears, a hot wind brushed his face. That sensations of this kind could overcome a person at a moment of the most intense happiness was something he had never realized before. It was a brief note on lined paper:

Darling Jep,

Runi and I are fine. We were in a refugee camp, but your friend Mr Naimul has picked us up from there and placed us with relatives of his. We are being extremely well looked after in their house. We are perfectly safe.

Your Jep, Asmani

Shahed remained standing beside Naimul's bed with the letter in his hand. Naimul was curled up in bed like an infant, lost in a deep and peaceful sleep.

62

"So it's you!" exclaimed Dhirendranath Ray Choudhury delightedly as soon as he had opened the door. "How are you, dear Shahed?"

"Not Shahed, sir," protested Naimul as he touched the professor's feet in respect, "It's Naimul."

Dhirendranath Ray Choudhury was not in the least disconcerted. "Of course, Naimul was the name that first came to mind," he explained, "only somehow I said Shahed. So where's that friend of yours?"

"He's on his way to India, to find his wife and daughter. He set out this morning."

Dhirendranath Ray Choudhury raised his eyebrows in feigned astonishment. "You don't say!" he exclaimed. "How very remarkable!"

Naimul smiled to himself. What an extraordinary fellow he was! He was quite out of step with all the affairs of the world, yet he was always very keen to conceal that fact.

"You know what, sir? I'm going to join you for lunch."

"Yes, yes, of course, of course you can. And we'll have something special. Look, you had better go to the shops and buy something. I don't have anything at home except rice and lentils. We could have hilsa fish, what do you say to that? Get them to cut it into pieces before you bring it home. We'll fry it in oil and eat it piping hot."

"I'm afraid fish is not on, sir," said Naimul. "Nobody in Bangladesh is eating fish these days."

"Why ever not? Why aren't they eating fish?"

"The army keep shooting people and throwing their bodies into the river. The fish in the rivers are feeding on decomposed corpses. That's why there's a ban on fish as food."

"But hilsa isn't a riverine fish, it's a pelagic species."

"Even if they're sea fish they're swimming in rivers when they're caught."

"That's a good point. However, why should fish eat human corpses? Are fish carnivorous? Pop into my library, would you, I think there are some books about fish in there. I need to look it up and see whether fish are carnivorous or not. I'm sure we'll find they don't eat animal proteins. They feed on mud, pondweed and that sort of stuff. And there we are, just think of it, giving up fish as food without bothering to look into the matter."

Naimul went, not to the library but straight to the kitchen. He was feeling like a cup of tea. "Would you like some tea, sir?" he called from the kitchen.

"What are you doing in my kitchen?" asked Dhirendranath Ray Choudhury indignantly. "Didn't I tell you to look for some works on ichthyology?"

Naimul put the kettle on to boil and then went to look for books about fish. He felt slightly annoyed with his old teacher. The professor had paid little attention to the fact that fish were off the menu because there were human corpses in every river; the thing that had aroused his interest was what fish normally ate.

"Naimul!"

"Yes, sir?"

"Have you found the books?"

"I'm looking, sir. Your books are very higgledy-piggledy."

"Books are allowed to be higgledy-piggledy. It's things like saris and suits which have to be stored neatly. By the way, did you get married all right?"

"Yes, sir."

"I got into terrible trouble that evening. You had given me the wrong address, and I kept wandering around looking for the house until ten at night. What's your wife called?"

"Moriam."

"A lovely name. Moriam, the mother of Jesus. You really must bring your wife to see me one day. But you'll have to let me know in advance so that I can have some decent clothes on. You see, I've got this habit of going around barechested. It's extremely rude for anyone to leave their torso uncovered when women are present."

"I shall bring her here, and I shall let you know in advance. Well, I've found a book."

"Very good. Bring the book here, and bring a pen and paper too."

"What do you want a pen and paper for, sir?"

"I shall make some notes. It's no use just running your eye over a printed page, you need to make notes. Then you have to reflect on what you have read."

"Listen, I'd like to stay with you for a few days, sir."

"Stay by all means."

"It won't be a bother for you?"

Dhirendranath Ray Choudhury gave no reply. He had already started to jot down some notes on the paper.

"Last night I was looking for somewhere to stay," said Naimul, "and I never even thought of your house."

Again Dhirendranath Ray Choudhury failed to reply.

The kettle was boiling and Naimul went off to make the tea. It was clear that until all the ichthyological details had been sorted out it would be impossible to get any sense out of this unworldly sage.

One can gain sanctity just by being near a holy person, without having to do anything to earn it. Naimul decided he should stick around the old man for a few days and stock up on virtue. This simple fellow had donated his entire life savings, his house and everything else he had inherited to Dhaka University. He was now living on the pension he received from the university. Occasionally his daughter sent money from Canada.

"Sir!"

"What?"

"I want to ask you something. Have you made this house over to the university?"

"Yes. But it won't be theirs until I die."

"And supposing the university wants to have it now, what'll you do?"

Dhirendranath Ray Choudhury became quite cross.

"That is a most unjust decision they have taken," he fulminated. "I told them they are to let me live in the house until I die. There's no written agreement, I admit, but it was a mutual understanding. Here, pass me the telephone, will you? I must speak to the Vice Chancellor. They have no right to suddenly land me in such an awkward spot."

"Just carry on with what you're doing, sir," said Naimul. "The university hasn't taken any such decision at all. Have your tea, sir, it's getting cold."

Dhirendranath Ray Choudhury sipped his tea and went on writing:

> Vernacular name: **Ruhi**
> Scientific name: *Labeo rohita*
> Food: Vegetarian. Also consumes mud.

Vernacular name: **Katol**
Scientific name: *Catla catla*
Food: Phytoplankton, pondweed, aquatic plants, small crustaceans and insects.

Vernacular name: **Mrigel**
Scientific name: *Cirrhinus mrigala*
Food: Decomposing aquatic vegetation, insects, remains of animal corpses, mud.

Vernacular name: **Chitol**
Scientific name: *Notopterus chitala*
Food: Carnivorous.

Having got that far Dhirendranath Ray Choudhury announced his verdict.
"We cannot eat fish. There is a distinct possibility that fish might consume human corpses. We shall have egg curry for lunch."

63

Pakistan army soldiers had got hold of Gourango and were taking him away. He was wearing a filthy pair of black trousers, and had nothing on the upper half of his body. His teeth, which hadn't seen a toothbrush in a long time, were discoloured. There were angry red lesions at the corners of his mouth. He was being led by a rope tied round his waist, but Gourango seemed entirely unconcerned and was smoking a cigarette with apparent enjoyment. A lieutenant had handed him the cigarette a short while ago, indeed he had even lit the cigarette for him with his lighter.

The soldiers were having a marvellous time with this raving lunatic they had found. The lieutenant kept chatting him up and creasing with laughter at his replies.

"Hey, are you a Hindu?"

"Yes, sir."

"Prove to me that you're a Hindu. Pull your trousers down."

Gourango promptly dropped his trousers and let him look. His face was wreathed in smiles.

"Where is your wife?"

"Soldiers took her away."

"What about your children?"

"Shooting. Dead."

As he uttered the word "dead" Gourango closed his eyes and hung out his tongue in a pantomime of dying. The soldiers were loving all of this. They were delighted by everything Gourango said or did.

"Who is Sheikh Mujib?"

"Leader, our great leader. *Joy Bangla!*"

"Are you a *Joy Bangla* supporter?"

"Yes, sir."

"You know what we do to *Joy Bangla* people?"

"Yes, sir, I do. You shoot them."

"So we'll shoot you, too."

"Yes, all right, sir."

"D'you want another cigarette?"

"Yes, please, sir."

The lieutenant gave him another cigarette, and once again lit it for him. He gave orders for the madman to be taken to the army mess. He could be tied to a tree and everyone could make fun of him. The madman knew some English, which was another point of interest.

"What is your name?" The lieutenant asked in English.

"My name is Gourango."

"What is the meaning of the name?"

"Fair skin."

"Say *Pakistan Zindabad*," ordered the lieutenant.

Gourango assumed a bashful voice. "*Joy Bangla!*" he said.

The lieutenant found even that very funny. Gourango was led away to the army mess.

64

An emergency meeting of staff officers was convening in the private office of the commander of 36th Brigade, Major General Jamshed. Those present included the commander of 93rd Brigade, Brigadier Qadir; the head of the tank regiment, Colonel Fazle Hamid; the air force chief, Air Commodore Enam Ahmed; Brigadier Qasim; Brigadier Bashir. Only the man in control of Narayanganj zone, Brigadier Manzoor, had not come; he had let it be known that he would arrive later with General Niazi.

The emergency staff meeting was supposed to have started at nine in the morning. It was now eleven minutes past ten, and the meeting wasn't yet under way. The reason: General Niazi had been held up. He had sent a message explaining that he was awaiting an urgent call from the commander-in-chief of the Pakistan army, General Gul Hassan, but so far the chief hadn't been able to get through from West Pakistan. So they were to wait for him.

"Couldn't we start discussing things among ourselves?" suggested Brigadier Bashir.

General Jamshed made no reply. Instead he poured himself a cup of tea from the teapot in front of him. Then a little accident occurred: the cup toppled over and tea spread all over the immaculate white tablecloth. A similar thing had happened at the previous staff meeting. Did this have some kind of significance? In wartime people seek meanings even in the smallest things. They look out for omens. The tank commander General Rommel, the Desert Fox, always used to study the omens before starting any operation.

General Jamshed's aide de camp came forward with a cloth to wipe up the tea which had spilled on the tablecloth, but Jamshed dismissed him with a wave of the hand. The tea was drawing a kind of map on the tablecloth, which maybe had a meaning. It looked very much like a map of England.

"How much longer are we going to have to wait?" asked Brigadier Qadir in annoyance, looking at his watch.

General Jamshed took his eyes off the map on the tablecloth and fixed them on Brigadier Qadir.

"Sir," said Qadir, "how about calling General Niazi again to check? He can't expect us to wait for ever. I have to go to Tongi, I've got a field meeting."

General Jamshed stretched his hand out to pick up the phone, and just at that moment it rang. It was General Niazi and his voice sounded cheerful. "Hello, Jamshed!"

"Yes, sir?"

"You can start your meeting. I'm not going to make it today."

"Right, sir."

"Give everyone there my warm congratulations for their heroic performance."

"Of course, I'll pass that on."

"They're highly committed soldiers, all of them, a credit to Pakistan."

"Yes, sir."

"Why do you sound so downcast? I suppose you were dreaming of your wife last night, were you? Servicemen always get depressed after dreaming about their wives. Ha ha! Hello? Jamshed?"

"Yes, sir?"

"Listen to this funny joke. You can share it with your officers, they'll love it. There was this Panjabi sergeant major called Mitha Khan. His pride and glory was one foot long. Listen to this carefully, one foot long. He told his wife to knit a sort of woollen sock to protect it. Can you hear me all right, Jamshed?"

"Yes, I can hear you."

"You remember how long it was?"

"One foot."

"Right. You have an exceptionally sharp memory. Anyway, listen to the story. Mitha Khan's wife knitted this woollen sock thing. And then... Hee hee!"

General Jamshed listened to the rest of the dirty story with all the patience he could muster. Maybe he ought to have given a polite laugh at the end, but in fact it was unnecessary because General Niazi himself laughed so heartily he nearly shattered the telephone. He didn't seem to need anyone else to laugh in agreement.

"How was the joke, Jamshed?"

"A good one."

"There's another rather similar one, a sort of modified version. I'll tell it to you some other time. Don't forget to remind me."

"Right. I'll remind you."

"I'm in a good mood today, have you noticed that?"

"But you're always in a good mood, sir."

"That's true enough; but there's a particular reason for my being cheerful today. The Chinese are coming!"

"We've been hearing talk like that for quite some time now."

"Ah, but there's a difference between the talk you heard earlier and the news today. They're going to arrive in hordes."

"Well, it'll be good if they do."

"Something's going to happen within the week. By the way, I know a terrific joke about the Chinese, would you like to hear it?"

"Oh, very well, go ahead."

But Niazi didn't get far with his story about the Chinese. The people at headquarters were trying to get through to him on the phone and he had to take the call.

General Jamshed started the emergency meeting. On the agenda was a discussion of the very latest situation. "What is the current state of morale among our men?" he asked, lighting a cigarette. Nobody offered a reply. "My impression is that morale in the ranks has sunk to its lowest point yet," Jamshed continued. "But why is that? The war has scarcely started. A few *mukti* are firing the odd shot here and there, but is that enough to bother us so much? Maybe a couple of border outposts are under strain, but nobody's managed to take any of them so far. Of course if India declares all out war we shall be put under a wee bit of pressure."

"A wee bit of pressure?" protested Air Commodore Enam Ahmed. "Aren't we being rather too sure of ourselves?"

"A true soldier will never consider himself inferior to his foe."

"General, are you suggesting I'm not a true soldier?"

"Why are you getting so excited for no reason? It's just like the air force to get excited. The army does all the real work, and everyone else just flaps around."

"Did you call this meeting in order to trade personal insults?"

"If you think this meeting is unnecessary you are free to leave," retorted General Jamshed.

Everyone was silent for a while. Then Colonel Fazle Hamid retrieved the situation.

"We have hard times ahead of us," he said. "Don't you think we should restrain our language and focus on the problems ahead?"

"I apologize for my little outburst," said General Jamshed. "To tell you the truth I'm feeling distinctly pessimistic, and when you're in a pessimistic mood you sometimes says wild things. Listen, we keep treating the *mukti* as if they were quite insignificant. But should we really be rating them so low? They are getting stronger all the time."

"They haven't got so strong that a powerful general like yourself needs to lose hope," sneered the air commodore.

General Jamshed spun his revolving chair to face the air commodore directly. "You've heard of a certain civilian called Kader Siddiqui? You surely know about him?"

"I don't believe I've ever heard of him."

"You ought to know the name. I'm having to tie down a large part of my 36th Brigade on his account. You've also had to attack his militia with your air force a number of times. And yet we can't touch him. If after all that you insist you've never even heard of him, then I really don't know what to say."

"I see no reason to lose heart if he's the only threat."

"You may see no reason, but I do. He has seized one of our ships crammed with munitions. In fact not only one. He now has no shortage of weapons."

"So today's emergency meeting is merely about him?"

"Others like him will soon spring up."

"That may be the case, but let's face that if and when the time comes. Fantasizing about what might possibly happen in the future is a waste of time."

"Very well, suppose you tell us what is not a waste of time?"

The meeting went silent again.

"I hear the Chinese may provide some assistance," said Brigadier Qasim eventually. "When might that assistance arrive?"

"What need do we have of assistance from the Chinese?" General Jamshed asked wearily. "Why should we look to the outside world for assistance while we've got super-heroes like Air Commodore Enam Ahmed on our side? Anyway, the business of today's meeting will have to be adjourned. We shall convene again very shortly with General Niazi present. Good day."

General Niazi was having a telephone conference with the commander-in-chief of the Pakistan Army, General Gul Hassan Khan. A Chinese ship bearing a consignment of arms and twenty medium sized tanks had docked at Chittagong port, and they were discussing how it was to be unloaded.

"Unload the arms, but send the tanks on to West Pakistan," Gul Hassan Khan was saying.

"But I need the tanks," objected General Niazi.

"How could you get any tanks from Chittagong to Dhaka? The railway link is closed, and all the road bridges have been sabotaged."

"How I get the tanks to Dhaka is my business."

"Kindly tell me how you would do it."

"That's entirely my business."

"Perhaps I have a right to know too."

"Both the arms and the tanks are intended for Eastern Command."

"But come to the point, how do you intend to shift the tanks from A to B?"

"I've already told you, that's my headache."

"Listen, General, you're to send all the tanks on to Karachi. And that is an order."

Gul Hassan Khan slammed down the telephone. In the event General Niazi disobeyed orders and had the entire shipment unloaded at Chittagong.*

The phone conversation had put General Niazi in a bad mood, but he didn't let it last long. He helped himself to a tot of vodka. Although vodka properly belonged to a cold climate it tasted very agreeable in the heat of East Bengal. If he made up his drink with plenty of ice and plenty of lemon, one sip of it was enough to give him a pleasant buzz. Then he would feel that a soldier's life was not such a bad one after all. He reflected that he had come to East Pakistan bearing a very big burden of responsibility, and he was carrying out his responsibility in an admirable way. The war would be over in a short time, and then his place in history would be assured. It would be mentioned in all the textbooks: in Pakistan's hour of need Tiger Niazi took the helm.

He was sipping his vodka hurriedly, one sip after another in rapid succession. One wasn't supposed to drink so rapidly, but it didn't seem to be doing any harm, on the contrary, he felt it clearing his head. The fog in his mind was being dissipated. He decided he would write his autobiography, eloquently describing the way he had brought East Pakistan to heel. He would adopt a humble tone while writing it, for all great heroes were modest; modesty was one of the hallmarks of heroism.

He would write his autobiography in English so that people of all countries could read it. The opening sentence would be: "*It was a monsoon of discontent.*"

Quite quickly General Niazi began to feel merry. It was no good being so merry on one's own, happiness always needed to be shared. So he phoned General Jamshed. He knew he had to pass some urgent instructions on to him; he couldn't remember what the instructions were, but doubtless it would all come back to him by and by in the course of his conversation. That was one of the great things about drinking: you forget everything, and then you remember it all over again.

"Hello, Jamshed!"

"Yes, sir."

"I'm planning to write my autobiography."

"Good idea, sir."

"It will be documentary evidence of how Pakistan was saved."

"Quite."

"I want to make the book enjoyable to read."

"That won't be hard for you, sir. You know any number of stories, and I presume they'll find their way into the book."

"They will. I shall make a special mention of the courageous rôle played by yourself and your heroic men in Eastern Command."

"Thank you, sir."

"There's no need to thank me. I shall give due recognition to all concerned. By the way, I have some important instructions for you. I'd forgotten what they were, but now I remember."

"Yes, sir?"

"Some tanks are being unloaded in Chittagong port. You are to arrange for them to be brought to Dhaka."

"How is that going to be possible, sir?"

"Look, I've given you an order. How things are done is your headache. All I ask is that the order should be carried out."

---

* *Memoir*, Gul Hassan Khan.

"I've got a little bit of bad news for you, sir," said General Jamshed after a silence.

"I'm not in the right mood for listening to bad news," growled Niazi. "Nevertheless go ahead, out with it."

"Kader Siddiqui has annihilated an entire company of ours. Some of our men have been taken captive."

"Who's Kader Siddiqui? Some chap from the Indian army?"

"No, sir. A civilian *mukti*."

"Well, you must bring him to me, dead or alive. That's an order, an official one."

General Niazi put down the phone. He was now in a vile mood. However after some minutes had passed the familiar rosy glow was restored, and he went on dreaming about his autobiography.

65

The Dhaleswari River, 12th August 1971.

A great convoy of seven ships was moving upriver. The ships were heading for the landing stage at Phulchori in the northern part of East Pakistan, where they were to unload their cargo of weapons, ammunition and provisions. From there the goods would be taken by road to the Pakistan army cantonments in Rangpur and Saidpur.

In charge of the convoy was Captain Amanullah, with Lieutenant Ataullah as his second in command. The vessels were carrying cargo and thus had nothing to do with the Pakistan navy. Instead there was a sizeable detachment of Pakistan army personnel on board, whose job was to conduct the ships safely to their destination. The crew were all Bengalis who knew the rivers and were steering the ships carefully, keeping to deep water.

Captain Amanullah and Lieutenant Ataullah were on the ship which bore the name S.U. Engineers LC3. It was a large freighter, and beside it sailed S.T. Razon, a tanker covered over with tarpaulin, which had Sergeant Rahim Khan on board.

Captain Amanullah was standing at the rail on the ship's deck. He felt rather as if he was going on a pleasant holiday boat trip for a change. It amused him to see how the people on the banks of the river scattered in terror when they saw the convoy coming. He had heard that the Bengalis were of a timorous disposition because they ate too much fish, and now he was seeing proof of this. People fled from their homes, fishermen out fishing abandoned their boats and nets and jumped into the river to escape. Captain Amanullah thought he couldn't really blame them; anyone would be scared if they saw a seven vessel convoy approaching. Anyway, it was fun to watch faint-hearted Bengalis dashing in all directions.

The ships were making their way very slowly. The river was not uniformly deep, and here and there sandbanks rose up out of the water. It was necessary to proceed cautiously, all the time gauging the depth of the bottom. It would have been better if they could have sailed a bit faster.

Lieutenant Ataullah came up on deck holding a camera. His aim was to get a few snaps of himself to send back home. He wanted to take the photos in such a way that most of the convoy would be visible in them. His elderly mother loved looking at photos of her son.

"Hello Mr Photographer!" said Captain Amanullah smiling. "If you go on taking photos at that rate you'll soon run out of film. But if you have any frames left please take one of me."

"Certainly, sir," said Lieutenant Ataullah.

"You must make it so that I look like Christopher Columbus."

"Right, sir. Let's not do it here, but up on the bridge. I can get a better picture from there, with most of the convoy in it."

"Okay, let's go."

Captain Amanullah had just placed his foot on the companionway to climb up to the bridge when a mortar shell crashed down on the ship. Before he could make out what was going on machine gun fire started raining down.

"What's happening?" he gasped in amazement. "Who could have the audacity to attack a whole convoy of ships?"

"We're passing through Kader Siddiqui's territory, sir," replied Lieutenant Ataullah. "It must be his private army which is attacking us. Nobody but Kader Siddiqui could do this!"

Meanwhile all hell had broken out. The ships at the rear were trying to retreat. The ship Captain Amanullah was on and the S.T. Razon were now out of sight of the other ships in the convoy. Such a heavy bombardment of mortar shells was battering the S.T. Razon, it was in danger of catching fire at any moment. The tanker was holding one hundred and eighty thousand gallons of diesel fuel.

From the ship's control room the captain contacted headquarters.

"We have been attacked. We have been attacked. Mortar shells are coming down on us like rain. Lieutenant Ataullah has been killed. Sergeant Rahim Khan has been killed."

"This is incredible!"

"Mayday! Mayday!"

"Turn the boat round and retreat. Under no circumstances must the ship fall into Kader Siddiqui's hands. It is packed with munitions."

"We've got stuck on a sandbank. Almost all our men have been killed. We need support from the air. We require support from the air force immediately."

"Air support is on its way. Do not let them get hold of those munitions."

"Kader Siddiqui's army is approaching. I can see them."

"Fend them off with heavy machine gun fire. Fighter planes are on their way."

"We have no gunners left alive."

While he was still talking a shell fired from a rocket launcher exploded over the ship with a deafening boom. Captain Amanullah plunged down into the river.[*]

---

[*] The man who, with extreme bravery, led the attack on the convoy in the area near Matikata was a distinguished soldier from Kader Siddiqui's brigade. His name was Muhammad Habibur Rahman. After the incident he became known as Habib the Ship Sinker. The Bangladesh Government later honoured him with the Bir Bikram medal. Before joining Kader Siddiqui's militia he had been a *habildar* (sergeant) in the East Bengal Regiment within the Pakistan army. – **Author**

66

Captain Jan-e-Rasul of the Pakistan army was sitting on the upper deck of a large double-decker river launch at Banaripara in Barisal District. His face was glum. Thirty soldiers, five men from the West Pakistan police force and a number of *razakar* volunteers were on board with him. Captain Jan-e-Rasul had been sent on a special mission, to wipe out a band of freedom fighters called the 'Hemayet Army'. Also on board was an informant who was to provide details of where the Hemayet Army was and how it was operating. Koyes Ali was the informant's name; he was a little under forty years of age, and had a goatee beard on his chin and a round cap made of woven rattan on his head. He had lined his eyelids with antimony, but some of this had become smudged so it looked rather as if he had picked up a black eye in a fight.

Captain Jan-e-Rasul was quickly losing patience with his informant. He was failing to extract any useful information from him, and was beginning to suspect that the man might actually be working as a spy for the Hemayet Army itself. The informant maintained they would be courting disaster if they moved anywhere at all in the launch. However the captain had been specifically ordered by higher command to set out in search of the enemy. Riverine operations were really the responsibility of the navy: they could easily come out in their gunboats, do the needful and return to port. So what was the point of sending an army patrol out on the river in a rickety launch? Captain Jan-e-Rasul suspected that these days the army was being run in a somewhat capricious manner. The men at the top were doing whatever came into their heads, and sending out orders by wireless with no heed for the consequences.

Koyes Ali brought out a little *paan* container from the pocket of his tunic and stuffed two wads of *paan* into his mouth at once.

"Have you decided what you're going to do, Major?" he asked, speaking in tolerable Urdu. That was one good thing, he knew some Urdu. Many informants could neither speak nor understand Urdu, so any communication with them had to be done through an interpreter. And interpreters invariably added their own embellishments to what was being said.

"Your name is Koyes Ali, is it?"
"Yes, sir."
"Where did you learn Urdu?"
"I worked in the army cantonment in Comilla for five years."
"What was your job?"
"I was a kitchen assistant."
"Why did you leave that job?"
"God is the one who determines our livelihood. He decreed that I could no longer make a living from the army, and thus it happened that my employment was terminated."
"Are you acquainted with the Hemayet Army?"
"Indeed I should be, for I'm distantly related."
"Related to whom?"
"To Hemayet Uddin. He had a wife whose name was Hazera Khatun. She was shot and killed in the war. He took a second wife, a Hindu girl called Soneka Rani Ray. His eldest son is Hasib Uddin, commonly known as Pappu."
"And you want to get Hemayet Uddin arrested?"
"Certainly I do."
"Why is that?"
"Don't we want to save Pakistan?"

"Is saving Pakistan your only reason for wanting to get him arrested?"
"There are other reasons. Family matters."
"Do you know where Hemayet Uddin is?"
"Indeed I do."
"If we go there will we find him?"
"He's a real dolphin, we have to bear that in mind."
"What's that, a dolphin?"
"An animal which lives in the river. It sometimes comes to the surface, then it dives down again."
"Well, can you show us the way to where he is now?"
"Let me sit beside the helmsman and I can guide him. Only we'll need to make our way into side channels, so we'll have to take account of the tides."
"Tides? On a river?"
"What do you expect? This whole delta is tidal. If you travel by river you have to take account of the tides."
"And if we do, when can we start?"
"After another hour."
"Right then, you can go now, we'll set off in an hour."

Captain Jan-e-Rasul brought out a map of the area round Barisal and spread it on the table in front of him. It was impossible to make anything whatever out of that map: all it showed was a vast network of waterways big and small. This was a dauntingly impenetrable zone. Anyone not intimately acquainted with the area would find it virtually impossible to make his way from one point to another. And he had been sent to a place like this in order to conduct a punitive raid on someone about whom practically no information was available. He knew the man had formerly been a non commissioned officer in the East Bengal Regiment, and for years had worked as an instructor at Abbotabad military academy in West Pakistan. And now he was a *mukti*, and a real pest. Apparently he had organized a sizeable army of his own, without even getting any help from India. This militia was confidently taking on the Pakistan army in full scale battles. None of your hit and run guerrilla stuff, real face to face clashes. The fact that the Pakistan army was taking the Hemayet Army at all seriously was in itself remarkable.

And now apparently the fellow had married a Hindu woman called Soneka Rani Ray. Well, he would marry a Hindu, wouldn't he, they were all half Hindu anyway. Captain Jan-e-Rasul had heard that the majority of East Pakistani Muslim men weren't even circumcised.

The launch, the M.V. Jamuna, set out after a delay of one and a half hours instead of just one hour. Koyes Ali was sitting beside the helmsman telling him which way to go. From Banaripara they were heading in the direction of Swarupkathi. The Hemayet Army's real plan was to attack the Pakistan army camp which had been set up in the grounds of the hermitage belonging to the Holy Man of Shorshina, and they were just waiting for the right moment.

Captain Jan-e-Rasul sent for Koyes Ali to go over the available details once again.

"You know the place where the Hemayet Army is hiding?"
"Certainly I do. It's a huge guava orchard. There's a kind of thicket there."
"Will Hemayet Uddin be with his fighters himself?"
"He always takes part in all his operations. So does his wife. She's a Hindu, and her name is Soneka Rani. She's from the Ray sub-caste."
"You've already told me his wife is a Hindu. Tell me something new."

"His wife joins in the fighting too. She knows how to use a rifle. She can also handle a light machine gun. At least, that's what I've heard, I haven't seen her myself. Would you care for some *paan*, sir?"

"I don't take *paan*."

Koyes Ali crammed two large wads of *paan* into his mouth.

"I'd better go and sit with the *sareng*," he said, chewing away contentedly. "He's from Chittagong and he doesn't know this area at all well."

"Off you go."

Shortly after Koyes Ali had gone to rejoin the *sareng* – the foreman of the crew, who was steering the vessel – the engine stopped working. It made a few coughing sounds, *kattack, kattack,* and was silent. The launch was in mid river. The river at this point was not at all wide. Just then a fishing boat came into view. The season for hilsa fishing had started, and fishermen were risking their lives to go out in search of a catch. Only when they heard the distinctive sound of a gunboat approaching would they quickly take refuge in a side channel.

When these fishermen saw the M.V. Jamuna they thought it was an ordinary public service launch. Indeed it had been made to look just as if it was. The soldiers were confined to the lower deck, with instructions that none of them was so much as to look out of the window, to make sure nobody from the outside would catch a glimpse of them. And both lower and upper decks were full of merchandise: coconuts, guavas, papayas and so on. There had been no need to load these goods specially, for the army had commandeered the vessel with cargo already on board.

On enquiry Captain Jan-e-Rasul was informed that there was some problem with the engine, which would be fixed within a short time. An hour later he was told that it hadn't been possible to repair the engine, but that a mechanic lived nearby and if the captain gave permission the *sareng* could go and fetch him. It didn't even matter if the mechanic was not at home, for as long as the *sareng* could borrow a couple of wrenches from his house he would be able to fix the engine himself.

"How long will that take?" demanded Jan-e-Rasul in considerable annoyance.

"Just the time to get there and back," replied the *sareng*. "One hour at most."

The captain gave permission for him to go. In fact there was nothing else he could do, he had no alternative. It wasn't even as if there was any other boat available which could take him back to base. Hardly a single launch was to be seen on the rivers these days. Nor did he have a wireless set on board which he could use to call for assistance.

The *sareng* was supposed to return within the hour. Nearly two hours had passed, and still there was no sign of him. It was after 5 p.m. and the day was nearly over. The light was starting to fade and dark clouds were building up in the sky. Captain Jan-e-Rasul sent for Koyes Ali, who came and stood in front of him with a contrite expression on his face.

"What's going on?" asked Jan-e-Rasul peevishly.

"Things aren't looking good," replied Koyes Ali in a flat voice.

"How do you mean, not looking good?"

"I reckon the *sareng* has done a bunker, together with his assistant."

"Why do you think that?"

"Just my impression. Putting two and two together I get four. Straightforward reckoning, nothing complex."

"Nothing complex?"

"No. As I told you earlier, the *sareng* is from Chittagong and doesn't know this area. So how would he know where to get hold of a local mechanic?"

"Why didn't you mention this to me this before?"

"I did think of saying something. Then I thought, no, it isn't right to be so suspicious minded. He travels around this area with his launch, maybe he does know where a mechanic lives."

"Supposing the *sareng* really has run away, what's to be done?"

"That's just what I've been thinking about, sir. And I've reached a conclusion. If you say the word I can explain."

"Do explain."

"Something tells me there's nothing really wrong with the engine. That fellow drove the boat onto a sandbank on purpose."

"What, are we stuck on a sandbank?"

"Yes. Anyway, there are some smaller launches at Shikarpur. If you will send someone with me I can go to Shikarpur by country boat and come back with a launch. This area is no good. It would be dangerous to remain stuck here in this launch at night. The Hemayet Army is not something to be trifled with."

"So you want to go and fetch a launch from Shikarpur?"

"I know a couple of launch owners there. However if you want to send anyone else, that's fine. The only point I want to make is that it would be extremely dangerous to hang around in this area after dark. Well, I shall be in the *sareng*'s room. Please let me know what you decide. I'm going to say my late afternoon prayers now. I don't mind performing any of the other prayers out of time, but not the *asr* prayer. You know, of course, Captain *sahib*, that on the Day of Judgment proceedings will start in the late afternoon, at the time of *asr*?"

Captain Jan-e-Rasul did not reply. He was examining Koyes Ali through narrowed eyes. He was now quite convinced that this fellow had played a part in getting the launch stranded on a sandbank in mid-river, a very big part. The man was operating in accordance with a plan. He had connived with the *sareng* to run the vessel aground. There were dense groves of coconut palms on either side of the river, and the Hemayet Army would have an easy time attacking from the cover they provided. He, on the other hand, was exposed, out in the open with no cover at all.

"Your name is Koyes Ali?"

"Yes, sir."

"Are you married?"

"Yes, sir."

"Have you any children?"

"Two sons and a daughter. I've put both my sons in a madrasah, a *hafiziya* madrasah; they are acquiring the Holy Quran by heart. The younger one has mastered five of the thirty sections, the elder one only one. My elder son isn't as sharp as the little one."

"I believe you're a member of the Hemayet Army. You led us here intentionally."

"You're quite mistaken in what you're thinking."

"I'm not going to argue with you. I'm going to make you stand on the cabin roof on the top deck. Then I'm going to shoot you and chuck your body into the river."

"You just do what you think right, but the master of life and death is God Himself. I may be fated to die here, and similarly so may all of you. Here's this launch stuck in mid-river, it's hardly conceivable the news hasn't already reached the Hemayet Army. The *sareng* who ran away will have taken the news with him."

"Come along, up onto the roof with you."

"Very well," replied Koyes Ali. "But before I die let me have the pleasure of eating a last wad of *paan*. I think I'll have one with spiced tobacco in it."

Captain Jan-e-Rasul shot Koyes Ali himself, blasting his head with a bullet fired from his revolver at short range. The moment before he pulled the trigger Koyes Ali spat out some *paan* juice and spoke his last words.

"The angel of death is coming for you all. He won't be long coming."

Shortly after sunset the Hemayet Army attacked the launch from the south side. Koyes Ali's lifeless body was still lying nearby. As the tide hadn't come in it hadn't yet been lifted up and carried away.[*]

---

[*] Mohammed Hemayet Uddin was awarded the Bir Bikram° medal for his outstanding acts of extreme bravery by the Bangladesh Government. However Koyes Ali's action has been neither recognized nor rewarded. Through the pages of this book I now record, on behalf of the whole nation, my profound respect for his achievement. The name Koyes Ali is not in fact correct; unfortunately I could not recall his real name. If any reader can supply his true name it will be substituted in future editions. I am unable to resist the temptation to add one more little detail. In *Sadhinatar Juddhe Khetabprapto Muktijoddha* (*Decorated Freedom Fighters of the War of Independence*) Md Abdul Hannan writes: "While the war was still going on the Mujibnagar Government° awarded Md Hemayet Uddin the rank of *subedar* and gave him the nickname of Himu." – **Author**

67

"What's your name?"
"My name is Mohammed Abu Taher."
"Tell me your name."
"My name is Mohammed Abu Taher."
"*Kya nam?*"
"Abu Taher."
"*Your name, what is it?*"
"Abu Taher, sir."
"What is your name?"
"My name is Mohammed Abu Taher."
"*Nam kya hay?*"
"Abu Taher."
"Tell me your name."
"Abu Taher, sir."

Mohammed Abu Taher was seated on a wooden chair. He was stark naked. A two hundred watt bulb was glaring above his head. Even with his eyes closed he couldn't escape from its penetrating rays. The fierce light was passing straight through his eyelids and into his skull, causing a sharp pinprick of agony in some dark recess of his brain. The agony seemed to stretch to infinity. How much suffering a simple light bulb can cause to a human being, he kept thinking bitterly.

His arms were tied to the arms of the chair, his legs to the chair legs. The legs were bound so tightly the rope was biting through the skin into his flesh. The strange thing was, he had no sensation in his legs at all. His mouth was drooling saliva; the drooling had started a short while ago. Two army intelligence officers were sitting opposite him. Their faces both looked the same to him, round faces, fair skinned, with a slight moustache under the nose. Somebody was standing behind Abu Taher as well. That person occasionally came into his field of vision, and he too looked very much like the others, though he was thinner and his face had pockmarks on it. Could they be triplets? Was it possible for three sons to be born together?

"What is your name?"
"My name is Mohammed Abu Taher."
"Tell me your name."
"Abu Taher."
"*Kya nam?*"
"Mohammed Abu Taher."
"Your name is – ?"
"Abu Taher, sir."
"*What is your name?*"
"My name is Mohammed Abu Taher."

They were going on and on, asking the same question all the time. How long had it been so far, a couple of days, a couple of years? Would they go on asking the same question for ever? What was the point of asking the same thing over and over again? A few minutes earlier Abu Taher had relieved himself while still tied to his chair, and his urine had trickled over the floor towards where the two in front of him were sitting. They had seen this but said nothing. They were smoking, lighting one cigarette after another, and the pall of tobacco smoke was unbearable, enough to make you want to throw up.

"Mohammed Abu Taher?"

"Yes, sir?"

"These *mukti* guerrillas who are operating in Dhaka city: do you know any of them?"

"No, sir."

"But you were involved in the looting of the branch of Habib Bank at Hatkhola in Motijheel. Who else was with you?"

"Sir, I wasn't involved in any looting of any bank."

"What is your occupation?"

"I'm a student at Dhaka University. I'm in the MSc Physics thesis group."

"Weren't you involved in the hijacking of that petrol tanker at Tikatuli?"

"No, sir."

"Now we're going to start sticking pins into the fingers of your right hand. We'll stop if you'll admit to your crimes."

"I haven't been involved in anything whatever connected with the *mukti bahini*, sir."

"You are one of three brothers. Where are the other two?"

"I don't know, sir."

"We have reason to believe they have joined the *mukti bahini*."

"I don't know what they have been doing, sir."

"Why didn't you join the *mukti bahini*?"

"I believe in Pakistan. India is our enemy. *Pakistan Zindabad! Qaid-e-Azam Zindabad!* Long live Liaquat Ali Khan°! Long live the memory of our great poet Iqbal°!"

The two intelligence branch men laughed out loud.

"Go on," said one to the other, still laughing, "stick those pins in!"

"God, please make me lose conscience," mumbled Abu Taher. "Merciful Allah, make me lose conscience. Make me faint away!"

What intense pain, what unbearable torment! A lot of flames seemed to suddenly blaze up in front of his eyes. The pain of stabbing steel pinpoints didn't seem to come from his fingers but from somewhere else.

"Water, sir! I must have water!"

"What is your name?"

"Abu Taher. Give me some water, sir!"

"A grenade was thrown at the vehicle of government minister Moulana Mohammed Ishaque at the traffic lights at the Medical College Hospital crossroads. Were you with the people who carried out that crime?"

"Water, water!"

"Answer my question. Were you with them?"

"Yes, sir."

"Were you in the Habib Bank looting incident?"

"Yes, sir, please, water, water!"

"Were you in the Tikatuli operation?"

"Yes, sir, a glass of water, I'm so thirsty!"

"Do you know where these guerrillas are hiding?"

"Yes, sir."

"If you can help us to seize two of those people we'll let you go. Just two, that's all we're asking. Will you cooperate?"

"Yes, sir. I must have water."

Abu Taher was allowed to drink some water. The lamp over his head was switched off. Another light was still on in the room, but Abu Taher couldn't see a thing; to him it seemed the room was in darkness. Was it as dark as this in one's tomb?

"Mohammed Abu Taher!"

"Yes, sir?"

"Here, have a cigarette."

"I don't smoke, sir."

"Never mind whether you smoke or not, take a puff of it. The way you are, your body will appreciate a shot of nicotine."

Abu Taher smoked his cigarette. He was holding it in his left hand; he couldn't raise his right hand because all its fingers were stuck full of pins. The pin in his middle finger hadn't gone in properly; it was sticking out awkwardly. For a moment he had an idea none of this was real. He was just having a horrible dream, he was about to have one of his fits – he always had nasty dreams just before a fit came on. When he woke up again everything would be all right.

"Mohammed Abu Taher!"

"Yes, sir."

"Many people confess to crimes just so as to escape from our treatment. Then when they are asked to take us to where the *mukti* are hanging out they are unable to take us anywhere, and we can't get hold of any *mukti*. In other words they simply waste our time. Now tell me, is it a good thing to waste our time?"

"No, sir."

"You're not wasting our time now, are you?"

"No, sir."

"If you can't lead us to anyone we'll reward you with a very special kind of punishment. The English word for it is *castration*. We shall excise both of your testicles. We'll make you into a eunuch. Do you know what a eunuch is?"

"Yes, sir."

"It would be best of all if we could make a eunuch of every single man in East Pakistan. Then a new race would emerge, a race of neuters. How would that be? Quite good, eh?"

"Yes, sir. It would be good."

"We shall go out in an hour's time, taking you with us. You will then show us where they all live. We aren't going to take those pins out of your hand, they can stay as they are. Okay?"

"Yes, sir."

"I notice one of the pins hasn't gone in properly. Shall I shove it in?"

"Please do, sir."

"No, well, let's leave it for now, I can do it when we get back from our outing."

"Right, sir."

"Would you like anything to eat before we go out? A slice of cake, some tea?"

"I'd like that, sir."

"No, I think we'd better leave it until we get back. Let's do our job first and then eat. Don't you think that's better?"

"Oh, yes, sir."

A bright blue Toyota car was cruising around visiting various places in Dhaka. It had special glass in its windows which prevented outsiders from seeing the people inside, but allowed the people inside to see everything outside. Abu Taher was sitting in the back seat with a blanket wrapped round him. Dribbles of saliva were still coming out of his mouth and he had a raging fever. He kept shivering violently all over. There was a man on either side of him. Abu Taher was pointing out houses to them and they were making notes. But Abu Taher was selecting the houses entirely at random. He had no connection whatever with any freedom fighters, and had absolutely no idea where any of them might or might not be hanging out.

"There, that house, sir."

"But it's a two storeyed building, which floor do you mean?"

"I'm not sure, sir."

"Have another look, are you sure this is the house?"

"Yes, sir."

"Where shall we go next?"

"To Purana Paltan."

"Purana Paltan?"

"Yes, sir."

"What's the name of the chap who lives there?"

"I don't know his name, sir. He comes and sleeps here at night."

"Alone, or are others with him?"

"I'm not sure, sir."

Abu Taher pointed out a total of five buildings in various parts of the city. That same night the army seized a total of nine men from those five buildings. None of them came home alive. And none of them had had any knowledge at all of the *mukti bahini*.

Those nine men mentioned other people's names. And so it went on, in a nightmarish chain reaction. Young men were seized for no rhyme or reason. They realized their only chance of survival was if they came up with some other names. They supplied names and pointed out houses. And the cycle went on.

At the same time rewards were being offered for running in 'miscreants', as an enticement to anyone willing to betray another person for the sake of money. The District Commissioner in every district had the power to offer a one thousand rupee reward to anyone facilitating the arrest of any freedom fighter. *

A. For information leading to the apprehension of an ordinary miscreant: Rs 500/-
B. For information leading to the apprehension of a miscreant in receipt of training from India: Rs 750/-
C. For information leading to the apprehension of a miscreant together with weapon or weapons: Rs 1000/-
D. For information leading to the apprehension of a commander of a miscreant group: Rs 2000/-
E. For information leading to the apprehension of a commander of a miscreant group together with a weapon or weapons: Rs 10,000/-

---

* Source: *Dainik Pakistan* newspaper.

68

Indira Gandhi, the only daughter of Jawaharlal Nehru, was generally called "Indira-ji" by the people of her country. This combination of her given name with the reverential '*ji*' conveyed a mixture of respect and affection.

It was 3rd December 1971. Indira-ji was about to give a speech at the Brigade Parade Ground in Calcutta. She was originally supposed to have come on 4th December, but she had brought forward her schedule by one day. Did this have some special significance? Was today the day? The great and historic day when she would announce India's official recognition of a new state, the republic of Bangladesh? When the Indian army would intervene and enter the battlefield on the side of the *mukti bahini* freedom fighters, when Bangladesh would become independent, when the millions of refugees living a wretched existence in a foreign land would at last be able to return to their homes?

The parade ground was milling with people, a great sea of people eagerly awaiting a big event. Everyone was longing to hear the speech in which India's official recognition of the People's Republic of Bangladesh would be announced.

Indira-ji began her speech. She spoke in a calm and apparently emotionless voice, and she said nothing new. She talked of the sufferings of the refugees. She made yet another appeal to the world powers to play a more active part in the search for a solution to the problem in East Pakistan. She concluded as calmly as she had begun. However at one point during the speech a small note had been passed to her, on reading which her brow had clouded over and a look of fury had glinted in her eyes; then she had quickly regained her composure and continued speaking as if nothing had happened.

What was written in the note was as follows: "Pakistan air force has carried out air raids on Amritsar, Pathankot, Srinagar, Avastipur, Jodhpur, Ambala and Agra. Pakistan army has started hostilities on Panjab border, and penetrated a short distance into Indian territory."

Indira Gandhi returned to Delhi. That very night, or more precisely in the early hours of 4th December, she addressed the nation from the Delhi studios of Akash Bani radio and made the kind of announcement everyone in East Bengal had been waiting for. Although she did not actually declare that India had recognized the state of Bangladesh, it became obvious that that was the way things were heading:

> "Today the war in Bangladesh has become a war on India ... Aggression must be met, and the people of India will meet it with fortitude and determination, with discipline and utmost unity."

In response to Indira Gandhi's announcement Yahya Khan issued a formal declaration of war, on the morning of 4th December. This is what he announced on radio:

> "Our enemy has once again challenged us ... March forward. Give the hardest blow of Allahu Akbar to the enemy."

Following Yahya Khan's declaration of war Indira Gandhi announced to the Indian parliament, the Lok Sabha:

> "This morning I received news that Pakistan has declared war on us. We are ready."

The entry on that day's events in *Keesing's Contemporary Archives* reads as follows:

> The Indian Army, linking up with the Mukti Bahini, entered East Pakistan on December 4 from five main directions: (1) the Comilla Sector, east of Dacca; (2) the Sylhet Sector, in the north-east of the

province; (3) the Mymensingh Sector, in the north; (4) the Rangpur-Dinajpur Sector, in the north-west; (5) the Jessore Sector, south-west of Dacca ...

Then began an extraordinary international chess game. The big powers got all excited and started vying with one another to establish relative positions of advantage.

On 5th December, at the behest of the United States government, an emergency session of the United Nations Security Council was convened. The US delegate George Bush* brought forward a motion demanding a ceasefire. Eleven nations voted in favour of the proposal, the United Kingdom and France abstained, and the Soviet Union used its veto to scupper it. "Don't any of you comprehend what is going on?" fulminated the Soviet delegate, Comrade Malikov. "Eighty-eight of the member states of the United Nations have populations well under ten million, yet more than that number of refugees have fled from East Pakistan to seek refuge in India."

An announcement on Radio Peking stated that China would afford every possible assistance to Pakistan. The Indian army would soon know the bitter taste of defeat.

Russia took steps to ensure that China could not go on the offensive, pushing through Ladakh straight into India, by posting one million troops on the USSR/Chinese border.

The US President Richard Nixon told reporters that what India was doing amounted to a malicious and illegal attempt to annexe part of the territory of another sovereign nation.

The US Seventh Fleet was at that time still stationed near North Vietnam. The decision was taken to relocate it in the Bay of Bengal, and accordingly it set sail in that direction. The fleet included the huge nuclear powered aircraft carrier Enterprise, an amphibious assault ship, a frigate and four destroyers equipped for firing guided missiles, and some landing craft.

In response the USSR moved twenty of its destroyers to the Indian Ocean, and sent a frigate equipped with missiles and a nuclear powered submarine with nuclear missile firing capability to the Bay of Bengal.

General Gul Hassan Khan telephoned his panicking subordinate General Niazi in Eastern Command and, speaking in Pushto, assured him that there was no need to worry, he should keep his nerve, allies of both the yellow and the white variety were on their way to help him, coming from north and south respectively.

President Yahya Khan also phoned Niazi and told him he could count on foreign support coming to his rescue any minute now.

"In what form will this foreign support come?" General Niazi wanted to know.

"I can't explain exactly what form it will come in, but foreign assistance is definitely on its way. There is no ambiguity about it, we are relying on highly secret and most reliable sources of information. Just make absolutely sure Dhaka doesn't fall. You must keep Dhaka in your hands, that's all. Help is on its way, significant help."

A meeting had been convened at the Governor's House. The Governor of East Pakistan, Dr Abdul Motaleb Malik, had a white prayer cap on his head; he had

---

* George Bush, a future President of the USA, and father of George W. Bush who was President when this book was being published in 2004. – **Author**

just that moment got up from his prayer mat. He had a confused and hopeless look on his face. General Niazi, however, was looking positively cheerful. Also present at the meeting were General Rao Farman Ali (the military advisor to the governor) and General Jamshed. General Jamshed appeared profoundly worried. Rao Farman Ali's face was neutral, as if he considered he personally had nothing to do with the events taking place around him.

"What is our position now?" asked Dr Malik in a plaintive little voice after clearing his throat nervously.

"Perfectly fine," declared Niazi. "The cowardly Indian army is attempting to advance on Dhaka. It's proving to be a real education for them. They are being taught new lessons at every step."

"May I know what the overall situation is?" asked Dr Malik.

"There's no need for you to think about the overall situation," growled General Jamshed. "It's not your job as governor to attend to what's going on on the war front. You should keep your eyes on civil affairs. You could be considering what to do in relation to the motion in favour of a ceasefire which has been put to the plenary session of the National Assembly."

"I had other plans in mind," piped Dr Malik in an even smaller voice.

"What plans?" demanded Rao Farman Ali severely.

Dr Malik was so overcome with embarrassment he couldn't speak.

"The chess game is very far advanced," said Farman Ali. "We've got past the mid game, and now we're in the endgame. But the endgame doesn't usually finish just like that, it goes on and on. And that's the position we're in now. Neither India nor Pakistan will achieve a victory, there will be a stalemate. Then it will be time to seek some kind of a settlement through the mediation of foreign powers."

"You are certain of that?" asked Dr Malik.

"Absolutely positive," replied Farman Ali. "A coalition government has already been formed with Nurul Amin, an East Pakistani, as prime minister and Zulfiqar Ali Bhutto as deputy prime minister. Don't you read anything into that? Look, this coalition government was formed after behind the scenes discussions. It's quite possible that it was set up after consultation with Indira Gandhi herself."

"But the way the Indian troops are advancing it looks as if they'll burst into Dhaka itself very soon," suggested Dr Malik.

"To get into Dhaka city," purred General Niazi, "will take them at the very least five years. Those Indians are lily-livered. There's no way they could brave our artillery and sneak into Dhaka. There's a good joke about why they're so cowardly, shall I tell you?"

The others remained silent; from their manner it was evident that none of them were in the right mood for listening to funny stories just then. But that didn't dampen Niazi's enthusiasm and he launched into his anecdote. "Physiologically, you see, cowardice is centred in the foreskin. We Muslims cut that bit off so we're fearless. The Hindus leave it on, so they're faint-hearted. You get it? Ha ha ha!"

The general laughed heartily, but his laughter found no echo in the throats of his companions. Then the wail of a siren was heard. Another air raid was imminent. The Indian air force was at it again! Everyone promptly got up and left the room.

It was late at night. Brigadier Abdul Qadir Khan, the Pakistan army officer in command of the Tangail sector, who was stationed at Elenga, had been passing his last few nights in sleepless torment. Now he was at the end of his tether, exhausted and depressed. One piece of ghastly news after another kept reaching him. It was a grand irony, the head of the liberation army in Tangail had the same name as him, Qadir. He was generally known as Kader Siddiqui. In his worst nightmare Qadir Khan saw himself being taken prisoner by Kader Siddiqui.

Would Kader Siddiqui treat him with respect? He didn't think so. To the freedom fighters all members of the Pakistan army were objects of hatred. The only person who would show due respect to a regular army officer was another officer of a regular army. If it came to surrender he would be better off surrendering to the Indian army. What should he do? What *could* he do?

All kinds of vague instructions were coming from higher command. At one moment they would say sit tight where you are, next moment they would advise you to beat a retreat and come to Dhaka. Dhaka had to be held at all costs. If East Pakistan was to be saved at all they must keep hold of Dhaka city.

How was he to get to Dhaka anyway? There was no way of doing it. The freedom fighters had destroyed every road bridge there was. Admittedly there was a good side to that, it meant that the Indian army was equally unable to reach Dhaka in a hurry; they would have to advance slowly on foot.

When Brigadier Qadir Khan sat down to his evening meal it was already two o'clock in the morning. A few dried-up chapatis and a dish of congealed beef curry awaited him. The meat was not properly cooked, it was as tough as nails. That was the way, of course: once things start going awry every single detail goes wrong. In the field kitchen cooking had ground to a halt; no doubt there was a problem with supplies or something like that, but he simply didn't want to know. His only concern was how to get to Dhaka – as quickly as possible.

Qadir Khan was just starting to chew a piece of chapati without any meat when some good news was delivered to him. He hadn't heard such excellent news for a very long time. Help had arrived from abroad: great multitudes of Chinese paratroopers were landing – yes, in Tangail itself!

"*Alhamdulillah!*" exclaimed Brigadier Qadir Khan. "Praise be to God! So they've showed up at last, have they? How many of them are there?"

"Any number! More and more are coming down."

"Make sure they are given a warm welcome on my behalf. I need to know what their plans are. I imagine they chose to come down in Tangail for a reason. They intend to deal with Kader Siddiqui at the very outset."

"That may well be the reason, sir."

"Not *may be*, that definitely is the reason. Now get in touch with headquarters and let them know the good news about the landing of these Chinese paratroopers. And one way or another see to it that I can communicate with the Chinese myself."

Qadir Khan finished his meal with great satisfaction. For some days he hadn't been in the mood for touching alcohol, but now he opened a bottle of rum and finished it by himself.

When Qadir Khan's men went to welcome the Chinese paratroopers they were shot down. For the paratroopers weren't Chinese after all, they were Indian.

By a twist of fate Brigadier Qadir Khan of the Pakistan army, officer in command of Tangail sector, was indeed captured by his namesake Kader Siddiqui. With him were two colonels, three majors and a lieutenant. All their troops had been massacred at Kalihati and Elenga. Only this small band of officers had escaped with their lives.

Kader Siddiqui did not mistreat his prisoners in any way, but handed them over to the Indian army.

69

6th December 1971. India had given official recognition to Bangladesh as an independent sovereign state. The liberation army and the Indian army were jointly advancing on Dhaka. All the Pakistani army positions outside of Dhaka were toppling like dominoes. In the air the Indian air force held unchallenged supremacy.

People who had been stuck in refugee camps in India, impatient to return to their homes, started pushing into Bangladesh even as fierce fighting went on. They were keen to celebrate the liberation of their country from inside.

Shortly after sunset that evening, in the midst of these rapidly changing circumstances, Shahed could be seen standing outside a homestead in a village near Barasat. In his hand he held a scrap of paper on which Naimul had scribbled an address. It had taken him a great deal of effort to get this far, but now at last he had traced the area, the village, the very house mentioned in the address. And he had suddenly run out of courage. He simply couldn't bring himself to knock on the door and ask, "Does a girl called Asmani live here?" He was terrified the answer would be "No, I've never heard of her," or else, "Oh yes, a girl of that name was here for a while, but she and her daughter have left. I've no idea where they went."

Suddenly Shahed realized he was thirsty, almost dying of thirst. Perhaps before trying to find Asmani he ought to ask someone to give him a glass of water.

It wasn't necessary for him to knock on the door, for it opened by itself. A gentle looking elderly man with a puzzled look on his face emerged and came up to Shahed.

"Who are you looking for?" asked the old man.

"I need some water," stammered Shahed shakily, "a glass of water."

"Well, do come inside and I'll get you some."

"Listen," babbled Shahed, "is there anyone called Asmani living round here? She has a little girl with her called Runi."

"Who are you, a relative of theirs?"

"I'm Runi's father."

Shahed was trembling all over. He thought he was about to faint. The old man stepped forward and took him by the hand.

"Your wife and daughter are here in my house. And they're quite all right. Asmani has just gone down to the pond at the back of the house. That's where your daughter spends most of her time. Do you want to go to them straight away, or have your water first?"

"Where's the pond?" murmured Shahed.

The old man led him through to the back garden. Shahed was stumbling along uncertainly, feeling he would never get as far as the pond; he would lose his balance and collapse long before that. He couldn't even breathe properly.

Not long afterwards Runi went down to the pond in search of her mother and chanced on a very odd scene. Mummy was clinging onto a strange man with wild hair and a beard, and kissing him passionately. Oh dear, how terribly embarrassing!

"Mum! What on earth are you up to!" yelled Runi. "Mum! Mum!"

70

Over and over again All India Radio was broadcasting an announcement made by the Chief of Staff of the Indian army, General Sam Manekshaw:

> "My troops have now surrounded Dhaka city. Pakistan army HQ is in the sights of our heavy artillery. I call on you to surrender. Your safety and proper treatment in accordance with international law are guaranteed."

> "My troops have now surrounded Dhaka city. Pakistan army HQ is in the sights of our heavy artillery. I call on you to surrender. Your safety and proper treatment in accordance with international law are guaranteed."

> "My troops have now surrounded Dhaka city. Pakistan army HQ is in the sights of our heavy artillery. I call on you to surrender. Your safety and proper treatment in accordance with international law are guaranteed."

> "My troops have now surrounded Dhaka city. Pakistan army HQ is in the sights of our heavy artillery. I call on you to surrender. Your safety and proper treatment in accordance with international law are guaranteed."

> "My troops have now surrounded Dhaka city. Pakistan army HQ is in the sights of our heavy artillery. I call on you to surrender. Your safety and proper treatment in accordance with international law are guaranteed."

71

Early in the morning of 14th December Moriam woke from a bizarre dream. Someone had knocked on the front door, making her nervous. "Who's there?" Moriam had asked. From the other side of the door had come a voice saying rather gruffly, "Mori, let me in." Even in her sleep Moriam had started quivering with excitement. He had returned, her hero had returned! He had kept his word: he had told her he would come back the day their country was liberated. And it was certainly about to be liberated, perhaps it would be set free that very day! Moriam had cautiously got out of bed. Everyone else was fast asleep. She was the only person awake, and that was a good thing; it was best for nobody else to be watching when she welcomed her beloved. Then the scene of the dream had abruptly changed, and she was in their old house. She had opened the door of her bedroom and there stood her father. In the dream she had not been aware that her father had been missing for months.

"Naimul's been hammering on the door for ages," he had said to her smiling. "Why don't you open the door? You're such a sleepy-head. A girl ought always to sleep as lightly as a bird. Anyway, go and open the door!"

Moriam had made a dash for the stairs, but then Mobarak Hussain had spoken again, reprovingly as before.

"You should tidy yourself up before you go. Change your sari! If after all this time your husband comes back to find you looking like a beggar, how do you think he'll feel? Where is your jewellery? Put it on. And if you can't find a decent sari put on your wedding one."

Moriam had changed her sari. In her dream she was able to do this very rapidly. Her light blue sari instantly turned into her wedding sari, and magically she was now wearing all her jewellery. The thing that slowed her down was putting on her eye liner; there wasn't enough light to see clearly by. Mobarak Hussain had become impatient and started banging on her bedroom door. And then his banging had woken Moriam up.

Tears came to Moriam's eyes. Had it all been a dream? Hadn't anyone really come and knocked on the door and called "Mori! Mori!"? The only bit in the dream which corresponded to reality had been the banging noise; but it hadn't been anyone banging on her bedroom door, it had been coming from much further away. She could hear it now, the sound of heavy artillery. The *mukti bahini* had surrounded Dhaka city, along with the Indian army, and it was they who were firing mortars. Was Naimul there with them? When they entered the city would he be somewhere in the midst of them? Surely he would. Moriam slipped cautiously out of bed. Her youngest sister Mafruha was there; she had been sleeping beside her. How beautiful she looked as she slept, she was getting more and more beautiful by the day. When Mafruha got married would her husband nickname her Maf, which meant 'pardon'? He might use 'Maf' as a pet form of Mafruha just as Naimul liked to call her 'Mori' instead of Moriam.

Their father had bungled things when naming them. All three of the names he had chosen were unsuitable for shortening. 'Mori' meant 'I die', 'Maf' meant 'pardon' and if you were to shorten Masuma's name you would get 'Ma', which meant 'mother'. What man would wish to call his wife 'mother'?

Moriam came out of her room and went to the kitchen. This was a new habit of hers, to go straight to the kitchen as soon as she got up in the morning. She would prepare two cups of tea and quickly go off with them to a quiet spot somewhere. One cup she would drink, the other she would set down in front of her – for Naimul. Such was her little game. Today she decided to take the cups up onto the roof. Probably the Indian fighter planes would come hurtling across the sky again today. She would enjoy watching their antics as she drank her tea.

Just as she was about to go up on the roof with her teacups she bumped into Kolimullah. She couldn't help staring in amazement. Just last night that man had had a big beard, and now he was clean shaven! He looked so odd.

"I'd started to get lice in my beard," explained Kolimullah, stroking his chin. "I had to get rid of it. Where are you off to with your tea, are you going up onto the roof? You shouldn't go up there now, the Indian planes are shooting at random. They've been killing off any number of civilians. Instead of going where the Pakistani soldiers are they keep flying over civilian areas. Er, why have you got *two* cups of tea?"

"I drink two cups, one after the other," said Moriam in embarrassment.

"Well, how about giving me one of them. I don't normally drink tea on an empty stomach, but suppose I try for once."

Very unwillingly Moriam surrendered one of her cups to him.

"Fearsome times are ahead," mused Kolimullah as he sipped the tea. "But nobody seems to realize that."

"Why will it be so fearsome?"

"The real battle is about to begin now, the battle for Dhaka. The Pakistan army is going to hold firm, there is no question of their letting go of the city. They've assembled all their forces in Dhaka; they have enough military strength to hold the city for a whole year. During that year negotiations will take place. Some kind of loose federation will be set up, that's what the foreign powers want."

"Won't our country become independent?"

"Goodness no, is gaining independence such a simple matter? No, it's very far from simple. The Indians are flying a few rickety old planes over our skies, and someone or other in Delhi called Manekshaw keeps screaming "Surrender!" To hear him you'd think the Pakistan army are going to chuck away their guns and put their arms up saying sorry, just because he's told them to. The Pakistan army isn't the kind of army which holds up its arms and says sorry. I'm telling you, sister, the world's top soldiers are: one, the Gurkha regiment and two, the Pakistan army. And the Indians know it. It's only our *mukti bahini* with their silly towels round their heads who don't recognize the fact."

"Oh," said Moriam bleakly.

"Listen, sister," said Kolimullah, "as soon as you've finished your tea you must wake everyone up. We've got work to do."

"What kind of work?"

"We're going to move out of this house back to your father's old place. I've a feeling it'll be much safer there. We'll have to get hold of enough rice and stuff to last us three months. And as soon as we're back in your old house we'll have to dig a bunker. It would be best of all if we could leave Dhaka altogether, but that's not feasible."

"But how are you going to move?" asked Moriam. "There's a curfew on."

"We can move during the curfew, that's no problem, I can arrange things. The rest of you just need to gather all your stuff together."

For the purpose of transporting his wife and in-laws back to their old house Kolimullah borrowed a special vehicle which was being used to seek out and abduct various intellectuals from all over Dhaka city.

At three o'clock in the afternoon this vehicle stopped in front of Professor Dhirendranath Ray Choudhury's bungalow. The professor had just sat down to eat his lunch. He had done the cooking himself, a simple dish, a kind of egg risotto. He had put a whole egg into his pan of boiling rice and added three green chillies. The egg had been boiled along with the rice and the chillies had been reduced to softness. He had then peeled the egg and mashed everything up together, adding some salt and half a tablespoon of pungent mustard oil. The result was as good as ambrosia, food for the gods. He could tell that from the smell, though he hadn't yet tasted it. Just as he was about to start eating there was a knock on the door. He went to open it and there was Kolimullah, bending down to touch his feet and giving him a respectful greeting.

"How are you, son?" asked Dhirendranath Ray Choudhury, beaming. He was assuming that the young man standing in front of him was one of his old pupils. Students had a habit of dropping in at awkward times.

"I'm quite well, sir," replied Kolimullah. "Do you recognize me?"

Dhirendranath Ray Choudhury could not recognize him at all, indeed he could hardly have been expected to, given that he had never seen him before. Nevertheless he smiled kindly and exclaimed, "How could I not recognize you? Of course I do!"

He had a reason for telling such lies. He knew from experience that if ever he confessed to not recognizing a student the young person concerned would be deeply hurt. One student of his had even been reduced to tears.

"What was your name, now, my son?"

"Kolimullah."

"Ah, yes. Kolimullah. Kolimullah. I remember quite clearly now. Have you eaten?"

"No, sir."

"Come along then, have pot luck with me. There isn't very much, actually, just a mixture of boiled rice and egg. But I have some more eggs, I can fry you some. I did have a tin of the most excellent ghee, but unfortunately I can't find it."

"I won't be able to stop and eat now, sir," said Kolimullah. "I came on urgent business."

"What business?"

"There's an army colonel who is keen to speak to you."

"What would an army colonel want with me?" asked Dhirendranath Ray Choudhury, perplexed.

"I don't know. However, there's no need to be nervous, sir, I'll be at your side."

"Which batch of mine were you in, now?" enquired the professor.

"We can't waste time talking, sir. Let's get the meeting over, then we can have a good chat."

"Then please wait just a couple of minutes while I finish my lunch. I'm really rather hungry, I didn't have any breakfast this morning."

"I'm afraid there's no time for eating, sir."

"Well, let me just put my shirt on then. I can't imagine what he wants with me. Was he by any chance a student of mine? I taught at Karachi University for two years. Professor Salam was one of my colleagues."

"Possibly he is an old pupil of yours," said Kolimullah. "The way he said, 'do bring the old professor to see me,' it did sound as if he might be a pupil of yours."

When Dhirendranath Ray Choudhury got into the vehicle he saw it was full of people, all of them looking extremely worried. Dhirendranath glanced at them and smiled in a friendly way. As he had forgotten his spectacles he couldn't recognize anyone. If he had had his glasses on he would have realized that he knew most of them. The cream of East Bengal's intelligentsia were sitting there in the van. And they were on their way to the slaughterhouse.

Kolimullah was sitting on a plain wooden chair in Mr Zohar's room. It was early evening and the light had been switched on. For the first time ever both of the room's windows were open. As before Mr Zohar was sitting at his desk, wrapped in his shawl. He had an open book in front of him and appeared to be absorbed in reading it. Although there was a hundred watt bulb illuminating the room he had placed two burning candles beside the book on his desk. From time to time a breath of wind came in through the windows and made the candle flames gutter; only then did Mr Zohar raise his eyes from the page to fix them on the candles.

Kolimullah cleared his throat to attract Mr Zohar's attention.

"How are you, Kolimullah?" asked Mr Zohar casually, without looking up.

"I'm fine, sir. How is your health, sir?"

"You're a poet, Kolimullah," said Mr Zohar without heeding his question, "so maybe you can tell me what a soul is?"

"Don't know, sir," replied Kolimullah.

"In the Holy Quran," said Mr Zohar, "the soul has been referred to as an *order of God*. By the way, do you believe in God?"

"Sir!" protested Kolimullah in discomfiture. "How can you question that? Surely I believe in God! I admit I don't say my prayers five times a day, but I certainly do believe in the deity. And I fast for the whole month of Ramadan."

Mr Zohar looked up from his book and turned his gaze on Kolimullah.

"I wonder... Would it be possible for one who really believed in God to commit such grotesque acts of betrayal as you have been guilty of in recent days?"

Kolimullah was completely taken aback by this rapier thrust. Privately he thought, what kind of talk is this, Zohar? Everything I've done, I've done it for you lot. I've just been carrying out your instructions. You gave me a list, I traced the people on it and brought them to you. What you did with them afterwards is none of my business. If anyone has been sinning it's you lot, not me.

"Listen to what this book says about the soul," continued Mr Zohar, and he proceeded to read the passage out in English. *"The experience of every soul becomes the experience of the divine mind; therefore, the divine mind has the knowledge of all beings."*

"Who wrote the book, sir?" asked Kolimullah.

"A Sufi, called Hazrat Enayet Khan."

Kolimullah pinned a fixed smile on his face and inwardly thought, Bihari bastard! Now you're studying Sufism, are you? Burning candles, eh, and getting pious!

"My belief in God," Mr Zohar went on, closing the book, "and in heaven and hell and all that stuff, is very limited. Even so, I sometimes think perhaps there's some truth in it. And if that's the case I shall go straight to hell."

"You can't say that, sir," objected Kolimullah. "The only one who can decide who will go to heaven and who to hell is God."

"I have no doubt at all that I'll go to hell," said Mr Zohar firmly. "And that doesn't bother me at all. What does bother me is the thought that people like you will be in there with me."

Kolimullah couldn't think what to reply. He had come in the hopes of wheedling some inside information out of Mr Zohar, but now he could see it was a mistake to have come.

"Kolimullah."

"Yes, sir."

"I've got some very bad news for you."

Kolimullah's heart sank. What was he talking about? What bad news?

Mr Zohar brought out a cigarette from the depths of his shawl and lit it at one of the candles. It was suddenly obvious he was burning candles purely for convenience, simply for lighting his cigarettes.

"Kolimullah!"

"Yes, sir?"

"Here's the bad news. Your country is going to gain independence. The Indian army hasn't got to Dhaka yet, but the *mukti bahini* have already entered the city."

"No! You can't mean that, sir!"

"To the best of my knowledge," continued Mr Zohar after taking a long drag at his cigarette, "President Yahya Khan has instructed General Niazi to surrender on suitably honourable terms. That is what will shortly take place. I extend my congratulations to you in advance: you are about to become a citizen of a newly independent country. And now look at me, a Bihari, a member of an outcast tribe with no homeland."

"I think I'll be going now, sir."

"You may go. When did you shave off your beard? Today?"

"Yes, sir. It had started to get lice in it."

"You have done well to cut it off. Quite a smart move."

Mr Zohar stopped talking and went back to reading his book.

Moriam had been up on the flat roof of the house all afternoon. Previously going up on the roof had given her a slightly scary feeling, but since this morning all sense of fear had departed. There were people on every roof, all staring up at the sky. Indian fighter jets kept passing over. They would come in low, roar overhead, vanish into the distance and then come back again. What fun it was to watch! Shouts could be heard from the roofs of some houses, '*Joy Bangla!*' Yes, people in Dhaka now had the courage to openly pronounce those words. '*Joy Bangla!*' To Moriam it seemed unbelievable, as if there was some mistake somewhere.

Safiya came up onto the roof carrying her baby son. Seeing Moriam she said, "Would you hold Babu for me a bit, please. I think he's got a temperature."

"Why don't you stay up here for a while, Mum?" asked Moriam as she took her little brother.

"It's nearly time for breaking the fast. I'm going to have my *iftar*," said Safiya.

"Oh, you're fasting, are you?"

"Yes."

"What for?"

"I'm fasting for the independence of our country."

"Oh, why didn't you tell me? I could have fasted with you. Mum, what do you think, will we get independence?"

"I don't understand things like politics."

"But what do you feel in your heart?"

Safiya didn't reply. She started to go back downstairs, but then turned, came up to Moriam again and said, "There, let me have Babu, I'll take him down with me."

"Why take him?" asked Moriam. "Let him stay, I'll hold him."

"But you're wearing a pretty sari, it'll get messed up."

"It'll be quite all right. Leave him with me. Mum, how do I look?"

"Oh, you look lovely, darling. Really pretty."

"Is it true, Mum, you must never wear your wedding sari any other day except your wedding anniversary because it's unlucky?"

"Who told you that?"

"I can't remember who told me, but if it is unlucky I'll change into a different sari."

Again Safiya made no reply. She had no idea whether wearing wedding saris on other days brought bad luck or not. If it really did, then of course it was better to avoid doing so. But dear Moriam, she had been so excited about putting hers on today, it would seem cruel to tell her to change out of it.

Moriam was walking up and down with her baby brother in her arms, from one end of the flat roof to the other, chatting to him all the time in a low murmur. By now everyone knew that the baby was blind, but Moriam had begun to realize he was stone deaf as well. However much she chattered at him he didn't react, he just made little sounds of his own at random. However if you tickled his stomach he would start laughing, and the sound of his laughter was delightful.

Moriam kept tickling the baby's stomach to make him laugh, and from time to time she murmured "Gutku! Hello, Gutku!" Nobody called the child Yahya any more; instead people used various nicknames. Moriam had taken to calling him Gutku.

"Gutku, listen, our country is going independent, did you know? Mmmm, independent! Do you understand what independent means? Independent means *Joy Bangla*. All the soldiers are going to go away. No-o-o, in fact they won't go away, we're going to slice them up into chips. Slice! Slice!"

Gutku laughed. He was laughing with pleasure, for Moriam, while going "Slice! Slice!", had used her hand to pretend she was passing a saw across his stomach.

"Did you notice I'm wearing my wedding sari? Why am I wearing it, come on, you tell me! If you can tell me I'll have to admit you're very clever. When our country's independent a very special man will come to our house. I'm wearing it for his sake. Come on, who is that special man, can you tell me? What is he to me? Stop laughing, you rascal, stop laughing and answer my question!"

Moriam leaned over the parapet; from there she could see far and wide. A curfew was still in force, yet people were out walking in the streets. There were no military vehicles to be seen anywhere. Had independence arrived?

Meanwhile Kolimullah was in his room. He was feeling rather unwell and had gone to lie down, all bundled up in the bedding. Masuma had come several times to feel him and see if he had a temperature. She always got into a state if anything was wrong with her husband, and the thing she found most upsetting was if he didn't want to talk. He had been unusually silent since the day before.

"Are you feeling awful?" asked Masuma. "Oy! Can you hear me?"

"I'm just feeling out of sorts," said Kolimullah. "It's nothing much."

"Shall I massage you?"

"No need."

"How about if I stroke your head?"

"Nope. Listen, why don't you pop off somewhere else while I just lie on my own for a while with my eyes closed."

"Let me stay with you," pleaded Masuma in a pathetic tone. "I won't talk, I'll just run my hands gently over your head and body, that'll make you feel better."

"There's no need for that at all. But what you could do is hand me my poetry writing book and a pencil, please."

Masuma at last felt a sense of relief. When Kolimullah had said he wanted to lie alone for a while with his eyes closed she had felt deeply hurt, for it sounded as though he must dislike her company. But now she could see that the case was rather different: the reason he had said those words was that he was busy composing poetry in his head. The wives of poetic types like him must often get confused in this way, she realized.

Masuma fetched the poetry notebook and two pencils, gave them to her husband and got into bed. Whether he liked it or not, even if it made him angry, she was going lie down and cling to him under the sheets. And she would rub her nose against his back, something she particularly loved doing, though she had no idea why.

Kolimullah was half lying, half sitting with the notebook and pencil in his hands, and Masuma was snuggling up close to him. Kolimullah was silent.

"What's the name of the poem?" asked Masuma in a sentimental tone.

"Quiet!" said Kolimullah. "Lie there and keep still. No talking."

"Sorry!" said Masuma. "I won't say anything more."

Kolimullah was trying to write a long poem about independence. He had got the first line, but the second line was eluding him. In circumstances like this one had to let the first line keep dancing around in one's mind, till eventually the second line would appear spontaneously.

Hail to the dawn, rainswept, lush leaved morn.

That was the first line. Here *dawn* meant independence, *rainswept, lush leaved* referred to the eternal spirit of Bengal.

Hail to the dawn, rainswept, lush leaved morn.

Masuma was ready to burst from having to keep quiet for so long. To release the tension she asked, "What are you writing the poem about?"

"Independence," said Kolimullah quietly, with no hint of annoyance.

"You haven't written any poems about me for a long time," ventured Masuma, emboldened by the calm tone of her husband's reply. "You could write the independence thing later, why don't you write a poem about me first?"

Kolimullah said nothing. A second line had just occurred to him, or at least the first half of it:

A whiff of gunpowder rides on the wind..

"Hey! Why don't you write a poem about me?"

"For goodness' sake, just pipe down, will you."

"First tell me when you're going to write a poem about me, then I'll pipe down. You haven't even got independence yet, and there you are writing about it. But you've got me already, I've been lying here beside you all this time, only you haven't even glanced at me. Independence is something you can't see, but you can see me."

Kolimullah looked at his wife. Masuma had a deep green sari on, and looked beautiful. Darker colours suit women with a light skin, he thought.

"Before you used to say our country would never become independent, but now it is actually going to get independence. Isn't it?"

Kolimullah gave no reply. Almost in a whisper Masuma said, "As long as you don't get cross with me, I'd like to ask you a question."

"All right, ask it."

"No, first promise you won't be cross. Lay your hand on me and say you won't be angry with me."

"I shall not be angry," promised Kolimullah with his hand on his wife's shoulder.

"You see, you've done a lot of things for the Pakistanis. Won't you get into trouble now?"

"No. I'm a chamaeleon."

"What do you mean?"

"A chamaeleon can change the colour of its skin. I can do the same. A person has to be able to do that in order to stay alive. Let me tell you a story. It's a Darwinian story, a story of survival."

Masuma kept gazing at her husband with worshipping eyes. She wasn't taking in a word of the story he was relating to her, she was too busy admiring his expression as he talked, just like an orator delivering a speech. A single phrase, "I love you, I love you," kept going round and round in her head, and she decided to keep repeating it until her husband had finished his lecture. Not only repeating it, but counting the number of repeats.

Kolimullah reached the end of his story. "What was it you were counting on your fingers?" he asked.

"Oh, nothing," said Masuma in embarrassment.

"Did you approve of my argument? Namely, the individual who is fit for society will survive; and the one who is ill fitted will fall by the wayside. How do you like it?"

"Oh, I do. I love everything you say."

"Ah, in that case I suggest you fetch a pair of scissors."

"Scissors? What for?"

"We're going to cut up your green sari and make a Bangladesh flag with it. The very day the country becomes independent we shall fly it. We need some red cloth too. Have you got a red sari anywhere?"

"Yes, I have!"

They closed the door and husband and wife set to, stitching together a Bangladesh flag with a circular red sun on a dark green background. Masuma was having the time of her life.

72

At nine o'clock in the morning of 16th December 1971 General Niazi received a short note on a slip of paper. It had been brought to him by the aide de camp of an Indian general, Major General Nagra. The note was only a couple of lines long, but it took General Niazi almost three minutes to absorb its contents. He muttered to himself and mopped his brow with his left hand.

"What does it say?" asked General Rao Farman Ali.

Niazi handed the note to him. After reading it Rao Farman Ali passed it on to General Jamshed.

The note read: *"Dear Abdullah, I am now at Mirpur bridge. My advice to you is that you should surrender to me. Send a representative."*

Niazi was already acquainted with Major General Nagra, who had been stationed for a number of years in Islamabad as Military Attaché to the Indian High Commission. The two had met there and become friends.

"Should we surrender to Nagra then?" asked General Rao Farman Ali, looking at General Niazi.

Niazi made no reply.

"Do you have any forces in reserve?" enquired Farman Ali.

Again Niazi gave no reply. He seemed to have become temporarily dumb. The chit had by now passed through the hands of everyone present and been returned to him. He was staring at the word 'Abdullah' in the note.

"Anything left in the bag?" called Rear Admiral Sharif in Panjabi, addressing Niazi. Niazi looked at General Jamshed. Immediate responsibility for the defence of Dhaka rested with him. Jamshed shook his head. The bag was empty. No tricks in reserve.

"If that's the case," said Sharif, "then the best thing is to do as Nagra suggests."

Rao Farman Ali nodded his head in agreement. For a while a deathly silence descended on the assembled company. Then it was broken by Rao Farman Ali.

"Well," he said, turning towards General Niazi, " perhaps it's time now for a few dirty jokes in Panjabi!"

But Niazi remained silent. For the first time in his life he was at a loss for a joke.

The old soldier who had won a Military Cross for bravery in the Second World War stood up with an ashen face. Rao Farman Ali stared at him.

"I'm going to Mirpur bridge," said General Jamshed.

"What for?" asked Admiral Sharif.

"To surrender," replied General Jamshed curtly. "I shall give General Nagra a courteous reception and bring him back here."

"I see."

"I can think of no alternative. Can any of you?"

Nobody answered.

Two vehicles rumbled along the roads of Dhaka early in the morning of 16th December. A thick mist was hanging over the city. A curfew was still in force and the streets were totally empty. The vehicles were heading for the headquarters of Pakistan Eastern Command. The first vehicle was a jeep, with Major General Jamshed sitting in it. The second was a staff car with a flag flying above it. Inside were Major General Nagra and Bangabir Kader Siddiqui. With his flowing hair and beard Kader Siddiqui resembled Che Guevara.

Niazi was waiting at headquarters. His wait ended when the door of his room opened and General Nagra came in. Niazi embraced Nagra, laid his head on his shoulder and started to weep bitterly. "It's the bastards in Rawalpindi who are responsible for this humiliation of mine," he moaned between sobs.

When Niazi had sufficiently overcome his emotion General Nagra introduced him to the man standing at his side. "Let me introduce you," he said quietly. "This is Tiger Siddiqui."

General Niazi and General Jamshed stared at Kader Siddiqui in amazement. It took some time for their astonishment to wane. Finally Niazi held out his hand to Kader Siddiqui.

Kader Siddiqui did not take Niazi's proffered hand. To the surprise of all present he announced in English, "I do not shake hands with the murderers of women and children."

Tiger Niazi waited for an Indian representative to arrive with instructions. To whom would he have to formally surrender, he wondered. What would be the terms of surrender? Where would the ceremony take place? He had heard that Lieutenant General Jacob was on his way to Dhaka by helicopter to arrange the whole process. Niazi couldn't work out whether he ought to go to the airport to receive General Jacob in person or send somebody else, and if so who.

Rumour had it that Lieutenant General Aurora was going to sign the deed of surrender on behalf of the Indian armed forces. And General Aurora was bringing his wife with him. It seemed she couldn't bear to miss the chance of seeing such an extraordinary event take place. When would Aurora arrive? Should he arrange lunch for him and his entourage? What kind of menu would be appropriate? Tiger Niazi's head was filled with all these minor concerns.

General Niazi signed the document of surrender at a ceremony on the open green of Dhaka racecourse. He removed his pistol from the holster on his belt and handed it over to Lieutenant General Aurora. The time was nineteen minutes past four p.m.

At that moment I, the author, was at a house in Jhigatola on the west side of Dhaka city, where I had been in hiding. My younger brother Mohammed Zafar Iqbal was also in Dhaka, but I didn't know that; I didn't even know whether he was still alive. With me in the one storey corrugated iron roofed bungalow in Jhigatola was my close friend Anis Sabet. A couple of years senior to me, he was one of the best and noblest individuals I have ever met. Let me say a few words about what we did on that special 16th December.

It suddenly seemed we had gone mad. Our world had turned upside down. An insistent buzzing like a cicada's stridulating call was filling our ears, deafening us. Anis Sabet threw himself down on the ground in front of the house and tossed to and fro as if in agony, weeping loudly as he did so.

I pulled him up onto his feet, and he said, "Come on, let's go out into the streets!" A moment earlier he had been crying, now he was laughing. We went out into the road and started running aimlessly. Anis was holding onto me with one firm hand as we ran.

Everyone in the city had come out of their homes, and people were acting crazy, doing whatever came into their heads, yelling, laughing, dancing, leaping all over the place. From time to time a deafening roar of 'Joy Bangla!' rent the air. There seemed to be a Bangladesh flag flying over every rooftop: I wondered where people could have been hiding their flags all this time.

When we reached the Jhigatola crossroads a crowd of people made us stop. They were obviously scared and they told us not to cross the main road, as a group of Biharis marooned in a nearby building were firing out of their upstairs windows at people in the street. "Oh, who cares about them!" said Anis. "Come on, Humayun, let's keep going!" So we continued on our way, entering a side road. Seeing us many others also plucked up courage and moved on.

When we had got as far as the Science Laboratory Anis stopped to buy two packets of biscuits. At that time I was penniless, and Anis was the one who controlled our budget. We hadn't eaten anything all day and were ravenous. I looked at Anis and said, "You know, I could manage a dish of pulao!"

"Of course!" said Anis. "We'll have some pulao! Pulao, pulao!" And we kept shouting "pulao! pulao!" like a couple of madmen. Passers by stared at us, but nobody was at all put out. Then we saw a rickshaw approaching. The occupant, a middle aged man, was standing in a precarious position on the passenger seat and rhythmically, almost devotionally chanting "Joy Bangla! Joy Bangla! Joy Bangla!" non-stop. Anis started crumbling the biscuits from his packet and I did the same; we marched along sprinkling biscuit crumbs left and right as we went. We had no idea where we were going. This was a day without any specific goal.

But enough of personal memories. I must return to the story.

A Bangladesh flag was flying over Moriam's family home. Moriam was wearing her wedding sari. She was a tiny bit upset because the sari had got a stain on it. She herself had splashed a drop of gravy onto it while cooking, and all her efforts to wash it off had been unsuccessful. And the stain was in such a place, there was no way of concealing it.

Moriam was sitting near the bottom of the stairs. She had had nothing to eat all day, though a great deal of food had been cooked, including various little extras like very thinly sliced potato fries and a thick pulp made with fire-scorched tomatoes. Those last two items were things Naimul particularly liked. Moriam had also made a chicken and new potato curry.

Her mother and sisters kept coming up to Moriam and begging her to have something to eat. This annoyed Moriam. It wasn't as if she was on hunger strike and needed persuasion to break her fast; no, she was quite ready to eat, when the time came.

Naimul had promised he would return on the day Bangladesh became independent. Moriam knew Naimul would keep his word. It might not be until late at night, but he would return; he would be standing there in front of the house, and he would call out in his solemn voice, "Mori! I've come home! Some people may not keep their promises, but I'm Naimul, I always keep my word!" And very likely he would also croon that English song about Annabel Lee or whoever it was.

When darkness had fallen Safiya came and took Moriam by the hand. "Darling," she said softly, "how long are you going to stay sitting here?"

"Mum," replied Moriam, "you can take my word for it, I'm going to stay sitting here until he comes."

At one o'clock in the morning Moriam was still sitting there, now with a sister on each side hugging her tightly.

"Go to bed now, you two," said Moriam eventually. "I shall sit here on my own."

"Why should you be on your own?" pleaded the youngest sister in a pained voice. "Let us sit here with you."

"No," said Moriam quite firmly. The other two got up and went away.

Hours passed. There! The figure of a young man with wild hair and beard was standing in front of the house in the early morning mist.

"That girl sitting at the bottom of the stairs," came his grave voice, "do I know her?" And the tall young man stood there with open arms.

"Mother! Look who's come!" screeched Moriam. "Look! Look who's come!"

Instantly Moriam was hugging him, rubbing her face avidly all over his chest

"Hey!" she laughed, "what do you mean embracing me like that, in front of everyone! Let go, naughty! I feel so embarrassed!"

Yet Naimul wasn't embracing his wife, his arms were still spread in readiness. The one who was doing all the hugging was Moriam herself.

Gentle reader, a story which concludes on our glorious Victory Day ought to have a happy ending, which is why I have concocted this final scene of joyful reunion..

But the real ending was not like that. Naimul did not keep his word. He was unable to return to the arms of his loving wife. His body lies buried somewhere in the great alluvial plain of East Bengal, and nobody knows where. His is but one of the countless unknown graves of fallen freedom fighters. That is good: let the soil of the motherland proudly embrace the mortal remains of her heroic sons. On moonlit nights beautiful patterns are traced on their graves, and a sad and solemn voice whispers, "Alas, my darlings!"

NOTES

page

5 Ratneswari
An unmistakeably Hindu name. In this way the author reveals that the family is a Hindu one. This explains why Ratneswari's father is nervous of an orthodox-looking Muslim like Irtazuddin, and why he does not return his *salaam*.

6 Awami League
Political party founded by Moulana Bhashani and other former members of the Muslim League in 1949, not long after the emergence of Pakistan. Its original name was All Pakistan Awami Muslim League; this was shortened to Awami League in 1953. Its early leaders were Moulana Bhashani and Shaheed Suhrawardy. Bhashani left the Awami League in 1958 to set up his National Awami Party. Suhrawardy died in 1963, after which his disciple Sheikh Mujibur Rahman became the undisputed leader of the party.

Bhutto
Zulfiqar Ali Bhutto (1928-1979), founder and leader of the Pakistan People's Party which was operative exclusively in West Pakistan.

seats
In the 1970 elections Sheikh Mujib's Awami League won 160 out of 162 of the parliamentary seats reserved for East Pakistan, plus all seven of the seats set aside for women, giving him an absolute majority in the Pakistan national assembly. Bhutto's party won 81 out of the 138 seats belonging to West Pakistan.

11 Sheikh Mujibur Rahman
Sheikh Mujibur Rahman (1920-1975) was the most prominent and popular politician in East Pakistan from 1963 onwards. After the collapse of the Agartala conspiracy trial, in which he had been the chief defendant, he led the Awami League to a landslide victory in the 1970 general elections. His election promise was to secure autonomy (not independence) for East Pakistan.

12 Joy Bangla, Joy Hind
Joy means victory, *Bangla* means Bengal (and also Bengali, the language). "*Joy Bangla*" became a rallying cry at Sheikh Mujibur Rahman's political meetings when regional autonomy was the main topic. It was then adopted as the war cry for the independence movement. It is still chanted at all kinds of political meetings and national celebrations. In the final years of British rule *Joy Hind* (or in standard transcription *Jay Hind*) had been the rallying cry of the Indian independence movement, but had been eschewed by those Indian Muslims who wished for a separate independent Muslim state.

15 Moulana Bhashani
Abdul Hamid Khan Bhashani (1880-1976), founder and leader of the National Awami Party. Bhashani had been the founder and first president of the Awami League, but later disagreed with its leader Shaheed Suhrawardy on basic policy matters (Suhrawardy was committed to the idea of a unified Pakistan, Bhashani wanted autonomy for the East wing) and left the AL to set up the NAP in 1958. His foresight in predicting a separate destiny for East Pakistan is referred to in his 1971 speech quoted on page 81. Bhashani acquired the religious title of Moulana because he was a devout Muslim who

351

had graduated from the Islamic academy at Deoband and was well versed in the teachings of the Quran and the Hadith. He was the only politician of his era whose educational background was non-colonial and who consistently fought for the interests of the ordinary peasants and workers of East Bengal.

17 **Murshidabad**
Murshidabad District in West Bengal lies between Bangladesh and Bihar. Shahed's boss Moin Arafi is a man of Bihari origin, not a Bengali.

Partition
When British rule over India came to an end in 1947 two separate independent states emerged: India (sometimes referred to as Hindustan), the majority of whose citizens were Hindus, and Pakistan with a majority population of Muslims. This political and territorial splitting of the former British colony is generally known as 'Partition'. It was accompanied by communal riots and large scale migration of Hindus from Pakistan and Muslims from Hindustan.

18 **Rage Kumar**
A play on the name of the legendary Indian film star Raj Kumar. In Bengali Asmani says *Rag Kumar* ('Anger Kumar').

21 **tui, apni**
In Bengali there are three modes for addressing another person, three ways of saying "you". *Apni* is the polite form, used to address a person of higher status than oneself, or a stranger; *tumi* is the familiar form, used to address a person of lower status than oneself, or someone with whom one has a bond of affection; *tui* is the intimate form, similar to *tumi* but implying a total absence of respect. *Tui* can be used mutually by very close friends, or by a parent to a child, but (unlike *tumi*) not by a child to a parent. Here, the still tenuous relationship between Gourango and Shahed does not justify the use of *tui*, but Gourango is too blinded by sentiment to appreciate this fact.

22 **Noy Bangla**
Noy means 'it is not'. The cynical Mr Dewan is suggesting "It is not Bengal" as an alternative to "Victory for Bengal".

23 **rasagolla**
A popular Bengali dessert item consisting of compacted balls of milk curd, slightly fortified with semolina and flavoured with cardamom, stewed in a thick sugary syrup. Sweetmeats of this kind are often brought as an offering when visiting someone else's home.

Moron Chand
Moron Chand Ghose, a long established Hindu confectioner's shop in Nawabpur Road, Old Dhaka, which at the time of this story was considered the best of its kind in the city.

Ittefaq
A respected Bengali language newspaper established in 1953 by Moulana Bhashani and Yar Mohammed Khan as a mouthpiece for their political party, the Awami League. It originally came out only once a week but soon became a daily paper. It is still in production today. *Ittifaq* is an Arabic word, used also in Urdu, meaning 'agreement' or 'concord'.

Rabindranath Tagore
Rabindranath Tagore (1861-1941), the best known and most highly revered of all Bengali poets, who also wrote plays, novels and short stories and composed numerous songs which form a special genre of their own.

24 **Saha**
Saha is the surname of a Hindu subcaste, typically small traders.

29 **Tagore songs**
Songs written by the poet Rabindranath Tagore (see note for page 32 above). Rabindranath was not an orthodox Hindu, but a member of the Brahma Samaj, some of whose doctrines and rituals were influenced by Christianity. His work is very highly esteemed by Bengalis of all political and religious persuasions. In 1967, in a narrow-minded move to eliminate so-called 'Hindu influence' the Pakistan government announced a ban on the transmission of Tagore songs on state radio. This contributed to the upsurge of Bengali nationalist feeling at that time, which fuelled Sheikh Mujib's campaign for regional autonomy.

Nazrul Islam
Kazi Nazrul Islam (1899-1976), the 'rebel poet', a most distinguished Muslim Bengali poet and song-writer.

Ayub Khan
Ayub Khan (1907-1974), Pakistan army general appointed chief martial law administrator in 1958, who then usurped Iskandar Mirza as president of Pakistan. As a benevolent dictator and shrewd player of international politics he brought stability and increased prosperity to the country and enhanced Pakistan's international standing. However neglect of East Pakistan's specific needs gave rise to steadily escalating discontent which eventually toppled his regime.

Fatima Jinnah
Fatima Jinnah (1893-1967) was the youngest sister of Muhammad Ali Jinnah (1876-1948), the statesman generally regarded as the founder of Pakistan. She was persuaded to stand in the 1964 presidential elections in opposition to Ayub Khan, the incumbent candidate, but lost to him.

points
The reference is to Sheikh Mujibur Rahman's famous 'Six Point Demand' of 1966 and the 'Eleven Point Demand' put forward by his supporters in early 1969. The demands all concerned autonomy for East Pakistan.

Agartala conspiracy
An alleged conspiracy involving Awami League politicians and others to mount an armed insurgency, backed by India, leading to the break-up of Pakistan. The supposed ringleader Sheikh Mujibur Rahman and other alleged conspirators were arrested by the Pakistan authorities in 1966. They were put on trial in 1968, but this provoked enormous unrest throughout East Pakistan. In early 1969 the trial had to be abandoned and the then president of Pakistan, Ayub Khan, was forced to resign. He handed over power to the Pakistan Army and General Yahya Khan became the new president.

30 **Asaduzzaman**
Amanullah Mohammed Asaduzzaman (1942-1969) was a student political activist shot dead by police in 1969 while demonstrating against Ayub Khan's regime and demanding the release of Sheikh Mujibur Rahman and the other alleged Agartala conspirators. His death further inflamed the general public unrest.

34 **Suhrawardy**
Huseyn Shaheed Suhrawardy (1892-1963), prominent Bengali Muslim politician. Before partition he was involved with the Muslim League in the movement to create a separate independent Muslim state. After partition he joined Moulana Bhashani's Pakistan Awami Muslim League (later known as the Awami League). He was for a while Prime Minister of Pakistan (1956-

1957). He was the political mentor of Sheikh Mujibur Rahman, but not in favour of provincial autonomy. Note his daughter's opposition to the independence movement (page 209).
Purnea District
Purnea District is in Bihar, a state in India contiguous to West Bengal. Many Muslim Biharis migrated to East Pakistan after partition. Most of them sided with the Pakistan government and army during the liberation war in 1971. When Bangladesh became independent some Biharis fled to the rump of Pakistan, others were interned in concentration camps.

36 **Shokhina**
Shokhina Khatun was a heroine of the liberation war, credited with having killed five pro-government *razakars* by herself. The reference here appears to be an anachronism, as she was unknown before the start of the war.

47 **Iqbal Hall**
A residential unit of Dhaka University.
Shah Kolim
Shah is a title applied to Muslim saints, and also used by ordinary Muslims claiming descent from one.

48 **Shamsur Rahman**
Shamsur Rahman (1929-2006), one of the foremost poets of East Pakistan and subsequently of Bangladesh.
Sukanta
Sukanta Bhattacharya (1926-1947), Bengali poet.

49 **Asad's Shirt**
This well known poem was written by Shamsur Rahman in memory of the activist Asaduzzaman (see note for page 30 above).

75 **Mori**
Mori in Bengali means 'I die'.

98 **sweepers**
The sanitation workers employed by Dhaka Municipality were low caste non-Bengali Hindus. Their occupation was hereditary. Their main function was to empty cesspits and clear garbage in the old city, though they were generally referred to as 'sweepers'. They were housed in purpose built 'colonies' or sets of apartment blocks owned by the municipality. The corporation garbage dump was situated at Dhalpur, outside the old city.

109 **Abdul Qadir Jilani**
Abdul Qadir Jilani ("Boro Pir"), a Muslim mystic saint active in Baghdad in the twelfth century and highly revered by many Bengali Muslims.

114 **Tarasangkar**
Tarasangkar Bandopadhyay (1898-1971), West Bengali novelist.

118 **Yunus**
Yunus is the biblical prophet Jonah, noted for his unshakeable faith. For more detail about the Yunus prayer, see page 149-150 of the novel.

119 **Shahid Minar**
The original Shahid Minar, or Martyrs' Monument, was built in the Nilkhet area of Dhaka city, close to the university, as a memorial to student activists who had been shot by police while campaigning for the recognition of Bengali as a national language of Pakistan in February 1952. The campaign was ultimately successful. The slaughtered activists have ever since been referred to as the language martyrs, and Language Martyrs' Day is observed

on 21st February every year. Nowadays there is a local Shahid Minar in every town.

120 **Major Zia**
Ziaur Rahman (1936-1981) was a major in the Pakistan army when the crackdown took place. Like most other Bengali servicemen posted in East Pakistan at that time he deserted from the Pakistan military and joined the embryonic Bangladesh liberation army. He became one of the chief figures in that force. After the liberation of Bangladesh he continued his career in the newly established Bangladesh army but retained an interest in political events. Disenchanted with Sheikh Mujibur Rahman's style of government, he joined in a military coup which arranged the assassination of Sheikh Mujib in August 1975. A counter-coup led by Brigadier Khaled Mosharraf (see note for page 251 below) was swiftly put down. Ziaur Rahman founded the Bangladesh Nationalist Party and became president of Bangladesh in 1977. He was assassinated in another military coup four years later.

127 **Major Siddiq Salik**
Siddiq Salik was the Public Relations Officer of the Pakistan armed services during the occupation of East Pakistan in 1971. Later he wrote, in Urdu, his own account of his experiences in that rôle, *Main ne Dhaka Dubte Dekha* ('I Saw Dhaka Sinking'), translated into English as *Witness to Surrender*. The book was used as a source by the present author (see his footnote on page 90).

139 **Begum Sufia Kamal**
Begum Sufia Kamal (1911-1999) was a prominent champion of democracy and of women's rights who spoke out against various oppressive measures adopted by the Pakistan government.
Nilima Ibrahim
Nilima Ibrahim (1921-2002), professor of Bengali, literary critic and novelist, also protested against oppressive policies of the Pakistan government.

141 **Procession for Peace**
Demonstrations in support of Yahya Khan's government and its military action in East Pakistan were organized by certain parties who opposed Sheikh Mujib and his plans for regional autonomy. Although condoning genocide these rallies were given the euphemistic title of *shanti misil* or 'peace demonstrations'. The names mentioned are those of well known figures who collaborated with the regime.
Ghulam Azam
Ghulam Azam (1922-2014) was the Ameer or leader of the Islamist party Jamaat-e-Islami in East Pakistan. He and his organization opposed the independence movement and cooperated fully with the Pakistan authorities in their efforts to crush it. He played an active rôle in setting up the Peace Committees (see note for page 216 below) and the network of *razakar* volunteers who collaborated with the military regime. The notorious paramilitary Al-Badar brigades (see note for page 293 below) were organized by the Jamaat-e-Islami with Azam's blessing. When Bangladesh became independent Azam fled into exile, living mainly in England, but continued to campaign for the reinstatement of Pakistani rule in East Bengal. In 1978 the government of Ziaur Rahman allowed him to return to Bangladesh and resume de facto leadership of Jamaat-e-Islami, which had been banned since 1972. In 2012, under an Awami

League government, he was finally tried by a war crimes tribunal and found guilty on several counts. He was spared the death sentence on account of his age and failing health.

142 **Jibonananda**
Jibonananda Das (1899-1954), Bengali poet who celebrated the natural beauty of Bengal.

160 **Ram and Laksman**
Rama, whose name is pronounced 'ram' in Bengali, was the mythical hero of the Hindu scriptural epic the Ramayana. Laksmana (in Bengal often written Laksman, actually pronounced 'lokkon') was his brother. The English word *rum* is also pronounced 'ram' in Bengali. Thus Gourango's thoughts wander from rum to Rama and thence to Laksmana.

171 **Atatul Kursi**
The 'verse of the throne', a verse in the second surah of the Quran which describes God and is held in great reverence by most Muslims. Many believe that reciting it, either mentally or aloud, will afford divine protection from evil.

Jonah
See note for page 118 above.

Colonel Jamshed
Jamshed Gulzar Kiani (at that time a captain, later a distinguished general) served as an army intelligence officer in Dhaka for a period during 1971. The character of Colonel Jamshed in the novel was possibly named after him.

177 **Jamaat-e-Islami**
The main Islamist political party in Pakistan. It still exists.

189 **malaun**
A corruption of the Arabic word *mal'ūn* meaning 'cursed' or 'accursed one'. This highly derogatory term is sometimes used by a Muslim to insult a Hindu.

O.C.
Officer in Charge – the usual title for the officer in charge of a police station.

190 **Komola**
Irtazuddin remembered that the young woman's name referred to a fruit. *Komola* is the word for an orange or similar citrus fruit in Bengali.

209 **Huseyn Shaheed Suhrawardy**
See note for page 34 above.

211 **razakar**
In pursuance of the martial law provision quoted here, a loose network of civilian vigilantes was set up in all areas of East Pakistan under government control. Their main task was to act as informants, bringing any suspected anti-state activity to the attention of the military, but they were also provided with arms and allowed to use them for offensive purposes. Thus any individual willing to collaborate with the authorities found a golden opportunity to settle scores with his personal enemies. A large number of innocent civilians were killed either directly by these vigilantes or by the Pakistan army after being denounced by them.

216 **Peace Committees**
All over Bangladesh those opponents of the independence movement who were willing to collaborate with the military authorities were organized into local Peace Committees. Their rôle was to gather intelligence for the

army and report anyone involved in anti-government activities. Innumerable Awami League supporters and others who sympathized with the independence movement, as well as those actively involved in it, were betrayed in this way, to be seized, tortured and killed.

Al-Badar brigades
See note for page 293 below.

221 **Shahid Minar, G.C. Dev, Iqbal Hall**
Nirmalendu Goon was visiting the sites of particular atrocities committed by the Pakistan army during the initial crackdown. The Shahid Minar (monument to Bengali language martyrs) had been razed to the ground. Professor G.C. Dev was one of the intellectuals sought out and murdered in cold blood on the night of the crackdown. Iqbal Hall (a residential unit of Dhaka University) was where a large number of students had been massacred during the same night.

222 **khatm-e-Yunus**
A series of repetitions of the 'Yunus prayer', *la ilaha illa anta subhanaka inni kuntu minaz zalimin*, customarily 125,000 times in total, performed as a penance in order to obtain deliverance from any kind of perilous situation.

244 **Ataul Goni Osmani**
Mohammed Ataul Gani Osmani (1918-1984) had served in the British Indian army and Pakistan army, reaching the rank of colonel, before retiring in 1967. He joined the Awami League and stood in the 1970 elections. Following the Pakistan army clampdown he was appointed commander-in-chief of the Bangladesh liberation forces.

Kazi Nazrul Islam
See note for page 29 above. At the time of the Bangladesh liberation war he was living in Calcutta. When Bangladesh became independent he moved to Dhaka as a protégé of the new state, and he remained there until his death five years later.

Munier Chowdhury
Munier Chowdhury (1925-1971), talented linguist and writer, lecturer in Bengali and English at Dhaka University. He played an important rôle in the Bengali language movement of 1952 and in the protest against the Radio Pakistan ban on Tagore songs in 1967. Along with a number of other prominent intellectuals he was abducted and murdered by the Pakistan army on 14th December 1971, scarcely forty-eight hours before the moment of Liberation.

Ranada Prasad Saha
R.P. Saha (1896-1971), successful Hindu entrepreneur of humble origins who became the most noted philanthropist in East Bengal. He founded the Kumudini Hospital, the Bharateswari Homes and the Kumudini Welfare Trust, all of which are still in operation. He and his son were detained by the martial authorities in April 1971. They were released after a couple of weeks but then taken back into army custody, never to be seen again.

Zainal Abedin
Zainal Abedin (1914-1976), an artist originally based in Calcutta and famous for his shocking and starkly realistic sketches of destitute people during the great Bengal Famine of 1943. After partition he moved to Dhaka where he founded the Institute of Fine Arts and championed painting as an art form.

250 **Agartala conspiracy case**
See note for page 29 above.
251 **Khaled Mosharraf**
Khaled Mosharraf (1937-1975) was a major in the Pakistan army at the time of the crackdown in East Pakistan. He immediately joined the liberation movement, becoming one of the sector commanders of the official liberation army. After Bangladesh had achieved independence he served in its regular army, rising to the rank of brigadier. Khaled Mosharraf was opposed to the military coup of August 1975 in which Sheikh Mujib was assassinated; he mounted a counter-coup three months later, but this was swiftly suppressed by associates of the man behind the first coup, Brigadier Ziaur Rahman. Khaled Mosharraf was killed and Ziaur Rahman went on to become President of Bangladesh.
Begum Jahanara Imam
Jahanara Imam (1929-1994), educationist and active promoter of girls' education, who lost her elder son and her husband in the troubles of 1971. For her efforts to gain proper recognition for the rôle played by freedom fighters and to keep their memory alive she was dubbed *Shahid Jononi* or 'Mother of Martyrs'. In 1978, when President Ziaur Rahman rehabilitated the most notorious war criminal Ghulam Azam for reasons of party political convenience, Jahanara Imam led public protests and set up a symbolic 'people's court' to examine his alleged war crimes. Her diary of the events of 1971, *Ekattorer Din-guli* ('The Days of 1971'), was published in 1986 and helped to revive public awareness of that period.
Rumi
Shafi Imam 'Rumi' (1951-1971), a student, enrolled in the official liberation army, trained in the Agartala area and went on to serve with distinction in the 'Crack Platoon' mentioned by the author, which harassed the Pakistan army within Dhaka city. Rumi, his younger brother and his father were all apprehended by Pakistan forces in August 1971 as a result of a tip-off. Rumi was tortured and killed. His father was tortured and released, but died shortly afterwards.
253 **Hasina**
Sheikh Hasina Wazed (1947-), elder daughter of Sheikh Mujib, later leader of the Awami League and sometime prime minister of Bangladesh.
Begum Sufia Kamal
See note for page 139 above.
281 **Bir Shrestha**
After Bangladesh had achieved independence the Bangladesh government compiled lists of those people who had fought in various different regular and paramilitary brigades in the war of liberation, and set up a system of decorations for bravery. There were four levels of award, Bir Shrestha, Bir Uttam, Bir Bikram and Bir Pratik. A list of the recipients of these honours was appended to the first edition of *Josna o Jononir Golpo*. There were only seven Bir Shrestha, all of whom were members of the regular armed forces. There were 68 Bir Uttam, 175 Bir Bikram and 426 Bir Pratik.
282 **Ziaur Rahman**
See note for page 120 above.
293 **Al-Badar brigades**
The paramilitary Al-Badar (or more correctly Al-Badr) organization was founded by members of the Jamaat-e-Islami party with the theoretical aim of promoting a truly Islamic way of life in East Pakistan. In practice the Al-

Badar brigades acted as a cat's paw for the Pakistan army and indulged in cruel persecution of anyone perceived as an enemy of Pakistan or an infidel. The Al-Badar gained a reputation for extreme ruthlessness and were greatly feared by civilians.

299 **Abdul Hamid Khan Bhashani**
See note for page 15 above.
Tajuddin Ahmad
Tajuddin Ahmad (1925-1975), one of Sheikh Mujibur Rahman's Awami League stalwarts, was instrumental in organizing and leading the Provisional Bangladesh Government in exile. He had the post of prime minister. Along with others of Sheikh Mujib's close associates he was arrested during the coup of August 1975, and murdered in jail.

301 **786**
786 is a number considered auspicious by some Muslims and often placed at the head of documents.

327 **Bir Bikram**
See note for page 281 above.
Mujibnagar
Mujibnagar was the name given to the place where the Provisional Bangladesh Government, or government in exile, was initially set up. This was a village in Kushtia District previously known as Baidyanathtala. The government in exile is often referred to as the Mujibnagar Government.

329 **Liaquat Ali Khan**
Liaquat Ali Khan (1895-1951), the first prime minister of Pakistan.
Iqbal
Muhammad Iqbal (1877-1938), a highly revered Indian Muslim poet who wrote in both Persian and Urdu. He was also an influential political thinker. In 1930 he put forward the idea that the Muslims of India constituted a nation of their own, which merited a separate system of governance. This "two nation theory" was later used by proponents of a separate state for Muslims.

GLOSSARY

adhan – Muslim call to prayer (Arabic *'aðān*) (pronounced *azan* in Bengali)
al-Badar – name of an Islamist paramilitary organization (Arabic *al-badr* = the full moon) (pronounced *al bodor* in Bengali)
alhamdulillah – 'praise to God' (Arabic *al-ḥamdu li l-lāhi*)
Allah – The Deity; God (Arabic *al-lāhu*)
Allahu – 'O God' (pronounced this way when calling directly to God in the vocative)
al-Shams – name of an Islamist paramilitary organization (Arabic *al-šams* = the sun)
apni – you (respectful form, like French *vous*)
Asharh – the third Bengali month (June-July) (rainy season)
Ashwin – the sixth Bengali month (September-October)
asr – late afternoon; one of the prescribed daily prayer times (Arabic *'aṣr*) (pronounced *asor* in Bengali)
as-salaamu alaikum – 'peace upon you'; the usual Muslim greeting (Arabic *al-salāmu 'alaikum*)
astaghfirullah – 'I seek pardon from God'; an expression of contrition or alarm (Arabic *'astaġfiru l-lāha*)
ayat – verse (of the Quran) (Arabic *'ayāh*)
ayatul kursi – 'the verse of the throne'; a verse of the Quran [2:225] which describes God; reciting it is considered by many Muslims as a way to obtain divine protection
Azrael – the name of the angel who visits humans to announce their imminent death
babu – father; respectful term for addressing a Hindu man
baby taxi – a kind of small open-sided taxi built on a motor scooter base
bahini – brigade, battalion, militia
Baisakh – the first Bengali month (April-May)
Bangal mulk – the land of Bengal (Urdu equivalent of '*Bangla desh*')
Bangabandhu – 'friend of Bengal', special title for Sheikh Mujibur Rahman
Bangabir – 'hero of Bengal', popular title for certain prominent liberation war heroes
Bangla – Bengal; Bengali (language)
Bangla desh – the land of Bengal
bari – homestead; ancestral village home
beai – father-in-law of one's son or daughter
betel leaf – leaf of the pepper vine *Piper betle*, chewed with betelnut as a stimulant (called *paan* in Bengali)
betelnut – the nut of the areca palm *Areca catechu*, chewed with betel leaf
bhabi – the wife of a *bhai*
bhai – brother; male cousin of same generation; social 'brother' like English 'mate'
bhai jan – respected elder brother
bharta – a savoury mash made with any vegetable, chopped raw onion and oil or ghee (pronounced *bhorta* in Bengali)
bhuna – a curry with a thick sauce
bidi – miniature conical cigar made with shredded tobacco rolled up in a tobacco leaf (pronounced *biri* in Bengali)
bir – hero (Sanskrit *vīra*)

birokto – bothered, annoyed, put out of mood
biryani – savoury dish of rice and meat cooked together (Persian *biryānī* = roast dish)
burqa – hood-like garment worn by some Muslim women to conceal their hair and face in public (Arabic *burquʻ*)
bou ma – 'mother bride'; affectionate term for addressing a daughter-in-law
chacha – uncle, in the sense of father's brother or father's bhai
Chaitra – the twelfth and last Bengali month (March-April)
Chakma – minority ethnic group related to certain Burmese tribes
chatim – large evergreen tree with horizontal branches, *Alstonia scholaris*, also known as the devil tree
chokh gelo – 'the eye went', common name for the hawk-cuckoo or brain fever bird *Cuculus varius*, whose three syllable call sounds like 'chokh gelo' or 'brain fever'
chorompotro – 'ultimatum'; name of a radio drama glorifying the liberation movement, beamed into Bangladesh from India
dab – the unripe fruit of the coconut palm, the liquid from inside which is much regarded as a health-giving drink
dacoit – armed robber
dal – leguminous seeds, pulses like lentils; the kinds of pottage or broth made from them are a basic element of the typical Bengali diet
daroga – senior police officer; officer in command of a police station
dhoti – traditional Indian male raiment; a kind of legging formed with a broad strip of white cotton wound in a specific way
dhul qarnain – 'owner of the two horns'; an epithet applied to Alexander the Great by ancient Arab historians (Arabic *ðū l-qarnaina*)
enegra – corruption of the trade name of a type of grenade, the Energa grenade
fajr – dawn; one of the prescribed daily prayer times (Arabic *fajr*) (pronounced *fozor* in Bengali)
ghee – semi-liquid clarified butter
hafiz – one who has memorized the entire Quran (Arabic *ḥāfiż* = keeper)
hafiziya – (madrasah) devoted to training students to become *hafiz*
haji – title for anyone who has performed the Hajj pilgrimage
hajj – the prescribed pilgrimage to Mecca (Arabic *ḥajj*) (pronounced *hoj* or *hoz* in Bengali)
haqqul ibada – 'true reality of worship'; piety in practice (Arabic *ḥaqqu l-ʻibāda*) (pronounced *hokkul ibadot* in Bengali)
hasnahena – an evergreen shrub, *Cestrum nocturnum*, with sweet scented flowers
hilsa – a species of fish, *Hilsa ilisha*, highly prized as food
houri – celestial maiden (Arabic *ḥūriya*)
ibada – worship (Arabic *ʻibāda*) (pronounced *ibadot* in Bengali)
iftar – food taken to break a fast (Arabic *ʼiftār* = opening)
imam – leader of congregational prayers, who stands in front of the rest of the congregation (Arabic *ʼimām* = leader)
inshallah – 'if God wishes'; customary qualification of any statement about the future, similar to *deo volente* (Arabic *ʼin šaʻa l-lāhu*)
istikhara – a special prayer for enlightenment (Arabic *istiḳāra* = request for good)
jaggery – a kind of unrefined brown sugar made from palm sap or sugar cane juice (called *gur* in Bengali)
janaza – funeral (Arabic *janāza*) (usually pronounce *jonoja* in Bengali)

jhal – spicy hot
jinn – a type of being similar to a human but usually invisible, in Muslim belief (Arabic *jinn*) (sometimes spelt 'djinn' in English)
joy – victory (Sanskrit *jaya*)
joy bangla – 'victory to Bengal'; Bengali nationalist rallying cry
juma – of or relating to congregational prayers; Friday, the congregational prayer day (Arabic *jum'a*) (pronounced *jum-ma* in Bengali)
Jyaistha – the second Bengali month (May-June)
kacchi biryani – a dish of rice cooked together with mutton, onions and spices; a type of biryani particularly associated with Dhaka
kadamba – a tall tree with straight trunk bearing yellow bobble flowers in summer, *Anthocephalus cadamba*
kalijira – a superior type of rice with a sweet flavour
kalima – Muslim declaration of faith in standard form (Arabic *kalima* = word; saying) (pronounced *kolima* in Bengali)
kalima tayyib – the first and shortest of the four standard declarations of faith which is *la ilaha illallahu, muhammadur rasulullah* (in Arabic *lā ilāha illā l-lāhu muḥammadu l-rasūlu l-lāhi*) meaning 'there is no deity except The Deity, and Muhammad is the messenger of The Deity') (*tayyib*, meaning 'good', is pronounced *toyob* in Bengali)
kamranga – a tree, *Averrhoa carambola*, whose succulent fruit is known variously as carambola and star fruit
Kartik – the seventh Bengali month (October-November)
katla – a species of fish of the carp family, *Catla catla*
khadim – warden or attendant at a Muslim saint's shrine (Arabic *ḵādim* = servant)
khichuri – a dish of rice and pulses cooked together, with onions and oil
kobi – poet
koel – a type of cuckoo with black plumage which parasitizes crows, *Eudynamys scolopacea*
koi – a species of fish with spiny fins, *Anabas testudineus* (not related to Japanese koi carp)
korma – a meat curry made with onions and ginger but no pungent spices (Persian *qormeh* = preserved meat)
kurta – a loose knee-length tunic with long sleeves worn by males (the indigenous variety is usually called *panjabi* in Bengali)
la ilaha illa anta subhanaka inni kuntu minaz zalimin – the 'Yunus prayer' (q.v.)
la ilaha illallah – part of the first *kalima* (q.v.), meaning 'there is no deity except The Deity (Allah)' (Arabic *lā ilāha illā l-lāhu*)
lathi – police baton used for crowd control
lungi – a type of skirt worn by males throughout south east Asia
madrasah – Islamic school (Arabic *madrasa* = place of study)
maghrib – the place of the setting sun, the West; name of the dusk prayer (Arabic *maġrib*) (usually pronounced *mogrib* or *mugrib* in Bengali)
malaun – accursed one (Arabic *mal'ūn*)
mashallah – 'whatever God wishes'; common Muslim interjection, expressing satisfaction with providence (Arabic *mā šā'a l-lāhu*)
monda – a kind of sweetmeat made of curd cheese
moulana – title of respect given to men well versed in Islamic teachings (Arabic *maula-nā* = our lord)
muezzin – person who sings out the call to prayer in advance of each prayer session at a mosque (Arabic *mu'aḏḏin*) (pronounced *mu-ajjin* in Bengali)

mukti – freedom; sometimes also used as shorthand for *mukti bahini* (freedom army) or *mukti joddha* (freedom fighter)
muri – puffed rice, prepared like popcorn
nafl – optional (in reference to prayers) (Arabic *nafl*) (pronounced *nofol* in Bengali)
nagkeshar – 'snake's mane' or 'snake stamen'; the ironwood tree *Mesua ferrea*, which bears somewhat rose-like flowers
namaz – prayers, in the sense of prescribed prayer rituals (Persian *namāz*)
niyya – formal intention (a requisite prelude to all Muslim prayers) (Arabic *niyya*) (pronounced *niyot* in Bengali)
O.C. – officer in charge; specifically the police officer in charge of a police station
paan – betel leaf, or a preparation of sliced areca nut with catechu, slaked lime and sometimes tobacco or spices wrapped in a betel leaf ready for chewing
paijama – loose baggy ankle-length drawers, normally made of white cotton
pak sarzamin shadbad – 'for our sacred territory rejoicing'; first line of the Pakistan national anthem
Panjabi – a native of Panjab in western India/Pakistan (also spelt *Punjab*, *Punjabi*)
panjabi – loose knee-length cotton tunic with long sleeves; a kind of *kurta*
paratha – a flaky type of flatbread fried in ghee or oil (pronounced *porota* in Bengali)
partition – the division of what had been British India into two new states, India (also known as 'Bharat' and 'Hindustan') and Pakistan
Pathan – a native of the North West Frontier Province of Pakistan, ethnically and culturally identical to a Pakhtun/Pashtun of Afghanistan
paturi – a dish created by steaming filleted fish with mustard and rice inside a banana leaf wrapper
peshkar – court clerk
pir – title given to a venerable Islamic spiritual leader with psychic powers (Persian *pīr* = old man)
pranama – salutation (Sanskrit *praṇāma*) (pronounced *pronam* in Bengali)
pulao – savoury dish of delicately spiced fried rice which may include saffron, sultanas and nuts and is usually garnished with fried onions (Persian *pilav*)
Qaid-e-azam – great leader; title given to Muhammad Ali Jinnah, the founder of Pakistan (Urdu/Persian, from Arabic *qā'id* = leader, *a'ẓam* = very great)
rakat – a constituent unit of ritual in Muslim prayers, consisting of recitation, a bowing and two prostrations, which is repeated a specified number of times, minimum three, at every prayer session (Arabic *rak'a* = a bowing, plural *raka'āt*)
rasagolla – a popular Bengali sweetmeat consisting of balls of curd cheese stewed in a thick syrup (pronounced *rosho-gul-la* in Bengali)
razakar – civilian vigilantes sanctioned and armed by the Pakistan military authorities (Persian *rezākār* = volunteer) (sometimes also pronounced *rezakar* in Bengali)
rijek – corruption of the word *rizq*; the provision of daily sustenance, which in Muslim belief has been divinely ordained in advance (Arabic *rizq*)
ruhi – a species of fish of the carp family, *Labeo rohita*, prized as food
rumali chapati – a large, thin, floppy type of flatbread
S.D.O. – Subdivisional Officer; civil servant in charge of a geographical Subdivision
S.D.P.O. – Subdivisional Police Officer; police officer in overall charge of the police force in a Subdivision, covering a number of police stations

sab – shortened form of *sahib* (pronounced *shab* in Bengali)
sadhu – Hindu ascetic or holy man (Sanskrit *sādhu*)
sahib – master; respectful form for addressing a Muslim man (Arabic *ṣāḥib*)
sal – a deciduous forest tree, *Shorea robusta*, common in hilly country
salaam – Muslim salutation or greeting (Arabic *salām*)
salaam alaikum – 'peace upon you', the usual Muslim greeting (Arabic *salāmu 'alaikum*) (the form *as-salaamu alaikum* is also used)
sandesh – a sweetmeat made of compressed dried milk and sugar, often formed into an attractive shape with a mould (pronounced *shondesh* in Bengali)
sareng – foreman of a boat crew
seer – a traditional Indian measure of weight, about 0.933 of a kilogram
shadhin bangla – 'independent Bengal'; name of a temporary radio service during the 1971 war of liberation
shefali – a small tree with fragrant white flowers, *Nyctanthes arbortristis*, also known as coral jasmine
shimul – a tall deciduous tree, *Bombax malabaricum*, whose striking scarlet flowers appear in late winter while it is leafless; also known as the silk cotton tree
shinni – food shared out at the end of any Muslim ceremony (a corruption of the Persian word *shirīnī*, meaning sweetmeats)
shiuli – variant of the name for the *shefali* tree (q.v.)
Shrabon – the fourth Bengali month (July-August) (rainy season)
shukur – 'thanks' (Arabic *šukr*)
shukur alhamdulillah – 'thanks and praise to God'; phrase used by Muslims to express relief and satisfaction
slamalekum – corruption of *salaam alaikum* (q.v.)
subedar – non-commissioned officer rank, equivalent to sergeant
sudra – lowest class of Hindus, associated with menial occupations
Sufi – adherent of a Muslim mystic sect or movement
surah – chapter of the Quran (Arabic *sūra*)
surma – antimony, a black substance used cosmetically for lining the eye
tehsil – local revenue collection (Arabic *taḥṣīl* = acquisition) (pronounced *toshil* in Bengali)
tehsildar – revenue collector
thana – police station, or the area under the care of a police station
tarif – renown, good reputation; used in Urdu as a euphemism for 'name' (Arabic *ta`rīf*)
tasbih – the act of repeating the phrase *subhanallah* ('glory to God'); hence, a set of beads similar to a Catholic rosary comprising one bead for each of the ninety-nine names of Allah, used for repeatedly praising the deity (Arabic *tasbīḥ*) (pronounced *tosbi* in Bengali)
tauba – exclamation used by Muslims to express contrition, or distance themselves from an unpleasant proposition (Arabic *tauba* = repentance)
tola – jeweller's measure of weight, equal to 180 grains
tui – you (intimate, disrespectful form)
tumi – you (intimate form)
union – a group of villages; the lowest tier of civil administration, roughly equivalent to a parish
utar – antidote; enchanted water (local dialect, not standard Bengali)
wa alaikum salaam, wa alaikum as-salaam – the standard reply to the greeting *salaam alaikum* or *as-salaamu alaikum* (q.v.)

witr – uneven, referring to those prayers which comprise an uneven number of *rakat* (Arabic *witr* = uneven number) (pronounced *betor* in Bengali)

ya gafurur rahim – exclamation of surprise or alarm (Arabic *yā ġafūru l-raḥīm* = o Merciful Pardoner)

ya nafsi – exclamation uttered at moments of panic (Arabic *ya nafsī* = o my self)

Yunus – Jonah

Yunus prayer – words from the Quran [21:87] said to have been uttered by Jonah when swallowed by the whale: *la ilaha illa anta subhanaka inni kuntu minaz zalimin*, 'there is no deity but You, may your name be magnified, and I am one of those who have gone astray.' (Arabic *lā ilāha illā anta subḥānaka, innī kuntu mina l-ḍālimīn)*

zamindar – rural land estate owner (Persian *zamīndār*) (*jomidar* in Bengali)

zarda – yellowed tobacco leaf prepared for oral use (pronounce *jorda* in Bengali)

zindabad – state of being alive; 'long may he/she/it live' (Urdu) (usually pronounced *jindabad* in Bengali)

CHARACTERS IN THE STORY
(real historical figures in bold type)

Abdul Hamid Khan Bhashani – veteran populist politician of East Bengal, founder of both the Awami League and the National Awami Party
Abdul Motaleb Malik – civilian Governor of East Pakistan, appointed in August 1971
Amir Abdullah Khan Niazi – Pakistan army general in charge of Eastern Command, successor to Tikka Khan
Ashiya – wife of headmaster Monsur
Asmani – wife of Shahed, mother of Runi
Ayesha – wife of Foyzur Rahman, author's mother
Babu – nickname of Yahya, son of Mobarak Hussain
Bacchu – nickname of Foyzur Rahman's eldest son, the author
Bacchu Miah – servant of Kolimullah
Basit, Muhammad – Pakistan army captain stationed at Nilganj
Begum Fazilatunnessa Mujib – wife of Sheikh Mujibur Rahman
Bhai Pagla – a self-styled mystic who operates a clairvoyance service
Bhashani [see Abdul Hamid Khan Bhashani]
Bhutto [see Zulfiqar Ali Bhutto]
Dewan, Asgar Ali – head clerk at Shahed's office
Dhirendranath Ray Choudhury – a retired professor of Dhaka University
Foyzur Rahman – senior police officer, father of the author
Gul Hassan Khan – commander in chief of the Pakistan army
Gourango – work colleague and friend of Shahed
Haribhajan Shaha – Gourango's father-in-law
Harun Majhi – a notorious robber in the Nilganj area where Irtazuddin lived
Hussain [see Mobarak Hussain]
Irtazuddin Kashempuri – rural school teacher, brother of Shahed
Jaheda – Kumkum's mother, wife of Motaleb
Jamila – first wife of Mobarak Hussain
Jamshed, Colonel – Pakistan Army intelligence officer
Jamshed, General – Pakistan Army officer
Kader Siddiqui – famed freedom fighter who organized his own army in Tangail District
Kalipad – English teacher at Nilganj high school; a Hindu
Kashempuri [see Irtazuddin Kashempuri]
Khaled Mosharraf – a former Pakistan army major, sector commander of Bangladesh liberation army
Kolimullah – a would-be poet and a shameless opportunist
Komola – Sadrul Amin's wife
Kongkon – child in the house where Shahed sheltered on the night of the crackdown
Kumkum – Asmani's friend, whose parents sheltered Asmani in wartime
Mafruha – youngest daughter of Mobarak Hussain
Masuma – middle daughter of Mobarak Hussain
Misri Babu – proprietor of Nirala Hotel in Agartala
Mobarak Hussain – rough but honest Inspector of Police based in Dhaka city
Modhu – headmaster Monsur's servant and school janitor
Mohammed Ataul Gani Osmani – retired Pakistan army colonel, commander-in-chief of the Bangladesh liberation army

Moin Arafi – Shahed's boss ('Mr B.Happy'), a Bihari
Monowara – woman in whose house Shahed took shelter, mother of Kongkon
Monsur – headmaster of Nilganj High School where Irtazuddin teaches
Moriam – eldest daughter of Mobarak Hussain
Moslem Uddin Sarkar – Mobarak Hussain's maternal uncle
Motaleb – Kumkum's father
Moulana Bhashani [see Abdul Hamid Khan Bhashani]
Mujib [see Sheikh Mujibur Rahman]
Naimul – Shahed's best friend, brilliant student, husband of Moriam
Niazi [see Amir Abdullah Khan Niazi]
Nilima – Gourango's wife
Nirmalendu Goon – a noted poet
Osmani [see Mohammed Ataul Gani Osmani]
Quddus – loyal retainer of Sarfaraz Miah's family
Rashid – Foyzur Rahman's fan puller
Runi – daughter of Asmani and Shahed
Runu – daughter of Nilima and Gourango
Sadrul Amin – Police Inspector in charge of Nilganj Police Station
Safiya – second wife of Mobarak Hussain
Saghir Uddin – maths teacher at Nilganj high school
Sarfaraz Miah – retired police officer, father of Motaleb, grandfather of Asmani's friend Kumkum, at whose village home Asmani and Runi find temporary shelter
Shahed – office employee, resident in Dhaka; brother of Irtazuddin, husband of Asmani and father of Runi
Shah Kolim – *nom de plume* of Kolimullah
Shahrukh Khan – officer of the Pakistan Inter Services Intelligence corps
Shamsur Rahman – foremost poet of East Pakistan
Sheikh Mujibur Rahman – leader of the Awami League, champion of autonomy for East Pakistan
Siddiq Salik – wartime public relations officer for the Pakistan armed forces
Sobahan – head of the family which sheltered Shahed during the initial crackdown
Tikka Khan – Pakistan army general, head of Eastern Command, responsible for the brutal military crackdown in March 1971
Yahya – Mobarak Hussain's infant son
Yahya Khan – Pakistan army general, President of Pakistan
Zafar Iqbal – second son of Foyzur Rahman, author's brother
Ziaur Rahman – a former Pakistan army major, sector commander of Bangladesh liberation army
Zohar – intelligence officer working for the Pakistan military authorities, a Bihari
Zulfiqar Ali Bhutto – leader of the Pakistan People's Party, runner up in the 1970 general elections, rival of Sheikh Mujib in the race to form a national government

CHRONOLOGY

Important events leading up to the emergence of Bangladesh as a separate state

1947 Partition of India following end of British rule. Pakistan established, with Muslim League as its main political party..
1949 All Pakistan Awami Muslim League founded. Prominent members include Moulana Bhashani, Shaheed Suhrawardy and Sheikh Mujibur Rahman.
1952 Movement to secure Bengali as a national language of Pakistan on a par with Urdu. Death of the six Language Martyrs.
1953 All Pakistan Awami Muslim League changes its name to Awami League.
1956 Shaheed Suhrawardy becomes prime minister of Pakistan (till 1957).
1958 General Ayub Khan becomes chief martial law administrator and president of Pakistan. Moulana Bhashani leaves Awami League to set up the National Awami Party with a more radical manifesto.
1963 Shaheed Suhrawardy dies, Sheikh Mujib becomes leader of Awami League.
1966 Launch of the six-point demand for equal status for East and West wings of Pakistan. Sheikh Mujib arrested and imprisoned.
1968 Start of the Agartala Conspiracy case against Sheikh Mujib and others. Widespread civil unrest in East Pakistan.
1969 (January) All-party Students' Action Committee presents eleven-point demand for greater autonomy and socio-economic advancement of East Pakistan. Riots. Death of the activist Asaduzzaman.
(February) Pakistan government drops the Agartala Conspiracy case and exonerates all the accused. Civil unrest continues.
(March) Round table conference of political parties convened by President Ayub. Awami League the strongest contender. Sheikh Mujib presents plan for federal system. Turmoil in East Pakistan. Ayub Khan resigns, Yahya Khan takes over as president and martial law administrator.
1970 A major cyclonic storm causes extensive damage and many deaths in southern areas of East Pakistan; the response by government is perceived as inadequate. A general election is held, in which the Awami League wins an outright majority of seats in the Pakistan National Assembly and 98% of the vote in East Pakistan.
1971 Great unrest continues in East Pakistan; government almost inoperative. President Yahya Khan fails to broker any political agreement or to convene the National Assembly.
(March 7th) Historic speech by Sheikh Mujib, calling for autonomy for East Pakistan.
(March 25th) Military clampdown (Operation Searchlight) by Pakistan army in Dhaka. Massacre of students and intellectuals.
(March 26th) Declaration of Independence of Bangladesh.
(April 17th) Bangladesh Provisional Government sworn in at Mujibnagar.
(December 4th) India and Pakistan declare war on each other.
(December 14th) Second massacre of Bengali intellectuals by Pakistan military.
(December 16th) Pakistan army in East Bengal surrenders to Indian army. People's Republic of Bangladesh achieves independence.

MAP

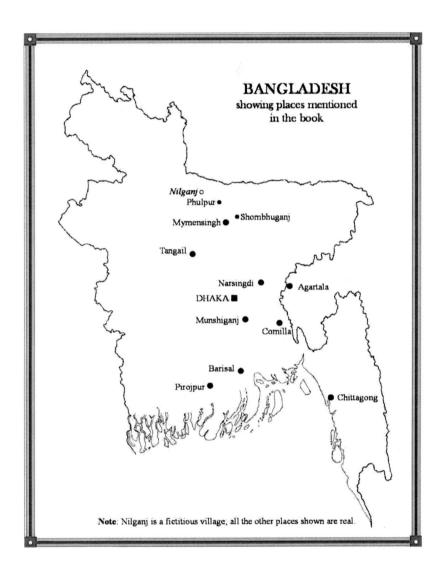

FEB 06 2018

CPSIA information can be obtained
at www.ICGtesting.com
Printed in the USA
LVOW10s1719190118
563158LV00012B/670/P

9 781539 381211